Chinese NUMEROLOGY

Once a week I do Chinese numerology readings over the radio, and people frequently express amazement that I can start interpreting their charts the instant I have their date of birth.
—Richard Webster

Virtually nothing has been published in the West that explains the traditional methods of constructing and interpreting numerology charts. In *Chinese Numerology*, author Richard Webster explains the 4,000 year-old origins of this revolutionary divination tool and teaches you how to use the traditional system. You'll also learn an easy-to-do Western variation that enables you to gain valuable insights about yourself and others very quickly.

Chinese Numerology is the first book in the West to explain and teach you how to:

- Draw a numerology chart in a matter of seconds and be able to interpret it accurately

- Discover future trends in your life by looking at your personal years, months and days. Is this a money year? Are you having a spiritual-growth year? Is this a good year to get married? Now you can predict the future of your own success

- Uncover your compatibility with another person using an easy, never-before-published technique

- Find out which famous people share the same numerology as you do

- Determine whether you have an arrow of loneliness, losses or confusion in your chart and what to do about it

- Learn three interlocking systems of numerology, all of which evolved from the days of Wu of Hsia in ancient China

About the Author

Richard Webster was born in New Zealand in 1946, where he still resides. He travels widely every year, lecturing and conducting workshops on psychic subjects around the world. He has written many books, mainly on psychic subjects, and also writes monthly magazine columns.

Richard is married with three children. His family is very supportive of his occupation, but his oldest son, after watching his father's career, has decided to become an accountant.

To Write to the Author

If you wish to contact the author or would like more information about this book, please write to the author in care of Llewellyn Worldwide, and we will forward your request. Both the author and publisher appreciate hearing from you. Llewellyn Worldwide cannot guarantee that every letter written to the author can be answered, but all will be forwarded. Please write to:

Richard Webster
℅ Llewellyn Worldwide
P.O. Box 64383, Dept. K804-4
St. Paul, MN 55164-0383, U.S.A.

Please enclose a self-addressed, stamped envelope for reply, or $1.00 to cover costs. If outside the U.S.A., enclose international postal reply coupon.

Chinese
NUMEROLOGY

4	9	2
3	5	7
8	1	6

Richard Webster

The Way to Prosperity & Fulfillment

1998
Llewellyn Publications
St. Paul, Minnesota 55164-0383
U.S.A.

FIRST EDITION
First Printing, 1998

Cover design: Anne Marie Garrison
Cover photo: © Arthur Montes De Oca
Editing and book design: Amy Rost

Library of Congress Cataloging In-Publication Data

Webster, Richard, 1946–
    Chinese numerology: the way to prosperity & fulfillment / Richard Webster.
        p. cm.
    Includes bibliographical references and index.
    ISBN 1-56718-804-4 (trade paper)
    1. Numerology.   2. Numerology—China.   I. Title.
BF1623.P9W37   1998
133.3'35'0951—dc21

Publisher's Note

Llewellyn Worldwide does not participate in, endorse, or have any authority or responsibility concerning private business transactions between our authors and the public. All mail addressed to the author is forwarded but the publisher cannot, unless specifically instructed by the author, give out an address or phone number. The publisher has not tested the techniques included in this book, and takes no position on their effectiveness.

Llewellyn Publications
A Division of Llewellyn Worldwide
P.O. Box 64383, Dept. K804-4
St. Paul, Minnesota 55164-0383

Printed in the U.S.A.

Other Books by Richard Webster

(Published by Llewellyn Publications)

101 Feng Shui Tips for the Home
(from the Feng Shui Series)

Spirit Guides & Angel Guardians

Astral Travel for Beginners

Aura Reading for Beginners

Seven Secrets to Success: A Story of Hope

Feng Shui for Beginners: Successful Living by Design

Dowsing for Beginners:
The Art of Discovering Water, Treasure, Gold, Oil, Artifacts

Numerology Magic

Omens, Oghams & Oracles: Divination in the Druidic Tradition

Revealing Hands: How to Read Palms

Forthcoming

Feng Shui Series:

Feng Shui for Apartment Living

Feng Shui for the Workplace

Feng Shui for Love and Romance

Feng Shui in the Garden

Dedication

For all my friends in
The Psychic Entertainers Association.

~

Contents

Introduction

It must have been an incredibly exciting and unexpected find that day, some 4,000 years ago. Wu of Hsia, later to become the first of the five mythical emperors of China, was working on the Hwang Ho (Yellow) River, trying to find a way to prevent the flooding that regularly devastated the communities sited along the lower and middle streams of the river.

In the course of this work, Wu found a tortoise shell. This, by itself, was a highly auspicious omen as the people of this time believed that God lived inside tortoise and turtle shells. However, this particular tortoise shell had extraordinary markings on it. Wu and his colleagues discovered that the tortoise shell contained a perfect, three-by-three magic square on its back. This square is known as the Lo Shu grid (Figure Intro A).

4	9	2
3	5	7
8	1	6

Figure Intro A.
The Lo Shu grid.

This square was remarkable because every horizontal, vertical, and diagonal row added up to fifteen. Fifteen is the number of days between the new moon and the full moon. The number five was highly regarded in ancient China and this magic square contained a five in the central position. No wonder Wu and his advisors were so excited by this find.

Wu was made emperor because he successfully solved the flooding problems, but his real claim to fame was his discovery of this tortoise shell. From this find ultimately evolved the I Ching, feng shui, the Nine Star Ki, geomancy, Chinese astrology, and Chinese numerology.[1]

Numerology appears to have developed independently in other parts of the world at around the same time. Over the years, different people have modernized it and made it more suitable for their way of life. Pythagoras is the most famous of these. (In fact, some authorities call the first system we will be covering here "The Arrows of Pythagoras.")[2] Chinese numerology gradually evolved into the three completely different systems discussed in this book.

The Western version of Chinese numerology is better known in Australasia than in other parts of the world. Its fame is largely due to the efforts of Hettie Templeton, who was instrumental in popularizing numerology in Australia in the 1930s, 1940s, and 1950s. She taught classes, conducted lectures, and gave frequent radio broadcasts. Her book on the subject is called *Numbers and Their Influence*, and at least two of her students have also written books on this system of numerology.[3] Consequently, most of the literature on this system of numerology has come from Australia and New Zealand.

I was introduced to Chinese numerology in 1978 by my late friend, Dr. David A. Phillips, in Sydney. Ten years earlier, I had received a numerology reading in Singapore that had confounded me with its detail and accuracy. I considered myself to be reasonably proficient in numerology, but knew nothing whatsoever about the system the Singapore numerologist used. Since then, I had been trying to find more information on Chinese numerology with little success. It was a great surprise to find that the man who owned the company that was distributing my early books in Australia was just as interested in numerology as I was. Not only that, but Dr. Phillips was also busy writing a book on the subject. He knew nothing about the Chinese origins, but was an authority on Pythagoras, and credited this system to him. We had many pleasant discussions arguing about the origins of this system of numerology.

The origins of the Western version of Chinese numerology are lost in the mists of time. I have found nothing in print on this subject prior to Hettie Templeton's book, which was published in 1940. She had been teaching this system for more than twenty years by this time, but unfortunately did not list in her book her sources of information.

The traditional Chinese system of numerology is still being used in most parts of Asia. I cover the basics of this system in chapter 9. Something I find very interesting is that I have met a

large number of numerologists in China and Hong Kong who use the Western version rather than the traditional Chinese method.

This book begins with a thorough explanation of the Western version of Chinese numerology. It is the easiest of the three systems to learn. Many numerologists around the world use this system and no other. However, I hope that you will be sufficiently interested to learn the more traditional Chinese methods as well. It is useful background material to know, even if you do ultimately choose to use just one of the systems. Once you have mastered the Western version of Chinese numerology you will find the traditional Chinese method and the Ki system much easier to understand.

I find Chinese numerology extremely useful in daily life. It enables me to quickly build up a complete picture of a person just as soon as I know his or her date of birth. Once a week I do Chinese numerology readings over the radio and people frequently express amazement that I can start interpreting their charts the instant I have their date of birth. Most divination systems take much longer to prepare and interpret. I know of no other system that can provide as much information with the same ease that Chinese numerology does.

I am sure that you will find the systems explained here to be fascinating and helpful in your everyday life.

1

Your Life Path Number

We start our exploration of numerology by working out our life path number. This is generally regarded as being the most important number in numerology, because it reveals our purpose in life. Most people have little idea of what they should be doing with their lives, and knowledge of this number, on its own, can transform lives.

There are eleven possible life path numbers: 1, 2, 3, 4, 5, 6, 7, 8, 9, 11, and 22. Eleven and 22 are called master numbers and contain more power than the other numbers.

We determine our life path number by adding up the digits in our date of birth and reducing the answer down to a single digit. If, when you reduce the numbers, the total comes to an 11 or 22, you stop at that point.

Here is an example. Let's imagine that we are doing a reading for a young man born on July 12, 1973. We construct a sum from his date of birth.

$$
\begin{array}{rl}
7 & \text{(month)} \\
12 & \text{(day)} \\
+\ \underline{1973} & \text{(year)} \\
1992 &
\end{array}
$$

$$1 + 9 + 9 + 2 = 21, \text{ and } 2 + 1 = \mathbf{3}$$

This man has a life path of 3.

Here is another example. A friend of mine was born on February 29, 1944.

$$\begin{array}{rl} 2 & \text{(month)} \\ 29 & \text{(day)} \\ + \underline{1944} & \text{(year)} \\ 1975 & \end{array}$$

and $1 + 9 + 7 + 5 = 22$

As we arrive at 22 while reducing, we stop at that point, rather than reduce it still further to a four. This is because 22 is one of the possible life path numbers.

My friend's date of birth illustrates another point. We need to ensure that we create a sum, rather than simply adding across, so we don't lose master numbers. If we add my friend's date of birth in a straight line, we get the following:

2 (month) + 2 + 9 (day) + 1 + 9 + 4 + 4 (year) = 31

and $3 + 1 = 4$

As you can see, by adding in a straight line we lost the master number. In practice, I usually add up the numbers in my head, but if my answer comes to a 2, 4, 11, or 22, I will double check by creating a sum on paper.

Meanings of the Life Path Numbers

Each of the life path numbers has a specific meaning.

1 Life Path

People with a life path number of 1 have to learn to stand on their own two feet and achieve something. They usually start out in life by being dependent, and gradually achieve a degree of independence as they mature. Ultimately, they often become pioneers, innovators, and leaders.

1 Life Path

~

Keyword:

Independence

Ones can be self-centered and like to be at the head of the line. Consequently, they are ambitious, progressive, determined, and stubborn. They have inquiring minds and considerable leadership qualities. They have executive skills and can rise through the ranks to the ultimate top position in their field. They have strong

personal needs that need to be met. Although this may be disguised to others, people on a 1 life path are aware of it themselves. Whatever their needs are, ones makes sure that they are met.

There is a negative side to the 1 life path. Some ones find it hard to achieve independence and seem overly dependent. Consequently, they will be taken advantage of by others and will deeply resent it, even though they feel powerless to prevent it.

Another negative side to this 1 life path is that people on it try to build themselves up by pulling others down. They have ego problems and think of themselves first, second, and always.

Famous people who have or had a 1 life path include Charlie Chaplin, Mikhail Gorbachev, Salvador Dali, Arthur C. Clarke, Ringo Starr, Danny De Vito, Sting, Florence Nightingale, and Richard Rogers.

George Washington (born February 22, 1732) is an example of someone with a 1 life path. He was born to a family of Virginia planters and had a rather haphazard formal education. He first had an opportunity to prove himself in the French and Indian War (1754–1763) where he made two expeditions into the Ohio country. In 1755 he became commander of the Virginia troops. In 1758 he was elected to the House of Burgesses, resigning his commission to do so. He was elected to the first Continental Congress in 1774. A year later he was elected to the second Congress, and that year (1775) became commander of the colonial forces.

In 1776, Washington and his men forced the British to give up Boston and, in the next five years, he became a popular and successful leader. He became president of the Constitutional Convention (1787) and two years later was overwhelmingly elected first president of the republic. He was reelected in 1792. Washington's life provides a perfect example of someone who knew what he wanted and went after it with unwavering determination.

Henry Ford (born July 30, 1863) is another excellent example of someone on a 1 life path. Once he made up his mind to do something he pursued it with incredible persistence. Like most ones, it took many years for him to become confident in his abilities and be able to stand on his own two feet. He was forty years old when he founded the Ford Motor Company in 1903. The famous Model T was launched in 1908. By 1913 his use of mass production enabled him to sell the car for $500. In 1927, at the age of fifty-four, he introduced the Model A, and five years later, introduced the V-8 engine. In 1941, at the age of seventy-eight, he signed the first union contract in the automobile industry.

~

Famous Ones:

Charlie Chaplin

Arthur C. Clarke

Salvador Dali

Danny De Vito

Henry Ford

Mikhail Gorbachev

Florence Nightingale

Sting

Richard Rogers

Ringo Starr

George Washington

2 Life Path

People with a life path number of 2 are able to make people feel at ease. They are gracious and charming and make wonderful hosts and hostesses. They are sensitive to the needs of others and find it easy to make friends. They prefer being in a permanent relationship to being on their own. They are sensitive, peace loving, and naturally intuitive. They make good friends and express their feelings well. They are not overly concerned with status or material needs. Consequently, they often find themselves in the "number two" position, rather than the "number one." They are content to be the power behind the throne. In this position they do not always receive the full recognition that they should, but they are usually content knowing that they have done a good job.

Occasionally you will find people who are using their 2 life path negatively. They will try desperately to become leaders, preferring to be mediocre in this role instead of outstanding in the number two position. Although they may achieve these aims, they will never feel comfortable or happy in the leadership role.

Famous people who have or had a 2 life path include Ronald Reagan, Madonna, Art Garfunkel, Jacqueline Onassis, Jamie Lee Curtis, Jules Verne, Bobby Fischer, and Andrew Lloyd Webber.

Singer Karen Carpenter (born March 2, 1950) was an example of someone with a 2 life path. Karen was by all accounts a charming person, but someone who needed continual encouragement from her family to go out on stage and perform. In 1965, her brother Richard formed an instrumental trio with Karen and their friend, Wes Jacobs. When she was just sixteen they competed in a battle of the bands at the Hollywood Bowl. Their group won, and they were given a recording contract with RCA.

The trio broke up after recording two LPs that were not released. A few years later, Herb Alpert liked Richard and Karen's demo tapes so much that he offered them a contract with A & M. Their first hit was their interpretation of the Beatles' hit "Ticket to Ride." This was followed by "Close to You," which sold a million copies in 1970. Other hits followed, but for Karen the high point was an invitation to perform at the White House in 1974.

In 1975 anorexia nervosa was taking its toll on Karen; the Carpenters had to cancel a European tour because she was too weak to perform. In 1980 she married, but the marriage did not last. In 1983 she started making public appearances again after an absence of several years. On February 4, 1983, she collapsed

without warning while visiting her parents. Doctors said that her long struggle with anorexia had weakened her heart. Obviously, the stresses and strains of her chosen career were too much for her. This is a common problem with people on a 2 life path.

Prince Philip (born June 10, 1921), husband of Great Britain's Queen Elizabeth II, is a perfect example of someone with a 2 life path. He can never be "number one," no matter what he does, but he plays an extremely effective role as "number two." Here he can be a peacemaker, diplomat, and someone who "soothes troubled waters."

3 Life Path

People with a life path number of 3 need to express themselves in some sort of way, ideally creatively. As this expression usually uses verbal skills, it can include singing, talking, or writing. Threes are usually excellent conversationalists and enjoy expressing all the joys of life. Communication is their forte. They have active, imaginative brains and are always full of ideas. However, they often lack the motivation to put them into play. People on this life path are friendly, sociable, and outgoing. They enjoy having others around them and cannot stand being on their own for very long. Their path is lighthearted and less serious than other paths.

Some people with a 3 life path use it negatively by being superficial and scatterbrained. They dabble in numerous areas, but never take anything very far. This lack of purpose distresses people close to them, particularly when they start overindulging in alcohol, drugs, and/or sex.

Many entertainers have a 3 life path. John Belushi, Bill Cosby, Billy Crystal, Alfred Hitchcock, Johnny Mercer, and Olivia Newton-John are all examples.

Judy Garland (born June 10, 1922) is also a good example of someone born on this life path. She made her stage debut at the age of three and first appeared on screen in 1936. International stardom came three years later when she played the part of Dorothy in the movie *The Wizard of Oz*. She was awarded a special Academy Award for her portrayal of this role.

She found the pressures of stardom increasingly hard to handle and the last fifteen years of her life saw drugs, suicide attempts, and breakdowns—all negative traits of a 3 life path. However, she pulled herself together many times and had successful comebacks that broke box office records in New York and London.

3 Life Path

~

Keyword:
Self-expression

~

Famous Threes:

John Belushi

Bill Cosby

Billy Crystal

Judy Garland

Alfred Hitchcock

Johnny Mercer

Olivia Newton-John

4 Life Path

People with a life path number of 4 need to work hard to achieve their goals. They are practical, reliable, conscientious, and well-organized people who enjoy keeping to routines. They are able to create order out of chaos. They are hard workers who enjoy seeing the results of their labor. Fours are prepared to patiently plod along for years, provided they can see that the effort is worthwhile. They are good with details and enjoy fine, complicated tasks. Inclined to being rigid and stubborn, they find it very hard to change their minds once it has been made up. They have strong likes and dislikes and are not afraid to express their views.

There are many people who use their 4 life path negatively. These people dislike their feelings of limitation and restriction, and try to fight them by becoming dominating and abusive. Their inability to see the larger picture costs them opportunities which results in increasing frustration.

Famous people who have or had a 4 life path include Joseph Patrick Kennedy, Jean Cocteau, Guglielmo Marconi, Fanny Brice, Robert Heinlein, and the Duchess of Windsor.

Sir Thomas Beecham (born April 29, 1879), the famous conductor, had a 4 life path. His first opportunity came almost accidentally when the Hallé orchestra visited his hometown of St. Helens, England, but its conductor was not available. The twenty-year-old Beecham stepped in and, with very little rehearsal, conducted. His ambition was to be a concert pianist, but after an injury to his wrist in 1904 he put this aside and concentrated on conducting. He made his first public performance in London in 1905, and a year later founded his own orchestra. In 1910 he conducted his first opera season at Covent Garden, performing many works that had not been heard in Britain before then.

During World War I, Beecham toured Britain with a small opera company for which he was knighted in 1916. In 1920 he produced a major opera season in London that almost bankrupted him. After this disaster he disappeared from public view until 1929 when he presented the first Delius Festival in London. In 1932 he founded the London Philharmonic Orchestra. During World War II he toured extensively in the United States and Australia. After his return to London in 1944 he founded the Royal Philharmonic Orchestra. Beecham remained busy conducting, writing, and touring until his death in 1961.

5 Life Path

People with a life path number of 5 are versatile and enjoy doing a wide variety of different things. They become restless and impatient when they feel restricted in any way. They enjoy travel, excitement, and anything that takes them out of their familiar routines. Fives are quick thinkers who enjoy solving problems. Early on in life they are inclined to dabble, but once they find their correct path, they frequently achieve a great deal. These people are always curious, enthusiastic, and forever young at heart.

The negative side of a 5 life path is overindulgence. These people often change directions and find it impossible to stick to anything for long. Many experiment with and overindulge in alcohol, drugs, and sex.

Famous people who have or had a 5 life path include Sir Isaac Newton, Mark Twain, Willie Nelson, Franklin D. Roosevelt, Eva Peron, Helen Keller, and Sir Arthur Conan Doyle.

Abraham Lincoln (born February 12, 1809) is another example of someone with a 5 life path. After a humble beginning he practiced as a lawyer in Illinois in the 1830s and 1840s. He entered the U.S. Congress in 1847 and became a Republican in 1856. Two years later he attempted to gain a seat in the Senate and failed. However, his debates had made him a nationally known figure, and he was elected president in 1860.

His entire period as president was occupied with the war against the southern states. Lincoln pronounced the slaves in these rebellious states free in 1863. He was assassinated in 1865, just days after the Union victory. His versatility, enthusiasm, and energy are all positive traits of the 5 life path.

5 Life Path

~

Keywords:
Freedom, variety

~

Famous Fives:
Sir Arthur Conan Doyle

Helen Keller

Abraham Lincoln

Willie Nelson

Sir Isaac Newton

Eva Peron

Franklin D. Roosevelt

Mark Twain

6 Life Path

People with a life path number of 6 are nurturing, caring, and responsible. They enjoy accepting other people's burdens and providing a shoulder for others to lean on. They particularly enjoy helping the people they care for. They become the members of the family that the others turn to when things are not going well. Sixes are capable of solving problems between others in such a way that everyone feels happy with the outcome. Sympathetic, loving, and kind, they are happiest when surrounded by their friends and loved ones. Sixes are often creative, usually in artistic fields.

It is rare to find people using their 6 life path negatively. However, sixes who accept everyone's responsibilities often end up being overwhelmed by everyone else's problems.

6 Life Path

~

Keywords:
Home and family responsibility

Famous people with a 6 life path include Richard Nixon, Dwight Eisenhower, Jawalharlal Nehru, Sylvester Stallone, Stevie Wonder, Hoagie Carmichael, John Lennon, and Thomas Edison.

Albert Einstein (born March 14, 1879) is an example of someone born on a 6 life path. In 1905, the same year that he gained his doctorate, Einstein published four research papers, each of which contained a new discovery in physics. He achieved international fame in 1919 when his theory of relativity was proven. He was awarded the Nobel Prize for Physics two years later for his photoelectric law and work in theoretical physics. He joined the Institute for Advanced Studies in Princeton, New Jersey, in 1933.

Elisabeth Kübler-Ross (born July 8, 1926) is an excellent contemporary example of someone who is using the humanitarian side of her 6 life path and spending her life helping others. She was born in Switzerland, where she later studied medicine. She emigrated to the United States in 1958 and quickly became known for her pioneering work in counseling the terminally ill. Her book *On Death and Dying* (1969) brought her worldwide recognition. She has also worked extensively with terminally ill children and, more recently, AIDS victims.

7 Life Path

People with a life path number of 7 need time by themselves to grow in knowledge and wisdom. They have their own special, unique approach to everything they do. This gives them great originality, but also means that they find it hard to make changes and adapt. It also can sometimes make it difficult for them to feel comfortable as part of a group.

Sevens prefer a few close friends to large groups of acquaintances. They can be hard to get to know initially as they protect themselves with barriers, but they make good friends once they fully trust the other person. Reserved, cautious, and introspective, sevens are spiritual people and their philosophy of life grows and develops as they go through life.

People on the negative side of their 7 life path find it impossible to get close to others and hide themselves away. They become increasingly introspective and self-centered.

Famous people who have or had a 7 life path include Queen Elizabeth II, Louis Pasteur, John F. Kennedy, Jim Henson, Oliver North, Bob Geldof, Mel Gibson, Johnny Cash, Lech Walesa, and Andy Warhol.

Sir Winston Churchill (born November 30, 1874) is another excellent example of someone born on a 7 life path. After a mediocre school life, he graduated from the Royal Military College at Sandhurst and served as a subaltern and war correspondent in Cuba, India, and South Africa. He entered politics in 1900 as a Conservative. Four years later, he crossed the floor and joined the Liberals. His promotion was rapid and he did much to strengthen the British navy before World War I. He served as a military officer in 1915 and 1916, before returning to parliament and finishing the war as Minister of Munitions.

After the war, Churchill became secretary of war, head of the Colonial Office, and Chancellor of the Exchequer. His greatest years were during World War II when, as prime minister from 1940 to 1945, he led Britain to triumphant victory. He was voted out of office in 1945, but returned as prime minister in 1951. He resigned in 1955.

Throughout his busy political career he kept writing (using the research qualities of his 7 life path).

Famous Sevens:
Johnny Cash
Sir Winston Churchill
Queen Elizabeth II
Bob Geldof
Mel Gibson
Jim Henson
John F. Kennedy
Oliver North
Louis Pasteur
Lech Walesa
Andy Warhol

8 Life Path

People with a life path number of 8 enjoy being involved in large-scale enterprises and want to reap the rewards of their success. They set worthwhile goals for themselves, then go out and achieve these goals. They are ambitious and determined and invariably achieve their aims. Eights live very much in the real world and have no time for dreamers. They are good at dealing with money, and once they achieve their financial goals they can be very generous. They are good judges of character. They have leadership capabilities and usually rise to positions of responsibility. Eights are inclined to be rigid and stubborn in outlook, though usually they cannot see this trait in themselves.

People who use their 8 life path negatively achieve large sums of money, but do so at the cost of health, happiness, and relationships. They can become intolerant, vengeful, and power-hungry.

Famous people who have or had an 8 life path include Ginger Rogers, Pablo Picasso, George Harrison, Barbra Streisand, Lyndon Baynes Johnson, Gene Kelly, Elizabeth Taylor, Jim Bakker, and Gene Wilder.

George Bernard Shaw (born July 26, 1856) is a good example of someone with an 8 life path. He was a product of a broken family, had a limited education, wrote five unpublished novels and, in 1895, believing he was a failure as a playwright, accepted a position

8 Life Path

Keyword:
Materialism

~

Famous Eights:

Jim Bakker

Andrew Carnegie

Lyndon Baynes Johnson

Gene Kelly

George Harrison

Ginger Rogers

Pablo Picasso

George Bernard Shaw

Barbra Streisand

Elizabeth Taylor

Gene Wilder

as a drama critic. Originally very shy, he managed to transform himself into a competent public speaker. He experienced a breakdown in 1898 and the following year experienced success for the first time—at the age of 43.

Andrew Carnegie (born November 25, 1835) is a perfect example of someone on an 8 life path who became a multimillionaire. He was born in Dunfernline, Scotland, and emigrated to the United States in 1848. At the age of fifteen, he began work in a cotton factory, the first of several menial jobs he had before joining the Pennsylvania Railroad in 1853. Carnegie had risen to the position of superintendent when he left in 1865 to work for himself. His company grew to become the largest iron and steel works in the United States, and he sold it in 1901 for an estimated $500 million.

He then began using the generous side of his 8 life path by giving away large amounts of money. These included more than 2,500 libraries in Britain, the United States, and Canada, as well as substantial gifts to American and Scottish universities, and the establishment of a number of charitable foundations. The largest of these is the Carnegie Corporation of New York, which Carnegie endowed with $125 million to support his benefactions after his death.

9 Life Path

9 Life Path

~

Keyword:

Humanitarianism

People with a life path number of 9 are inclined to be self-sacrificing. Sensitive, caring people with a strong need to serve others, they enjoy helping others and frequently give much more than they receive in return. Consequently, they can easily be taken advantage of by others. Nines are romantics at heart and are profoundly disappointed when their deep, true love is not returned. These humanitarian aims of the nine are usually slightly detached and universal in scope. Nine is the third creative number and these people often express their creativity in writing, though it can come out in many different ways.

You will find many negative people on a 9 life path. This is because it is so difficult to remain selfless and giving in a materialistic world. These people try taking instead of giving. They never find any satisfaction in this, as they are fighting their true nature.

Famous people who have or had a 9 life path include Shirley MacLaine, Dustin Hoffman, Harrison Ford, Patrick Swayze, Benazir Bhutto, Jimmy Carter, Jack Nicklaus, Nelson Rockefeller, Carl Jung, and Carlos Castenada.

Albert Schweitzer (born January 14, 1875) is an example of someone on a 9 life path. He could have achieved success in a number of fields, but chose to live in a small village in Africa spending his life in humanitarian work. He is remembered as a theologian, philosopher, musician, author, and mission doctor.

Schweitzer received his doctorate in philosophy in 1899. The following year he was awarded a doctorate in theology. His first book on theology, published in 1906, made him an international figure in this field. At the same time he was developing as a musician. This career began with a series of organ concerts in Strasbourg in 1893. His first publication in music was *J. S. Bach: le musicien-poète*, which appeared in 1905.

In the same year, he announced his intention to become a mission doctor. He gave up his university appointments to study medicine, graduating in 1913. He and his wife immediately sailed for French Equatorial Africa where they spent most of the rest of their lives building and operating a hospital for the native people. Schweitzer was interned during World War I, but returned to Africa in 1924 to rebuild his hospital on a new site a few miles away from his original one. The hospital grew, and in 1963 he was looking after 350 patients at the hospital and another 150 at the adjacent leper colony. Throughout his life, he continued to publish books and make recordings of J. S. Bach's music. He also gave innumerable lectures and recitals.

Mahatma Gandhi (born October 2, 1869) is another excellent example of someone who used the positive side of his 9 life path throughout his life. In India he is considered the father of the country, and in the rest of the world he is remembered for his policy of non-violence.

Gandhi was educated in India and England. He went to South Africa in 1893 where he was appalled at the racial discrimination. He campaigned for equality and after a series of challenges to the South African government he was imprisoned. Returning to India, he entered politics in 1919. He led the Indian National Congress party in a campaign of nonviolent noncooperation. They were repressed throughout World War II, but his efforts paid off in 1947 when India became independent. He was assassinated on January 30, 1948.

Famous Nines:

Benazir Bhutto

Jimmy Carter

Carlos Castenada

Harrison Ford

Mahatma Gandhi

Dustin Hoffman

Carl Jung

Shirley MacLaine

Jack Nicklaus

Nelson Rockefeller

Albert Schweitzer

Patrick Swayze

The Master Number Life Paths

In numerology, 11 and 22 are considered master numbers. They belong to highly evolved souls—people who have already learned the easy lessons in past incarnations and now have some of the more challenging lessons to learn. (In the East most people believe in reincarnation.) People with a master number life path have been reincarnated many times and now have the opportunity to really make their mark on the world. Unfortunately, many people on a master number path find it too difficult to handle and achieve just a fraction of their potential.

There is always a degree of nervous tension associated with master numbers, which also makes it difficult for these people to achieve their aims. It is rare for people with a master number path to achieve success early on in life. Usually, they start off reflecting more of the potential of a two or four, but gradually become more confident and sure of themselves, and the master number characteristics become more and more apparent. Usually, they achieve the most success late in life.

11 Life Path

11 Life Path

~

Keyword:

Idealism

People with a life path number of 11 are idealistic. They are frequently visionaries; they have access to unique ideas and are dreamers rather than doers. However, they are extremely capable at whatever they do, and with sufficient motivation, can achieve anything. Because their ideas are not always practical, they need to evaluate them carefully before attempting to pursue them. Elevens are always intuitive and caring.

People who use the negative side of their 11 life path are impractical dreamers who achieve little and live in a world where it is hard to separate reality from fantasy.

~

Famous Elevens:

Hans Christian Anderson

Harry Houdini

Beatrix Potter

There have been very few people born with an 11 life path in the last 200 years. This is because during this period, most of the birth dates have reduced down to a 2, rather than 11. However, we will see a lot more from now on. (An example is the son of a friend of mine who was born on March 30, 1985.) It is not surprising that we will see many more of these people in the twenty-first century, as we will then be well inside the Age of Aquarius.

Famous people who have or had an 11 life path include Hans Christian Anderson and Beatrix Potter.

Harry Houdini (born March 24, 1874) is an example of someone on an 11 life path. He was definitely an ideas man, and

managed to make enough ideas work to ensure a lasting reputation. Even today, more than seventy years after his death, he will be the first, and possibly only, name to come to mind if you ask someone to name a magician.

Houdini was the son of a rabbi who emigrated from Hungary to the United States. His real name was Erik Weisz. He adopted the stage name Houdini in honor of his idol, the famous French magician Robert-Houdin. He began his performance career as a trapeze artist and became an escape artist when he found he could get much more publicity for his incredible feats as an escapologist.

In addition to his feats as a magician, he also campaigned against charlatan mediums. He was very close to his mother and, when she died, he tried to contact her by visiting mediums. To his dismay, he found many were using simple magic tricks, and he exposed them with relentless vigor. However, he also made an agreement with his wife that whichever of them died first would try to communicate with the survivor. For ten years after his death his widow, Bessie, held a séance every year on the anniversary of his death. (Sadly, this experiment was not a success.)

22 Life Path

People with a life path number of 22 are able to achieve anything they set their minds on. Usually, their goal is something large in scope. They have a great deal of ability and need to channel it constructively. Elevens are often dreamers; twenty-twos also have the dreams, but then make them happen. These people are practical, usually unconventional, and frequently charismatic. They are able to excite and motivate others with their words and actions.

The negative side of a 22 life path is selfishness. Twenty-twos use their considerable abilities for their own ends and totally ignore the needs of others. Sometimes they are aware of this trait, but find it difficult to move onto a more positive track.

Famous people who have or had a 22 life path include Elton John, Arnold Schwarzenegger, Marie Curie, and Marcel Marceau.

Comedian Lenny Bruce (born October 13, 1925) was an example of someone with a life path number of 22. He was a man of enormous potential and promise, but he found the pressures too hard to handle and destroyed himself with drugs. He was largely self-educated, as he dropped out of high school and joined the Navy in 1942. He was discharged after convincing Navy psychiatrists that he was homosexual.

22 Life Path

~

Keywords:

Master builder

~

Famous Twenty-Twos:

Lenny Bruce

Marie Curie

Bill Gates

Elton John

Marcel Marceau

Arnold Schwarzenegger

Margaret Thatcher

With the help of his mother he began to get bookings in night-clubs and in 1948 was "discovered" when he appeared on "Arthur Godfrey's Talent Scouts." He gradually became more and more popular, but in 1964 he was arrested on a charge of obscenity. After this he was constantly harassed by the police and became more and more depressed. In 1965 he was $40,000 in debt. He died from a narcotics overdose on August 3, 1966.

Margaret Thatcher (born October 13, 1925) is another good example of someone with a 22 life path. She had a modest start in life, but climbed through the ranks in politics to rule Great Britain for many years.

2

The Day of Birth

The day of the month that you were born is also examined when doing a numerological analysis. Each day has its own special quality or vibration. It is becoming increasingly common in the East for labor to be induced so that babies will be born on a day that the parents consider auspicious.

I must admit that before each of our three children was born I drew up numerological charts for all the days the baby was likely to be born on. This enabled me to say, for instance, "If the baby is born on Tuesday he or she will be like this…" and then describe the character traits. This made an interesting exercise, but at no time was I tempted to have labor induced so that our babies would be born on a certain day. I believe that we are born when we are meant to be born, and I do not like the idea of interfering with this.

The vibrations of the day of birth are not nearly as strong or important as the life path number. The day of birth modifies the qualities of the life path. For example, people who have a 7 life path are likely to be quiet and introspective. However, if they were born on the 3rd, 12th, 21st, or 30th of the month they would gain some of the outgoing, expressive qualities of the 3, and would be much more communicative than most people with a 7 life path.

Qualities of Specific Days

1st of the Month

People born on the 1st of the month gain pure 1 energy. They gain logic, energy, enthusiasm, independence, and analytical ability. They are likely to repress their emotions for fear of revealing a weakness. They are natural leaders who enjoy opportunities to display their skills.

2nd of the Month

People born on the 2nd day of the month are friendly, loving, helpful, idealistic, emotional, intuitive, and occasionally moody. Although they like people, they often feel nervous in large groups. They sometimes get downhearted and need constant reassurance from others. They prefer working in partnerships to being on their own.

3rd of the Month

People born on the 3rd of the month are outgoing, imaginative, sociable communicators. They express all the joys of life and are generally highly popular. They are often better at coming up with ideas than they are at carrying them out. They are restless and frequently have more than one major relationship in their lives. They have a talent with words and are likely to be most successful in any field where this talent could be utilized. (Teaching and sales are two good examples of such fields.)

4th of the Month

People born on the 4th of the month are well-organized people who enjoy challenges. They also have a close love of home, family, and country. They are stubborn and find it very hard to change their minds once they have made a decision. They are conscientious, highly responsible, and prepared to work hard and long for what they want.

5th of the Month

People born on the 5th day of the month are versatile and outgoing. They usually need to learn to concentrate their energies, because they have a desire to try everything. These people enjoy

mixing with like-minded associates and often do well in business. They are sociable, well-adjusted people with good brains. They need freedom and variety in their lives.

6th of the Month

People born on the 6th of the month are positive, caring, generous humanitarians. They are generally happiest when helping others. They enjoy the responsibilities of marriage and family life. They have good minds, strong emotions, and great sensitivity. They are not afraid to show their feelings to others.

7th of the Month

People born on the 7th of the month are sensitive, secretive, intuitive people who like to work things out for themselves. They enjoy spending time on their own in research and study. They love their friends with great intensity, but find it hard to give and receive affection. They have their own unique way of doing things.

8th of the Month

People born on the 8th of the month make natural business people. They enjoy dealing with money and finance, and are able to come up with excellent money-making ideas. They are ambitious, motivated, and practical. They are prepared to work hard for what they get, as long as they consider the goal to be a worthwhile one.

9th of the Month

People born on the 9th of the month are natural humanitarians, who often get trampled on by others who take their efforts for granted. They frequently get trapped in marriages where they give much more than they receive. This can be regarded as a learning experience, as they generally enjoy giving more than receiving. They have rich imaginations and are usually happiest working in creative fields. They are broadminded, tolerant, and idealistic.

10th of the Month

People born on the 10th of the month are positive, determined, creative people who know how to sell themselves and their ideas to others. They are able to successfully manage a number of activities at the same time, and often need to be forced to take time off for

relaxation. They are independent, ambitious, confident, and seldom reveal their true feelings.

11th of the Month

We have already discussed master numbers in chapter 1. People born on the 11th come up with great ideas, but are seldom able to carry them through and make them happen. These people are highly intuitive and extremely capable, but their nervousness and high-strung temperament make it hard for them to achieve their goals. Their emotions carry them quickly from one extreme to the other. They have the potential to inspire others with their ideas.

12th of the Month

People born on the 12th of the month gain 3 energy (as 1 + 2 = 3), but they also gain the individual energies of both 1 and 2. This makes them more complex than people born on the 3rd of the month. They are excellent at selling themselves and their ideas to others. They are charming, amusing, and excellent conversationalists. Their wonderful imaginations cause them to frequently embellish the truth. They have the potential to channel their excellent imaginations into creative endeavors. They are inclined to be impatient and want everything immediately.

13th of the Month

Those born on the 13th of the month are hard working, methodical people who have the potential to become very successful. They are cautious, stubborn, disciplined, and tenacious. They are good with the details, sometimes at the expense of the overall picture. Although they ultimately do well, they often feel frustrated, restricted, and hemmed in by circumstances.

14th of the Month

People born on the 14th of the month are adventurous, courageous, adaptable, and always ready to try something new and different. They are naturally intuitive. They are easily led by others and should avoid overindulging in alcohol, drugs, and sex. They enjoy working with others, and can work extremely hard when necessary, but not usually for long periods of time.

15th of the Month

People born on the 15th of the month are understanding and loyal. They tend to be creative, especially in the field of music. They instinctively know when someone needs a shoulder to lean on and are the first to offer help. They are loving, demonstrative, and easy to get along with. They are responsible, but like to keep a degree of independence at the same time. They are sympathetic, helpful, and conscientious.

16th of the Month

People born on the 16th of the month are reserved, cautious, and introspective. They find it hard to express their thoughts and feelings, and tend to retreat into themselves rather than face potentially difficult situations. They also find it hard to give and receive love and affection. They gradually build up a strong faith or philosophy of life. They are often interested in technical or scientific subjects, and enjoy researching and finding things out for themselves.

17th of the Month

People born on the 17th of the month are good with money and finances. They work steadily towards their goals with great determination. They invariably get what they want in the end, although they usually experience a number of setbacks along the way. They are confident, reliable, realistic, and have the necessary talents to handle large-scale projects.

18th of the Month

People born on the 18th of the month are good administrators and natural humanitarians. Often they are able to combine these qualities and make a career in a philanthropic field. Despite their desire to help others, they frequently have problems in their personal lives and need to learn that charity begins at home. They are sympathetic, tolerant, understanding, and use a creative approach to problem solving.

19th of the Month

People born on the 19th of the month are responsible, idealistic, and ambitious. Their emotions can let them down at times, because these emotions always win over logic. They are versatile and prefer to work with as little interference from others as possible.

20th of the Month

People born on the 20th of the month are friendly, articulate, and easy to get along with. They prefer quiet lives and tend to avoid the hustle and bustle of modern life as much as possible. They often express themselves well with words on paper. They can be moody, and need the support of close friends and family.

21st of the Month

People born on the 21st of the month are intelligent, amusing, and creative. However, they tend to worry about small things, and are often nervous and moody. They can be on top of the world one minute, and down in the dumps the next. They have definite verbal skills and could do well in any career involving their voice.

22nd of the Month

Because 22 is a master number, people born on the 22nd are extremely capable, but have major ups and downs in their lives. This is because they have access to energies and vibrations that most of the rest of us never experience, and consequently sometimes suffer nervous and physical exhaustion. However, usually in later life, they are capable of achieving much more than most people. They are highly intuitive, but inclined to nervousness.

23rd of the Month

People born on the 23rd of the month are sensitive, sympathetic, understanding, independent people who enjoy helping others. They are versatile and enjoy challenges of all sorts.

24th of the Month

People born on the 24th of the month are caring, motivated, and enthusiastic. Their positive, often dramatic approach to achieving their goals enables them to achieve more in five minutes than others manage in years.

25th of the Month

People born on the 25th of the month are intuitive, gentle, and need time on their own. They are easily hurt and tend to withdraw when this happens. They are hard to get close to, but once a friendship with them has been formed, it lasts forever.

26th of the Month

People born on the 26th of the month are rigid, stubborn, and motivated to achieve. They have the knack of taking a simple idea and making money from it. They can be very generous.

27th of the Month

People born on the 27th of the month are determined, trusting, and passionate. They enjoy change and variety. They enjoy responsibility and opportunities to serve others.

28th of the Month

People born on the 28th of the month are affectionate and freedom-loving. They do not like being told what to do and are usually happiest when they are their own boss.

29th of the Month

People born on the 29th day of the month experience the energies of both the 2 and the 9, of course, but they also receive the greater potential of the 11 (as $2 + 9 = 11$). Consequently, these people often lead lives that are either up or down. Their potential is obvious to everyone except themselves. They are inspired dreamers who find it difficult to make their wonderful visions come true.

30th of the Month

People born on the 30th of the month are intelligent, creative, and loving. However, they lack motivation and try to get by on charm rather than make use of their considerable abilities. They achieve most when in partnership with someone who provides frequent encouragement and prompts them into action.

31st of the Month

People born on the 31st of the month possess good business, organizational, and managerial skills. They generally start at the bottom of the ladder and slowly, but steadily, rise through the ranks. They value their friendships and are willing to help others who need it. They have good memories and never forget a favor or a slight.

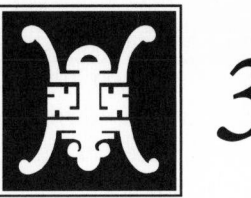

3

The Lo Shu Grid

The magic square on the tortoise's back was called the Lo Shu grid. It was a perfect three by three magic square (Figure 3A).

4	9	2
3	5	7
8	1	6

Figure 3A.

Every row, horizontally, vertically, and diagonally, added up to fifteen.

In the Far East numerology is still done using the original Lo Shu positions, and we will be looking at that later (in chapter 10). In the West, though, the grid is used in a slightly different way. Any 1s in the person's full date of birth are placed in the bottom left-hand square (Figure 3B). Any 2s are placed in the square immediately above this, and any 3s go in the top left-hand square.

1		

Figure 3B.

The three squares in the middle house any 4s in the bottom square, any 5s in the middle, and any 6s in the top. Naturally, the right-hand side boxes contain any sevens (in the bottom square), any eights (in the middle) and the nines (in the top). The correct positions for each number are shown in

3	6	9
2	5	8
1	4	7

Figure 3C.

Figure 3C. (This is simply to show where each number goes.) It is impossible to have a chart in which every single square is filled. Similarly, it is impossible for anyone who has ever lived to

have a completely empty chart. Empty charts are waiting for people who have not yet come into the world. The chart only comes to life when a baby is born.

We will use the two examples from the previous chapter to illustrate completed charts. The young man born on July 12, 1973,

3		*9*
2		
11		*77*

Figure 3D.

will have the chart that is shown in Figure 3D. The 7 of July is placed in the bottom right-hand square, as this is where any 7s go. The 1 and 2 from the 12th are placed in the bottom and middle left-hand squares, respectively. The 1 from the 1973 is placed in the bottom left-hand square. The 9 is placed in the top right-hand square, the 7 in the bottom right-hand square, and the 3 in the top left-hand square.

Let's try another example. This time we will use the lady born on February 29, 1944 (Figure 3E). The 2 from February is placed in the middle left-hand square. Another 2 is then placed in the same square (from the 29). The 9 from the

		99
22		
1	*44*	

Figure 3E.

29th is placed in the top right-hand square. Finally the numbers from the year are put into position: the 1 in the bottom left-hand square, the 9 in the top right-hand square, and the two 4s in the bottom square on the middle row.

Here is another example. Someone born on May 27, 1948, will have the chart shown in Figure 3F.

		9
2	*5*	*8*
1	*4*	*7*

Figure 3F.

All people born in the twentieth century will have at least one 1 and one 9 in their chart, but there is an almost limitless combination of the other numbers. Everybody born in the twenty-first century will have at least one 2 in their chart. You will find many similar charts, but it is unusual to find two identical charts except, of course, for people born on the exact same day.

The chart can be looked at in a number of different ways. The top row (made up of the numbers 3, 6, and 9) can represent the head of a person. The middle row (numbers 2, 5, and 8) represents the body. Finally, the bottom row (numbers 1, 4, and 7) represents the legs and feet.

Consequently, the top row is usually regarded as the Mental Plane. It encompasses thinking, creating, imagining, and analyzing.

The middle row is called the Emotional Plane. After all, the heart is in the body. This plane includes spirituality, intuition, feelings, and emotions.

The bottom row is called the Practical Plane. This encompasses physical labor, the ability to be good with one's hands, and the ability be practical in everyday life. To use the head-body-legs analogy again, the feet are firmly placed on the ground in the Practical Plane (Figure 3G).

Mental
Emotional
Practical

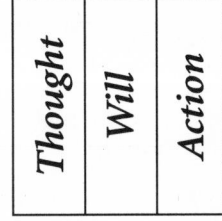

Figure 3G.

The vertical rows are also interpreted. The first of these (numbers 1, 2, and 3) is the Thought Plane. This reveals the person's ability at coming up with ideas, creating things, and carrying them through to fruition.

The middle vertical row (numbers 4, 5, and 6) is the Will Plane. This gives the determination and persistence to succeed.

The final vertical row (numbers 7, 8, and 9) is the Action Plane. This shows the person's ability at putting their thoughts into action (Figure 3H).

Thought	*Will*	*Action*

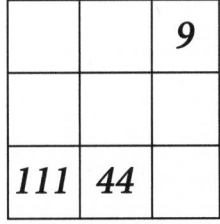

Figure 3H.

The three vertical rows make a natural progression. First of all, the person has to come up with an idea (Thought Plane). He or she has to have determination and persistence (Will Plane), otherwise the idea will never be acted upon. The planning is done at this stage. Finally, the person needs to be able to put the idea and the determination into action (Action Plane).

Every number in the chart has a meaning.

The Number 0

There is no position in the chart for zeros. They are simply ignored. Cliff Richard, whose chart is shown in Figure 3I, has two zeros in his date of birth (October 14, 1940). We insert the 1s, 4s, and 9 in their correct positions in the chart, but forget about the two zeros. One of the most interesting people I have ever met was a retired naval commander who was born on October 14, 1910. This meant that his chart consisted solely of four

		9
111	*44*	

Figure 3I.
Cliff Richard (October 14, 1940).

1s and one 9. Even more interesting will be the people born on February 20, 2020, as their chart will consist of just one number!

The Number 1

One is situated in the bottom left-hand corner at the start of the Practical Plane. It provides a valuable clue as to how the person reacts and communicates with others.

One 1

People with just one 1 in their chart find it hard to express their innermost feelings. They may be good communicators in other ways, but find it hard to allow their inner self to emerge. They often find it hard to see the other person's point of view.

Senator Edward Kennedy (born February 22, 1932) is a good example of a person with one 1 in his chart (Figure 3J). He obviously expresses himself extremely well in Congress, but finds it difficult to talk about his innermost feelings with the people he loves the most. Note his 22 day number.

3		9
2222		
1		

Figure 3J.
Edward Kennedy (February 22, 1932).

Two 1s

People with two 1s in their chart are able to express themselves easily and fluently. They have a balanced outlook on life and are able to assess situations in an impartial manner. They can understand the other person's point of view as well as their own. This is regarded as being the perfect number of 1s to have in a chart. The late President John F. Kennedy (born May 29, 1917) is an example of someone with two 1s in his chart (Figure 3K).

		99
2	5	
11		7

Figure 3K.
John F. Kennedy (January 27, 1917).

Three 1s

People with three 1s in their chart fall into two types. Usually, they are chatterboxes who never stop talking. However, you also sometimes find people with three 1s who are quiet and introspective.

Interestingly enough, many of these people can be both, and which one they are at any given time depends on the situation.

People with three 1s are generally happy, outgoing people, and many prominent entertainers have this combination in their chart. Cliff Richard (born October 14, 1940) is an example of someone with three 1s in his chart (see Figure 3I, page 29).

Four 1s

People with four 1s in their chart find it extremely difficult to express themselves verbally. They are sensitive, caring people who are frequently misunderstood. They also find it very hard to relax and unwind. The late Princess Grace of Monaco (born November 12, 1929) is an example of someone with four 1s in her chart (Figure 3L).

		9
1111	44	

Figure 3L.
Princess Grace of Monaco (November 12, 1929).

Five, Six, or Seven 1s

People with five or more 1s in their chart experience enormous difficulties in expressing themselves verbally. They are frequently misunderstood and often direct their expressive skills into an area they find less painful, such as writing, painting or dancing. Some people with this combination overindulge in food, drugs or alcohol. The late prime minister of India, Indira Gandhi (born November 19, 1917) is an example of someone with five 1s in her chart (Figure 3M).

		99
111 11		7

Figure 3M.
Indira Gandhi (November 19, 1917).

The Number 2

Two is the first number on the Emotional Plane. It reveals how sensitive and intuitive the person is. This century, it is the third most common number in Chinese numerology charts. Everyone born in the twenty-first century will have at least one 2 in their charts. This can be taken as a sign of the coming of the Age of Aquarius as everyone will possess caring, sensitive, and intuitive qualities. How—and if—they use these traits is another matter, of course.

One 2

People with one 2 in their charts are sensitive and intuitive. Unfortunately, they are also easily hurt. They are able to sum other people up at a glance, and have an uncanny ability at detecting insincerity. Nostradamus, the celebrated sixteenth-century psychic, who was born December 14, 1503, had one 2 in his chart (Figure 3N).

3		
2	5	
111	4	

Figure 3N.
Nostradamus
(December 14, 1503).

Two 2s

People with two 2s in their chart are highly intelligent, sensitive, and intuitive. Unlike people with only one 2, they are able to make good use of their intuition. They can easily detect the motivations of others and be able to assess others at a glance. The late Jacqueline Onassis (born July 28, 1929) is an example of someone with two 2s in her chart (Figure 3O).

		99
22		8
1		7

Figure 3O.
Jacqueline Onassis
(July 28, 1929).

Three 2s

People with three 2s in their chart experience an overabundance of this sensitive, intuitive energy and can easily be hurt. They may give the impression of being aloof, because they live in a world of their own feelings, and often prefer being on their own instead of spending time with others who might hurt their feelings. Elizabeth Taylor (born February 27, 1932) is an example of someone with three 2s in her chart (Figure 3P).

3		9
222		
1		7

Figure 3P.
Elizabeth Taylor
(February 27, 1932).

Four 2s

People with four 2s in their chart are impatient and inclined to overreact to small problems. They are extremely sensitive and frequently prefer time by themselves, rather than risk being hurt by others. Louis Pasteur (born December 27, 1822) is an example of someone with four 2s in his chart (Figure 3Q). Edward Kennedy (see Figure 3J, page 30) is another example.

2222		8
11		7

Figure 3Q.
Louis Pasteur
(December 27, 1822).

Five 2s

People with five 2s are very rare, which is fortunate, as they find life extremely difficult. They are overly sensitive; they suffer constantly from self-doubt and lack of confidence and trust in others.

Next century it will be possible to find people with six twos (February 22, 2022), and these people will find this incredible sensitivity almost impossible to handle.

The Number 3

Three is found in the top left-hand position of the chart, at the start of the Mental Plane. It is the final number of the Thought Row and the first number of the Mental Plane. Consequently, it is largely related to intellectual capacity. It is a positive, happy number. Three also relates to memory and the ability to think clearly and logically.

One 3

People with one 3 in their chart possess good, creative brains and an excellent memory. They keep their feet on the ground and have a positive approach concerning reaching their goals. They are able to inspire others with their optimism and honesty. Elvis Presley (born January 8, 1935) is an example of someone with one 3 in his chart (Figure 3R).

3		9
	5	8
11		

Figure 3R.
Elvis Presley (January 8, 1935).

Two 3s

People with two 3s in their chart possess good imaginations. They are mentally alert and usually creative. They enjoy flouting convention and may appear to be slightly eccentric. Many people with this combination become writers, as they have the ability to channel their creative imagination and express their ideas in words. Mikhail Gorbachev (born March 2, 1931) is an example of someone with two 3s in his chart (Figure 3S).

33		9
2		
11		

Figure 3S.
Mikhail Gorbachev (March 2, 1931).

Three 3s

People with three 3s in their chart live inside their rich imagina-tions. They often find it hard to relate well with others and can appear self-absorbed and remote. They possess excellent mental ability, but frequently spend their lives in a world of dreams. They find it hard to listen to others and can be argumentative and petty at times. Richard Chamberlain, the actor, has three 3s in his chart. He was born on March 31, 1935 (Figure 3T).

333		9
	5	
11		

Figure 3T.
Richard Chamberlain (March 31, 1935).

Four 3s

People with four 3s in their chart are impractical, overly imagi-native, and fearful. All of these things make it hard for them to function well in every-day life.

This combination is found very rarely. The next time it will occur is March 3, 2033 (Figure 3U). It will appear again on the 13th, 23rd, and 31st of the same month.

3333		
2		

Figure 3U.
People born on March 3, 2033, will have four 3s in their charts.

The Number 4

Four is a practical, hard-working number that represents order and balance. People with this number in their charts are usually neat, tidy, and good with details.

One 4

People with one 4 in their charts are practical and usually good with their hands. They enjoy "hands-on" type occupations and get impatient with imaginative ideas and theo-ries. They have the ability to organize others and carry out plans to perfection. A single 4 also relates to music and handicrafts. Liza Minelli (born March 12, 1946) is an exam-ple of someone with a single 4 in her chart (Figure 3V).

3	6	9
2		
11	4	

Figure 3V.
Liza Minelli (March 12, 1946).

Two 4s

People with two 4s in their chart are inclined to become overly involved in physical and materialistic activities at the expense of other activities. They have excellent organizational skills, and love starting a task at the beginning and carrying it through to the end. They are conscientious, accurate, and tidy people. They often have considerable creative ability in their hands and enjoy making beautiful objects. Priscilla Presley (born May 24, 1946) is an example of someone with two 4s in her chart (Figure 3W).

	6	9
2	5	
1	44	

Figure 3W.

Priscilla Presley (May 24, 1946).

Three 4s

People with three 4s in their chart are involved almost exclusively with physical activities, and find it hard to pay attention to other areas of their lives. They are well organized, self-disciplined, and hard-working. Their abilities are obvious to others, but people with three 4s frequently find it difficult to accept their natural talents and waste years working in the wrong fields. Shirley MacLaine (born April 24, 1934) is an example of someone with three 4s in her chart (Figure 3X).

3		9
2		
1	444	

Figure 3X.

Shirley MacLaine (April 24, 1934).

Four 4s

People with four 4s in their chart are very hard to find. Last time this chart occurred was on April 24, 1944 (Figure 3Y). It will not occur again until 2044. These people are totally immersed in physical activities and find it difficult to understand other people who are interested in intellectual or spiritual matters. They possess enormous ability at anything involving their hands. People with four 4s are susceptible to damage to the lower limbs.

		9
2		
1	4444	

Figure 3Y.

April 24, 1944: The last time four 4s occurred in a chart.

The Number 5

Five is placed in the central position of the chart, and denotes balance and emotional stability. However, it also relates to freedom, so people with a 5 in their charts need a certain amount of room around them and are likely to run if they feel overly restricted.

One 5

People with one 5 in their charts are emotionally well balanced.

		9
2	5	
1111	4	

Figure 3Z.
Goldie Hawn
(November 21, 1945).

They are compassionate, understanding, and caring. They are able to motivate and inspire others to achieve much more than would have otherwise been possible. Goldie Hawn, the actress, was born November 21, 1945, which gives her one 5 in her chart (Figure 3Z). (Also note the four 1s.)

Two 5s

People with two 5s in their chart are intense and determined. They

3		9
	55	
11		

Figure 3AA.
Stevie Wonder
(May 13, 1950).

have a great deal of drive and enthusiasm. They have problems harnessing their emotions, which can lead to outbursts that are later regretted. This often creates difficulties in home and family life. Stevie Wonder (born May 13, 1950) is an example of someone with two 5s in his chart (Figure 3AA).

Three 5s

People with three 5s in their chart are prone to speaking without thinking and can hurt others unwittingly. They have a great deal of

		9
	555	
111		

Figure 3BB.
Paul Samuelson
(May 15, 1915).

drive and energy, but these qualities need to be carefully channeled. They enjoy change, adventure, excitement, and often take unnecessary risks. Paul Samuelson, the economist, who was born May 15, 1915, is an example of someone with three 5s in his chart (Figure 3BB).

Four 5s

People with four 5s in their chart are hard to find, because this combination occurs just three times every hundred years. The next time this combination occurs will be May 5, 2055 (Figure 3CC). This combination is a dangerous one as it provides the potential for accidents. People with four 5s need to slow down and think before acting.

2	5555	

Figure 3CC.
Four 5s will next appear in the chart for May 5, 2055.

The Number 6

The number 6, located in the center of the top row, relates to creativity and love of home and family.

One 6

People with one 6 in their charts have a great love for their home and loved ones. They enjoy domestic responsibilities and also possess considerable creative potential. They make good parents and ultimately become the person everyone comes to in the family when things are not going well. They are often insecure and worry about being widowed and left on their own. Ginger Rogers (born July 16, 1911) is an example of someone with one 6 in her chart (Figure 3DD).

	6	9
1111		7

Figure 3DD.
Ginger Rogers (July 16, 1911).

Two 6s

People with two 6s in their chart are inclined to worry unnecessarily about their home and family. The nervous strain this creates means that they need more rest than most people. They enjoy creative activities and are happiest surrounded by beautiful things. They are usually over-protective and find it hard to let their children stand on their own two feet. Jerry Lewis (born March 16, 1926) is an example of someone with two 6s in his chart (Figure 3EE).

3	66	9
2		
11		

Figure 3EE
Jerry Lewis (March 16, 1926).

Three 6s

People with three 6s in their chart are inclined to be overly protective and possessive of their loved ones. They also have considerable creative potential, which provides a useful release for their emotional tension. They are inclined to look more on the negative side of life than the positive, and need constant encouragement. Stress and worry can be a problem for these people. Mike Tyson, the boxer (born June 30, 1966), is an example of someone with three 6s in his chart (Figure 3FF).

3	*666*	*9*
1		

Figure 3FF.
Mike Tyson
(June 30, 1966).

Four 6s

People with four 6s in their chart are highly creative, but they find it hard to channel this energy in the early part of their life. Everything affects them emotionally, which makes it hard for them to fit in to everyday life. There are just three days every century where people with four 6s are born. The most recent of these was June 26, 1966 (Figure 3GG).

	66 66	*9*
2		
1		

Figure 3GG.
June 26, 1966, the most recent day with three 6s in its chart.

The Number 7

The number 7 is situated in the bottom right-hand corner of the chart. It represents sacrifice, usually learning the hard way, through a disappointment or a loss.

One 7

People with one 7 in their chart are likely to learn through losses of love, possessions, or health. As they learn from these experiences they usually become more and more interested in metaphysical or spiritual pursuits. Elisabeth Kübler-Ross (born July 8, 1926) is an example of a person with one 7 in her chart (Figure 3HH).

	6	9
2		8
1		7

Figure 3HH.
Elisabeth
Kübler-Ross
(July 8, 1926).

Two 7s

People with two 7s in their chart grow in knowledge and wisdom by losing either love, health, or money. Ultimately, this is likely to lead to an interest in the psychic or occult worlds. They have analytical brains, which makes them good at solving intricate technical problems.

Edgar Cayce (born March 18, 1877) is an example of someone with two 7s in his chart (Figure 3II). Both Ludwig van Beethoven (born December 17, 1770) and Wolfgang Amadeus Mozart (born January 27, 1756) had two sevens in their charts.

3		
		88
11		77

Figure 3II.
Edgar Cayce (March 18, 1877).

Three 7s

People with three 7s in their chart often lead sad lives caused by major disappointments and setbacks in the areas of love, health, and money. Frequently, these people develop tremendous reserves of inner strength as a result of these difficulties. Poet William Wordsworth (born April 7, 1770) is an example of someone with three 7s in his chart (Figure 3JJ).

1	4	777

Figure 3JJ.
William Wordsworth (April 7, 1770).

Four 7s

People with four 7s in their chart have to learn through major lessons involving loss of love, health, and finances. Fortunately, there are only three days every century when this combination occurs. The most recent of these was July 27, 1977 (Figure 3KK).

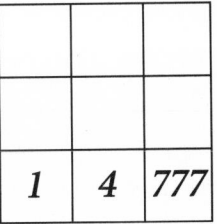

		9
2		
1		77 77

Figure 3KK.
July 27, 1977, the most recent date with four 7s in its chart.

The Number 8

The number eight relates to attention to detail.

One 8

People with one 8 in their charts are methodical, conscientious, and good with details. However, surprisingly, they usually find it

Figure 3LL.
Napoleon Bonaparte (August 15, 1769).

hard to finish the tasks they begin. They have restless, active minds and need constant mental challenges. Napoleon Bonaparte (born August 15, 1769) is an example of someone who has a single 8 in his chart (Figure 3LL).

Two 8s

People with two 8s in their chart are extremely perceptive and conscientious. They prefer to experience things for themselves, rather than take too much on trust. They have fixed views and opinions and find it hard to change their minds after decisions have been made. Bertrand Russell, the great British philosopher (born May 18, 1872), is an example of someone with two 8s in his chart (Figure 3MM).

Figure 3MM.
Bertrand Russell (May 18, 1872).

Three 8s

People with three 8s in their chart are conscientious, rigid, and frequently restless. They develop more purpose in life about the time they reach age forty and after that make rapid progress. They can do extremely well in the fields of business and finance. They can be overly materialistic and need to learn that possessions cannot bring lasting happiness. Author Jules Verne (born February 8, 1828) is an example of someone with three 8s in his chart (Figure 3NN).

Figure 3NN.
Jules Verne (February 8, 1828).

Four 8s

People with four 8s in their chart are extremely restless and have a strong need for change and variety in their lives. Once they find something they really want to pursue, their progress can be a joy to behold. Until then, though, they are likely to lead rather aimless, pointless lives. This combination occurs just three times every century. The most recent was August 28, 1988. Lawrence of Arabia (born August 15, 1888) is an example of someone with four 8s in his chart (Figure 3OO).

Figure 3OO.
Lawrence of Arabia (August 15, 1888).

The Number 9

Everybody born in the twentieth century has at least one 9 in his or her chart. It is a humanitarian number, representing idealism, valor, and ambition.

One 9

People with one 9 in their chart are ambitious and have a strong desire to improve themselves. The number 9 is on both the Mental Plane and the Action Line. This is one reason humankind has achieved such a great deal in the twentieth century. However, it appears that many of us still need to learn to be humanitarians. It is not hard to find someone to act as an example of one 9 in their chart. Mother Teresa (born August 27, 1910) is a striking example, exemplifying all the humanitarian qualities of the number 9 (Figure 3PP).

		9
2		8
11		7

Figure 3PP.
Mother Teresa
(August 27, 1910).

Two 9s

People with two 9s in their chart are idealistic, intelligent, and inclined to be critical of others. Because they are highly intelligent they sometimes tend to look down on others who are not similarly blessed. They need to learn to mix with people from all levels of society. Entertainer Michael Jackson (born August 29, 1958) is an example of someone with two 9s in his chart (Figure 3QQ).

		99
2	5	88
1		

Figure 3QQ.
Michael Jackson
(August 29, 1958).

Three 9s

People with three 9s in their chart are idealistic, caring, and intelligent. They are inclined to exaggerate and "make mountains out of molehills." They learn to handle this better as they mature. When they are making good use of their mental capabilities, they are happy and positive. However, they quickly become frustrated and despondent when they feel that they are caught in a rut. Billy Joel (born May 9, 1949) is an example of someone with three 9s in his chart (Figure 3RR).

		999
4	5	
1		

Figure 3RR.
Billy Joel
(May 9, 1949).

Four or five 9s

People with four or five 9s in their chart are highly intelligent, but find it hard to live in the everyday world. They frequently retreat into a world of their own imagination. If they can learn to harness the enormous amount of power and energy at their disposal they can become a real force for good in the world.

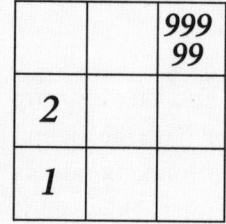

Figure 3SS.
September 29, 1999: the last time this millennium five 9s appear in a chart.

Five 9s are exceptionally rare. The next time five nines will appear will be September 29, 1999 (Figure 3SS). It will not occur again after that until September 9, 2999!

Missing Numbers

Numbers that are completely missing from the chart indicate lessons that the person has to learn in this lifetime. Knowing what numbers our friends and families are missing in their charts allows us to know what they are struggling to learn. This enables us to be more understanding and supportive. Without this knowledge we might criticize others for their performance in certain areas. This never works. By knowing their missing numbers we can encourage and help them in their difficult areas.

Everyone has at least one number missing in his or her chart.

Number 1

Next century we will again find people without the number 1 in their charts. This has been impossible for the last thousand years. People missing the number 1 will find it difficult to express their individuality, and will be more concerned with helping and nurturing others. They will be almost entirely without an ego. They will need to develop a creative outlet of some sort as this will allow them to express their emotions constructively.

Number 2

People without the number 2 in their charts are lacking sensitivity and intuition. Consequently, they will make many mistakes by ignoring the still, small, quiet voice within. They are inclined to be impatient and unpunctual. There is a tendency in these people to try to justify their actions, rather than admit they have made a

mistake. These people need to learn to achieve balance in their life. Roald Dahl (born September 13, 1916), author of *Willie Wonka and the Chocolate Factory*, is an example of someone without a 2 in his chart (Figure 3TT).

3	6	99
111		

Figure 3TT.
Roald Dahl
(September 13, 1916).

Number 3

People without the number 3 in their charts lack confidence and find it hard to express themselves. They are inclined to underestimate themselves and be overly self-effacing. They find it hard to think logically when faced with distractions. They need to learn to accept themselves as they are, then move forward gaining in confidence and self-esteem at every step. Diana, Princess of Wales (born July 1, 1961) is an example of someone without a 3 in her chart (Figure 3UU).

	6	9
111		7

Figure 3UU.
Diana, Princess of Wales
(July 1, 1961).

Number 4

People missing the number 4 find it difficult to work to a set routine. They are frequently disorganized and lacking in motivation. Consequently, they seldom achieve much until they have altered the way they look at life. They need to learn to be better organized and to work for what they want. Because 4 is the number of dexterity, people lacking it are seldom good with their hands. As they develop more patience and tolerance life becomes easier for them. Emily Brontë (born August 20, 1818) is an example of someone without a 4 in her chart (Figure 3VV).

2		888
11		

Figure 3VV.
Emily Brontë
(August 20, 1818).

Number 5

People missing the number 5 find it hard to set goals; they lack drive and versatility. They need constant motivation from others. These people need to learn to set realistic goals and to complete them before starting on others. A missing number 5 is very common. Thomas Edison (born February 11, 1847) is an example of someone without a 5 in his chart (Figure 3WW).

2		8
111	4	7

Figure 3WW.
Thomas Edison
(February 11, 1847).

Number 6

People missing the number 6 need to learn to give more of themselves. They tend to hide their innermost feelings from others. This usually relates to difficulties with one of their parents (often the father) in early life. These people experience problems in their relationships until they learn to be more open and free. Willie Nelson (born April 30, 1933) is an example of someone without a 6 in his chart (Figure 3XX).

333		9
1	4	

Figure 3XX.

Willie Nelson (April 30, 1933).

Number 7

People missing the number 7 are inclined to be inconsiderate of other people's feelings. They are disorganized in their everyday life. They have little or no interest in spiritual or metaphysical matters. They find it hard to be self-sufficient and dislike being left on their own. They need to learn to express their inner feelings and become more relaxed around others. Sir Isaac Newton (born December 25, 1642) is an example of someone without a 7 in his chart (Figure 3YY).

	6	
222	5	
11	4	

Figure 3YY.

Sir Isaac Newton (December 25, 1642).

Number 8

People missing the number 8 are poor at handling their financial matters. They can be overly careless or too trusting and suffer financially as a result. They also tend to lack motivation and leave tasks unfinished. They need to learn to control a natural impulsiveness and think before acting. Mick Jagger (born July 26, 1943) is an example of someone without an 8 in his chart (Figure 3ZZ).

3	6	9
2		
1	4	7

Figure 3ZZ.

Mick Jagger (July 26, 1943).

Number 9

It is impossible for anyone born in the twentieth century to be missing this number, but many people born in the twenty-first century will not have it. People missing the number 9 tend to overlook the feelings and needs of others. They are detached and

oblivious to what is going on in the lives of others. They need to learn to give of themselves, and to become true humanitarians. Bertrand Russell (born May 18, 1872) is an example of someone without a 9 in his chart (see Figure 3MM, page 40).

As you can see, there is an enormous range of possible combinations and in the next chapter we will start to interpret these combinations.

4

The Arrows of Strength and Weakness

There are fifteen arrows or lines that can appear in the chart. The arrows of strength occur when three numbers appear together in a row, horizontally, vertically, or diagonally. The arrows of weakness occur when three empty boxes appear together in a row, again horizontally, vertically, or diagonally.

These arrows are sometimes known as the Arrows of Pythagoras. It is possible that Pythagoras did use them, but if so, they were lost—at least to the Western world—until the 1930s when they were rediscovered by Dr. Hettie Templeton and published in her book *Numbers and Their Influence.*[1]

Arrows do not appear in every chart. Wolfgang Amadeus Mozart (born January 27, 1756) did not have any arrows in his chart (Figure 4A). However, most charts do have them and when they appear they provide a valuable clue as to the person's makeup and personality. Some people have more than one arrow in their chart and, providing these are arrows of strength, they indicate significant capabilities and strength of character.

	6	
2	5	
11		77

Figure 4A.
Wolfgang Amadeus Mozart (January 27, 1756).

However, it is not always what we are given that counts. I have encountered many people with remarkable charts who have achieved little in life, and also met people with apparently difficult charts who have persevered and overcome their limitations. Later on, we will look at

the chart of Indira Gandhi, who is an excellent example of some-one with an extremely difficult chart who went on to make her mark on the world.

The Arrows of Strength

The arrows of strength are regarded as positive influences in the chart. However, the mere presence of them does not ensure that the person will make good use of them. They should be regarded as natural talents that still need further development. They indicate the areas where the person can quickly move ahead.

The Arrow of Determination

This arrow is made up of the diagonal numbers 1, 5, and 9. It is frequently found, as everyone born during the 1950s possesses it. As its name indicates, it makes people born with it determined and persistent. They are also enterprising, intense, and progressive. They are patient and prepared to wait for whatever it is they have set their minds on.

However, it is not always easy to be patient for long periods of time, and these people need to learn to control their temper. This is particularly the case if the number 4 is missing from their chart.

Figure 4B.
Margaret Thatcher
(October 13, 1925).

Margaret Thatcher (born October 13, 1925) is a good example of someone with an arrow of determination (Figure 4B). She needed to develop patience and persistence in the long years before she achieved power.

The Arrow of Compassion

This arrow is made up of the diagonal numbers 3, 5, and 7. People with this combination develop a strong faith and philosophy of life. This is normally caused by life's experiences; consequently these people often lead sad lives. However, as they mature, they develop an inner serenity and a strong faith that sustains and comforts them. Many people with this arrow have a strong interest in music.

This arrow is sometimes known as the arrow of mysticism. It is interesting to note that everyone born in the twentieth century

with an arrow of compassion will also have the arrow of determination.

Elton John (born March 25, 1947) is a good example of someone with an arrow of compassion (Figure 4C). His faith and philosophy come across vividly in much of his musical work.

Figure 4C.
Elton John
(March 25, 1947).

The Arrow of Intellect

The arrow of intellect is made up of the horizontal row of 3, 6, and 9. These are all the mental numbers and give those who possess them a good mind and excellent memory. These people are inclined to use their intellect at the expense of their emotions. They may also tend to look down on people who are not their intellectual equals. Apart from this, they are well balanced and enjoy helping others. Home and family are important to them.

George Orwell (born June 25, 1903) is a good example of someone with an arrow of intellect (Figure 4D). Orwell also had the arrows of determination and the planner in his chart, so he was gifted with enormous potential. His literary career took off when he published *Down and Out in Paris and London* in 1933. Today he is best known for his satirical books, but he also wrote more general works and a series of essays on leading authors and their works.

Figure 4D.
George Orwell
(June 25, 1903).

The Arrow of Emotional Balance

The arrow of emotional balance is composed of the numbers 2, 5, and 8 in the Emotional Plane. People with this combination in their charts are understanding, compassionate, and emotionally well balanced. They can easily understand and empathize with other people's points of view. They are also very natural healers. This is an extremely strong arrow because of the presence of the 5. When people with this arrow decide to do something they don't stop halfway. They achieve their goals.

The celebrated actor Sean Connery (born August 25, 1930) is a good example of someone with an arrow of emotional balance (Figure 4E) in his chart.

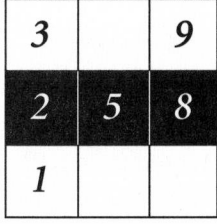

Figure 4E.
Sean Connery
(August 25, 1930).

The Arrow of Practicality

The arrow of practicality is made up of the numbers 1, 4, and 7 on the Practical Plane. Not surprisingly, people with this arrow in their charts are capable with their hands. This may simply mean they work hard, but they can also express it as some form of creativity. These people are usually the "salt of the earth," being down to earth, capable, practical, and easy to get along with. This arrow usually relates to physical talents, but it can also be related to mental dexterity as well. These people are prepared to work long and hard for anything that they believe in.

Winston Churchill (born November 30, 1874) is a good example of a person with the arrow of practicality (Figure 4F). Despite his privileged background and upbringing, he always had the "common touch" and related well with others. He also enjoyed working with his hands, constructing enormous brick walls and painting pictures.

3		
		8
111	*4*	*7*

Figure 4F.
Winston Churchill
(November 30, 1874).

The Arrow of the Planner

The arrow of the planner consists of the first vertical column: numbers 1, 2, and 3. People with this combination have at least one number in each of the Mental, Emotional, and Practical Planes. They are well-organized people who enjoy planning ahead and achieving their goals. Their weakness is in being undisciplined with the details. These people express themselves well and enjoy lengthy discussions on subjects that interest them. They can also be studious and completely immerse themselves in their studies, becoming oblivious to everything around them.

Andrew Lloyd Webber, the famous British composer of musicals (born March 22, 1948), is a good example of someone with the arrow of the planner (Figure 4G).

3		*9*
22		*8*
1	*4*	

Figure 4G.
Andrew Lloyd
Webber
(March 22, 1948).

The Arrow of Willpower

The arrow of willpower is a vertical column comprising the numbers 4, 5, and 6. It is an uncommon arrow, but one that gives considerable strength and endurance. People with this arrow in their charts are inclined to be self-centered, dynamic, and unbelievably persistent. They tend to be unaware of the feelings of others and

can unwittingly hurt others in their drive to reach their own goals. However, they make extremely good friends. Once someone with this arrow becomes your friend, nothing will break the friendship. These people often experience major problems in their lives, but remain positive and optimistic. Invariably, they find resolutions.

Film star Gregory Peck (born April 5, 1916) is a good example of someone with the arrow of willpower (Figure 4H).

Figure 4H.
Gregory Peck
(April 5, 1916).

The Arrow of Activity

The arrow of activity comprises the numbers 7, 8, and 9. People with this arrow in their charts need to express themselves through action. They need to be busy, either physically or mentally. They dislike confined spaces and prefer being outdoors with plenty of room around them. They have a tendency to be nervous and express themselves well with words on paper.

Richard Simmons (born July 12, 1948) is an interesting example of someone with the arrow of activity (Figure 4I).

Figure 4I.
Richard Simmons
(July 12, 1948).

The Arrows of Weakness

The arrows of weakness reveal the areas in the chart where the person needs to make the greatest effort. We are all able to make changes in our lives and improve ourselves in many different ways. These arrows show where we should start.

The Arrow of Indecision

Nobody has had this arrow for the last thousand years as it is made up of a line of spaces created by a missing 1, 5, and 9 in the chart. However, in the twenty-first century we will start to see people with this arrow again. One is a self-centered number, which means that everybody born in the last thousand years has put themselves first. Everybody born in the twenty-first century will have a 2 in their charts. (Two is a caring, nurturing, intuitive number, which portends good things for humanity in the next thousand years.)

People with an arrow of indecision will be likeable, caring people who want to do the right thing. Consequently, they will find it difficult to make decisions where it is impossible to please everybody.

The Arrow of Skepticism

The arrow of skepticism is made up of spaces where the numbers 3, 5, and 7 would appear. People with this combination in their charts like to see things demonstrated or proven, rather than accepting things on trust. They usually have a conservative approach to religion and are likely to simply accept the beliefs of their parents without questioning them in any way. These people are loving, honest, and fair, but frequently find it difficult to express these feelings to others. They are idealists and have strong visionary capabilities that can make them highly intuitive.

President Abraham Lincoln (born February 12, 1809) is a good example of someone with the arrow of skepticism in his chart (Figure 4J).

Figure 4J.
Abraham Lincoln (February 12, 1809).

■		*9*
22	■	*8*
11		■

The Arrow of Poor Memory

Nobody born in the twentieth century can have this arrow as it is made up of the absence of the numbers 3, 6, and 9 in the chart. However, it will reappear again in the twenty-first century.

The absence of the mental numbers does not indicate a low intellect. In fact, the opposite is frequently the case and many people with this combination have been very quick and witty. What it means is that the mental faculties tend to fade as the person gets older. This comes out as forgetfulness and absent-mindedness. People with this arrow usually learn slowly as children, but catch up later on. Then, in later life, their intellect gradually deserts them. This can be averted if they keep themselves mentally alert and stimulated with a variety of hobbies and interests.

Bertrand Russell (born May 18, 1872) is an interesting example of someone with the arrow of poor memory (Figure 4K). He is generally regarded as being an intellectual giant and his achievements were incredible. However, his memory gradually deserted him as he aged.

Figure 4K.
Bertrand Russell (May 18, 1872).

■	■	■
2	*5*	*88*
11		*7*

W. Somerset Maugham, the great British writer (born January 25, 1874), is another example of someone with this arrow (Figure 4L). (Incidentally, his chart also contained the arrows of emotional balance and practicality.) His last great success before his death in 1964 was *The Razor's Edge*, which was published in 1944.

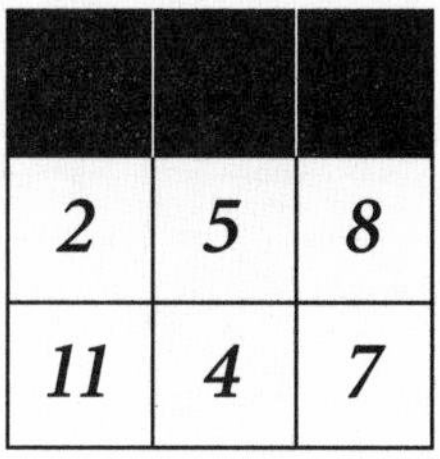

Figure 4L

W. Somerset Maugham (January 25, 1874).

The Arrow of Emotional Sensitivity

The arrow of emotional sensitivity indicates an absence of the numbers 2, 5, and 8. This means that there are no numbers on the Emotional Plane to provide protection in this area of life. Consequently, people with this arrow in their charts are overly sensitive and easily hurt. They soon learn how to hide their feelings. These people are also very capable of supporting and nurturing others, particularly those who deserve their help. People with this arrow are usually shy as children, though most overcome this as they mature. Some, unfortunately, have an inferiority complex that lasts through their lifetime.

Diana, Princess of Wales (born July 1, 1961) is an example of someone with the arrow of emotional sensitivity (Figure 4M).

Figure 4M.

Diana, Princess of Wales (July 1, 1961).

The Arrow of Impracticality

This is another arrow that has not appeared for the last thousand years, as it is created by an absence of the numbers 1, 4, and 7 in the chart. However, it will start to appear again with people born in the twenty-first century.

These people have no numbers in the Practical Plane, so they will lead their lives mainly in a world of logic and emotion. They will be impractical, idealistic, and find it hard to function in everyday life. However, these people will excel in theoretical, rather than practical, pursuits.

The Arrow of Frustrations

This arrow is made from the absence of the numbers 4, 5, and 6 in the chart. This effectively divides the chart in two, with numbers on both sides but nothing in the middle. People with this

arrow experience more than their fair share of setbacks, disappointments, and frustrations. This is usually their own fault as they expect more from others than they should. Until they learn to accept other people as they are, they are doomed to continual frustration and disillusionment.

3		9
222		
1		7

Figure 4N.
**Elizabeth Taylor
(February 27, 1932).**

Elizabeth Taylor (born February 27, 1932) is an example of someone with the arrow of frustrations in her chart (Figure 4N).

The Arrow of Hesitation

This arrow is made from the absence of the numbers 7, 8, and 9 in the chart. Consequently, nobody born in the twentieth century is able to have this arrow, but it will occur again shortly.

People with this arrow lack motivation, are disorganized in their thinking, and fail to make plans. Because of this, they seldom achieve much until they learn self-discipline and set some worthwhile goals for themselves. Once they do this, they can then become pioneers and innovators. Their lateral thinking skills, original ideas, and dedication can open the doorways to new advances.

	6	
222	5	
11	4	

Figure 4O.
**Sir Isaac Newton
(December 25, 1642).**

Sir Isaac Newton (born December 25, 1642) is an example of someone with the arrow of hesitation in his chart (Figure 4O).

By combining the interpretations of the arrows with the meanings of the numbers, we can start to give character readings for our relatives and friends. Two sample readings are included in the next chapter.

5

Character Analysis

We now know enough to give a pen-portrait for any date of birth. Let's use a man born on May 29, 1917, as an example (Figure 5A).

		99
2	5	
11		7

Figure 5A.
Chart for a man born May 29, 1917.

He has a life path number of 7. This means that his purpose in this lifetime is to gain knowledge and wisdom and to grow spiritually. He will need to spend time in quiet contemplation. He will have a slightly different way of looking at the world, which will give him access to unique solutions.

His day number is a 29, which reduces to create an 11 master number. This gives him access to a wide variety of ideas and the potential to achieve greatness.

This chart contains the arrow of determination, so we know he will be persistent and determined in achieving his life's goals.

This man has two 9s in the Mental Plane. He will be idealistic and a deep thinker. Because he is naturally bright, he will need to ensure that he does not look down on people who are less intelligent.

The single 5 gives him emotional balance, compassion, and considerable strength of character. The single 2 in the same plane makes him naturally intuitive, but easily hurt. This number also makes him a good judge of character. He would have a natural talent at understanding the needs of others.

The single 7 in the Practical Plane shows that he has to learn through a loss or sacrifice of some sort.

Next, the two 1s make it easy for him to express himself. They also give him a balanced outlook and the ability to see both sides of a situation.

Finally, this man is missing four numbers in his chart: 3, 4, 6, and 8. Therefore, he needs to learn to express himself, be loyal, work to a set routine, be responsible with home and family, and use money wisely.

This man was President John F. Kennedy.

Here is another example. This is a chart of a woman born on November 19, 1917 (Figure 5B).

Figure 5B.
Chart for a woman born November 19, 1917.

		99
11 *111*		7

Her life path number is 3. She needs to express herself in some way in this lifetime. This could be singing, writing, talking, or some other form of communication.

Her day number of 19 reduces to a 1. This lady will always see herself as an individual. She will be responsible, ambitious, and also somewhat idealistic.

The first thing we notice in her chart are the two arrows of weakness. The arrow of emotional sensitivity shows that she is extremely sensitive. Despite her 3 life path, she was probably shy as a child and is easily hurt emotionally during her lifetime.

The arrow of frustrations shows that she often expects more of others than they want or are able to give. She has to develop willpower.

The two 9s on the Mental Plane show that she has a good brain, coupled with a great deal of idealism. Being naturally bright, she, like President Kennedy, has to learn to be tolerant of people who are not as intelligent as she is.

The single 7 shows that she has to learn through a loss, setback, or sacrifice.

She has a large number of missing numbers in her chart. All of these, except for the 3, are covered by the arrows of frustration and emotional sensitivity. The missing 3 shows that she has to learn loyalty, develop healthy self-esteem, and not sell herself short.

The most interesting part of this chart, though, are the five 1s. This lady finds it incredibly hard to express what she really feels. She is frequently misunderstood and probably frequently feels isolated and lonely.

Yet this woman became leader of India in 1966. Her name was Indira Gandhi.

Mrs. Gandhi's chart is a perfect example of someone who overcame many of the obstacles and difficulties shown in her chart and made a mark on the world. She certainly experienced her share of losses and setbacks. She lost her husband, a son, and power. However, she rebounded every time.

It is interesting to note the number of world leaders, past and present, who had what would appear to be major defects in their charts. They provide excellent proof of the adage "It's not what you're given, it's what you do with it that's important." You might like to construct the charts of Ronald Reagan (February 6, 1911) and Margaret Thatcher (October 13, 1925) to see this for yourself.

You will also find people who have what appear to be wonderful charts who accomplish little in their lives. This could relate to the fact that if it is given easily, it is not always utilized. Certainly, we all appreciate things more if we have had to make a considerable effort to achieve them.

I enjoy searching out interesting looking charts. For example, how would you interpret a chart for someone born February 2, 2000? It is almost 900 years since anyone had a chart consisting of just one number.

How would you interpret the chart of someone born April 20, 1889 (Figure 5C)? This is Adolf Hitler's date of birth. Obviously, many other people were also born on this same day. Yet most of them were probably very average people. What went wrong in the case of Adolf Hitler? He used his 5 life path number negatively, misusing freedom. Although a brilliant orator, he had just one 1 in his chart, making it very difficult to express his innermost feelings. The one 2

		9
2		88
1	4	

Figure 5C.
Adolf Hitler
(April 20, 1889).

made him sensitive and easily hurt. The single 4 shows he was prepared to work hard for what he wanted. The two 8s show attention to detail, but also made him rigid and stubborn. The arrow of skepticism showed that he did not accept much on trust and liked to have things demonstrated or proven.

All of these traits can be used positively, but the suspicious nature created by the arrow of skepticism and the single 2, combined with the rigidity and stubbornness of the 4 and 8s, along with the negative traits of his 5 life path, turned Adolf Hitler into a monster who tried to take over the world.

If you are interested in history, it is an interesting exercise to explore the characteristics of people from the past. For instance, how much of Mozart's musical genius came from the two 7s in his

date of birth? He was born January 27, 1756. They certainly provided originality, but how much was also supplied by the intuition of the single 2, the emotional balance of the 5, and the intellectual ability of the 6? Of course, Mozart was a mixture of all of these things, and it is the combination that is important, not the individual numbers in the chart.

When giving readings for others it is important to accentuate the positive. Naturally, we all have both positive and negative traits in our characters. However, nothing is gained by concentrating on the negative traits. Obviously, when giving a reading, I would mention areas the person should work on improving, but I would also talk about the person's positive characteristics. Consequently, both positive and negative traits would be mentioned, but by far the greatest emphasis would be on the positive side. After all, my purpose is to send my clients away feeling that they can overcome their obstacles and achieve their goals.

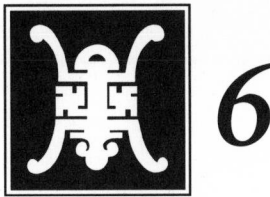 *6*

Exploring the Future

We can now explore the future trends of a person's life by looking at personal years and the pyramids (sometimes known as pinnacles). These show the various influences surrounding a person at any given time.

Personal Years and the Epicycle

According to numerology, we live our lives in nine-year cycles. This is known as the Epicycle. Each year contains a different energy, and if we work with the energy, or tone, of the year we will progress smoothly and quickly. Conversely, if we fight the tone of the year, we will struggle all year long.

It is a simple matter to determine what personal year you are in. You simply create a sum, just as we did to determine the life path number, but instead of using the year of birth, we use the current year.

For example, in chapter 1 we used as our example a young man born on July 12, 1973. In 1997 he experienced a 9 personal year. This is because:

$$
\begin{array}{rl}
7 & \text{(month)} \\
12 & \text{(day)} \\
+ \ \underline{1997} & \text{(year)} \\
2016 &
\end{array}
$$

and $2 + 0 + 1 + 6 = 9$

As we lead our lives in nine-year cycles, the following year he will experience a 1 personal year again:

$$7 \quad \text{(month)}$$
$$12 \quad \text{(day)}$$
$$+ \underline{1998} \quad \text{(year)}$$
$$2017$$

$$2 + 0 + 1 + 7 = 10$$

and $1 + 0 = 1$

Here is another example, this time a lady born on August 25, 1962. In 1999 she will experience a 7 personal year.

$$8 \quad \text{(month)}$$
$$25 \quad \text{(day)}$$
$$+ \underline{1999} \quad \text{(year)}$$
$$2032$$

and $2 + 0 + 3 + 2 = 7$

If the sum is 11 or 22, reduce it further to 2 or 4. Personal years that reduce down to an 11 or 22 have more power and potential than personal years that do not reduce in the same way.

Once we know the personal year someone is in we also know the energies that are surrounding this person at the time, and can interpret them to understand what is going on in his or her life.

1 Personal Year

Keywords:

New starts
Enthusiasm
Energy

This is a year of new starts. You will have more enthusiasm and energy this year than you will have had for many years. Anything you start now is likely to remain important for a long time. You may start several new activities this year, but will have enough enthusiasm and energy to sustain them all.

2 Personal Year

Keywords:

Patient waiting

This is a slower, gentler year. In many ways it is a consolidation year. In a 1 personal year you can go shooting off in all directions. The 2 personal year brings everything back to more manageable proportions. The keywords for this year are "patient waiting." These two words do not fit together very well; it is often hard to patiently wait. You will be tempted to push in an attempt to make things happen. This works in a 1 personal year, but is a waste of time and energy in a 2 year. This is a year to exercise patience, to

trust your intuition, and to enjoy pleasant times with people you love. By doing this, at the end of the year you will find yourself pretty much where you want to be.

3 Personal Year

This is a pleasant, happy, carefree year. Ideally, you will be able to have the whole year off to play and enjoy life. Unfortunately, this is unlikely to be the case, so you will have to work hard, even though most of your thoughts will be on pleasant, fun activities. This is a good year to spend time with old friends, to make new friends, to take up new hobbies and interests, or to pay more attention to existing interests. You may have several short-lived interests come and go during the year.

Keywords:

Pleasant

Happy

Carefree

4 Personal Year

After a year of fun, you will be wanting to get involved in something more serious. A 4 personal year is a year of hard work. If you set a specific goal for yourself at the start of the year, you will find that you will have achieved it by the end of the year. You will probably still be pleased that the year is over, but will also have something to show for it. If you have no specific goal in mind, you will find the tone of year to be serious, heavy, and restricting. This is why most people consider the 4 personal year to be the most difficult year of the Epicycle.

Keywords:

Hard work

Goals achieved

5 Personal Year

This is a year of change and variety. After the seriousness of the 4 personal year you will be ready to do something exciting and different. This is the perfect year to change anything in your life that you are not happy with—be it career, home, partner, or even country. You have to be prepared to expect the unexpected. Consequently, you are likely to find yourself doing things that you never thought possible. If you have always wanted to go bungee jumping, but never quite got around to it, this is the year to do it!

Keywords:

Change

Variety

Expect the unexpected

6 Personal Year

This is the year for home and family. It is the perfect year to get married (or divorced). This is because the numbers simply "are." They are neither good nor bad. Consequently, if a relationship is going really well, this is a wonderful year to make it permanent.

Keywords:

Home and family

Conversely, if a relationship is foundering, this is the best year for the couple to part. Because it is also a year of family, it is an excellent year to have a baby and to spend time with loved ones. It is also a year when you will be involved in helping others in some way and deriving great pleasure from it. It is a good year for moving or for making alterations to your existing home. You may redecorate or beautify your house and garden in some way. Most of your thoughts and energies will be directed toward your home and the people you love.

7 Personal Year

Keywords:

Learning
Wisdom
Inner development

A 7 personal year is a quieter, gentler year. You will want more time than usual by yourself to think about things, to learn, or to meditate. Many people carry on with their education in some sort of way during a 7 personal year. Even if this is not formal study, you will be learning and growing in knowledge and wisdom this year. It is an excellent year to make plans and to analyze things. Many people become interested in spiritual or philosophical pursuits in a 7 year. This year is a sabbatical year in many ways. You will be less interested in striving after material possessions and more interested in developing inwardly.

8 Personal Year

Keywords:

Money
Rewards

This is the money year. It is a year of hard work, but with a financial payoff. In this year you reap the rewards for all the hard work you have done over the last decade. If you have done little, you will receive little. Money matters will tend to go your way in an 8 personal year. If you buy something, you will buy it at a good price. If you sell something, you will receive a good price for it. Make sure to take a little bit of time off during the year to relax and unwind. Many people are inclined to overwork during an 8 year and experience health problems as a result.

9 Personal Year

Keywords:

Reevaluation
Letting go
Looking ahead

This is the final year of the nine-year Epicycle. It is a reevaluation year. You will be looking back over the last nine years and letting go of things that have outworn their use. It is never easy to let go of things, so this may be a painful and difficult task. You will also be looking ahead, figuring out where to go from here. During the year you will be given a number of false leads, but in the last three months of this year it will become much clearer as to where you want to go in the next nine years.

Personal Months

We can also determine our personal months once we know our personal year. All we do is add the number of the month to the personal year and bring it down to a single digit.

For example, someone who is currently in a 3 personal year would be in a 5 personal month in February (3 + 2 = 5). In November, he or she would also be in a 5 personal month (3 + 11 = 14, and 1 + 4 = 5). Naturally, as there are twelve months every year, but only nine personal months, three personal months are repeated. The personal month numbers for January, February, and March are repeated in October, November, and December.

The interpretations for the personal months are the same as for the personal years, but have much less power because they last for just one month. They are also modified by the personal year number. For instance, if someone was in a 5 personal year, he or she would be experiencing change and variety. However, during that year this person would experience a 7 personal month in both February and November. A 7 personal month is a quiet, thinking, contemplative time. This may appear to be at odds with the tone of the year, but in fact, the time spent alone thinking or meditating may lead to changes and new directions.

Personal Days

It is even possible to determine personal days by adding the day of the month to the personal month number. For example, on March 24, someone in a 7 personal month would be in a 4 personal day (2 + 4 (day) + 7 (personal month) = 13, and 1 + 3 = 4.

Obviously, the strength of a personal day is miniscule compared to the strength of the personal year, but knowledge of it can be useful. For instance, if you were planning to sign a contract or agreement involving a large amount of money, it might be a good idea to do it on an 8 personal day.

Years ago I met a numerologist in India who advised people on their personal hours! He would suggest that someone visit the dentist at 3:00 P.M. and buy a pair of shoes at 11:00 A.M. Although personal hours can be worked out easily by adding the hour to the personal day number, I think this is taking the subject too far.

Pyramids

In addition to the nine-year Epicycle and personal months and days, we can also look at the trends of people's entire lives by looking at their pyramids.

We start by drawing a diagram similar to Figure 6A. At the base of the two inner pyramids in this diagram we insert the person's date of birth. However, before doing this, we reduce each of the digits of the person's day, month, and year of birth to a single number (unless, of course, it reduces down to an 11 or 22).

Figure 6A.

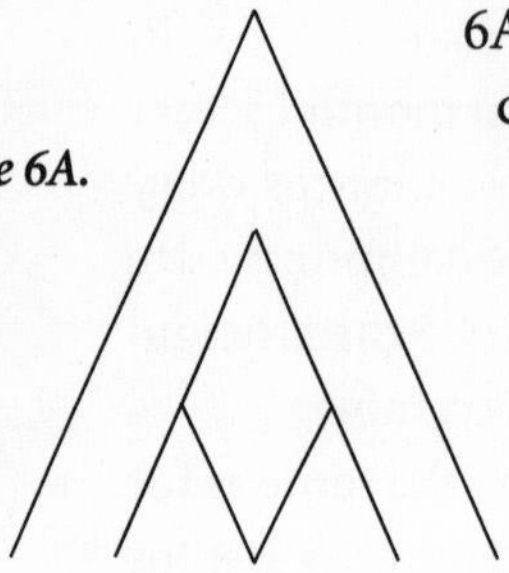

Our example of someone born on July 12, 1973, is shown in Figure 6B. First, we place his month of birth below the left-hand side of the inner pyramid. We place his day of birth (12, which reduces to a 3) below the right-hand side of the same pyramid. Finally, we place his year of birth (1973, which reduces to a 2) below the right-hand side of the second inner pyramid.

Figure 6B.

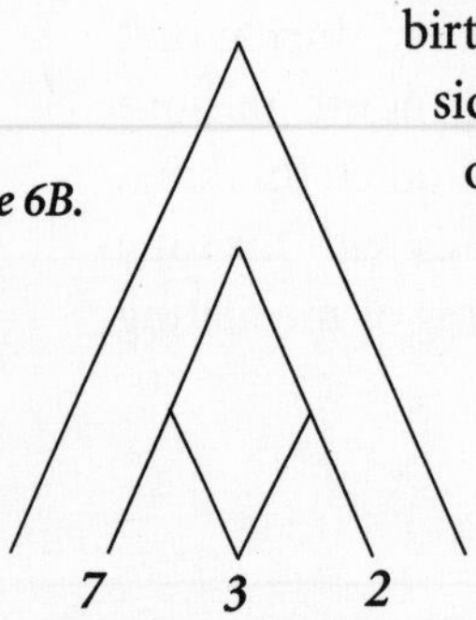

7   3   2

We then work out the other numbers required by a process of addition. We add the person's month and day of birth together and place that at the top of the left-hand inner pyramid. In our example, we add 7 (month) to 3 (day), which gives us 10, and, as you know, 1 + 0 = 1. We place the number 1 at the top of this pyramid. (Naturally, if the addition resulted in a master number we would not reduce it down to a 2 or a 4.)

We do the same with the other pyramid, adding the person's day and year together. In our example we add 3 and 2 together, and place the answer—5—at the top of the second pyramid.

There is another pyramid resting on top of the bottom two. We add the two numbers at the top of the bottom pyramids and place the answer, reduced to a single digit, at the top of this pyramid. In our example, we add up 1 and 5 and place the number 6 at the top.

Figure 6C.

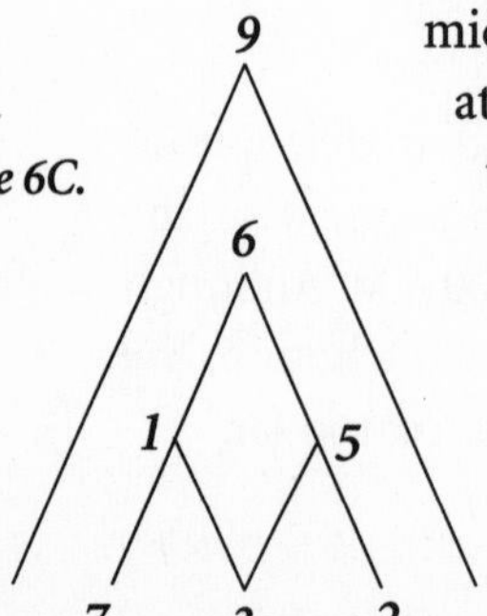

9

6

1   5

7   3   2

Finally, we add the month and year numbers together, and place the answer at the top of the outermost pyramid. In our example, we add 7 (month) and 2 (year), which gives us 9. This number is placed at the very top. Our final result should look like Figure 6C.

We now have to add time to our chart to make it useable. The first important year is placed at the top of the first pyramid. This shows the age at which the person reaches maturity, numerologically speaking. We determine what age this will be by subtracting the person's life path number from 36. In this instance, both 11 and 22 are reduced to a 2 and a 4 to determine this age. This is the only time in this system of numerology that master numbers get reduced. Consequently, someone with an 11 life path reaches maturity at the age of 34, not 25. Someone with a 22 life path reaches maturity at 32, and not 14.

To return to our example, this person has a life path number of 3. By subtracting 3 from 36, we get 33. This age is placed next to the 1 that is already at the top of the first pyramid.

As we lead our lives in nine-year cycles, the next important age is nine years after the person reaches maturity numerologically. In our example, this will be at the age of 42. This is placed alongside the number 5 at the top of the second pyramid.

The number 51 (42 + 9 years) is placed at the top of the next pyramid, beside the number 6 that is already there.

The number 60 is placed at the very top of the chart, next to, or above, the 9.

We now return to the bottom of the chart and put the number 69 (51 + 9 years) beside the number 7 (day of birth). In the same way, 78 is placed next to the 3 (month) and 87 is placed next to the 2 (year) (Figure 6D).

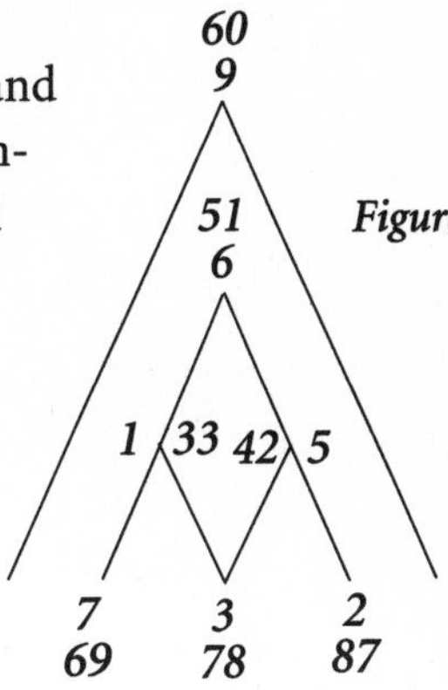

If we want to carry on even further we mentally place 96 (87 + 9 years) beside the age at which he reached maturity (33) and go around the entire chart again.

Figure 6D.

It is important to realize that these numbers all mark periods of time. They have nothing whatsoever to do with how long the person will live. However, they do show what the person is working towards during each cycle.

All of the ages indicated on the chart are important years in terms of the person's life. They always correspond to either a 9 or a 1 personal year. In fact, almost everyone experiences part of both of these years at the age indicated on the chart. The only exceptions are people who were born at the very start or end of the year.

The transition between one pyramid and the next usually happens very quickly. A few months before one cycle ends, the person begins to experience a taste of the next cycle of experience. The

influence of the ending pyramid is seldom felt more than a month after it ends. Consequently, the changes can be rather abrupt at times, particularly if the two numbers are completely different from each other.

The First Cycle

This cycle is from birth up to the time the person reaches maturity, numerologically speaking. This age is anywhere between twenty-seven and thirty-five. It is probably impossible for an eighteen- or twenty-year-old to realize that they do not reach maturity for another x number of years, as they usually consider themselves to be highly mature already. However, in numerology it is assumed that the person is still growing and learning and is not properly considered adult until they reach the first pyramid.

From birth up to this age, the person is heading toward, and learning all about, the number that is at the first pyramid. In our example, this young man is heading toward a 1. This is the number of independence and attainment. He is likely to start out in life by being dependent, and will gradually become more and more independent. By the time he reaches the age of thirty-three, he will be able to stand firmly on his own two feet. He is also likely to have attained something worthwhile.

The Second Cycle

This is the first of the nine-year-cycle pyramids. The first pyramid (from birth to maturity) is often a limiting one. In the second cycle the person is able to be more productive. During this period he or she is learning the qualities of the number that is alongside the next important age. In our example, our young man is heading toward a 5. This means he will experience change and variety in these years. This could indicate a change of career and/or location in this period. He will probably do some overseas travel.

The Third Cycle

This is the first of the two maturity cycles. It is usually more productive and successful than the second cycle. At this stage the person is in his or her middle years and should have some idea of where he or she is going. This cycle begins somewhere between the ages of thirty-six and forty-four. The old saying "Life begins at 40" is generally proven in this cycle. It is amazing the number of people who finally work out what they want to do with their

lives by the end of the second cycle, and actually do it in the third and later cycles.

The Fourth Cycle

This cycle usually leads up to the retirement years. The feelings people experience in this cycle depend on what they achieved in the previous two cycles. Because their children have grown up and left home, people in this age group are able to rediscover each other. They are generally better off financially at this stage than ever before. They have reached the peak as far as their career is concerned, and they should be making plans for what they want to do in their retirement years.

The Fifth, Sixth, and Seventh Cycles

For most people these are the retirement years. Hopefully, they have prepared for their retirement throughout their working lives and are able to enjoy productive and happy retirements. These are often known as the years of fulfillment, as people in these years are able to forget the strains and struggles to achieve, and are able to spend time in quieter, more pleasant activities. They have a wealth of wisdom to offer the younger generations and, as long as they remain fit and active, are able to thoroughly enjoy these final years.

It is possible that numbers do not change every nine years. If a number is repeated, it means the lesson is not fully learned in just one cycle, and the person has to repeat that cycle. Usually, the lesson is learned in the final cycle where the number appears. (Just for interest, construct the pyramids for someone born September 9, 1971. This person has nothing but 9s all the way through his or her life. The need to be a humanitarian and help others less fortunate is obviously an extremely difficult lesson for this person to learn.)

For most people the pyramid number changes every nine years. This means that the lesson is learned during the nine-year period. However, the same number may appear again in a later pyramid. This means that although the lesson was learned in the nine years where the number first appeared, the knowledge was gradually forgotten and the lesson needs to be learned again.

Awareness of your personal years, personal months, personal days, and the pyramids can be extremely useful in making plans for the future and for undertaking different tasks at the right times. Obviously, it is much easier and far less stressful to work with our numbers than to fight against them.

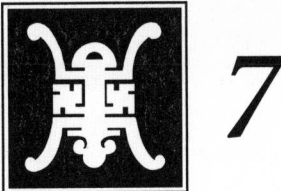

7

The Inclusion

We can give a good personality reading by placing the date of birth inside our chart. We can expand on this reading considerably by converting the letters of our names into numbers and placing these into a chart. This is done very easily using the following:

1	2	3	4	5	6	7	8	9
A	B	C	D	E	F	G	H	I
J	K	L	M	N	O	P	Q	R
S	T	U	V	W	X	Y	Z	

As an example, let's use the name Arthur Conan Doyle, the spiritualist and celebrated author of the Sherlock Holmes mysteries. We place a 1 under the letter A, as A is in the 1 column in the chart. R has a 9 placed underneath it. The T a 2, and so on right through the name. Here is the finished result:

ARTHUR CONAN DOYLE
1928 39 36515 46735

Once we have done this, we determine the quantity of each number. Sir Arthur Conan Doyle has:

Number of 1s: 2	Number of 4s: 1	Number of 7s: 1
Number of 2s: 1	Number of 5s: 3	Number of 8s: 1
Number of 3s: 3	Number of 6s: 2	Number of 9s: 2

These numbers can then be placed in the chart in the usual way.

In the 1 box, we place two 1s, as Sir Arthur had two 1s in his name. In the 2 box, we insert the number 2, as he had just one 2 in his name. Box 3 is given three 3s, and so on, until all the boxes have been filled. The finished result, once all the squares have been filled in, is shown in Figure 7A.

333	66	99
2	555	8
11	4	7

Figure 7A.
Sir Arthur Conan Doyle.

Let's do another example before we start interpreting the chart. Our second example is an imaginary person called Olive Lee Brown.

OLIVE LEE BROWN
6 3945 355 29 6 5 5

Number of 1s: 0   Number of 4s: 1   Number of 7s: 0
Number of 2s: 1   Number of 5s: 5   Number of 8s: 0
Number of 3s: 2   Number of 6s: 2   Number of 9s: 2

33	66	99
2	555 55	
	4	

Figure 7B.
Olive Lee Brown.

Once we have filled in Olive's chart (Figure 7B) we find that she is missing three numbers—the 1, 7, and 8. I usually leave these boxes empty, but some numerologists like to insert a 0 (zero) in each one. Use whichever version you prefer.

Olive also has several 5s in her chart.

The Meanings of the Numbers

We can interpret the example charts using the following meanings.

Number 1

Number 1

~

Keywords:

Independence Ego

The absence of the number 1 in the chart shows a lack of confidence, drive, and motivation. People without 1s are inclined to be timid and afraid to speak what is on their minds.

A reasonable number of 1s is determined by looking at all the numbers in the chart. Arthur Conan Doyle had a reasonable number of 1s in his chart (see Figure 7A, above), as the other squares all contained one, two, or three of their respective numbers. It is impossible to give a specific figure for a reasonable number, as this is determined by the length of the name. However, two, three, or four 1s would usually be regarded as ample.

People with a reasonable number of 1s have confidence, ambition, pride, and originality. They are prepared to stand on their own two feet and go after whatever it is they want.

People with too many 1s in their chart (at the expense of the other numbers) are overly dominant and try to force their desires on others. They are inclined to be brutish, overbearing, and inconsiderate.

Number 2

The absence of the number 2 in the chart shows a lack of people skills, making it hard to associate and get on well with others. People without any 2s are overly sensitive and blame their mistakes on others.

People with a reasonable number of 2s get along well with others. They can very quickly make other people feel at ease. They are tactful, diplomatic, and intuitive.

People with too many 2s are usually overly emotional and find it hard to stand up for themselves.

Number 2

~

Keywords:

Tact
Diplomacy

Number 3

People lacking the number 3 in their charts are self-centered, withdrawn, and introspective. Their lives lack fun and spontaneity.

People with a reasonable number of 3s in their chart are friendly, outgoing, and sociable. They find it easy to get along with others. They appreciate nice things and often possess a creative talent of some sort.

People with too many 3s are inclined to be boastful, egotistical, and have many great ideas that are never put into practice.

Number 3

~

Keywords:

Self-expression
Communication

Number 4

People without the number 4 in their charts tend to avoid hard work, particularly manual labor.

People with a reasonable number of 4s are prepared to work for what they want. They do not mind working hard and actually enjoy challenges. They are usually conscientious and good with the details.

People with too many 4s in their chart tend to get themselves overloaded with work. They can become so immersed in the details that they completely forget the overall picture.

Number 4

~

Keywords:

Limitations
Restrictions
Hard work

Number 5

Number 5

~

Keywords:

Change
Freedom
Variety

People without the number 5 in their charts find it hard to accept change. They want everything to stay the way it always was. They lead limited, restricted lives.

People with a reasonable number of 5s use their time wisely. They know when to work and when to take time off to play. They enjoy change and variety in their lives.

People with too many 5s in their chart do not know how to use freedom wisely and tend to overindulge. They frequently hurt the people who love them by abusing alcohol, drugs, or sex.

Number 6

Number 6

~

Keywords:

Home
Responsibility
Humanitarianism

People lacking the number 6 in their charts find it hard to handle responsibility. They have unrealistic desires for perfection in their home and family life.

People with a reasonable number of 6s in their chart are able to handle responsibility and adjust to changing situations in their home and family life. They live in the real world and keep their feet on the ground.

People with too many 6s in their chart are overly concerned with home and family matters. They fuss and worry unnecessarily about all the members of the family. They often end up being taken for granted and used by others.

Number 7

Number 7

~

Keywords:

Analysis
Wisdom
Spirituality

People lacking the number 7 in their charts pay no attention to philosophical or spiritual truths. They are inclined to be impatient, impulsive, and have no time for people developing along more spiritual lines. However, as they get older they usually become searchers for some sort of faith or philosophy that they can accept. An absence of the number 7 is very common.

People with a reasonable number of 7s in their chart are understanding, compassionate, and have beliefs that they live by. They have good minds and are interested in learning.

People with too many 7s in their chart are hard to find. The more 7s in the chart, the more spiritually aware the person is.

Number 8

People without the number 8 in their charts are careless with money and possessions. At the same time, they frequently have a strong desire for money, which is constantly frustrated.

People with a reasonable number of 8s in their chart are interested in progressing financially, but they keep this in perspective. They move ahead slowly, but steadily, gradually becoming more and more financially secure.

People with too many 8s in their chart are obsessed with money, power, and possessions. They will do anything they can to obtain these things, and this is frequently done at the expense of relationships.

Number 8

~

Keywords:
Materialism
Money
Power

Number 9

It is rare to find people without the number 9 in their charts. These people have not learned how to be compassionate and caring. Usually, the lesson is learned during this incarnation.

People with a reasonable number of 9s in their chart are caring people who understand, support, and assist others.

People with too many 9s are determined people who believe that they know the only correct way of doing things. Therefore, they seldom listen to others and have to learn the hard way. Often, they become very involved in trying to solve the problems of the world.

Number 9

~

Keywords:
Humanitarianism

Evaluating the Chart

Now we can look at the two charts we drew up at the start of this chapter. Sir Arthur Conan Doyle has an extremely well-balanced chart. He has no missing numbers. All the boxes are filled with one, two, or three numbers. However, there is an emphasis on the Mental Plane (the top row), because he has seven numbers there, compared to five on the Emotional Plane and four on the Practical Plane. Obviously, he was more suited to intellectual work than he was to manual labor.

He also has seven numbers on the arrow of determination. This shows that he was motivated and persistent. When he knew what he wanted, he would persevere until he got there.

Sir Arthur also had seven numbers on the arrow of spirituality. His interest in spiritualism is well known, and there is no doubt that his faith was strong and sincere.

With a strong, well-balanced chart showing so much potential, it is not surprising that Sir Arthur achieved lasting fame for his creativity.

Now, let's look at Olive's chart. I deliberately chose her as her chart is in striking contrast to Conan Doyle's well-balanced one.

Olive is missing three numbers: 1, 7, and 8. She is lacking in confidence and drive, and probably leans heavily on others for support (lack of 1s). She has no faith or interest in philosophy (lack of 7s). As she progresses through life she is likely to become more interested in finding a personal philosophy or faith. She is also careless with money and finances, but at the same time wants more money (lack of 8s).

She has too many 5s at the expense of the other numbers. (This is a common occurrence.) She could hurt others by misusing her freedom, and could easily become over-attached to sex, drugs, or alcohol.

She has six numbers on both the Mental and Emotional Planes, but only one on the Practical Plane. She is not likely to be good with her hands, but will have a good brain. The arrow of the intellect is perfectly balanced (with two numbers in each position). She also has seven numbers on the 1-5-9 diagonal, but they do not form an arrow of determination, as the diagonal is lacking any numbers in the 1 position.

So far we have dwelt on poor Olive's failings. We must also take into account the reasonable numbers of 2, 3, 6, and 9 in her chart. She is likely to cooperate and be happiest at home, surrounded by loved ones (number 2). The presence of this 2 also makes her diplomatic, tactful, and intuitive. She can express herself well when she chooses to (number 3). She can accept home and family responsibility (number 6), and she cares for humanity in general (number 9).

Olive is an imaginary person. If I were doing a reading for her, I would be as encouraging as possible and try to help build up her self-esteem and confidence. I would encourage her to become involved in a career that used her excellent brain, but was not directly involved with money or finance. If she were single, she would probably still be living at home with her parents. I would encourage her to go out and socialize to give her as much opportunity as possible to meet potential partners. This is because she would be happier married rather than on her own (numbers 2 and 6). She would definitely express herself best inside a close relationship, too. Finally, she is more likely to gain more confidence and self-esteem inside a close relationship than on her own.

Name Changes

If you are considering changing your name for any reason, it is a good idea to complete the Inclusion for both the old and the new names to see what you "gain" and what you "lose."

You need to remember that in numerology we choose our own names for the experiences we need in this lifetime. Consequently, the chart constructed from the original name at birth always remains, no matter how many times the name is changed. However, the new chart, from the new name, acts as an "over vibration" and can make the person's life easier or harder, depending on what numbers have been gained or lost.

Let's assume that Olive Lee Brown marries Jonathan Hayton and changes her name. Her married name now fills up all the missing numbers in her chart.

OLIVE LEE HAYTON
6 3945 355 8 17205

Number of 1s: 1	Number of 4s: 1	Number of 7s: 1
Number of 2s: 1	Number of 5s: 4	Number of 8s: 1
Number of 3s: 2	Number of 6s: 1	Number of 9s: 1

Obviously, this new name will make her life easier as she has at least one number in every position. However, as her birth name remains the most important one, she must not forget that she still needs to learn the lessons of 1, 7, and 8. These lessons will be much easier to learn with her new name.

Of course, she might have married Jason O'Neil. In this case, her new name will create more empty spaces than her original name did.

OLIVE LEE O'NEIL
6 3945 355 6 5 593

Number of 1s: 0	Number of 4s: 1	Number of 7s: 0
Number of 2s: 0	Number of 5s: 5	Number of 8s: 0
Number of 3s: 3	Number of 6s: 2	Number of 9s: 2

Her maiden name was missing the numbers 1, 7, and 8. Her new name is missing the numbers 1, 2, 7, and 8. This new name is likely to make her life a little bit harder, because she will still be grappling with the lessons of 1, 7, and 8, and will also have a new lesson created by the missing number 2. However, this new lesson

will be minor compared to the others, and will apply only as long as she uses the name.

Naturally, we can change our names for a variety of reasons. Marriage is the most common, but we can also change our names to receive the energies we need at a given time. If you wish to do this, experiment with a number of names and see which one "feels" right for you. Then work out the Inclusion and see if the new name is likely to make your life easier or harder.

Remember that no matter how many times we change our names, the name we are given at birth remains constant, and provides the lessons we need to learn in this lifetime.

The Inclusion rewards serious study as it provides such great insight into people's character and motivations. By knowing other people's strengths and weaknesses you are in an excellent position to help and guide them. Always be kind and gentle when helping other people analyze their charts. No matter what you discover in other people's Inclusionss, you can never know exactly how other people feel, because you can never be them.

8

Compatibility

Numerology provides a wonderful way of determining personality and predicting the trends for the future. This method is also particularly useful for determining compatibility.

I believe that almost any relationship can be made to work providing there is love and goodwill on both sides. However, some relationships appear to work incredibly smoothly with little apparent effort, while others seem to require constant work. Naturally, all relationships need work, but some need a great deal more than others, and unfortunately, most of the hard work is usually done by just one of the partners. We can use numerology to help avoid mistakes and choose the right partner.

Many years ago, a friend of mine was teaching a numerology class. He had just gone through a painful divorce and was getting his life back into order again. While talking about compatibility, he asked one of the students for her date of birth. As he wrote it on the board he said, "My goodness, you'd be perfect for me!" He then proceeded to draw his chart alongside hers and told the class how this particular partnership would work. After the class he took the lady for a cup of coffee and twelve months later they got married! My friend died a couple of years ago, but the final twelve years of his life were by far his happiest because he finally found the right partner. Even though he was a professional numerologist, he had not used numerology to assess his two previous relationships until it

was too late. In the numerology class, he assessed his and his future wife's compatibility before he even knew her name!

The Chinese system of determining compatibility is extremely easy to do. There are three steps:

1. We look to see if the charts constructed from each person's date of birth are similar, with each partner giving the other a number that he or she does not already have.

2. We look at the life path numbers to see how compatible they are.

3. We look at the personal years to see if the the two people are in step with each other as they go through life.

Ideally, we want both people to have similar charts, but each should contain a number that the other does not have. In Figures 8A and 8B, we have a good example of this. Bill, the husband, was born July 21, 1948, and his wife Alice was born two years later on April 27, 1950. They both have the numbers 1, 2, 4, 7, and 9 in their charts.

		9
2		8
11	4	7

Figure 8A.
Husband Bill
(July 21, 1948).

		9
2	5	
1	4	7

Figure 8B.
Wife Alice
(April 27, 1950).

For compatibility purposes we take no account of the number of times an individual number appears. Bill, in this example, has two 1s and Alice has one. Naturally, this will affect how they communicate with each other, but it is not taken into account in this quick assessment.

The important factor here is that the husband is able to give the wife 8 energy that she does not have in her chart, and she is able to give him the 5 energy he is lacking. Consequently, they are each able to offer something that the other person does not already have. This helps to keep the relationship vibrant and exciting.

We totally ignore the meanings of these numbers, but simply check to see that each is giving one number to the other. It does not matter what number is given to the other, just as long as each is providing a different number.

Once we have done this, we then look at Figure 8C, which shows the compatibility ratings of the life path numbers. In this example, Bill has a 5 life path and Alice, a 1. On the chart, this combination rates an A. This is the best possible combination, and bodes well for the future happiness of this couple.

Life Path	1	2	3	4	5	6	7	8	9	11	22
1	B	C	D	A	A	C	A	B	D	D	C
2	C	B	B	A	C	A	B	D	B	B	A
3	D	B	A	C	C	A	C	A	A	C	B
4	A	A	C	B	D	B	A	A	D	C	B
5	A	C	C	C	B	C	C	D	B	B	C
6	C	A	A	B	C	A	C	C	A	B	D
7	A	B	C	A	C	C	B	D	C	B	A
8	B	D	C	A	D	C	D	C	C	B	A
9	D	B	A	C	B	A	B	C	A	B	B
11	D	B	C	C	B	B	B	B	B	B	A
22	C	A	B	B	C	D	A	A	B	A	B

Figure 8C.

Life path compatibilities.

"A" indicates the most compatible life paths; "D" indicates the least compatible life paths.

In this compatibility chart of life path numbers, A is regarded as being the most favorable and D as the most difficult. However, do not despair if your particular relationship is rated as D. This is only one of the factors that are considered in determining compatibility. Also remember what I said at the start of the chapter about love and goodwill on both sides.

The final step is to look at the personal years. In 1998, Bill will be in a 1 personal year. He will be starting on a whole new cycle of experience, and will be making new starts with plenty of enthusiasm and energy. Alice will be entering a 4 personal year in 1998. She will be wanting to work hard and achieve a worthwhile goal. This certainly sounds highly compatible. He will provide the ideas and the enthusiasm, and she will be able to provide much of the hard work.

However, look at the same couple three years later, in 2001. Bill will be entering a 4 personal year and will be wanting to work hard to achieve something worthwhile. Alice will be entering a 7 personal year and will want time on her own to think about things and to grow in knowledge and wisdom. Is this compatible? Actually, yes, because they have good, compatible charts and compatible life path numbers. However, they will have to make adjustments for each other in the year 2001. He will have to be prepared to let her have sufficient time on her own, and she will have to let him have sufficient time to tackle the hard work he wants to do. This will probably be easier for Alice than for Bill, as he is likely to want reassurance and support at times during the year.

Most couples are in step some years and out of step other years. The best combination is when both partners have the same personal years. This means that if one of them wants to take an overseas trip (probably in a 5 personal year) the other will be just as enthusiastic.

The most difficult combination occurs when the couple is one year apart in their personal years. When one of them is in a 4 personal year and wanting to work hard to achieve a goal, the other will be in a 3 year and will want to have fun and play. The following year, the first person will want to do something exciting and different but the partner will now be in a 4 year and will want to work hard.

It is also important to realize that we all put out different energies in different personal years. In a 2 or 6 personal year we are likely to be sending out more romantic signals than we do in other years. This can make us more attractive to others, who may not have been interested in us if we had been in another personal year.

Let's look at another combination, that of George Burns, born January 20, 1896 (Figure 8D), and Gracie Allen, born July 26, 1902 (Figure 8E). George provided Gracie with an 8, and she gave him a 7. They each gave equally to the relationship. Their life path numbers were the same—a 9. This is an excellent combination. Both were prepared to give of themselves.

	6	9
2		8
11		

Figure 8D.
George Burns
(January 20, 1896).

	6	9
22		
1		7

Figure 8E.
Gracie Allen
(July 26, 1902).

Finally, their personal years were three steps apart. When George was in a 2 personal year, Gracie was in a 5 personal year. This means that in some years they were out of step, but in other years harmonized wonderfully. The year they were married, 1926, was a perfect year for them to get married: she was in a 6 personal year and he was in a 3 year. It is not surprising that this became one of the most successful and enduring of all show business partnerships.

Difficult Combinations

There are many possible combinations that can prove difficult. The most obvious is if the two people have the same numbers in their chart. The couple shown in Figures 8F and 8G is an example of this. Jared was born June 28, 1955. Rachel, his wife, was born August 5, 1962. From a compatibility point of view, their charts are identical. (Jared's chart contains one more 5 than Rachel's, but this is ignored in compatibility analysis.)

	6	9
2	55	8
1		

Figure 8F.
Jared
(June 28, 1955).

This means that they would have a great deal in common initially, but the relationship would gradually become stale and boring. This is why it is important for each partner to offer something (a number) that the other does not already have.

	6	9
2	5	8
1		

Figure 8G.
Rachel
(August 5, 1962).

Incidentally, people with virtually identical charts make wonderful platonic friends. After all, "Birds of a feather flock together." We like our friends to be like us, and someone with the same numbers (maybe in different quantities) is likely to make a very good friend.

Now let's look at a lopsided relationship. Chuck was born June 5, 1960. Mary was born May 28, 1967. When we look at their charts (Figures 8H and 8I) we see that Mary is not gaining any numbers from Chuck that she does not already have. However, he is gaining three numbers (2, 7, and 8) from her. Chuck is getting the benefit of these numbers, but is totally unable to reciprocate because he has no numbers to give back in return. In this relationship, Mary would gradually feel that she was giving much, much more than she was getting back in return. Consequently, this relationship is a lopsided one.

	66	9
	5	
1		

Figure 8H.
Chuck
(June 5, 1960).

It is interesting to note that many of these lopsided relationships work well. This occurs when one of the partners has a need to give of oneself. These people may moan and groan about the necessity of forever giving, but deep down they actually enjoy it.

	6	9
2	5	8
1		7

Figure 8I.
Mary
(May 28, 1967).

Chuck and Mary's relationship could well survive because of this. Mary has a life path number of 2, so will be much happier in a relationship than she would be on her own. Chuck has a 9 life path, which means he will be a caring, concerned person, though he is likely to put much of his time and energy into helping people in the community. He is likely to be somewhat detached at home. This will frustrate Mary, but she will probably learn to live with it.

Western Methods of Compatibility

It is possible to combine the Eastern and Western methods of numerology to gain even further insights into compatibility.

In the previous chapter we turned the letters of our name into numbers. Here, all the letters of the name are again turned into numbers, added up, and reduced down to a single digit (except, of course, in the case of master numbers) to create a new number known as the Expression. This number represents the person's natural abilities, in other words, what he or she is good at.

By adding up all the vowels in a person's name and bringing them down to a single digit we create a number known as the Soul Urge. This represents the person's motivation and what they love doing.

There is another number that can be created from the person's name. This is the Personality number, and it is created by adding up all the consonants in a person's name and reducing them down to a single digit. The characteristics of this number are the first things that strangers, meeting you for the first time, will notice.

The Personality number is not used in compatibility analysis, but the Expression and Soul Urge numbers are.

There are a few rules to keep in mind:

1. The full name that the person was given at birth is the one that is used. It does not matter if William Cecil Moriarty is known to his friends as Bill or Cec. For compatibility purposes we use his full name.

2. The letter *Y* is usually classified as being a vowel. If it acts as a vowel, as in *Yvonne*, or is unpronounced, as in *Kay*, it is classified as a vowel. However, if the letter *Y* is pronounced, as in *Yolande*, it is classified as a consonant.

3. Master numbers (11 and 22) are left as they are. They do not get reduced down to a single digit.

Let's use the name *Barbara Evelyn Sadgrove* as an example. We turn all the letters into numbers, using the chart in the previous chapter. We place the vowels above the name and the consonants below.

```
  1   1 1 5 5 7   1     6 5
BARBARA  EVELYN  SADGROVE
2 92 9    4 3 51  479 1
```

Notice that the *Y* in *Evelyn* was classified as a vowel, not as a consonant.

Once we have done this, we add up the numbers in each individual word in the name, and bring them down to a single digit (unless, of course, we find a master number along the way).

```
                  8           3
                ⏜          ⏜
      3    17 (1+7)    12 (1+2)
    ⏜    ⏜        ⏜
  1   1  1 5 5 7   1     6 5
BARBARA  EVELYN  SADGROVE
2 92 9    4 3 51  479 1
  ⏝      ⏝    ⏝
  22      12 (1+2) 25 (2+5)
             ⏝      ⏝
             3         7
```

If you look at the vowels first, you will see that the three 1s in the name *Barbara* total a 3. In *Evelyn*, the vowels totalled 17, and 1 + 7 = 8. The vowels in *Sadgrove* total 12 and 1 + 2 = 3.

We then do the same thing with the consonants. Notice that the consonants of the name *Barbara* total 22 and are not reduced down to a 4.

Now we can work out Barbara's Expression and Soul Urge numbers. Her Expression is the total of all the numbers in her name, so we add up both the vowels and the consonants:

3 + 8 + 3 (the vowels) + 22 + 3 + 7 (the consonants) = 46

4 + 6 = 10, then 1 + 0 = **1**

Barbara's Expression number is reached by reducing the total of 46 to a single digit (4 + 6 = 10, and 1 + 0 = 1).

Her Soul Urge number is worked out by reducing the total of all the vowels to a single digit:

$3 + 8 + 3 = 14$ and $1 + 4 = 5$

Barbara has an Expression number of 1 and a Soul Urge number of 5.

Let us now assume that she was born July 27, 1953. This gives her a life path number of 7 and a birthday number of 9 ($2 + 7 = 9$). Barbara's four main numbers are listed in the following order:

Life Path: 7
Expression: 1
Soul Urge: 5
Birthday: 9

In Western numerology, the life path is considered to represent about 40 percent of the person's makeup. The Expression represents 30 percent, the Soul Urge 20 percent, and the Birthday 10 percent. These are approximate figures only, but are used to show the relative importance of each number.

For compatibility we want both people in a relationship to have one of these four numbers in common. Consequently, Barbara will relate well to people who have any one of the numbers 7, 1, 5, or 9 as one of their four main numbers.

Usually, it is better if the numbers go diagonally, rather than in a straight line. Barbara would be likely to relate better to someone who had the number 7 as their Expression, Soul Urge, or Birthday, rather than someone who also had a 7 life path. However, even if it does go in a straight line, there is a definite bond. (Look at the shared 9 life path that George Burns and Gracie Allen had.)

There is one major exception. This is when two people have the same Soul Urge number. This creates a marriage that is made in heaven. Sadly, this does not occur very often. These two people will live for each other; they almost have no need for anyone else. No matter what problems beset them, they have each other and will ride any storms secure in each other's arms.

No one knows why someone becomes strongly attracted to one person and not to another. Fortunately, the mysterious attraction that makes two people fall in love with each other will always remain a wonderful mystery. Compatibility analysis can be of great help in understanding part of this mystery. But the real secret will forever remain just that: a secret.

Here are a few interesting combinations for you to analyze:

Ferdinand Marcos (born September 11, 1917) and Imelda Marcos (born July 2, 1931).

John F. Kennedy (born May 29, 1917) and Jacqueline Bouvier (born July 28, 1929).

Aristotle Onassis (born January 20, 1906) and Jacqueline Bouvier Kennedy (born July 28, 1929).

Carlo Ponti (born December 11, 1910) and Sophia Loren (born September 20, 1934).

Ronald Reagan (born February 6, 1911) and Nancy Davis (born July 6, 1921).

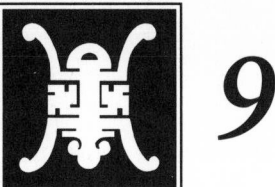 *9*

Numerology in the East

In most of the Far East, numerology is done on the same Lo Shu grid that we have been using. People in the East use the arrows that we use, but place the numbers in their original positions in Wu's three by three magic square. To complicate things still further, they use the lunar calendar rather than the solar calendar we use in the West.

The lunar calendar is an interesting one. Because it is based on the cycles of the moon, each month consists of either twenty-nine or thirty days.[1] Every so often there are thirteen months in a lunar calendar, because twelve lunar months do not add up to the 365 days of the solar calendar. This extra month is known as a leap month. The ancient scholars discovered that after three solar years, the lunar calendar was some thirty-three days behind the movement of the sun. This created an impossible situation for cultures largely dependent on agriculture, so the leap month was added to correct the situation.[2] The astronomers discovered that a nineteen-year cycle with seven leap months kept both the solar and lunar calendars aligned. In the solar calendar, the seasons are kept in their correct positions by having the winter solstice occur in the eleventh month. Consequently, in the lunar calendar the new year starts on the second new moon after the winter solstice. Because the Chinese New Year starts on a different date every year, people who were born in January or February in the West may find that they were born in the previous year in the Chinese lunar system.

The lunar calendar contains between 353 and 355 days in a normal year, and between 380 and 385 days in a leap year.

There are no life path numbers in the Eastern system. Life path numbers are believed to have been discovered by Pythagoras some 2,500 years ago when he modernized numerology for the West, and there is no direct equivalent in the East.

In the Western version of this chart the three planes are known as the Mental (top horizontal row), Emotional (middle row), and Practical (bottom row) planes (see chapter 3, page 29). In the East the top row is called the Intellectual Plane, the middle row is known as the Spiritual Plane and the bottom row is the Material Plane (Figure 9A). The differences are subtle. The top row relates to the intellect in both cases. The middle row, despite the different names, relates to the person's feelings, emotions, and intuition. While the bottom row in the West relates to people's physical expression, particularly their skills and talents with their hands, in the East the bottom row relates to financial and business success. However, the negative aspects of this plane are identical, indicating egotism, boastfulness, materialism, and vulgar displays of wealth.

| Intellectual |
| Spiritual |
| Material |

Figure 9A.

In the East the planes are also looked at in another way, relating them to weather and agriculture. This is not surprising as the weather had a major impact on the well-being of everyone living in a purely agricultural nation 4,000 years ago.

The top horizontal row represents sunshine and rain, both necessary for the crops to grow. The middle horizontal row represents the crops that are produced from the soil. Finally, the bottom row represents the soil itself.

The vertical columns also have meanings. The left-hand column represents thought. The middle vertical column represents activity, and the third, right-hand column represents strength (Figure 9B).

| Thought | Activity | Strength |

Figure 9B.

We can look at all the numbers in the chart using these horizontal and vertical meanings. Let's take the number 4 as an example. It is in an excellent position on both the rows of sunlight and thought in the Lo Shu chart (Figure 9C). As you will see shortly, number 4 has the keywords *logic*, *caution*, and *intelligence*. The thought is

4	9	2
3	5	7
8	1	6

Figure 9C.
The Lo Shu chart.

bathed in sunshine, indicating happiness. Consequently, the thinking is likely to be positive. However, the heat of the sun prevents
impulsiveness, making the person with the 4 cautious. By being
cautious, he or she has more time for thinking things through
before acting, and this can be an indication of high intelligence.

Naturally, we also receive different charts using the lunar calendar. For instance, I was born December 9, 1946; my Western
numerology chart is shown in Figure 9D.
Converting my date to the lunar calendar
changes my date of birth to November 16,
1946. I construct the Lo Shu chart shown in
Figure 9E by placing the two 1s from
November in the middle square in the bottom row. (This is the position where all the
1s go in the Lo Shu grid, as shown in Figure
9C on the previous page.) I place a third 1
in this box (from the 16 day number) and
then place the 6 in the right-hand position
on the bottom row.

	6	99
2		
11	4	

Figure 9D

**Author's Western
chart (based on his
solar birthday,
December 9, 1946).**

4	9	
1111	66	

Figure 9E.

**Author's Lo Shu
chart (based on his
lunar birthday,
November 16, 1946).**

Finally, the year is added. The 1 goes in
the middle square in the bottom row. The 9
is placed into the middle box in the top row.
The 4 goes alongside it, in the left-hand square in the top row.
Finally, the 6 is placed with the 6 that is already there in the right-
hand square in the bottom row.

As you can see, my lunar chart (Figure 9E) is quite different
from my solar one (Figure 9D). Does this mean that if I were living in Malaysia, for instance, I would be a different person than
the one I am in the West?

The short answer is no, of course. The meanings of the numbers change in the East. As well as taking the meanings of each
individual number, the reader also looks at each one using his
knowledge of the five elements of Chinese astrology and feng shui.
In addition, combinations of numbers are often more important
than the individual numbers. This is why, in the East, the absence
of a number is not necessarily negative. Chinese numerology is
concerned with balance, and combinations can provide good balance, even when many other numbers are missing from the chart.
Also, missing numbers can be "cured" by using the five elements of
Chinese astrology.

In the West, the only combinations that are looked at in great
depth are the arrows. However, in the East all sorts of other group-
ings are examined to see if they are auspicious or inauspicious.

Eastern Meanings of the Numbers

Here are the meanings of the individual numbers as they are used in the East.

Number 1

One is in the central position on the material plane. It is considered to be a positive number as it indicates someone with the potential to make money and enjoy a good lifestyle.

People with one 1 in the chart will do reasonably well financially. The potential for monetary success increases dramatically if the other two numbers in the material plane (8 and 6) are present, creating the arrow of prosperity (see page 98).

People with two 1s in their chart are destined to do well financially. They are also inclined to be lucky. If the chart contains two or three 7s, as well as the arrow of prosperity, the person will be extremely versatile and be able to achieve great success in a number of areas.

People with three 1s are financially successful and blessed with a positive, happy approach to life. The amount of luck the person can expect to receive increases markedly if the chart also includes the arrow of prosperity. If the chart also contains two 7s, the person will be extremely fortunate. Three 1s are considered the ideal number to have in Eastern numerology.

People with four or more 1s concentrate on the pursuit of wealth and possessions to the exclusion of almost everything else. This obsession on money creates a one-sided person who finds little or no happiness in other areas of life. This is modified if the person has numbers on the Spiritual Plane (3, 5, or 7).

Number 2

Number 2 is in the top right-hand square on the Mental Plane. It is the least auspicious number of the intellect, as it occurs so frequently. Next century its importance will diminish even further, as all people will have at least one 2 in their chart. In Eastern numerology, 2 is regarded as a negative or neutral number, unless it is found in company with the numbers 4 and 9, creating the arrow of the intellect (see page 97). When found with the number 3, it denotes someone who loves to argue and squabble.

People with just one 2 in the Mental Plane of their chart have very average minds. They seldom come up with original thoughts

on their own. People with one 2, plus the numbers 4 and 9, creating the arrow of the intellect, have the potential to do well in the fields of law, philosophy, and literature. People with one 2, plus the numbers 5 and 8, creating the arrow of determination (see page 96), are mentally strong. They are stable, decisive, and determined.

Two 2s on the Mental Plane are considered highly negative, unless they are accompanied by either, or both, the numbers 4 and 9. Two 2s on their own produce a lack of energy and the potential for illness. However, when the two 2s are found as part of the arrows of the intellect or determination, the interpretation is much more positive. This enhances the mental faculties and gives the person a good, clear mind and an excellent memory.

Three 2s are considered most unfortunate, unless they are supported by the arrows of the intellect or determination. Three 2s on their own are an indication of major illness. This is averted if the person also has the arrow of prosperity (8, 1, and 6) in the chart.

Four or more 2s are even less auspicious. Apart from the potential of health problems, people with this combination can often be arrogant, sarcastic, and rude. They are inclined to overreact to everything that happens to them, and they instinctively blame others for their mistakes.

Number 3

Number 3 is the first of the spiritual numbers and is found in the left-hand position of the middle row of the chart. In Western numerology, 3 is related to logic. In the East, it is concerned with sensitivity and intuition.

People with one 3 in their chart need the assistance of the numbers 5 and 7 (creating the arrow of spirituality; see page 97) or 8 and 4 (creating the arrow of the planner; see page 98). Without one or both of these numbers, people with one 3 are easily hurt and suffer from stress. They find it hard to survive in competitive fields. One 3, combined with an 8, shows that the person has someone they can rely on for comfort, support, and guidance.

People with two 3s are intelligent, sensitive, and intuitive. They are well balanced, well adjusted, and easily get along with others. They are perceptive and can understand the motivations of others. They make good friends. If the two 3s are part of the arrow of spirituality the person will develop a strong faith and philosophy of life.

People with three 3s are over-sensitive. They live in an imaginary dream world of their own making, and are constantly hurt by

Number 3

~

Concerned with spirituality, sensitivity, and intuition.

the real or imagined actions of others. If the three 3s are part of the arrow of spirituality, the interpretation is softened considerably. These people are intellectual, spiritually inclined, and intuitive. Once they learn how to exist in the real world they can make significant progress.

People with four or more 3s are impatient, reckless, and impulsive. These qualities are not helped much even when they make up part of the arrow of spirituality. In fact, these people's intuition can be extremely unreliable. Oddly enough, the intuitive faculties are aided more when the person has an arrow of the planner than when the arrow of spirituality is present.

Number 4

Four is an interesting number in the East. This is because the word *four* sounds like the word *death* in some Chinese dialects. Consequently, it is frequently considered to be a negative number. However, in some circumstances it can be favorable.[3] In Eastern numerology the number 4 is in the top left-hand square of the Mental Plane and is found in people with high intelligence.

People with one 4 in their chart are logical, cautious, and intelligent. These qualities can be utilized in a variety of fields, and these are determined by the other numbers in the chart.

People with two 4s are inclined to be stubborn, intolerant, and certain of their own correctness. This is tempered if the chart also contains numbers in the Spiritual Plane (3, 5, and 7). People with two 4s have excellent brains and use them well. However, they are also inclined to consider themselves superior to others and need to learn to get along better with other people.

People with three 4s in their chart are extremely stubborn and inflexible. They find it hard to get along with others who are less intelligent than they are, and often lead sad and lonely lives.

It is very rare to find people with four 4s in their chart. This creates an unbalanced chart. These people find it hard to understand themselves and have major difficulties in getting along with others.

Number 5

The number 5 occupies the central position in the chart. In Western numerology, it is the balance number. In the East, it reveals the intensity of the person's feelings and emotions.

People with one 5 in their chart are emotionally well balanced. They instinctively make the right decisions, particularly if their

Number 4

~

Frequently negative, but sometimes favorable; indicates high intelligence.

charts also contain either the arrows of spirituality or willpower (see page 97). If the single 5 is accompanied by the numbers 2 and 3, the person is inclined to work more on the negative side of his or her capabilities and be unfeeling and unsympathetic. However, if the numbers 2 and 3 are absent, people with a single 5 can demonstrate great strength of character.

People with two 5s in their chart are enthusiastic, eager, and full of life. They enjoy challenges and are happiest when demonstrating their capabilities. They are determined, confident, and ambitious. These qualities are enhanced if the two 5s make up part of the arrow of willpower (1, 5, and 9). However, the two 5s can also be negative if these people do not find a suitable outlet for their abilities. These people sometimes overindulge in drink, drugs, and sex.

People with three 5s are inclined to be overpowering and domineering. They find it hard to get on with others until they have this under control.

It is very rare to find people with four 5s. These people have a tremendous intensity of emotional power that they cannot control. In extreme cases this can even lead to suicide.

Number 6

The number 6 is in the right-hand square in the Material Plane. Because it is on the Material Plane, it represents financial satisfaction and a comfortable lifestyle.

People with one 6 in their chart are inclined to be lucky in small ways. When it is part of the arrow of prosperity (see page 98), it virtually guarantees a life free of financial problems. When it is on its own, without the numbers 8 and 1, it indicates that the person can do well financially in a creative field.

The creative potential of a single 6 is often directed toward the home. These people are family-minded and enjoy living and working in pleasing environments. As their fortunes improve, people with a single 6 often start helping less fortunate people in the community. This trait is particularly emphasized if the 6 forms part of the arrow of action (see page 99).

People with two 6s are highly creative, but lack confidence in their abilities. They worry unnecessarily, and it can take a long time for them to recover from even small setbacks. These people work best with gentle support and encouragement from their loved ones.

People with three 6s are inclined to worry all the time about their loved ones. This is taken even further by people with four 6s. Both of these combinations are helped enormously if they make

Number 5

⁓

Reveals the intensity of feelings and emotions.

Number 6

⁓

Represents financial satisfaction and a comfortable lifestyle.

up part of the arrow of prosperity. In these instances, financial success takes the edge off the worry. Numbers on the spiritual plane also help people with three or more 6s.

Number 7

The number seven is placed in the right-hand square of the Spiritual Plane. Until the year 2003 it is the reigning number in Chinese numerology.[4] Consequently, the presence of a 7 in the chart is an indication of good fortune from the years 1983 to 2003. It represents spirituality, intuition, and a developing faith. People with a 7 in their charts become more and more aware of its influence once they reach middle age. In the earlier years it is usually ignored.

A single 7 in the chart, without the numbers 3 and 5, represents someone who seeks perfection and is interested in searching out hidden truths. If the single 7 makes up part of the arrow of spirituality (3, 5, and 7; see page 97) it indicates someone who is likely to make a career in a spiritual or humanitarian field. However, if there are two or more 3s or 5s in the arrow, the person is inclined to be overly dogmatic and often loses the big picture because of too much interest in the details. A single 7 accompanied by an arrow of prosperity (see page 98) indicates someone who is both successful and caring.

People with two 7s are inclined to enjoy the pomp and display of the spiritual life more than the spirituality itself. These people can become very successful materially, but often experience vague feelings of guilt about their success.

People with three 7s fall into two different types. Usually, they are model citizens who conform and work hard to achieve their goals. Unfortunately, some suffer badly from depression caused by overanalyzing their philosophies of life. This second type is usually found in people with the arrow of suspicion (an absence of 4, 5, and 6; see page 99).

It is very rare to find someone with four 7s. (People born on the 7th, 17th and 27th of July, 1977 are the only examples this century.) Unfortunately, they are likely to act on the negative side of their potential as the weight of all the 7s unbalances the chart.

Number 8

Eight occupies an excellent position in the chart, being in the left-hand square at the start of the Material Plane. Because 8 represents money to the Chinese, it has always been a popular number. Also,

in feng shui, we will be entering a twenty-year cycle of the number 8 from the year 2004.[4] The presence of an 8 in the chart indicates financial success and good fortune. The years 2004 to 2023 will be especially fortunate for people with an 8 in their chart.

A single 8 in the chart, without the numbers 1 and 6, represents efficiency, money, and attention to detail. When it is combined with the numbers 1 and 6 to create the arrow of prosperity (see page 98), it represents significant financial success and a happy life. This happiness is increased if the chart also contains the numbers 5 and 7.

People with two 8s do very well in business. Consequently, they usually retire in a very comfortable position. They have shrewd brains and are able to quickly analyze and seize opportunities that come their way. However, they need to make sure that they also pay attention to the non-materialistic aspects of life to create balance, harmonious relationships, and peace of mind.

It is rare to find people with three or more 8s in their chart. Three 8s is regarded as being a positive combination, even though it can be a difficult one to handle early on in life. These people find it hard to succeed financially in their younger years. They generally need to make mistakes first and, once they have learned from these, start to forge ahead in their forties. By this stage they have sufficient maturity and wisdom to take advantage of the good opportunities and leave the others alone.

Number 9

Nine is considered highly auspicious in Eastern numerology, because it symbolizes completion and a synthesis of heaven and earth. As in Western numerology, it is also considered a number of the intellect. The presence of a 9 in a chart also indicates prosperity in the distant future. This is because in Eastern numerology we start a twenty-year cycle of 9 in the year 2024.

Everybody born this century has at least one 9 in their chart. This symbolizes idealism, humanitarianism, and ambition. In previous centuries, people with a single 9 in their charts often entered politics or the government service. It was common for lawyers and judges to have a single 9 in their chart.

People with two 9s in their chart have good brains and enjoy learning. They are serious thinkers and enjoy working in fields that are intellectually stimulating. The only negative aspect of two 9s is that these people usually think entirely with their heads, ignoring the heart. This is not the case if they also have the arrow of spirituality in their chart (see page 97).

Number 8

~

Indicates money, financial success, and good fortune.

Number 9

~

Symbolizes completion; indicates prosperity in the distant future

People with three 9s are idealistic and highly intelligent. They are ambitious and have a strong desire to excel academically. However, this overemphasis of 9s can sometimes produce people who are arrogant and have a bad temper. This is particularly the case if the chart also contains the arrows of loneliness and/or losses (see pages 100 and 101).

The Arrows

You will have realized by now the special emphasis that the arrows have in the East. Remember that although some of the arrows have the same name and take the same position on the grid, they do contain different numbers. The following are the meanings of the different arrows as they are interpreted in the Far East.

The Arrows of Strength

The Arrow of Determination

Figure 9F.
May 18, 1926: chart with the arrow of determination.

This arrow is found in the same position as in the West, and is made up of the numbers 8, 5, and 2. People with this arrow are patient, persistent, and determined. They are happy to bide their time until the moment is right, then act with decisiveness. No matter what happens to them they never lose sight of their goals.

Someone born May 18, 1926, in the lunar calendar would have the arrow of determination (Figure 9F).

The Arrow of Emotional Balance

This arrow follows the path of the Arrow of Compassion in the Western chart, and consists of the numbers 4, 5, and 6.

Figure 9G.
April 15, 1966: chart with the arrow of emotional balance.

People with this arrow are compassionate, caring people who often make a career out of helping others. They are sensitive, often intuitive, and have an uncanny ability to understand other people's needs. These people can appear to be shy, particularly in the growing-up years. As children, they are well behaved, quiet, and gentle.

A person born April 15, 1966, in the lunar calendar would have the arrow of emotional balance (Figure 9G).

The Arrow of Spirituality

This arrow is particularly interesting as it is made up of the numbers 3, 5, and 7, the same numbers as in the Western version of this same arrow. However, instead of crossing the chart diagonally from the top left to the bottom right, it occupies the central, horizontal row.

The interpretation of this arrow is virtually identical to that used in the West. It emphasizes the feelings, emotions, and spiritual aspects of the people who have it. It indicates a serious approach to life and an inner calm and serenity that seldom appears before middle age.

A person born March 17, 1953, in the lunar calendar would have the arrow of spirituality (Figure 9H).

Figure 9H.
March 17, 1953: chart with the arrow of spirituality.

The Arrow of Intellect

This arrow is in the same position as it is in the Western grid, but the numbers it comprises are 4, 9, and 2. The presence of these three numbers gives intellectual ability and an excellent memory. This arrow belongs to people who are analytical, articulate, and logical, but who sometimes consider themselves to be superior to others.

Next century we will find a few people who do not have any numbers on the Spiritual or Material Planes. These people will be so overwhelmed by their thoughts that they run the risk of becoming mentally unbalanced. They will find it very hard to relax and unwind, and they will need constant support and help from others.

Someone born April 12, 1919, in the lunar calendar would have the arrow of intellect (Figure 9I).

4	99	2
	111	

Figure 9I.
April 12, 1919: chart with the arrow of intellect.

The Arrow of Willpower

This arrow is in the same position as it is in the Western grid, but contains the numbers 1, 5, and 9. (These numbers make up the arrow of determination in the Western version of the chart.)

People with this arrow are stubborn, persistent, and determined. They are inclined to be argumentative and have strong opinions on a variety of subjects. This arrow is regarded as a symbol of success, because people with it steadily persist until they reach their ultimate goals.

Someone with a lunar birthday of September 15, 1955, would have the arrow of willpower (Figure 9J).

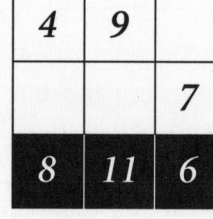

Figure 9J.
September 15, 1955: chart with the arrow of willpower.

The Arrow of Prosperity

This arrow is in the bottom horizontal row, in the same position as the arrow of practicality on the Western chart. It is made up of the numbers 8, 1, and 6.

People with the arrow of prosperity excel in the business and commercial worlds. They are interested in money for its own sake, and are not usually interested in the higher values of life.

People who have the arrow of prosperity, but also have no numbers on the Spiritual Plane, are cold, calculating, and unfeeling. They achieve great material success, but do so by ignoring the feelings and needs of others.

A person born June 18, 1974, in the lunar calendar would have the arrow of prosperity (Figure 9K).

Figure 9K.
June 18, 1974: chart with the arrow of prosperity.

The Arrow of the Planner

This arrow is in the same position in both the solar and lunar charts. However, in the Eastern chart it consists of the numbers 8, 3, and 4.

The basic meaning of this arrow is similar in both charts, but the Chinese idea of a planner is someone who is shrewd, cunning, and not very ethical. Consequently, it is sometimes known, fairly or not, as the "Politician's Arrow."

Someone born May 18, 1943, in the lunar calendar would have the arrow of the planner (Figure 9L).

Figure 9L.
May 18, 1943: chart with the arrow of the planner.

The Arrow of Action

This arrow occupies the same position as the arrow of activity in the Western chart. This is not surprising, as one of the keywords for this arrow is *action*. It consists of the numbers 6, 7, and 2.

People with this arrow need to be busy, and love physical activities. They enjoy exercise and participating in sports. They have tremendous reserves of energy and are happiest when expending it on some physical challenge.

A person born July 12, 1960, in the lunar calendar would have the arrow of action (Figure 9M).

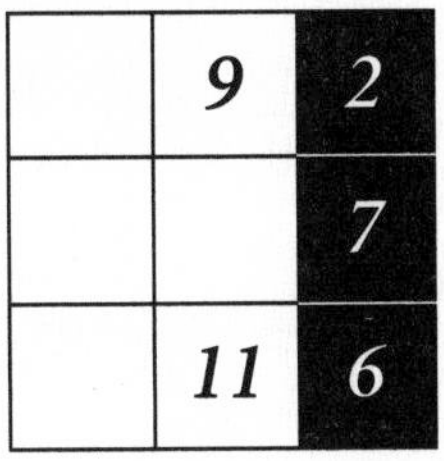

Figure 9M.
July 12, 1960: chart with the arrow of action.

The Arrows of Weakness

The Arrow of Frustrations

The arrow of frustrations in the Western chart is an absence of the numbers 4, 5, and 6. In the East, it is a diagonal arrow created by the absence of the numbers 8, 5, and 2.

This arrow indicates many setbacks and frustrations. In the East it is regarded as a sign of consistent failure. People who have this arrow should try to learn from every experience and think carefully before acting.

Someone born on June 19, 1934, in the lunar calendar would have the arrow of frustrations (Figure 9N).

Figure 9N.
June 19, 1934: chart with the arrow of frustrations.

The Arrow of Suspicion

This arrow is created by an absence of the numbers 4, 5, and 6, the same numbers that create the arrow of frustrations in the Western numerology chart.

In the East, this arrow indicates people who are suspicious, cynical, and moody. They are inclined to worry and dwell on the negative side of life. A numerologist in Hong Kong told me that he felt this arrow revealed a "gray person," indicating someone who always lives in the shade and never comes out into the full light of day.

Figure 9O.
July 12, 1932: chart with the arrow of suspicion.

Someone born July 12, 1932, in the lunar calendar would have the arrow of suspicion (Figure 9O, previous page).

The Arrow of Loneliness

This arrow consists of the absence of the numbers 3, 5, and 7. It takes up the center, horizontal row where the arrow of emotional sensitivity is in the Western chart.

This arrow denotes a lack of feelings. People with this arrow are so intent on achieving their goals that they forget their friends and family, and consequently lack joy, love, and laughter in their lives. They usually suffer enormously from loneliness in their old age.

Figure 9P.
August 18, 1946: chart with the arrow of loneliness.

Someone born August 18, 1946, in the lunar calendar would have the arrow of loneliness (Figure 9P).

The Arrow of Apathy

This arrow is created when the chart lacks the numbers 2, 7, and 6. This arrow is in the same position as the arrow of inactivity in the Western chart, and its meaning is very similar.

People with the arrow of apathy lack motivation and fail to grasp opportunities, even when freely handed to them. These people are indecisive, frightened of taking risks, and generally achieve only a fraction of what they could do if they applied themselves.

Figure 9Q.
May 14, 1983: chart with the arrow of apathy.

Someone born May 14, 1983, in the lunar calendar would have the arrow of apathy (Figure 9Q).

The Arrow of Confusion

This arrow is caused by a lack of the numbers 8, 3, and 4 in the chart. It occupies the left-hand vertical column.

People with this arrow are not logical, methodical, or organized. They live from day to day, seldom making long-term plans. When they do, they usually sabotage the plans before they bear fruit.

Figure 9R.
July 12, 1975: chart with the arrow of confusion.

Someone born July 12, 1975, in the lunar calendar has the arrow of confusion (Figure 9R).

The Arrow of Losses

This arrow is created by an absence of the numbers 8, 1, and 6. Consequently, nobody has had this arrow in their charts for the last thousand years, but it will appear again in the twenty-first century. These people will try to make money by participating in get-rich-quick schemes. They will constantly fail in these, and will not realize until middle age that if they had put the same amount of effort into a single, worthwhile goal they would have achieved success.

People born April 23, 2035, in the lunar calendar will have the arrow of losses (Figure 9S).

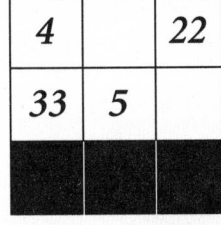

Figure 9S.
April 23, 2035: chart with the arrow of losses.

The Arrow of Indecision

This arrow is created by an absence of the number 1, 5, and 9. No one has had this arrow for the last one thousand years, but we will start to see it in the twenty-first century.

People with this arrow have a desperate desire to be accepted and liked. Consequently, they can be easily led and swayed by others. They will find it extremely hard to stand up for what they believe in as they want to please everyone and are unable to express views that other people might not accept (Figure 9T).

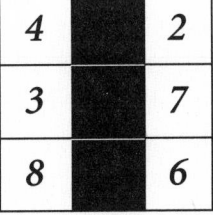

Figure 9T.
July 8, 2346: chart with the arrow of indecision.

The Arrow of Poor Memory

This arrow is created by an absence of the numbers 4, 9, and 2. This arrow will not be found until the thirty-first century. Everyone born in the last century has had a 9 in his or her chart and everyone born in the next one thousand years will have a 2.

People with this arrow start out in life with strong intellectual capabilities that gradually weaken as the person matures. These people are also frequently overwhelmed by the vivid nature of their thoughts and can suffer from mental imbalance.

Figure 9U.
May 6, 3087: chart with the arrow of poor memory.

The Four Small Arrows

In the Far East, there are also four small arrows created by joining the four middle numbers of the outside horizontal and vertical rows. These are the small arrows joining the numbers 1 and 3, 3 and 9, 9 and 7, and 7 and 1.

The Arrow of Detail and Deceit

This is the arrow created when the chart contains both a 1 and a 3.

	9	
■		7
	■	6

Figure 9V.
March 13, 1967: chart with the arrow of detail and deceit.

People with this combination enjoy the details of things. In fact, if there is more than one of each number the person is inclined to be a perfectionist.

There is a negative side to this arrow. People with it are inclined to be dishonest when it suits them. They may lie about something or conceal the truth to protect themselves. In China this is sometimes known as the Criminal Line,[5] but in my experience it belongs more to people who lie, rather than people who commit robberies or crimes of violence.

Someone born March 13, 1967, in the lunar calendar would have the arrow of detail and deceit (Figure 9V).

The Arrow of Litigation

This arrow is created when the chart contains both the numbers 3 and 9. People with this combination are inclined to argue and become involved in disputes of all kinds. If

	9	
3	5	7
8	1	

Figure 9W.
July 3, 1985: chart with the arrow of litigation.

these get too serious they have to be settled in a court of law, which is why this combination is known as the arrow of litigation.

Someone born July 3, 1985, in the lunar calendar would have the arrow of litigation (Figure 9W).

The Arrow of Peace of Mind

This arrow is created when the chart contains both a 9 and a 7. People with this combination are positive, confident, and have a strong faith. The logic of the 9 helps the spirituality of the 7, and

vice versa. These people can face up to difficult situations with equanimity, confident that everything will work out for the best.

Someone born July 8, 1966, in the lunar calendar would have the arrow of peace of mind (Figure 9X).

Figure 9X.
July 8, 1966: a chart with the arrow of peace of mind.

Arrow of Science

People with charts that contain the numbers 1 and 7 are interested in the mysteries of the world we live in. They enjoy searching for the hidden truths and can become so involved with their studies that they get lost in research. They are usually interested in the sciences (frequently those that concern the oceans), which is how this arrow got its name.

Figure 9Y.
May 27, 1974: a chart with the arrow of science.

Someone born May 27, 1974, in the lunar calendar would have the arrow of science (Figure 9Y).

Numerology Cures

In Eastern numerology it is believed that missing numbers in the chart can be "cured" or corrected if you surround yourself with objects made of the element that belongs to that particular number. Usually, only one or two of the empty spaces in a chart are "cured." A good example would be someone with a chart that contains the numbers 8 and 1. The addition of a 6 would complete the arrow of prosperity. Naturally, someone with this particular chart would be interested in having something to fill in this empty space on the chart.

If an entire row is missing, as is the case with charts containing the arrows of frustration, suspicion, loneliness, apathy, confusion and losses, just one number in the row would be "cured" to eliminate the arrow of weakness.

The Five Elements

In Chinese astrology there are five elements: wood, fire, earth, metal, and water. Everything in the world can be categorized as belonging to one of these elements. These elements can be both productive and destructive.[6]

The productive cycle goes:

> **Wood** burns, creating **fire.**
> This leaves **earth,** out of which comes **metal.**
> **Metal** liquifies like **water.**
> **Water** nurtures **wood.**

The destructive cycle is:

> **Wood** draws from **earth.**
> **Earth** pollutes **water.**
> **Water** puts out **fire.**
> **Fire** melts **metal.**
> **Metal** can chop and destroy **wood.**

Each element is assigned a number:

> 1 relates to water
> 2 relates to earth
> 3 relates to wood
> 4 relates to wood
> 5 relates to earth
> 6 relates to metal
> 7 relates to metal
> 8 relates to earth
> 9 relates to fire

Wood

If you are missing the numbers 3 or 4 in your chart you may want to "cure" this lack by surrounding yourself with wood. You may choose living wood, such as trees, shrubs, potted plants, or even grass. You may prefer to use objects made of wood, such as furniture and decorative ornaments. Because the element wood is also frequently known as "tree," the most effective cures are made of living wood.

Fire

If the number 9 is missing from your chart you may want to surround yourself with bright objects, particularly objects that give out light. Anything red also relates to fire.

Earth

A lack of earth is common in numerology charts, as it represents the three numbers that make up the arrow of determination—8, 5, and 2. (As you already know, the lack of these numbers creates the arrow of frustration.) To compensate for the lack of any or all of these numbers, you can surround yourself with objects that come from the ground, but are not metal. Quartz crystals make a particularly useful "cure."

Metal

The numbers 6 and 7 relate to metal. If either of these are missing from the chart, an effective remedy is for the person to surround him or herself with any objects made from metal. A ring or bracelet made from gold or silver makes a very effective "cure." The element metal is also frequently known as gold basically meaning money. Consequently, metal coins can also be considered a "cure."

Water

Water relates to the number 1. Naturally, it is impossible for anyone born in the last thousand years to be missing this number. However, many people born in the twenty-first century will need a "cure," as they will not have this number in their charts. Anything that is blue or black will be effective. Naturally, water itself makes the best remedy. An aquarium, a small pond or a view over a lake or the ocean also make excellent "cures."

An interesting side benefit of these cures is that each element also relates to a desirable quality. It is believed that you can enhance your ability in these areas by surrounding yourself with objects that relate to the correct element.

- **Wood** relates to creativity.
- **Fire** relates to enthusiasm, excitement, and motivation.

- **Earth** relates to stability and the ability to reach one's goals.

- **Metal** relates to valor and the ability to stand up for oneself.

- **Water** relates to communication with others.

If you feel you are lacking in any of these areas, experiment by surrounding yourself with objects that relate to the correct element and observe your gradual but steady progress.

10

The Ki

Two completely different systems of numerology evolved from Wu's magic square. So far we have looked at both the Western and Eastern interpretations of Chinese numerology. There is also another Chinese system, known as the Ki, which also evolved from Wu's Lo Shu grid.

The Ki system, sometimes known as the Nine Star Ki or Nine House Divination, starts with the same magic square, but the numbers change position every year creating nine different combinations (Figure 10A, following page). Only the original square can be described as a magic square, as each horizontal, vertical, and diagonal row adds up to fifteen. Although the other squares do not have each horizontal, vertical, and diagonal adding up to the same total, they do follow a pattern. In each case, every row adds up to a certain number, or alternatively, that specific number plus a multiple of nine.[1]

The Ki system is based on the ancient Chinese concept of yin and yang. Yin and yang are the opposite polarities in the universe. Male and female is an example. The Chinese Taoists considered that the entire universe, and everything in it, could be classified as being yin or yang. Yin and yang are the opposite forces in nature. The markings on the back of Wu's tortoise were black and white. The odd numbers were white (yin) and the even ones were black (yang).[2] Originally, yin and yang described two sides of a mountain. Yin was the shady, northern side, and yang described the sunny, southern side.[3] Because of

8	4	6
7	9	2
3	5	1

7	3	5
6	8	1
2	4	9

6	2	4
5	7	9
1	3	8

5	1	3
4	6	8
9	2	7

4	9	2
3	5	7
8	1	6

3	8	1
2	4	6
7	9	5

Figure 10A.

In the Ki, the numbers change position every year, creating nine different combinations.

2	7	9
1	3	5
6	8	4

1	6	8
9	2	4
5	7	3

9	5	7
8	1	3
4	6	2

this, they came to mean light and dark, white and black, day and night, and countless other opposites. Even today the Chinese delight in creating yin and yang combinations.

The Ki system also uses the five basic elements of wood, fire, earth, metal, and water that were discussed briefly in chapter 9. All of the numbers from 1 to 9 are assigned to an element. Wood relates to the numbers 3 and 4; fire has number 9; earth has 2, 5, and 8; metal 6 and 7; and water has number 1 (Figure 10B). Each number also relates to a color:

Wood	Fire	Earth
4	**9**	**2**
Wood	Earth	Metal
3	**5**	**7**
Earth	Water	Metal
8	**1**	**6**

Figure 10B.

1 is white water
2 is black earth
3 is turquoise tree (wood)
4 is green tree (wood)
5 is yellow earth

6 is white metal
7 is red metal
8 is white earth
9 is purple fire

In fact, many of the ancient Ki squares that still survive show the colors in each square, rather than the number.[4]

There are three important numbers in the Ki system of numerology: the Natal Year number, the Natal Month number, and the House number.

The Natal Year Number

The Natal Year number is found by looking up your year of birth in Figure 10C.

Year	Number	Year	Number	Year	Number	Year	Number
1901	9	1931	6	1961	3	1991	9
1902	8	1932	5	1962	2	1992	8
1903	7	1933	4	1963	1	1993	7
1904	6	1934	3	1964	9	1994	6
1905	5	1935	2	1965	8	1995	5
1906	4	1936	1	1966	7	1996	4
1907	3	1937	9	1967	6	1997	3
1908	2	1938	8	1968	5	1998	2
1909	1	1939	7	1969	4	1999	1
1910	9	1940	6	1970	3	2000	9
1911	8	1941	5	1971	2	2001	8
1912	7	1942	4	1972	1	2002	7
1913	6	1943	3	1973	9	2003	6
1914	5	1944	2	1974	8	2004	5
1915	4	1945	1	1975	7	2005	4
1916	3	1946	9	1976	6	2006	3
1917	2	1947	8	1977	5	2007	2
1918	1	1948	7	1978	4	2008	1
1919	9	1949	6	1979	3	2009	9
1920	8	1950	5	1980	2	2010	8
1921	7	1951	4	1981	1	2011	7
1922	6	1952	3	1982	9	2012	6
1923	5	1953	2	1983	8	2013	5
1924	4	1954	1	1984	7	2014	4
1925	3	1955	9	1985	6	2015	3
1926	2	1956	8	1986	5	2016	2
1927	1	1957	7	1987	4	2017	1
1928	9	1958	6	1988	3	2018	9
1929	8	1959	5	1989	2	2019	8
1930	7	1960	4	1990	1	2020	7

Figure 10C.

Natal numbers for years 1901 to 2020.

The Chinese New Year is approximately February 4, so if you were born between January 1 and February 5, your Natal Year number is probably that of the previous year. You can determine which year you are in by looking at Figure 10D; this figure gives the dates on which the New Year starts for every date in the twentieth century.

Year	Date	Year	Date	Year	Date	Year	Date
1901	Feb. 4	1926	Feb. 4	1951	Feb. 5	1976	Feb. 5
1902	Feb. 5	1927	Feb. 5	1952	Feb. 5	1977	Feb. 4
1903	Feb. 5	1928	Feb. 5	1953	Feb. 4	1978	Feb. 4
1904	Feb. 5	1929	Feb. 4	1954	Feb. 4	1979	Feb. 4
1905	Feb. 4	1930	Feb. 4	1955	Feb. 5	1980	Feb. 5
1906	Feb. 5	1931	Feb. 5	1956	Feb. 5	1981	Feb. 4
1907	Feb. 5	1932	Feb. 5	1957	Feb. 4	1982	Feb. 4
1908	Feb. 5	1933	Feb. 4	1958	Feb. 4	1983	Feb. 4
1909	Feb. 4	1934	Feb. 4	1959	Feb. 4	1984	Feb. 4
1910	Feb. 5	1935	Feb. 5	1960	Feb. 5	1985	Feb. 4
1911	Feb. 5	1936	Feb. 5	1961	Feb. 4	1986	Feb. 4
1912	Feb. 5	1937	Feb. 4	1962	Feb. 4	1987	Feb. 4
1913	Feb. 4	1938	Feb. 4	1963	Feb. 4	1988	Feb. 4
1914	Feb. 5	1939	Feb. 5	1964	Feb. 5	1989	Feb. 4
1915	Feb. 5	1940	Feb. 5	1965	Feb. 4	1990	Feb. 4
1916	Feb. 5	1941	Feb. 4	1966	Feb. 4	1991	Feb. 4
1917	Feb. 4	1942	Feb. 4	1967	Feb. 4	1992	Feb. 4
1918	Feb. 5	1943	Feb. 5	1968	Feb. 5	1993	Feb. 4
1919	Feb. 5	1944	Feb. 5	1969	Feb. 4	1994	Feb. 4
1920	Feb. 5	1945	Feb. 4	1970	Feb. 4	1995	Feb. 4
1921	Feb. 4	1946	Feb. 4	1971	Feb. 4	1996	Feb. 4
1922	Feb. 5	1947	Feb. 5	1972	Feb. 5	1997	Feb. 4
1923	Feb. 5	1948	Feb. 5	1973	Feb. 4	1998	Feb. 4
1924	Feb. 5	1949	Feb. 4	1974	Feb. 4	1999	Feb. 4
1925	Feb. 4	1950	Feb. 4	1975	Feb. 4	2000	Feb. 4

Figure 10D.
Lunar Year
Starting Dates.

There is also an easy method of working out your Natal Year number without using the chart. All you do is add up the last two numbers of your year of birth and reduce them down to a single digit. This number is then subtracted from ten.

Here is an example. If you were born in 1967 you add the 6 and the 7, and then reduce the total to a single digit:

$$6 + 7 = 13, \text{ and } 1 + 3 = \mathbf{4}$$

We now subtract the 4 from 10 and discover that your Natal Year number is a 6:

$$10 - 4 = \mathbf{6}$$

Likewise, if you were born in 1989, you add the 8 and 9 together, creating 17, and reduce it to a single digit—8. This is subtracted from 10, giving you a Natal Year number of 2.

Master numbers also get reduced to a single digit. If you were born in 1974, you add the 7 and 4 to get an 11. This is reduced to a 2, then subtracted from 10, giving you an 8 Natal Year number.

Remember that if you were born on, say, January 29, 1952, your Natal Year number is a 4, not a 3, as you are considered being born in the previous year.

In the next century the formula will change. Instead of subtracting from 10, we subtract from 9. Consequently, someone born in 2015 will have a Natal Year number of 3.

$$1 + 5 = 6, \text{ and } 9 - 6 = \mathbf{3}$$

Naturally, we will have years where we subtract 9 from 9 and receive a zero answer (2009 and 2018 are examples). Whenever this occurs, it is classified as a 9 Natal Year. Consequently, someone born in 2009 will have a 9 Natal Year number.

Your chart is derived from the original Lo Shu magic square, but has your Natal Year number in the central position. The nine variations of this chart are shown in Figure 10A (page 108).

Before starting to interpret the Natal Year numbers, we will also work out our Natal Month number.

The Natal Month Number

The Natal Year number is the most important number in the Ki system and governs our adult life. The Natal Month number is the most important number until about the age of eighteen, so its influence is primarily during our growing-up years. However, it is always there, the child within us. In moments of crisis or stress we

are likely to revert back to the feelings and responses of our Natal Month number.

In the same way, if a young child is forced by circumstances to be independent, he or she is likely to exhibit more of the qualities of the Natal Year number than of the Natal Month number. Also, the Natal Month number can become the dominant number again when the person becomes dependent on others, as in old age.

Unfortunately, there is no simple formula for determining the Natal Month number. First of all, you need to determine what month you were born. This is because the Chinese use the lunar calendar and their months change at different times from ours. If you were born early in the month, it is quite likely that in this system you are considered as being born in the previous month.

For instance, if you were born October 8, 1959, in the Ki system you are considered as being born in September. Marilyn Monroe was born June 1, 1926. If we were constructing a Ki chart for her we would consider her as being born in May.

The chart for determining your month of birth is shown in Figure 10E. Figure 10F (page 115) also shows your Natal Month number.

Your Natal Month chart is the one shown in Figure 10A (page 108) that has your Natal Month number in the central position.

Year	Feb.	Mar.	Apr.	May	Jun.	Jul.	Aug.	Sep.	Oct.	Nov.	Dec.	Jan.
1900	4	6	5	6	6	8	8	8	9	8	7	6
1901	4	6	5	6	6	8	8	8	9	8	8	6
1902	5	6	6	6	7	8	8	9	9	8	8	6
1903	5	7	6	7	7	8	9	9	9	9	8	7
1904	5	6	5	6	6	8	8	8	9	8	7	6
1905	4	6	5	6	6	8	8	8	9	8	7	6
1906	5	6	6	6	7	8	8	9	9	8	8	6
1907	5	7	6	7	7	8	9	9	9	8	8	7
1908	5	6	5	6	6	7	8	8	9	8	7	6
1909	4	6	5	6	6	8	8	8	9	8	8	6
1910	5	6	6	6	7	8	8	8	9	8	8	6
1911	5	7	6	7	7	8	9	9	9	8	8	7
1912	5	6	5	6	6	7	8	8	9	8	7	6
1913	4	6	5	6	6	8	8	8	9	8	8	6
1914	5	6	6	6	7	8	8	8	9	8	8	6
1915	5	7	6	7	7	8	9	9	9	8	8	7
1916	5	6	5	6	6	7	8	8	9	8	7	6

Figure 10E.
Dates the Months Change.
(Continued on the following two pages.)

Year	Feb.	Mar.	Apr.	May	Jun.	Jul.	Aug.	Sep.	Oct.	Nov.	Dec.	Jan.
1917	4	6	5	6	6	8	8	8	9	8	8	6
1918	5	6	6	6	6	8	8	8	9	8	8	6
1919	5	7	6	7	7	8	9	9	9	8	8	7
1920	5	6	5	6	6	7	8	8	9	8	7	6
1921	4	6	5	6	6	8	8	8	9	8	8	6
1922	5	6	5	6	6	8	8	8	9	8	8	6
1923	5	7	6	6	7	8	9	9	9	8	8	7
1924	5	6	5	6	6	7	8	8	8	8	7	6
1925	4	6	5	6	6	8	8	8	9	8	8	6
1926	4	6	5	6	6	8	8	8	9	8	8	6
1927	5	6	6	6	7	8	8	9	9	8	8	6
1928	5	6	5	6	6	7	8	8	8	8	7	6
1929	4	6	5	6	6	8	8	8	9	8	7	6
1930	4	6	5	6	6	8	8	9	9	8	8	6
1931	5	6	6	6	7	8	8	9	9	8	8	6
1932	5	6	5	6	6	7	8	8	8	8	7	6
1933	4	6	5	6	6	8	8	8	9	8	7	6
1934	4	6	5	6	6	8	8	8	9	8	8	6
1935	5	6	6	6	7	8	8	9	9	8	8	6
1936	5	6	5	6	6	7	8	8	8	8	7	6
1937	4	6	5	6	6	8	8	8	9	8	7	6
1938	4	6	5	6	7	8	8	8	9	8	8	6
1939	5	6	6	6	6	8	8	8	9	8	8	6
1940	5	6	5	6	6	7	8	8	8	8	7	6
1941	4	6	5	6	6	7	8	8	9	8	7	6
1942	4	6	5	6	6	8	8	8	9	8	8	6
1943	5	6	6	6	7	8	8	8	9	8	8	6
1944	5	6	5	6	6	7	8	8	8	7	7	6
1945	4	6	5	6	6	7	8	8	9	8	7	6
1946	4	6	5	6	6	8	8	8	9	8	8	6
1947	5	6	6	6	6	8	8	8	9	8	8	6
1948	5	6	5	6	6	7	8	8	8	7	7	6
1949	4	6	5	6	6	7	8	8	9	8	7	6
1950	4	6	5	6	6	8	8	8	9	8	8	6
1951	5	6	6	6	6	8	8	8	9	8	8	6
1952	5	6	5	6	6	7	8	8	8	7	7	6
1953	4	6	5	6	6	7	8	8	9	8	7	6
1954	4	6	5	6	6	8	8	8	9	8	8	6
1955	5	6	6	6	6	8	8	8	9	8	8	6
1956	5	5	5	5	6	7	7	8	8	7	7	5
1957	4	6	5	6	6	7	8	8	8	8	7	6
1958	4	6	5	6	6	8	8	8	9	8	7	6

Figure 10E (continued).

Dates the Months Change.

Year	Feb.	Mar.	Apr.	May	Jun.	Jul.	Aug.	Sep.	Oct.	Nov.	Dec.	Jan.
1959	4	6	5	6	6	8	8	8	9	8	8	6
1960	5	5	5	5	6	7	7	8	8	7	7	5
1961	4	6	5	6	6	7	8	8	8	8	7	6
1962	4	6	5	6	6	7	8	8	9	8	7	6
1963	4	6	5	6	6	8	8	8	9	8	8	6
1964	5	5	5	5	6	7	7	7	8	7	7	5
1965	4	6	5	6	6	7	8	8	8	8	7	6
1966	4	6	5	6	6	7	8	8	9	8	7	6
1967	4	6	5	6	6	8	8	8	9	8	8	6
1968	5	5	5	5	6	7	7	7	8	7	7	5
1969	4	6	5	6	6	7	8	8	8	7	7	6
1970	4	6	5	6	6	7	8	8	9	8	7	6
1971	4	6	5	6	6	8	8	8	9	8	8	6
1972	5	5	5	5	5	7	7	7	8	7	7	5
1973	4	6	5	6	6	7	8	8	8	7	7	6
1974	4	6	5	6	6	7	8	8	9	8	7	6
1975	4	6	7	6	6	8	8	8	9	8	8	6
1976	5	5	5	5	5	7	7	7	8	7	7	5
1977	4	6	5	5	6	7	8	8	8	7	7	6
1978	4	6	5	6	6	7	8	8	9	8	7	6
1979	4	6	5	6	6	8	8	8	9	8	8	6
1980	5	5	4	5	5	7	7	7	8	7	7	5
1981	4	6	5	5	6	7	7	8	8	7	7	6
1982	4	6	5	6	6	7	8	8	8	8	7	6
1983	4	6	5	6	6	8	8	8	9	8	7	6
1984	4	5	4	5	5	7	7	7	8	7	7	5
1985	4	5	5	5	6	7	7	8	8	7	7	5
1986	4	6	5	6	6	7	8	8	8	8	7	6
1987	4	6	5	6	6	8	8	8	9	8	7	6
1988	4	5	4	5	5	7	7	7	8	7	7	5
1989	4	5	5	5	6	7	7	8	8	7	7	5
1990	4	6	5	6	6	7	8	8	9	8	7	6
1991	4	6	5	6	6	7	8	8	9	8	7	6
1992	4	5	4	5	5	7	7	7	8	7	7	5
1993	4	5	5	5	6	7	7	8	8	7	7	5
1994	4	6	5	6	6	7	8	8	8	7	7	6
1995	4	6	5	6	6	7	8	8	9	8	7	6
1996	4	5	4	5	5	7	7	7	8	7	7	5
1997	4	5	5	5	6	7	7	7	8	7	7	5
1998	4	6	5	6	6	7	8	8	8	7	7	5
1999	4	6	5	6	6	7	8	8	9	8	7	6
2000	4	5	4	5	5	7	7	7	8	7	7	6

Figure 10E (continued).

Dates the Months Change.

If your Natal Year number is: Your Natal Month number is:	1, 4, or 7	2, 5, or 8	3, 6, or 9	For birthdays between:
	8	2	5	Feb. 4 to March 5
	7	1	4	March 6 to April 5
	6	9	3	April 5 to May 5
	5	8	2	May 6 to June 5
	4	7	1	June 6 to July 7
	3	6	9	July 8 to August 7
	2	5	8	August 8 to Sept. 7
	1	4	7	Sept. 8 to Oct. 8
	9	3	6	Oct. 9 to Nov. 7
	8	2	5	Nov. 8 to Dec. 7
	7	1	4	Dec. 8 to Jan. 5
	6	9	3	Jan. 6 to Feb. 3

Figure 10F.
Determining Natal Month numbers.

House Number

The House number is the third of the major numbers in Ki numerology. This number depicts the house, or square, that your Natal Year number is in when you look at your Natal Month chart.

Let's assume we are working out the chart for a man born September 21, 1947. His Natal Year chart will have an 8 in the central position (Figure 10G). Naturally, his Natal Month number of 4 is also in the central position of his Natal Month chart (Figure 10H). We look for the position of his Natal Year number in his Natal Month chart. It is in the central position in the top row. We now look at this same position in the Lo Shu chart (Figure 10I, next page) to see what number is in that exact same position. It is

7	3	5
6	8	1
2	4	9

Figure 10G.
Natal Year chart for a man born on September 21, 1947.

3	(8)	1
2	4	6
7	9	5

Figure 10H.
Natal Month chart for a man born on September 21, 1947.

Figure 10I.

Lo Shu chart and House number for a man born on September 21, 1947.

the number 9. Therefore, this person's House number is 9.

This means that this person has a Natal Year number of 8, a Natal Month number of 4, and a House number of 9. This chart belongs to Stephen King.

Let's do another example. This time it is a woman born February 27, 1932. Her Natal Year number is 5. Her Natal Month number is 2, and her House number is 8. The House number was obtained by looking at her Natal Month chart and seeing what position her Natal Year number was occupying. It was in the bottom left-hand corner. We then look at the Universal chart and see what number is in that space and find it is an 8. This is the House number. The chart we have just done belongs to Elizabeth Taylor.

Here is one final example. Marilyn Monroe was born June 1, 1926. This means that she had a 2 Natal Year number, an 8 Natal Month number, and an 8 House number. (As she was born June 1, we consider that she was born in May. Consequently, she had an 8 Natal Month number, rather than the 7 she would have had if she had been born later in the month.)

There are 108 possible combinations of the three main numbers in the Ki system. In the next chapter we will learn the meanings of each number.

Summary

To determine the person's Natal Year number we:

1. Add up the last two numbers of the person's year of birth and reduce them down to a single digit.

2. We subtract this digit from 10 (if the person was born in the twentieth century; we subtract from 9 if the person was born in the twenty-first century).

3. The answer we obtain is the person's Natal Year number.

To determine the person's Natal Month number we:

1. Determine which month the person was born according to the Chinese calendar. This is shown in Figure 10E (pages 112 to 114).

2. Determine your Natal Month number from Figure 10F.

If your birthday is after the 9th of any month, you can determine your Natal Month number in a different way. Do not use this shortcut if you were born in the first nine days of any month.

If your Natal Year number is 1, 4, or 7 your Natal Month number is:

> 6 if you were born in January
> 8 if you were born in February
> 7 if you were born in March
> 6 if you were born in April
> 5 if you were born in May
> 4 if you were born in June
> 3 if you were born in July
> 2 if you were born in August
> 1 if you were born in September
> 9 if you were born in October
> 8 if you were born in November
> 7 if you were born in December

If your Natal Year number is 2, 5, or 8 your Natal Month number is:

> 9 if you were born in January
> 2 if you were born in February
> 1 if you were born in March
> 9 if you were born in April
> 8 if you were born in May
> 7 if you were born in June
> 6 if you were born in July
> 5 if you were born in August
> 4 if you were born in September
> 3 if you were born in October
> 2 if you were born in November
> 1 if you were born in December

If your Natal Year number is 3, 6, or 9 your Natal Month number is:

> 3 if you were born in January
> 5 if you were born in February
> 4 if you were born in March
> 3 if you were born in April
> 2 if you were born in May
> 1 if you were born in June
> 9 if you were born in July
> 8 if you were born in August
> 7 if you were born in September
> 6 if you were born in October
> 5 if you were born in November
> 4 if you were born in December

To determine the person's House number we:

1. Look for the position of the Natal Year number on the Natal Month chart.

2. Note the number at the same position on the Lo Shu chart. This number is the House number.

This completes the mathematics for basic Ki. We will look at the interpretations for each number in the next chapter.

11

Meanings of the Numbers

Each number in the Ki system relates to a color, an element, and one of the eight trigrams from the I Ching, and is either yin or yang (female or male) in nature.

With adults, the traits of these numbers are most apparent in the Natal Year number, which represents approximately 45 percent of the person's makeup. The Natal Month number represents approximately 30 percent of the person's makeup.[1] (However, it is the most important number for people under the age of eighteen, and for people who are basically immature. It can also become the most important number when the person is under great stress or pressure.) The House number represents the final 25 percent.

Most people are a mixture of two or three different numbers. It is rare to find people who have all three numbers the same. Examples are some people born in a 5 Natal Year who also have 5 Natal Month and House numbers. (People born between August 8 and September 7, 1995, are examples.)

If you were born August 3, 1953, you would have a Natal Year number of 2, a Natal Month number of 6, and a House number of 1. When interpreting this, most attention would be placed on the characteristics of the Natal Year, followed by the Natal Month, with the House number also being important, but having the least effect.

Meanings of the Numbers

Number 1

> Color: White
> Element: Water
> Trigram: K'an

People born in a White Water year are adaptable, easy to get along with, and usually gentle. They have active, often creative, brains. They are perceptive and able to quickly assess both sides of a situation. However, they are cautious and seldom reveal everything that they are thinking about. They are deep thinkers and inclined to listen rather than talk. It is not always easy to know what they are thinking about, and they are extremely good at keeping secrets. They enjoy solitude and quiet times on their own. They do well in business and invariably rise to a position at or near the top. They enjoy variety and often travel extensively in the course of their lives. One is a yang, or male, number.

Number 2

> Color: Black
> Element: Earth
> Trigram: K'un

People born in a Black Soil year are stable, well balanced, and thoughtful. They are generally outgoing and enjoy social activities. They also work well as part of a team. They do not expect any handouts, and are prepared to work hard for what they want. Consequently, they are usually most successful later on in life. They are stubborn and resistant to change. They find it hard to delegate, as they are often perfectionists and believe that no one can do the task as well as they can. They are good with details. They are compassionate, understanding, and supportive. They have a strong need to be appreciated by others, and will work long and hard, providing their effort is rewarded by sufficient acknowledgment and attention. They enjoy good food and have a tendency to put on weight as they get older. Two is a yin, or female, number.

Number 3

Color: Green
Element: Wood
Trigram: Chen

People born in a Bright Green Tree year (sometimes referred to as the Turquoise or Jade Wood year) are idealistic and emotional. They are quick thinkers who frequently skim over the surface, gaining superficial knowledge instead of a deep understanding of the subject. They are generous and kind. They are ambitious and often achieve success at a young age. They are impulsive people who possess a great deal of energy. However, this energy can sometimes be spread thinly over too wide an area. Because they are so emotional, these people can become very angry when frustrated. Although they normally seek marriage, threes basically remain independent. This independence also means that they usually prefer self-employment to being a part of someone else's corporation. Alternatively, a position as an "ideas person" would be ideal for them. They find it hard to hold onto money, because they enjoy a good time and are also extremely generous. Three is a yang number.

Number 4

Color: Green
Element: Wood
Trigram: Sun

People born in a Green Wood year are practical, independent, thoughtful, and ambitious. They are a constant source of fresh, new ideas, which makes them fun to be around. They are strong proponents of justice and make their views heard when they feel that personal freedoms are being attacked. However, they do this in a charming manner that does not cause offense. They are not good with details, preferring the overall view. Consequently, in business they need other people to take care of the details. They are inclined to procrastinate, which leads to frantic, last-minute attempts to finish the task on time. This creates tension, and these people find it hard to work in stressful situations. Four is a yin number.

Number 5

Color: Yellow
Element: Earth
Trigrams: K'un and Ken

People born in a Yellow Soil year are practical realists. They are gentle and easy to get along with, but they have a strong core inside. They have definite views on the things that are important to them. Because of this, they can appear to be very stubborn. Although they outwardly appear confident and responsible, inside they often feel insecure and unsure of themselves. They often gravitate to leadership positions, even though they are strongly independent and don't find it easy to work as part of a team. They are responsible. Five is in the center of the Universal Chart, and is also in the middle of the nine-year cycle. Consequently, both yin and yang energies are present.

Number 6

Color: White
Element: Metal
Trigram: Ch'ien

People born in a White Metal year are self-disciplined and controlled. They are analytical, logical, and inward looking. This can sometimes make it hard for them to relate well with others. They have strong views and can appear to be unyielding to others. They are hardest on themselves and often blame themselves for mistakes. They are hardworking and frequently take on more than they can comfortably handle. This hard work usually leads to material success, but they do need to ensure that they take sufficient time off for play. They are careful with money and do not like spending it on things that they consider unimportant. They are interested in technology and often work in technical fields. They have a strong sense of responsibility that starts early on in life. They are family-oriented and enjoy helping and supporting the young and elderly members of the family. They usually have a strong, traditional faith and enjoy being part of and working for a group of like-minded people. Six is a yang number.

Number 7

Color: Red
Element: Metal
Trigram: Tui

Red Metal is like molten metal, and people born in this year experience many changes in their lives. They often find it hard to stand on their own two feet but, once independence is achieved, they make rapid progress. They are quick thinkers, but can be overly changeable, making it hard for them to focus on their major goals. They are survivors, though; no matter what happens to them, they always come out of the situation smiling. They are good communicators and enjoy talking, whether they know anything about the subject or not. They dislike arguments and stressful situations, and will say exactly what other people want to hear, rather than what may be on their minds. They want to be liked and find it hard to say "no." Seven is a yin number.

Number 8

Color: White
Element: Earth
Trigram: Ken

People born in a White Earth year are stable and responsible. They enjoy carrying on family traditions and need the love and support of their families. They are methodical and careful. This means that they are not as quick at completing tasks as others, which can sometimes cause problems. However, they are perfectionists who enjoy tasks that test and challenge their abilities. They need to remain aware of the full picture and guard against getting lost in the details. They are generally reserved, but when they speak their minds they say exactly what they mean. This honesty and frankness lands them in trouble at times. They are tenacious and stubborn. They are conservative by nature and dislike change. They present a calm, dispassionate exterior to others, but deep down are highly sensitive. They progress steadily throughout life, achieving their greatest successes in middle age. They are often financially successful, though this is not generally apparent, as they do not display their wealth to others. Eight is a yang number.

Number 9

Color: Purple
Element: Fire
Trigram: Li

People born in a Purple Fire year are bright, cheerful, and full of ideas. They have good taste and enjoy working and living in attractive surroundings. They are usually better at starting tasks than they are at completing them. Their enthusiasm is inclined to falter if the task cannot be completed in a reasonable length of time. They are likely to be noticed, if not for their attractive appearance, for their humor and charm. They can be outspoken at times. They always give the impression that everything is going well with their lives, even when this is not the case. They have leadership capabilities and can easily motivate and inspire others. Money is not their strong point. They tend to live up to their income and find it hard to save. Nine is a yin number.

Putting It Together

Now that we know the meanings of the numbers in the Ki system, we are ready to give character readings to our friends and family.

Here is a sample reading for a man born September 23, 1920. He has a Natal Year number of 8, a Natal Month number of 4, and a House number of 9. We might say:

"You are a stable and responsible person. You are happiest when you have the love and support of your family. You are usually methodical and careful. You like to do things properly and are prepared to spend as much time as necessary to do a really good job.

"Although you put on a bright, positive front to the world, you can also be reserved at times. However, when you do speak your mind you say exactly what you mean. You don't suffer fools gladly. Your frankness and honesty has got you into trouble at times. Even though you sometimes say exactly what you feel, deep down you are very sensitive.

"Money is important to you only in terms of what it can do to make your life better. You are not an extravagant or showy sort of person. (All of the above comes from his Natal Year number. Now we start using the Natal Month number.) However, having said that, you can be a good spender at times.

"You are practical, independent, thoughtful and ambitious. You are always full of ideas, and these make you great fun to be around. When you speak your mind you do it in a charming manner that wins people over to your point of view. You are not always good with the details of things, preferring the overall view. This means that in business you should make use of other people to take care of the details. When you procrastinate, as you do now and again, you end up feeling tense and stressed. (Now we add the qualities of his House number.)

"You are definitely an ideas person. You get very enthusiastic about things, so much so that at times you have not always finished everything you started because you've gone off on a tangent and started something new. Fortunately, you have a strong Natal Year number, which means that you do complete the important tasks.

"You have the ability to please and captivate others with your humor and charming personality. Other people notice you and you enjoy that. You have a natural good taste and enjoy living and working in attractive surroundings.

"You like people to think that you are in total control all the time. You put on a bright face even when you are feeling sad. You always manage to give the impression that everything is going well with your life, even when this may not be the case."

This man's name is Mickey Rooney.

12

The Nine Houses

Because the numbers change position in the Ki system all the time, it is very easy to determine future trends.

Each box in the three-by-three magic square contains a house. Over a period of time, the Natal Year and Natal Month numbers move around the chart, giving us the opportunity to experience the different energies each house gives to the two main numbers.

In 1997, for instance, the universal chart for the year will be the one that contains 3 in the center position. In 1998, it will be the chart that has a 2 in this position. The year 1999 contains a 1; 2000 a 9; 2001 an 8, and so on.

Also, every month the monthly charts change. The number in the center of these monthly charts is shown in Figure 12A (next page).

Naturally, because we can work out where our numbers will be in the magic square for any date, we are able to use the Ki system to know what energies will be around us at any given time. This knowledge allows us to make important decisions at the right times and to live in harmony with the universe.

If you are looking at the yearly trends, pay particular attention to the house your Natal Year number is in. Then look at the month number and finally the House number.

Naturally, there are monthly and even daily cycles as well. The possible variations of these are immense. In practice, I seldom look at the daily cycles unless I am planning to do

If the yearly chart contains 1, 4, or 7 in the central position:
    January will have a 6 in the center.
    February will have an 8.
    March will have a 7.
    April will have a 6.
    May will have a 5.
    June will have a 4.
    July will have a 3.
    August will have a 2.
    September will have a 1.
    October will have a 9.
    November will have an 8.
    December will have a 7.

If the yearly chart contains 3, 6, or 9 in the central position:
    January will have a 3 in the center.
    February will have a 5.
    March will have a 4.
    April will have a 3.
    May will have a 2.
    June will have a 1.
    July will have a 9.
    August will have an 8.
    September will have a 7.
    October will have a 6.
    November will have a 5.
    December will have a 4.

If the yearly chart contains 2, 5, or 8 in the central position:
    January will have a 2 in the center.
    February will have a 2.
    March will have a 1.
    April will have a 9.
    May will have an 8.
    June will have a 7.
    July will have a 6.
    August will have a 5.
    September will have a 6.
    October will have a 5.
    November will have a 4.
    December will have a 3.

Figure 12A.
**Determining
monthly charts.**

something important and want to choose the most auspicious day for it. However, each year I work out my yearly and monthly cycles as a guide.

Favorable and Unfavorable Positions

As your natal numbers move around the chart they are going to spend time in each house. Some of these houses will be especially good for you, and you will experience this as a time when everything seems to go your way. At other times, your natal numbers will reside in unfavorable houses, and this is when everything will seem to conspire against you, making it impossible to move ahead.

The easiest way to determine the favorable and unfavorable houses is to look at the elements controlling each position. For instance, if your Natal Year number is a 2, 5, or 8, all of which are earth numbers, you will find it easy to move ahead when your natal number is in any of the earth houses. You would also prosper when your natal number was in House 9, as that is a fire house, and fire produces earth. However, you would not fare so well when your natal number was in House 1, as this is a water house and water can be polluted by earth.

In the same way, wood people (3 and 4) should be cautious when in the houses of fire (9) and metal (6 and 7), because these can both destroy wood.

It is an interesting exercise to follow your natal numbers through a nine-year period and determine the different energies you will experience at each stage.

Magic Square Directions

The magic square also shows directions (Figure 12B). These directions remain constant, of course, but the numbers inside the square change all the time. The positions of our Natal Year and Natal Month in the chart show us the best directions for us to travel at that time. This is particularly emphasized if the number is inside a positive house. When the Natal Year or Natal

	SE	S	SW	
E	4	9	2	
	3	5	7	W
	8	1	6	
	NE	N	NW	

Figure 12B.
Directions as shown by the magic square.

Month number is inside House 5 (the center of the chart), travel is not advised.

The Meanings of the Houses

Each year the basic chart changes, and as a result your Natal Year numbers change positions. The places, or houses, they arrive in can be interpreted to give you some idea of the nature of the year. (Naturally, you can also do this on a monthly basis, if you wish.) Each house has a meaning.

House 1

~

Element: *Water*

Color: *White*

Direction: *North*

When your Natal Year or Month number is in this house you need to be patient and cautious. It is a time to think, reflect, and make future plans. It is often a time when money problems arise. Pay attention to details and do not overextend yourself, particularly financially.

Although you will spend some time with friends and loved ones, you will also seek out periods to be by yourself. Make sure that you let your family and friends know what you are doing to avoid any misunderstandings.

Most of your development at this time will be inner development. It is a good time to trust your intuition and to develop this side of your makeup.

House 2

~

Element: *Earth*

Color: *Black*

Direction: *Southwest*

This is a time of slow and steady progress. Your fortunes will improve, and you will be feeling positive about all aspects of your life. However, the deep thinking that began in House 1 is still continuing, so bide your time and avoid making impulsive decisions. It is not a good time to start on anything new, but you can improve and stabilize existing ventures. Seek advice from others on matters that you are not sure about. Stress is likely, so make sure you allow sufficient time to relax and unwind. Make sure that you keep in touch with close friends and family.

House 3

This is a time of new beginnings. Your enthusiasm and energy levels will be high, and your creativity will blossom. You will have a strong desire to make things happen and will be feeling optimistic and positive. Even though you will be impatient to start, make sure that your ideas are good and workable before getting them underway. This is an excellent time for travel and for starting new ventures. It is also a good time for love and romance. Avoid nervous tension, and exercise and eat wisely.

~

Element: *Wood*

Color: *Turquoise*

Direction: *East*

House 4

When your natal numbers are in this house you will start to reap the rewards of your hard work. You will have a clear idea of what you want to achieve, and this focus makes it much easier to reach your goals. You will be working on developing things that you began last year, and you will find that you will move forward smoothly. It is also a good time for love and friendships.

You will be able to express yourself well, and will possess a confident and mature outlook. This is a time of success.

~

Element: *Wood*

Color: *Green*

Direction:
Southeast

House 5

This house is sometimes referred to as the House of Disaster, but this is usually an overstatement. Unexpected happenings occur when your natal numbers appear in this position, but these can be good as well as bad. During this year you should pause, take stock of your life, and make plans for future progress. Be cautious and well disciplined, and avoid impulsive actions. Undue haste and impatience may cause problems.

This is not a good year for travel. Five is in the center position and you should stay "centered" this year—in other words, as close to home as possible.

Naturally, when you were born your Natal Year number was in House 5. Consequently, it remains your most important house, and every nine years, when your Natal Year number appears in it, you tend to reap what you have sown. This makes it a karmic house, as well. The Ki system, just like the other systems of numerology, works in nine-year cycles. Naturally, all the other numbers are also in the same positions they were in when you were born. This means that for this year, you evaluate how your life is progressing and look both backward and forward.

~

Element: *Earth*

Color: *Yellow*

Direction: *Center*

Speaking generally, matters go more smoothly in the first half of this year than they do in the second. This is just as true with love and romance as it is with other areas of your life.

House 6

~

Element: *Metal*

Color: *White*

Direction:
Northwest

This is a time when you are able to move ahead strongly. The tide is going your way, and you should seize the opportunities that present themselves. Hard work done in the past will pay off now. However, do not overwork and allow sufficient time for relaxation. It is a good period for spending time with friends, providing you do not overindulge in food or drink.

On the negative side, avoid being petty or arrogant, and realize that other people may sometimes be right in their views. Avoid disagreements and concentrate on your own goals. It is a waste to spend this fruitful time on small-minded matters.

House 7

~

Element: *Metal*

Color: *Red*

Direction: *West*

At this time, matters will go your way, apparently without any effort. In actuality, you will be reaping rewards for things that you did in the past. Although everything appears to happen easily, you will still need to pay attention to details to ensure that you make the most of this time. This is a good period for creativity, for partnerships, and for money. It is not a good time for starting anything new, but it provides an excellent opportunity to capitalize on your past efforts.

House 8

~

Element: *Earth*

Color: *White*

Direction:
Northeast

This is a period where you appear to mark time. In fact, you are inwardly progressing, but may not be fully aware of it. It is a good time to carry on with your education, perhaps exploring a subject that you have not had time to properly examine in the past. It is a moderate year financially. You may find a strong desire to improve your physical fitness. All relationships blossom at this time.

By the end of the year there is a strong possibility that you will have changed direction. This could be a change of occupation, home, or way of thinking. However, this will happen so gradually, almost imperceptibly, that it could be a surprise when it occurs. This change will open up new directions for you and eliminate many past frustrations.

House 9

This marks a time when all matters in your life are lit up. On the positive side, this could bring fame, fortune, and great success. On the negative side, something you have tried to keep hidden may somehow be revealed, causing distress and embarrassment. If your dealings with others are honest and you have nothing to be ashamed about, you will find this a period of great joy.

You are likely to make new friends and be exposed to new experiences during this year. Make sure that you do one thing at a time, rather than trying to do everything all at once. Long-term relationships fare well this year, provided you pay attention to them. It is not a good year for short-term, superficial relationships.

Element: *Fire*

Color: *Purple*

Direction: *South*

13

Conclusion

I hope that you will put the information you have learned about Chinese numerology into practice in your life. You will find it helpful to you in many different ways.

We have covered three variations of numerology—the Eastern and Western versions of Chinese numerology, and the Nine Star Ki system—all of which come originally from Wu's tortoise. Experiment with all three and decide which one you like best. I have found that my students usually prefer one method over the others, but use the other two when they feel it would be more suitable.

I usually construct charts using the Westernized version, as it uses the Western solar calendar and is quick and easy to do, without the need to look anything up. On my regular radio show I use this method exclusively. However, I also often use the Ki system along with it, because of the extra insights it offers.

I seldom use the traditional Chinese system, except when traveling in Asia or when I have an Asian client. This is because until now it has been extremely difficult to find conversion charts in the West. When in Asian countries, or when with an Asian client, this is not a problem, as the people I deal with already know their lunar birthdays. However, because this book contains the solar and lunar conversion chart for the entire twentieth century (see the appendix), it is likely that I'll make more and more use of traditional Chinese numerology.

Experiment with all three systems. Work out the numbers of your family and friends and see which method or methods you prefer. Then do charts for as many people as you can. As you construct and interpret these charts you will be learning all the time. For instance, you may find an arrow of determination in the chart of someone you thought was always meek and mild. Ask this person about it, and you will learn the different ways in which the arrows can be used. I have a friend who always appears to be bending and yielding to others, but she has an arrow of determination in her chart. When I asked her about this, she laughed and told me that she bent only as much as suited her, and in fact, almost invariably got her own way. Yet she did it in such a charming manner that no one realized what was happening.

I wish you every success in numerology, no matter which method you ultimately decide to use.

Appendix: Solar-Lunar Conversion Chart

Converting Solar Calandar Dates to Lunar Calendar Dates

In the solar calendar, most months consist of either thirty or thirty-one days, with February as the sole exception. In the lunar calendar the months consist of either twenty-nine or thirty days. However, in certain years months repeat themselves, creating thirteen month years. The first example of this occurs on September 24, 1900 when the lunar month of August starts to repeat itself.

In the following table, the months are printed before the days. Consequently, 8/3 represents August 3 and not March 8.

Solar Date	Lunar Date							
1900		1/15	12/15	2/1	1/2	2/19	1/20
		1/16	12/16	2/2	1/3	2/20	1/21
		1/17	12/17	2/3	1/4	2/21	1/22
		1/18	12/18	2/4	1/5	2/22	1/23
1/1	12/1/1899	1/19	12/19	2/5	1/6	2/23	1/24
1/2	12/2	1/20	12/20	2/6	1/7	2/24	1/25
1/3	12/3	1/21	12/21	2/7	1/8	2/25	1/26
1/4	12/4	1/22	12/22	2/8	1/9	2/26	1/27
1/5	12/5	1/23	12/23	2/9	1/10	2/27	1/28
1/6	12/6	1/24	12/24	2/10	1/11	2/28	1/29
1/7	12/7	1/25	12/25	2/11	1/12		
1/8	12/8	1/26	12/26	2/12	1/13	3/1	2/1
1/9	12/9	1/27	12/27	2/13	1/14	3/2	2/2
1/10	12/10	1/28	12/28	2/14	1/15	3/3	2/3
1/11	12/11	1/29	12/29	2/15	1/16	3/4	2/4
1/12	12/12	1/30	12/30	2/16	1/17	3/5	2/5
1/13	12/13	1/31	1/1/1900	2/17	1/18	3/6	2/6
1/14	12/14			2/18	1/19	3/7	2/7

Solar	Lunar	Solar	Lunar	Solar	Lunar	Solar	Lunar	Solar	Lunar
3/8	2/8	5/5	4/7	7/2	6/6	8/30	8/6	10/27	9/5
3/9	2/9	5/6	4/8	7/3	6/7	8/31	8/7	10/28	9/6
3/10	2/10	5/7	4/9	7/4	6/8			10/29	9/7
3/11	2/11	5/8	4/10	7/5	6/9	9/1	8/8	10/30	9/8
3/12	2/12	5/9	4/11	7/6	6/10	9/2	8/9	10/31	9/9
3/13	2/13	5/10	4/12	7/7	6/11	9/3	8/10		
3/14	2/14	5/11	4/13	7/8	6/12	9/4	8/11	11/1	9/10
3/15	2/15	5/12	4/14	7/9	6/13	9/5	8/12	11/2	9/11
3/16	2/16	5/13	4/15	7/10	6/14	9/6	8/13	11/3	9/12
3/17	2/17	5/14	4/16	7/11	6/15	9/7	8/14	11/4	9/13
3/18	2/18	5/15	4/17	7/12	6/16	9/8	8/15	11/5	9/14
3/19	2/19	5/16	4/18	7/13	6/17	9/9	8/16	11/6	9/15
3/20	2/20	5/17	4/19	7/14	6/18	9/10	8/17	11/7	9/16
3/21	2/21	5/18	4/20	7/15	6/19	9/11	8/18	11/8	9/17
3/22	2/22	5/19	4/21	7/16	6/20	9/12	8/19	11/9	9/18
3/23	2/23	5/20	4/22	7/17	6/21	9/13	8/20	11/10	9/19
3/24	2/24	5/21	4/23	7/18	6/22	9/14	8/21	11/11	9/20
3/25	2/25	5/22	4/24	7/19	6/23	9/15	8/22	11/12	9/21
3/26	2/26	5/23	4/25	7/20	6/24	9/16	8/23	11/13	9/22
3/27	2/27	5/24	4/26	7/21	6/25	9/17	8/24	11/14	9/23
3/28	2/28	5/25	4/27	7/22	6/26	9/18	8/25	11/15	9/24
3/29	2/29	5/26	4/28	7/23	6/27	9/19	8/26	11/16	9/25
3/30	2/30	5/27	4/29	7/24	6/28	9/20	8/27	11/17	9/26
3/31	3/1	5/28	5/1	7/25	6/29	9/21	8/28	11/18	9/27
		5/29	5/2	7/26	7/1	9/22	8/29	11/19	9/28
4/1	3/2	5/30	5/3	7/27	7/2	9/23	8/30	11/20	9/29
4/2	3/3	5/31	5/4	7/28	7/3	9/24	8/1	11/21	9/30
4/3	3/4			7/29	7/4	9/25	8/2	11/22	10/1
4/4	3/5	6/1	5/5	7/30	7/5	9/26	8/3	11/23	10/2
4/5	3/6	6/2	5/6	7/31	7/6	9/27	8/4	11/24	10/3
4/6	3/7	6/3	5/7			9/28	8/5	11/25	10/4
4/7	3/8	6/4	5/8	8/1	7/7	9/29	8/6	11/26	10/5
4/8	3/9	6/5	5/9	8/2	7/8	9/30	8/7	11/27	10/6
4/9	3/10	6/6	5/10	8/3	7/9			11/28	10/7
4/10	3/11	6/7	5/11	8/4	7/10	10/1	8/8	11/29	10/8
4/11	3/12	6/8	5/12	8/5	7/11	10/2	8/9	11/30	10/9
4/12	3/13	6/9	5/13	8/6	7/12	10/3	8/10		
4/13	3/14	6/10	5/14	8/7	7/13	10/4	8/11	12/1	10/10
4/14	3/15	6/11	5/15	8/8	7/14	10/5	8/12	12/2	10/11
4/15	3/16	6/12	5/16	8/9	7/15	10/6	8/13	12/3	10/12
4/16	3/17	6/13	5/17	8/10	7/16	10/7	8/14	12/4	10/13
4/17	3/18	6/14	5/18	8/11	7/17	10/8	8/15	12/5	10/14
4/18	3/19	6/15	5/19	8/12	7/18	10/9	8/16	12/6	10/15
4/19	3/20	6/16	5/20	8/13	7/19	10/10	8/17	12/7	10/16
4/20	3/21	6/17	5/21	8/14	7/20	10/11	8/18	12/8	10/17
4/21	3/22	6/18	5/22	8/15	7/21	10/12	8/19	12/9	10/18
4/22	3/23	6/19	5/23	8/16	7/22	10/13	8/20	12/10	10/19
4/23	3/24	6/20	5/24	8/17	7/23	10/14	8/21	12/11	10/20
4/24	3/25	6/21	5/25	8/18	7/24	10/15	8/22	12/12	10/21
4/25	3/26	6/22	5/26	8/19	7/25	10/16	8/23	12/13	10/22
4/26	3/27	6/23	5/27	8/20	7/26	10/17	8/24	12/14	10/23
4/27	3/28	6/24	5/28	8/21	7/27	10/18	8/25	12/15	10/24
4/28	3/29	6/25	5/29	8/22	7/28	10/19	8/26	12/16	10/25
4/29	4/1	6/26	5/30	8/23	7/29	10/20	8/27	12/17	10/26
4/30	4/2	6/27	6/1	8/24	7/30	10/21	8/28	12/18	10/27
		6/28	6/2	8/25	8/1	10/22	8/29	12/19	10/28
5/1	4/3	6/29	6/3	8/26	8/2	10/23	9/1	12/20	10/29
5/2	4/4	6/30	6/4	8/27	8/3	10/24	9/2	12/21	10/30
5/3	4/5			8/28	8/4	10/25	9/3	12/22	11/1
5/4	4/6	7/1	6/5	8/29	8/5	10/26	9/4	12/23	11/2

Solar	Lunar
12/24	11/3
12/25	11/4
12/26	11/5
12/27	11/6
12/28	11/7
12/29	11/8
12/30	11/9
12/31	11/10

Solar Date	Lunar Date
1901	
1/1	11/11
1/2	11/12
1/3	11/13
1/4	11/14
1/5	11/15
1/6	11/16
1/7	11/17
1/8	11/18
1/9	11/19
1/10	11/20
1/11	11/21
1/12	11/22
1/13	11/23
1/14	11/24
1/15	11/25
1/16	11/26
1/17	11/27
1/18	11/28
1/19	11/29
1/20	12/1
1/21	12/2
1/22	12/3
1/23	12/4
1/24	12/5
1/25	12/6
1/26	12/7
1/27	12/8
1/28	12/9
1/29	12/10
1/30	12/11
1/31	12/12
2/1	12/13
2/2	12/14
2/3	12/15
2/4	12/16
2/5	12/17
2/6	12/18
2/7	12/19
2/8	12/20
2/9	12/21
2/10	12/22
2/11	12/23
2/12	12/24
2/13	12/25
2/14	12/26

Solar	Lunar	Solar	Lunar	Solar	Lunar	Solar	Lunar	Solar	Lunar	Solar	Lunar
2/15	12/27	4/14	2/26	6/11	4/25	8/8	6/24	10/5	8/23	12/2	10/22
2/16	12/28	4/15	2/27	6/12	4/26	8/9	6/25	10/6	8/24	12/3	10/23
2/17	12/29	4/16	2/28	6/13	4/27	8/10	6/26	10/7	8/25	12/4	10/24
2/18	12/30	4/17	2/29	6/14	4/28	8/11	6/27	10/8	8/26	12/5	10/25
2/19	1/1/1901	4/18	2/30	6/15	4/29	8/12	6/28	10/9	8/27	12/6	10/26
2/20	1/2	4/19	3/1	6/16	5/1	8/13	6/29	10/10	8/28	12/7	10/27
2/21	1/3	4/20	3/2	6/17	5/2	8/14	7/1	10/11	8/29	12/8	10/28
2/22	1/4	4/21	3/3	6/18	5/3	8/15	7/2	10/12	9/1	12/9	10/29
2/23	1/5	4/22	3/4	6/19	5/4	8/16	7/3	10/13	9/2	12/10	10/30
2/24	1/6	4/23	3/5	6/20	5/5	8/17	7/4	10/14	9/3	12/11	11/1
2/25	1/7	4/24	3/6	6/21	5/6	8/18	7/5	10/15	9/4	12/12	11/2
2/26	1/8	4/25	3/7	6/22	5/7	8/19	7/6	10/16	9/5	12/13	11/3
2/27	1/9	4/26	3/8	6/23	5/8	8/20	7/7	10/17	9/6	12/14	11/4
2/28	1/10	4/27	3/9	6/24	5/9	8/21	7/8	10/18	9/7	12/15	11/5
		4/28	3/10	6/25	5/10	8/22	7/9	10/19	9/8	12/16	11/6
3/1	1/11	4/29	3/11	6/26	5/11	8/23	7/10	10/20	9/9	12/17	11/7
3/2	1/12	4/30	3/12	6/27	5/12	8/24	7/11	10/21	9/10	12/18	11/8
3/3	1/13			6/28	5/13	8/25	7/12	10/22	9/11	12/19	11/9
3/4	1/14	5/1	3/13	6/29	5/14	8/26	7/13	10/23	9/12	12/20	11/10
3/5	1/15	5/2	3/14	6/30	5/15	8/27	7/14	10/24	9/13	12/21	11/11
3/6	1/16	5/3	3/15			8/28	7/15	10/25	9/14	12/22	11/12
3/7	1/17	5/4	3/16	7/1	5/16	8/29	7/16	10/26	9/15	12/23	11/13
3/8	1/18	5/5	3/17	7/2	5/17	8/30	7/17	10/27	9/16	12/24	11/14
3/9	1/19	5/6	3/18	7/3	5/18			10/28	9/17	12/25	11/15
3/10	1/20	5/7	3/19	7/4	5/19	8/31	7/18	10/29	9/18	12/26	11/16
3/11	1/21	5/8	3/20	7/5	5/20	9/1	7/19	10/30	9/19	12/27	11/17
3/12	1/22	5/9	3/21	7/6	5/21	9/2	7/20	10/31	9/20	12/28	11/18
3/13	1/23	5/10	3/22	7/7	5/22	9/3	7/21			12/29	11/19
3/14	1/24	5/11	3/23	7/8	5/23	9/4	7/22	11/1	9/21	12/30	11/20
3/15	1/25	5/12	3/24	7/9	5/24	9/5	7/23	11/2	9/22	12/31	11/21
3/16	1/26	5/13	3/25	7/10	5/25	9/6	7/24	11/3	9/23		
3/17	1/27	5/14	3/26	7/11	5/26	9/7	7/25	11/4	9/24		
3/18	1/28	5/15	3/27	7/12	5/27	9/8	7/26	11/5	9/25	Solar	Lunar
3/19	1/29	5/16	3/28	7/13	5/28	9/9	7/27	11/6	9/26	Date	Date
3/20	2/1	5/17	3/29	7/14	5/29	9/10	7/28	11/7	9/27	**1902**	
3/21	2/2	5/18	4/1	7/15	5/30	9/11	7/29	11/8	9/28	1/1	11/22
3/22	2/3	5/19	4/2	7/16	6/1	9/12	7/30	11/9	9/29	1/2	11/23
3/23	2/4	5/20	4/3	7/17	6/2	9/13	8/1	11/10	9/30	1/3	11/24
3/24	2/5	5/21	4/4	7/18	6/3	9/14	8/2	11/11	10/1	1/4	11/25
3/25	2/6	5/22	4/5	7/19	6/4	9/15	8/3	11/12	10/2	1/5	11/26
3/26	2/7	5/23	4/6	7/20	6/5	9/16	8/4	11/13	10/3	1/6	11/27
3/27	2/8	5/24	4/7	7/21	6/6	9/17	8/5	11/14	10/4	1/7	11/28
3/28	2/9	5/25	4/8	7/22	6/7	9/18	8/6	11/15	10/5	1/8	11/29
3/29	2/10	5/26	4/9	7/23	6/8	9/19	8/7	11/16	10/6	1/9	11/30
3/30	2/11	5/27	4/10	7/24	6/9	9/20	8/8	11/17	10/7	1/10	12/1
3/31	2/12	5/28	4/11	7/25	6/10	9/21	8/9	11/18	10/8	1/11	12/2
		5/29	4/12	7/26	6/11	9/22	8/10	11/19	10/9	1/12	12/3
4/1	2/13	5/30	4/13	7/27	6/12	9/23	8/11	11/20	10/10	1/13	12/4
4/2	2/14	5/31	4/14	7/28	6/13	9/24	8/12	11/21	10/11	1/14	12/5
4/3	2/15			7/29	6/14	9/25	8/13	11/22	10/12	1/15	12/6
4/4	2/16	6/1	4/15	7/30	6/15	9/26	8/14	11/23	10/13	1/16	12/7
4/5	2/17	6/2	4/16	7/31	6/16	9/27	8/15	11/24	10/14	1/17	12/8
4/6	2/18	6/3	4/17			9/28	8/16	11/25	10/15	1/18	12/9
4/7	2/19	6/4	4/18	8/1	6/17	9/29	8/17	11/26	10/16	1/19	12/10
4/8	2/20	6/5	4/19	8/2	6/18	9/30	8/18	11/27	10/17	1/20	12/11
4/9	2/21	6/6	4/20	8/3	6/19			11/28	10/18	1/21	12/12
4/10	2/22	6/7	4/21	8/4	6/20	10/1	8/19	11/29	10/19	1/22	12/13
4/11	2/23	6/8	4/22	8/5	6/21	10/2	8/20	11/30	10/20	1/23	12/14
4/12	2/24	6/9	4/23	8/6	6/22	10/3	8/21			1/24	12/15
4/13	2/25	6/10	4/24	8/7	6/23	10/4	8/22	12/1	10/21		

Solar	Lunar	Solar	Lunar	Solar	Lunar	Solar	Lunar	Solar	Lunar	Solar	Lunar
1/25	12/16	3/24	2/15	5/21	4/14	7/18	6/14	9/14	8/13	11/11	10/12
1/26	12/17	3/25	2/16	5/22	4/15	7/19	6/15	9/15	8/14	11/12	10/13
1/27	12/18	3/26	2/17	5/23	4/16	7/20	6/16	9/16	8/15	11/13	10/14
1/28	12/19	3/27	2/18	5/24	4/17	7/21	6/17	9/17	8/16	11/14	10/15
1/29	12/20	3/28	2/19	5/25	4/18	7/22	6/18	9/18	8/17	11/15	10/16
1/30	12/21	3/29	2/20	5/26	4/19	7/23	6/19	9/19	8/18	11/16	10/17
1/31	12/22	3/30	2/21	5/27	4/20	7/24	6/20	9/20	8/19	11/17	10/18
		3/31	2/22	5/28	4/21	7/25	6/21	9/21	8/20	11/18	10/19
2/1	12/23			5/29	4/22	7/26	6/22	9/22	8/21	11/19	10/20
2/2	12/24	4/1	2/23	5/30	4/23	7/27	6/23	9/23	8/22	11/20	10/21
2/3	12/25	4/2	2/24	5/31	4/24	7/28	6/24	9/24	8/23	11/21	10/22
2/4	12/26	4/3	2/25			7/29	6/25	9/25	8/24	11/22	10/23
2/5	12/27	4/4	2/26	6/1	4/25	7/30	6/26	9/26	8/25	11/23	10/24
2/6	12/28	4/5	2/27	6/2	4/26	7/31	6/26	9/27	8/26	11/24	10/25
2/7	12/29	4/6	2/28	6/3	4/27			9/28	8/27	11/25	10/26
2/8	1/1	4/7	2/29	6/4	4/28	8/1	6/27	9/29	8/28	11/26	10/27
2/9	1/2	4/8	3/1	6/5	4/29	8/2	6/28	9/30	8/29	11/27	10/28
2/10	1/3	4/9	3/2	6/6	5/1	8/3	6/29			11/28	10/29
2/11	1/4	4/10	3/3	6/7	5/2	8/4	7/1	10/1	8/30	11/29	10/30
2/12	1/5	4/11	3/4	6/8	5/3	8/5	7/2	10/2	9/1	11/31	11/1
2/13	1/6	4/12	3/5	6/9	5/4	8/6	7/3	10/3	9/2		
2/14	1/7	4/13	3/6	6/10	5/5	8/7	7/4	10/4	9/3	12/1	11/2
2/15	1/8	4/14	3/7	6/11	5/6	8/8	7/5	10/5	9/4	12/2	11/3
2/16	1/9	4/15	3/8	6/12	5/7	8/9	7/6	10/6	9/5	12/3	11/4
2/17	1/10	4/16	3/9	6/13	5/8	8/10	7/7	10/7	9/6	12/4	11/5
2/18	1/11	4/17	3/10	6/14	5/9	8/11	7/8	10/8	9/7	12/5	11/6
2/19	1/12	4/18	3/11	6/15	5/10	8/12	7/9	10/9	9/8	12/6	11/7
2/20	1/13	4/19	3/12	6/16	5/11	8/13	7/10	10/10	9/9	12/7	11/8
2/21	1/14	4/20	3/13	6/17	5/12	8/14	7/11	10/11	9/10	12/8	11/9
2/22	1/15	4/21	3/14	6/18	5/13	8/15	7/12	10/12	9/11	12/9	11/10
2/23	1/16	4/22	3/15	6/19	5/14	8/16	7/13	10/13	9/12	12/10	11/11
2/24	1/17	4/23	3/16	6/20	5/15	8/17	7/14	10/14	9/13	12/11	11/12
2/25	1/18	4/24	3/17	6/21	5/16	8/18	7/15	10/15	9/14	12/13	11/13
2/26	1/19	4/25	3/18	6/22	5/17	8/19	7/16	10/16	9/15	12/14	11/14
2/27	1/20	4/26	3/19	6/23	5/18	8/20	7/17	10/17	9/16	12/15	11/15
2/28	1/21	4/27	3/20	6/24	5/19	8/21	7/18	10/18	9/17	12/16	11/16
		4/28	3/21	6/25	5/20	8/22	7/19	10/19	9/18	12/17	11/17
3/1	1/22	4/29	3/22	6/26	5/21	8/23	7/20	10/20	9/19	12/18	11/18
3/2	1/23	4/30	3/23	6/27	5/22	8/24	7/21	10/21	9/20	12/19	11/19
3/3	1/24			6/28	5/23	8/25	7/22	10/22	9/21	12/20	11/20
3/4	1/25	5/1	3/24	6/29	5/24	8/26	7/23	10/23	9/22	12/21	11/21
3/5	1/26	5/2	3/25	6/30	5/25	8/27	7/24	10/24	9/23	12/22	11/22
3/6	1/27	5/3	3/26			8/28	7/25	10/25	9/24	12/23	11/23
3/7	1/28	5/4	3/27	7/1	5/26	8/29	7/26	10/26	9/25	12/24	11/24
3/8	1/29	5/5	3/28	7/2	5/27	8/30	7/27	10/27	9/26	12/25	11/25
3/9	1/30	5/6	3/29	7/3	5/28	8/31	7/28	10/28	9/27	12/26	11/26
3/10	2/1	5/7	3/30	7/4	5/29			10/29	9/28	12/27	11/27
3/11	2/2	5/8	4/1	7/5	6/1	9/1	7/29	10/30	9/29	12/28	11/28
3/12	2/3	5/9	4/2	7/6	6/2	9/2	8/1	10/31	10/1	12/29	11/29
3/13	2/4	5/10	4/3	7/7	6/3	9/3	8/2			12/30	12/1
3/14	2/5	5/11	4/4	7/8	6/4	9/4	8/3	11/1	10/2	12/31	12/2
3/15	2/6	5/12	4/5	7/9	6/5	9/5	8/4	11/2	10/3		
3/16	2/7	5/13	4/6	7/10	6/6	9/6	8/5	11/3	10/4		
3/17	2/8	5/14	4/7	7/11	6/7	9/7	8/6	11/4	10/5	Solar	Lunar
3/18	2/9	5/15	4/8	7/12	6/8	9/8	8/7	11/5	10/6	Date	Date
3/19	2/10	5/16	4/9	7/13	6/9	9/9	8/8	11/6	10/7		
3/20	2/11	5/17	4/10	7/14	6/10	9/10	8/9	11/7	10/8	**1903**	
3/21	2/12	5/18	4/11	7/15	6/11	9/11	8/10	11/8	10/9	1/1	12/3
3/22	2/13	5/19	4/12	7/16	6/12	9/12	8/11	11/9	10/10	1/2	12/4
3/23	2/14	5/20	4/13	7/17	6/13	9/13	8/12	11/10	10/11	1/3	12/5

Solar	Lunar	Solar	Lunar	Solar	Lunar	Solar	Lunar	Solar	Lunar	Solar	Lunar
1/4	12/6	3/3	2/5	5/1	4/5	6/28	5/4	8/25	7/3	10/22	9/3
1/5	12/7	3/4	2/6	5/2	4/6	6/29	5/5	8/26	7/4	10/23	9/4
1/6	12/8	3/5	2/7	5/3	4/7	6/30	5/6	8/27	7/5	10/24	9/5
1/7	12/9	3/6	2/8	5/4	4/8			8/28	7/6	10/25	9/6
1/8	12/10	3/7	2/9	5/5	4/9	7/1	5/7	8/29	7/7	10/26	9/7
1/9	12/11	3/8	2/10	5/6	4/10	7/2	5/8	8/30	7/8	10/27	9/8
1/10	12/12	3/9	2/11	5/7	4/11	7/3	5/9	8/31	7/9	10/28	9/9
1/11	12/13	3/10	2/12	5/8	4/12	7/4	5/10			10/29	9/10
1/12	12/14	3/11	2/13	5/9	4/13	7/5	5/11	9/1	7/10	10/30	9/11
1/13	12/15	3/12	2/14	5/10	4/14	7/6	5/12	9/2	7/11	10/31	9/12
1/14	12/16	3/13	2/15	5/11	4/15	7/7	5/13	9/3	7/12		
1/15	12/17	3/14	2/16	5/12	4/16	7/8	5/14	9/4	7/13	11/1	9/13
1/16	12/18	3/15	2/17	5/13	4/17	7/9	5/15	9/5	7/14	11/2	9/14
1/17	12/19	3/16	2/18	5/14	4/18	7/10	5/16	9/6	7/15	11/3	9/15
1/18	12/20	3/17	2/19	5/15	4/19	7/11	5/17	9/7	7/16	11/4	9/16
1/19	12/21	3/18	2/20	5/16	4/20	7/12	5/18	9/8	7/17	11/5	9/17
1/20	12/22	3/19	2/21	5/17	4/21	7/13	5/19	9/9	7/18	11/6	9/18
1/21	12/23	3/20	2/22	5/18	4/22	7/14	5/20	9/10	7/19	11/7	9/19
1/22	12/24	3/21	2/23	5/19	4/23	7/15	5/21	9/11	7/20	11/8	9/20
1/23	12/25	3/22	2/24	5/20	4/24	7/16	5/22	9/12	7/21	11/9	9/21
1/24	12/26	3/23	2/25	5/21	4/25	7/17	5/23	9/13	7/22	11/10	9/22
1/25	12/27	3/24	2/26	5/22	4/26	7/18	5/24	9/14	7/23	11/11	9/23
1/26	12/28	3/25	2/27	5/23	4/27	7/19	5/25	9/15	7/24	11/12	9/24
1/27	12/29	3/26	2/28	5/24	4/28	7/20	5/26	9/16	7/25	11/13	9/25
1/28	12/30	3/27	2/29	5/25	4/29	7/21	5/27	9/17	7/26	11/14	9/26
1/29	1/1	3/28	2/30	5/26	4/30	7/22	5/28	9/18	7/27	11/15	9/27
1/30	1/2	3/29	3/1	5/27	5/1	7/23	5/29	9/19	7/28	11/16	9/28
1/31	1/3	3/30	3/2	5/28	5/2	7/24	6/1	9/20	7/29	11/17	9/29
		3/31	3/3	5/29	5/3	7/25	6/2	9/21	8/1	11/18	9/30
2/1	1/4			5/30	5/4	7/26	6/3	9/22	8/2	11/19	10/1
2/2	1/5	4/1	3/4	5/31	5/5	7/27	6/4	9/23	8/3	11/20	10/2
2/3	1/6	4/2	3/5			7/28	6/5	9/24	8/4	11/21	10/3
2/4	1/7	4/3	3/6	6/1	5/6	7/29	6/6	9/25	8/5	11/22	10/4
2/5	1/8	4/4	3/7	6/2	5/7	7/30	6/7	9/26	8/6	11/23	10/5
2/6	1/9	4/5	3/8	6/3	5/8	7/31	6/8	9/27	8/7	11/24	10/6
2/7	1/10	4/6	3/9	6/4	5/9			9/28	8/8	11/25	10/7
2/8	1/11	4/7	3/10	6/5	5/10	8/1	6/9	9/29	8/9	11/26	10/8
2/9	1/12	4/8	3/11	6/6	5/11	8/2	6/10	9/30	8/10	11/27	10/9
2/10	1/13	4/9	3/12	6/7	5/12	8/3	6/11			11/28	10/10
2/11	1/14	4/10	3/13	6/8	5/13	8/4	6/12	10/1	8/11	11/29	10/11
2/12	1/15	4/11	3/14	6/9	5/14	8/5	6/13	10/2	8/12	11/30	10/12
2/13	1/16	4/12	3/15	6/10	5/15	8/6	6/14	10/3	8/13		
2/14	1/17	4/13	3/16	6/11	5/16	8/7	6/15	10/4	8/14	12/1	10/13
2/15	1/18	4/14	3/17	6/12	5/17	8/8	6/16	10/5	8/15	12/2	10/14
2/16	1/19	4/15	3/18	6/13	5/18	8/9	6/17	10/6	8/16	12/3	10/15
2/17	1/20	4/16	3/19	6/14	5/19	8/10	6/18	10/7	8/17	12/4	10/16
2/18	1/21	4/17	3/20	6/15	5/20	8/11	6/19	10/8	8/18	12/5	10/17
2/19	1/22	4/18	3/21	6/16	5/21	8/12	6/20	10/9	8/19	12/6	10/18
2/20	1/23	4/19	3/22	6/17	5/22	8/13	6/21	10/10	8/20	12/7	10/19
2/21	1/24	4/20	3/23	6/18	5/23	8/14	6/22	10/11	8/21	12/8	10/20
2/22	1/25	4/21	3/24	6/19	5/24	8/15	6/23	10/12	8/22	12/9	10/21
2/23	1/26	4/22	3/25	6/20	5/25	8/16	6/24	10/13	8/23	12/10	10/22
2/24	1/27	4/23	3/26	6/21	5/26	8/17	6/25	10/14	8/24	12/11	10/23
2/25	1/28	4/24	3/27	6/22	5/27	8/18	6/26	10/15	8/25	12/12	10/24
2/26	1/29	4/25	3/28	6/23	5/28	8/19	6/27	10/16	8/26	12/13	10/25
2/27	2/1	4/26	3/29	6/24	5/29	8/20	6/28	10/17	8/27	12/14	10/26
2/28	2/2	4/27	4/1	6/25	5/1	8/21	6/29	10/18	8/28	12/15	10/27
		4/28	4/2	*(Leap month)*		8/22	6/30	10/19	8/29	12/16	10/28
3/1	2/3	4/29	4/3	6/26	5/2	8/23	7/1	10/20	9/1	12/17	10/29
3/2	2/4	4/30	4/4	6/27	5/3	8/24	7/2	10/21	9/2	12/18	10/30

Solar	Lunar	Solar	Lunar	Solar	Lunar	Solar	Lunar	Solar	Lunar	Solar	Lunar
12/19	11/1	2/10	12/25	4/8	2/23	6/5	4/22	8/2	6/21	9/30	8/21
12/20	11/2	2/11	12/26	4/9	2/24	6/6	4/23	8/3	6/22		
12/21	11/3	2/12	12/27	4/10	2/25	6/7	4/24	8/4	6/23	10/1	8/22
12/22	11/4	2/13	12/28	4/11	2/26	6/8	4/25	8/5	6/24	10/2	8/23
12/23	11/5	2/14	12/29	4/12	2/27	6/9	4/26	8/6	6/25	10/3	8/24
12/24	11/6	2/15	12/30	4/13	2/28	6/10	4/27	8/7	6/26	10/4	8/25
12/25	11/7	2/16	1/1	4/14	2/29	6/11	4/28	8/8	6/27	10/5	8/26
12/26	11/8	2/17	1/2	4/15	2/30	6/12	4/29	8/9	6/28	10/6	8/27
12/27	11/9	2/18	1/3	4/16	3/1	6/13	4/30	8/10	6/29	10/7	8/28
12/28	11/10	2/19	1/4	4/17	3/2	6/14	5/1	8/11	7/1	10/8	8/29
12/29	11/11	2/20	1/5	4/18	3/3	6/15	5/2	8/12	7/2	10/9	9/1
12/30	11/12	2/21	1/6	4/19	3/4	6/16	5/3	8/13	7/3	10/10	9/2
12/31	11/13	2/22	1/7	4/20	3/5	6/17	5/4	8/14	7/4	10/11	9/3
		2/23	1/8	4/21	3/6	6/18	5/5	8/15	7/5	10/12	9/4
		2/24	1/9	4/22	3/7	6/19	5/6	8/16	7/6	10/13	9/5
Solar	**Lunar**	2/25	1/10	4/23	3/8	6/20	5/7	8/17	7/7	10/14	9/6
Date	**Date**	2/26	1/11	4/24	3/9	6/21	5/8	8/18	7/8	10/15	9/7
		2/27	1/12	4/25	3/10	6/22	5/9	8/19	7/9	10/16	9/8
1904		2/28	1/13	4/26	3/11	6/23	5/10	8/20	7/10	10/17	9/9
1/1	11/14	2/29	1/14	4/27	3/12	6/24	5/11	8/21	7/11	10/18	9/10
1/2	11/15			4/28	3/13	6/25	5/12	8/22	7/12	10/19	9/11
1/3	11/16	3/1	1/15	4/29	3/14	6/26	5/13	8/23	7/13	10/20	9/12
1/4	11/17	3/2	1/16	4/30	3/15	6/27	5/14	8/24	7/14	10/21	9/13
1/5	11/18	3/3	1/17			6/28	5/15	8/25	7/15	10/22	9/14
1/6	11/19	3/4	1/18	5/1	3/16	6/29	5/16	8/26	7/16	10/23	9/15
1/7	11/20	3/5	1/19	5/2	3/17	6/30	5/17	8/27	7/17	10/24	9/16
1/8	11/21	3/6	1/20	5/3	3/18			8/28	7/18	10/25	9/17
1/9	11/22	3/7	1/21	5/4	3/19	7/1	5/18	8/29	7/19	10/26	9/18
1/10	11/23	3/8	1/22	5/5	3/20	7/2	5/19	8/30	7/20	10/27	9/19
1/11	11/24	3/9	1/23	5/6	3/21	7/3	5/20	8/31	7/21	10/28	9/20
1/12	11/25	3/10	1/24	5/7	3/22	7/4	5/21			10/29	9/21
1/13	11/26	3/11	1/25	5/8	3/23	7/5	5/22	9/1	7/22	10/30	9/22
1/14	11/27	3/12	1/26	5/9	3/24	7/6	5/23	9/2	7/23	10/31	9/23
1/15	11/28	3/13	1/27	5/10	3/25	7/7	5/24	9/3	7/24		
1/16	11/29	3/14	1/28	5/11	3/26	7/8	5/25	9/4	7/25	11/1	9/24
1/17	12/1	3/15	1/29	5/12	3/27	7/9	5/26	9/5	7/26	11/2	9/25
1/18	12/2	3/16	1/30	5/13	3/28	7/10	5/27	9/6	7/27	11/3	9/26
1/19	12/3	3/17	2/1	5/14	3/29	7/11	5/28	9/7	7/28	11/4	9/27
1/20	12/4	3/18	2/2	5/15	4/1	7/12	5/29	9/8	7/29	11/5	9/28
1/21	12/5	3/19	2/3	5/16	4/2	7/13	6/1	9/9	7/30	11/6	9/29
1/22	12/6	3/20	2/4	5/17	4/3	7/14	6/2	9/10	8/1	11/7	10/1
1/23	12/7	3/21	2/5	5/18	4/4	7/15	6/3	9/11	8/2	11/8	10/2
1/24	12/8	3/22	2/6	5/19	4/5	7/16	6/4	9/12	8/3	11/9	10/3
1/25	12/9	3/23	2/7	5/20	4/6	7/17	6/5	9/13	8/4	11/10	10/4
1/26	12/10	3/24	2/8	5/21	4/7	7/18	6/6	9/14	8/5	11/11	10/5
1/27	12/11	3/25	2/9	5/22	4/8	7/19	6/7	9/15	8/6	11/12	10/6
1/28	12/12	3/26	2/10	5/23	4/9	7/20	6/8	9/16	8/7	11/13	10/7
1/29	12/13	3/27	2/11	5/24	4/10	7/21	6/9	9/17	8/8	11/14	10/8
1/30	12/14	3/28	2/12	5/25	4/11	7/22	6/10	9/18	8/9	11/15	10/9
1/31	12/15	3/29	2/13	5/26	4/12	7/23	6/11	9/19	8/10	11/16	10/10
		3/30	2/14	5/27	4/13	7/24	6/12	9/20	8/11	11/17	10/11
2/1	12/16	3/31	2/15	5/28	4/14	7/25	6/13	9/21	8/12	11/18	10/12
2/2	12/17			5/29	4/15	7/26	6/14	9/22	8/13	11/19	10/13
2/3	12/18	4/1	2/16	5/30	4/16	7/27	6/15	9/23	8/14	11/20	10/14
2/4	12/19	4/2	2/17	5/31	4/17	7/28	6/16	9/24	8/15	11/21	10/15
2/5	12/20	4/3	2/18			7/29	6/17	9/25	8/16	11/22	10/16
2/6	12/21	4/4	2/19	6/1	4/18	7/30	6/18	9/26	8/17	11/23	10/17
2/7	12/22	4/5	2/20	6/2	4/19	7/31	6/19	9/27	8/18	11/24	10/18
2/8	12/23	4/6	2/21	6/3	4/20			9/28	8/19	11/25	10/19
2/9	12/24	4/7	2/22	6/4	4/21	8/1	6/20	9/29	8/20	11/26	10/20

Solar	Lunar	Solar	Lunar	Solar	Lunar	Solar	Lunar	Solar	Lunar	Solar	Lunar
11/27	10/21	1/19	12/14	3/18	2/13	5/15	4/12	7/12	6/10	9/8	8/10
11/28	10/22	1/20	12/15	3/19	2/14	5/16	4/13	7/13	6/11	9/9	8/11
11/29	10/23	1/21	12/16	3/20	2/15	5/17	4/14	7/14	6/12	9/10	8/12
11/30	10/24	1/22	12/17	3/21	2/16	5/18	4/15	7/15	6/13	9/11	8/13
		1/23	12/18	3/22	2/17	5/19	4/16	7/16	6/14	9/12	8/14
12/1	10/25	1/24	12/19	3/23	2/18	5/20	4/17	7/17	6/15	9/13	8/15
12/2	10/26	1/25	12/20	3/24	2/19	5/21	4/18	7/18	6/16	9/14	8/16
12/3	10/27	1/26	12/21	3/25	2/20	5/22	4/19	7/19	6/17	9/15	8/17
12/4	10/28	1/27	12/22	3/26	2/21	5/23	4/20	7/20	6/18	9/16	8/18
12/5	10/29	1/28	12/23	3/27	2/22	5/24	4/21	7/21	6/19	9/17	8/19
12/6	10/30	1/29	12/24	3/28	2/23	5/25	4/22	7/22	6/20	9/18	8/20
12/7	11/1	1/30	12/25	3/29	2/24	5/26	4/23	7/23	6/21	9/19	8/21
12/8	11/2	1/31	12/26	3/30	2/25	5/27	4/24	7/24	6/22	9/20	8/22
12/9	11/3			3/31	2/26	5/28	4/25	7/25	6/23	9/21	8/23
12/10	11/4	2/1	12/27			5/29	4/26	7/26	6/24	9/22	8/24
12/11	11/5	2/2	12/28	4/1	2/27	5/30	4/27	7/27	6/25	9/23	8/25
12/12	11/6	2/3	12/29	4/2	2/28	5/31	4/28	7/28	6/26	9/24	8/26
12/13	11/7	2/4	1/1	4/3	2/29			7/29	6/27	9/25	8/27
12/14	11/8	2/5	1/2	4/4	2/30	6/1	4/29	7/30	6/28	9/26	8/28
12/15	11/9	2/6	1/3	4/5	3/1	6/2	4/30	7/31	6/29	9/27	8/29
12/16	11/10	2/7	1/4	4/6	3/2	6/3	5/1			9/28	8/30
12/17	11/11	2/8	1/5	4/7	3/3	6/4	5/2	8/1	7/1	9/29	9/1
12/18	11/12	2/9	1/6	4/8	3/4	6/5	5/3	8/2	7/2	9/30	9/2
12/19	11/13	2/10	1/7	4/9	3/5	6/6	5/4	8/3	7/3		
12/20	11/14	2/11	1/8	4/10	3/6	6/7	5/5	8/4	7/4	10/1	9/3
12/21	11/15	2/12	1/9	4/11	3/7	6/8	5/6	8/5	7/5	10/2	9/4
12/22	11/16	2/13	1/10	4/12	3/8	6/9	5/7	8/6	7/6	10/3	9/5
12/23	11/17	2/14	1/11	4/13	3/9	6/10	5/8	8/7	7/7	10/4	9/6
12/24	11/18	2/15	1/12	4/14	3/10	6/11	5/9	8/8	7/8	10/5	9/7
12/25	11/19	2/16	1/13	4/15	3/11	6/12	5/10	8/9	7/9	10/6	9/8
12/26	11/20	2/17	1/14	4/16	3/12	6/13	5/11	8/10	7/10	10/7	9/9
12/27	11/21	2/18	1/15	4/17	3/13	6/14	5/12	8/11	7/11	10/8	9/10
12/28	11/22	2/19	1/16	4/18	3/14	6/15	5/13	8/12	7/12	10/9	9/11
12/29	11/23	2/20	1/17	4/19	3/15	6/16	5/14	8/13	7/13	10/10	9/12
12/30	11/24	2/21	1/18	4/20	3/16	6/17	5/15	8/14	7/14	10/11	9/13
12/31	11/25	2/22	1/19	4/21	3/17	6/18	5/16	8/15	7/15	10/12	9/14
		2/23	1/20	4/22	3/18	6/19	5/17	8/16	7/16	10/13	9/15
		2/24	1/21	4/23	3/19	6/20	5/18	8/17	7/17	10/14	9/16
Solar	**Lunar**	2/25	1/22	4/24	3/20	6/21	5/19	8/18	7/18	10/15	9/17
Date	**Date**	2/26	1/23	4/25	3/21	6/22	5/20	8/19	7/19	10/16	9/18
1905		2/27	1/24	4/26	3/22	6/23	5/21	8/20	7/20	10/17	9/19
1/1	11/26	2/28	1/25	4/27	3/23	6/24	5/22	8/21	7/21	10/18	9/20
1/2	11/27			4/28	3/24	6/25	5/23	8/22	7/22	10/19	9/21
1/3	11/28	3/1	1/26	4/29	3/25	6/26	5/24	8/23	7/23	10/20	9/22
1/4	11/29	3/2	1/27	4/30	3/26	6/27	5/25	8/24	7/24	10/21	9/23
1/5	11/30	3/3	1/28			6/28	5/26	8/25	7/25	10/22	9/24
1/6	12/1	3/4	1/29	5/1	3/27	6/29	5/27	8/26	7/26	10/23	9/25
1/7	12/2	3/5	1/30	5/2	3/28	6/30	5/28	8/27	7/27	10/24	9/26
1/8	12/3	3/6	2/1	5/3	3/29			8/28	7/28	10/25	9/27
1/9	12/4	3/7	2/2	5/4	4/1	7/1	5/29	8/29	7/29	10/26	9/28
1/10	12/5	3/8	2/3	5/5	4/2	7/2	5/30	8/30	8/1	10/27	9/29
1/11	12/6	3/9	2/4	5/6	4/3	7/3	6/1	8/31	8/2	10/28	10/1
1/12	12/7	3/10	2/5	5/7	4/4	7/4	6/2			10/29	10/2
1/13	12/8	3/11	2/6	5/8	4/5	7/5	6/3	9/1	8/3	10/30	10/3
1/14	12/9	3/12	2/7	5/9	4/6	7/6	6/4	9/2	8/4	10/31	10/4
1/15	12/10	3/13	2/8	5/10	4/7	7/7	6/5	9/3	8/5		
1/16	12/11	3/14	2/9	5/11	4/8	7/8	6/6	9/4	8/6	11/1	10/5
1/17	12/12	3/15	2/10	5/12	4/9	7/9	6/7	9/5	8/7	11/2	10/6
1/18	12/13	3/16	2/11	5/13	4/10	7/10	6/8	9/6	8/8	11/3	10/7
		3/17	2/12	5/14	4/11	7/11	6/9	9/7	8/9	11/4	10/8

Solar	Lunar	Solar Date	Lunar Date	Solar	Lunar	Solar	Lunar	Solar	Lunar	Solar	Lunar
11/5	10/9	**1906**		2/25	2/3	4/24	4/1	6/20	4/29	8/17	6/28
11/6	10/10			2/26	2/4	4/25	4/2	6/21	4/30	8/18	6/29
11/7	10/11			2/27	2/5	4/26	4/3	6/22	5/1	8/19	6/30
11/8	10/12			2/28	2/6	4/27	4/4	6/23	5/2	8/20	7/1
11/9	10/13	1/1	12/7			4/28	4/5	6/24	5/3	8/21	7/2
11/10	10/14	1/2	12/8	3/1	2/7	4/29	4/6	6/25	5/4	8/22	7/3
11/11	10/15	1/3	12/9	3/2	2/8	4/30	4/7	6/26	5/5	8/23	7/4
11/12	10/16	1/4	12/10	3/3	2/9			6/27	5/6	8/24	7/5
11/13	10/17	1/5	12/11	3/4	2/10	5/1	4/8	6/28	5/7	8/25	7/6
11/14	10/18	1/6	12/12	3/5	2/11	5/2	4/9	6/29	5/8	8/26	7/7
11/15	10/19	1/7	12/13	3/6	2/12	5/3	4/10	6/30	5/9	8/27	7/8
11/16	10/20	1/8	12/14	3/7	2/13	5/4	4/11			8/28	7/9
11/17	10/21	1/9	12/15	3/8	2/14	5/5	4/12	7/1	5/10	8/29	7/10
11/18	10/22	1/10	12/16	3/9	2/15	5/6	4/13	7/2	5/11	8/30	7/11
11/19	10/23	1/11	12/17	3/10	2/16	5/7	4/14	7/3	5/12	8/31	7/12
11/20	10/24	1/12	12/18	3/11	2/17	5/8	4/15	7/4	5/13		
11/21	10/25	1/13	12/19	3/12	2/18	5/9	4/16	7/5	5/14	9/1	7/13
11/22	10/26	1/14	12/20	3/13	2/19	5/10	4/17	7/6	5/15	9/2	7/14
11/23	10/27	1/15	12/21	3/14	2/20	5/11	4/18	7/7	5/16	9/3	7/15
11/24	10/28	1/16	12/22	3/15	2/21	5/12	4/19	7/8	5/17	9/4	7/16
11/25	10/29	1/17	12/23	3/16	2/22	5/13	4/20	7/9	5/18	9/5	7/17
11/26	10/30	1/18	12/24	3/17	2/23	5/14	4/21	7/10	5/19	9/6	7/18
11/27	11/1	1/19	12/25	3/18	2/24	5/15	4/22	7/11	5/20	9/7	7/19
11/28	11/2	1/20	12/26	3/19	2/25	5/16	4/23	7/12	5/21	9/8	7/20
11/29	11/3	1/21	12/27	3/20	2/26	5/17	4/24	7/13	5/22	9/9	7/21
11/30	11/4	1/22	12/28	3/21	2/27	5/18	4/25	7/14	5/23	9/10	7/22
		1/23	12/29	3/22	2/28	5/19	4/26	7/15	5/24	9/11	7/23
12/1	11/5	1/24	12/30	3/23	2/29	5/20	4/27	7/16	5/25	9/12	7/24
12/2	11/6	1/25	1/1	3/24	2/30	5/21	4/28	7/17	5/26	9/13	7/25
12/3	11/7	1/26	1/2	3/25	3/1	5/22	4/29	7/18	5/27	9/14	7/26
12/4	11/8	1/27	1/3	3/26	3/2	5/23	4/1	7/19	5/28	9/15	7/27
12/5	11/9	1/28	1/4	3/27	3/3	*(Leap month)*		7/20	5/29	9/16	7/28
12/6	11/10	1/29	1/5	3/28	3/4	5/24	4/2	7/21	6/1	9/17	7/29
12/7	11/11	1/30	1/6	3/29	3/5	5/25	4/3	7/22	6/2	9/18	8/1
12/8	11/12	1/31	1/7	3/30	3/6	5/26	4/4	7/23	6/3	9/19	8/2
12/9	11/13			3/31	3/7	5/27	4/5	7/24	6/4	9/20	8/3
12/10	11/14	2/1	1/8			5/28	4/6	7/25	6/5	9/21	8/4
12/11	11/15	2/2	1/9	4/1	3/8	5/29	4/7	7/26	6/6	9/22	8/5
12/12	11/16	2/3	1/10	4/2	3/9	5/30	4/8	7/27	6/7	9/23	8/6
12/13	11/17	2/4	1/11	4/3	3/10	5/31	4/9	7/28	6/8	9/24	8/7
12/14	11/18	2/5	1/12	4/4	3/11			7/29	6/9	9/25	8/8
12/15	11/19	2/6	1/13	4/5	3/12	6/1	4/10	7/30	6/10	9/26	8/9
12/16	11/20	2/7	1/14	4/6	3/13	6/2	4/11	7/31	6/11	9/27	8/10
12/17	11/21	2/8	1/15	4/7	3/14	6/3	4/12			9/28	8/11
12/18	11/22	2/9	1/16	4/8	3/15	6/4	4/13	8/1	6/12	9/29	8/12
12/19	11/23	2/10	1/17	4/9	3/16	6/5	4/14	8/2	6/13	9/30	8/13
12/20	11/24	2/11	1/18	4/10	3/17	6/6	4/15	8/3	6/14		
12/21	11/25	2/12	1/19	4/11	3/18	6/7	4/16	8/4	6/15	10/1	8/14
12/22	11/26	2/13	1/20	4/12	3/19	6/8	4/17	8/5	6/16	10/2	8/15
12/23	11/27	2/14	1/21	4/13	3/20	6/9	4/18	8/6	6/17	10/3	8/16
12/24	11/28	2/15	1/22	4/14	3/21	6/10	4/19	8/7	6/18	10/4	8/17
12/25	11/29	2/16	1/23	4/15	3/22	6/11	4/20	8/8	6/19	10/5	8/18
12/26	12/1	2/17	1/24	4/16	3/23	6/12	4/21	8/9	6/20	10/6	8/19
12/27	12/2	2/18	1/25	4/17	3/24	6/13	4/22	8/10	6/21	10/7	8/20
12/28	12/3	2/19	1/26	4/18	3/25	6/14	4/23	8/11	6/22	10/8	8/21
12/29	12/4	2/20	1/27	4/19	3/26	6/15	4/24	8/12	6/23	10/9	8/22
12/20	12/5	2/21	1/28	4/20	3/27	6/16	4/25	8/13	6/24	10/10	8/23
12/31	12/6	2/22	1/29	4/21	3/28	6/17	4/26	8/14	6/25	10/11	8/24
		2/23	2/1	4/22	3/29	6/18	4/27	8/15	6/26	10/12	8/25
		2/24	2/2	4/23	3/30	6/19	4/28	8/16	6/27	10/13	8/26

Solar	Lunar
10/14	8/27
10/15	8/28
10/16	8/29
10/17	8/30
10/18	9/1
10/19	9/2
10/20	9/3
10/21	9/4
10/21	9/5
10/22	9/6
10/23	9/7
10/24	9/8
10/25	9/9
10/26	9/10
10/27	9/11
10/28	9/12
10/29	9/13
10/30	9/14
10/31	9/15
11/1	9/16
11/2	9/17
11/3	9/18
11/4	9/19
11/5	9/20
11/6	9/21
11/7	9/22
11/8	9/23
11/9	9/24
11/10	9/25
11/11	9/26
11/12	9/27
11/13	9/28
11/14	9/29
11/15	9/30
11/16	10/1
11/17	10/2
11/18	10/3
11/19	10/4
11/20	10/5
11/21	10/6
11/22	10/7
11/23	10/8
11/24	10/9
11/25	10/10
11/26	10/11
11/27	10/12
11/28	10/13
11/29	10/14
11/30	10/15
12/1	10/16
12/2	10/17
12/3	10/18
12/4	10/19
12/5	10/20
12/6	10/21
12/7	10/22
12/8	10/23
12/9	10/24

Solar	Lunar
12/10	10/25
12/11	10/26
12/12	10/27
12/13	10/28
12/14	10/29
12/15	10/30
12/16	11/1
12/17	11/2
12/18	11/3
12/19	11/4
12/20	11/5
12/21	11/6
12/22	11/7
12/23	11/8
12/24	11/9
12/25	11/10
12/26	11/11
12/27	11/12
12/28	11/13
12/29	11/14
12/30	11/15
12/31	11/16

Solar Date / **Lunar Date**

1907

Solar	Lunar
1/1	11/17
1/2	11/18
1/3	11/19
1/4	11/20
1/5	11/21
1/6	11/22
1/7	11/23
1/8	11/24
1/9	11/25
1/10	11/26
1/11	11/27
1/12	11/28
1/13	11/29
1/14	12/1
1/15	12/2
1/16	12/3
1/17	12/4
1/18	12/5
1/19	12/6
1/20	12/7
1/21	12/8
1/22	12/9
1/23	12/10
1/24	12/11
1/25	12/12
1/26	12/13
1/27	12/14
1/28	12/15
1/29	12/16
1/30	12/17
1/31	12/18

Solar	Lunar
2/1	12/19
2/2	12/20
2/3	12/21
2/4	12/22
2/5	12/23
2/6	12/24
2/7	12/25
2/8	12/26
2/9	12/27
2/10	12/28
2/11	12/29
2/12	12/30
2/13	1/1
	(1907)
2/14	1/2
2/15	1/3
2/16	1/4
2/17	1/5
2/18	1/6
2/19	1/7
2/20	1/8
2/21	1/9
2/22	1/10
2/23	1/11
2/24	1/12
2/25	1/13
2/26	1/14
2/27	1/15
2/18	1/16
3/1	1/17
3/2	1/18
3/3	1/19
3/4	1/20
3/5	1/21
3/6	1/22
3/7	1/23
3/8	1/24
3/9	1/25
3/10	1/26
3/11	1/27
3/12	1/28
3/13	1/29
3/14	2/1
3/15	2/2
3/16	2/3
3/17	2/4
3/18	2/5
3/19	2/6
3/20	2/7
3/21	2/8
3/22	2/9
3/23	2/10
3/24	2/11
3/25	2/12
3/26	2/13
3/27	2/14
3/28	2/15
3/29	2/16
3/20	2/17

Solar	Lunar
3/31	2/18
4/1	2/19
4/2	2/20
4/3	2/21
4/4	2/22
4/5	2/23
4/6	2/24
4/7	2/25
4/8	2/26
4/9	2/27
4/10	2/28
4/11	2/29
4/12	2/30
4/13	3/1
4/14	3/2
4/15	3/3
4/16	3/4
4/17	3/5
4/18	3/6
4/19	3/7
4/20	3/8
4/21	3/9
4/22	3/10
4/23	3/11
4/24	3/12
4/25	3/13
4/26	3/14
4/27	3/15
4/28	3/16
4/29	3/17
4/30	3/18
5/1	3/19
5/2	3/20
5/3	3/21
5/4	3/22
5/5	3/23
5/6	3/24
5/7	3/25
5/8	3/26
5/9	3/27
5/10	3/28
5/11	3/29
5/12	4/1
5/13	4/2
5/14	4/3
5/15	4/4
5/16	4/5
5/17	4/6
5/18	4/7
5/19	4/8
5/20	4/9
5/21	4/10
5/22	4/11
5/23	4/12
5/24	4/13
5/25	4/14
5/26	4/15
5/27	4/16

Solar	Lunar
5/28	4/17
5/29	4/18
5/30	4/19
5/31	4/20
6/1	4/21
6/2	4/22
6/3	4/23
6/4	4/24
6/5	4/25
6/6	4/26
6/7	4/27
6/8	4/28
6/9	4/29
6/10	4/30
6/11	5/1
6/12	5/2
6/13	5/3
6/14	5/4
6/15	5/5
6/16	5/6
6/17	5/7
6/18	5/8
6/19	5/9
6/20	5/10
6/21	5/11
6/22	5/12
6/23	5/13
6/24	5/14
6/25	5/15
6/26	5/16
6/27	5/17
6/28	5/18
6/29	5/19
6/30	5/20
7/1	5/21
7/2	5/22
7/3	5/23
7/4	5/24
7/5	5/25
7/6	5/26
7/7	5/27
7/8	5/28
7/9	5/29
7/10	6/1
7/11	6/2
7/12	6/3
7/13	6/4
7/14	6/5
7/15	6/6
7/16	6/7
7/17	6/8
7/18	6/9
7/19	6/10
7/20	6/11
7/21	6/12
7/22	6/13
7/23	6/14
7/24	6/15

Solar	Lunar
7/25	6/16
7/26	6/17
7/27	6/18
7/28	6/19
7/29	6/20
7/30	6/21
7/31	6/22
8/1	6/23
8/2	6/24
8/3	6/25
8/4	6/26
8/5	6/27
8/6	6/28
8/7	6/29
8/8	6/30
8/9	7/1
8/10	7/2
8/11	7/3
8/12	7/4
8/13	7/5
8/14	7/6
8/15	7/7
8/16	7/8
8/17	7/9
8/18	7/10
8/19	7/11
8/20	7/12
8/21	7/13
8/22	7/14
8/23	7/15
8/24	7/16
8/25	7/17
8/26	7/18
8/27	7/19
8/28	7/20
8/29	7/21
8/30	7/22
8/31	7/23
9/1	7/24
9/2	7/25
9/3	7/26
9/4	7/27
9/5	7/28
9/6	7/29
9/7	7/30
9/8	8/1
9/9	8/2
9/10	8/3
9/11	8/4
9/12	8/5
9/13	8/6
9/14	8/7
9/15	8/8
9/16	8/9
9/17	8/10
9/18	8/11
9/19	8/12
9/20	8/13

Solar	Lunar
9/21	8/14
9/22	8/15
9/23	8/16
9/24	8/17
9/25	8/18
9/26	8/19
9/27	8/20
9/28	8/21
9/29	8/22
9/30	8/23
10/1	8/24
10/2	8/25
10/3	8/26
10/4	8/27
10/5	8/28
10/6	8/29
10/7	9/1
10/8	9/2
10/9	9/3
10/10	9/4
10/11	9/5
10/12	9/6
10/13	9/7
10/14	9/8
10/15	9/9
10/16	9/10
10/17	9/11
10/18	9/12
10/19	9/13
10/20	9/14
10/21	9/15
10/22	9/16
10/23	9/17
10/24	9/18
10/25	9/19
10/26	9/20
10/27	9/21
10/28	9/22
10/29	9/23
10/30	9/24
10/31	9/25
11/1	9/26
11/2	9/27
11/3	9/28
11/4	9/29
11/5	9/30
11/6	10/1
11/7	10/2
11/8	10/3
11/9	10/4
11/10	10/5
11/11	10/6
11/12	10/7
11/13	10/8
11/14	10/9
11/15	10/10
11/16	10/11
11/17	10/12

Solar	Lunar
11/18	10/13
11/19	10/14
11/20	10/15
11/21	10/16
11/22	10/17
11/23	10/18
11/24	10/19
11/25	10/20
11/26	10/21
11/27	10/22
11/28	10/23
11/29	10/24
11/30	10/25
12/1	10/26
12/2	10/27
12/3	10/28
12/4	10/29
12/5	11/1
12/6	11/2
12/7	11/3
12/8	11/4
12/9	11/5
12/10	11/6
12/11	11/7
12/12	11/8
12/13	11/9
12/14	11/10
12/15	11/11
12/16	11/12
12/17	11/12
12/18	11/13
12/19	11/14
12/20	11/15
12/21	11/16
12/22	11/17
12/23	11/18
12/24	11/19
12/25	11/20
12/26	11/21
12/27	11/22
12/28	11/23
12/29	11/24
12/30	11/25
12/31	11/26

Solar Date	Lunar Date
1908	
1/1	11/27
1/2	11/28
1/3	11/29
1/4	12/1
1/5	12/2
1/6	12/3
1/7	12/4
1/8	12/5
1/9	12/6

Solar	Lunar
1/10	12/7
1/11	12/8
1/12	12/9
1/13	12/10
1/14	12/11
1/15	12/12
1/16	12/13
1/17	12/14
1/18	12/15
1/19	12/16
1/20	12/17
1/21	12/18
1/22	12/19
1/23	12/20
1/24	12/21
1/25	12/22
1/26	12/23
1/27	12/24
1/28	12/25
1/29	12/26
1/30	12/27
1/31	12/28
2/1	12/29
2/2	1/1
	(1908)
2/3	1/2
2/4	1/3
2/5	1/4
2/6	1/5
2/7	1/6
2/8	1/7
2/9	1/8
2/10	1/9
2/11	1/10
2/12	1/11
2/13	1/12
2/14	1/13
2/15	1/14
2/16	1/15
2/17	1/16
2/18	1/17
2/19	1/18
2/20	1/19
2/21	1/20
2/22	1/21
2/23	1/22
2/24	1/23
2/25	1/24
2/26	1/25
2/27	1/26
2/28	1/27
2/29	1/28
3/1	1/29
3/2	1/30
3/3	2/1
3/4	2/2
3/5	2/3
3/6	2/4

Solar	Lunar
3/7	2/5
3/8	2/6
3/9	2/7
3/10	2/8
3/11	2/9
3/12	2/10
3/13	2/11
3/14	2/12
3/15	2/13
3/16	2/14
3/17	2/15
3/18	2/16
3/19	2/17
3/20	2/18
3/21	2/19
3/22	2/20
3/23	2/21
3/24	2/22
3/25	2/23
3/26	2/24
3/27	2/25
3/28	2/26
3/29	2/27
3/30	2/28
3/31	2/29
4/1	3/1
4/2	3/2
4/3	3/3
4/4	3/4
4/5	3/5
4/6	3/6
4/7	3/7
4/8	3/8
4/9	3/9
4/10	3/10
4/11	3/11
4/12	3/12
4/13	3/13
4/14	3/14
4/15	3/15
4/16	3/16
4/17	3/17
4/18	3/18
4/19	3/19
4/20	3/20
4/21	3/21
4/22	3/22
4/23	3/23
4/24	3/24
4/25	3/25
4/26	3/26
4/27	3/27
4/28	3/28
4/29	3/29
4/30	4/1
5/1	4/2
5/2	4/3
5/3	4/4

Solar	Lunar
5/4	4/5
5/5	4/6
5/6	4/7
5/7	4/8
5/8	4/9
5/9	4/10
5/10	4/11
5/11	4/12
5/12	4/13
5/13	4/14
5/14	4/15
5/15	4/16
5/16	4/17
5/17	4/18
5/18	4/19
5/19	4/20
5/20	4/21
5/21	4/22
5/22	4/23
5/23	4/24
5/24	4/25
5/25	4/26
5/26	4/27
5/27	4/28
5/28	4/29
5/29	4/30
5/30	5/1
5/31	5/2
6/1	5/3
6/2	5/4
6/3	5/5
6/4	5/6
6/5	5/7
6/6	5/8
6/7	5/9
6/8	5/10
6/9	5/11
6/10	5/12
6/11	5/13
6/12	5/14
6/13	5/15
6/14	5/16
6/15	5/17
6/16	5/18
6/17	5/19
6/18	5/20
6/19	5/21
6/20	5/22
6/21	5/23
6/22	5/24
6/23	5/25
6/24	5/26
6/25	5/27
6/26	5/28
6/27	5/29
6/28	5/30
6/29	6/1
6/30	6/2

Solar	Lunar
7/1	6/3
7/2	6/4
7/3	6/5
7/4	6/6
7/5	6/7
7/6	6/8
7/7	6/9
7/8	6/10
7/9	6/11
7/10	6/12
7/11	6/13
7/12	6/14
7/13	6/15
7/14	6/16
7/15	6/17
7/16	6/18
7/17	6/19
7/18	6/20
7/19	6/21
7/20	6/22
7/21	6/23
7/22	6/24
7/23	6/25
7/24	6/26
7/25	6/27
7/26	6/28
7/27	6/29
7/28	7/1
7/29	7/2
7/30	7/3
7/31	7/4
8/1	7/5
8/2	7/6
8/3	7/7
8/4	7/8
8/5	7/9
8/6	7/10
8/7	7/11
8/8	7/12
8/9	7/13
8/10	7/14
8/11	7/15
8/12	7/16
8/13	7/17
8/14	7/17
8/15	7/18
8/16	7/19
8/17	7/20
8/18	7/21
8/19	7/22
8/20	7/23
8/21	7/24
8/22	7/25
8/23	7/26
8/24	7/27
8/25	7/28
8/26	7/29
8/27	8/1
8/28	8/2

Solar	Lunar	Solar	Lunar	Solar	Lunar	Solar	Lunar	Solar	Lunar	Solar	Lunar
8/29	8/3	10/26	10/2	12/23	12/1	2/13	1/23	4/11	2/21	6/8	4/21
8/30	8/4	10/27	10/3	12/24	12/2	2/14	1/24	4/12	2/22	6/9	4/22
8/31	8/5	10/28	10/4	12/25	12/3	2/15	1/25	4/13	2/23	6/10	4/23
		10/29	10/5	12/26	12/4	2/16	1/26	4/14	2/24	6/11	4/24
9/1	8/6	10/30	10/6	12/27	12/5	2/17	1/27	4/15	2/25	6/12	4/25
9/2	8/7	10/31	10/7	12/28	12/6	2/18	1/28	4/16	2/26	6/13	4/26
9/3	8/8			12/29	12/7	2/19	1/29	4/17	2/27	6/14	4/27
9/4	8/9	11/1	10/8	12/30	12/8	2/20	2/1	4/18	2/28	6/15	4/28
9/5	8/10	11/2	10/9	12/31	12/9	2/21	2/2	4/19	2/29	6/16	4/29
9/6	8/11	11/3	10/10			2/22	2/3	4/20	3/1	6/17	4/30
9/7	8/12	11/4	10/11			2/23	2/4	4/21	3/2	6/18	5/1
9/8	8/13	11/5	10/12	**Solar**	**Lunar**	2/24	2/5	4/22	3/3	6/19	5/2
9/9	8/14	11/6	10/13	**Date**	**Date**	2/25	2/6	4/23	3/4	6/20	5/3
9/10	8/15	11/7	10/14			2/26	2/7	4/24	3/5	6/21	5/4
9/11	8/16	11/8	10/15	**1909**		2/27	2/8	4/25	3/6	6/22	5/5
9/12	8/17	11/9	10/16	1/1	12/10	2/28	2/9	4/26	3/7	6/23	5/6
9/13	8/18	11/10	10/17	1/2	12/11			4/27	3/8	6/24	5/7
9/14	8/19	11/11	10/18	1/3	12/12	3/1	2/10	4/28	3/9	6/25	5/8
9/15	8/20	11/12	10/19	1/4	12/13	3/2	2/11	4/29	3/10	6/26	5/9
9/16	8/21	11/13	10/20	1/5	12/14	3/3	2/12	4/30	3/11	6/27	5/10
9/17	8/22	11/14	10/21	1/6	12/15	3/4	2/13			6/28	5/11
9/18	8/23	11/15	10/22	1/7	12/16	3/5	2/14	5/1	3/12	6/29	5/12
9/19	8/24	11/16	10/23	1/8	12/17	3/6	2/15	5/2	3/13	6/30	5/13
9/20	8/25	11/17	10/24	1/9	12/18	3/7	2/16	5/3	3/14		
9/21	8/26	11/18	10/25	1/10	12/19	3/8	2/17	5/4	3/15	7/1	5/14
9/22	8/27	11/19	10/26	1/11	12/20	3/9	2/18	5/5	3/16	7/2	5/15
9/23	8/28	11/20	10/27	1/12	12/21	3/10	2/19	5/6	3/17	7/3	5/16
9/24	8/29	11/21	10/28	1/13	12/22	3/11	2/20	5/7	3/18	7/4	5/17
9/25	9/1	11/22	10/29	1/14	12/23	3/12	2/21	5/8	3/19	7/5	5/18
9/26	9/2	11/23	10/30	1/15	12/24	3/13	2/22	5/9	3/20	7/6	5/19
9/27	9/3	11/24	11/1	1/16	12/25	3/14	2/23	5/10	3/21	7/7	5/20
9/28	9/4	11/25	11/2	1/17	12/26	3/15	2/24	5/11	3/22	7/8	5/21
9/29	9/5	11/26	11/3	1/18	12/27	3/16	2/25	5/12	3/23	7/9	5/22
9/30	9/6	11/27	11/4	1/19	12/28	3/17	2/26	5/13	3/24	7/10	5/23
		11/28	11/5	1/20	12/29	3/18	2/27	5/14	3/25	7/11	5/24
10/1	9/7	11/29	11/6	1/21	12/30	3/19	2/28	5/15	3/26	7/12	5/25
10/2	9/8	11/30	11/7	1/22	1/1	3/20	2/29	5/16	3/27	7/13	5/26
10/3	9/9				(1909)	3/21	2/30	5/17	3/28	7/14	5/27
10/4	9/10	12/1	11/8	1/23	1/2	3/22	2/1	5/18	3/29	7/15	5/28
10/5	9/11	12/2	11/9	1/24	1/3	*(Leap Month)*		5/19	4/1	7/16	5/29
10/6	9/12	12/3	11/10	1/25	1/4	3/23	2/2	5/20	4/2	7/17	6/1
10/7	9/13	12/4	11/11	1/26	1/5	3/24	2/3	5/21	4/3	7/18	6/2
10/8	9/14	12/5	11/12	1/27	1/6	3/25	2/4	5/22	4/4	7/19	6/3
10/9	9/15	12/6	11/13	1/28	1/7	3/26	2/5	5/23	4/5	7/20	6/4
10/10	9/16	12/7	11/14	1/29	1/8	3/27	2/6	5/24	4/6	7/21	6/5
10/11	9/17	12/8	11/15	1/30	1/9	3/28	2/7	5/25	4/7	7/22	6/6
10/12	9/18	12/9	11/16	1/31	1/10	3/29	2/8	5/26	4/8	7/23	6/7
10/13	9/19	12/10	11/17			3/30	2/9	5/27	4/9	7/24	6/8
10/14	9/20	12/11	11/18	2/1	1/11	3/31	2/10	5/28	4/10	7/25	6/9
10/15	9/21	12/12	11/19	2/2	1/12			5/29	4/11	7/26	6/10
10/16	9/22	12/13	11/20	2/3	1/13	4/1	2/11	5/30	4/12	7/27	6/11
10/17	9/23	12/14	11/21	2/4	1/14	4/2	2/12	5/31	4/13	7/28	6/12
10/18	9/24	12/15	11/22	2/5	1/15	4/3	2/13			7/29	6/13
10/19	9/25	12/16	11/23	2/6	1/16	4/4	2/14	6/1	4/14	7/30	6/14
10/20	9/26	12/17	11/24	2/7	1/17	4/5	2/15	6/2	4/15	7/31	6/15
10/21	9/27	12/18	11/25	2/8	1/18	4/6	2/16	6/3	4/16		
10/22	9/28	12/19	11/26	2/9	1/19	4/7	2/17	6/4	4/17	8/1	6/16
10/23	9/29	12/20	11/27	2/10	1/20	4/8	2/18	6/5	4/18	8/2	6/17
10/24	9/30	12/21	11/28	2/11	1/21	4/9	2/19	6/6	4/19	8/3	6/18
10/25	10/1	12/22	11/29	2/12	1/22	4/10	2/20	6/7	4/20	8/4	6/19

Solar	Lunar	Solar	Lunar	Solar	Lunar	Solar	Lunar	Solar	Lunar	Solar	Lunar
8/5	6/20	10/2	8/19	11/30	10/18	1/22	12/12	3/20	2/10	5/17	4/9
8/6	6/21	10/3	8/20			1/23	12/13	3/21	2/11	5/18	4/10
8/7	6/22	10/4	8/21	12/1	10/19	1/24	12/14	3/22	2/12	5/19	4/11
8/8	6/23	10/5	8/22	12/2	10/20	1/25	12/15	3/23	2/13	5/20	4/12
8/9	6/24	10/6	8/23	12/3	10/21	1/26	12/16	3/24	2/14	5/21	4/13
8/10	6/25	10/7	8/24	12/4	10/22	1/27	12/17	3/25	2/15	5/22	4/14
8/11	6/26	10/8	8/25	12/5	10/23	1/28	12/18	3/26	2/16	5/23	4/15
8/12	6/27	10/9	8/26	12/6	10/24	1/29	12/19	3/27	2/17	5/24	4/16
8/13	6/28	10/10	8/27	12/7	10/25	1/30	12/20	3/28	2/18	5/25	4/17
8/14	6/29	10/11	8/28	12/8	10/26	1/31	12/21	3/29	2/19	5/26	4/18
8/15	6/30	10/12	8/29	12/9	10/27			3/30	2/20	5/27	4/19
8/16	7/1	10/13	8/30	12/10	10/28	2/1	12/22	3/31	2/21	5/28	4/20
8/17	7/2	10/14	9/1	12/11	10/29	2/2	12/23			5/29	4/21
8/18	7/3	10/15	9/2	12/12	10/30	2/3	12/24	4/1	2/22	5/30	4/22
8/19	7/4	10/16	9/3	12/13	11/1	2/4	12/25	4/2	2/23	5/31	4/23
8/20	7/5	10/17	9/4	12/14	11/2	2/5	12/26	4/3	2/24		
8/21	7/6	10/18	9/5	12/15	11/3	2/6	12/27	4/4	2/25	6/1	4/24
8/22	7/7	10/19	9/6	12/16	11/4	2/7	12/28	4/5	2/26	6/2	4/25
8/23	7/8	10/20	9/7	12/17	11/5	2/8	12/29	4/6	2/27	6/3	4/26
8/24	7/9	10/21	9/8	12/18	11/6	2/9	12/30	4/7	2/28	6/4	4/27
8/25	7/10	10/22	9/9	12/19	11/7	2/10	1/1	4/8	2/29	6/5	4/28
8/26	7/11	10/23	9/10	12/20	11/8		(1910)	4/9	2/30	6/6	4/29
8/27	7/12	10/24	9/11	12/21	11/9	2/11	1/2	4/10	3/1	6/7	5/1
8/28	7/13	10/25	9/12	12/22	11/10	2/12	1/3	4/11	3/2	6/8	5/2
8/29	7/14	10/26	9/13	12/23	11/11	2/13	1/4	4/12	3/3	6/9	5/3
8/30	7/15	10/27	9/14	12/24	11/12	2/14	1/5	4/13	3/4	6/10	5/4
8/31	7/16	10/28	9/15	12/25	11/13	2/15	1/6	4/14	3/5	6/11	5/5
		10/29	9/16	12/26	11/14	2/16	1/7	4/15	3/6	6/12	5/6
9/1	7/17	10/30	9/17	12/27	11/15	2/17	1/8	4/16	3/7	6/13	5/7
9/2	7/18	10/31	9/18	12/28	11/16	2/18	1/9	4/17	3/8	6/14	5/8
9/3	7/19			12/29	11/17	2/19	1/10	4/18	3/9	6/15	5/9
9/4	7/20	11/1	9/19	12/30	11/18	2/20	1/11	4/19	3/10	6/16	5/10
9/5	7/21	11/2	9/20	12/31	11/19	2/21	1/12	4/20	3/11	6/17	5/11
9/6	7/22	11/3	9/21			2/22	1/13	4/21	3/12	6/18	5/12
9/7	7/23	11/4	9/22			2/23	1/14	4/22	3/13	6/19	5/13
9/8	7/24	11/5	9/23	**Solar**	**Lunar**	2/24	1/15	4/23	3/14	6/20	5/14
9/9	7/25	11/6	9/24	**Date**	**Date**	2/25	1/16	4/24	3/15	6/21	5/15
9/10	7/26	11/7	9/25			2/26	1/17	4/25	3/16	6/22	5/16
9/11	7/27	11/8	9/26	**1910**		2/27	1/18	4/26	3/17	6/23	5/17
9/12	7/28	11/9	9/27	1/1	11/20	2/28	1/19	4/27	3/18	6/24	5/18
9/13	7/29	11/10	9/28	1/2	11/21			4/28	3/19	6/25	5/19
9/14	8/1	11/11	9/29	1/3	11/22	3/1	1/20	4/29	3/20	6/26	5/20
9/15	8/2	11/12	9/30	1/4	11/23	3/2	1/21	4/30	3/21	6/27	5/21
9/16	8/3	11/13	10/1	1/5	11/24	3/3	1/22			6/28	5/22
9/17	8/4	11/14	10/2	1/6	11/25	3/4	1/23	5/1	3/22	6/29	5/23
9/18	8/5	11/15	10/3	1/7	11/26	3/5	1/24	5/2	3/23	6/30	5/24
9/19	8/6	11/16	10/4	1/8	11/27	3/6	1/25	5/3	3/24		
9/20	8/7	11/17	10/5	1/9	11/28	3/7	1/26	5/4	3/25	7/1	5/25
9/21	8/8	11/18	10/6	1/10	11/29	3/8	1/27	5/5	3/26	7/2	5/26
9/22	8/9	11/19	10/7	1/11	12/1	3/9	1/28	5/6	3/27	7/3	5/27
9/23	8/10	11/20	10/8	1/12	12/2	3/10	1/29	5/7	3/28	7/4	5/28
9/24	8/11	11/21	10/9	1/13	12/3	3/11	2/1	5/8	3/29	7/5	5/29
9/25	8/12	11/22	10/10	1/14	12/4	3/12	2/2	5/9	4/1	7/6	5/30
9/26	8/13	11/23	10/11	1/15	12/5	3/13	2/3	5/10	4/2	7/7	6/1
9/27	8/14	11/24	10/12	1/16	12/6	3/14	2/4	5/11	4/3	7/8	6/2
9/28	8/15	11/25	10/13	1/17	12/7	3/15	2/5	5/12	4/4	7/9	6/3
9/29	8/16	11/26	10/14	1/18	12/8	3/16	2/6	5/13	4/5	7/10	6/4
9/30	8/17	11/27	10/15	1/19	12/9	3/17	2/7	5/14	4/6	7/11	6/5
		11/28	10/16	1/20	12/10	3/18	2/8	5/15	4/7	7/12	6/6
10/1	8/18	11/29	10/17	1/21	12/11	3/19	2/9	5/16	4/8	7/13	6/7

Solar	Lunar	Solar	Lunar	Solar	Lunar	Solar Date	Lunar Date	Solar	Lunar	Solar	Lunar
7/14	6/8	9/10	8/7	11/7	10/6			2/24	1/26	4/23	3/25
7/15	6/9	9/11	8/8	11/8	10/7			2/25	1/27	4/24	3/26
7/16	6/10	9/12	8/9	11/9	10/8			2/26	1/28	4/25	3/27
7/17	6/11	9/13	8/10	11/10	10/9	**1911**		2/27	1/29	4/26	3/28
7/18	6/12	9/14	8/11	11/11	10/10	1/1	12/1	2/28	1/30	4/27	3/29
7/19	6/13	9/15	8/12	11/12	10/11	1/2	12/2			4/28	3/30
7/20	6/14	9/16	8/13	11/13	10/12	1/3	12/3	3/1	2/1	4/29	4/1
7/21	6/15	9/17	8/14	11/14	10/13	1/4	12/4	3/2	2/2	4/30	4/2
7/22	6/16	9/18	8/15	11/15	10/14	1/5	12/5	3/3	2/3		
7/23	6/17	9/19	8/16	11/16	10/15	1/6	12/6	3/4	2/4	5/1	4/3
7/24	6/18	9/20	8/17	11/17	10/16	1/7	12/7	3/5	2/5	5/2	4/4
7/25	6/19	9/21	8/18	11/18	10/17	1/8	12/8	3/6	2/6	5/3	4/5
7/26	6/20	9/22	8/19	11/19	10/18	1/9	12/9	3/7	2/7	5/4	4/6
7/27	6/21	9/23	8/20	11/20	10/19	1/10	12/10	3/8	2/8	5/5	4/7
7/28	6/22	9/24	8/21	11/21	10/20	1/11	12/11	3/9	2/9	5/6	4/8
7/29	6/23	9/25	8/22	11/22	10/21	1/12	12/12	3/10	2/10	5/7	4/9
7/30	6/24	9/26	8/23	11/23	10/22	1/13	12/13	3/11	2/11	5/8	4/10
7/31	6/25	9/27	8/24	11/24	10/23	1/14	12/14	3/12	2/12	5/9	4/11
		9/28	8/25	11/25	10/24	1/15	12/15	3/13	2/13	5/10	4/12
8/1	6/26	9/29	8/26	11/26	10/25	1/16	12/16	3/14	2/14	5/11	4/13
8/2	6/27	9/30	8/27	11/27	10/26	1/17	12/17	3/15	2/15	5/12	4/14
8/3	6/28			11/28	10/27	1/18	12/18	3/16	2/16	5/13	4/15
8/4	6/29	10/1	8/28	11/29	10/28	1/19	12/19	3/17	2/17	5/14	4/16
8/5	6/30	10/2	8/29	11/30	10/29	1/20	12/20	3/18	2/18	5/15	4/17
8/6	7/1	10/3	9/1			1/21	12/21	3/19	2/19	5/16	4/18
8/7	7/2	10/4	9/2	12/1	10/30	1/22	12/22	3/20	2/20	5/17	4/19
8/8	7/3	10/5	9/3	12/2	11/1	1/23	12/23	3/21	2/21	5/18	4/20
8/9	7/4	10/6	9/4	12/3	11/2	1/24	12/24	3/22	2/22	5/19	4/21
8/10	7/5	10/7	9/5	12/4	11/3	1/25	12/25	3/23	2/23	5/20	4/22
8/11	7/6	10/8	9/6	12/5	11/4	1/26	12/26	3/24	2/24	5/21	4/23
8/12	7/7	10/9	9/7	12/6	11/5	1/27	12/27	3/25	2/25	5/22	4/24
8/13	7/8	10/10	9/8	12/7	11/6	1/28	12/28	3/26	2/26	5/23	4/25
8/14	7/9	10/11	9/9	12/8	11/7	1/29	12/29	3/27	2/27	5/24	4/26
8/15	7/10	10/12	9/10	12/9	11/8	1/30	1/1	3/28	2/28	5/25	4/27
8/16	7/11	10/13	9/11	12/10	11/9		(1911)	3/29	2/29	5/26	4/28
8/17	7/12	10/14	9/12	12/11	11/10	1/31	1/2	3/30	3/1	5/27	4/29
8/18	7/13	10/15	9/13	12/12	11/11			3/31	3/2	5/28	5/1
8/19	7/14	10/16	9/14	12/13	11/12	2/1	1/3			5/29	5/2
8/20	7/15	10/17	9/15	12/14	11/13	2/2	1/4	4/1	3/3	5/30	5/3
8/21	7/16	10/18	9/16	12/15	11/14	2/3	1/5	4/2	3/4	5/31	5/4
8/22	7/17	10/19	9/17	12/16	11/15	2/4	1/6	4/3	3/5		
8/23	7/18	10/20	9/18	12/17	11/16	2/5	1/7	4/4	3/6	6/1	5/5
8/24	7/19	10/21	9/19	12/18	11/17	2/6	1/8	4/5	3/7	6/2	5/6
8/25	7/20	10/22	9/20	12/19	11/18	2/7	1/9	4/6	3/8	6/3	5/7
8/26	7/21	10/23	9/21	12/20	11/19	2/8	1/10	4/7	3/9	6/4	5/8
8/27	7/22	10/24	9/22	12/21	11/20	2/9	1/11	4/8	3/10	6/5	5/9
8/28	7/23	10/25	9/23	12/22	11/21	2/10	1/12	4/9	3/11	6/6	5/10
8/29	7/24	10/26	9/24	12/23	11/22	2/11	1/13	4/10	3/12	6/7	5/11
8/30	7/25	10/27	9/25	12/24	11/23	2/12	1/14	4/11	3/13	6/8	5/12
8/31	7/26	10/28	9/26	12/25	11/24	2/13	1/15	4/12	3/14	6/9	5/13
		10/29	9/27	12/26	11/25	2/14	1/16	4/13	3/15	6/10	5/14
9/1	7/27	10/30	9/28	12/27	11/26	2/15	1/17	4/14	3/16	6/11	5/15
9/2	7/28	10/31	9/29	12/28	11/27	2/16	1/18	4/15	3/17	6/12	5/16
9/3	7/29			12/29	11/28	2/17	1/19	4/16	3/18	6/13	5/17
9/4	8/1	11/1	9/30	12/30	11/29	2/18	1/20	4/17	3/19	6/14	5/18
9/5	8/2	11/2	10/1	12/31	11/30	2/19	1/21	4/18	3/20	6/15	5/19
9/6	8/3	11/3	10/2			2/20	1/22	4/19	3/21	6/16	5/20
9/7	8/4	11/4	10/3			2/21	1/23	4/20	3/22	6/17	5/21
9/8	8/5	11/5	10/4			2/22	1/24	4/21	3/23	6/18	5/22
9/9	8/6	11/6	10/5			2/23	1/25	4/22	3/24	6/19	5/23

Solar	Lunar
6/20	5/24
6/21	5/25
6/22	5/26
6/23	5/27
6/24	5/28
6/25	5/29
6/26	6/1
6/27	6/2
6/28	6/3
6/29	6/4
6/30	6/5
7/1	6/6
7/2	6/7
7/3	6/8
7/4	6/9
7/5	6/10
7/6	6/11
7/7	6/12
7/8	6/13
7/9	6/14
7/10	6/15
7/11	6/16
7/12	6/17
7/13	6/18
7/14	6/19
7/15	6/20
7/16	6/21
7/17	6/22
7/18	6/23
7/19	6/24
7/20	6/25
7/21	6/26
7/22	6/27
7/23	6/28
7/24	6/29
7/25	6/30
7/26	6/1
(Leap Month)	
7/27	6/2
7/28	6/3
7/29	6/4
7/30	6/5
7/31	6/6
8/1	6/7
8/2	6/8
8/3	6/9
8/4	6/10
8/5	6/11
8/6	6/12
8/7	6/13
8/8	6/14
8/9	6/15
8/10	6/16
8/11	6/17
8/12	6/18
8/13	6/19
8/14	6/20
8/15	6/21

Solar	Lunar
8/16	6/22
8/17	6/23
8/18	6/24
8/19	6/25
8/20	6/26
8/21	6/27
8/22	6/28
8/23	6/29
8/24	7/1
8/25	7/2
8/26	7/3
8/27	7/4
8/28	7/5
8/29	7/6
8/30	7/7
8/31	7/8
9/1	7/9
9/2	7/10
9/3	7/11
9/4	7/12
9/5	7/13
9/6	7/14
9/7	7/15
9/8	7/16
9/9	7/17
9/10	7/18
9/11	7/19
9/12	7/20
9/13	7/21
9/14	7/22
9/15	7/23
9/16	7/24
9/17	7/25
9/18	7/26
9/19	7/27
9/20	7/28
9/21	7/29
9/22	8/1
9/23	8/2
9/24	8/3
9/25	8/4
9/26	8/5
9/27	8/6
9/28	8/7
9/29	8/8
9/30	8/9
10/1	8/10
10/2	8/11
10/3	8/12
10/4	8/13
10/5	8/14
10/6	8/15
10/7	8/16
10/8	8/17
10/9	8/18
10/10	8/19
10/11	8/20
10/12	8/21

Solar	Lunar
10/13	8/22
10/14	8/23
10/15	8/24
10/16	8/25
10/17	8/26
10/18	8/27
10/19	8/28
10/20	8/29
10/21	8/30
10/22	9/1
10/23	9/2
10/24	9/3
10/25	9/4
10/26	9/5
10/27	9/6
10/28	9/7
10/29	9/8
10/30	9/9
10/31	9/10
11/1	9/11
11/2	9/12
11/3	9/13
11/4	9/14
11/5	9/15
11/6	9/16
11/7	9/17
11/8	9/18
11/9	9/19
11/10	9/20
11/11	9/21
11/12	9/22
11/13	9/23
11/14	9/24
11/15	9/25
11/16	9/26
11/17	9/27
11/18	9/28
11/19	9/29
11/20	9/30
11/21	10/1
11/22	10/2
11/23	10/3
11/24	10/4
11/25	10/5
11/26	10/6
11/27	10/7
11/28	10/8
11/29	10/9
11/30	10/10
12/1	10/11
12/2	10/12
12/3	10/13
12/4	10/14
12/5	10/15
12/6	10/16
12/7	10/17
12/8	10/18
12/9	10/19

Solar	Lunar
12/10	10/20
12/11	10/21
12/12	10/22
12/13	10/23
12/14	10/24
12/15	10/25
12/16	10/26
12/17	10/27
12/18	10/28
12/19	10/29
12/20	11/1
12/21	11/2
12/22	11/3
12/23	11/4
12/24	11/5
12/25	11/6
12/26	11/7
12/27	11/8
12/28	11/9
12/29	11/10
12/30	11/11
12/31	11/12

Solar Date	Lunar Date
1912	
1/1	11/13
1/2	11/14
1/3	11/15
1/4	11/16
1/5	11/17
1/6	11/18
1/7	11/19
1/8	11/20
1/9	11/21
1/10	11/22
1/11	11/23
1/12	11/24
1/13	11/25
1/14	11/26
1/15	11/27
1/16	11/28
1/17	11/29
1/18	11/30
1/19	12/1
1/20	12/2
1/21	12/3
1/22	12/4
1/23	12/5
1/24	12/6
1/25	12/7
1/26	12/8
1/27	12/9
1/28	12/10
1/29	12/11
1/30	12/12
1/31	12/13

Solar	Lunar
2/1	12/14
2/2	12/15
2/3	12/16
2/4	12/17
2/5	12/18
2/6	12/19
2/7	12/20
2/8	12/21
2/9	12/22
2/10	12/23
2/11	12/24
2/12	12/25
2/13	12/26
2/14	12/27
2/15	12/28
2/16	12/29
2/17	12/30
2/18	1/1
	(1912)
2/19	1/2
2/20	1/3
2/21	1/4
2/22	1/5
2/23	1/6
2/24	1/7
2/25	1/8
2/26	1/9
2/27	1/10
2/28	1/11
2/29	1/12
3/1	1/13
3/2	1/14
3/3	1/15
3/4	1/16
3/5	1/17
3/6	1/18
3/7	1/19
3/8	1/20
3/9	1/21
3/10	1/22
3/11	1/23
3/12	1/24
3/13	1/25
3/14	1/26
3/15	1/27
3/16	1/28
3/17	1/29
3/18	1/30
3/19	2/1
3/20	2/2
3/21	2/3
3/22	2/4
3/23	2/5
3/24	2/6
3/25	2/7
3/26	2/8
3/27	2/9
3/28	2/10
3/29	2/11

Solar	Lunar
3/30	2/12
3/31	2/13
4/1	2/14
4/2	2/15
4/3	2/16
4/4	2/17
4/5	2/18
4/6	2/19
4/7	2/20
4/8	2/21
4/9	2/22
4/10	2/23
4/11	2/24
4/12	2/25
4/13	2/26
4/14	2/27
4/15	2/28
4/16	2/29
4/17	3/1
4/18	3/2
4/19	3/3
4/20	3/4
4/21	3/5
4/22	3/6
4/23	3/7
4/24	3/8
4/25	3/9
4/26	3/10
4/27	3/11
4/28	3/12
4/29	3/13
4/30	3/14
5/1	3/15
5/2	3/16
5/3	3/17
5/4	3/18
5/5	3/19
5/6	3/20
5/7	3/21
5/8	3/22
5/9	3/23
5/10	3/24
5/11	3/25
5/12	3/26
5/13	3/27
5/14	3/28
5/15	3/29
5/16	3/30
5/17	4/1
5/18	4/2
5/19	4/3
5/20	4/4
5/21	4/5
5/22	4/6
5/23	4/7
5/24	4/8
5/25	4/9
5/26	4/10

Solar	Lunar	Solar	Lunar	Solar	Lunar	Solar	Lunar	Solar	Lunar	Solar	Lunar
5/27	4/11	7/24	6/11	9/20	8/10	11/17	10/9	1/9	12/3	3/7	1/30
5/28	4/12	7/25	6/12	9/21	8/11	11/18	10/10	1/10	12/4	3/8	2/1
5/29	4/13	7/26	6/13	9/22	8/12	11/19	10/11	1/11	12/5	3/9	2/2
5/30	4/14	7/27	6/14	9/23	8/13	11/20	10/12	1/12	12/6	3/10	2/3
5/31	4/15	7/28	6/15	9/24	8/14	11/21	10/13	1/13	12/7	3/11	2/4
		7/29	6/16	9/25	8/15	11/22	10/14	1/14	12/8	3/12	2/5
6/1	4/16	7/30	6/17	9/26	8/16	11/23	10/15	1/15	12/9	3/13	2/6
6/2	4/17	7/31	6/18	9/27	8/17	11/24	10/16	1/16	12/10	3/14	2/7
6/3	4/18			9/28	8/18	11/25	10/17	1/17	12/11	3/15	2/8
6/4	4/19	8/1	6/19	9/29	8/19	11/26	10/18	1/18	12/12	3/16	2/9
6/5	4/20	8/2	6/20	9/30	8/20	11/27	10/19	1/19	12/13	3/17	2/10
6/6	4/21	8/3	6/21			11/28	10/20	1/20	12/14	3/18	2/11
6/7	4/22	8/4	6/22	10/1	8/21	11/29	10/21	1/21	12/15	3/19	2/12
6/8	4/23	8/5	6/23	10/2	8/22	11/30	10/22	1/22	12/16	3/20	2/13
6/9	4/24	8/6	6/24	10/3	8/23			1/23	12/17	3/21	2/14
6/10	4/25	8/7	6/25	10/4	8/24	12/1	10/23	1/24	12/18	3/22	2/15
6/11	4/26	8/8	6/26	10/5	8/25	12/2	10/24	1/25	12/19	3/23	2/16
6/12	4/27	8/9	6/27	10/6	8/26	12/3	10/25	1/26	12/20	3/24	2/17
6/13	4/28	8/10	6/28	10/7	8/27	12/4	10/26	1/27	12/21	3/25	2/18
6/14	4/29	8/11	6/29	10/8	8/28	12/5	10/27	1/28	12/22	3/26	2/19
6/15	5/1	8/12	6/30	10/9	8/29	12/6	10/28	1/29	12/23	3/27	2/20
6/16	5/2	8/13	7/1	10/10	9/1	12/7	10/29	1/30	12/24	3/28	2/21
6/17	5/3	8/14	7/2	10/11	9/2	12/8	10/30	1/31	12/25	3/29	2/22
6/18	5/4	8/15	7/3	10/12	9/3	12/9	11/1			3/30	2/23
6/19	5/5	8/16	7/4	10/13	9/4	12/10	11/2	2/1	12/26	3/31	2/24
6/20	5/6	8/17	7/5	10/14	9/5	12/11	11/3	2/2	12/27		
6/21	5/7	8/18	7/6	10/15	9/6	12/12	11/4	2/3	12/28	4/1	2/25
6/22	5/8	8/19	7/7	10/16	9/7	12/13	11/5	2/4	12/29	4/2	2/26
6/23	5/9	8/20	7/8	10/17	9/8	12/14	11/6	2/5	12/30	4/3	2/27
6/24	5/10	8/21	7/9	10/18	9/9	12/15	11/7	2/6	1/1	4/4	2/28
6/25	5/11	8/22	7/10	10/19	9/10	12/16	11/8		(1913)	4/5	2/29
6/26	5/12	8/23	7/11	10/20	9/11	12/17	11/9	2/7	1/2	4/6	2/30
6/27	5/13	8/24	7/12	10/21	9/12	12/18	11/10	2/8	1/3	4/7	3/1
6/28	5/14	8/25	7/13	10/22	9/13	12/19	11/11	2/9	1/4	4/8	3/2
6/29	5/15	8/26	7/14	10/23	9/14	12/20	11/12	2/10	1/5	4/9	3/3
6/30	5/16	8/27	7/15	10/24	9/15	12/21	11/13	2/11	1/6	4/10	3/4
		8/28	7/16	10/25	9/16	12/22	11/14	2/12	1/7	4/11	3/5
7/1	5/17	8/29	7/17	10/26	9/17	12/23	11/15	2/13	1/8	4/12	3/6
7/2	5/18	8/30	7/18	10/27	9/18	12/24	11/16	2/14	1/9	4/13	3/7
7/3	5/19	8/31	7/19	10/28	9/19	12/25	11/17	2/15	1/10	4/14	3/8
7/4	5/20			10/29	9/20	12/26	11/18	2/16	1/11	4/15	3/9
7/5	5/21	9/1	7/20	10/30	9/21	12/27	11/19	2/17	1/12	4/16	3/10
7/6	5/22	9/2	7/21	10/31	9/22	12/28	11/20	2/18	1/13	4/17	3/11
7/7	5/23	9/3	7/22			12/29	11/21	2/19	1/14	4/18	3/12
7/8	5/24	9/4	7/23	11/1	9/23	12/30	11/22	2/20	1/15	4/19	3/13
7/9	5/25	9/5	7/24	11/2	9/24	12/31	11/23	2/21	1/16	4/20	3/14
7/10	5/26	9/6	7/25	11/3	9/25			2/22	1/17	4/21	3/15
7/11	5/27	9/7	7/26	11/4	9/26			2/23	1/18	4/22	3/16
7/12	5/28	9/8	7/27	11/5	9/27	Solar	Lunar	2/24	1/19	4/23	3/17
7/13	5/29	9/9	7/28	11/6	9/28	Date	Date	2/25	1/20	4/24	3/18
7/14	6/1	9/10	7/29	11/7	9/29	**1913**		2/26	1/21	4/25	3/19
7/15	6/2	9/11	8/1	11/8	9/30	1/1	11/24	2/27	1/22	4/26	3/20
7/16	6/3	9/12	8/2	11/9	10/1	1/2	11/25	2/28	1/23	4/27	3/21
7/17	6/4	9/13	8/3	11/10	10/2	1/3	11/26			4/28	3/22
7/18	6/5	9/14	8/4	11/11	10/3	1/4	11/27	3/1	1/24	4/29	3/23
7/19	6/6	9/15	8/5	11/12	10/4	1/5	11/28	3/2	1/25	4/30	3/24
7/20	6/7	9/16	8/6	11/13	10/5	1/6	11/29	3/3	1/26		
7/21	6/8	9/17	8/7	11/14	10/6	1/7	12/1	3/4	1/27	5/1	3/25
7/22	6/9	9/18	8/8	11/15	10/7	1/8	12/2	3/5	1/28	5/2	3/26
7/23	6/10	9/19	8/9	11/16	10/8			3/6	1/29	5/3	3/27

Solar	Lunar
5/4	3/28
5/5	3/29
5/6	4/1
5/7	4/2
5/8	4/3
5/9	4/4
5/10	4/5
5/11	4/6
5/12	4/7
5/13	4/8
5/14	4/9
5/15	4/10
5/16	4/11
5/17	4/12
5/18	4/13
5/19	4/14
5/20	4/15
5/21	4/16
5/22	4/17
5/23	4/18
5/24	4/19
5/25	4/20
5/26	4/21
5/27	4/22
5/28	4/23
5/29	4/24
5/30	4/25
5/31	4/26
6/1	4/27
6/2	4/28
6/3	4/29
6/4	4/30
6/5	5/1
6/6	5/2
6/7	5/3
6/8	5/4
6/9	5/5
6/10	5/6
6/11	5/7
6/12	5/8
6/13	5/9
6/14	5/10
6/15	5/11
6/16	5/12
6/17	5/13
6/18	5/14
6/19	5/15
6/20	5/16
6/21	5/17
6/22	5/18
6/23	5/19
6/24	5/20
6/25	5/21
6/26	5/22
6/27	5/23
6/28	5/24
6/29	5/25
6/30	5/26

Solar	Lunar
7/1	5/27
7/2	5/28
7/3	5/29
7/4	6/1
7/5	6/2
7/6	6/3
7/7	6/4
7/8	6/5
7/9	6/6
7/10	6/7
7/11	6/8
7/12	6/9
7/13	6/10
7/14	6/11
7/15	6/12
7/16	6/13
7/17	6/14
7/18	6/15
7/19	6/16
7/20	6/17
7/21	6/18
7/22	6/19
7/23	6/20
7/24	6/21
7/25	6/22
7/26	6/23
7/27	6/24
7/28	6/25
7/29	6/26
7/30	6/27
7/31	6/28
8/1	6/29
8/2	7/1
8/3	7/2
8/4	7/3
8/5	7/4
8/6	7/5
8/7	7/6
8/8	7/7
8/9	7/8
8/10	7/9
8/11	7/10
8/12	7/11
8/13	7/12
8/14	7/13
8/15	7/14
8/16	7/15
8/17	7/16
8/18	7/17
8/19	7/18
8/20	7/19
8/21	7/20
8/22	7/21
8/23	7/22
8/24	7/23
8/25	7/24
8/26	7/25
8/27	7/26
8/28	7/27

Solar	Lunar
8/29	7/28
8/30	7/29
8/31	7/30
9/1	8/1
9/2	8/2
9/3	8/3
9/4	8/4
9/5	8/5
9/6	8/6
9/7	8/7
9/8	8/8
9/9	8/9
9/10	8/10
9/11	8/11
9/12	8/12
9/13	8/13
9/14	8/14
9/15	8/15
9/16	8/16
9/17	8/17
9/18	8/18
9/19	8/19
9/20	8/20
9/21	8/21
9/22	8/22
9/23	8/23
9/24	8/24
9/25	8/25
9/26	8/26
9/27	8/27
9/28	8/28
9/29	8/29
9/30	9/1
10/1	9/2
10/2	9/3
10/3	9/4
10/4	9/5
10/5	9/6
10/6	9/7
10/7	9/8
10/8	9/9
10/9	9/10
10/10	9/11
10/11	9/12
10/12	9/13
10/13	9/14
10/14	9/15
10/15	9/16
10/16	9/17
10/17	9/18
10/18	9/19
10/19	9/20
10/20	9/21
10/21	9/22
10/22	9/23
10/23	9/24
10/24	9/25
10/25	9/26

Solar	Lunar
10/26	9/27
10/27	9/28
10/28	9/29
10/29	10/1
10/30	10/2
10/31	10/3
11/1	10/4
11/2	10/5
11/3	10/6
11/4	10/7
11/5	10/8
11/6	10/9
11/7	10/10
11/8	10/11
11/9	10/12
11/10	10/13
11/11	10/14
11/12	10/15
11/13	10/16
11/14	10/17
11/15	10/18
11/16	10/19
11/17	10/20
11/18	10/21
11/19	10/22
11/20	10/23
11/21	10/24
11/22	10/25
11/23	10/26
11/24	10/27
11/25	10/28
11/26	10/29
11/27	10/30
11/28	11/1
11/29	11/2
11/30	11/3
12/1	11/4
12/2	11/5
12/3	11/6
12/4	11/7
12/5	11/8
12/6	11/9
12/7	11/10
12/8	11/11
12/9	11/12
12/10	11/13
12/11	11/14
12/12	11/15
12/13	11/16
12/14	11/17
12/15	11/18
12/16	11/19
12/17	11/20
12/18	11/21
12/19	11/22
12/20	11/23
12/21	11/24
12/22	11/25

Solar Date	Lunar Date
12/23	11/26
12/24	11/27
12/25	11/28
12/26	11/29
12/27	12/1
12/28	12/2
12/29	12/3
12/30	12/4
12/31	12/5
1914	
1/1	12/6
1/2	12/7
1/3	12/8
1/4	12/9
1/5	12/10
1/6	12/11
1/7	12/12
1/8	12/13
1/9	12/14
1/10	12/15
1/11	12/16
1/12	12/17
1/13	12/18
1/14	12/19
1/15	12/20
1/16	12/21
1/17	12/22
1/18	12/23
1/19	12/24
1/20	12/25
1/21	12/26
1/22	12/27
1/23	12/28
1/24	12/29
1/25	12/30
1/26	1/1 (1914)
1/27	1/2
1/28	1/3
1/29	1/4
1/30	1/5
1/31	1/6
2/1	1/7
2/2	1/8
2/3	1/9
2/4	1/10
2/5	1/11
2/6	1/12
2/7	1/13
2/8	1/14
2/9	1/15
2/10	1/16
2/11	1/17
2/12	1/18

Solar	Lunar
2/13	1/19
2/14	1/20
2/15	1/21
2/16	1/22
2/17	1/23
2/18	1/24
2/19	1/25
2/20	1/26
2/21	1/27
2/22	1/28
2/23	1/29
2/24	1/30
2/25	2/1
2/26	2/2
2/27	2/3
2/28	2/4
3/1	2/5
3/2	2/6
3/3	2/7
3/4	2/8
3/5	2/9
3/6	2/10
3/7	2/11
3/8	2/12
3/9	2/13
3/10	2/14
3/11	2/15
3/12	2/16
3/13	2/17
3/14	2/18
3/15	2/19
3/16	2/20
3/17	2/21
3/18	2/22
3/19	2/23
3/20	2/24
3/21	2/25
3/22	2/26
3/23	2/27
3/24	2/28
3/25	2/29
3/26	2/30
3/27	3/1
3/28	3/2
3/29	3/3
3/30	3/4
3/31	3/5
4/1	3/6
4/2	3/7
4/3	3/8
4/4	3/9
4/5	3/10
4/6	3/11
4/7	3/12
4/8	3/13
4/9	3/14
4/10	3/15
4/11	3/16

Solar	Lunar	Solar	Lunar	Solar	Lunar	Solar	Lunar	Solar	Lunar	Solar	Lunar
4/12	3/17	6/9	5/16	8/5	6/14	10/2	8/13	11/30	10/14	1/22	12/8
4/13	3/18	6/10	5/17	8/6	6/15	10/3	8/14			1/23	12/9
4/14	3/19	6/11	5/18	8/7	6/16	10/4	8/15	12/1	10/15	1/24	12/10
4/15	3/20	6/12	5/19	8/8	6/17	10/5	8/16	12/2	10/16	1/25	12/11
4/16	3/21	6/13	5/20	8/9	6/18	10/6	8/17	12/3	10/17	1/26	12/12
4/17	3/22	6/14	5/21	8/10	6/19	10/7	8/18	12/4	10/18	1/27	12/13
4/18	3/23	6/15	5/22	8/11	6/20	10/8	8/19	12/5	10/19	1/28	12/14
4/19	3/24	6/16	5/23	8/12	6/21	10/9	8/20	12/6	10/20	1/29	12/15
4/20	3/25	6/17	5/24	8/13	6/22	10/10	8/21	12/7	10/21	1/30	12/16
4/21	3/26	6/18	5/25	8/14	6/23	10/11	8/22	12/8	10/22	1/31	12/17
4/22	3/27	6/19	5/26	8/15	6/24	10/12	8/23	12/9	10/23		
4/23	3/28	6/20	5/27	8/16	6/25	10/13	8/24	12/10	10/24	2/1	12/18
4/24	3/29	6/21	5/28	8/17	6/26	10/14	8/25	12/11	10/25	2/2	12/19
4/25	4/1	6/22	5/29	8/18	6/27	10/15	8/26	12/12	10/26	2/3	12/20
4/26	4/2	6/23	5/1	8/19	6/28	10/16	8/27	12/13	10/27	2/4	12/21
4/27	4/3	(Leap Month)		8/20	6/29	10/17	8/28	12/14	10/28	2/5	12/22
4/28	4/4	6/24	5/2	8/21	7/1	10/18	8/29	12/15	10/29	2/6	12/23
4/29	4/5	6/25	5/3	8/22	7/2	10/19	9/1	12/16	10/30	2/7	12/24
4/30	4/6	6/26	5/4	8/23	7/3	10/20	9/2	12/17	11/1	2/8	12/25
		6/27	5/5	8/24	7/4	10/21	9/3	12/18	11/2	2/9	12/26
5/1	4/7	6/28	5/6	8/25	7/5	10/22	9/4	12/19	11/3	2/10	12/27
5/2	4/8	6/29	5/7	8/26	7/6	10/23	9/5	12/20	11/4	2/11	12/28
5/3	4/9	6/30	5/8	8/27	7/7	10/24	9/6	12/21	11/5	2/12	12/29
5/4	4/10			8/28	7/8	10/25	9/7	12/22	11/6	2/13	12/30
5/5	4/11	7/1	5/9	8/29	7/9	10/26	9/8	12/23	11/7	2/14	1/1
5/6	4/12	7/2	5/10	8/30	7/10	10/27	9/9	12/24	11/8		(1915)
5/7	4/13	7/3	5/11	8/31	7/11	10/28	9/10	12/25	11/9	2/15	1/2
5/8	4/14	7/4	5/12			10/29	9/11	12/26	11/10	2/16	1/3
5/9	4/15	7/5	5/13	9/1	7/12	10/30	9/12	12/27	11/11	2/17	1/4
5/10	4/16	7/6	5/14	9/2	7/13	10/31	9/13	12/28	11/12	2/18	1/5
5/11	4/17	7/7	5/15	9/3	7/14			12/29	11/13	2/19	1/6
5/12	4/18	7/8	5/16	9/4	7/15			12/30	11/14	2/20	1/7
5/13	4/19	7/9	5/17	9/5	7/16	11/1	9/14	12/31	11/15	2/21	1/8
5/14	4/20	7/10	5/18	9/6	7/17	11/2	9/15			2/22	1/9
5/15	4/21	7/11	5/19	9/7	7/18	11/3	9/16			2/23	1/10
5/16	4/22	7/12	5/20	9/8	7/19	11/4	9/17	Solar	Lunar	2/24	1/11
5/17	4/23	7/13	5/21	9/9	7/20	11/5	9/18	Date	Date	2/25	1/12
5/18	4/24	7/14	5/22	9/10	7/21	11/6	9/19	**1915**		2/26	1/13
5/19	4/25	7/15	5/23	9/11	7/22	11/7	9/20	1/1	11/16	2/27	1/14
5/20	4/26	7/16	5/24	9/12	7/23	11/8	9/21	1/2	11/17	2/28	1/15
5/21	4/27	7/17	5/25	9/13	7/24	11/9	9/22	1/3	11/18		
5/22	4/28	7/18	5/26	9/14	7/25	11/10	9/23	1/4	11/19	3/1	1/16
5/23	4/29	7/19	5/27	9/15	7/26	11/11	9/24	1/5	11/20	3/2	1/17
5/24	4/30	7/20	5/28	9/16	7/27	11/12	9/25	1/6	11/21	3/3	1/18
5/25	5/1	7/21	5/29	9/17	7/28	11/13	9/26	1/7	11/22	3/4	1/19
5/26	5/2	7/22	5/30	9/18	7/29	11/14	9/27	1/8	11/23	3/5	1/20
5/27	5/3	7/23	6/1	9/19	7/30	11/15	9/28	1/9	11/24	3/6	1/21
5/28	5/4	7/24	6/2	9/20	8/1	11/16	9/29	1/10	11/25	3/7	1/22
5/29	5/5	7/25	6/3	9/21	8/2	11/17	10/1	1/11	11/26	3/8	1/23
5/30	5/6	7/26	6/4	9/22	8/3	11/18	10/2	1/12	11/27	3/9	1/24
5/31	5/7	7/27	6/5	9/23	8/4	11/19	10/3	1/13	11/28	3/10	1/25
		7/28	6/6	9/24	8/5	11/20	10/4	1/14	11/29	3/11	1/26
6/1	5/8	7/29	6/7	9/25	8/6	11/21	10/5	1/15	12/1	3/12	1/27
6/2	5/9	7/30	6/8	9/26	8/7	11/22	10/6	1/16	12/2	3/13	1/28
6/3	5/10	7/31	6/9	9/27	8/8	11/23	10/7	1/17	12/3	3/14	1/29
6/4	5/11			9/28	8/9	11/24	10/8	1/18	12/4	3/15	1/30
6/5	5/12	8/1	6/10	9/29	8/10	11/25	10/9	1/19	12/5	3/16	2/1
6/6	5/13	8/2	6/11	9/30	8/11	11/26	10/10	1/20	12/6	3/17	2/2
6/7	5/14	8/3	6/12			11/27	10/11	1/21	12/7	3/18	2/3
6/8	5/15	8/4	6/13	10/1	8/12	11/28	10/12			3/19	2/4
						11/29	10/13				

The sixth column group is headed **Solar Date / Lunar Date** (year **1916**).

Solar	Lunar	Solar	Lunar	Solar	Lunar	Solar	Lunar	Solar	Lunar	Solar	Lunar
3/20	2/5	5/17	4/4	7/14	6/3	9/10	8/2	11/7	10/1		
3/21	2/6	5/18	4/5	7/15	6/4	9/11	8/3	11/8	10/2		
3/22	2/7	5/19	4/6	7/16	6/5	9/12	8/4	11/9	10/3		
3/23	2/8	5/20	4/7	7/17	6/6	9/13	8/5	11/10	10/4	1/1	11/26
3/24	2/9	5/21	4/8	7/18	6/7	9/14	8/6	11/11	10/5	1/2	11/27
3/25	2/10	5/22	4/9	7/19	6/8	9/15	8/7	11/12	10/6	1/3	11/28
3/26	2/11	5/23	4/10	7/20	6/9	9/16	8/8	11/13	10/7	1/4	11/29
3/27	2/12	5/24	4/11	7/21	6/10	9/17	8/9	11/14	10/8	1/5	12/2
3/28	2/13	5/25	4/12	7/22	6/11	9/18	8/10	11/15	10/9	1/6	12/3
3/29	2/14	5/26	4/13	7/23	6/12	9/19	8/11	11/16	10/10	1/7	12/4
3/30	2/15	5/27	4/14	7/24	6/13	9/20	8/12	11/17	10/11	1/8	12/5
3/31	2/16	5/28	4/15	7/25	6/14	9/21	8/13	11/18	10/12	1/9	12/6
		5/29	4/16	7/26	6/15	9/22	8/14	11/19	10/13	1/10	12/7
4/1	2/17	5/30	4/17	7/27	6/16	9/23	8/15	11/20	10/14	1/11	12/8
4/2	2/18	5/31	4/18	7/28	6/17	9/24	8/16	11/21	10/15	1/12	12/9
4/3	2/19			7/29	6/18	9/25	8/17	11/22	10/16	1/13	12/10
4/4	2/20	6/1	4/19	7/30	6/19	9/26	8/18	11/23	10/17	1/14	12/11
4/5	2/21	6/2	4/20	7/31	6/20	9/27	8/19	11/24	10/18	1/15	12/12
4/6	2/22	6/3	4/21			9/28	8/20	11/25	10/19	1/16	12/13
4/7	2/23	6/4	4/22	8/1	6/21	9/29	8/21	11/26	10/20	1/17	12/14
4/8	2/24	6/5	4/23	8/2	6/22	9/30	8/22	11/27	10/21	1/18	12/15
4/9	2/25	6/6	4/24	8/3	6/23			11/28	10/22	1/19	12/16
4/10	2/26	6/7	4/25	8/4	6/24	10/1	8/23	11/29	10/23	1/20	12/17
4/11	2/27	6/8	4/26	8/5	6/25	10/2	8/24	11/30	10/23	1/21	12/18
4/12	2/28	6/9	4/27	8/6	6/26	10/3	8/25			1/22	12/19
4/13	2/29	6/10	4/28	8/7	6/27	10/4	8/26	12/1	10/24	1/23	12/20
4/14	3/1	6/11	4/29	8/8	6/28	10/5	8/27	12/2	10/25	1/24	12/21
4/15	3/2	6/12	4/30	8/9	6/29	10/6	8/28	12/3	10/26	1/25	12/22
4/16	3/3	6/13	5/1	8/10	6/30	10/7	8/29	12/4	10/27	1/26	12/23
4/17	3/4	6/14	5/2	8/11	7/1	10/8	8/30	12/5	10/28	1/27	12/24
4/18	3/5	6/15	5/3	8/12	7/2	10/9	9/1	12/6	10/29	1/28	12/25
4/19	3/6	6/16	5/4	8/13	7/3	10/10	9/2	12/7	11/1	1/29	12/26
4/20	3/7	6/17	5/5	8/14	7/4	10/11	9/3	12/8	11/2	1/30	12/27
4/21	3/8	6/18	5/6	8/15	7/5	10/12	9/4	12/9	11/3	1/31	12/28
4/22	3/9	6/19	5/7	8/16	7/6	10/13	9/5	12/10	11/4		
4/23	3/10	6/20	5/8	8/17	7/7	10/14	9/6	12/11	11/5	2/1	12/29
4/24	3/11	6/21	5/9	8/18	7/8	10/15	9/7	12/12	11/6	2/2	12/30
4/25	3/12	6/22	5/10	8/19	7/9	10/16	9/8	12/13	11/7	2/3	1/1 (1916)
4/26	3/13	6/23	5/11	8/20	7/10	10/17	9/9	12/14	11/8		
4/27	3/14	6/24	5/12	8/21	7/11	10/18	9/10	12/15	11/9	2/4	1/2
4/28	3/15	6/25	5/13	8/22	7/12	10/19	9/11	12/16	11/10	2/5	1/3
4/29	3/16	6/26	5/14	8/23	7/13	10/20	9/12	12/17	11/11	2/6	1/4
4/30	3/17	6/27	5/15	8/24	7/14	10/21	9/13	12/18	11/12	2/7	1/5
		6/28	5/16	8/25	7/15	10/22	9/14	12/19	11/13	2/8	1/6
5/1	3/18	6/29	5/17	8/26	7/16	10/23	9/15	12/20	11/14	2/9	1/7
5/2	3/19	6/30	5/18	8/27	7/17	10/24	9/16	12/21	11/15	2/10	1/8
5/3	3/20			8/28	7/18	10/25	9/17	12/22	11/16	2/11	1/9
5/4	3/21	7/1	5/19	8/29	7/19	10/26	9/18	12/23	11/17	2/12	1/10
5/5	3/22	7/2	5/20	8/30	7/20	10/27	9/19	12/24	11/18	2/13	1/11
5/6	3/23	7/3	5/21	8/31	7/21	10/28	9/20	12/25	11/19	2/14	1/12
5/7	3/24	7/4	5/22			10/29	9/21	12/26	11/20	2/15	1/13
5/8	3/25	7/5	5/23	9/1	7/22	10/30	9/22	12/27	11/21	2/16	1/14
5/9	3/26	7/6	5/24	9/2	7/23	10/31	9/23	12/28	11/22	2/17	1/15
5/10	3/27	7/7	5/25	9/3	7/24			12/29	11/23	2/18	1/16
5/11	3/28	7/8	5/26	9/4	7/25	11/1	9/24	12/30	11/24	2/19	1/17
5/12	3/29	7/9	5/27	9/5	7/26	11/2	9/25	12/31	11/25	2/20	1/18
5/13	3/30	7/10	5/28	9/6	7/27	11/3	9/26			2/21	1/19
5/14	4/1	7/11	5/29	9/7	7/28	11/4	9/27			2/22	1/20
5/15	4/2	7/12	6/1	9/8	7/29	11/5	9/28			2/23	1/21
5/16	4/3	7/13	6/2	9/9	8/1	11/6	9/29				

Solar	Lunar	Solar	Lunar	Solar	Lunar	Solar	Lunar	Solar	Lunar	Solar	Lunar
2/24	1/22	4/23	3/21	6/20	5/20	8/17	7/19	10/14	9/18	12/11	11/17
2/25	1/23	4/24	3/22	6/21	5/21	8/18	7/20	10/15	9/19	12/12	11/18
2/26	1/24	4/25	3/23	6/22	5/22	8/19	7/21	10/16	9/20	12/13	11/19
2/27	1/25	4/26	3/24	6/23	5/23	8/20	7/22	10/17	9/21	12/14	11/20
2/28	1/26	4/27	3/25	6/24	5/24	8/21	7/23	10/18	9/22	12/15	11/21
		4/28	3/26	6/25	5/25	8/22	7/24	10/19	9/23	12/16	11/22
3/1	1/27	4/29	3/27	6/26	5/26	8/23	7/25	10/20	9/24	12/17	11/23
3/2	1/28	4/30	3/28	6/27	5/27	8/24	7/26	10/21	9/25	12/18	11/24
3/3	1/29			6/28	5/28	8/25	7/27	10/22	9/26	12/19	11/25
3/4	2/1	5/1	3/29	6/29	5/29	8/26	7/28	10/23	9/27	12/20	11/26
3/5	2/2	5/2	4/1	6/30	6/1	8/27	7/29	10/24	9/28	12/21	11/27
3/6	2/3	5/3	4/2			8/28	8/1	10/25	9/29	12/22	11/28
3/7	2/4	5/4	4/3	7/1	6/2	8/29	8/2	10/26	9/30	12/23	11/29
3/8	2/5	5/5	4/4	7/2	6/3	8/30	8/3	10/27	10/1	12/24	11/30
3/9	2/6	5/6	4/5	7/3	6/4	8/31	8/4	10/28	10/2	12/25	12/1
3/10	2/7	5/7	4/6	7/4	6/5			10/29	10/3	12/26	12/2
3/11	2/8	5/8	4/7	7/5	6/6	9/1	8/5	10/30	10/4	12/27	12/3
3/12	2/9	5/9	4/8	7/6	6/7	9/2	8/6	10/31	10/5	12/28	12/4
3/13	2/10	5/10	4/9	7/7	6/8	9/3	8/7			12/29	12/5
3/14	2/11	5/11	4/10	7/8	6/9	9/4	8/8	11/1	10/6	12/30	12/6
3/15	2/12	5/12	4/11	7/9	6/10	9/5	8/9	11/2	10/7	12/31	12/7
3/16	2/13	5/13	4/12	7/10	6/11	9/6	8/10	11/3	10/8		
3/17	2/14	5/14	4/13	7/11	6/12	9/7	8/11	11/4	10/9		
3/18	2/15	5/15	4/14	7/12	6/13	9/8	8/12	11/5	10/10	Solar	Lunar
3/19	2/16	5/16	4/15	7/13	6/14	9/9	8/13	11/6	10/11	Date	Date
3/20	2/17	5/17	4/16	7/14	6/15	9/10	8/14	11/7	10/12		
3/21	2/18	5/18	4/17	7/15	6/16	9/11	8/15	11/8	10/13		
3/22	2/19	5/19	4/18	7/16	6/17	9/12	8/16	11/9	10/14	1917	
3/23	2/20	5/20	4/19	7/17	6/18	9/13	8/17	11/10	10/15	1/1	12/8
3/24	2/21	5/21	4/20	7/18	6/19	9/14	8/18	11/11	10/16	1/2	12/9
3/25	2/22	5/22	4/21	7/19	6/20	9/15	8/19	11/12	10/17	1/3	12/10
3/26	2/23	5/23	4/22	7/20	6/21	9/16	8/20	11/13	10/18	1/4	12/11
3/27	2/24	5/24	4/23	7/21	6/22	9/17	8/21	11/14	10/19	1/5	12/12
3/28	2/25	5/25	4/24	7/22	6/23	9/18	8/22	11/15	10/20	1/6	12/13
3/29	2/26	5/26	4/25	7/23	6/24	9/19	8/23	11/16	10/21	1/7	12/14
3/30	2/27	5/27	4/26	7/24	6/25	9/20	8/24	11/17	10/22	1/8	12/15
3/31	2/28	5/28	4/27	7/25	6/26	9/21	8/25	11/18	10/23	1/9	12/16
		5/29	4/28	7/26	6/27	9/22	8/26	11/19	10/24	1/10	12/17
4/1	2/29	5/30	4/29	7/27	6/28	9/23	8/27	11/20	10/25	1/11	12/18
4/2	2/30	5/31	4/30	7/28	6/29	9/24	8/28	11/21	10/26	1/12	12/19
4/3	3/1			7/29	6/30	9/25	8/29	11/22	10/27	1/13	12/20
4/4	3/2	6/1	5/1	7/30	7/1	9/26	8/30	11/23	10/28	1/14	12/21
4/5	3/3	6/2	5/2	7/31	7/2	9/27	9/1	11/24	10/29	1/15	12/22
4/6	3/4	6/3	5/3			9/28	9/2	11/25	11/1	1/16	12/23
4/7	3/5	6/4	5/4	8/1	7/3	9/29	9/3	11/26	11/2	1/17	12/24
4/8	3/6	6/5	5/5	8/2	7/4	9/30	9/4	11/27	11/3	1/18	12/25
4/9	3/7	6/6	5/6	8/3	7/5			11/28	11/4	1/19	12/26
4/10	3/8	6/7	5/7	8/4	7/6	10/1	9/5	11/29	11/5	1/20	12/27
4/11	3/9	6/8	5/8	8/5	7/7	10/2	9/6	11/30	11/6	1/21	12/28
4/12	3/10	6/9	5/9	8/6	7/8	10/3	9/7			1/22	12/29
4/13	3/11	6/10	5/10	8/7	7/9	10/4	9/8	12/1	11/7	1/23	12/30
4/14	3/12	6/11	5/11	8/8	7/10	10/5	9/9	12/2	11/8	1/24	1/1
4/15	3/13	6/12	5/12	8/9	7/11	10/6	9/10	12/3	11/9		(1917)
4/16	3/14	6/13	5/13	8/10	7/12	10/7	9/11	12/4	11/10	1/25	1/2
4/17	3/15	6/14	5/14	8/11	7/13	10/8	9/12	12/5	11/11	1/26	1/3
4/18	3/16	6/15	5/15	8/12	7/14	10/9	9/13	12/6	11/12	1/27	1/4
4/19	3/17	6/16	5/16	8/13	7/15	10/10	9/14	12/7	11/13	1/28	1/5
4/20	3/18	6/17	5/17	8/14	7/16	10/11	9/15	12/8	11/14	1/29	1/6
4/21	3/19	6/18	5/18	8/15	7/17	10/12	9/16	12/9	11/15	1/30	1/7
4/22	3/20	6/19	5/19	8/16	7/18	10/13	9/17	12/10	11/16	1/31	1/8

Solar Date	Lunar Date	Solar Date	Lunar Date	Solar Date	Lunar Date	Solar Date	Lunar Date	Solar Date	Lunar Date	Solar Date	Lunar Date
2/1	1/9	3/31	2/9	5/28	4/8	7/25	6/7	9/21	8/6	11/18	10/4
2/2	1/10			5/29	4/9	7/26	6/8	9/22	8/7	11/19	10/5
2/3	1/11	4/1	2/10	5/30	4/10	7/27	6/9	9/23	8/8	11/20	10/6
2/4	1/12	4/2	2/11	5/31	4/11	7/28	6/10	9/24	8/9	11/21	10/7
2/5	1/13	4/3	2/12			7/29	6/11	9/25	8/10	11/22	10/8
2/6	1/14	4/4	2/13	6/1	4/12	7/30	6/12	9/26	8/11	11/23	10/9
2/7	1/15	4/5	2/14	6/2	4/13	7/31	6/13	9/27	8/12	11/24	10/10
2/8	1/16	4/6	2/15	6/3	4/14			9/28	8/13	11/25	10/11
2/9	1/17	4/7	2/16	6/4	4/15	8/1	6/14	9/29	8/14	11/26	10/12
2/10	1/18	4/8	2/17	6/5	4/16	8/2	6/15	9/30	8/15	11/27	10/13
2/11	1/19	4/9	2/18	6/6	4/17	8/3	6/16			11/28	10/14
2/12	1/20	4/10	2/19	6/7	4/18	8/4	6/17	10/1	8/16	11/29	10/15
2/13	1/21	4/11	2/20	6/8	4/19	8/5	6/18	10/2	8/17	11/30	10/16
2/14	1/22	4/12	2/21	6/9	4/20	8/6	6/19	10/3	8/18		
2/15	1/23	4/13	2/22	6/10	4/21	8/7	6/20	10/4	8/19	12/1	10/17
2/16	1/24	4/14	2/23	6/11	4/22	8/8	6/21	10/5	8/20	12/2	10/18
2/17	1/25	4/15	2/24	6/12	4/23	8/9	6/22	10/6	8/21	12/3	10/19
2/18	1/26	4/16	2/25	6/13	4/24	8/10	6/23	10/7	8/22	12/4	10/20
2/19	1/27	4/17	2/26	6/14	4/25	8/11	6/24	10/8	8/23	12/5	10/21
2/20	1/28	4/18	2/27	6/15	4/26	8/12	6/25	10/9	8/24	12/6	10/22
2/21	1/29	4/19	2/28	6/16	4/27	8/13	6/26	10/10	8/25	12/7	10/23
2/22	2/1	4/20	2/29	6/17	4/28	8/14	6/27	10/11	8/26	12/8	10/24
2/23	2/2	4/21	3/1	6/18	4/29	8/15	6/28	10/12	8/27	12/9	10/25
2/24	2/3	4/22	3/2	6/19	5/1	8/16	6/29	10/13	8/28	12/10	10/26
2/25	2/4	4/23	3/3	6/20	5/2	8/17	6/30	10/14	8/29	12/11	10/27
2/26	2/5	4/24	3/4	6/21	5/3	8/18	7/1	10/15	8/30	12/12	10/28
2/27	2/6	4/25	3/5	6/22	5/4	8/19	7/2	10/16	9/1	12/13	10/29
2/28	2/7	4/26	3/6	6/23	5/5	8/20	7/3	10/17	9/2	12/14	11/1
		4/27	3/7	6/24	5/6	8/21	7/4	10/18	9/3	12/15	11/2
3/1	2/8	4/28	3/8	6/25	5/7	8/22	7/5	10/19	9/4	12/16	11/3
3/2	2/9	4/29	3/9	6/26	5/8	8/23	7/6	10/20	9/5	12/17	11/4
3/3	2/10	4/30	3/10	6/27	5/9	8/24	7/7	10/21	9/6	12/18	11/5
3/4	2/11			6/28	5/10	8/25	7/8	10/22	9/7	12/19	11/6
3/5	2/12	5/1	3/11	6/29	5/11	8/26	7/9	10/23	9/8	12/20	11/7
3/6	2/13	5/2	3/12	6/30	5/12	8/27	7/10	10/24	9/9	12/21	11/8
3/7	2/14	5/3	3/13			8/28	7/11	10/25	9/10	12/22	11/9
3/8	2/15	5/4	3/14	7/1	5/13	8/29	7/12	10/26	9/11	12/23	11/10
3/9	2/16	5/5	3/15	7/2	5/14	8/30	7/13	10/27	9/12	12/24	11/11
3/10	2/17	5/6	3/16	7/3	5/15	8/31	7/14	10/28	9/13	12/25	11/12
3/11	2/18	5/7	3/17	7/4	5/16			10/29	9/14	12/26	11/13
3/12	2/19	5/8	3/18	7/5	5/17	9/1	7/15	10/30	9/15	12/27	11/14
3/13	2/20	5/9	3/19	7/6	5/18	9/2	7/16	10/31	9/16	12/28	11/15
3/14	2/21	5/10	3/20	7/7	5/19	9/3	7/17			12/29	11/16
3/15	2/22	5/11	3/21	7/8	5/20	9/4	7/18	11/1	9/17	12/30	11/17
3/16	2/23	5/12	3/22	7/9	5/21	9/5	7/19	11/2	9/18	12/31	11/18
3/17	2/24	5/13	3/23	7/10	5/22	9/6	7/20	11/3	9/19		
3/18	2/25	5/14	3/24	7/11	5/23	9/7	7/21	11/4	9/20		
3/19	2/26	5/15	3/25	7/12	5/24	9/8	7/22	11/5	9/21	Solar Date	Lunar Date
3/20	2/27	5/16	3/26	7/13	5/25	9/9	7/23	11/6	9/22		
3/21	2/28	5/17	3/27	7/14	5/26	9/10	7/24	11/7	9/23	**1918**	
3/22	2/29	5/18	3/28	7/15	5/27	9/11	7/25	11/8	9/24	1/1	11/19
3/23	2/1	5/19	3/29	7/16	5/28	9/12	7/26	11/9	9/25	1/2	11/20
(Leap Month)		5/20	3/30	7/17	5/29	9/13	7/27	11/10	9/26	1/3	11/21
3/24	2/2	5/21	4/1	7/18	5/30	9/14	7/28	11/11	9/27	1/4	11/22
3/25	2/3	5/22	4/2	7/19	6/1	9/15	7/29	11/12	9/28	1/5	11/23
3/26	2/4	5/23	4/3	7/20	6/2	9/16	8/1	11/13	9/29	1/6	11/24
3/27	2/5	5/24	4/4	7/21	6/3	9/17	8/2	11/14	9/30	1/7	11/25
3/28	2/6	5/25	4/5	7/22	6/4	9/18	8/3	11/15	10/1	1/8	11/26
3/29	2/7	5/26	4/6	7/23	6/5	9/19	8/4	11/16	10/2	1/9	11/27
3/30	2/8	5/27	4/7	7/24	6/6	9/20	8/5	11/17	10/3		

Solar	Lunar	Solar	Lunar	Solar	Lunar	Solar	Lunar	Solar	Lunar	Solar	Lunar
1/10	11/28	3/8	1/26	5/5	3/25	7/2	5/24	8/30	7/24	10/27	9/23
1/11	11/29	3/9	1/27	5/6	3/26	7/3	5/25	8/31	7/25	10/28	9/24
1/12	11/30	3/10	1/28	5/7	3/27	7/4	5/26			10/29	9/25
1/13	12/1	3/11	1/29	5/8	3/28	7/5	5/27	9/1	7/26	10/30	9/26
1/14	12/2	3/12	1/30	5/9	3/29	7/6	5/28	9/2	7/27	10/31	9/27
1/15	12/3	3/13	2/1	5/10	4/1	7/7	5/29	9/3	7/28		
1/16	12/4	3/14	2/2	5/11	4/2	7/8	6/1	9/4	7/29	11/1	9/28
1/17	12/5	3/15	2/3	5/12	4/3	7/9	6/2	9/5	8/1	11/2	9/29
1/18	12/6	3/16	2/4	5/13	4/4	7/10	6/3	9/6	8/2	11/3	9/30
1/19	12/7	3/17	2/5	5/14	4/5	7/11	6/4	9/7	8/3	11/4	10/1
1/20	12/8	3/18	2/6	5/15	4/6	7/12	6/5	9/8	8/4	11/5	10/2
1/21	12/9	3/19	2/7	5/16	4/7	7/13	6/6	9/9	8/5	11/6	10/3
1/22	12/10	3/20	2/8	5/17	4/8	7/14	6/7	9/10	8/6	11/7	10/4
1/23	12/11	3/21	2/9	5/18	4/9	7/15	6/8	9/11	8/7	11/8	10/5
1/24	12/12	3/22	2/10	5/19	4/10	7/16	6/9	9/12	8/8	11/9	10/6
1/25	12/13	3/23	2/11	5/20	4/11	7/17	6/10	9/13	8/9	11/10	10/7
1/26	12/14	3/24	2/12	5/21	4/12	7/18	6/11	9/14	8/10	11/11	10/8
1/27	12/15	3/25	2/13	5/22	4/13	7/19	6/12	9/15	8/11	11/12	10/9
1/28	12/16	3/26	2/14	5/23	4/14	7/20	6/13	9/16	8/12	11/13	10/10
1/29	12/17	3/27	2/15	5/24	4/15	7/21	6/14	9/17	8/13	11/14	10/11
1/30	12/18	3/28	2/16	5/25	4/16	7/22	6/15	9/18	8/14	11/15	10/12
1/31	12/19	3/29	2/17	5/26	4/17	7/23	6/16	9/19	8/15	11/16	10/13
		3/30	2/18	5/27	4/18	7/24	6/17	9/20	8/16	11/17	10/14
2/1	12/20	3/31	2/19	5/28	4/19	7/25	6/18	9/21	8/17	11/18	10/15
2/2	12/21			5/29	4/20	7/26	6/19	9/22	8/18	11/19	10/16
2/3	12/22	4/1	2/20	5/30	4/21	7/27	6/20	9/23	8/19	11/20	10/17
2/4	12/23	4/2	2/21	5/31	4/22	7/28	6/21	9/24	8/20	11/21	10/18
2/5	12/24	4/3	2/22			7/29	6/22	9/25	8/21	11/22	10/19
2/6	12/25	4/4	2/23	6/1	4/23	7/30	6/23	9/26	8/22	11/23	10/20
2/7	12/26	4/5	2/24	6/2	4/24	7/31	6/24	9/27	8/23	11/24	10/21
2/8	12/27	4/6	2/25	6/3	4/25			9/28	8/24	11/25	10/22
2/9	12/28	4/7	2/26	6/4	4/26	8/1	6/25	9/29	8/25	11/26	10/23
2/10	12/29	4/8	2/27	6/5	4/27	8/2	6/26	9/30	8/26	11/27	10/24
2/11	1/1	4/9	2/28	6/6	4/28	8/3	6/27			11/28	10/25
	(1918)	4/10	2/29	6/7	4/29	8/4	6/28	10/1	8/27	11/29	10/26
2/12	1/2	4/11	3/1	6/8	4/30	8/5	6/29	10/2	8/28	11/30	10/27
2/13	1/3	4/12	3/2	6/9	5/1	8/6	6/30	10/3	8/29		
2/14	1/4	4/13	3/3	6/10	5/2	8/7	7/1	10/4	8/30	12/1	10/28
2/15	1/5	4/14	3/4	6/11	5/3	8/8	7/2	10/5	9/1	12/2	10/29
2/16	1/6	4/15	3/5	6/12	5/4	8/9	7/3	10/6	9/2	12/3	11/1
2/17	1/7	4/16	3/6	6/13	5/5	8/10	7/4	10/7	9/3	12/4	11/2
2/18	1/8	4/17	3/7	6/14	5/6	8/11	7/5	10/8	9/4	12/5	11/3
2/19	1/9	4/18	3/8	6/15	5/7	8/12	7/6	10/9	9/5	12/6	11/4
2/20	1/10	4/19	3/9	6/16	5/8	8/13	7/7	10/10	9/6	12/7	11/5
2/21	1/11	4/20	3/10	6/17	5/9	8/14	7/8	10/11	9/7	12/8	11/6
2/22	1/12	4/21	3/11	6/18	5/10	8/15	7/9	10/12	9/8	12/9	11/7
2/23	1/13	4/22	3/12	6/19	5/11	8/16	7/10	10/13	9/9	12/10	11/8
2/24	1/14	4/23	3/13	6/20	5/12	8/17	7/11	10/14	9/10	12/11	11/9
2/25	1/15	4/24	3/14	6/21	5/13	8/18	7/12	10/15	9/11	12/12	11/10
2/26	1/16	4/25	3/15	6/22	5/14	8/19	7/13	10/16	9/12	12/13	11/11
2/27	1/17	4/26	3/16	6/23	5/15	8/20	7/14	10/17	9/13	12/14	11/12
2/28	1/18	4/27	3/17	6/24	5/16	8/21	7/15	10/18	9/14	12/15	11/13
		4/28	3/18	6/25	5/17	8/22	7/16	10/19	9/15	12/16	11/14
3/1	1/19	4/29	3/19	6/26	5/18	8/23	7/17	10/20	9/16	12/17	11/15
3/2	1/20	4/30	3/20	6/27	5/19	8/24	7/18	10/21	9/17	12/18	11/16
3/3	1/21			6/28	5/20	8/25	7/19	10/22	9/18	12/19	11/17
3/4	1/22	5/1	3/21	6/29	5/21	8/26	7/20	10/23	9/19	12/20	11/18
3/5	1/23	5/2	3/22	6/30	5/22	8/27	7/21	10/24	9/20	12/21	11/19
3/6	1/24	5/3	3/23			8/28	7/22	10/25	9/21	12/22	11/20
3/7	1/25	5/4	3/24	7/1	5/23	8/29	7/23	10/26	9/22	12/23	11/21

Solar	Lunar	Solar	Lunar	Solar	Lunar	Solar	Lunar	Solar	Lunar	Solar	Lunar
12/24	11/22	2/14	1/14	4/13	3/13	6/10	5/13	8/7	7/12	10/3	8/10
12/25	11/23	2/15	1/15	4/14	3/14	6/11	5/14	8/8	7/13	10/4	8/11
12/26	11/24	2/16	1/16	4/15	3/15	6/12	5/15	8/9	7/14	10/5	8/12
12/27	11/25	2/17	1/17	4/16	3/16	6/13	5/16	8/10	7/15	10/6	8/13
12/28	11/26	2/18	1/18	4/17	3/17	6/14	5/17	8/11	7/16	10/7	8/14
12/29	11/27	2/19	1/19	4/18	3/18	6/15	5/18	8/12	7/17	10/8	8/15
12/30	11/28	2/20	1/20	4/19	3/19	6/16	5/19	8/13	7/18	10/9	8/16
12/31	11/29	2/21	1/21	4/20	3/20	6/17	5/20	8/14	7/19	10/10	8/17
		2/22	1/22	4/21	3/21	6/18	5/21	8/15	7/20	10/11	8/18
		2/23	1/23	4/22	3/22	6/19	5/22	8/16	7/21	10/12	8/19
Solar Date	Lunar Date	2/24	1/24	4/23	3/23	6/20	5/23	8/17	7/22	10/13	8/20
		2/25	1/25	4/24	3/24	6/21	5/24	8/18	7/23	10/14	8/21
1919		2/26	1/26	4/25	3/25	6/22	5/25	8/19	7/24	10/15	8/22
1/1	11/30	2/27	1/27	4/26	3/26	6/23	5/26	8/20	7/25	10/16	8/23
1/2	12/1	2/28	1/28	4/27	3/27	6/24	5/27	8/21	7/26	10/17	8/24
1/3	12/2			4/28	3/28	6/25	5/28	8/22	7/27	10/18	8/25
1/4	12/3	3/1	1/29	4/29	3/29	6/26	5/29	8/23	7/28	10/19	8/26
1/5	12/4	3/2	2/1	4/30	4/1	6/27	5/30	8/24	7/29	10/20	8/27
1/6	12/5	3/3	2/2			6/28	6/1	8/25	7/1	10/21	8/28
1/7	12/6	3/4	2/3	5/1	4/2	6/29	6/2	*(Leap Month)*		10/22	8/29
1/8	12/7	3/5	2/4	5/2	4/3	6/30	6/3	8/26	7/2	10/23	8/30
1/9	12/8	3/6	2/5	5/3	4/4			8/27	7/3	10/24	9/1
1/10	12/9	3/7	2/6	5/4	4/5	7/1	6/4	8/28	7/4	10/25	9/2
1/11	12/10	3/8	2/7	5/5	4/6	7/2	6/5	8/29	7/5	10/26	9/3
1/12	12/11	3/9	2/8	5/6	4/7	7/3	6/6	8/30	7/6	10/27	9/4
1/13	12/12	3/10	2/9	5/7	4/8	7/4	6/7	8/31	7/7	10/28	9/5
1/14	12/13	3/11	2/10	5/8	4/9	7/5	6/8			10/29	9/6
1/15	12/14	3/12	2/11	5/9	4/10	7/6	6/9	9/1	7/8	10/30	9/7
1/16	12/15	3/13	2/12	5/10	4/11	7/7	6/10	9/2	7/9	10/31	9/8
1/17	12/16	3/14	2/13	5/11	4/12	7/8	6/11	9/3	7/10		
1/18	12/17	3/15	2/14	5/12	4/13	7/9	6/12	9/4	7/11		
1/19	12/18	3/16	2/15	5/13	4/14	7/10	6/13	9/5	7/12	11/1	9/9
1/20	12/19	3/17	2/16	5/14	4/15	7/11	6/14	9/6	7/13	11/2	9/10
1/21	12/20	3/18	2/17	5/15	4/16	7/12	6/15	9/7	7/14	11/3	9/11
1/22	12/21	3/19	2/18	5/16	4/17	7/13	6/16	9/8	7/15	11/4	9/12
1/23	12/22	3/20	2/19	5/17	4/18	7/14	6/17	9/9	7/16	11/5	9/13
1/24	12/23	3/21	2/20	5/18	4/19	7/15	6/18	9/10	7/17	11/6	9/14
1/25	12/24	3/22	2/21	5/19	4/20	7/16	6/19	9/11	7/18	11/7	9/15
1/26	12/25	3/23	2/22	5/20	4/21	7/17	6/20	9/12	7/19	11/8	9/16
1/27	12/26	3/24	2/23	5/21	4/22	7/18	6/21	9/13	7/20	11/9	9/17
1/28	12/27	3/25	2/24	5/22	4/23	7/19	6/22	9/14	7/21	11/10	9/18
1/29	12/28	3/26	2/25	5/23	4/24	7/20	6/23	9/15	7/22	11/11	9/19
1/30	12/29	3/27	2/26	5/24	4/25	7/21	6/24	9/16	7/23	11/12	9/20
1/31	12/30	3/28	2/27	5/25	4/26	7/22	6/25	9/17	7/24	11/13	9/21
		3/29	2/28	5/26	4/27	7/23	6/26	9/18	7/25	11/14	9/22
		3/30	2/29	5/27	4/28	7/24	6/27	9/19	7/26	11/15	9/23
2/1	1/1	3/31	2/30	5/28	4/29	7/25	6/28	9/20	7/27	11/16	9/24
	(1919)			5/29	5/1	7/26	6/29	9/21	7/28	11/17	9/25
2/2	1/2	4/1	3/1	5/30	5/2	7/27	7/1	9/22	7/29	11/18	9/26
2/3	1/3	4/2	3/2	5/31	5/3	7/28	7/2	9/23	7/30	11/19	9/27
2/4	1/4	4/3	3/3			7/29	7/3	9/24	8/1	11/20	9/28
2/5	1/5	4/4	3/4	6/1	5/4	7/30	7/4	9/25	8/2	11/21	9/29
2/6	1/6	4/5	3/5	6/2	5/5	7/31	7/5	9/26	8/3	11/22	10/1
2/7	1/7	4/6	3/6	6/3	5/6			9/27	8/4	11/23	10/2
2/8	1/8	4/7	3/7	6/4	5/7	8/1	7/6	9/28	8/5	11/24	10/3
2/9	1/9	4/8	3/8	6/5	5/8	8/2	7/7	9/29	8/6	11/25	10/4
2/10	1/10	4/9	3/9	6/6	5/9	8/3	7/8	9/30	8/7	11/26	10/5
2/11	1/11	4/10	3/10	6/7	5/10	8/4	7/9			11/27	10/6
2/12	1/12	4/11	3/11	6/8	5/11	8/5	7/10	10/1	8/8	11/28	10/7
2/13	1/13	4/12	3/12	6/9	5/12	8/6	7/11	10/2	8/9	11/29	10/8
										11/30	10/9

Solar	Lunar	Solar	Lunar	Solar	Lunar	Solar	Lunar	Solar	Lunar	Solar	Lunar
12/1	10/10	1/24	12/4	3/21	2/2	5/18	4/1	7/15	5/30	9/11	7/29
12/2	10/11	1/25	12/5	3/22	2/3	5/19	4/2	7/16	6/1	9/12	8/1
12/3	10/12	1/26	12/6	3/23	2/4	5/20	4/3	7/17	6/2	9/13	8/2
12/4	10/13	1/27	12/7	3/24	2/5	5/21	4/4	7/18	6/3	9/14	8/3
12/5	10/14	1/28	12/8	3/25	2/6	5/22	4/5	7/19	6/4	9/15	8/4
12/6	10/15	1/29	12/9	3/26	2/7	5/23	4/6	7/20	6/5	9/16	8/5
12/7	10/16	1/30	12/10	3/27	2/8	5/24	4/7	7/21	6/6	9/17	8/6
12/8	10/17	1/31	12/11	3/28	2/9	5/25	4/8	7/22	6/7	9/18	8/7
12/9	10/18			3/29	2/10	5/26	4/9	7/23	6/8	9/19	8/8
12/10	10/19	2/1	12/12	3/30	2/11	5/27	4/10	7/24	6/9	9/20	8/9
12/11	10/20	2/2	12/13	3/31	2/12	5/28	4/11	7/25	6/10	9/21	8/10
12/12	10/21	2/3	12/14			5/29	4/12	7/26	6/11	9/22	8/11
12/13	10/22	2/4	12/15	4/1	2/13	5/30	4/13	7/27	6/12	9/23	8/12
12/14	10/23	2/5	12/16	4/2	2/14	5/31	4/14	7/28	6/13	9/24	8/13
12/15	10/24	2/6	12/17	4/3	2/15			7/29	6/14	9/25	8/14
12/16	10/25	2/7	12/18	4/4	2/16	6/1	4/15	7/30	6/15	9/26	8/15
12/17	10/26	2/8	12/19	4/5	2/17	6/2	4/16	7/31	6/16	9/27	8/16
12/18	10/27	2/9	12/20	4/6	2/18	6/3	4/17			9/28	8/17
12/19	10/28	2/10	12/21	4/7	2/19	6/4	4/18	8/1	6/17	9/29	8/18
12/20	10/29	2/11	12/22	4/8	2/20	6/5	4/19	8/2	6/18	9/30	8/19
12/21	10/30	2/12	12/23	4/9	2/21	6/6	4/20	8/3	6/19		
12/22	11/1	2/13	12/24	4/10	2/22	6/7	4/21	8/4	6/20	10/1	8/20
12/23	11/2	2/14	12/25	4/11	2/23	6/8	4/22	8/5	6/21	10/2	8/21
12/24	11/3	2/15	12/26	4/12	2/24	6/9	4/23	8/6	6/22	10/3	8/22
12/25	11/4	2/16	12/27	4/13	2/25	6/10	4/24	8/7	6/23	10/4	8/23
12/26	11/5	2/17	12/28	4/14	2/26	6/11	4/25	8/8	6/24	10/5	8/24
12/27	11/6	2/18	12/29	4/15	2/27	6/12	4/26	8/9	6/25	10/6	8/25
12/28	11/7	2/19	12/30	4/16	2/28	6/13	4/27	8/10	6/26	10/7	8/26
12/29	11/8	2/20	1/1 (1920)	4/17	2/29	6/14	4/28	8/11	6/27	10/8	8/27
12/30	11/9			4/18	2/30	6/15	4/29	8/12	6/28	10/9	8/28
12/31	11/10	2/21	1/2	4/19	3/1	6/16	5/1	8/13	6/29	10/10	8/29
		2/22	1/3	4/20	3/2	6/17	5/2	8/14	7/1	10/11	8/30
		2/23	1/4	4/21	3/3	6/18	5/3	8/15	7/2	10/12	9/1
Solar	**Lunar**	2/24	1/5	4/22	3/4	6/19	5/4	8/16	7/3	10/13	9/2
Date	**Date**	2/25	1/6	4/23	3/5	6/20	5/5	8/17	7/4	10/14	9/3
		2/26	1/7	4/24	3/6	6/21	5/6	8/18	7/5	10/15	9/4
1920		2/27	1/8	4/25	3/7	6/22	5/7	8/19	7/6	10/16	9/5
1/1	11/11	2/28	1/9	4/26	3/8	6/23	5/8	8/20	7/7	10/17	9/6
1/2	11/12	2/29	1/10	4/27	3/9	6/24	5/9	8/21	7/8	10/18	9/7
1/3	11/13			4/28	3/10	6/25	5/10	8/22	7/9	10/19	9/8
1/4	11/14	3/1	1/11	4/29	3/11	6/26	5/11	8/23	7/10	10/20	9/9
1/5	11/15	3/2	1/12	4/30	3/12	6/27	5/12	8/24	7/11	10/21	9/10
1/6	11/16	3/3	1/13			6/28	5/13	8/25	7/12	10/22	9/11
1/7	11/17	3/4	1/14	5/1	3/13	6/29	5/14	8/26	7/13	10/23	9/12
1/8	11/18	3/5	1/15	5/2	3/14	6/30	5/15	8/27	7/14	10/24	9/13
1/9	11/19	3/6	1/16	5/3	3/15			8/28	7/15	10/25	9/14
1/10	11/20	3/7	1/17	5/4	3/16	7/1	5/16	8/29	7/16	10/26	9/15
1/11	11/21	3/8	1/18	5/5	3/17	7/2	5/17	8/30	7/17	10/27	9/16
1/12	11/22	3/9	1/19	5/6	3/18	7/3	5/18	8/31	7/18	10/28	9/17
1/13	11/23	3/10	1/20	5/7	3/19	7/4	5/19			10/29	9/18
1/14	11/24	3/11	1/21	5/8	3/20	7/5	5/20	9/1	7/19	10/30	9/19
1/15	11/25	3/12	1/22	5/9	3/21	7/6	5/21	9/2	7/20	10/31	9/20
1/16	11/26	3/13	1/23	5/10	3/22	7/7	5/22	9/3	7/21		
1/17	11/27	3/14	1/24	5/11	3/23	7/8	5/23	9/4	7/22	11/1	9/21
1/18	11/28	3/15	1/25	5/12	3/24	7/9	5/24	9/5	7/23	11/2	9/22
1/19	11/29	3/16	1/26	5/13	3/25	7/10	5/25	9/6	7/24	11/3	9/23
1/20	11/30	3/17	1/27	5/14	3/26	7/11	5/26	9/7	7/25	11/4	9/24
1/21	12/1	3/18	1/28	5/15	3/27	7/12	5/27	9/8	7/26	11/5	9/25
1/22	12/2	3/19	1/29	5/16	3/28	7/13	5/28	9/9	7/27	11/6	9/26
1/23	12/3	3/20	2/1	5/17	3/29	7/14	5/29	9/10	7/28	11/7	9/27

Solar	Lunar	Solar Date	Lunar Date	Solar	Lunar	Solar	Lunar	Solar	Lunar	Solar	Lunar
11/8	9/28			2/24	1/17	4/23	3/16	6/20	5/15	8/17	7/14
11/9	9/29		**1921**	2/25	1/18	4/24	3/17	6/21	5/16	8/18	7/15
11/10	9/30			2/26	1/19	4/25	3/18	6/22	5/17	8/19	7/16
11/11	10/1			2/27	1/20	4/26	3/19	6/23	5/18	8/20	7/17
11/12	10/2	1/1	11/23	2/28	1/21	4/27	3/20	6/24	5/19	8/21	7/18
11/13	10/3	1/2	11/24			4/28	3/21	6/25	5/20	8/22	7/19
11/14	10/4	1/3	11/25	3/1	1/22	4/29	3/22	6/26	5/21	8/23	7/20
11/15	10/5	1/4	11/26	3/2	1/23	4/30	3/23	6/27	5/22	8/24	7/21
11/16	10/6	1/5	11/27	3/3	1/24			6/28	5/23	8/25	7/22
11/17	10/7	1/6	11/28	3/4	1/25	5/1	3/24	6/29	5/24	8/26	7/23
11/18	10/8	1/7	11/29	3/5	1/26	5/2	3/25	6/30	5/25	8/27	7/24
11/19	10/9	1/8	11/30	3/6	1/27	5/3	3/26			8/28	7/25
11/20	10/10	1/9	12/1	3/7	1/28	5/4	3/27	7/1	5/26	8/29	7/26
11/21	10/11	1/10	12/2	3/8	1/29	5/5	3/28	7/2	5/27	8/30	7/27
11/22	10/12	1/11	12/3	3/9	1/30	5/6	3/29	7/3	5/28	8/31	7/28
11/23	10/13	1/12	12/4	3/10	2/1	5/7	3/30	7/4	5/29		
11/24	10/14	1/13	12/5	3/11	2/2	5/8	4/1	7/5	6/1	9/1	7/29
11/25	10/15	1/14	12/6	3/12	2/3	5/9	4/2	7/6	6/2	9/2	8/1
11/26	10/16	1/15	12/7	3/13	2/4	5/10	4/3	7/7	6/3	9/3	8/2
11/27	10/17	1/16	12/8	3/14	2/5	5/11	4/4	7/8	6/4	9/4	8/3
11/28	10/18	1/17	12/9	3/15	2/6	5/12	4/5	7/9	6/5	9/5	8/4
11/29	10/19	1/18	12/10	3/16	2/7	5/13	4/6	7/10	6/6	9/6	8/5
11/30	10/20	1/19	12/11	3/17	2/8	5/14	4/7	7/11	6/7	9/7	8/6
		1/20	12/12	3/18	2/9	5/15	4/8	7/12	6/8	9/8	8/7
12/1	10/21	1/21	12/13	3/19	2/10	5/16	4/9	7/13	6/9	9/9	8/8
12/2	10/22	1/22	12/14	3/20	2/11	5/17	4/10	7/14	6/10	9/10	8/9
12/3	10/23	1/23	12/15	3/21	2/12	5/18	4/11	7/15	6/11	9/11	8/10
12/4	10/24	1/24	12/16	3/22	2/13	5/19	4/12	7/16	6/12	9/12	8/11
12/5	10/25	1/25	12/17	3/23	2/14	5/20	4/13	7/17	6/13	9/13	8/12
12/6	10/26	1/26	12/18	3/24	2/15	5/21	4/14	7/18	6/14	9/14	8/13
12/7	10/27	1/27	12/19	3/25	2/16	5/22	4/15	7/19	6/15	9/15	8/14
12/8	10/28	1/28	12/20	3/26	2/17	5/23	4/16	7/20	6/16	9/16	8/15
12/9	10/29	1/29	12/21	3/27	2/18	5/24	4/17	7/21	6/17	9/17	8/16
12/10	11/1	1/30	12/22	3/28	2/19	5/25	4/18	7/22	6/18	9/18	8/17
12/11	11/2	1/31	12/23	3/29	2/20	5/26	4/19	7/23	6/19	9/19	8/18
12/12	11/3			3/30	2/21	5/27	4/20	7/24	6/20	9/20	8/19
12/13	11/4	2/1	12/24	3/31	2/22	5/28	4/21	7/25	6/21	9/21	8/20
12/14	11/5	2/2	12/25			5/29	4/22	7/26	6/22	9/22	8/21
12/15	11/6	2/3	12/26	4/1	2/23	5/30	4/23	7/27	6/23	9/23	8/22
12/16	11/7	2/4	12/27	4/2	2/24	5/31	4/24	7/28	6/24	9/24	8/23
12/17	11/8	2/5	12/28	4/3	2/25			7/29	6/25	9/25	8/24
12/18	11/9	2/6	12/29	4/4	2/26	6/1	4/25	7/30	6/26	9/26	8/25
12/19	11/10	2/7	12/30	4/5	2/27	6/2	4/26	7/31	6/27	9/27	8/26
12/20	11/11	2/8	1/1 (1921)	4/6	2/28	6/3	4/27			9/28	8/27
12/21	11/12			4/7	2/29	6/4	4/28	8/1	6/28	9/29	8/28
12/22	11/13	2/9	1/2	4/8	3/1	6/5	4/29	8/2	6/29	9/30	8/29
12/23	11/14	2/10	1/3	4/9	3/2	6/6	5/1	8/3	6/30		
12/24	11/15	2/11	1/4	4/10	3/3	6/7	5/2	8/4	7/1	10/1	9/1
12/25	11/16	2/12	1/5	4/11	3/4	6/8	5/3	8/5	7/2	10/2	9/2
12/26	11/17	2/13	1/6	4/12	3/5	6/9	5/4	8/6	7/3	10/3	9/3
12/27	11/18	2/14	1/7	4/13	3/6	6/10	5/5	8/7	7/4	10/4	9/4
12/28	11/19	2/15	1/8	4/14	3/7	6/11	5/6	8/8	7/5	10/5	9/5
12/29	11/20	2/16	1/9	4/15	3/8	6/12	5/7	8/9	7/6	10/6	9/6
12/30	11/21	2/17	1/10	4/16	3/9	6/13	5/8	8/10	7/7	10/7	9/7
12/31	11/22	2/18	1/11	4/17	3/10	6/14	5/9	8/11	7/8	10/8	9/8
		2/19	1/12	4/18	3/11	6/15	5/10	8/12	7/9	10/9	9/9
		2/20	1/13	4/19	3/12	6/16	5/11	8/13	7/10	10/10	9/10
		2/21	1/14	4/20	3/13	6/17	5/12	8/14	7/11	10/11	9/11
		2/22	1/15	4/21	3/14	6/18	5/13	8/15	7/12	10/12	9/12
		2/23	1/16	4/22	3/15	6/19	5/14	8/16	7/13	10/13	9/13

Solar	Lunar	Solar	Lunar	Solar	Lunar	Solar	Lunar	Solar	Lunar	Solar	Lunar
10/14	9/14	12/11	11/13	2/1	1/5	4/1	3/5	5/30	5/4	7/26	6/3
10/15	9/15	12/12	11/14	2/2	1/6	4/2	3/6	5/31	5/5	7/27	6/4
10/16	9/16	12/13	11/15	2/3	1/7	4/3	3/7			7/28	6/5
10/17	9/17	12/14	11/16	2/4	1/8	4/4	3/8	6/1	5/6	7/29	6/6
10/18	9/18	12/15	11/17	2/5	1/9	4/5	3/9	6/2	5/7	7/30	6/7
10/19	9/19	12/16	11/18	2/6	1/10	4/6	3/10	6/3	5/8	7/31	6/8
10/20	9/20	12/17	11/19	2/7	1/11	4/7	3/11	6/4	5/9		
10/21	9/21	12/18	11/20	2/8	1/12	4/8	3/12	6/5	5/10	8/1	6/9
10/22	9/22	12/19	11/21	2/9	1/13	4/9	3/13	6/6	5/11	8/2	6/10
10/23	9/23	12/20	11/22	2/10	1/14	4/10	3/14	6/7	5/12	8/3	6/11
10/24	9/24	12/21	11/23	2/11	1/15	4/11	3/15	6/8	5/13	8/4	6/12
10/25	9/25	12/22	11/24	2/12	1/16	4/12	3/16	6/9	5/14	8/5	6/13
10/26	9/26	12/23	11/25	2/13	1/17	4/13	3/17	6/10	5/15	8/6	6/14
10/27	9/27	12/24	11/26	2/14	1/18	4/14	3/18	6/11	5/16	8/7	6/15
10/28	9/28	12/25	11/27	2/15	1/19	4/15	3/19	6/12	5/17	8/8	6/16
10/29	9/29	12/26	11/28	2/16	1/20	4/16	3/20	6/13	5/18	8/9	6/17
10/30	9/30	12/27	11/29	2/17	1/21	4/17	3/21	6/14	5/19	8/10	6/18
10/31	10/1	12/28	11/30	2/18	1/22	4/18	3/22	6/15	5/20	8/11	6/19
		12/29	12/1	2/19	1/23	4/19	3/23	6/16	5/21	8/12	6/20
11/1	10/2	12/30	12/2	2/20	1/24	4/20	3/24	6/17	5/22	8/13	6/21
11/2	10/3	12/31	12/3	2/21	1/25	4/21	3/25	6/18	5/23	8/14	6/22
11/3	10/4			2/22	1/26	4/22	3/26	6/19	5/24	8/15	6/23
11/4	10/5			2/23	1/27	4/23	3/27	6/20	5/25	8/16	6/24
11/5	10/6	Solar	Lunar	2/24	1/28	4/24	3/28	6/21	5/26	8/17	6/25
11/6	10/7	Date	Date	2/25	1/29	4/25	3/29	6/22	5/27	8/18	6/26
11/7	10/8			2/26	1/30	4/26	3/30	6/23	5/28	8/19	6/27
11/8	10/9	1922		2/27	2/1	4/27	4/1	6/24	5/29	8/20	6/28
11/9	10/10	1/1	12/4	2/28	2/2	4/28	4/2	6/25	5/1	8/21	6/29
11/10	10/11	1/2	12/5			4/29	4/3	*(Leap Month)*		8/22	6/30
11/11	10/12	1/3	12/6	3/1	2/3	4/30	4/4	6/26	5/2	8/23	7/1
11/12	10/13	1/4	12/7	3/2	2/4			6/27	5/3	8/24	7/2
11/13	10/14	1/5	12/8	3/3	2/5	5/1	4/5	6/28	5/4	8/25	7/3
11/14	10/15	1/6	12/9	3/4	2/6	5/2	4/6	6/29	5/5	8/26	7/4
11/15	10/16	1/7	12/10	3/5	2/7	5/3	4/7	6/30	5/6	8/27	7/5
11/16	10/17	1/8	12/11	3/6	2/8	5/4	4/8			8/28	7/6
11/17	10/18	1/9	12/12	3/7	2/9	5/5	4/9	7/1	5/7	8/29	7/7
11/18	10/19	1/10	12/13	3/8	2/10	5/6	4/10	7/2	5/8	8/30	7/8
11/19	10/20	1/11	12/14	3/9	2/11	5/7	4/11	7/3	5/9	8/31	7/9
11/20	10/21	1/12	12/15	3/10	2/12	5/8	4/12	7/4	5/10		
11/21	10/22	1/13	12/16	3/11	2/13	5/9	4/13	7/5	5/11	9/1	7/10
11/22	10/23	1/14	12/17	3/12	2/14	5/10	4/14	7/6	5/12	9/2	7/11
11/23	10/24	1/15	12/18	3/13	2/15	5/11	4/15	7/7	5/13	9/3	7/12
11/24	10/25	1/16	12/19	3/14	2/16	5/12	4/16	7/8	5/14	9/4	7/13
11/25	10/26	1/17	12/20	3/15	2/17	5/13	4/17	7/9	5/15	9/5	7/14
11/26	10/27	1/18	12/21	3/16	2/18	5/14	4/18	7/10	5/16	9/6	7/15
11/27	10/28	1/19	12/22	3/17	2/19	5/15	4/19	7/11	5/17	9/7	7/16
11/28	10/29	1/20	12/23	3/18	2/20	5/16	4/20	7/12	5/18	9/8	7/17
11/29	11/1	1/21	12/24	3/19	2/21	5/17	4/21	7/13	5/19	9/9	7/18
11/30	11/2	1/22	12/25	3/20	2/22	5/18	4/22	7/14	5/20	9/10	7/19
		1/23	12/26	3/21	2/23	5/19	4/23	7/15	5/21	9/11	7/20
12/1	11/3	1/24	12/27	3/22	2/24	5/20	4/24	7/16	5/22	9/12	7/21
12/2	11/4	1/25	12/28	3/23	2/25	5/21	4/25	7/17	5/23	9/13	7/22
12/3	11/5	1/26	12/29	3/24	2/26	5/22	4/26	7/18	5/24	9/14	7/23
12/4	11/6	1/27	12/30	3/25	2/27	5/23	4/27	7/19	5/25	9/15	7/24
12/5	11/7	1/28	1/1	3/26	2/28	5/24	4/28	7/20	5/26	9/16	7/25
12/6	11/8		(1922)	3/27	2/29	5/25	4/29	7/21	5/27	9/17	7/26
12/7	11/9	1/29	1/2	3/28	3/1	5/26	4/30	7/22	5/28	9/18	7/27
12/8	11/10	1/30	1/3	3/29	3/2	5/27	5/1	7/23	5/29	9/19	7/28
12/9	11/11	1/31	1/4	3/30	3/3	5/28	5/2	7/24	6/1	9/20	7/29
12/10	11/12			3/31	3/4	5/29	5/3	7/25	6/2	9/21	8/1

Solar	Lunar	Solar	Lunar	Solar	Lunar	Solar	Lunar	Solar	Lunar	Solar	Lunar
9/22	8/2	11/19	10/1	1/10	11/24	3/8	1/21	5/5	3/20	7/2	5/19
9/23	8/3	11/20	10/2	1/11	11/25	3/9	1/22	5/6	3/21	7/3	5/20
9/24	8/4	11/21	10/3	1/12	11/26	3/10	1/23	5/7	3/22	7/4	5/21
9/25	8/5	11/22	10/4	1/13	11/27	3/11	1/24	5/8	3/23	7/5	5/22
9/26	8/6	11/23	10/5	1/14	11/28	3/12	1/25	5/9	3/24	7/6	5/23
9/27	8/7	11/24	10/6	1/15	11/29	3/13	1/26	5/10	3/25	7/7	5/24
9/28	8/8	11/25	10/7	1/16	11/30	3/14	1/27	5/11	3/26	7/8	5/25
9/29	8/9	11/26	10/8	1/17	12/1	3/15	1/28	5/12	3/27	7/9	5/26
9/30	8/10	11/27	10/9	1/18	12/2	3/16	1/29	5/13	3/28	7/10	5/27
		11/28	10/10	1/19	12/3	3/17	2/1	5/14	3/29	7/11	5/28
10/1	8/11	11/29	10/11	1/20	12/4	3/18	2/2	5/15	3/30	7/12	5/29
10/2	8/12	11/30	10/12	1/21	12/5	3/19	2/3	5/16	4/1	7/13	5/30
10/3	8/13	11/31	10/13	1/22	12/6	3/20	2/4	5/17	4/2	7/14	6/1
10/4	8/14			1/23	12/7	3/21	2/5	5/18	4/3	7/15	6/2
10/5	8/15	12/1	10/14	1/24	12/8	3/22	2/6	5/19	4/4	7/16	6/3
10/6	8/16	12/2	10/15	1/25	12/9	3/23	2/7	5/20	4/5	7/17	6/4
10/7	8/17	12/3	10/16	1/26	12/10	3/24	2/8	5/21	4/6	7/18	6/5
10/8	8/18	12/4	10/17	1/27	12/11	3/25	2/9	5/22	4/7	7/19	6/6
10/9	8/19	12/5	10/18	1/28	12/12	3/26	2/10	5/23	4/8	7/20	6/7
10/10	8/20	12/6	10/19	1/29	12/13	3/27	2/11	5/24	4/9	7/21	6/8
10/11	8/21	12/7	10/20	1/30	12/14	3/28	2/12	5/25	4/10	7/22	6/9
10/12	8/22	12/8	10/21	1/31	12/15	3/29	2/13	5/26	4/11	7/23	6/10
10/13	8/23	12/9	10/22			3/30	2/14	5/27	4/12	7/24	6/11
10/14	8/24	12/10	10/23	2/1	12/16	3/31	2/15	5/28	4/13	7/25	6/12
10/15	8/25	12/11	10/24	2/2	12/17			5/29	4/14	7/26	6/13
10/16	8/26	12/12	10/25	2/3	12/18	4/1	2/16	5/30	4/15	7/27	6/14
10/17	8/27	12/13	10/26	2/4	12/19	4/2	2/17	5/31	4/16	7/28	6/15
10/18	8/28	12/14	10/27	2/5	12/20	4/3	2/18			7/29	6/16
10/19	8/29	12/15	10/28	2/6	12/21	4/4	2/19	6/1	4/17	7/30	6/17
10/20	9/1	12/16	10/29	2/7	12/22	4/5	2/20	6/2	4/18	7/31	6/18
10/21	9/2	12/17	10/30	2/8	12/23	4/6	2/21	6/3	4/19		
10/22	9/3	12/18	11/1	2/9	12/24	4/7	2/22	6/4	4/20	8/1	6/19
10/23	9/4	12/19	11/2	2/10	12/25	4/8	2/23	6/5	4/21	8/2	6/20
10/24	9/5	12/20	11/3	2/11	12/26	4/9	2/24	6/6	4/22	8/3	6/21
10/25	9/6	12/21	11/4	2/12	12/27	4/10	2/25	6/7	4/23	8/4	6/22
10/26	9/7	12/22	11/5	2/13	12/28	4/11	2/26	6/8	4/24	8/5	6/23
10/27	9/8	12/23	11/6	2/14	12/29	4/12	2/27	6/9	4/25	8/6	6/24
10/28	9/9	12/24	11/7	2/15	12/30	4/13	2/28	6/10	4/26	8/7	6/25
10/29	9/10	12/25	11/8	2/16	1/1	4/14	2/29	6/11	4/27	8/8	6/26
10/30	9/11	12/26	11/9		(1923)	4/15	2/30	6/12	4/28	8/9	6/27
10/31	9/12	12/27	11/10	2/17	1/2	4/16	3/1	6/13	4/29	8/10	6/28
		12/28	11/11	2/18	1/3	4/17	3/2	6/14	5/1	8/11	6/29
11/1	9/13	12/29	11/12	2/19	1/4	4/18	3/3	6/15	5/2	8/12	7/1
11/2	9/14	12/30	11/13	2/20	1/5	4/19	3/4	6/16	5/3	8/13	7/2
11/3	9/15	12/31	11/14	2/21	1/6	4/20	3/5	6/17	5/4	8/14	7/3
11/4	9/16			2/22	1/7	4/21	3/6	6/18	5/5	8/15	7/4
11/5	9/17			2/23	1/8	4/22	3/7	6/19	5/6	8/16	7/5
11/6	9/18	Solar	Lunar	2/24	1/9	4/23	3/8	6/20	5/7	8/17	7/6
11/7	9/19	Date	Date	2/25	1/10	4/24	3/9	6/21	5/8	8/18	7/7
11/8	9/20			2/26	1/11	4/25	3/10	6/22	5/9	8/19	7/8
11/9	9/21	1923		2/27	1/12	4/26	3/11	6/23	5/10	8/20	7/9
11/10	9/22	1/1	11/15	2/28	1/13	4/27	3/12	6/24	5/11	8/21	7/10
11/11	9/23	1/2	11/16			4/28	3/13	6/25	5/12	8/22	7/11
11/12	9/24	1/3	11/17	3/1	1/14	4/29	3/14	6/26	5/13	8/23	7/12
11/13	9/25	1/4	11/18	3/2	1/15	4/30	3/15	6/27	5/14	8/24	7/13
11/14	9/26	1/5	11/19	3/3	1/16			6/28	5/15	8/25	7/14
11/15	9/27	1/6	11/20	3/4	1/17	5/1	3/16	6/29	5/16	8/26	7/15
11/16	9/28	1/7	11/21	3/5	1/18	5/2	3/17	6/30	5/17	8/27	7/16
11/17	9/29	1/8	11/22	3/6	1/19	5/3	3/18			8/28	7/17
11/18	9/30	1/9	11/23	3/7	1/20	5/4	3/19	7/1	5/18	8/29	7/18

Solar	Lunar	Solar	Lunar	Solar	Lunar	Solar	Lunar	Solar	Lunar	Solar	Lunar
8/30	7/19	10/27	9/18	12/24	11/17	2/14	1/10	4/12	3/9	6/9	5/8
8/31	7/20	10/28	9/19	12/25	11/18	2/15	1/11	4/13	3/10	6/10	5/9
		10/29	9/20	12/26	11/19	2/16	1/12	4/14	3/11	6/11	5/10
9/1	7/21	10/30	9/21	12/27	11/20	2/17	1/13	4/15	3/12	6/12	5/11
9/2	7/22	10/31	9/22	12/28	11/21	2/18	1/14	4/16	3/13	6/13	5/12
9/3	7/23			12/29	11/22	2/19	1/15	4/17	3/14	6/14	5/13
9/4	7/24	11/1	9/23	12/30	11/23	2/20	1/16	4/18	3/15	6/15	5/14
9/5	7/25	11/2	9/24	12/31	11/24	2/21	1/17	4/19	3/16	6/16	5/15
9/6	7/26	11/3	9/25			2/22	1/18	4/20	3/17	6/17	5/16
9/7	7/27	11/4	9/26			2/23	1/19	4/21	3/18	6/18	5/17
9/8	7/28	11/5	9/27	**Solar**	**Lunar**	2/24	1/20	4/22	3/19	6/19	5/18
9/9	7/29	11/6	9/28	**Date**	**Date**	2/25	1/21	4/23	3/20	6/20	5/19
9/10	7/30	11/7	9/29	**1924**		2/26	1/22	4/24	3/21	6/21	5/20
9/11	8/1	11/8	10/1	1/1	11/25	2/27	1/23	4/25	3/22	6/22	5/21
9/12	8/2	11/9	10/2	1/2	11/26	2/28	1/24	4/26	3/23	6/23	5/22
9/13	8/3	11/10	10/3	1/3	11/27	2/29	1/25	4/27	3/24	6/24	5/23
9/14	8/4	11/11	10/4	1/4	11/28			4/28	3/25	6/25	5/24
9/15	8/5	11/12	10/5	1/5	11/29	3/1	1/26	4/29	3/26	6/26	5/25
9/16	8/6	11/13	10/6	1/6	12/1	3/2	1/27	4/30	3/27	6/27	5/26
9/17	8/7	11/14	10/7	1/7	12/2	3/3	1/28			6/28	5/27
9/18	8/8	11/15	10/8	1/8	12/3	3/4	1/29	5/1	3/28	6/29	5/28
9/19	8/9	11/16	10/9	1/9	12/4	3/5	1/30	5/2	3/29	6/30	5/29
9/20	8/10	11/17	10/10	1/10	12/5	3/6	2/1	5/3	3/30		
9/21	8/11	11/18	10/11	1/11	12/6	3/7	2/2	5/4	4/1	7/1	5/30
9/22	8/12	11/19	10/12	1/12	12/7	3/8	2/3	5/5	4/2	7/2	6/1
9/23	8/13	11/20	10/13	1/13	12/8	3/9	2/4	5/6	4/3	7/3	6/2
9/24	8/14	11/21	10/14	1/14	12/9	3/10	2/5	5/7	4/4	7/4	6/3
9/25	8/15	11/22	10/15	1/15	12/10	3/11	2/6	5/8	4/5	7/5	6/4
9/26	8/16	11/23	10/16	1/16	12/11	3/12	2/7	5/9	4/6	7/6	6/5
9/27	8/17	11/24	10/17	1/17	12/12	3/13	2/8	5/10	4/7	7/7	6/6
9/28	8/18	11/25	10/18	1/18	12/13	3/14	2/9	5/11	4/8	7/8	6/7
9/29	8/19	11/26	10/19	1/19	12/14	3/15	2/10	5/12	4/9	7/9	6/8
9/30	8/20	11/27	10/20	1/20	12/15	3/16	2/11	5/13	4/10	7/10	6/9
		11/28	10/21	1/21	12/16	3/17	2/12	5/14	4/11	7/11	6/10
10/1	8/21	11/29	10/22	1/22	12/17	3/18	2/13	5/15	4/12	7/12	6/11
10/2	8/22	11/30	10/23	1/23	12/18	3/19	2/14	5/16	4/13	7/13	6/12
10/3	8/23			1/24	12/19	3/20	2/15	5/17	4/14	7/14	6/13
10/4	8/24	12/1	10/24	1/25	12/20	3/21	2/16	5/18	4/15	7/15	6/14
10/5	8/25	12/2	10/25	1/26	12/21	3/22	2/17	5/19	4/16	7/16	6/15
10/6	8/26	12/3	10/26	1/27	12/22	3/23	2/18	5/20	4/17	7/17	6/16
10/7	8/27	12/4	10/27	1/28	12/23	3/24	2/19	5/21	4/18	7/18	6/17
10/8	8/28	12/5	10/28	1/29	12/24	3/25	2/20	5/22	4/19	7/19	6/18
10/9	8/29	12/6	10/29	1/30	12/25	3/26	2/21	5/23	4/20	7/20	6/19
10/10	9/1	12/7	10/30	1/31	12/26	3/27	2/22	5/24	4/21	7/21	6/20
10/11	9/2	12/8	11/1			3/28	2/23	5/25	4/22	7/22	6/21
10/12	9/3	12/9	11/2			3/29	2/24	5/26	4/23	7/23	6/22
10/13	9/4	12/10	11/3	2/1	12/27	3/30	2/25	5/27	4/24	7/24	6/23
10/14	9/5	12/11	11/4	2/2	12/28	3/31	2/26	5/28	4/25	7/25	6/24
10/15	9/6	12/12	11/5	2/3	12/29			5/29	4/26	7/26	6/25
10/16	9/7	12/13	11/6	2/4	12/30	4/1	2/27	5/30	4/27	7/27	6/26
10/17	9/8	12/14	11/7	2/5	1/1	4/2	2/28	5/31	4/28	7/28	6/27
10/18	9/9	12/15	11/8		(1924)	4/3	2/29			7/29	6/28
10/19	9/10	12/16	11/9	2/6	1/2	4/4	3/1	6/1	4/29	7/30	6/30
10/20	9/11	12/17	11/10	2/7	1/3	4/5	3/2	6/2	5/1	7/31	6/30
10/21	9/12	12/18	11/11	2/8	1/4	4/6	3/3	6/3	5/2		
10/22	9/13	12/19	11/12	2/9	1/5	4/7	3/4	6/4	5/3	8/1	7/1
10/23	9/14	12/20	11/13	2/10	1/6	4/8	3/5	6/5	5/4	8/2	7/2
10/24	9/15	12/21	11/14	2/11	1/7	4/9	3/6	6/6	5/5	8/3	7/3
10/25	9/16	12/22	11/15	2/12	1/8	4/10	3/7	6/7	5/6	8/4	7/4
10/26	9/17	12/23	11/16	2/13	1/9	4/11	3/8	6/8	5/7	8/5	7/5

8/6	7/6
8/7	7/7
8/8	7/8
8/9	7/9
8/10	7/10
8/11	7/11
8/12	7/12
8/13	7/13
8/14	7/14
8/15	7/15
8/16	7/16
8/17	7/17
8/18	7/18
8/19	7/19
8/20	7/20
8/21	7/21
8/22	7/22
8/23	7/23
8/24	7/24
8/25	7/25
8/26	7/26
8/27	7/27
8/28	7/28
8/29	7/29
8/30	8/1
8/31	8/2
9/1	8/3
9/2	8/4
9/3	8/5
9/4	8/6
9/5	8/7
9/6	8/8
9/7	8/9
9/8	8/10
9/9	8/11
9/10	8/12
9/11	8/13
9/12	8/14
9/13	8/15
9/14	8/16
9/15	8/17
9/16	8/18
9/17	8/19
9/18	8/20
9/19	8/21
9/20	8/22
9/21	8/23
9/22	8/24
9/23	8/25
9/24	8/26
9/25	8/27
9/26	8/28
9/27	8/29
9/28	8/30
9/29	9/1
9/30	9/2
10/1	9/3
10/2	9/4
10/3	9/5
10/4	9/6
10/5	9/7
10/6	9/8
10/7	9/9
10/8	9/10
10/9	9/11
10/10	9/12
10/11	9/13
10/12	9/14
10/13	9/15
10/14	9/16
10/15	9/17
10/16	9/18
10/17	9/19
10/18	9/20
10/19	9/21
10/20	9/22
10/21	9/23
10/22	9/24
10/23	9/25
10/24	9/26
10/25	9/27
10/26	9/28
10/27	9/29
10/28	10/1
10/29	10/2
10/30	10/3
10/31	10/4
11/1	10/5
11/2	10/6
11/3	10/7
11/4	10/8
11/5	10/9
11/6	10/10
11/7	10/11
11/8	10/12
11/9	10/13
11/10	10/14
11/11	10/15
11/12	10/16
11/13	10/17
11/14	10/18
11/15	10/19
11/16	10/20
11/17	10/21
11/18	10/22
11/19	10/23
11/20	10/24
11/21	10/25
11/22	10/26
11/23	10/27
11/24	10/28
11/25	10/29
11/26	10/30
11/27	11/1
11/28	11/2
11/29	11/3
11/30	11/4
12/1	11/5
12/2	11/6
12/3	11/7
12/4	11/8
12/5	11/9
12/6	11/10
12/7	11/11
12/8	11/12
12/9	11/13
12/10	11/14
12/11	11/15
12/12	11/16
12/13	11/17
12/14	11/18
12/15	11/19
12/16	11/20
12/17	11/21
12/18	11/22
12/19	11/23
12/20	11/24
12/21	11/25
12/22	11/26
12/23	11/27
12/24	11/28
12/25	11/29
12/26	12/1
12/27	12/2
12/28	12/3
12/29	12/4
12/30	12/5
12/31	12/6
Solar Date	**Lunar Date**
1925	
1/1	12/7
1/2	12/8
1/3	12/9
1/4	12/10
1/5	12/11
1/6	12/12
1/7	12/13
1/8	12/14
1/9	12/15
1/10	12/16
1/11	12/17
1/12	12/18
1/13	12/19
1/14	12/20
1/15	12/21
1/16	12/22
1/17	12/23
1/18	12/24
1/19	12/25
1/20	12/26
1/21	12/27
1/22	12/28
1/23	12/29
1/24	12/30
1/25	1/1 (1925)
1/26	1/2
1/27	1/3
1/28	1/4
1/29	1/5
1/30	1/6
1/31	1/7
2/1	1/8
2/2	1/9
2/3	1/10
2/4	1/11
2/5	1/12
2/6	1/13
2/7	1/14
2/8	1/15
2/9	1/16
2/10	1/17
2/11	1/18
2/12	1/19
2/13	1/20
2/14	1/21
2/15	1/22
2/16	1/23
2/17	1/24
2/18	1/25
2/19	1/26
2/20	1/27
2/21	1/28
2/22	1/29
2/23	2/1
2/24	2/2
2/25	2/3
2/26	2/4
2/27	2/5
2/28	2/6
3/1	2/7
3/2	2/8
3/3	2/9
3/4	2/10
3/5	2/11
3/6	2/12
3/7	2/13
3/8	2/14
3/9	2/15
3/10	2/16
3/11	2/17
3/12	2/18
3/13	2/19
3/14	2/20
3/15	2/21
3/16	2/22
3/17	2/23
3/18	2/24
3/19	2/25
3/20	2/26
3/21	2/27
3/22	2/28
3/23	2/29
3/24	3/1
3/25	3/2
3/26	3/3
3/27	3/4
3/28	3/5
3/29	3/6
3/30	3/7
3/31	3/8
4/1	3/9
4/2	3/10
4/3	3/11
4/4	3/12
4/5	3/13
4/6	3/14
4/7	3/15
4/8	3/16
4/9	3/17
4/10	3/18
4/11	3/19
4/12	3/20
4/13	3/21
4/14	3/22
4/15	3/23
4/16	3/24
4/17	3/25
4/18	3/26
4/19	3/27
4/20	3/28
4/21	3/29
4/22	3/30
4/23	4/1
4/24	4/2
4/25	4/3
4/26	4/4
4/27	4/5
4/28	4/6
4/29	4/7
4/30	4/8
5/1	4/9
5/2	4/10
5/3	4/11
5/4	4/12
5/5	4/13
5/6	4/14
5/7	4/15
5/8	4/16
5/9	4/17
5/10	4/18
5/11	4/19
5/12	4/20
5/13	4/21
5/14	4/22
5/15	4/23
5/16	4/24
5/17	4/25
5/18	4/26
5/19	4/27
5/20	4/28
5/21	4/29
5/22	4/1
(Leap Month)	
5/23	4/2
5/24	4/3
5/25	4/4
5/26	4/5
5/27	4/6
5/28	4/7
5/29	4/8
5/30	4/9
5/31	4/10
6/1	4/11
6/2	4/12
6/3	4/13
6/4	4/14
6/5	4/15
6/6	4/16
6/7	4/17
6/8	4/18
6/9	4/19
6/10	4/20
6/11	4/21
6/12	4/22
6/13	4/23
6/14	4/24
6/15	4/25
6/16	4/26
6/17	4/27
6/18	4/28
6/19	4/29
6/20	4/30
6/21	5/1
6/22	5/2
6/23	5/3
6/24	5/4
6/25	5/5
6/26	5/6
6/27	5/7
6/28	5/8
6/29	5/9
6/30	5/10
7/1	5/11
7/2	5/12
7/3	5/13
7/4	5/14
7/5	5/15
7/6	5/16
7/7	5/17
7/8	5/18
7/9	5/19
7/10	5/20
7/11	5/21
7/12	5/22
7/13	5/23
7/14	5/24

Solar	Lunar	Solar	Lunar	Solar	Lunar	Solar Date	Lunar Date	Solar	Lunar	Solar	Lunar
7/15	5/25	9/11	7/24	11/7	9/22			2/24	1/12	4/23	3/12
7/16	5/26	9/12	7/25	11/8	9/23			2/25	1/13	4/24	3/13
7/17	5/27	9/13	7/26	11/9	9/24	**1926**		2/26	1/14	4/25	3/14
7/18	5/28	9/14	7/27	11/10	9/25			2/27	1/15	4/26	3/15
7/19	5/29	9/15	7/28	11/11	9/26	1/1	11/17	2/28	1/16	4/27	3/16
7/20	5/30	9/16	7/29	11/12	9/27	1/2	11/18			4/28	3/17
7/21	6/1	9/17	7/30	11/13	9/28	1/3	11/19	3/1	1/17	4/29	3/18
7/22	6/2	9/18	8/1	11/14	9/29	1/4	11/20	3/2	1/18	4/30	3/19
7/23	6/3	9/19	8/2	11/15	9/30	1/5	11/21	3/3	1/19		
7/24	6/4	9/20	8/3	11/16	10/1	1/6	11/22	3/4	1/20	5/1	3/20
7/25	6/5	9/21	8/4	11/17	10/2	1/7	11/23	3/5	1/21	5/2	3/21
7/26	6/6	9/22	8/5	11/18	10/3	1/8	11/24	3/6	1/22	5/3	3/22
7/27	6/7	9/23	8/6	11/19	10/4	1/9	11/25	3/7	1/23	5/4	3/23
7/28	6/8	9/24	8/7	11/20	10/5	1/10	11/26	3/8	1/24	5/5	3/24
7/29	6/9	9/25	8/8	11/21	10/6	1/11	11/27	3/9	1/25	5/6	3/25
7/30	6/10	9/26	8/9	11/22	10/7	1/12	11/28	3/10	1/26	5/7	3/26
7/31	6/11	9/27	8/10	11/23	10/8	1/13	11/29	3/11	1/27	5/8	3/27
		9/28	8/11	11/24	10/9	1/14	12/1	3/12	1/28	5/9	3/28
8/1	6/12	9/29	8/12	11/25	10/10	1/15	12/2	3/13	1/29	5/10	3/29
8/2	6/13	9/30	8/13	11/26	10/11	1/16	12/3	3/14	2/1	5/11	3/30
8/3	6/14			11/27	10/12	1/17	12/4	3/15	2/2	5/12	4/1
8/4	6/15	10/1	8/14	11/28	10/13	1/18	12/5	3/16	2/3	5/13	4/2
8/5	6/16	10/2	8/15	11/29	10/14	1/19	12/6	3/17	2/4	5/14	4/3
8/6	6/17	10/3	8/16	11/30	10/15	1/20	12/7	3/18	2/5	5/15	4/4
8/7	6/18	10/4	8/17			1/21	12/8	3/19	2/6	5/16	4/5
8/8	6/19	10/5	8/18	12/1	10/16	1/22	12/9	3/20	2/7	5/17	4/6
8/9	6/20	10/6	8/19	12/2	10/17	1/23	12/10	3/21	2/8	5/18	4/7
8/10	6/21	10/7	8/20	12/3	10/18	1/24	12/11	3/22	2/9	5/19	4/8
8/11	6/22	10/8	8/21	12/4	10/19	1/25	12/12	3/23	2/10	5/20	4/9
8/12	6/23	10/9	8/22	12/5	10/20	1/26	12/13	3/24	2/11	5/21	4/10
8/13	6/24	10/10	8/23	12/6	10/21	1/27	12/14	3/25	2/12	5/22	4/11
8/14	6/25	10/11	8/24	12/7	10/22	1/28	12/15	3/26	2/13	5/23	4/12
8/15	6/26	10/12	8/25	12/8	10/23	1/29	12/16	3/27	2/14	5/24	4/13
8/16	6/27	10/13	8/26	12/9	10/24	1/30	12/17	3/28	2/15	5/25	4/14
8/17	6/28	10/14	8/27	12/10	10/25	1/31	12/18	3/29	2/16	5/26	4/15
8/18	6/29	10/15	8/28	12/11	10/26			3/30	2/17	5/27	4/16
8/19	7/1	10/16	8/29	12/12	10/27	2/1	12/19	3/31	2/18	5/28	4/17
8/20	7/2	10/17	8/30	12/13	10/28	2/2	12/20			5/29	4/18
8/21	7/3	10/18	9/1	12/14	10/29	2/3	12/21	4/1	2/19	5/30	4/19
8/22	7/4	10/19	9/2	12/15	10/30	2/4	12/22	4/2	2/20	5/31	4/20
8/23	7/5	10/20	9/3	12/16	11/1	2/5	12/23	4/3	2/21		
8/24	7/6	10/21	9/4	12/17	11/2	2/6	12/24	4/4	2/22	6/1	4/21
8/25	7/7	10/22	9/5	12/18	11/3	2/7	12/25	4/5	2/23	6/2	4/22
8/26	7/8	10/23	9/6	12/19	11/4	2/8	12/26	4/6	2/24	6/3	4/23
8/27	7/9	10/24	9/7	12/20	11/5	2/9	12/27	4/7	2/25	6/4	4/24
8/28	7/10	10/25	9/8	12/21	11/6	2/10	12/28	4/8	2/26	6/5	4/25
8/29	7/11	10/25	9/9	12/22	11/7	2/11	12/29	4/9	2/27	6/6	4/26
8/30	7/12	10/26	9/10	12/23	11/8	2/12	12/30	4/10	2/28	6/7	4/27
8/31	7/13	10/27	9/11	12/24	11/9	2/13	1/1 (1926)	4/11	2/29	6/8	4/28
		10/28	9/12	12/25	11/10			4/12	3/1	6/9	4/29
9/1	7/14	10/29	9/13	12/26	11/11	2/14	1/2	4/13	3/2	6/10	5/1
9/2	7/15	10/30	9/14	12/27	11/12	2/15	1/3	4/14	3/3	6/11	5/2
9/3	7/16	10/31	9/15	12/28	11/13	2/16	1/4	4/15	3/4	6/12	5/3
9/4	7/17			12/29	11/14	2/17	1/5	4/16	3/5	6/13	5/4
9/5	7/18	11/1	9/16	12/30	11/15	2/18	1/6	4/17	3/6	6/14	5/5
9/6	7/19	11/2	9/17	12/31	11/16	2/19	1/7	4/18	3/7	6/15	5/6
9/7	7/20	11/3	9/18			2/20	1/8	4/19	3/8	6/16	5/7
9/8	7/21	11/4	9/19			2/21	1/9	4/20	3/9	6/17	5/8
9/9	7/22	11/5	9/20			2/22	1/10	4/21	3/10	6/18	5/9
9/10	7/23	11/6	9/21			2/23	1/11	4/22	3/11	6/19	5/10

Solar	Lunar	Solar	Lunar	Solar	Lunar	Solar	Lunar	Solar	Lunar	Solar	Lunar
6/20	5/11	8/17	7/10	10/14	9/8	12/11	11/7	2/2	1/1	4/1	2/29
6/21	5/12	8/18	7/11	10/15	9/9	12/12	11/8		(1927)	4/2	3/1
6/22	5/13	8/19	7/12	10/16	9/10	12/13	11/9	2/3	1/2	4/3	3/2
6/23	5/14	8/20	7/13	10/17	9/11	12/14	11/10	2/4	1/3	4/4	3/3
6/24	5/15	8/21	7/14	10/18	9/12	12/15	11/11	2/5	1/4	4/5	3/4
6/25	5/16	8/22	7/15	10/19	9/13	12/16	11/12	2/6	1/5	4/6	3/5
6/26	5/17	8/23	7/16	10/20	9/14	12/17	11/13	2/7	1/6	4/7	3/6
6/27	5/18	8/24	7/17	10/21	9/15	12/18	11/14	2/8	1/7	4/8	3/7
6/28	5/19	8/25	7/18	10/22	9/16	12/19	11/15	2/9	1/8	4/9	3/8
6/29	5/20	8/26	7/19	10/23	9/17	12/20	11/16	2/10	1/9	4/10	3/9
6/30	5/21	8/27	7/20	10/24	9/18	12/21	11/17	2/11	1/10	4/11	3/10
		8/28	7/21	10/25	9/19	12/22	11/18	2/12	1/11	4/12	3/11
7/1	5/22	8/29	7/22	10/26	9/20	12/23	11/19	2/13	1/12	4/13	3/12
7/2	5/23	8/30	7/23	10/27	9/21	12/24	11/20	2/14	1/13	4/14	3/13
7/3	5/24	8/31	7/24	10/28	9/22	12/25	11/21	2/15	1/14	4/15	3/14
7/4	5/25			10/29	9/23	12/26	11/22	2/16	1/15	4/16	3/15
7/5	5/26	9/1	7/25	10/30	9/24	12/27	11/23	2/17	1/16	4/17	3/16
7/6	5/27	9/2	7/26	10/31	9/25	12/28	11/24	2/18	1/17	4/18	3/17
7/7	5/28	9/3	7/27			12/29	11/25	2/19	1/18	4/19	3/18
7/8	5/29	9/4	7/28	11/1	9/26	12/30	11/26	2/20	1/19	4/20	3/19
7/9	5/30	9/5	7/29	11/2	9/27	12/31	11/27	2/21	1/20	4/21	3/20
7/10	6/1	9/6	7/30	11/3	9/28			2/22	1/21	4/22	3/21
7/11	6/2	9/7	8/1	11/4	9/29			2/23	1/22	4/23	3/22
7/12	6/3	9/8	8/2	11/5	10/1			2/24	1/23	4/24	3/23
7/13	6/4	9/9	8/3	11/6	10/2	Solar	Lunar	2/25	1/24	4/25	3/24
7/14	6/5	9/10	8/4	11/7	10/3	Date	Date	2/26	1/25	4/26	3/25
7/15	6/6	9/11	8/5	11/8	10/4			2/27	1/26	4/27	3/26
7/16	6/7	9/12	8/6	11/9	10/5	1927		2/28	1/27	4/28	3/27
7/17	6/8	9/13	8/7	11/10	10/6	1/1	11/28			4/29	3/28
7/18	6/9	9/14	8/8	11/11	10/7	1/2	11/29	3/1	1/28	4/30	3/29
7/19	6/10	9/15	8/9	11/12	10/8	1/3	11/30	3/2	1/29		
7/20	6/11	9/16	8/10	11/13	10/9	1/4	12/1	3/3	1/30	5/1	4/1
7/21	6/12	9/17	8/11	11/14	10/10	1/5	12/2	3/4	2/1	5/2	4/2
7/22	6/13	9/18	8/12	11/15	10/11	1/6	12/3	3/5	2/2	5/3	4/3
7/23	6/14	9/19	8/13	11/16	10/12	1/7	12/4	3/6	2/3	5/4	4/4
7/24	6/15	9/20	8/14	11/17	10/13	1/8	12/5	3/7	2/4	5/5	4/5
7/25	6/16	9/21	8/15	11/18	10/14	1/9	12/6	3/8	2/5	5/6	4/6
7/26	6/17	9/22	8/16	11/19	10/15	1/10	12/7	3/9	2/6	5/7	4/7
7/27	6/18	9/23	8/17	11/20	10/16	1/11	12/8	3/10	2/7	5/8	4/8
7/28	6/19	9/24	8/18	11/21	10/17	1/12	12/9	3/11	2/8	5/9	4/9
7/29	6/20	9/25	8/19	11/22	10/18	1/13	12/10	3/12	2/9	5/10	4/10
7/30	6/21	9/26	8/20	11/23	10/19	1/14	12/11	3/13	2/10	5/11	4/11
7/31	6/22	9/27	8/21	11/24	10/20	1/15	12/12	3/14	2/11	5/12	4/12
		9/28	8/22	11/25	10/21	1/16	12/13	3/15	2/12	5/13	4/13
8/1	6/23	9/29	8/23	11/26	10/22	1/17	12/14	3/16	2/13	5/14	4/14
8/2	6/24	9/30	8/24	11/27	10/23	1/18	12/15	3/17	2/14	5/15	4/15
8/3	6/25			11/28	10/24	1/19	12/16	3/18	2/15	5/16	4/16
8/4	6/26	10/1	8/25	11/29	10/25	1/20	12/17	3/19	2/16	5/17	4/17
8/5	6/27	10/2	8/26	11/30	10/26	1/21	12/18	3/20	2/17	5/18	4/18
8/6	6/28	10/3	8/27			1/22	12/19	3/21	2/18	5/19	4/19
8/7	6/29	10/4	8/28	12/1	10/27	1/23	12/20	3/22	2/19	5/20	4/20
8/8	7/1	10/5	8/29	12/2	10/28	1/24	12/21	3/23	2/20	5/21	4/21
8/9	7/2	10/6	8/30	12/3	10/29	1/25	12/22	3/24	2/21	5/22	4/22
8/10	7/3	10/7	9/1	12/4	10/30	1/26	12/23	3/25	2/22	5/23	4/23
8/11	7/4	10/8	9/2	12/5	11/1	1/27	12/24	3/26	2/23	5/24	4/24
8/12	7/5	10/9	9/3	12/6	11/2	1/28	12/25	3/27	2/24	5/25	4/25
8/13	7/6	10/10	9/4	12/7	11/3	1/29	12/26	3/28	2/25	5/26	4/26
8/14	7/7	10/11	9/5	12/8	11/4	1/30	12/27	3/29	2/26	5/27	4/27
8/15	7/8	10/12	9/6	12/9	11/5	1/31	12/28	3/30	2/27	5/28	4/28
8/16	7/9	10/13	9/7	12/10	11/6	2/1	12/29	3/31	2/28	5/29	4/29

Solar	Lunar	Solar	Lunar	Solar	Lunar	Solar	Lunar	Solar	Lunar	Solar	Lunar
5/30	4/30	7/27	6/29	9/23	8/28	11/20	10/27	1/12	12/20	3/9	2/18
5/31	5/1	7/28	6/30	9/24	8/29	11/21	10/28	1/13	12/21	3/10	2/19
		7/29	7/1	9/25	8/30	11/22	10/29	1/14	12/22	3/11	2/20
6/1	5/2	7/30	7/2	9/26	9/1	11/23	10/30	1/15	12/23	3/12	2/21
6/2	5/3	7/31	7/3	9/27	9/2	11/24	11/1	1/16	12/24	3/13	2/22
6/3	5/4			9/28	9/3	11/25	11/2	1/17	12/25	3/14	2/23
6/4	5/5	8/1	7/4	9/29	9/4	11/26	11/3	1/18	12/26	3/15	2/24
6/5	5/6	8/2	7/5	9/30	9/5	11/27	11/4	1/19	12/27	3/16	2/25
6/6	5/7	8/3	7/6			11/28	11/5	1/20	12/28	3/17	2/26
6/7	5/8	8/4	7/7	10/1	9/6	11/29	11/6	1/21	12/29	3/18	2/27
6/8	5/9	8/5	7/8	10/2	9/7	11/30	11/7	1/22	12/30	3/19	2/28
6/9	5/10	8/6	7/9	10/3	9/8			1/23	1/1	3/20	2/29
6/10	5/11	8/7	7/10	10/4	9/9	12/1	11/8		(1928)	3/21	2/30
6/11	5/12	8/8	7/11	10/5	9/10	12/2	11/9	1/24	1/2	3/22	2/1
6/12	5/13	8/9	7/12	10/6	9/11	12/3	11/10	1/25	1/3	*(Leap Month)*	
6/13	5/14	8/10	7/13	10/7	9/12	12/4	11/11	1/26	1/4	3/23	2/2
6/14	5/15	8/11	7/14	10/8	9/13	12/5	11/12	1/27	1/5	3/24	2/3
6/15	5/16	8/12	7/15	10/9	9/14	12/6	11/13	1/28	1/6	3/25	2/4
6/16	5/17	8/13	7/16	10/10	9/15	12/7	11/14	1/29	1/7	3/26	2/5
6/17	5/18	8/14	7/17	10/11	9/16	12/8	11/15	1/30	1/8	3/27	2/6
6/18	5/19	8/15	7/18	10/12	9/17	12/9	11/16	1/31	1/9	3/28	2/7
6/19	5/20	8/16	7/19	10/13	9/18	12/10	11/17			3/29	2/8
6/20	5/21	8/17	7/20	10/14	9/19	12/11	11/18	2/1	1/10	3/30	2/9
6/21	5/22	8/18	7/21	10/15	9/20	12/12	11/19	2/2	1/11	3/31	2/10
6/22	5/23	8/19	7/22	10/16	9/21	12/13	11/20	2/3	1/12		
6/23	5/24	8/20	7/23	10/17	9/22	12/14	11/21	2/4	1/13	4/1	2/11
6/24	5/25	8/21	7/24	10/18	9/23	12/15	11/22	2/5	1/14	4/2	2/12
6/25	5/26	8/22	7/25	10/19	9/24	12/16	11/23	2/6	1/15	4/3	2/13
6/26	5/27	8/23	7/26	10/20	9/25	12/17	11/24	2/7	1/16	4/4	2/14
6/27	5/28	8/24	7/27	10/21	9/26	12/18	11/25	2/8	1/17	4/5	2/15
6/28	5/29	8/25	7/28	10/22	9/27	12/19	11/26	2/9	1/18	4/6	2/16
6/29	6/1	8/26	7/29	10/23	9/28	12/20	11/27	2/10	1/19	4/7	2/17
6/30	6/2	8/27	8/1	10/24	9/29	12/21	11/28	2/11	1/20	4/8	2/18
		8/28	8/2	10/25	10/1	12/22	11/29	2/12	1/21	4/9	2/19
7/1	6/3	8/29	8/3	10/26	10/2	12/23	11/30	2/13	1/22	4/10	2/20
7/2	6/4	8/30	8/4	10/27	10/3	12/24	12/1	2/14	1/23	4/11	2/21
7/3	6/5	8/31	8/5	10/28	10/4	12/25	12/2	2/15	1/24	4/12	2/22
7/4	6/6			10/29	10/5	12/26	12/3	2/16	1/25	4/13	2/23
7/5	6/7	9/1	8/6	10/30	10/6	12/27	12/4	2/17	1/26	4/14	2/24
7/6	6/8	9/2	8/7	10/31	10/7	12/28	12/5	2/18	1/27	4/15	2/25
7/7	6/9	9/3	8/8			12/29	12/6	2/19	1/28	4/16	2/26
7/8	6/10	9/4	8/9	11/1	10/8	12/30	12/7	2/20	1/29	4/17	2/27
7/9	6/11	9/5	8/10	11/2	10/9	12/31	12/8	2/21	2/1	4/18	2/28
7/10	6/12	9/6	8/11	11/3	10/10			2/22	2/2	4/19	2/29
7/11	6/13	9/7	8/12	11/4	10/11			2/23	2/3	4/20	3/1
7/12	6/14	9/8	8/13	11/5	10/12	**Solar**	**Lunar**	2/24	2/4	4/21	3/2
7/13	6/15	9/9	8/14	11/6	10/13	**Date**	**Date**	2/25	2/5	4/22	3/3
7/14	6/16	9/10	8/15	11/7	10/14	**1928**		2/26	2/6	4/23	3/4
7/15	6/17	9/11	8/16	11/8	10/15	1/1	12/9	2/27	2/7	4/24	3/5
7/16	6/18	9/12	8/17	11/9	10/16	1/2	12/10	2/28	2/8	4/25	3/6
7/17	6/19	9/13	8/18	11/10	10/17	1/3	12/11	2/29	2/9	4/26	3/7
7/18	6/20	9/14	8/19	11/11	10/18	1/4	12/12			4/27	3/8
7/19	6/21	9/15	8/20	11/12	10/19	1/5	12/13	3/1	2/10	4/28	3/9
7/20	6/22	9/16	8/21	11/13	10/20	1/6	12/14	3/2	2/11	4/29	3/10
7/21	6/23	9/17	8/22	11/14	10/21	1/7	12/15	3/3	2/12	4/30	3/11
7/22	6/24	9/18	8/23	11/15	10/22	1/8	12/16	3/4	2/13		
7/23	6/25	9/19	8/24	11/16	10/23	1/9	12/17	3/5	2/14	5/1	3/12
7/24	6/26	9/20	8/25	11/17	10/24	1/10	12/18	3/6	2/15	5/2	3/13
7/25	6/27	9/21	8/26	11/18	10/25	1/11	12/19	3/7	2/16	5/3	3/14
7/26	6/28	9/22	8/27	11/19	10/26			3/8	2/17	5/4	3/15

Solar	Lunar	Solar	Lunar	Solar	Lunar	Solar	Lunar	Solar	Lunar	Solar	Lunar
5/5	3/16	7/2	5/15	8/30	7/16	10/27	9/15	12/24	11/13	2/14	1/5
5/6	3/17	7/3	5/16	8/31	7/17	10/28	9/16	12/25	11/14	2/15	1/6
5/7	3/18	7/4	5/17			10/29	9/17	12/26	11/15	2/16	1/7
5/8	3/19	7/5	5/18	9/1	7/18	10/30	9/18	12/27	11/16	2/17	1/8
5/9	3/20	7/6	5/19	9/2	7/19	10/31	9/19	12/28	11/17	2/18	1/9
5/10	3/21	7/7	5/20	9/3	7/20			12/29	11/18	2/19	1/10
5/11	3/22	7/8	5/21	9/4	7/21	11/1	9/20	12/30	11/19	2/20	1/11
5/12	3/23	7/9	5/22	9/5	7/22	11/2	9/21	12/31	11/20	2/21	1/12
5/13	3/24	7/10	5/23	9/6	7/23	11/3	9/22			2/22	1/13
5/14	3/25	7/11	5/24	9/7	7/24	11/4	9/23			2/23	1/14
5/15	3/26	7/12	5/25	9/8	7/25	11/5	9/24	**Solar**	**Lunar**	2/24	1/15
5/16	3/27	7/13	5/26	9/9	7/26	11/6	9/25	**Date**	**Date**	2/25	1/16
5/17	3/28	7/14	5/27	9/10	7/27	11/7	9/26			2/26	1/17
5/18	3/29	7/15	5/28	9/11	7/28	11/8	9/27	**1929**		2/27	1/18
5/19	4/1	7/16	5/29	9/12	7/29	11/9	9/28	1/1	11/21	2/28	1/19
5/20	4/2	7/17	6/1	9/13	7/30	11/10	9/29	1/2	11/22		
5/21	4/3	7/18	6/2	9/14	8/1	11/11	9/30	1/3	11/23	3/1	1/20
5/22	4/4	7/19	6/3	9/15	8/2	11/12	10/1	1/4	11/24	3/2	1/21
5/23	4/5	7/20	6/4	9/16	8/3	11/13	10/2	1/5	11/25	3/3	1/22
5/24	4/6	7/21	6/5	9/17	8/4	11/14	10/3	1/6	11/26	3/4	1/23
5/25	4/7	7/22	6/6	9/18	8/5	11/15	10/4	1/7	11/27	3/5	1/24
5/26	4/8	7/23	6/7	9/19	8/6	11/16	10/5	1/8	11/28	3/6	1/25
5/27	4/9	7/24	6/8	9/20	8/7	11/17	10/6	1/9	11/29	3/7	1/26
5/28	4/10	7/25	6/9	9/21	8/8	11/18	10/7	1/10	11/30	3/8	1/27
5/29	4/11	7/26	6/10	9/22	8/9	11/19	10/8	1/11	12/1	3/9	1/28
5/30	4/12	7/27	6/11	9/23	8/10	11/20	10/9	1/12	12/2	3/10	1/29
5/31	4/13	7/28	6/12	9/24	8/11	11/21	10/10	1/13	12/3	3/11	2/1
		7/29	6/13	9/25	8/12	11/22	10/11	1/14	12/4	3/12	2/2
6/1	4/14	7/30	6/14	9/26	8/13	11/23	10/12	1/15	12/5	3/13	2/3
6/2	4/15	7/31	6/15	9/27	8/14	11/24	10/13	1/16	12/6	3/14	2/4
6/3	4/16			9/28	8/15	11/25	10/14	1/17	12/7	3/15	2/5
6/4	4/17	8/1	6/16	9/29	8/16	11/26	10/15	1/18	12/8	3/16	2/6
6/5	4/18	8/2	6/17	9/30	8/17	11/27	10/16	1/19	12/9	3/17	2/7
6/6	4/19	8/3	6/18			11/28	10/17	1/20	12/10	3/18	2/8
6/7	4/20	8/4	6/19	10/1	8/18	11/29	10/18	1/21	12/11	3/19	2/9
6/8	4/21	8/5	6/20	10/2	8/19	11/30	10/19	1/22	12/12	3/20	2/10
6/9	4/22	8/6	6/21	10/3	8/20			1/23	12/13	3/21	2/11
6/10	4/23	8/7	6/22	10/4	8/21	12/1	10/20	1/24	12/14	3/22	2/12
6/11	4/24	8/8	6/23	10/5	8/22	12/2	10/21	1/25	12/15	3/23	2/13
6/12	4/25	8/9	6/24	10/6	8/23	12/3	10/22	1/26	12/16	3/24	2/14
6/13	4/26	8/10	6/25	10/7	8/24	12/4	10/23	1/27	12/17	3/25	2/15
6/14	4/27	8/11	6/26	10/8	8/25	12/5	10/24	1/28	12/18	3/26	2/16
6/15	4/28	8/12	6/27	10/9	8/26	12/6	10/25	1/29	12/19	3/27	2/17
6/16	4/29	8/13	6/28	10/10	8/27	12/7	10/26	1/30	12/20	3/28	2/18
6/17	4/30	8/14	6/29	10/11	8/28	12/8	10/27	1/31	12/21	3/29	2/19
6/18	5/1	8/15	7/1	10/12	8/29	12/9	10/28			3/30	2/20
6/19	5/2	8/16	7/2	10/13	9/1	12/10	10/29	2/1	12/22	3/31	2/21
6/20	5/3	8/17	7/3	10/14	9/2	12/11	10/30	2/2	12/23		
6/21	5/4	8/18	7/4	10/15	9/3	12/12	11/1	2/3	12/24	4/1	2/22
6/22	5/5	8/19	7/5	10/16	9/4	12/13	11/2	2/4	12/25	4/2	2/23
6/23	5/6	8/20	7/6	10/17	9/5	12/14	11/3	2/5	12/26	4/3	2/24
6/24	5/7	8/21	7/7	10/18	9/6	12/15	11/4	2/6	12/27	4/4	2/25
6/25	5/8	8/22	7/8	10/19	9/7	12/16	11/5	2/7	12/28	4/5	2/26
6/26	5/9	8/23	7/9	10/20	9/8	12/17	11/6	2/8	12/29	4/6	2/27
6/27	5/10	8/24	7/10	10/21	9/9	12/18	11/7	2/9	12/30	4/7	2/28
6/28	5/11	8/25	7/11	10/22	9/10	12/19	11/8	2/10	1/1	4/8	2/29
6/29	5/12	8/26	7/12	10/23	9/11	12/20	11/9		(1929)	4/9	2/30
6/30	5/13	8/27	7/13	10/24	9/12	12/21	11/10	2/11	1/2	4/10	3/1
		8/28	7/14	10/25	9/13	12/22	11/11	2/12	1/3	4/11	3/2
7/1	5/14	8/29	7/15	10/26	9/14	12/23	11/12	2/13	1/4	4/12	3/3

Solar	Lunar	Solar	Lunar	Solar	Lunar	Solar	Lunar	Solar	Lunar	Solar	Lunar
4/13	3/4	6/10	5/4	8/7	7/3	10/4	9/2	12/1	11/1	1/24	12/25
4/14	3/5	6/11	5/5	8/8	7/4	10/5	9/3	12/2	11/2	1/25	12/26
4/15	3/6	6/12	5/6	8/9	7/5	10/6	9/4	12/3	11/3	1/26	12/27
4/16	3/7	6/13	5/7	8/10	7/6	10/7	9/5	12/4	11/4	1/27	12/28
4/17	3/8	6/14	5/8	8/11	7/7	10/8	9/6	12/5	11/5	1/28	12/29
4/18	3/9	6/15	5/9	8/12	7/8	10/9	9/7	12/6	11/6	1/29	12/30
4/19	3/10	6/16	5/10	8/13	7/9	10/10	9/8	12/7	11/7	1/30	1/1
4/20	3/11	6/17	5/11	8/14	7/10	10/11	9/9	12/8	11/8		(1930)
4/21	3/12	6/18	5/12	8/15	7/11	10/12	9/10	12/9	11/9	1/31	1/2
4/22	3/13	6/19	5/13	8/16	7/12	10/13	9/11	12/10	11/10		
4/23	3/14	6/20	5/14	8/17	7/13	10/14	9/12	12/11	11/11	2/1	1/3
4/24	3/15	6/21	5/15	8/18	7/14	10/15	9/13	12/12	11/12	2/2	1/4
4/25	3/16	6/22	5/16	8/19	7/15	10/16	9/14	12/13	11/13	2/3	1/5
4/26	3/17	6/23	5/17	8/20	7/16	10/17	9/15	12/14	11/14	2/4	1/6
4/27	3/18	6/24	5/18	8/21	7/17	10/18	9/16	12/15	11/15	2/5	1/7
4/28	3/19	6/25	5/19	8/22	7/18	10/19	9/17	12/16	11/16	2/6	1/8
4/29	3/20	6/26	5/20	8/23	7/19	10/20	9/18	12/17	11/17	2/7	1/9
4/30	3/21	6/27	5/21	8/24	7/20	10/21	9/19	12/18	11/18	2/8	1/10
		6/28	5/22	8/25	7/21	10/22	9/20	12/19	11/19	2/9	1/11
5/1	3/22	6/29	5/23	8/26	7/22	10/23	9/21	12/20	11/20	2/10	1/12
5/2	3/23	6/30	5/24	8/27	7/23	10/24	9/22	12/21	11/21	2/11	1/13
5/3	3/24			8/28	7/24	10/25	9/23	12/22	11/22	2/12	1/14
5/4	3/25	7/1	5/25	8/29	7/25	10/26	9/24	12/23	11/23	2/13	1/15
5/5	3/26	7/2	5/26	8/30	7/26	10/27	9/25	12/24	11/24	2/14	1/16
5/6	3/27	7/3	5/27	8/31	7/27	10/28	9/26	12/25	11/25	2/15	1/17
5/7	3/28	7/4	5/28			10/29	9/27	12/26	11/26	2/16	1/18
5/8	3/29	7/5	5/29	9/1	7/28	10/30	9/28	12/27	11/27	2/17	1/19
5/9	4/1	7/6	5/30	9/2	7/29	10/31	9/29	12/28	11/28	2/18	1/20
5/10	4/2	7/7	6/1	9/3	8/1			12/29	11/29	2/19	1/21
5/11	4/3	7/8	6/2	9/4	8/2	11/1	10/1	12/30	11/30	2/20	1/22
5/12	4/4	7/9	6/3	9/5	8/3	11/2	10/2	12/31	12/1	2/21	1/23
5/13	4/5	7/10	6/4	9/6	8/4	11/3	10/3			2/22	1/24
5/14	4/6	7/11	6/5	9/7	8/5	11/4	10/4			2/23	1/25
5/15	4/7	7/12	6/6	9/8	8/6	11/5	10/5	**Solar**	**Lunar**	2/24	1/26
5/16	4/8	7/13	6/7	9/9	8/7	11/6	10/6	**Date**	**Date**	2/25	1/27
5/17	4/9	7/14	6/8	9/10	8/8	11/7	10/7			2/26	1/28
5/18	4/10	7/15	6/9	9/11	8/9	11/8	10/8	**1930**		2/27	1/29
5/19	4/11	7/16	6/10	9/12	8/10	11/9	10/9	1/1	12/2	2/28	2/1
5/20	4/12	7/17	6/11	9/13	8/11	11/10	10/10	1/2	12/3		
5/21	4/13	7/18	6/12	9/14	8/12	11/11	10/11	1/3	12/4	3/1	2/2
5/22	4/14	7/19	6/13	9/15	8/13	11/12	10/12	1/4	12/5	3/2	2/3
5/23	4/15	7/20	6/14	9/16	8/14	11/13	10/13	1/5	12/6	3/3	2/4
5/24	4/16	7/21	6/15	9/17	8/15	11/14	10/14	1/6	12/7	3/4	2/5
5/25	4/17	7/22	6/16	9/18	8/16	11/15	10/15	1/7	12/8	3/5	2/6
5/26	4/18	7/23	6/17	9/19	8/17	11/16	10/16	1/8	12/9	3/6	2/7
5/27	4/19	7/24	6/18	9/20	8/18	11/17	10/17	1/9	12/10	3/7	2/8
5/28	4/20	7/25	6/19	9/21	8/19	11/18	10/18	1/10	12/11	3/8	2/9
5/29	4/21	7/26	6/20	9/22	8/20	11/19	10/19	1/11	12/12	3/9	2/10
5/30	4/22	7/27	6/21	9/23	8/21	11/20	10/20	1/12	12/13	3/10	2/11
5/31	4/23	7/28	6/22	9/24	8/22	11/21	10/21	1/13	12/14	3/11	2/12
		7/29	6/23	9/25	8/23	11/22	10/22	1/14	12/15	3/12	2/13
6/1	4/24	7/30	6/24	9/26	8/24	11/23	10/23	1/15	12/16	3/13	2/14
6/2	4/25	7/31	6/25	9/27	8/25	11/24	10/24	1/16	12/17	3/14	2/15
6/3	4/26			9/28	8/26	11/25	10/25	1/17	12/18	3/15	2/16
6/4	4/27	8/1	6/26	9/29	8/27	11/26	10/26	1/18	12/19	3/16	2/17
6/5	4/28	8/2	6/27	9/30	8/28	11/27	10/27	1/19	12/20	3/17	2/18
6/6	4/29	8/3	6/28			11/28	10/28	1/20	12/21	3/18	2/19
6/7	5/1	8/4	6/30	10/1	8/29	11/29	10/29	1/21	12/22	3/19	2/20
6/8	5/2	8/5	7/1	10/2	8/30	11/30	10/30	1/22	12/23	3/20	2/21
6/9	5/3	8/6	7/2	10/3	9/1			1/23	12/24	3/21	2/22

Solar	Lunar	Solar	Lunar	Solar	Lunar	Solar	Lunar	Solar	Lunar	Solar	Lunar
3/22	2/23	5/20	4/22	7/18	6/22	9/13	7/21	11/10	9/20	1/2	11/14
3/23	2/24	5/21	4/23	7/19	6/23	9/14	7/22	11/11	9/21	1/3	11/15
3/24	2/25	5/22	4/24	7/20	6/24	9/15	7/23	11/12	9/22	1/4	11/16
3/25	2/26	5/23	4/25	7/21	6/25	9/16	7/24	11/13	9/23	1/5	11/17
3/26	2/27	5/24	4/26	7/22	6/26	9/17	7/25	11/14	9/24	1/6	11/18
3/28	2/28	5/25	4/27	7/23	6/27	9/18	7/26	11/15	9/25	1/7	11/19
3/29	2/29	5/26	4/28	7/24	6/28	9/19	7/27	11/16	9/26	1/8	11/20
3/30	3/1	5/27	4/29	7/25	6/29	9/20	7/28	11/17	9/27	1/9	11/21
3/31	3/2	5/28	5/1	7/26	6/1	9/21	7/29	11/18	9/28	1/10	11/22
		5/29	5/2	*(Leap Month)*		9/22	8/1	11/19	9/29	1/11	11/23
4/1	3/3	5/30	5/3	7/27	6/2	9/23	8/2	11/20	10/1	1/12	11/24
4/2	3/4	5/31	5/4	7/28	6/3	9/24	8/3	11/21	10/2	1/13	11/25
4/3	3/5			7/29	6/4	9/25	8/4	11/22	10/3	1/14	11/26
4/4	3/6	6/1	5/5	7/30	6/5	9/26	8/5	11/23	10/4	1/15	11/27
4/5	3/7	6/2	5/6	7/31	6/6	9/27	8/6	11/24	10/5	1/16	11/28
4/6	3/8	6/3	5/7			9/28	8/7	11/25	10/6	1/17	11/29
4/7	3/9	6/4	5/8	8/1	6/7	9/29	8/8	11/26	10/7	1/18	11/30
4/8	3/10	6/5	5/9	8/2	6/8	9/30	8/9	11/27	10/8	1/19	12/1
4/9	3/11	6/6	5/10	8/3	6/9			11/28	10/9	1/20	12/2
4/10	3/12	6/7	5/11	8/4	6/10	10/1	8/10	11/29	10/10	1/21	12/3
4/11	3/13	6/8	5/12	8/5	6/11	10/2	8/11	11/30	10/11	1/22	12/4
4/12	3/14	6/9	5/13	8/6	6/12	10/3	8/12			1/23	12/5
4/13	3/15	6/10	5/14	8/7	6/13	10/4	8/13	12/1	10/12	1/24	12/6
4/14	3/16	6/11	5/15	8/8	6/14	10/5	8/14	12/2	10/13	1/25	12/7
4/15	3/17	6/12	5/16	8/9	6/15	10/6	8/15	12/3	10/14	1/26	12/8
4/16	3/18	6/13	5/17	8/10	6/16	10/7	8/16	12/4	10/15	1/27	12/9
4/17	3/19	6/14	5/18	8/11	6/17	10/8	8/17	12/5	10/16	1/28	12/10
4/18	3/20	6/15	5/19	8/12	6/18	10/9	8/18	12/6	10/17	1/29	12/11
4/19	3/21	6/16	5/20	8/13	6/19	10/10	8/19	12/7	10/18	1/30	12/12
4/20	3/22	6/17	5/21	8/14	6/20	10/11	8/20	12/8	10/19	1/31	12/13
4/21	3/23	6/18	5/22	8/15	6/21	10/12	8/21	12/9	10/20		
4/22	3/24	6/19	5/23	8/16	6/22	10/13	8/22	12/10	10/21	2/1	12/14
4/23	3/25	6/20	5/24	8/17	6/23	10/14	8/23	12/11	10/22	2/2	12/15
4/24	3/26	6/21	5/25	8/18	6/24	10/15	8/24	12/12	10/23	2/3	12/16
4/25	3/27	6/22	5/26	8/19	6/25	10/16	8/25	12/13	10/24	2/4	12/17
4/26	3/28	6/23	5/27	8/20	6/26	10/17	8/26	12/14	10/25	2/5	12/18
4/27	3/29	6/24	5/28	8/21	6/27	10/18	8/27	12/15	10/26	2/6	12/19
4/28	3/30	6/25	5/29	8/22	6/28	10/19	8/28	12/16	10/27	2/7	12/20
4/29	4/1	6/26	6/1	8/23	6/29	10/20	8/29	12/17	10/28	2/8	12/21
4/30	4/2	6/27	6/2	8/24	7/1	10/21	8/30	12/18	10/28	2/9	12/22
		6/28	6/3	8/25	7/2	10/22	9/1	12/19	10/29	2/10	12/23
5/1	4/3	6/29	6/4	8/26	7/3	10/23	9/2	12/20	11/1	2/11	12/24
5/2	4/4	6/30	6/5	8/27	7/4	10/24	9/3	12/21	11/2	2/12	12/25
5/3	4/5			8/28	7/5	10/25	9/4	12/22	11/3	2/13	12/26
5/4	4/6	7/1	6/6	8/29	7/6	10/26	9/5	12/23	11/4	2/14	12/27
5/5	4/7	7/2	6/7	8/30	7/7	10/27	9/6	12/24	11/5	2/15	12/28
5/6	4/8	7/3	6/8	8/31	7/8	10/28	9/7	12/25	11/6	2/16	12/29
5/7	4/9	7/4	6/9			10/29	9/8	12/26	11/7	2/17	1/1
5/8	4/10	7/5	6/10	9/1	7/9	10/30	9/9	12/27	11/8		(1931)
5/9	4/11	7/6	6/11	9/2	7/10	10/31	9/10	12/28	11/9	2/18	1/2
5/10	4/12	7/8	6/12	9/3	7/11			12/29	11/10	2/19	1/3
5/11	4/13	7/9	6/13	9/4	7/12	11/1	9/11	12/30	11/11	2/20	1/4
5/12	4/14	7/10	6/14	9/5	7/13	11/2	9/12	12/31	11/12	2/21	1/5
5/13	4/15	7/11	6/15	9/6	7/14	11/3	9/13			2/22	1/6
5/14	4/16	7/12	6/16	9/7	7/15	11/4	9/14			2/23	1/7
5/15	4/17	7/13	6/17	9/8	7/16	11/5	9/15			2/24	1/8
5/16	4/18	7/14	6/18	9/9	7/17	11/6	9/16	**Solar**	**Lunar**	2/25	1/9
5/17	4/19	7/15	6/19	9/10	7/18	11/7	9/17	**Date**	**Date**	2/26	1/10
5/18	4/20	7/16	6/20	9/11	7/19	11/8	9/18	**1931**		2/27	1/11
5/19	4/21	7/17	6/21	9/12	7/20	11/9	9/19	1/1	11/13	2/28	1/12

Solar	Lunar	Solar	Lunar	Solar	Lunar	Solar	Lunar	Solar	Lunar	Solar	Lunar
3/1	1/13	4/29	3/12	6/26	5/11	8/23	7/10	10/20	9/10	12/17	11/9
3/2	1/14	4/30	3/13	6/27	5/12	8/24	7/11	10/21	9/11	12/18	11/10
3/3	1/15			6/28	5/13	8/25	7/12	10/22	9/12	12/19	11/11
3/4	1/16	5/1	3/14	6/29	5/14	8/26	7/13	10/23	9/13	12/20	11/12
3/5	1/17	5/2	3/15	6/30	5/15	8/27	7/14	10/24	9/14	12/21	11/13
3/6	1/18	5/3	3/16			8/28	7/15	10/25	9/15	12/22	11/14
3/7	1/19	5/4	3/17	7/1	5/16	8/29	7/16	10/26	9/16	12/23	11/15
3/8	1/20	5/5	3/18	7/2	5/17	8/30	7/17	10/27	9/17	12/24	11/16
3/9	1/21	5/6	3/19	7/3	5/18	8/31	7/18	10/28	9/18	12/25	11/17
3/10	1/22	5/7	3/20	7/4	5/19			10/29	9/19	12/26	11/18
3/11	1/23	5/8	3/21	7/5	5/20	9/1	7/19	10/30	9/20	12/27	11/19
3/12	1/24	5/9	3/22	7/6	5/21	9/2	7/20	10/31	9/21	12/28	11/20
3/13	1/25	5/10	3/23	7/7	5/22	9/3	7/21			12/29	11/21
3/14	1/26	5/11	3/24	7/8	5/23	9/4	7/22	11/1	9/22	12/30	11/22
3/15	1/27	5/12	3/25	7/9	5/24	9/5	7/23	11/2	9/23	12/31	11/23
3/16	1/28	5/13	3/26	7/10	5/25	9/6	7/24	11/3	9/24		
3/17	1/29	5/14	3/27	7/11	5/26	9/7	7/25	11/4	9/25		
3/18	1/30	5/15	3/28	7/12	5/27	9/8	7/26	11/5	9/26		
3/19	2/1	5/16	3/29	7/13	5/28	9/9	7/27	11/6	9/27	**Solar**	**Lunar**
3/20	2/2	5/17	4/1	7/14	5/29	9/10	7/28	11/7	9/28	**Date**	**Date**
3/21	2/3	5/18	4/2	7/15	6/1	9/11	7/29	11/8	9/29		
3/22	2/4	5/19	4/3	7/16	6/2	9/12	8/1	11/9	9/30	**1932**	
3/23	2/5	5/20	4/4	7/17	6/3	9/13	8/2	11/10	10/1	1/1	11/24
3/24	2/6	5/21	4/5	7/18	6/4	9/14	8/3	11/11	10/2	1/2	11/25
3/25	2/7	5/22	4/6	7/19	6/5	9/15	8/4	11/12	10/3	1/3	11/26
3/26	2/8	5/23	4/7	7/20	6/6	9/16	8/5	11/13	10/4	1/4	11/27
3/27	2/9	5/24	4/8	7/21	6/7	9/17	8/6	11/14	10/5	1/5	11/28
3/28	2/10	5/25	4/9	7/22	6/8	9/18	8/7	11/15	10/6	1/6	11/29
3/29	2/11	5/26	4/10	7/23	6/9	9/19	8/8	11/16	10/7	1/7	11/30
3/30	2/12	5/27	4/11	7/24	6/10	9/20	8/9	11/17	10/8	1/8	12/1
3/31	2/13	5/28	4/12	7/25	6/11	9/21	8/10	11/18	10/9	1/9	12/2
		5/29	4/13	7/26	6/12	9/22	8/11	11/19	10/10	1/10	12/3
4/1	2/14	5/30	4/14	7/27	6/13	9/23	8/12	11/20	10/11	1/11	12/4
4/2	2/15	5/31	4/15	7/28	6/14	9/24	8/13	11/21	10/12	1/12	12/5
4/3	2/16			7/29	6/15	9/25	8/14	11/22	10/13	1/13	12/6
4/4	2/17	6/1	4/16	7/30	6/16	9/26	8/15	11/23	10/14	1/14	12/7
4/5	2/18	6/2	4/17	7/31	6/17	9/27	8/16	11/24	10/15	1/15	12/8
4/6	2/19	6/3	4/18			9/28	8/17	11/25	10/16	1/16	12/9
4/7	2/20	6/4	4/19	8/1	6/18	9/29	8/18	11/26	10/17	1/17	12/10
4/8	2/21	6/5	4/20	8/2	6/19	9/30	8/19	11/27	10/18	1/18	12/11
4/9	2/22	6/6	4/21	8/3	6/20			11/28	10/19	1/19	12/12
4/10	2/23	6/7	4/22	8/4	6/21	10/1	8/20	11/29	10/20	1/20	12/13
4/11	2/24	6/8	4/23	8/5	6/22	10/2	8/21	11/30	10/21	1/21	12/14
4/12	2/25	6/9	4/24	8/6	6/23	10/3	8/22			1/22	12/15
4/13	2/26	6/10	4/25	8/7	6/24	10/4	8/23	12/1	10/22	1/23	12/16
4/14	2/27	6/11	4/26	8/8	6/25	10/5	8/24	12/2	10/23	1/24	12/17
4/15	2/28	6/12	4/27	8/9	6/26	10/6	8/25	12/3	10/24	1/25	12/18
4/16	2/29	6/13	4/28	8/10	6/27	10/7	8/26	12/4	10/25	1/26	12/19
4/17	2/30	6/14	4/29	8/11	6/28	10/8	8/27	12/5	10/26	1/27	12/20
4/18	3/1	6/15	4/30	8/12	6/29	10/9	8/28	12/6	10/27	1/28	12/21
4/19	3/2	6/16	5/1	8/13	6/30	10/10	8/29	12/7	10/28	1/29	12/22
4/20	3/3	6/17	5/2	8/14	7/1	10/11	9/1	12/8	10/29	1/30	12/23
4/21	3/4	6/18	5/3	8/15	7/2	10/12	9/2	12/9	11/1	1/31	12/24
4/22	3/5	6/19	5/4	8/16	7/3	10/13	9/3	12/10	11/2		
4/23	3/6	6/20	5/5	8/17	7/4	10/14	9/4	12/11	11/3	2/1	12/25
4/24	3/7	6/21	5/6	8/18	7/5	10/15	9/5	12/12	11/4	2/2	12/26
4/25	3/8	6/22	5/7	8/19	7/6	10/16	9/6	12/13	11/5	2/3	12/27
4/26	3/9	6/23	5/8	8/20	7/7	10/17	9/7	12/14	11/6	2/4	12/28
4/27	3/10	6/24	5/9	8/21	7/8	10/18	9/8	12/15	11/7	2/5	12/29
4/28	3/11	6/25	5/10	8/22	7/9	10/19	9/9	12/16	11/8		

Solar	Lunar	Solar	Lunar	Solar	Lunar	Solar	Lunar	Solar	Lunar	Solar	Lunar
2/6	1/1	4/3	2/28	6/1	4/27	7/30	6/27	9/26	8/26	11/23	10/26
	(1932)	4/4	2/29	6/2	4/28	7/31	6/28	9/27	8/27	11/24	10/27
2/7	1/2	4/5	2/30	6/3	4/29			9/28	8/28	11/25	10/28
2/8	1/3	4/6	3/1	6/4	5/1	8/1	6/29	9/29	8/29	11/26	10/29
2/9	1/4	4/7	3/2	6/5	5/2	8/2	7/1	9/30	9/1	11/27	10/30
2/10	1/5	4/8	3/3	6/6	5/3	8/3	7/2			11/28	11/1
2/11	1/6	4/9	3/4	6/7	5/4	8/4	7/3	10/1	9/2	11/29	11/2
2/12	1/7	4/10	3/5	6/8	5/5	8/5	7/4	10/2	9/3	11/30	11/3
2/13	1/8	4/11	3/6	6/9	5/6	8/6	7/5	10/3	9/4		
2/14	1/9	4/12	3/7	6/10	5/7	8/7	7/6	10/4	9/5	12/1	11/4
2/15	1/10	4/13	3/8	6/11	5/8	8/8	7/7	10/5	9/6	12/2	11/5
2/16	1/11	4/14	3/9	6/12	5/9	8/9	7/8	10/6	9/7	12/3	11/6
2/17	1/12	4/15	3/10	6/13	5/10	8/10	7/9	10/7	9/8	12/4	11/7
2/18	1/13	4/16	3/11	6/14	5/11	8/11	7/10	10/8	9/9	12/5	11/8
2/19	1/14	4/17	3/12	6/15	5/12	8/12	7/11	10/9	9/10	12/6	11/9
2/20	1/15	4/18	3/13	6/16	5/13	8/13	7/12	10/10	9/11	12/7	11/10
2/21	1/16	4/19	3/14	6/17	5/14	8/14	7/13	10/11	9/12	12/8	11/11
2/22	1/17	4/20	3/15	6/18	5/15	8/15	7/14	10/12	9/13	12/9	11/12
2/23	1/18	4/21	3/16	6/19	5/16	8/16	7/15	10/13	9/14	12/10	11/13
2/24	1/19	4/22	3/17	6/20	5/17	8/17	7/16	10/14	9/15	12/11	11/14
2/25	1/20	4/23	3/18	6/21	5/18	8/18	7/17	10/15	9/16	12/12	11/15
2/26	1/21	4/24	3/19	6/22	5/19	8/19	7/18	10/16	9/17	12/13	11/16
2/27	1/22	4/25	3/20	6/23	5/20	8/20	7/19	10/17	9/18	12/14	11/17
2/28	1/23	4/26	3/21	6/24	5/21	8/21	7/20	10/18	9/19	12/15	11/18
2/29	1/24	4/27	3/22	6/25	5/22	8/22	7/21	10/19	9/20	12/16	11/19
		4/28	3/23	6/26	5/23	8/23	7/22	10/20	9/21	12/17	11/20
3/1	1/25	4/29	3/24	6/27	5/24	8/24	7/23	10/21	9/22	12/18	11/21
3/2	1/26	4/30	3/25	6/28	5/25	8/25	7/24	10/22	9/23	12/19	11/22
3/3	1/27			6/29	5/26	8/26	7/25	10/23	9/24	12/20	11/23
3/4	1/28	5/1	3/26	6/30	5/27	8/27	7/26	10/24	9/25	12/21	11/24
3/5	1/29	5/2	3/27			8/28	7/27	10/25	9/26	12/22	11/25
3/6	1/30	5/3	3/28	7/1	5/28	8/29	7/28	10/26	9/27	12/23	11/26
3/7	2/1	5/4	3/29	7/2	5/29	8/30	7/29	10/27	9/28	12/24	11/27
3/8	2/2	5/5	3/30	7/3	5/30	8/31	7/30	10/28	9/29	12/25	11/28
3/9	2/3	5/6	4/1	7/4	6/1			10/29	10/1	12/26	11/29
3/10	2/4	5/7	4/2	7/5	6/2	9/1	8/1	10/30	10/2	12/27	12/1
3/11	2/5	5/8	4/3	7/6	6/3	9/2	8/2	10/31	10/3	12/28	12/2
3/12	2/6	5/9	4/4	7/7	6/4	9/3	8/3			12/29	12/3
3/13	2/7	5/10	4/5	7/8	6/5	9/4	8/4	11/1	10/4	12/30	12/4
3/14	2/8	5/11	4/6	7/9	6/6	9/5	8/5	11/2	10/5	12/31	12/5
3/15	2/9	5/12	4/7	7/10	6/7	9/6	8/6	11/3	10/6		
3/16	2/10	5/13	4/8	7/11	6/8	9/7	8/7	11/4	10/7		
3/17	2/11	5/14	4/9	7/12	6/9	9/8	8/8	11/5	10/8	Solar Date	Lunar Date
3/18	2/12	5/15	4/10	7/13	6/10	9/9	8/9	11/6	10/9		
3/19	2/13	5/16	4/11	7/14	6/11	9/10	8/10	11/7	10/10	1933	
3/20	2/14	5/17	4/12	7/15	6/12	9/11	8/11	11/8	10/11	1/1	12/6
3/21	2/15	5/18	4/13	7/16	6/13	9/12	8/12	11/9	10/12	1/2	12/7
3/22	2/16	5/19	4/14	7/17	6/14	9/13	8/13	11/10	10/13	1/3	12/8
3/23	2/17	5/20	4/15	7/18	6/15	9/14	8/14	11/11	10/14	1/4	12/9
3/24	2/18	5/21	4/16	7/19	6/16	9/15	8/15	11/12	10/15	1/5	12/10
3/25	2/19	5/22	4/17	7/20	6/17	9/16	8/16	11/13	10/16	1/6	12/11
3/26	2/20	5/23	4/18	7/21	6/18	9/17	8/17	11/14	10/17	1/7	12/12
3/27	2/21	5/24	4/19	7/22	6/19	9/18	8/18	11/15	10/18	1/8	12/13
3/28	2/22	5/25	4/20	7/23	6/20	9/19	8/19	11/16	10/19	1/9	12/14
3/29	2/23	5/26	4/21	7/24	6/21	9/20	8/20	11/17	10/20	1/10	12/15
3/30	2/24	5/27	4/22	7/25	6/22	9/21	8/21	11/18	10/21	1/11	12/16
3/31	2/25	5/28	4/23	7/26	6/23	9/22	8/22	11/19	10/22	1/12	12/17
		5/29	4/24	7/27	6/24	9/23	8/23	11/20	10/23	1/13	12/18
4/1	2/26	5/30	4/25	7/28	6/25	9/24	8/24	11/21	10/24	1/14	12/19
4/2	2/27	5/31	4/26	7/29	6/26	9/25	8/25	11/22	10/25		

Solar	Lunar
1/15	12/20
1/16	12/21
1/17	12/22
1/18	12/23
1/19	12/24
1/20	12/25
1/21	12/26
1/22	12/27
1/23	12/28
1/24	12/29
1/25	12/30
1/26	1/1 (1933)
1/27	1/2
1/28	1/3
1/29	1/4
1/30	1/5
1/31	1/6
2/1	1/7
2/2	1/8
2/3	1/9
2/4	1/10
2/5	1/11
2/6	1/12
2/7	1/13
2/8	1/14
2/9	1/15
2/10	1/16
2/11	1/17
2/12	1/18
2/13	1/19
2/14	1/20
2/15	1/21
2/16	1/22
2/17	1/23
2/18	1/24
2/19	1/25
2/20	1/26
2/21	1/27
2/22	1/28
2/23	1/29
2/24	2/1
2/25	2/2
2/26	2/3
2/27	2/4
2/28	2/5
3/1	2/6
3/2	2/7
3/3	2/8
3/4	2/9
3/5	2/10
3/6	2/11
3/7	2/12
3/8	2/13
3/9	2/14
3/10	2/15
3/11	2/16
3/12	2/17

Solar	Lunar
3/13	2/18
3/14	2/19
3/15	2/20
3/16	2/21
3/17	2/22
3/18	2/23
3/19	2/24
3/20	2/25
3/21	2/26
3/22	2/27
3/23	2/28
3/24	2/29
3/25	2/30
3/26	3/1
3/27	3/2
3/28	3/3
3/29	3/4
3/30	3/5
3/31	3/6
4/1	3/7
4/2	3/8
4/3	3/9
4/4	3/10
4/5	3/11
4/6	3/12
4/7	3/13
4/8	3/14
4/9	3/15
4/10	3/16
4/11	3/17
4/12	3/18
4/13	3/19
4/14	3/20
4/15	3/21
4/16	3/22
4/17	3/23
4/18	3/24
4/19	3/25
4/20	3/26
4/21	3/27
4/22	3/28
4/23	3/29
4/24	3/30
4/25	4/1
4/26	4/2
4/27	4/3
4/28	4/4
4/29	4/5
4/30	4/6
5/1	4/7
5/2	4/8
5/3	4/9
5/4	4/10
5/5	4/11
5/6	4/12
5/7	4/13
5/8	4/14
5/9	4/15

Solar	Lunar
5/10	4/16
5/11	4/17
5/12	4/18
5/13	4/19
5/14	4/20
5/15	4/21
5/16	4/22
5/17	4/23
5/18	4/24
5/19	4/25
5/20	4/26
5/21	4/27
5/22	4/28
5/23	4/29
5/24	5/1
5/25	5/2
5/26	5/3
5/27	5/4
5/28	5/5
5/29	5/6
5/30	5/7
5/31	5/8
6/1	5/9
6/2	5/10
6/3	5/11
6/4	5/12
6/5	5/13
6/6	5/14
6/7	5/15
6/8	5/16
6/9	5/17
6/10	5/18
6/11	5/19
6/12	5/20
6/13	5/21
6/14	5/22
6/15	5/23
6/16	5/24
6/17	5/25
6/18	5/26
6/19	5/27
6/20	5/28
6/21	5/29
6/22	5/30
6/23	5/1 *(Leap Month)*
6/24	5/2
6/25	5/3
6/26	5/4
6/27	5/5
6/28	5/6
6/29	5/7
6/30	5/8
7/1	5/9
7/2	5/10
7/3	5/11
7/4	5/12
7/5	5/13

Solar	Lunar
7/6	5/14
7/7	5/15
7/8	5/16
7/9	5/17
7/10	5/18
7/11	5/19
7/12	5/20
7/13	5/21
7/14	5/22
7/15	5/23
7/16	5/24
7/17	5/25
7/18	5/26
7/19	5/27
7/20	5/28
7/21	5/29
7/22	5/30
7/23	6/1
7/24	6/2
7/25	6/3
7/26	6/4
7/27	6/5
7/28	6/6
7/29	6/7
7/30	6/8
7/31	6/9
8/1	6/10
8/2	6/11
8/3	6/12
8/4	6/13
8/5	6/14
8/6	6/15
8/7	6/16
8/8	6/17
8/9	6/18
8/10	6/19
8/11	6/20
8/12	6/21
8/13	6/22
8/14	6/23
8/15	6/24
8/16	6/25
8/17	6/26
8/18	6/27
8/19	6/28
8/20	6/29
8/21	7/1
8/22	7/2
8/23	7/3
8/24	7/4
8/25	7/5
8/26	7/6
8/27	7/7
8/28	7/8
8/29	7/9
8/30	7/10
8/31	7/11
9/1	7/12

Solar	Lunar
9/2	7/13
9/3	7/14
9/4	7/15
9/5	7/16
9/6	7/17
9/7	7/18
9/8	7/19
9/9	7/20
9/10	7/21
9/11	7/22
9/12	7/23
9/13	7/24
9/14	7/25
9/15	7/26
9/16	7/27
9/17	7/28
9/18	7/29
9/19	7/30
9/20	8/1
9/21	8/2
9/22	8/3
9/23	8/4
9/24	8/5
9/25	8/6
9/26	8/7
9/27	8/8
9/28	8/9
9/29	8/10
9/30	8/11
10/1	8/12
10/2	8/13
10/3	8/14
10/4	8/15
10/5	8/16
10/6	8/17
10/7	8/18
10/8	8/19
10/9	8/20
10/10	8/21
10/11	8/22
10/12	8/23
10/13	8/24
10/14	8/25
10/15	8/26
10/16	8/27
10/17	8/28
10/18	8/29
10/19	9/1
10/20	9/2
10/21	9/3
10/22	9/4
10/23	9/5
10/24	9/6
10/25	9/7
10/26	9/8
10/27	9/9
10/28	9/10
10/29	9/11
10/30	9/12

Solar	Lunar
10/31	9/13
11/1	9/14
11/2	9/15
11/3	9/16
11/4	9/17
11/5	9/18
11/6	9/19
11/7	9/20
11/8	9/21
11/9	9/22
11/10	9/23
11/11	9/24
11/12	9/25
11/13	9/26
11/14	9/27
11/15	9/28
11/16	9/29
11/17	9/30
11/18	10/1
11/19	10/2
11/20	10/3
11/21	10/4
11/22	10/5
11/23	10/6
11/24	10/7
11/25	10/8
11/26	10/9
11/27	10/10
11/28	10/11
11/29	10/12
11/30	10/13
12/1	10/14
12/2	10/15
12/3	10/16
12/4	10/17
12/5	10/18
12/6	10/19
12/7	10/20
12/8	10/21
12/9	10/22
12/10	10/23
12/11	10/24
12/12	10/25
12/13	10/26
12/14	10/27
12/15	10/28
12/16	10/29
12/17	11/1
12/18	11/2
12/19	11/3
12/20	11/4
12/21	11/5
12/22	11/6
12/23	11/7
12/24	11/8
12/25	11/9
12/26	11/10
12/27	11/11

Solar Date	Lunar Date	Solar Date	Lunar Date	Solar Date	Lunar Date	Solar Date	Lunar Date	Solar Date	Lunar Date	Solar Date	Lunar Date
12/28	11/12	2/18	1/5	4/17	3/4	6/14	5/3	8/11	7/2	10/8	9/1
12/29	11/13	2/19	1/6	4/18	3/5	6/15	5/4	8/12	7/3	10/9	9/2
12/30	11/14	2/20	1/7	4/19	3/6	6/16	5/5	8/13	7/4	10/10	9/3
12/31	11/15	2/21	1/8	4/20	3/7	6/17	5/6	8/14	7/5	10/11	9/4
		2/22	1/9	4/21	3/8	6/18	5/7	8/15	7/6	10/12	9/5
		2/23	2/10	4/22	3/9	6/19	5/8	8/16	7/7	10/13	9/6
1934		2/24	2/11	4/23	3/10	6/20	5/9	8/17	7/8	10/14	9/7
1/1	11/16	2/25	2/12	4/24	3/11	6/21	5/10	8/18	7/9	10/15	9/8
1/2	11/17	2/26	2/13	4/25	3/12	6/22	5/11	8/19	7/10	10/16	9/9
1/3	11/18	2/27	2/14	4/26	3/13	6/23	5/12	8/20	7/11	10/17	9/10
1/4	11/19	2/28	2/15	4/27	3/14	6/24	5/13	8/21	7/12	10/18	9/11
1/5	11/20			4/28	3/15	6/25	5/14	8/22	7/13	10/19	9/12
1/6	11/21	3/1	2/16	4/29	3/16	6/26	5/15	8/23	7/14	10/20	9/13
1/7	11/22	3/2	2/17	4/30	3/17	6/27	5/16	8/24	7/15	10/21	9/14
1/8	11/23	3/3	2/18			6/28	5/17	8/25	7/16	10/22	9/15
1/9	11/24	3/4	2/19	5/1	3/18	6/29	5/18	8/26	7/17	10/23	9/16
1/10	11/25	3/5	2/20	5/2	3/19	6/30	5/19	8/27	7/18	10/24	9/17
1/11	11/26	3/6	2/21	5/3	3/20			8/28	7/19	10/25	9/18
1/12	11/27	3/7	2/22	5/4	3/21	7/1	5/20	8/29	7/20	10/26	9/19
1/13	11/28	3/8	2/23	5/5	3/22	7/2	5/21	8/30	7/21	10/27	9/20
1/14	11/29	3/9	2/24	5/6	3/23	7/3	5/22	8/31	7/22	10/28	9/21
1/15	12/1	3/10	2/25	5/7	3/24	7/4	5/23			10/29	9/22
1/16	12/2	3/11	2/26	5/8	3/25	7/5	5/24	9/1	7/23	10/30	9/23
1/17	12/3	3/12	2/27	5/9	3/26	7/6	5/25	9/2	7/24	10/31	9/24
1/18	12/4	3/13	2/28	5/10	3/27	7/7	5/26	9/3	7/25		
1/19	12/5	3/14	2/29	5/11	3/28	7/8	5/27	9/4	7/26	11/1	9/25
1/20	12/6	3/15	2/1	5/12	3/29	7/9	5/28	9/5	7/27	11/2	9/26
1/21	12/7	3/16	2/2	5/13	4/1	7/10	5/29	9/6	7/28	11/3	9/27
1/22	12/8	3/17	2/3	5/14	4/2	7/11	5/30	9/7	7/29	11/4	9/28
1/23	12/9	3/18	2/4	5/15	4/3	7/12	6/1	9/8	7/30	11/5	9/29
1/24	12/10	3/19	2/5	5/16	4/4	7/13	6/2	9/9	8/1	11/6	9/30
1/25	12/11	3/20	2/6	5/17	4/5	7/14	6/3	9/10	8/2	11/7	10/1
1/26	12/12	3/21	2/7	5/18	4/6	7/15	6/4	9/11	8/3	11/8	10/2
1/27	12/13	3/22	2/8	5/19	4/7	7/16	6/5	9/12	8/4	11/9	10/3
1/28	12/14	3/23	2/9	5/20	4/8	7/17	6/6	9/13	8/5	11/10	10/4
1/29	12/15	3/24	2/10	5/21	4/9	7/18	6/7	9/14	8/6	11/11	10/5
1/30	12/16	3/25	2/11	5/22	4/10	7/19	6/8	9/15	8/7	11/12	10/6
1/31	12/17	3/26	2/12	5/23	4/11	7/20	6/9	9/16	8/8	11/13	10/7
		3/27	2/13	5/24	4/12	7/21	6/10	9/17	8/9	11/14	10/8
		3/28	2/14	5/25	4/13	7/22	6/11	9/18	8/10	11/15	10/9
		3/29	2/15	5/26	4/14	7/23	6/12	9/19	8/11	11/16	10/10
		3/30	2/16	5/27	4/15	7/24	6/13	9/20	8/12	11/17	10/11
2/1	12/18	3/31	2/17	5/28	4/16	7/25	6/14	9/21	8/13	11/18	10/12
2/2	12/19			5/29	4/17	7/26	6/15	9/22	8/14	11/19	10/13
2/3	12/20	4/1	2/18	5/30	4/18	7/27	6/16	9/23	8/15	11/20	10/14
2/4	12/21	4/2	2/19	5/31	4/19	7/28	6/17	9/24	8/16	11/21	10/15
2/5	12/22	4/3	2/20			7/29	6/18	9/25	8/17	11/22	10/16
2/6	12/23	4/4	2/21	6/1	4/20	7/30	6/19	9/26	8/18	11/23	10/17
2/7	12/24	4/5	2/22	6/2	4/21	7/31	6/20	9/27	8/19	11/24	10/18
2/8	12/25	4/6	2/23	6/3	4/22			9/28	8/20	11/25	10/19
2/9	12/26	4/7	2/24	6/4	4/23	8/1	6/21	9/29	8/21	11/26	10/20
2/10	12/27	4/8	2/25	6/5	4/24	8/2	6/22	9/30	8/22	11/27	10/21
2/11	12/28	4/9	2/26	6/6	4/25	8/3	6/23			11/28	10/22
2/12	12/29	4/10	2/27	6/7	4/26	8/4	6/24	10/1	8/23	11/29	10/23
2/13	12/30	4/11	2/28	6/8	4/27	8/5	6/25	10/2	8/24	11/30	10/24
2/14	1/1 (1934)	4/12	2/29	6/9	4/28	8/6	6/26	10/3	8/25		
2/15	1/2	4/13	2/30	6/10	4/29	8/7	6/27	10/4	8/26	12/1	10/25
2/16	1/3	4/14	3/1	6/11	4/30	8/8	6/28	10/5	8/27	12/2	10/26
2/17	1/4	4/15	3/2	6/12	5/1	8/9	6/29	10/6	8/28	12/3	10/27
		4/16	3/3	6/13	5/2	8/10	7/1	10/7	8/29	12/4	10/28

Solar Date	Lunar Date
12/5	10/29
12/6	10/30
12/7	11/1
12/8	11/2
12/9	11/3
12/10	11/4
12/11	11/5
12/12	11/6
12/13	11/7
12/14	11/8
12/15	11/9
12/16	11/10
12/17	11/11
12/18	11/12
12/19	11/13
12/20	11/14
12/21	11/15
12/22	11/16
12/23	11/17
12/24	11/18
12/25	11/19
12/26	11/20
12/27	11/21
12/28	11/22
12/29	11/23
12/30	11/24
12/31	11/25

Solar Date	Lunar Date
1935	
1/1	11/26
1/2	11/27
1/3	11/28
1/4	11/29
1/5	12/1
1/6	12/2
1/7	12/3
1/8	12/4
1/9	12/5
1/10	12/6
1/11	12/7
1/12	12/8
1/13	12/9
1/14	12/10
1/15	12/11
1/16	12/12
1/17	12/13
1/18	12/14
1/19	12/15
1/20	12/16
1/21	12/17
1/22	12/18
1/23	12/19
1/24	12/20
1/25	12/21
1/26	12/22
1/27	12/23

Solar Date	Lunar Date
1/28	12/24
1/29	12/25
1/30	12/26
1/31	12/27
2/1	12/28
2/2	12/29
2/3	12/30
2/4	1/1 (1935)
2/5	1/2
2/6	1/3
2/7	1/4
2/8	1/5
2/9	1/6
2/10	1/7
2/11	1/8
2/12	1/9
2/13	1/10
2/14	1/11
2/15	1/12
2/16	1/13
2/17	1/14
2/18	1/15
2/19	1/16
2/20	1/17
2/21	1/18
2/22	1/19
2/23	1/20
2/24	1/21
2/25	1/22
2/26	1/23
2/27	1/24
2/28	1/25
3/1	1/26
3/2	1/27
3/3	1/28
3/4	1/29
3/5	2/1
3/6	2/2
3/7	2/3
3/8	2/4
3/9	2/5
3/10	2/6
3/11	2/7
3/12	2/8
3/13	2/9
3/14	2/10
3/15	2/11
3/16	2/12
3/17	2/13
3/18	2/14
3/19	2/15
3/20	2/16
3/21	2/17
3/22	2/18
3/23	2/19
3/24	2/20
3/25	2/21

Solar Date	Lunar Date
3/26	2/22
3/27	2/23
3/28	2/24
3/29	2/25
3/30	2/26
3/31	2/27
4/1	2/28
4/2	2/29
4/3	3/1
4/4	3/2
4/5	3/3
4/6	3/4
4/7	3/5
4/8	3/6
4/9	3/7
4/10	3/8
4/11	3/9
4/12	3/10
4/13	3/11
4/14	3/12
4/15	3/13
4/16	3/14
4/17	3/15
4/18	3/16
4/19	3/17
4/20	3/18
4/21	3/19
4/22	3/20
4/23	3/21
4/24	3/22
4/25	3/23
4/26	3/24
4/27	3/25
4/28	3/26
4/29	3/27
4/30	3/28
5/1	3/29
5/2	3/30
5/3	4/1
5/4	4/2
5/5	4/3
5/6	4/4
5/7	4/5
5/8	4/6
5/9	4/7
5/10	4/8
5/11	4/9
5/12	4/10
5/13	4/11
5/14	4/12
5/15	4/13
5/16	4/14
5/17	4/15
5/18	4/16
5/19	4/17
5/20	4/18
5/21	4/19
5/22	4/20

Solar Date	Lunar Date
5/23	4/21
5/24	4/22
5/25	4/23
5/26	4/24
5/27	4/25
5/28	4/26
5/29	4/27
5/30	4/28
5/31	4/29
6/1	5/1
6/2	5/2
6/3	5/3
6/4	5/4
6/5	5/5
6/6	5/6
6/7	5/7
6/8	5/8
6/9	5/9
6/10	5/10
6/11	5/11
6/12	5/12
6/13	5/13
6/14	5/14
6/15	5/15
6/16	5/16
6/17	5/17
6/18	5/18
6/19	5/19
6/20	5/20
6/21	5/21
6/22	5/22
6/23	5/23
6/24	5/24
6/25	5/25
6/26	5/26
6/27	5/27
6/28	5/28
6/29	5/29
6/30	5/30
7/1	6/1
7/2	6/2
7/3	6/3
7/4	6/4
7/5	6/5
7/6	6/6
7/7	6/7
7/8	6/8
7/9	6/9
7/10	6/10
7/11	6/11
7/12	6/12
7/13	6/13
7/14	6/14
7/15	6/15
7/16	6/16
7/17	6/17
7/18	6/18
7/19	6/19

Solar Date	Lunar Date
7/20	6/20
7/21	6/21
7/22	6/22
7/23	6/23
7/24	6/24
7/25	6/25
7/26	6/26
7/27	6/27
7/28	6/28
7/29	6/29
7/30	7/1
7/31	7/2
8/1	7/3
8/2	7/4
8/3	7/5
8/4	7/6
8/5	7/7
8/6	7/8
8/7	7/9
8/8	7/10
8/9	7/11
8/10	7/12
8/11	7/13
8/12	7/14
8/13	7/15
8/14	7/16
8/15	7/17
8/16	7/18
8/17	7/19
8/18	7/20
8/19	7/21
8/20	7/22
8/21	7/23
8/22	7/24
8/23	7/25
8/24	7/26
8/25	7/27
8/26	7/28
8/27	7/29
8/28	7/30
8/29	8/1
8/30	8/2
8/31	8/3
9/1	8/4
9/2	8/5
9/3	8/6
9/4	8/7
9/5	8/8
9/6	8/9
9/7	8/10
9/8	8/11
9/9	8/12
9/10	8/13
9/11	8/14
9/12	8/15
9/13	8/16
9/14	8/17
9/15	8/18

Solar Date	Lunar Date
9/16	8/19
9/17	8/20
9/18	8/21
9/19	8/22
9/20	8/23
9/21	8/24
9/22	8/25
9/23	8/26
9/24	8/27
9/25	8/28
9/26	8/29
9/27	8/30
9/28	9/1
9/29	9/2
9/30	9/3
10/1	9/4
10/2	9/5
10/3	9/6
10/4	9/7
10/5	9/8
10/6	9/9
10/7	9/10
10/8	9/11
10/9	9/12
10/10	9/13
10/11	9/14
10/12	9/15
10/13	9/16
10/14	9/17
10/15	9/18
10/16	9/19
10/17	9/20
10/18	9/21
10/19	9/22
10/20	9/23
10/21	9/24
10/22	9/25
10/23	9/26
10/24	9/27
10/25	9/28
10/26	9/29
10/27	10/1
10/28	10/2
10/29	10/3
10/30	10/4
10/31	10/5
11/1	10/6
11/2	10/7
11/3	10/8
11/4	10/9
11/5	10/10
11/6	10/11
11/7	10/12
11/8	10/13
11/9	10/14
11/10	10/15
11/11	10/16
11/12	10/17

Solar	Lunar	Solar	Lunar	Solar	Lunar	Solar	Lunar	Solar	Lunar	Solar	Lunar
11/13	10/18	1/5	12/11	3/2	2/9	4/29	3/9	6/26	5/8	8/23	7/7
11/14	10/19	1/6	12/12	3/3	2/10	4/30	3/10	6/27	5/9	8/24	7/8
11/15	10/20	1/7	12/13	3/4	2/11			6/28	5/10	8/25	7/9
11/16	10/21	1/8	12/14	3/5	2/12	5/1	3/11	6/29	5/11	8/26	7/10
11/17	10/22	1/9	12/15	3/6	2/13	5/2	3/12	6/30	5/12	8/27	7/11
11/18	10/23	1/10	12/16	3/7	2/14	5/3	3/13			8/28	7/12
11/19	10/24	1/11	12/17	3/8	2/15	5/4	3/14	7/1	5/13	8/29	7/13
11/20	10/25	1/12	12/18	3/9	2/16	5/5	3/15	7/2	5/14	8/30	7/14
11/21	10/26	1/13	12/19	3/10	2/17	5/6	3/16	7/3	5/15	8/31	7/15
11/22	10/27	1/14	12/20	3/11	2/18	5/7	3/17	7/4	5/16		
11/23	10/28	1/15	12/21	3/12	2/19	5/8	3/18	7/5	5/17	9/1	7/16
11/24	10/29	1/16	12/22	3/13	2/20	5/9	3/19	7/6	5/18	9/2	7/17
11/25	10/30	1/17	12/23	3/14	2/21	5/10	3/20	7/7	5/19	9/3	7/18
11/26	11/1	1/18	12/24	3/15	2/22	5/11	3/21	7/8	5/20	9/4	7/19
11/27	11/2	1/19	12/25	3/16	2/23	5/12	3/22	7/9	5/21	9/5	7/20
11/28	11/3	1/20	12/26	3/17	2/24	5/13	3/23	7/10	5/22	9/6	7/21
11/29	11/4	1/21	12/27	3/18	2/25	5/14	3/24	7/11	5/23	9/7	7/22
11/30	11/5	1/22	12/28	3/19	2/26	5/15	3/25	7/12	5/24	9/8	7/23
		1/23	12/29	3/20	2/27	5/16	3/26	7/13	5/25	9/9	7/24
12/1	11/6	1/24	1/1	3/21	2/28	5/17	3/27	7/14	5/26	9/10	7/25
12/2	11/7		(1936)	3/22	2/29	5/18	3/28	7/15	5/27	9/11	7/26
12/3	11/8	1/25	1/2	3/23	3/1	5/19	3/29	7/16	5/28	9/12	7/27
12/4	11/9	1/26	1/3	3/24	3/2	5/20	3/30	7/17	5/29	9/13	7/28
12/5	11/10	1/27	1/4	3/25	3/3	5/21	4/1	7/18	6/1	9/14	7/29
12/6	11/11	1/28	1/5	3/26	3/4	5/22	4/2	7/19	6/2	9/15	7/30
12/7	11/12	1/29	1/6	3/27	3/5	5/23	4/3	7/20	6/3	9/16	8/1
12/8	11/13	1/30	1/7	3/28	3/6	5/24	4/4	7/21	6/4	9/17	8/2
12/9	11/14	1/31	1/8	3/29	3/7	5/25	4/5	7/22	6/5	9/18	8/3
12/10	11/15			3/30	3/8	5/26	4/6	7/23	6/6	9/19	8/4
12/11	11/16	2/1	1/9	3/31	3/9	5/27	4/7	7/24	6/7	9/20	8/5
12/12	11/17	2/2	1/10			5/28	4/8	7/25	6/8	9/21	8/6
12/13	11/18	2/3	1/11	4/1	3/10	5/29	4/9	7/26	6/9	9/22	8/7
12/14	11/19	2/4	1/12	4/2	3/11	5/30	4/10	7/27	6/10	9/23	8/8
12/15	11/20	2/5	1/13	4/3	3/12	5/31	4/11	7/28	6/11	9/24	8/9
12/16	11/21	2/6	1/14	4/4	3/13			7/29	6/12	9/25	8/10
12/17	11/22	2/7	1/15	4/5	3/14	6/1	4/12	7/30	6/13	9/26	8/11
12/18	11/23	2/8	1/16	4/6	3/15	6/2	4/13	7/31	6/14	9/27	8/12
12/19	11/24	2/9	1/17	4/7	3/16	6/3	4/14			9/28	8/13
12/20	11/25	2/10	1/18	4/8	3/17	6/4	4/15	8/1	6/15	9/29	8/14
12/21	11/26	2/11	1/19	4/9	3/18	6/5	4/16	8/2	6/16	9/30	8/15
12/22	11/27	2/12	1/20	4/10	3/19	6/6	4/17	8/3	6/17		
12/23	11/28	2/13	1/21	4/11	3/20	6/7	4/18	8/4	6/18	10/1	8/16
12/24	11/29	2/14	1/22	4/12	3/21	6/8	4/19	8/5	6/19	10/2	8/17
12/25	11/30	2/15	1/23	4/13	3/22	6/9	4/20	8/6	6/20	10/3	8/18
12/26	12/1	2/16	1/24	4/14	3/23	6/10	4/21	8/7	6/21	10/4	8/19
12/27	12/2	2/17	1/25	4/15	3/24	6/11	4/22	8/8	6/22	10/5	8/20
12/28	12/3	2/18	1/26	4/16	3/25	6/12	4/23	8/9	6/23	10/6	8/21
12/29	12/4	2/19	1/27	4/17	3/26	6/13	4/24	8/10	6/24	10/7	8/22
12/30	12/5	2/20	1/28	4/18	3/27	6/14	4/25	8/11	6/25	10/8	8/23
12/31	12/6	2/21	1/29	4/19	3/28	6/15	4/26	8/12	6/26	10/9	8/24
		2/22	1/30	4/20	3/29	6/16	4/27	8/13	6/27	10/10	8/25
		2/23	2/1	4/21	3/1	6/17	4/28	8/14	6/28	10/11	8/26
Solar	Lunar	2/24	2/2	(Leap Month)		6/18	4/29	8/15	6/29	10/12	8/27
Date	Date	2/25	2/3	4/22	3/2	6/19	5/1	8/16	6/30	10/13	8/28
1936		2/26	2/4	4/23	3/3	6/20	5/2	8/17	7/1	10/14	8/29
1/1	12/7	2/27	2/5	4/24	3/4	6/21	5/3	8/18	7/2	10/15	9/1
1/2	12/8	2/28	2/6	4/25	3/5	6/22	5/4	8/19	7/3	10/16	9/2
1/3	12/9	2/29	2/7	4/26	3/6	6/23	5/5	8/20	7/4	10/17	9/3
1/4	12/10	3/1	2/8	4/27	3/7	6/24	5/6	8/21	7/5	10/18	9/4
				4/28	3/8	6/25	5/7	8/22	7/6	10/19	9/5

Solar	Lunar	Solar	Lunar	Solar	Lunar	Solar	Lunar	Solar	Lunar	Solar	Lunar
10/20	9/6	12/17	11/4	2/8	12/27	4/6	2/25	6/3	4/25	8/1	6/25
10/21	9/7	12/18	11/5	2/9	12/28	4/7	2/26	6/4	4/26	8/2	6/26
10/22	9/8	12/19	11/6	2/10	12/29	4/8	2/27	6/5	4/27	8/3	6/27
10/23	9/9	12/20	11/7	2/11	1/1	4/9	2/28	6/6	4/28	8/4	6/28
10/24	9/10	12/21	11/8		(1937)	4/10	2/29	6/7	4/29	8/5	6/29
10/25	9/11	12/22	11/9	2/12	1/2	4/11	3/1	6/8	4/30	8/6	7/1
10/26	9/12	12/23	11/10	2/13	1/3	4/12	3/2	6/9	5/1	8/7	7/2
10/27	9/13	12/24	11/11	2/14	1/4	4/13	3/3	6/10	5/2	8/8	7/3
10/28	9/14	12/25	11/12	2/15	1/5	4/14	3/4	6/11	5/3	8/9	7/4
10/29	9/15	12/26	11/13	2/16	1/6	4/15	3/5	6/12	5/4	8/10	7/5
10/30	9/16	12/27	11/14	2/17	1/7	4/16	3/6	6/13	5/5	8/11	7/6
10/31	9/17	12/28	11/15	2/18	1/8	4/17	3/7	6/14	5/6	8/12	7/7
		12/29	11/16	2/19	1/9	4/18	3/8	6/15	5/7	8/13	7/8
11/1	9/18	12/30	11/17	2/20	1/10	4/19	3/9	6/16	5/8	8/14	7/9
11/2	9/19	12/31	11/18	2/21	1/11	4/20	3/10	6/17	5/9	8/15	7/10
11/3	9/20			2/22	1/12	4/21	3/11	6/18	5/10	8/16	7/11
11/4	9/21			2/23	1/13	4/22	3/12	6/19	5/11	8/17	7/12
11/5	9/22	Solar	Lunar	2/24	1/14	4/23	3/13	6/20	5/12	8/18	7/13
11/6	9/23	Date	Date	2/25	1/15	4/24	3/14	6/21	5/13	8/19	7/14
11/7	9/24			2/26	1/16	4/25	3/15	6/22	5/14	8/20	7/15
11/8	9/25	**1937**		2/27	1/17	4/26	3/16	6/23	5/15	8/21	7/16
11/9	9/26	1/1	11/19	2/28	1/18	4/27	3/17	6/24	5/16	8/22	7/17
11/10	9/27	1/2	11/20			4/28	3/18	6/25	5/17	8/23	7/18
11/11	9/28	1/3	11/21	3/1	1/19	4/29	3/19	6/26	5/18	8/24	7/19
11/12	9/29	1/4	11/22	3/2	1/20	4/30	3/20	6/27	5/19	8/25	7/20
11/13	9/30	1/5	11/23	3/3	1/21			6/28	5/20	8/26	7/21
11/14	10/1	1/6	11/24	3/4	1/22	5/1	3/21	6/29	5/21	8/27	7/22
11/15	10/2	1/7	11/25	3/5	1/23	5/2	3/22	6/30	5/22	8/28	7/23
11/16	10/3	1/8	11/26	3/6	1/24	5/3	3/23			8/29	7/24
11/17	10/4	1/9	11/27	3/7	1/25	5/4	3/24	7/1	5/23	8/30	7/25
11/18	10/5	1/10	11/28	3/8	1/26	5/5	3/25	7/2	5/24	8/31	7/26
11/19	10/6	1/11	11/29	3/9	1/27	5/6	3/26	7/3	5/25		
11/20	10/7	1/12	11/30	3/10	1/28	5/7	3/27	7/4	5/26	9/1	7/27
11/21	10/8	1/13	12/1	3/11	1/29	5/8	3/28	7/5	5/27	9/2	7/28
11/22	10/9	1/14	12/2	3/12	1/30	5/9	3/29	7/6	5/28	9/3	7/29
11/23	10/10	1/15	12/3	3/13	2/1	5/10	4/1	7/7	5/29	9/4	7/30
11/24	10/11	1/16	12/4	3/14	2/2	5/11	4/2	7/8	6/1	9/5	8/1
11/25	10/12	1/17	12/5	3/15	2/3	5/12	4/3	7/9	6/2	9/6	8/2
11/26	10/13	1/18	12/6	3/16	2/4	5/13	4/4	7/10	6/3	9/7	8/3
11/27	10/14	1/19	12/7	3/17	2/5	5/14	4/5	7/11	6/4	9/8	8/4
11/28	10/15	1/20	12/8	3/18	2/6	5/15	4/6	7/12	6/5	9/9	8/5
11/29	10/16	1/21	12/9	3/19	2/7	5/16	4/7	7/13	6/6	9/10	8/6
11/30	10/17	1/22	12/10	3/20	2/8	5/17	4/8	7/14	6/7	9/11	8/7
		1/23	12/11	3/21	2/9	5/18	4/9	7/15	6/8	9/12	8/8
12/1	10/18	1/24	12/12	3/22	2/10	5/19	4/10	7/16	6/9	9/13	8/9
12/2	10/19	1/25	12/13	3/23	2/11	5/20	4/11	7/17	6/10	9/14	8/10
12/3	10/20	1/26	12/14	3/24	2/12	5/21	4/12	7/18	6/11	9/15	8/11
12/4	10/21	1/27	12/15	3/25	2/13	5/22	4/13	7/19	6/12	9/16	8/12
12/5	10/22	1/28	12/16	3/26	2/14	5/23	4/14	7/20	6/13	9/17	8/13
12/6	10/23	1/29	12/17	3/27	2/15	5/24	4/15	7/21	6/14	9/18	8/14
12/7	10/24	1/30	12/18	3/28	2/16	5/25	4/16	7/22	6/15	9/19	8/15
12/8	10/25	1/31	12/19	3/29	2/17	5/26	4/17	7/23	6/16	9/20	8/16
12/9	10/26			3/30	2/18	5/27	4/18	7/24	6/17	9/21	8/17
12/10	10/27	2/1	12/20	3/31	2/19	5/28	4/19	7/25	6/18	9/22	8/18
12/11	10/28	2/2	12/21			5/29	4/20	7/26	6/19	9/23	8/19
12/12	10/29	2/3	12/22	4/1	2/20	5/30	4/21	7/27	6/20	9/24	8/20
12/13	10/30	2/4	12/23	4/2	2/21	5/31	4/22	7/28	6/21	9/25	8/21
12/14	11/1	2/5	12/24	4/3	2/22			7/29	6/22	9/26	8/22
12/15	11/2	2/6	12/25	4/4	2/23	6/1	4/23	7/30	6/23	9/27	8/23
12/16	11/3	2/7	12/26	4/5	2/24	6/2	4/24	7/31	6/24	9/28	8/24

Solar	Lunar	Solar	Lunar	Solar	Lunar	Solar	Lunar	Solar	Lunar	Solar	Lunar
9/29	8/25	11/26	10/24	1/18	12/17	3/16	2/15	5/13	4/14	7/10	6/13
9/30	8/26	11/27	10/25	1/19	12/18	3/17	2/16	5/14	4/15	7/11	6/14
		11/28	10/26	1/20	12/19	3/18	2/17	5/15	4/16	7/12	6/15
10/1	8/27	11/29	10/27	1/21	12/20	3/19	2/18	5/16	4/17	7/13	6/16
10/2	8/28	11/30	10/28	1/22	12/21	3/20	2/19	5/17	4/18	7/14	6/17
10/3	8/29			1/23	12/22	3/21	2/20	5/18	4/19	7/15	6/18
10/4	9/1	12/1	10/29	1/24	12/23	3/22	2/21	5/19	4/20	7/16	6/19
10/5	9/2	12/2	10/30	1/25	12/24	3/23	2/22	5/20	4/21	7/17	6/20
10/6	9/3	12/3	11/1	1/26	12/25	3/24	2/23	5/21	4/22	7/18	6/21
10/7	9/4	12/4	11/2	1/27	12/26	3/25	2/24	5/22	4/23	7/19	6/22
10/8	9/5	12/5	11/3	1/28	12/27	3/26	2/25	5/23	4/24	7/20	6/23
10/9	9/6	12/6	11/4	1/29	12/28	3/27	2/26	5/24	4/25	7/21	6/24
10/10	9/7	12/7	11/5	1/30	12/29	3/28	2/27	5/25	4/26	7/22	6/25
10/11	9/8	12/8	11/6	1/31	1/1	3/29	2/28	5/26	4/27	7/23	6/26
10/12	9/9	12/9	11/7		(1938)	3/30	2/29	5/27	4/28	7/24	6/27
10/13	9/10	12/10	11/8			3/31	2/30	5/28	4/29	7/25	6/28
10/14	9/11	12/11	11/9	2/1	1/2			5/29	5/1	7/26	6/29
10/15	9/12	12/12	11/10	2/2	1/3	4/1	3/1	5/30	5/2	7/27	7/1
10/16	9/13	12/13	11/11	2/3	1/4	4/2	3/2	5/31	5/3	7/28	7/2
10/17	9/14	12/14	11/12	2/4	1/5	4/3	3/3			7/29	7/3
10/18	9/15	12/15	11/13	2/5	1/6	4/4	3/4	6/1	5/4	7/30	7/4
10/19	9/16	12/16	11/14	2/6	1/7	4/5	3/5	6/2	5/5	7/31	7/5
10/20	9/17	12/17	11/15	2/7	1/8	4/6	3/6	6/3	5/6		
10/21	9/18	12/18	11/16	2/8	1/9	4/7	3/7	6/4	5/7	8/1	7/6
10/22	9/19	12/19	11/17	2/9	1/10	4/8	3/8	6/5	5/8	8/2	7/7
10/23	9/20	12/20	11/18	2/10	1/11	4/9	3/9	6/6	5/9	8/3	7/8
10/24	9/21	12/21	11/19	2/11	1/12	4/10	3/10	6/7	5/10	8/4	7/9
10/25	9/22	12/22	11/20	2/12	1/13	4/11	3/11	6/8	5/11	8/5	7/10
10/26	9/23	12/23	11/21	2/13	1/14	4/12	3/12	6/9	5/12	8/6	7/11
10/27	9/24	12/24	11/22	2/14	1/15	4/13	3/13	6/10	5/13	8/7	7/12
10/28	9/25	12/25	11/23	2/15	1/16	4/14	3/14	6/11	5/14	8/8	7/13
10/29	9/26	12/26	11/24	2/16	1/17	4/15	3/15	6/12	5/15	8/9	7/14
10/30	9/27	12/27	11/25	2/17	1/18	4/16	3/16	6/13	5/16	8/10	7/15
10/31	9/28	12/28	11/26	2/18	1/19	4/17	3/17	6/14	5/17	8/11	7/16
		12/29	11/27	2/19	1/20	4/18	3/18	6/15	5/18	8/12	7/17
11/1	9/29	12/30	11/28	2/20	1/21	4/19	3/19	6/16	5/19	8/13	7/18
11/2	9/30	12/31	11/29	2/21	1/22	4/20	3/20	6/17	5/20	8/14	7/19
11/3	10/1			2/22	1/23	4/21	3/21	6/18	5/21	8/15	7/20
11/4	10/2			2/23	1/24	4/22	3/22	6/19	5/22	8/16	7/21
11/5	10/3	Solar	Lunar	2/24	1/25	4/23	3/23	6/20	5/23	8/17	7/22
11/6	10/4	Date	Date	2/25	1/26	4/24	3/24	6/21	5/24	8/18	7/23
11/7	10/5	1938		2/26	1/27	4/25	3/25	6/22	5/25	8/19	7/24
11/8	10/6	1/1	30/11	2/27	1/28	4/26	3/26	6/23	5/26	8/20	7/25
11/9	10/7	1/2	12/1	2/28	1/29	4/27	3/27	6/24	5/27	8/21	7/26
11/10	10/8	1/3	12/2			4/28	3/28	6/25	5/28	8/22	7/27
11/11	10/9	1/4	12/3	3/1	1/30	4/29	3/29	6/26	5/29	8/23	7/28
11/12	10/10	1/5	12/4	3/2	2/1	4/30	4/1	6/27	5/30	8/24	7/29
11/13	10/11	1/6	12/5	3/3	2/2			6/28	6/1	8/25	7/1
11/14	10/12	1/7	12/6	3/4	2/3	5/1	4/2	6/29	6/2	(Leap Month)	
11/15	10/13	1/8	12/7	3/5	2/4	5/2	4/3	6/30	6/3	8/26	7/2
11/16	10/14	1/9	12/8	3/6	2/5	5/3	4/4			8/27	7/3
11/17	10/15	1/10	12/9	3/7	2/6	5/4	4/5	7/1	6/4	8/28	7/4
11/18	10/16	1/11	12/10	3/8	2/7	5/5	4/6	7/2	6/5	8/29	7/5
11/19	10/17	1/12	12/11	3/9	2/8	5/6	4/7	7/3	6/6	8/30	7/6
11/20	10/18	1/13	12/12	3/10	2/9	5/7	4/8	7/4	6/7	8/31	7/7
11/21	10/19	1/14	12/13	3/11	2/10	5/8	4/9	7/5	6/8		
11/22	10/20	1/15	12/14	3/12	2/11	5/9	4/10	7/6	6/9	9/1	7/8
11/23	10/21	1/16	12/15	3/13	2/12	5/10	4/11	7/7	6/10	9/2	7/9
11/24	10/22	1/17	12/16	3/14	2/13	5/11	4/12	7/8	6/11	9/3	7/10
11/25	10/23			3/15	2/14	5/12	4/13	7/9	6/12	9/4	7/11

Solar Date	Lunar Date	Solar Date	Lunar Date	Solar Date	Lunar Date	Solar Date	Lunar Date	Solar Date	Lunar Date	Solar Date	Lunar Date
9/5	7/12	11/2	9/11	12/31	11/10	2/21	1/3	4/20	3/1	6/17	5/1
9/6	7/13	11/3	9/12			2/22	1/4	4/21	3/2	6/18	5/2
9/7	7/14	11/4	9/13			2/23	1/5	4/22	3/3	6/19	5/3
9/8	7/15	11/5	9/14	**Solar**	**Lunar**	2/24	1/6	4/23	3/4	6/20	5/4
9/9	7/16	11/6	9/15	**Date**	**Date**	2/25	1/7	4/24	3/5	6/21	5/5
9/10	7/17	11/7	9/16			2/26	1/8	4/25	3/6	6/22	5/6
9/11	7/18	11/8	9/17	**1939**		2/27	1/9	4/26	3/7	6/23	5/7
9/12	7/19	11/9	9/18	1/1	11/11	2/28	1/10	4/27	3/8	6/24	5/8
9/13	7/20	11/10	9/19	1/2	11/12			4/28	3/9	6/25	5/9
9/14	7/21	11/11	9/20	1/3	11/13	3/1	1/11	4/29	3/10	6/26	5/10
9/15	7/22	11/12	9/21	1/4	11/14	3/2	1/12	4/30	3/11	6/27	5/11
9/16	7/23	11/13	9/22	1/5	11/15	3/3	1/13			6/28	5/12
9/17	7/24	11/14	9/23	1/6	11/16	3/4	1/14	5/1	3/12	6/29	5/13
9/18	7/25	11/15	9/24	1/7	11/17	3/5	1/15	5/2	3/13	6/30	5/14
9/19	7/26	11/16	9/25	1/8	11/18	3/6	1/16	5/3	3/14		
9/20	7/27	11/17	9/26	1/9	11/19	3/7	1/17	5/4	3/15	7/1	5/15
9/21	7/28	11/18	9/27	1/10	11/20	3/8	1/18	5/5	3/16	7/2	5/16
9/22	7/29	11/19	9/28	1/11	11/21	3/9	1/19	5/6	3/17	7/3	5/17
9/23	7/30	11/20	9/29	1/12	11/22	3/10	1/20	5/7	3/18	7/4	5/18
9/24	8/1	11/21	9/30	1/13	11/23	3/11	1/21	5/8	3/19	7/5	5/19
9/25	8/2	11/22	10/1	1/14	11/24	3/12	1/22	5/9	3/20	7/6	5/20
9/26	8/3	11/23	10/2	1/15	11/25	3/13	1/23	5/10	3/21	7/7	5/21
9/27	8/4	11/24	10/3	1/16	11/26	3/14	1/24	5/11	3/22	7/8	5/22
9/28	8/5	11/25	10/4	1/17	11/27	3/15	1/25	5/12	3/23	7/9	5/23
9/29	8/6	11/26	10/5	1/18	11/28	3/16	1/26	5/13	3/24	7/10	5/24
9/30	8/7	11/27	10/6	1/19	11/29	3/17	1/27	5/14	3/25	7/11	5/25
		11/28	10/7	1/20	12/1	3/18	1/28	5/15	3/26	7/12	5/26
10/1	8/8	11/29	10/8	1/21	12/2	3/19	1/29	5/16	3/27	7/13	5/27
10/2	8/9	11/30	10/9	1/22	12/3	3/20	1/30	5/17	3/28	7/14	5/28
10/3	8/10			1/23	12/4	3/21	2/1	5/18	3/29	7/15	5/29
10/4	8/11	12/1	10/10	1/24	12/5	3/22	2/2	5/19	4/1	7/16	5/30
10/5	8/12	12/2	10/11	1/25	12/6	3/23	2/3	5/20	4/2	7/17	6/1
10/6	8/13	12/3	10/12	1/26	12/7	3/24	2/4	5/21	4/3	7/18	6/2
10/7	8/14	12/4	10/13	1/27	12/8	3/25	2/5	5/22	4/4	7/19	6/3
10/8	8/15	12/5	10/14	1/28	12/9	3/26	2/6	5/23	4/5	7/20	6/4
10/9	8/16	12/6	10/15	1/29	12/10	3/27	2/7	5/24	4/6	7/21	6/5
10/10	8/17	12/7	10/16	1/30	12/11	3/28	2/8	5/25	4/7	7/22	6/6
10/11	8/18	12/8	10/17	1/31	12/12	3/29	2/9	5/26	4/8	7/23	6/7
10/12	8/19	12/9	10/18			3/30	2/10	5/27	4/9	7/24	6/8
10/13	8/20	12/10	10/19	2/1	12/13	3/31	2/11	5/28	4/10	7/25	6/9
10/14	8/21	12/11	10/20	2/2	12/14			5/29	4/11	7/26	6/10
10/15	8/22	12/12	10/21	2/3	12/15	4/1	2/12	5/30	4/12	7/27	6/11
10/16	8/23	12/13	10/22	2/4	12/16	4/2	2/13	5/31	4/13	7/28	6/12
10/17	8/24	12/14	10/23	2/5	12/17	4/3	2/14			7/29	6/13
10/18	8/25	12/15	10/24	2/6	12/18	4/4	2/15	6/1	4/14	7/30	6/14
10/19	8/26	12/16	10/25	2/7	12/19	4/5	2/16	6/2	4/15	7/31	6/15
10/20	8/27	12/17	10/26	2/8	12/20	4/6	2/17	6/3	4/16		
10/21	8/28	12/18	10/27	2/9	12/21	4/7	2/18	6/4	4/17	8/1	6/16
10/22	8/29	12/19	10/28	2/10	12/22	4/8	2/19	6/5	4/18	8/2	6/17
10/23	9/1	12/20	10/29	2/11	12/23	4/9	2/20	6/6	4/19	8/3	6/18
10/24	9/2	12/21	10/30	2/12	12/24	4/10	2/21	6/7	4/20	8/4	6/19
10/25	9/3	12/22	11/1	2/13	12/25	4/11	2/22	6/8	4/21	8/5	6/20
10/26	9/4	12/23	11/2	2/14	12/26	4/12	2/23	6/9	4/22	8/6	6/21
10/27	9/5	12/24	11/3	2/15	12/27	4/13	2/24	6/10	4/23	8/7	6/22
10/28	9/6	12/25	11/4	2/16	12/28	4/14	2/25	6/11	4/24	8/8	6/23
10/29	9/7	12/26	11/5	2/17	12/29	4/15	2/26	6/12	4/25	8/9	6/24
10/30	9/8	12/27	11/6	2/18	12/30	4/16	2/27	6/13	4/26	8/10	6/25
10/31	9/9	12/28	11/7	2/19	1/1 (1939)	4/17	2/28	6/14	4/27	8/11	6/26
		12/29	11/8			4/18	2/29	6/15	4/28	8/12	6/27
11/1	9/10	12/30	11/9	2/20	1/2	4/19	2/30	6/16	4/29	8/13	6/28

Solar	Lunar	Solar	Lunar	Solar	Lunar	Solar	Lunar	Solar	Lunar	Solar	Lunar
8/14	6/29	10/11	8/29	12/8	10/28	1/31	12/23	3/28	2/20	5/25	4/19
8/15	7/1	10/12	8/30	12/9	10/29			3/29	2/21	5/26	4/20
8/16	7/2	10/13	9/1	12/10	10/30	2/1	12/24	3/30	2/22	5/27	4/21
8/17	7/3	10/14	9/2	12/11	11/1	2/2	12/25	3/31	2/23	5/28	4/22
8/18	7/4	10/15	9/3	12/12	11/2	2/3	12/26			5/29	4/23
8/19	7/5	10/16	9/4	12/13	11/3	2/4	12/27	4/1	2/24	5/30	4/24
8/20	7/6	10/17	9/5	12/14	11/4	2/5	12/28	4/2	2/25	5/31	4/25
8/21	7/7	10/18	9/6	12/15	11/5	2/6	12/29	4/3	2/26		
8/22	7/8	10/19	9/7	12/16	11/6	2/7	12/30	4/4	2/27	6/1	4/26
8/23	7/9	10/20	9/8	12/17	11/7	2/8	1/1	4/5	2/28	6/2	4/27
8/24	7/10	10/21	9/9	12/18	11/8		(1940)	4/6	2/29	6/3	4/28
8/25	7/11	10/22	9/10	12/19	11/9	2/9	1/2	4/7	2/30	6/4	4/29
8/26	7/12	10/23	9/11	12/20	11/10	2/10	1/3	4/8	3/1	6/5	4/30
8/27	7/13	10/24	9/12	12/21	11/11	2/11	1/4	4/9	3/2	6/6	5/1
8/28	7/14	10/25	9/13	12/22	11/12	2/12	1/5	4/10	3/3	6/7	5/2
8/29	7/15	10/26	9/14	12/23	11/13	2/13	1/6	4/11	3/4	6/8	5/3
8/30	7/16	10/27	9/15	12/24	11/14	2/14	1/7	4/12	3/5	6/9	5/4
8/31	7/17	10/28	9/16	12/25	11/15	2/15	1/8	4/13	3/6	6/10	5/5
		10/29	9/17	12/26	11/16	2/16	1/9	4/14	3/7	6/11	5/6
9/1	7/18	10/30	9/18	12/27	11/17	2/17	1/10	4/15	3/8	6/12	5/7
9/2	7/19	10/31	9/19	12/28	11/18	2/18	1/11	4/16	3/9	6/13	5/8
9/3	7/20			12/29	11/19	2/19	1/12	4/17	3/10	6/14	5/9
9/4	7/21	11/1	9/20	12/30	11/20	2/20	1/13	4/18	3/11	6/15	5/10
9/5	7/22	11/2	9/21	12/31	11/21	2/21	1/14	4/19	3/12	6/16	5/11
9/6	7/23	11/3	9/22			2/22	1/15	4/20	3/13	6/17	5/12
9/7	7/24	11/4	9/23			2/23	1/16	4/21	3/14	6/18	5/13
9/8	7/25	11/5	9/24	**Solar**	**Lunar**	2/24	1/17	4/22	3/15	6/19	5/14
9/9	7/26	11/6	9/25	**Date**	**Date**	2/25	1/18	4/23	3/16	6/20	5/15
9/10	7/27	11/7	9/26			2/26	1/19	4/24	3/17	6/21	5/16
9/11	7/28	11/8	9/27	**1940**		2/27	1/20	4/25	3/18	6/22	5/17
9/12	7/29	11/9	9/28	1/1	11/22	2/28	1/21	4/26	3/19	6/23	5/18
9/13	8/1	11/10	9/29	1/2	11/23	2/29	1/22	4/27	3/20	6/24	5/19
9/14	8/2	11/11	10/1	1/3	11/24			4/28	3/21	6/25	5/20
9/15	8/3	11/12	10/2	1/4	11/25	3/1	1/23	4/29	3/22	6/26	5/21
9/16	8/4	11/13	10/3	1/5	11/26	3/2	1/24	4/30	3/23	6/27	5/22
9/17	8/5	11/14	10/4	1/6	11/27	3/3	1/25			6/28	5/23
9/18	8/6	11/15	10/5	1/7	11/28	3/4	1/26	5/1	3/24	6/29	5/24
9/19	8/7	11/16	10/6	1/8	11/29	3/5	1/27	5/2	3/25	6/30	5/25
9/20	8/8	11/17	10/7	1/9	12/1	3/6	1/28	5/3	3/26		
9/21	8/9	11/18	10/8	1/10	12/2	3/7	1/29	5/4	3/27	7/1	5/26
9/22	8/10	11/19	10/9	1/11	12/3	3/8	1/30	5/5	3/28	7/2	5/27
9/23	8/11	11/20	10/10	1/12	12/4	3/9	2/1	5/6	3/29	7/3	5/28
9/24	8/12	11/21	10/11	1/13	12/5	3/10	2/2	5/7	4/1	7/4	5/29
9/25	8/13	11/22	10/12	1/14	12/6	3/11	2/3	5/8	4/2	7/5	6/1
9/26	8/14	11/23	10/13	1/15	12/7	3/12	2/4	5/9	4/3	7/6	6/2
9/27	8/15	11/24	10/14	1/16	12/8	3/13	2/5	5/10	4/4	7/7	6/3
9/28	8/16	11/25	10/15	1/17	12/9	3/14	2/6	5/11	4/5	7/8	6/4
9/29	8/17	11/26	10/16	1/18	12/10	3/15	2/7	5/12	4/6	7/9	6/5
9/30	8/18	11/27	10/17	1/19	12/11	3/16	2/8	5/13	4/7	7/10	6/6
		11/28	10/18	1/20	12/12	3/17	2/9	5/14	4/8	7/11	6/7
10/1	8/19	11/29	10/19	1/21	12/13	3/18	2/10	5/15	4/9	7/12	6/8
10/2	8/20	11/30	10/20	1/22	12/14	3/19	2/11	5/16	4/10	7/13	6/9
10/3	8/21			1/23	12/15	3/20	2/12	5/17	4/11	7/14	6/10
10/4	8/22	12/1	10/21	1/24	12/16	3/21	2/13	5/18	4/12	7/15	6/11
10/5	8/23	12/2	10/22	1/25	12/17	3/22	2/14	5/19	4/13	7/16	6/12
10/6	8/24	12/3	10/23	1/26	12/18	3/23	2/15	5/20	4/14	7/17	6/13
10/7	8/25	12/4	10/24	1/27	12/19	3/24	2/16	5/21	4/15	7/18	6/14
10/8	8/26	12/5	10/25	1/28	12/20	3/25	2/17	5/22	4/16	7/19	6/15
10/9	8/27	12/6	10/26	1/29	12/21	3/26	2/18	5/23	4/17	7/20	6/16
10/10	8/28	12/7	10/27	1/30	12/22	3/27	2/19	5/24	4/18	7/21	6/17

Solar	Lunar	Solar	Lunar	Solar	Lunar	Solar	Lunar	Solar	Lunar	Solar	Lunar
7/22	6/18	9/18	8/17	11/15	10/16	1/7	12/10	3/5	2/8	5/2	4/7
7/23	6/19	9/19	8/18	11/16	10/17	1/8	12/11	3/6	2/9	5/3	4/8
7/24	6/20	9/20	8/19	11/17	10/18	1/9	12/12	3/7	2/10	5/4	4/9
7/25	6/21	9/21	8/20	11/18	10/19	1/10	12/13	3/8	2/11	5/5	4/10
7/26	6/22	9/22	8/21	11/19	10/20	1/11	12/14	3/9	2/12	5/6	4/11
7/27	6/23	9/23	8/22	11/20	10/21	1/12	12/15	3/10	2/13	5/7	4/12
7/28	6/24	9/24	8/23	11/21	10/22	1/13	12/16	3/11	2/14	5/8	4/13
7/29	6/25	9/25	8/24	11/22	10/23	1/14	12/17	3/12	2/15	5/9	4/14
7/30	6/26	9/26	8/25	11/23	10/24	1/15	12/18	3/13	2/16	5/10	4/15
7/31	6/27	9/27	8/26	11/24	10/25	1/16	12/19	3/14	2/17	5/11	4/16
		9/28	8/27	11/25	10/26	1/17	12/20	3/15	2/18	5/12	4/17
8/1	6/28	9/29	8/28	11/26	10/27	1/18	12/21	3/16	2/19	5/13	4/18
8/2	6/29	9/30	8/29	11/27	10/28	1/19	12/22	3/17	2/20	5/14	4/19
8/3	6/30			11/28	10/29	1/20	12/23	3/18	2/21	5/15	4/20
8/4	7/1	10/1	9/1	11/29	11/1	1/21	12/24	3/19	2/22	5/16	4/21
8/5	7/2	10/2	9/2	11/30	11/2	1/22	12/25	3/20	2/23	5/17	4/22
8/6	7/3	10/3	9/3			1/23	12/26	3/21	2/24	5/18	4/23
8/7	7/4	10/4	9/4	12/1	11/3	1/24	12/27	3/22	2/25	5/19	4/24
8/8	7/5	10/5	9/5	12/2	11/4	1/25	12/28	3/23	2/26	5/20	4/25
8/9	7/6	10/6	9/6	12/3	11/5	1/26	12/29	3/24	2/27	5/21	4/26
8/10	7/7	10/7	9/7	12/4	11/6	1/27	1/1	3/25	2/28	5/22	4/27
8/11	7/8	10/8	9/8	12/5	11/7		(1941)	3/26	2/29	5/23	4/28
8/12	7/9	10/9	9/9	12/6	11/8	1/28	1/2	3/27	2/30	5/24	4/29
8/13	7/10	10/10	9/10	12/7	11/9	1/29	1/3	3/28	3/1	5/25	4/30
8/14	7/11	10/11	9/11	12/8	11/10	1/30	1/4	3/29	3/2	5/26	5/1
8/15	7/12	10/12	9/12	12/9	11/11	1/31	1/5	3/30	3/3	5/27	5/2
8/16	7/13	10/13	9/13	12/10	11/12			3/31	3/4	5/28	5/3
8/17	7/14	10/14	9/14	12/11	11/13	2/1	1/6			5/29	5/4
8/18	7/15	10/15	9/15	12/12	11/14	2/2	1/7	4/1	3/5	5/30	5/5
8/19	7/16	10/16	9/16	12/13	11/15	2/3	1/8	4/2	3/6	5/31	5/6
8/20	7/17	10/17	9/17	12/14	11/16	2/4	1/9	4/3	3/7		
8/21	7/18	10/18	9/18	12/15	11/17	2/5	1/10	4/4	3/8	6/1	5/7
8/22	7/19	10/19	9/19	12/16	11/18	2/6	1/11	4/5	3/9	6/2	5/8
8/23	7/20	10/20	9/20	12/17	11/19	2/7	1/12	4/6	3/10	6/3	5/9
8/24	7/21	10/21	9/21	12/18	11/20	2/8	1/13	4/7	3/11	6/4	5/10
8/25	7/22	10/22	9/22	12/19	11/21	2/9	1/14	4/8	3/12	6/5	5/11
8/26	7/23	10/23	9/23	12/20	11/22	2/10	1/15	4/9	3/13	6/6	5/12
8/27	7/24	10/24	9/24	12/21	11/23	2/11	1/16	4/10	3/14	6/7	5/13
8/28	7/25	10/25	9/25	12/22	11/24	2/12	1/17	4/11	3/15	6/8	5/14
8/29	7/26	10/26	9/26	12/23	11/25	2/13	1/18	4/12	3/16	6/9	5/15
8/30	7/27	10/27	9/27	12/24	11/26	2/14	1/19	4/13	3/17	6/10	5/16
8/31	7/28	10/28	9/28	12/25	11/27	2/15	1/20	4/14	3/18	6/11	5/17
		10/29	9/29	12/26	11/28	2/16	1/21	4/15	3/19	6/12	5/18
9/1	7/29	10/30	9/30	12/27	11/29	2/17	1/22	4/16	3/20	6/13	5/19
9/2	8/1	10/31	10/1	12/28	11/30	2/18	1/23	4/17	3/21	6/14	5/20
9/3	8/2			12/29	12/1	2/19	1/24	4/18	3/22	6/15	5/21
9/4	8/3	11/1	10/2	12/30	12/2	2/20	1/25	4/19	3/23	6/16	5/22
9/5	8/4	11/2	10/3	12/31	12/3	2/21	1/26	4/20	3/24	6/17	5/23
9/6	8/5	11/3	10/4			2/22	1/27	4/21	3/25	6/18	5/24
9/7	8/6	11/4	10/5			2/23	1/28	4/22	3/26	6/19	5/25
9/8	8/7	11/5	10/6	Solar	Lunar	2/24	1/29	4/23	3/27	6/20	5/26
9/9	8/8	11/6	10/7	Date	Date	2/25	1/30	4/24	3/28	6/21	5/27
9/10	8/9	11/7	10/8			2/26	2/1	4/25	3/29	6/22	5/28
9/11	8/10	11/8	10/9	1941		2/27	2/2	4/26	4/1	6/23	5/29
9/12	8/11	11/9	10/10	1/1	12/4	2/28	2/3	4/27	4/2	6/24	5/30
9/13	8/12	11/10	10/11	1/2	12/5			4/28	4/3	6/25	6/1
9/14	8/13	11/11	10/12	1/3	12/6	3/1	2/4	4/29	4/4	6/26	6/2
9/15	8/14	11/12	10/13	1/4	12/7	3/2	2/5	4/30	4/5	6/27	6/3
9/16	8/15	11/13	10/14	1/5	12/8	3/3	2/6			6/28	6/4
9/17	8/16	11/14	10/15	1/6	12/9	3/4	2/7	5/1	4/6	6/29	6/5

6/30	6/6	8/26	7/4	10/23	9/4	12/20	11/3	2/11	12/26	4/9	2/24
		8/27	7/5	10/24	9/5	12/21	11/4	2/12	12/27	4/10	2/25
7/1	6/7	8/28	7/6	10/25	9/6	12/22	11/5	2/13	12/28	4/11	2/26
7/2	6/8	8/29	7/7	10/26	9/7	12/23	11/6	2/14	12/29	4/12	2/27
7/3	6/9	8/30	7/8	10/27	9/8	12/24	11/7	2/15	1/1	4/13	2/28
7/4	6/10	8/31	7/9	10/28	9/9	12/25	11/8		(1942)	4/14	2/29
7/5	6/11			10/29	9/10	12/26	11/9	2/16	1/2	4/15	3/1
7/6	6/12	9/1	7/10	10/30	9/11	12/27	11/10	2/17	1/3	4/16	3/2
7/7	6/13	9/2	7/11	10/31	9/12	12/28	11/11	2/18	1/4	4/17	3/3
7/8	6/14	9/3	7/12			12/29	11/12	2/19	1/5	4/18	3/4
7/9	6/15	9/4	7/13	11/1	9/13	12/30	11/13	2/20	1/6	4/19	3/5
7/10	6/16	9/5	7/14	11/2	9/14	12/31	11/14	2/21	1/7	4/20	3/6
7/11	6/17	9/6	7/15	11/3	9/15			2/22	1/8	4/21	3/7
7/12	6/18	9/7	7/16	11/4	9/16			2/23	1/9	4/22	3/8
7/13	6/19	9/8	7/17	11/5	9/17	**Solar**	**Lunar**	2/24	1/10	4/23	3/9
7/14	6/20	9/9	7/18	11/6	9/18	**Date**	**Date**	2/25	1/11	4/24	3/10
7/15	6/21	9/10	7/19	11/7	9/19			2/26	1/12	4/25	3/11
7/16	6/22	9/11	7/20	11/8	9/20	**1942**		2/27	1/13	4/26	3/12
7/17	6/23	9/12	7/21	11/9	9/21	1/1	11/15	2/28	1/14	4/27	3/13
7/18	6/24	9/13	7/22	11/10	9/22	1/2	11/16			4/28	3/14
7/19	6/25	9/14	7/23	11/11	9/23	1/3	11/17	3/1	1/15	4/29	3/15
7/20	6/26	9/15	7/24	11/12	9/24	1/4	11/18	3/2	1/16	4/30	3/16
7/21	6/27	9/16	7/25	11/13	9/25	1/5	11/19	3/3	1/17		
7/22	6/28	9/17	7/26	11/14	9/26	1/6	11/20	3/4	1/18	5/1	3/17
7/23	6/29	9/18	7/27	11/15	9/27	1/7	11/21	3/5	1/19	5/2	3/18
7/24	6/1	9/19	7/28	11/16	9/28	1/8	11/22	3/6	1/20	5/3	3/19
(Leap Month)		9/20	7/29	11/17	9/29	1/9	11/23	3/7	1/21	5/4	3/20
7/25	6/2	9/21	8/1	11/18	9/30	1/10	11/24	3/8	1/22	5/5	3/21
7/26	6/3	9/22	8/2	11/19	10/1	1/11	11/25	3/9	1/23	5/6	3/22
7/27	6/4	9/23	8/3	11/20	10/2	1/12	11/26	3/10	1/24	5/7	3/23
7/28	6/5	9/24	8/4	11/21	10/3	1/13	11/27	3/11	1/25	5/8	3/24
7/29	6/6	9/25	8/5	11/22	10/4	1/14	11/28	3/12	1/26	5/9	3/25
7/30	6/7	9/26	8/6	11/23	10/5	1/15	11/29	3/13	1/27	5/10	3/26
7/31	6/8	9/27	8/7	11/24	10/6	1/16	11/30	3/14	1/28	5/11	3/27
		9/28	8/8	11/25	10/7	1/17	12/1	3/15	1/29	5/12	3/28
8/1	6/9	9/29	8/9	11/26	10/8	1/18	12/2	3/16	1/30	5/13	3/29
8/2	6/10	9/30	8/10	11/27	10/9	1/19	12/3	3/17	2/1	5/14	3/30
8/3	6/11			11/28	10/10	1/20	12/4	3/18	2/2	5/15	4/1
8/4	6/12	10/1	8/11	11/29	10/11	1/21	12/5	3/19	2/3	5/16	4/2
8/5	6/13	10/2	8/12	11/30	10/12	1/22	12/6	3/20	2/4	5/17	4/3
8/6	6/14	10/3	8/13			1/23	12/7	3/21	2/5	5/18	4/4
8/7	6/15	10/4	8/14	12/1	10/13	1/24	12/8	3/22	2/6	5/19	4/5
8/8	6/16	10/5	8/15	12/2	10/14	1/25	12/9	3/23	2/7	5/20	4/6
8/9	6/17	10/6	8/16	12/3	10/15	1/26	12/10	3/24	2/8	5/21	4/7
8/10	6/18	10/7	8/17	12/4	10/16	1/27	12/11	3/25	2/9	5/22	4/8
8/11	6/19	10/8	8/18	12/5	10/17	1/28	12/12	3/26	2/10	5/23	4/9
8/12	6/20	10/9	8/19	12/6	10/18	1/29	12/13	3/27	2/11	5/24	4/10
8/13	6/21	10/10	8/20	12/7	10/19	1/30	12/14	3/28	2/12	5/25	4/11
8/14	6/22	10/11	8/21	12/8	10/20	1/31	12/15	3/29	2/13	5/26	4/12
8/15	6/23	10/12	8/22	12/9	10/21			3/30	2/14	5/27	4/13
8/16	6/24	10/13	8/23	12/10	10/22	2/1	12/16	3/31	2/15	5/28	4/14
8/17	6/25	10/14	8/24	12/11	10/23	2/2	12/17			5/29	4/15
8/18	6/26	10/15	8/25	12/12	10/24	2/3	12/18	4/1	2/16	5/30	4/16
8/19	6/27	10/16	8/26	12/13	10/25	2/4	12/19	4/2	2/17	5/31	4/17
8/20	6/28	10/17	8/27	12/14	10/26	2/5	12/20	4/3	2/18		
8/21	6/29	10/18	8/28	12/15	10/27	2/6	12/21	4/4	2/19	6/1	4/18
8/22	6/30	10/19	8/29	12/16	10/28	2/7	12/22	4/5	2/20	6/2	4/19
8/23	7/1	10/20	9/1	12/17	10/29	2/8	12/23	4/6	2/21	6/3	4/20
8/24	7/2	10/21	9/2	12/18	11/1	2/9	12/24	4/7	2/22	6/4	4/21
8/25	7/3	10/22	9/3	12/19	11/2	2/10	12/25	4/8	2/23	6/5	4/22

Solar	Lunar	Solar	Lunar	Solar	Lunar	Solar	Lunar	Solar	Lunar	Solar	Lunar
6/6	4/23	8/3	6/22	10/1	8/22	11/29	10/22	1/21	12/16	3/19	2/14
6/7	4/24	8/4	6/23	10/2	8/23	11/30	10/23	1/22	12/17	3/20	2/15
6/8	4/25	8/5	6/24	10/3	8/24			1/23	12/18	3/21	2/16
6/9	4/26	8/6	6/25	10/4	8/25	12/1	10/24	1/24	12/19	3/22	2/17
6/10	4/27	8/7	6/26	10/5	8/26	12/2	10/25	1/25	12/20	3/23	2/18
6/11	4/28	8/8	6/27	10/6	8/27	12/3	10/26	1/26	12/21	3/24	2/19
6/12	4/29	8/9	6/28	10/7	8/28	12/4	10/27	1/27	12/22	3/25	2/20
6/13	4/30	8/10	6/29	10/8	8/29	12/5	10/28	1/28	12/23	3/26	2/21
6/14	5/1	8/11	6/30	10/9	8/30	12/6	10/29	1/29	12/24	3/27	2/22
6/15	5/2	8/12	7/1	10/10	9/1	12/7	10/30	1/30	12/25	3/28	2/23
6/16	5/3	8/13	7/2	10/11	9/2	12/8	11/1	1/31	12/26	3/29	2/24
6/17	5/4	8/14	7/3	10/12	9/3	12/9	11/2			3/30	2/25
6/18	5/5	8/15	7/4	10/13	9/4	12/10	11/3	2/1	12/27	3/31	2/26
6/19	5/6	8/16	7/5	10/14	9/5	12/11	11/4	2/2	12/28		
6/20	5/7	8/17	7/6	10/15	9/6	12/12	11/5	2/3	12/29	4/1	2/27
6/21	5/8	8/18	7/7	10/16	9/7	12/13	11/6	2/4	12/30	4/2	2/28
6/22	5/9	8/19	7/8	10/17	9/8	12/14	11/7	2/5	1/1	4/3	2/29
6/23	5/10	8/20	7/9	10/18	9/9	12/15	11/8		(1943)	4/4	2/30
6/24	5/11	8/21	7/10	10/19	9/10	12/16	11/9	2/6	1/2	4/5	3/1
6/25	5/12	8/22	7/11	10/20	9/11	12/17	11/10	2/7	1/3	4/6	3/2
6/26	5/13	8/23	7/12	10/21	9/12	12/18	11/11	2/8	1/4	4/7	3/3
6/27	5/14	8/24	7/13	10/22	9/13	12/19	11/12	2/9	1/5	4/8	3/4
6/28	5/15	8/25	7/14	10/23	9/14	12/20	11/13	2/10	1/6	4/9	3/5
6/29	5/16	8/26	7/15	10/24	9/15	12/21	11/14	2/11	1/7	4/10	3/6
6/30	5/17	8/27	7/16	10/25	9/16	12/22	11/15	2/12	1/8	4/11	3/7
		8/28	7/17	10/26	9/17	12/23	11/16	2/13	1/9	4/12	3/8
7/1	5/18	8/29	7/18	10/27	9/18	12/24	11/17	2/14	1/10	4/13	3/9
7/2	5/19	8/30	7/19	10/28	9/19	12/25	11/18	2/15	1/11	4/14	3/10
7/3	5/20	8/31	7/20	10/29	9/20	12/26	11/19	2/16	1/12	4/15	3/11
7/4	5/21			10/30	9/21	12/27	11/20	2/17	1/13	4/16	3/12
7/5	5/22	9/1	7/21	10/31	9/22	12/28	11/21	2/18	1/14	4/17	3/13
7/6	5/23	9/2	7/22			12/29	11/22	2/19	1/15	4/18	3/14
7/7	5/24	9/3	7/23	11/1	9/23	12/30	11/23	2/20	1/16	4/19	3/15
7/8	5/25	9/4	7/24	11/2	9/24	12/31	11/24	2/21	1/17	4/20	3/16
7/9	5/26	9/5	7/25	11/3	9/25			2/22	1/18	4/21	3/17
7/10	5/27	9/6	7/26	11/4	9/26			2/23	1/19	4/22	3/18
7/11	5/28	9/7	7/27	11/5	9/27	Solar	Lunar	2/24	1/20	4/23	3/19
7/12	5/29	9/8	7/28	11/6	9/28	Date	Date	2/25	1/21	4/24	3/20
7/13	6/1	9/9	7/29	11/7	9/29	1943		2/26	1/22	4/25	3/21
7/14	6/2	9/10	8/1	11/8	10/1	1/1	11/25	2/27	1/23	4/26	3/22
7/15	6/3	9/11	8/2	11/9	10/2	1/2	11/26	2/28	1/24	4/27	3/23
7/16	6/4	9/12	8/3	11/10	10/3	1/3	11/27			4/28	3/24
7/17	6/5	9/13	8/4	11/11	10/4	1/4	11/28	3/1	1/25	4/29	3/25
7/18	6/6	9/14	8/5	11/12	10/5	1/5	11/29	3/2	1/26	4/30	3/26
7/19	6/7	9/15	8/6	11/13	10/6	1/6	12/1	3/3	1/27		
7/20	6/8	9/16	8/7	11/14	10/7	1/7	12/2	3/4	1/28	5/1	3/27
7/21	6/9	9/17	8/8	11/15	10/8	1/8	12/3	3/5	1/29	5/2	3/28
7/22	6/10	9/18	8/9	11/16	10/9	1/9	12/4	3/6	2/1	5/3	3/29
7/23	6/11	9/19	8/10	11/17	10/10	1/10	12/5	3/7	2/2	5/4	4/1
7/24	6/12	9/20	8/11	11/18	10/11	1/11	12/6	3/8	2/3	5/5	4/2
7/25	6/13	9/21	8/12	11/19	10/12	1/12	12/7	3/9	2/4	5/6	4/3
7/26	6/14	9/22	8/13	11/20	10/13	1/13	12/8	3/10	2/5	5/7	4/4
7/27	6/15	9/23	8/14	11/21	10/14	1/14	12/9	3/11	2/6	5/8	4/5
7/28	6/16	9/24	8/15	11/22	10/15	1/15	12/10	3/12	2/7	5/9	4/6
7/29	6/17	9/25	8/16	11/23	10/16	1/16	12/11	3/13	2/8	5/10	4/7
7/30	6/18	9/26	8/17	11/24	10/17	1/17	12/12	3/14	2/9	5/11	4/8
7/31	6/19	9/27	8/18	11/25	10/18	1/18	12/13	3/15	2/10	5/12	4/9
		9/28	8/19	11/26	10/19	1/19	12/14	3/16	2/11	5/13	4/10
8/1	6/20	9/29	8/20	11/27	10/20	1/20	12/15	3/17	2/12	5/14	4/11
8/2	6/21	9/30	8/21	11/28	10/21			3/18	2/13	5/15	4/12

Solar	Lunar	Solar	Lunar	Solar	Lunar	Solar	Lunar	Solar Date	Lunar Date	Solar	Lunar
5/16	4/13	7/13	6/12	9/9	8/10	11/6	10/9	Solar	Lunar	2/24	2/1
5/17	4/14	7/14	6/13	9/10	8/11	11/7	10/10	Date	Date	2/25	2/2
5/18	4/15	7/15	6/14	9/11	8/12	11/8	10/11	1944		2/26	2/3
5/19	4/16	7/16	6/15	9/12	8/13	11/9	10/12			2/27	2/4
5/20	4/17	7/17	6/16	9/13	8/14	11/10	10/13	1/1	12/6	2/28	2/5
5/21	4/18	7/18	6/17	9/14	8/15	11/11	10/14	1/2	12/7	2/29	2/6
5/22	4/19	7/19	6/18	9/15	8/16	11/12	10/15	1/3	12/8		
5/23	4/20	7/20	6/19	9/16	8/17	11/13	10/16	1/4	12/9	3/1	2/7
5/24	4/21	7/21	6/20	9/17	8/18	11/14	10/17	1/5	12/10	3/2	2/8
5/25	4/22	7/22	6/21	9/18	8/19	11/15	10/18	1/6	12/11	3/3	2/9
5/26	4/23	7/23	6/22	9/19	8/20	11/16	10/19	1/7	12/12	3/4	2/10
5/27	4/24	7/24	6/23	9/20	8/21	11/17	10/20	1/8	12/13	3/5	2/11
5/28	4/25	7/25	6/24	9/21	8/22	11/18	10/21	1/9	12/14	3/6	2/12
5/29	4/26	7/26	6/25	9/22	8/23	11/19	10/22	1/10	12/15	3/7	2/13
5/30	4/27	7/27	6/26	9/23	8/24	11/20	10/23	1/11	12/16	3/8	2/14
5/31	4/28	7/28	6/27	9/24	8/25	11/21	10/24	1/12	12/17	3/9	2/15
		7/29	6/28	9/25	8/26	11/22	10/25	1/13	12/18	3/10	2/16
6/1	4/29	7/30	6/29	9/26	8/27	11/23	10/26	1/14	12/19	3/11	2/17
6/2	4/30	7/31	6/30	9/27	8/28	11/24	10/27	1/15	12/20	3/12	2/18
6/3	5/1			9/28	8/29	11/25	10/28	1/16	12/21	3/13	2/19
6/4	5/2	8/1	7/1	9/29	9/1	11/26	10/29	1/17	12/22	3/14	2/20
6/5	5/3	8/2	7/2	9/30	9/2	11/27	11/1	1/18	12/23	3/15	2/21
6/6	5/4	8/3	7/3			11/28	11/2	1/19	12/24	3/16	2/22
6/7	5/5	8/4	7/4	10/1	9/3	11/29	11/3	1/20	12/25	3/17	2/23
6/8	5/6	8/5	7/5	10/2	9/4	11/30	11/4	1/21	12/26	3/18	2/24
6/9	5/7	8/6	7/6	10/3	9/5			1/22	12/27	3/19	2/25
6/10	5/8	8/7	7/7	10/4	9/6	12/1	11/5	1/23	12/28	3/20	2/26
6/11	5/9	8/8	7/8	10/5	9/7	12/2	11/6	1/24	12/29	3/21	2/27
6/12	5/10	8/9	7/9	10/6	9/8	12/3	11/7	1/25	1/1	3/22	2/28
6/13	5/11	8/10	7/10	10/7	9/9	12/4	11/8		(1944)	3/23	2/29
6/14	5/12	8/11	7/11	10/8	9/10	12/5	11/9	1/26	1/2	3/24	3/1
6/15	5/13	8/12	7/12	10/9	9/11	12/6	11/10	1/27	1/3	3/25	3/2
6/16	5/14	8/13	7/13	10/10	9/12	12/7	11/11	1/28	1/4	3/26	3/3
6/17	5/15	8/14	7/14	10/11	9/13	12/8	11/12	1/29	1/5	3/27	3/4
6/18	5/16	8/15	7/15	10/12	9/14	12/9	11/13	1/30	1/6	3/28	3/5
6/19	5/17	8/16	7/16	10/13	9/15	12/10	11/14	1/31	1/7	3/29	3/6
6/20	5/18	8/17	7/17	10/14	9/16	12/11	11/15			3/30	3/7
6/21	5/19	8/18	7/18	10/15	9/17	12/12	11/16	2/1	1/8	3/31	3/8
6/22	5/20	8/19	7/19	10/16	9/18	12/13	11/17	2/2	1/9		
6/23	5/21	8/20	7/20	10/17	9/19	12/14	11/18	2/3	1/10	4/1	3/9
6/24	5/22	8/21	7/21	10/18	9/20	12/15	11/19	2/4	1/11	4/2	3/10
6/25	5/23	8/22	7/22	10/19	9/21	12/16	11/20	2/5	1/12	4/3	3/11
6/26	5/24	8/23	7/23	10/20	9/22	12/17	11/21	2/6	1/13	4/4	3/12
6/27	5/25	8/24	7/24	10/21	9/23	12/18	11/22	2/7	1/14	4/5	3/13
6/28	5/26	8/25	7/25	10/22	9/24	12/19	11/23	2/8	1/15	4/6	3/14
6/29	5/27	8/26	7/26	10/23	9/25	12/20	11/24	2/9	1/16	4/7	3/15
6/30	5/28	8/27	7/27	10/24	9/26	12/21	11/25	2/10	1/17	4/8	3/16
		8/28	7/28	10/25	9/27	12/22	11/26	2/11	1/18	4/9	3/17
7/1	5/29	8/29	7/29	10/26	9/28	12/23	11/27	2/12	1/19	4/10	3/18
7/2	6/1	8/30	7/30	10/27	9/29	12/24	11/28	2/13	1/20	4/11	3/19
7/3	6/2	8/31	8/1	10/28	9/30	12/25	11/29	2/14	1/21	4/12	3/20
7/4	6/3			10/29	10/1	12/26	11/30	2/15	1/22	4/13	3/21
7/5	6/4	9/1	8/2	10/30	10/2	12/27	12/1	2/16	1/23	4/14	3/22
7/6	6/5	9/2	8/3	10/31	10/3	12/28	12/2	2/17	1/24	4/15	3/23
7/7	6/6	9/3	8/4			12/29	12/3	2/18	1/25	4/16	3/24
7/8	6/7	9/4	8/5	11/1	10/4	12/30	12/4	2/19	1/26	4/17	3/25
7/9	6/8	9/5	8/6	11/2	10/5	12/31	12/5	2/20	1/27	4/18	3/26
7/10	6/9	9/6	8/7	11/3	10/6			2/21	1/28	4/19	3/27
7/11	6/10	9/7	8/8	11/4	10/7			2/22	1/29	4/20	3/28
7/12	6/11	9/8	8/9	11/5	10/8			2/23	1/30	4/21	3/29

Solar	Lunar		Solar	Lunar		Solar	Lunar
4/22	3/30		6/18	4/28		8/15	6/27
4/23	4/1		6/19	4/29		8/16	6/28
4/24	4/2		6/20	4/30		8/17	6/29
4/25	4/3		6/21	5/1		8/18	6/30
4/26	4/4		6/22	5/2		8/19	7/1
4/27	4/5		6/23	5/3		8/20	7/2
4/28	4/6		6/24	5/4		8/21	7/3
4/29	4/7		6/25	5/5		8/22	7/4
4/30	4/8		6/26	5/6		8/23	7/5
			6/27	5/7		8/24	7/6
5/1	4/9		6/28	5/8		8/25	7/7
5/2	4/10		6/29	5/9		8/26	7/8
5/3	4/11		6/30	5/10		8/27	7/9
5/4	4/12					8/28	7/10
5/5	4/13		7/1	5/11		8/29	7/11
5/6	4/14		7/2	5/12		8/30	7/12
5/7	4/15		7/3	5/13		8/31	7/13
5/8	4/16		7/4	5/14			
5/9	4/17		7/5	5/15		9/1	7/14
5/10	4/18		7/6	5/16		9/2	7/15
5/11	4/19		7/7	5/17		9/3	7/16
5/12	4/20		7/8	5/18		9/4	7/17
5/13	4/21		7/9	5/19		9/5	7/18
5/14	4/22		7/10	5/20		9/6	7/19
5/15	4/23		7/11	5/21		9/7	7/20
5/16	4/24		7/12	5/22		9/8	7/21
5/17	4/25		7/13	5/23		9/9	7/22
5/18	4/26		7/14	5/24		9/10	7/23
5/19	4/27		7/15	5/25		9/11	7/24
5/20	4/28		7/16	5/26		9/12	7/25
5/21	4/29		7/17	5/27		9/13	7/26
5/22	4/1		7/18	5/28		9/14	7/27
(Leap Month)			7/19	5/29		9/15	7/28
5/23	4/2		7/20	6/1		9/16	7/29
5/24	4/3		7/21	6/2		9/17	8/1
5/25	4/4		7/22	6/3		9/18	8/2
5/26	4/5		7/23	6/4		9/19	8/3
5/27	4/6		7/24	6/5		9/20	8/4
5/28	4/7		7/25	6/6		9/21	8/5
5/29	4/8		7/26	6/7		9/22	8/6
5/30	4/9		7/27	6/8		9/23	8/7
5/31	4/10		7/28	6/9		9/24	8/8
			7/29	6/10		9/25	8/9
6/1	4/11		7/30	6/11		9/66	8/10
6/2	4/12		7/31	6/12		9/27	8/11
6/3	4/13					9/28	8/12
6/4	4/14		8/1	6/13		9/29	8/13
6/5	4/15		8/2	6/14		9/30	8/14
6/6	4/16		8/3	6/15			
6/7	4/17		8/4	6/16		10/1	8/15
6/8	4/18		8/5	6/17		10/2	8/16
6/9	4/19		8/6	6/18		10/3	8/17
6/10	4/20		8/7	6/19		10/4	8/18
6/11	4/21		8/8	6/20		10/5	8/19
6/12	4/22		8/9	6/21		10/6	8/20
6/13	4/23		8/10	6/22		10/7	8/21
6/14	4/24		8/11	6/23		10/8	8/22
6/15	4/25		8/12	6/24		10/9	8/23
6/16	4/26		8/13	6/25		10/10	8/24
6/17	4/27		8/14	6/26		10/11	8/25

Solar	Lunar		Solar	Lunar		Solar	Lunar
10/12	8/26		12/9	10/24		2/1	12/19
10/13	8/27		12/10	10/25		2/2	12/20
10/14	8/28		12/11	10/26		2/3	12/21
10/15	8/29		12/12	10/27		2/4	12/22
10/16	8/30		12/13	10/28		2/5	12/23
10/17	9/1		12/14	10/29		2/6	12/24
10/18	9/2		12/15	11/1		2/7	12/25
10/19	9/3		12/16	11/2		2/8	12/26
10/20	9/4		12/17	11/3		2/9	12/27
10/21	9/5		12/18	11/4		2/10	12/28
10/22	9/6		12/19	11/5		2/11	12/29
10/23	9/7		12/20	11/6		2/12	12/30
10/24	9/8		12/21	11/7		2/13	1/1
10/25	9/9		12/22	11/8			(1945)
10/26	9/10		12/23	11/9		2/14	1/2
10/27	9/11		12/24	11/10		2/15	1/3
10/28	9/12		12/25	11/11		2/16	1/4
10/29	9/13		12/26	11/12		2/17	1/5
10/30	9/14		12/27	11/13		2/18	1/6
10/31	9/15		12/28	11/14		2/19	1/7
			12/29	11/15		2/20	1/8
11/1	9/16		12/30	11/16		2/21	1/9
11/2	9/17		12/31	11/17		2/22	1/10
11/3	9/18					2/23	1/11
11/4	9/19					2/24	1/12
11/5	9/20		**Solar**	**Lunar**		2/25	1/13
11/6	9/21		**Date**	**Date**		2/26	1/14
11/7	9/22					2/27	1/15
11/8	9/23		**1945**			2/28	1/16
11/9	9/24		1/1	11/18			
11/10	9/25		1/2	11/19		3/1	1/17
11/11	9/26		1/3	11/20		3/2	1/18
11/12	9/27		1/4	11/21		3/3	1/19
11/13	9/28		1/5	11/22		3/4	1/20
11/14	9/29		1/6	11/23		3/5	1/21
11/15	9/30		1/7	11/24		3/6	1/22
11/16	10/1		1/8	11/25		3/7	1/23
11/17	10/2		1/9	11/26		3/8	1/24
11/18	10/3		1/10	11/27		3/9	1/25
11/19	10/4		1/11	11/28		3/10	1/26
11/20	10/5		1/12	11/29		3/11	1/27
11/21	10/6		1/13	11/30		3/12	1/28
11/22	10/7		1/14	12/1		3/13	1/29
11/23	10/8		1/15	12/2		3/14	2/1
11/24	10/9		1/16	12/3		3/15	2/2
11/25	10/10		1/17	12/4		3/16	2/3
11/26	10/11		1/18	12/5		3/17	2/4
11/27	10/12		1/19	12/6		3/18	2/5
11/28	10/13		1/20	12/7		3/19	2/6
11/29	10/14		1/21	12/8		3/20	2/7
11/30	10/15		1/22	12/9		3/21	2/8
			1/23	12/10		3/22	2/9
12/1	10/16		1/24	12/11		3/23	2/10
12/2	10/17		1/25	12/12		3/24	2/11
12/3	10/18		1/26	12/13		3/25	2/12
12/4	10/19		1/27	12/14		3/26	2/13
12/5	10/20		1/28	12/15		3/27	2/14
12/6	10/21		1/29	12/16		3/28	2/15
12/7	10/22		1/30	12/17		3/29	2/16
12/8	10/23		1/31	12/18		3/30	2/17

3/31	2/18
4/1	2/19
4/2	2/20
4/3	2/21
4/4	2/22
4/5	2/23
4/6	2/24
4/7	2/25
4/8	2/26
4/9	2/27
4/10	2/28
4/11	2/29
4/12	3/1
4/13	3/2
4/14	3/3
4/15	3/4
4/16	3/5
4/17	3/6
4/18	3/7
4/19	3/8
4/20	3/9
4/21	3/10
4/22	3/11
4/23	3/12
4/24	3/13
4/25	3/14
4/26	3/15
4/27	3/16
4/28	3/17
4/29	3/18
4/30	3/19
5/1	3/20
5/2	3/21
5/3	3/22
5/4	3/23
5/5	3/24
5/6	3/25
5/7	3/26
5/8	3/27
5/9	3/28
5/10	3/29
5/11	3/30
5/12	4/1
5/13	4/2
5/14	4/3
5/15	4/4
5/16	4/5
5/17	4/6
5/18	4/7
5/19	4/8
5/20	4/9
5/21	4/10
5/22	4/11
5/23	4/12
5/24	4/13
5/25	4/14
5/26	4/15
5/27	4/16

5/28	4/17
5/29	4/18
5/30	4/19
5/31	4/20
6/1	4/21
6/2	4/22
6/3	4/23
6/4	4/24
6/5	4/25
6/6	4/26
6/7	4/27
6/8	4/28
6/9	4/29
6/10	5/1
6/11	5/2
6/12	5/3
6/13	5/4
6/14	5/5
6/15	5/6
6/16	5/7
6/17	5/8
6/18	5/9
6/19	5/10
6/20	5/11
6/21	5/12
6/22	5/13
6/23	5/14
6/24	5/15
6/25	5/16
6/26	5/17
6/27	5/18
6/28	5/19
6/29	5/20
6/30	5/21
7/1	5/22
7/2	5/23
7/3	5/24
7/4	5/25
7/5	5/26
7/6	5/27
7/7	5/28
7/8	5/29
7/9	6/1
7/10	6/2
7/11	6/3
7/12	6/4
7/13	6/5
7/14	6/6
7/15	6/7
7/16	6/8
7/17	6/9
7/18	6/10
7/19	6/11
7/20	6/12
7/21	6/13
7/22	6/14
7/23	6/15
7/24	6/16

7/25	6/17
7/26	6/18
7/27	6/19
7/28	6/20
7/29	6/21
7/30	6/22
7/31	6/23
8/1	6/24
8/2	6/25
8/3	6/26
8/4	6/27
8/5	6/28
8/6	6/29
8/7	6/30
8/8	7/1
8/9	7/2
8/10	7/3
8/11	7/4
8/12	7/5
8/13	7/6
8/14	7/7
8/15	7/8
8/16	7/9
8/17	7/10
8/18	7/11
8/19	7/12
8/20	7/13
8/21	7/14
8/22	7/15
8/23	7/16
8/24	7/17
8/25	7/18
8/26	7/19
8/27	7/20
8/28	7/21
8/29	7/22
8/30	7/23
8/31	7/24
9/1	7/25
9/2	7/26
9/3	7/27
9/4	7/28
9/5	7/29
9/6	8/1
9/7	8/2
9/8	8/3
9/9	8/4
9/10	8/5
9/11	8/6
9/12	8/7
9/13	8/8
9/14	8/9
9/15	8/10
9/16	8/11
9/17	8/12
9/18	8/13
9/19	8/14
9/20	8/15

9/21	8/16
9/22	8/17
9/23	8/18
9/24	8/19
9/25	8/20
9/26	8/21
9/27	8/22
9/28	8/23
9/29	8/24
9/30	8/25
10/1	8/26
10/2	8/27
10/3	8/28
10/4	8/29
10/5	8/30
10/6	9/1
10/7	9/2
10/8	9/3
10/9	9/4
10/10	9/5
10/11	9/6
10/12	9/7
10/13	9/8
10/14	9/9
10/15	9/10
10/16	9/11
10/17	9/12
10/18	9/13
10/19	9/14
10/20	9/15
10/21	9/16
10/22	9/17
10/23	9/18
10/24	9/19
10/25	9/20
10/26	9/21
10/27	9/22
10/28	9/23
10/29	9/24
10/30	9/25
10/31	9/26
11/1	9/27
11/2	9/28
11/3	9/29
11/4	9/30
11/5	10/1
11/6	10/2
11/7	10/3
11/8	10/4
11/9	10/5
11/10	10/6
11/11	10/7
11/12	10/8
11/13	10/9
11/14	10/10
11/15	10/11
11/16	10/12
11/17	10/13

11/18	10/14
11/19	10/15
11/20	10/16
11/21	10/17
11/22	10/18
11/23	10/19
11/24	10/20
11/25	10/21
11/26	10/22
11/27	10/23
11/28	10/24
11/29	10/25
11/30	10/26
12/1	10/27
12/2	10/28
12/3	10/29
12/4	10/30
12/5	11/1
12/6	11/2
12/7	11/3
12/8	11/4
12/9	11/5
12/10	11/6
12/11	11/7
12/12	11/8
12/13	11/9
12/14	11/10
12/15	11/11
12/16	11/12
12/17	11/13
12/18	11/14
12/19	11/15
12/20	11/16
12/21	11/17
12/22	11/18
12/23	11/19
12/24	11/20
12/25	11/21
12/26	11/22
12/27	11/23
12/28	11/24
12/29	11/25
12/30	11/26
12/31	11/27

Solar Date	**Lunar Date**
1946	
1/1	11/28
1/2	11/29
1/3	12/1
1/4	12/2
1/5	12/3
1/6	12/4
1/7	12/5
1/8	12/6
1/9	12/7
1/10	12/8
1/11	12/9
1/12	12/10
1/13	12/11
1/14	12/12
1/15	12/13
1/16	12/14
1/17	12/15
1/18	12/16
1/19	12/17
1/20	12/18
1/21	12/19
1/22	12/20
1/23	12/21
1/24	12/22
1/25	12/23
1/26	12/24
1/27	12/25
1/28	12/26
1/29	12/27
1/30	12/28
1/31	12/29
2/1	12/30
2/2	1/1
	(1946)
2/3	1/2
2/4	1/3
2/5	1/4
2/6	1/5
2/7	1/6
2/8	1/7
2/9	1/8
2/10	1/9
2/11	1/10
2/12	1/11
2/13	1/12
2/14	1/13
2/15	1/14
2/16	1/15
2/17	1/16
2/18	1/17
2/19	1/18
2/20	1/19
2/21	1/20
2/22	1/21
2/23	1/22
2/24	1/23
2/25	1/24
2/26	1/25
2/27	1/26
2/28	1/27
3/1	1/28
3/2	1/29
3/3	1/30
3/4	2/1
3/5	2/2
3/6	2/3
3/7	2/4

Solar	Lunar	Solar	Lunar	Solar	Lunar	Solar	Lunar	Solar	Lunar	Solar Date	Lunar Date
3/8	2/5	5/5	4/5	7/2	6/4	8/30	8/4	10/27	10/3	12/24	12/2
3/9	2/6	5/6	4/6	7/3	6/5	8/31	8/5	10/28	10/4	12/25	12/3
3/10	2/7	5/7	4/7	7/4	6/6			10/29	10/5	12/26	12/4
3/11	2/8	5/8	4/8	7/5	6/7	9/1	8/6	10/30	10/6	12/27	12/5
3/12	2/9	5/9	4/9	7/6	6/8	9/2	8/7	10/31	10/7	12/28	12/6
3/13	2/10	5/10	4/10	7/7	6/9	9/3	8/8			12/29	12/7
3/14	2/11	5/11	4/11	7/8	6/10	9/4	8/9	11/1	10/8	12/30	12/8
3/15	2/12	5/12	4/12	7/9	6/11	9/5	8/10	11/2	10/9	12/31	12/9
3/16	2/13	5/13	4/13	7/10	6/12	9/6	8/11	11/3	10/10		
3/17	2/14	5/14	4/14	7/11	6/13	9/7	8/12	11/4	10/11		
3/18	2/15	5/15	4/15	7/12	6/14	9/8	8/13	11/5	10/12	**Solar Date**	**Lunar Date**
3/19	2/16	5/16	4/16	7/13	6/15	9/9	8/14	11/6	10/13		
3/20	2/17	5/17	4/17	7/14	6/16	9/10	8/15	11/7	10/14	**1947**	
3/21	2/18	5/18	4/18	7/15	6/17	9/11	8/16	11/8	10/15	1/1	12/10
3/22	2/19	5/19	4/19	7/16	6/18	9/12	8/17	11/9	10/16	1/2	12/11
3/23	2/20	5/20	4/20	7/17	6/19	9/13	8/18	11/10	10/17	1/3	12/12
3/24	2/21	5/21	4/21	7/18	6/20	9/14	8/19	11/11	10/18	1/4	12/13
3/25	2/22	5/22	4/22	7/19	6/21	9/15	8/20	11/12	10/19	1/5	12/14
3/26	2/23	5/23	4/23	7/20	6/22	9/16	8/21	11/13	10/20	1/6	12/15
3/27	2/24	5/24	4/24	7/21	6/23	9/17	8/22	11/14	10/21	1/7	12/16
3/28	2/25	5/25	4/25	7/22	6/24	9/18	8/23	11/15	10/22	1/8	12/17
3/29	2/26	5/26	4/26	7/23	6/25	9/19	8/24	11/16	10/23	1/9	12/18
3/30	2/27	5/27	4/27	7/24	6/26	9/20	8/25	11/17	10/24	1/10	12/19
3/31	2/28	5/28	4/28	7/25	6/27	9/21	8/26	11/18	10/25	1/11	12/20
		5/29	4/29	7/26	6/28	9/22	8/27	11/19	10/26	1/12	12/21
4/1	2/29	5/30	4/30	7/27	6/29	9/23	8/28	11/20	10/27	1/13	12/22
4/2	3/1	5/31	5/1	7/28	7/1	9/24	8/29	11/21	10/28	1/14	12/23
4/3	3/2			7/29	7/2	9/25	9/1	11/22	10/29	1/15	12/24
4/4	3/3	6/1	5/2	7/30	7/3	9/26	9/2	11/23	10/30	1/16	12/25
4/5	3/4	6/2	5/3	7/31	7/4	9/27	9/3	11/24	11/1	1/17	12/26
4/6	3/5	6/3	5/4			9/28	9/4	11/25	11/2	1/18	12/27
4/7	3/6	6/4	5/5	8/1	7/5	9/29	9/5	11/26	11/3	1/19	12/28
4/8	3/7	6/5	5/6	8/2	7/6	9/30	9/6	11/27	11/4	1/20	12/29
4/9	3/8	6/6	5/7	8/3	7/7			11/28	11/5	1/21	12/30
4/10	3/9	6/7	5/8	8/4	7/8	10/1	9/7	11/29	11/6	1/22	1/1
4/11	3/10	6/8	5/9	8/5	7/9	10/2	9/8	11/30	11/7		(1947)
4/12	3/11	6/9	5/10	8/6	7/10	10/3	9/9			1/23	1/2
4/13	3/12	6/10	5/11	8/7	7/11	10/4	9/10	12/1	11/8	1/24	1/3
4/14	3/13	6/11	5/12	8/8	7/12	10/5	9/11	12/2	11/9	1/25	1/4
4/15	3/14	6/12	5/13	8/9	7/13	10/6	9/12	12/3	11/10	1/26	1/5
4/16	3/15	6/13	5/14	8/10	7/14	10/7	9/13	12/4	11/11	1/27	1/6
4/17	3/16	6/14	5/15	8/11	7/15	10/8	9/14	12/5	11/12	1/28	1/7
4/18	3/17	6/15	5/16	8/12	7/16	10/9	9/15	12/6	11/13	1/29	1/8
4/19	3/18	6/16	5/17	8/13	7/17	10/10	9/16	12/7	11/14	1/30	1/9
4/20	3/19	6/17	5/18	8/14	7/18	10/11	9/17	12/8	11/15	1/31	1/10
4/21	3/20	6/18	5/19	8/15	7/19	10/12	9/18	12/9	11/16		
4/22	3/21	6/19	5/20	8/16	7/20	10/13	9/19	12/10	11/17	2/1	1/11
4/23	3/22	6/20	5/21	8/17	7/21	10/14	9/20	12/11	11/18	2/2	1/12
4/24	3/23	6/21	5/22	8/18	7/22	10/15	9/21	12/12	11/19	2/3	1/13
4/25	3/24	6/22	5/23	8/19	7/23	10/16	9/22	12/13	11/20	2/4	1/14
4/26	3/25	6/23	5/24	8/20	7/24	10/17	9/23	12/14	11/21	2/5	1/15
4/27	3/26	6/24	5/25	8/21	7/25	10/18	9/24	12/15	11/22	2/6	1/16
4/28	3/27	6/25	5/26	8/22	7/26	10/19	9/25	12/16	11/23	2/7	1/17
4/29	3/28	6/26	5/27	8/23	7/27	10/20	9/26	12/17	11/24	2/8	1/18
4/30	3/29	6/27	5/28	8/24	7/28	10/21	9/27	12/18	11/25	2/9	1/19
		6/28	5/29	8/25	7/29	10/22	9/28	12/19	11/26	2/10	1/20
5/1	4/1	6/29	6/1	8/26	7/30	10/23	9/29	12/20	11/27	2/11	1/21
5/2	4/2	6/30	6/2	8/27	8/1	10/24	9/30	12/21	11/28	2/12	1/22
5/3	4/3			8/28	8/2	10/25	10/1	12/22	11/29	2/13	1/23
5/4	4/4	7/1	6/3	8/29	8/3	10/26	10/2	12/23	12/1		

Solar	Lunar	Solar	Lunar	Solar	Lunar	Solar	Lunar	Solar	Lunar	Solar	Lunar
2/14	1/24	4/12	2/21	6/9	4/21	8/6	6/20	10/3	8/19	12/1	10/19
2/15	1/25	4/13	2/22	6/10	4/22	8/7	6/21	10/4	8/20	12/2	10/20
2/16	1/26	4/14	2/23	6/11	4/23	8/8	6/22	10/5	8/21	12/3	10/21
2/17	1/27	4/15	2/24	6/12	4/24	8/9	6/23	10/6	8/22	12/4	10/22
2/18	1/28	4/16	2/25	6/13	4/25	8/10	6/24	10/7	8/23	12/5	10/23
2/19	1/29	4/17	2/26	6/14	4/26	8/11	6/25	10/8	8/24	12/6	10/24
2/20	1/30	4/18	2/27	6/15	4/27	8/12	6/26	10/9	8/25	12/7	10/25
2/21	2/1	4/19	2/28	6/16	4/28	8/13	6/27	10/10	8/26	12/8	10/26
2/22	2/2	4/20	2/29	6/17	4/29	8/14	6/28	10/11	8/27	12/9	10/27
2/23	2/3	4/21	3/1	6/18	4/30	8/15	6/29	10/12	8/28	12/10	10/28
2/24	2/4	4/22	3/2	6/19	5/1	8/16	7/1	10/13	8/29	12/11	10/29
2/25	2/5	4/23	3/3	6/20	5/2	8/17	7/2	10/14	9/1	12/12	11/1
2/26	2/6	4/24	3/4	6/21	5/3	8/18	7/3	10/15	9/2	12/13	11/2
2/27	2/7	4/25	3/5	6/22	5/4	8/19	7/4	10/16	9/3	12/14	11/3
2/28	2/8	4/26	3/6	6/23	5/5	8/20	7/5	10/17	9/4	12/15	11/4
		4/27	3/7	6/24	5/6	8/21	7/6	10/18	9/5	12/16	11/5
3/1	2/9	4/28	3/8	6/25	5/7	8/22	7/7	10/19	9/6	12/17	11/6
3/2	2/10	4/29	3/9	6/26	5/8	8/23	7/8	10/20	9/7	12/18	11/7
3/3	2/11	4/30	3/10	6/27	5/9	8/24	7/9	10/21	9/8	12/19	11/8
3/4	2/12			6/28	5/10	8/25	7/10	10/22	9/9	12/20	11/9
3/5	2/13	5/1	3/11	6/29	5/11	8/26	7/11	10/23	9/10	12/21	11/10
3/6	2/14	5/2	3/12	6/30	5/12	8/27	7/12	10/24	9/11	12/22	11/11
3/7	2/15	5/3	3/13			8/28	7/13	10/25	9/12	12/23	11/12
3/8	2/16	5/4	3/14	7/1	5/13	8/29	7/14	10/26	9/13	12/24	11/13
3/9	2/17	5/5	3/15	7/2	5/14	8/30	7/15	10/27	9/14	12/25	11/14
3/10	2/18	5/6	3/16	7/3	5/15	8/31	7/16	10/28	9/15	12/26	11/15
3/11	2/19	5/7	3/17	7/4	5/16			10/29	9/16	12/27	11/16
3/12	2/20	5/8	3/18	7/5	5/17	9/1	7/17	10/30	9/17	12/28	11/17
3/13	2/21	5/9	3/19	7/6	5/18	9/2	7/18	10/31	9/18	12/29	11/18
3/14	2/22	5/10	3/20	7/7	5/19	9/3	7/19			12/30	11/19
3/15	2/23	5/11	3/21	7/8	5/20	9/4	7/20	11/1	9/19	12/31	11/20
3/16	2/24	5/12	3/22	7/9	5/21	9/5	7/21	11/2	9/20		
3/17	2/25	5/13	3/23	7/10	5/22	9/6	7/22	11/3	9/21		
3/18	2/26	5/14	3/24	7/11	5/23	9/7	7/23	11/4	9/22	Solar	Lunar
3/19	2/27	5/15	3/25	7/12	5/24	9/8	7/24	11/5	9/23	Date	Date
3/20	2/28	5/16	3/26	7/13	5/25	9/9	7/25	11/6	9/24		
3/21	2/29	5/17	3/27	7/14	5/26	9/10	7/26	11/7	9/25	**1948**	
3/22	2/30	5/18	3/28	7/15	5/27	9/11	7/27	11/8	9/26	1/1	11/21
3/23	2/1	5/19	3/29	7/16	5/28	9/12	7/28	11/9	9/27	1/2	11/22
(Leap Month)		5/20	4/1	7/17	5/29	9/13	7/29	11/10	9/28	1/3	11/23
3/24	2/2	5/21	4/2	7/18	6/1	9/14	7/30	11/11	9/29	1/4	11/24
3/25	2/3	5/22	4/3	7/19	6/2	9/15	8/1	11/12	9/30	1/5	11/25
3/26	2/4	5/23	4/4	7/20	6/3	9/16	8/2	11/13	10/1	1/6	11/26
3/27	2/5	5/24	4/5	7/21	6/4	9/17	8/3	11/14	10/2	1/7	11/27
3/28	2/6	5/25	4/6	7/22	6/5	9/18	8/4	11/15	10/3	1/8	11/28
3/29	2/7	5/26	4/7	7/23	6/6	9/19	8/5	11/16	10/4	1/9	11/29
3/30	2/8	5/27	4/8	7/24	6/7	9/20	8/6	11/17	10/5	1/10	11/30
3/31	2/9	5/28	4/9	7/25	6/8	9/21	8/7	11/18	10/6	1/11	12/1
		5/29	4/10	7/26	6/9	9/22	8/8	11/19	10/7	1/12	12/2
4/1	2/10	5/30	4/11	7/27	6/10	9/23	8/9	11/20	10/8	1/13	12/3
4/2	2/11	5/31	4/12	7/28	6/11	9/24	8/10	11/21	10/9	1/14	12/4
4/3	2/12			7/29	6/12	9/25	8/11	11/22	10/10	1/15	12/5
4/4	2/13	6/1	4/13	7/30	6/13	9/26	8/12	11/23	10/11	1/16	12/6
4/5	2/14	6/2	4/14	7/31	6/14	9/27	8/13	11/24	10/12	1/17	12/7
4/6	2/15	6/3	4/15			9/28	8/14	11/25	10/13	1/18	12/8
4/7	2/16	6/4	4/16	8/1	6/15	9/29	8/15	11/26	10/14	1/19	12/9
4/8	2/17	6/5	4/17	8/2	6/16	9/30	8/16	11/27	10/15	1/20	12/10
4/9	2/18	6/6	4/18	8/3	6/17			11/28	10/16	1/21	12/11
4/10	2/19	6/7	4/19	8/4	6/18	10/1	8/17	11/29	10/17	1/22	12/12
4/11	2/20	6/8	4/20	8/5	6/19	10/2	8/18	11/30	10/18	1/23	12/13

1/24	12/14	3/21	2/11	5/18	4/10	7/15	6/9	9/11	8/9	11/8	10/8
1/25	12/15	3/22	2/12	5/19	4/11	7/16	6/10	9/12	8/10	11/9	10/9
1/26	12/16	3/23	2/13	5/20	4/12	7/17	6/11	9/13	8/11	11/10	10/10
1/27	12/17	3/24	2/14	5/21	4/13	7/18	6/12	9/14	8/12	11/11	10/11
1/28	12/18	3/25	2/15	5/22	4/14	7/19	6/13	9/15	8/13	11/12	10/12
1/29	12/19	3/26	2/16	5/23	4/15	7/20	6/14	9/16	8/14	11/13	10/13
1/30	12/20	3/27	2/17	5/24	4/16	7/21	6/15	9/17	8/15	11/14	10/14
1/31	12/21	3/28	2/18	5/25	4/17	7/22	6/16	9/18	8/16	11/15	10/15
		3/29	2/19	5/26	4/18	7/23	6/17	9/19	8/17	11/16	10/16
2/1	12/22	3/30	2/20	5/27	4/19	7/24	6/18	9/20	8/18	11/17	10/17
2/2	12/23	3/31	2/21	5/28	4/20	7/25	6/19	9/21	8/19	11/18	10/18
2/3	12/24			5/29	4/21	7/26	6/20	9/22	8/20	11/19	10/19
2/4	12/25	4/1	2/22	5/30	4/22	7/27	6/21	9/23	8/21	11/20	10/20
2/5	12/26	4/2	2/23	5/31	4/23	7/28	6/22	9/24	8/22	11/21	10/21
2/6	12/27	4/3	2/24			7/29	6/23	9/25	8/23	11/22	10/22
2/7	12/28	4/4	2/25	6/1	4/24	7/30	6/24	9/26	8/24	11/23	10/23
2/8	12/29	4/5	2/26	6/2	4/25	7/31	6/25	9/27	8/25	11/24	10/24
2/9	12/30	4/6	2/27	6/3	4/26			9/28	8/26	11/25	10/25
2/10	1/1	4/7	2/28	6/4	4/27	8/1	6/26	9/29	8/27	11/26	10/26
	(1948)	4/8	2/29	6/5	4/28	8/2	6/27	9/30	8/28	11/27	10/27
2/11	1/2	4/9	3/1	6/6	4/29	8/3	6/28			11/28	10/28
2/12	1/3	4/10	3/2	6/7	5/1	8/4	6/29	10/1	8/29	11/29	10/29
2/13	1/4	4/11	3/3	6/8	5/2	8/5	7/1	10/2	8/30	11/30	10/30
2/14	1/5	4/12	3/4	6/9	5/3	8/6	7/2	10/3	9/1		
2/15	1/6	4/13	3/5	6/10	5/4	8/7	7/3	10/4	9/2	12/1	11/1
2/16	1/7	4/14	3/6	6/11	5/5	8/8	7/4	10/5	9/3	12/2	11/2
2/17	1/8	4/15	3/7	6/12	5/6	8/9	7/5	10/6	9/4	12/3	11/3
2/18	1/9	4/16	3/8	6/13	5/7	8/10	7/6	10/7	9/5	12/4	11/4
2/19	1/10	4/17	3/9	6/14	5/8	8/11	7/7	10/8	9/6	12/5	11/5
2/20	1/11	4/18	3/10	6/15	5/9	8/12	7/8	10/9	9/7	12/6	11/6
2/21	1/12	4/19	3/11	6/16	5/10	8/13	7/9	10/10	9/8	12/7	11/7
2/22	1/13	4/20	3/12	6/17	5/11	8/14	7/10	10/11	9/9	12/8	11/8
2/23	1/14	4/21	3/13	6/18	5/12	8/15	7/11	10/12	9/10	12/9	11/9
2/24	1/15	4/22	3/14	6/19	5/13	8/16	7/12	10/13	9/11	12/10	11/10
2/25	1/16	4/23	3/15	6/20	5/14	8/17	7/13	10/14	9/12	12/11	11/11
2/26	1/17	4/24	3/16	6/21	5/15	8/18	7/14	10/15	9/13	12/12	11/12
2/27	1/18	4/25	3/17	6/22	5/16	8/19	7/15	10/16	9/14	12/13	11/13
2/28	1/19	4/26	3/18	6/23	5/17	8/20	7/16	10/17	9/15	12/14	11/14
2/29	1/20	4/27	3/19	6/24	5/18	8/21	7/17	10/18	9/16	12/15	11/15
		4/28	3/20	6/25	5/19	8/22	7/18	10/19	9/17	12/16	11/16
3/1	1/21	4/29	3/21	6/26	5/20	8/23	7/19	10/20	9/18	12/17	11/17
3/2	1/22	4/30	3/22	6/27	5/21	8/24	7/20	10/21	9/19	12/18	11/18
3/3	1/23			6/28	5/22	8/25	7/21	10/22	9/20	12/19	11/19
3/4	1/24	5/1	3/23	6/29	5/23	8/26	7/22	10/23	9/21	12/20	11/20
3/5	1/25	5/2	3/24	6/30	5/24	8/27	7/23	10/24	9/22	12/21	11/21
3/6	1/26	5/3	3/25			8/28	7/24	10/25	9/23	12/22	11/22
3/7	1/27	5/4	3/26	7/1	5/25	8/29	7/25	10/26	9/24	12/23	11/23
3/8	1/28	5/5	3/27	7/2	5/26	8/30	7/26	10/27	9/25	12/24	11/24
3/9	1/29	5/6	3/28	7/3	5/27	8/31	7/27	10/28	9/26	12/25	11/25
3/10	1/30	5/7	3/29	7/4	5/28			10/29	9/27	12/26	11/26
3/11	2/1	5/8	3/30	7/5	5/29	9/1	7/28	10/30	9/28	12/27	11/27
3/12	2/2 .	5/9	4/1	7/6	5/30	9/2	7/29	10/31	9/29	12/28	11/28
3/13	2/3	5/10	4/2	7/7	6/1	9/3	8/1			12/29	11/29
3/14	2/4	5/11	4/3	7/8	6/2	9/4	8/2	11/1	10/1	12/30	12/1
3/15	2/5	5/12	4/4	7/9	6/3	9/5	8/3	11/2	10/2	12/31	12/2
3/16	2/6	5/13	4/5	7/10	6/4	9/6	8/4	11/3	10/3		
3/17	2/7	5/14	4/6	7/11	6/5	9/7	8/5	11/4	10/4		
3/18	2/8	5/15	4/7	7/12	6/6	9/8	8/6	11/5	10/5		
3/19	2/9	5/16	4/8	7/13	6/7	9/9	8/7	11/6	10/6		
3/20	2/10	5/17	4/9	7/14	6/8	9/10	8/8	11/7	10/7		

Solar Date	Lunar Date	Solar	Lunar	Solar	Lunar	Solar	Lunar	Solar	Lunar	Solar	Lunar
		2/24	1/27	4/23	3/26	6/20	5/24	8/17	7/23	10/13	8/22
		2/25	1/28	4/24	3/27	6/21	5/25	8/18	7/24	10/14	8/23
1949		2/26	1/29	4/25	3/28	6/22	5/26	8/19	7/25	10/15	8/24
		2/27	1/30	4/26	3/29	6/23	5/27	8/20	7/26	10/16	8/25
1/1	12/3	2/28	2/1	4/27	3/30	6/24	5/28	8/21	7/27	10/17	8/26
1/2	12/4			4/28	4/1	6/25	5/29	8/22	7/28	10/18	8/27
1/3	12/5	3/1	2/2	4/29	4/2	6/26	6/1	8/23	7/29	10/19	8/28
1/4	12/6	3/2	2/3	4/30	4/3	6/27	6/2	8/24	7/1	10/20	8/29
1/5	12/7	3/3	2/4			6/28	6/3	(Leap Month)		10/21	8/30
1/6	12/8	3/4	2/5	5/1	4/4	6/29	6/4	8/25	7/2	10/22	9/1
1/7	12/9	3/5	2/6	5/2	4/5	6/30	6/5	8/26	7/3	10/23	9/2
1/8	12/10	3/6	2/7	5/3	4/6			8/27	7/4	10/24	9/3
1/9	12/11	3/7	2/8	5/4	4/7	7/1	6/6	8/28	7/5	10/25	9/4
1/10	12/12	3/8	2/9	5/5	4/8	7/2	6/7	8/29	7/6	10/26	9/5
1/11	12/13	3/9	2/10	5/6	4/9	7/3	6/8	8/30	7/7	10/27	9/6
1/12	12/14	3/10	2/11	5/7	4/10	7/4	6/9	8/31	7/8	10/28	9/7
1/13	12/15	3/11	2/12	5/8	4/11	7/5	6/10			10/29	9/8
1/14	12/16	3/12	2/13	5/9	4/12	7/6	6/11	9/1	7/9	10/30	9/9
1/15	12/17	3/13	2/14	5/10	4/13	7/7	6/12	9/2	7/10	10/31	9/10
1/16	12/18	3/14	2/15	5/11	4/14	7/8	6/13	9/3	7/11		
1/17	12/19	3/15	2/16	5/12	4/15	7/9	6/14	9/4	7/12	11/1	9/11
1/18	12/20	3/16	2/17	5/13	4/16	7/10	6/15	9/5	7/13	11/2	9/12
1/19	12/21	3/17	2/18	5/14	4/17	7/11	6/16	9/6	7/14	11/3	9/13
1/20	12/22	3/18	2/19	5/15	4/18	7/12	6/17	9/7	7/15	11/4	9/14
1/21	12/23	3/19	2/20	5/16	4/19	7/13	6/18	9/8	7/16	11/5	9/15
1/22	12/24	3/20	2/21	5/17	4/20	7/14	6/19	9/9	7/17	11/6	9/16
1/23	12/25	3/21	2/22	5/18	4/21	7/15	6/20	9/10	7/18	11/7	9/17
1/24	12/26	3/22	2/23	5/19	4/22	7/16	6/21	9/11	7/19	11/8	9/18
1/25	12/27	3/23	2/24	5/20	4/23	7/17	6/22	9/12	7/20	11/9	9/19
1/26	12/28	3/24	2/25	5/21	4/24	7/18	6/23	9/13	7/21	11/10	9/20
1/27	12/29	3/25	2/26	5/22	4/25	7/19	6/24	9/14	7/22	11/11	9/21
1/28	12/30	3/26	2/27	5/23	4/26	7/20	6/25	9/15	7/23	11/12	9/22
1/29	1/1	3/27	2/28	5/24	4/27	7/21	6/26	9/16	7/24	11/13	9/23
	(1949)	3/28	2/29	5/25	4/28	7/22	6/27	9/17	7/25	11/14	9/24
1/30	1/2	3/29	3/1	5/26	4/29	7/23	6/28	9/18	7/26	11/15	9/25
1/31	1/3	3/30	3/2	5/27	4/30	7/24	6/29	9/19	7/27	11/16	9/26
		3/31	3/3	5/28	5/1	7/25	6/30	9/20	7/28	11/17	9/27
2/1	1/4			5/29	5/2	7/26	7/1	9/21	7/29	11/18	9/28
2/2	1/5	4/1	3/4	5/30	5/3	7/27	7/2	9/22	8/1	11/19	9/29
2/3	1/6	4/2	3/5	5/31	5/4	7/28	7/3	9/23	8/2	11/20	10/1
2/4	1/7	4/3	3/6			7/29	7/4	9/24	8/3	11/21	10/2
2/5	1/8	4/4	3/7	6/1	5/5	7/30	7/5	9/25	8/4	11/22	10/3
2/6	1/9	4/5	3/8	6/2	5/6	7/31	7/6	9/26	8/5	11/23	10/4
2/7	1/10	4/6	3/9	6/3	5/7			9/27	8/6	11/24	10/5
2/8	1/11	4/7	3/10	6/4	5/8	8/1	7/7	9/28	8/7	11/25	10/6
2/9	1/12	4/8	3/11	6/5	5/9	8/2	7/8	9/29	8/8	11/26	10/7
2/10	1/13	4/9	3/12	6/6	5/10	8/3	7/9	9/30	8/9	11/27	10/8
2/11	1/14	4/10	3/13	6/7	5/11	8/4	7/10			11/28	10/9
2/12	1/15	4/11	3/14	6/8	5/12	8/5	7/11	10/1	8/10	11/29	10/10
2/13	1/16	4/12	3/15	6/9	5/13	8/6	7/12	10/2	8/11	11/30	10/11
2/14	1/17	4/13	3/16	6/10	5/14	8/7	7/13	10/3	8/12		
2/15	1/18	4/14	3/17	6/11	5/15	8/8	7/14	10/4	8/13	12/1	10/12
2/16	1/19	4/15	3/18	6/12	5/16	8/9	7/15	10/5	8/14	12/2	10/13
2/17	1/20	4/16	3/19	6/13	5/17	8/10	7/16	10/6	8/15	12/3	10/14
2/18	1/21	4/17	3/20	6/14	5/18	8/11	7/17	10/7	8/16	12/4	10/15
2/19	1/22	4/18	3/21	6/15	5/19	8/12	7/18	10/8	8/17	12/5	10/16
2/20	1/23	4/19	3/22	6/16	5/20	8/13	7/19	10/9	8/18	12/6	10/17
2/21	1/24	4/20	3/23	6/17	5/21	8/14	7/20	10/10	8/19	12/7	10/18
2/22	1/25	4/21	3/24	6/18	5/22	8/15	7/21	10/11	8/20	12/8	10/19
2/23	1/26	4/22	3/25	6/19	5/23	8/16	7/22	10/12	8/21	12/9	10/20

Solar	Lunar	Solar	Lunar	Solar	Lunar	Solar	Lunar	Solar	Lunar	Solar	Lunar
12/10	10/21	2/1	12/15	3/31	2/14	5/28	4/12	7/25	6/11	9/21	8/10
12/11	10/22	2/2	12/16			5/29	4/13	7/26	6/12	9/22	8/11
12/12	10/23	2/3	12/17	4/1	2/15	5/30	4/14	7/27	6/13	9/23	8/12
12/13	10/24	2/4	12/18	4/2	2/16	5/31	4/15	7/28	6/14	9/24	8/13
12/14	10/25	2/5	12/19	4/3	2/17			7/29	6/15	9/25	8/14
12/15	10/26	2/6	12/20	4/4	2/18	6/1	4/16	7/30	6/16	9/26	8/15
12/16	10/27	2/7	12/21	4/5	2/19	6/2	4/17	7/31	6/17	9/27	8/16
12/17	10/28	2/8	12/22	4/6	2/20	6/3	4/18			9/28	8/17
12/18	10/29	2/9	12/23	4/7	2/21	6/4	4/19	8/1	6/18	9/29	8/18
12/19	10/30	2/10	12/24	4/8	2/22	6/5	4/20	8/2	6/19	9/30	8/19
12/20	11/1	2/11	12/25	4/9	2/23	6/6	4/21	8/3	6/20		
12/21	11/2	2/12	12/26	4/10	2/24	6/7	4/22	8/4	6/21	10/1	8/20
12/22	11/3	2/13	12/27	4/11	2/25	6/8	4/23	8/5	6/22	10/2	8/21
12/23	11/4	2/14	12/28	4/12	2/26	6/9	4/24	8/6	6/23	10/3	8/22
12/24	11/5	2/15	12/29	4/13	2/27	6/10	4/25	8/7	6/24	10/4	8/23
12/25	11/6	2/16	12/30	4/14	2/28	6/11	4/26	8/8	6/25	10/5	8/24
12/26	11/7	2/17	1/1	4/15	2/29	6/12	4/27	8/9	6/26	10/6	8/25
12/27	11/8		(1950)	4/16	2/30	6/13	4/28	8/10	6/27	10/7	8/26
12/28	11/9	2/18	1/2	4/17	3/1	6/14	4/29	8/11	6/28	10/8	8/27
12/29	11/10	2/19	1/3	4/18	3/2	6/15	5/1	8/12	6/29	10/9	8/28
12/30	11/11	2/20	1/4	4/19	3/3	6/16	5/2	8/13	6/30	10/10	8/29
12/31	11/12	2/21	1/5	4/20	3/4	6/17	5/3	8/14	7/1	10/11	9/1
		2/22	1/6	4/21	3/5	6/18	5/4	8/15	7/2	10/12	9/2
		2/23	1/7	4/22	3/6	6/19	5/5	8/16	7/3	10/13	9/3
Solar	**Lunar**	2/24	1/8	4/23	3/7	6/20	5/6	8/17	7/4	10/14	9/4
Date	**Date**	2/25	1/9	4/24	3/8	6/21	5/7	8/18	7/5	10/15	9/5
		2/26	1/10	4/25	3/9	6/22	5/8	8/19	7/6	10/16	9/6
1950		2/27	1/11	4/26	3/10	6/23	5/9	8/20	7/7	10/17	9/7
1/1	11/13	2/28	1/12	4/27	3/11	6/24	5/10	8/21	7/8	10/18	9/8
1/2	11/14			4/28	3/12	6/25	5/11	8/22	7/9	10/19	9/9
1/3	11/15	3/1	1/13	4/29	3/13	6/26	5/12	8/23	7/10	10/20	9/10
1/4	11/16	3/2	1/14	4/30	3/14	6/27	5/13	8/24	7/11	10/21	9/11
1/5	11/17	3/3	1/15			6/28	5/14	8/25	7/12	10/22	9/12
1/6	11/18	3/4	1/16	5/1	3/15	6/29	5/15	8/26	7/13	10/23	9/13
1/7	11/19	3/5	1/17	5/2	3/16	6/30	5/16	8/27	7/14	10/24	9/14
1/8	11/20	3/6	1/18	5/3	3/17			8/28	7/15	10/25	9/15
1/9	11/21	3/7	1/19	5/4	3/18	7/1	5/17	8/29	7/16	10/26	9/16
1/10	11/22	3/8	1/20	5/5	3/19	7/2	5/18	8/30	7/17	10/27	9/17
1/11	11/23	3/9	1/21	5/6	3/20	7/3	5/19	8/31	7/18	10/28	9/18
1/12	11/24	3/10	1/22	5/7	3/21	7/4	5/20			10/29	9/19
1/13	11/25	3/11	1/23	5/8	3/22	7/5	5/21	9/1	7/19	10/30	9/20
1/14	11/26	3/12	1/24	5/9	3/23	7/6	5/22	9/2	7/20	10/31	9/21
1/15	11/27	3/13	1/25	5/10	3/24	7/7	5/23	9/3	7/21		
1/16	11/28	3/14	1/26	5/11	3/25	7/8	5/24	9/4	7/22	11/1	9/22
1/17	11/29	3/15	1/27	5/12	3/26	7/9	5/25	9/5	7/23	11/2	9/23
1/18	12/1	3/16	1/28	5/13	3/27	7/10	5/26	9/6	7/24	11/3	9/24
1/19	12/2	3/17	1/29	5/14	3/28	7/11	5/27	9/7	7/25	11/4	9/25
1/20	12/3	3/18	2/1	5/15	3/29	7/12	5/28	9/8	7/26	11/5	9/26
1/21	12/4	3/19	2/2	5/16	3/30	7/13	5/29	9/9	7/27	11/6	9/27
1/22	12/5	3/20	2/3	5/17	4/1	7/14	5/30	9/10	7/28	11/7	9/28
1/23	12/6	3/21	2/4	5/18	4/2	7/15	6/1	9/11	7/29	11/8	9/29
1/24	12/7	3/22	2/5	5/19	4/3	7/16	6/2	9/12	8/1	11/9	9/30
1/25	12/8	3/23	2/6	5/20	4/4	7/17	6/3	9/13	8/2	11/10	10/1
1/26	12/9	3/24	2/7	5/21	4/5	7/18	6/4	9/14	8/3	11/11	10/2
1/27	12/10	3/25	2/8	5/22	4/6	7/19	6/5	9/15	8/4	11/12	10/3
1/28	12/11	3/26	2/9	5/23	4/7	7/20	6/6	9/16	8/5	11/13	10/4
1/29	12/12	3/27	2/10	5/24	4/8	7/21	6/7	9/17	8/6	11/14	10/5
1/30	12/13	3/28	2/11	5/25	4/9	7/22	6/8	9/18	8/7	11/15	10/6
1/31	12/14	3/29	2/12	5/26	4/10	7/23	6/9	9/19	8/8	11/16	10/7
		3/30	2/13	5/27	4/11	7/24	6/10	9/20	8/9	11/17	10/8

Solar	Lunar	Solar	Lunar	Solar	Lunar	Solar	Lunar	Solar	Lunar	Solar	Lunar
11/18	10/9	1/10	12/3	3/8	2/1	5/5	3/30	7/2	5/28	8/30	7/28
11/19	10/10	1/11	12/4	3/9	2/2	5/6	4/1	7/3	5/29	8/31	7/29
11/20	10/11	1/12	12/5	3/10	2/3	5/7	4/2	7/4	6/1		
11/21	10/12	1/13	12/6	3/11	2/4	5/8	4/3	7/5	6/2	9/1	8/1
11/22	10/13	1/14	12/7	3/12	2/5	5/9	4/4	7/6	6/3	9/2	8/2
11/23	10/14	1/15	12/8	3/13	2/6	5/10	4/5	7/7	6/4	9/3	8/3
11/24	10/15	1/16	12/9	3/14	2/7	5/11	4/6	7/8	6/5	9/4	8/4
11/25	10/16	1/17	12/10	3/15	2/8	5/12	4/7	7/9	6/6	9/5	8/5
11/26	10/17	1/18	12/11	3/16	2/9	5/13	4/8	7/10	6/7	9/6	8/6
11/27	10/18	1/19	12/12	3/17	2/10	5/14	4/9	7/11	6/8	9/7	8/7
11/28	10/19	1/20	12/13	3/18	2/11	5/15	4/10	7/12	6/9	9/8	8/8
11/29	10/20	1/21	12/14	3/19	2/12	5/16	4/11	7/13	6/10	9/9	8/9
11/30	10/21	1/22	12/15	3/20	2/13	5/17	4/12	7/14	6/11	9/10	8/10
		1/23	12/16	3/21	2/14	5/18	4/13	7/15	6/12	9/11	8/11
12/1	10/22	1/24	12/17	3/22	2/15	5/19	4/14	7/16	6/13	9/12	8/12
12/2	10/23	1/25	12/18	3/23	2/16	5/20	4/15	7/17	6/14	9/13	8/13
12/3	10/24	1/26	12/19	3/24	2/17	5/21	4/16	7/18	6/15	9/14	8/14
12/4	10/25	1/27	12/20	3/25	2/18	5/22	4/17	7/19	6/16	9/15	8/15
12/5	10/26	1/28	12/21	3/26	2/19	5/23	4/18	7/20	6/17	9/16	8/16
12/6	10/27	1/29	12/22	3/27	2/20	5/24	4/19	7/21	6/18	9/17	8/17
12/7	10/28	1/30	12/23	3/28	2/21	5/25	4/20	7/22	6/19	9/18	8/18
12/8	10/29	1/31	12/24	3/29	2/22	5/26	4/21	7/23	6/20	9/19	8/19
12/9	11/1			3/30	2/23	5/27	4/22	7/24	6/21	9/20	8/20
12/10	11/2	2/1	12/25	3/31	2/24	5/28	4/23	7/25	6/22	9/21	8/21
12/11	11/3	2/2	12/26			5/29	4/24	7/26	6/23	9/22	8/22
12/12	11/4	2/3	12/27	4/1	2/25	5/30	4/25	7/27	6/24	9/23	8/23
12/13	11/5	2/4	12/28	4/2	2/26	5/31	4/26	7/28	6/25	9/24	8/24
12/14	11/6	2/5	12/29	4/3	2/27			7/29	6/26	9/25	8/25
12/15	11/7	2/6	1/1	4/4	2/28			7/30	6/27	9/26	8/26
12/16	11/8		(1951)	4/5	2/29	6/1	4/27	7/31	6/28	9/27	8/27
12/17	11/9	2/7	1/2	4/6	3/1	6/2	4/28			9/28	8/28
12/18	11/10	2/8	1/3	4/7	3/2	6/3	4/29	8/1	6/29	9/29	8/29
12/19	11/11	2/9	1/4	4/8	3/3	6/4	4/30	8/2	6/30	9/30	8/30
12/20	11/12	2/10	1/5	4/9	3/4	6/5	5/1	8/3	7/1		
12/21	11/13	2/11	1/6	4/10	3/5	6/6	5/2	8/4	7/2	10/1	9/1
12/22	11/14	2/12	1/7	4/11	3/6	6/7	5/3	8/5	7/3	10/2	9/2
12/23	11/15	2/13	1/8	4/12	3/7	6/8	5/4	8/6	7/4	10/3	9/3
12/24	11/16	2/14	1/9	4/13	3/8	6/9	5/5	8/7	7/5	10/4	9/4
12/25	11/17	2/15	1/10	4/14	3/9	6/10	5/6	8/8	7/6	10/5	9/5
12/26	11/18	2/16	1/11	4/15	3/10	6/11	5/7	8/9	7/7	10/6	9/6
12/27	11/19	2/17	1/12	4/16	3/11	6/12	5/8	8/10	7/8	10/7	9/7
12/28	11/20	2/18	1/13	4/17	3/12	6/13	5/9	8/11	7/9	10/8	9/8
12/29	11/21	2/19	1/14	4/18	3/13	6/14	5/10	8/12	7/10	10/9	9/9
12/30	11/22	2/20	1/15	4/19	3/14	6/15	5/11	8/13	7/11	10/10	9/10
12/31	11/23	2/21	1/16	4/20	3/15	6/16	5/12	8/14	7/12	10/11	9/11
		2/22	1/17	4/21	3/16	6/17	5/13	8/15	7/13	10/12	9/12
		2/23	1/18	4/22	3/17	6/18	5/14	8/16	7/14	10/13	9/13
Solar	Lunar	2/24	1/19	4/23	3/18	6/19	5/15	8/17	7/15	10/14	9/14
Date	Date	2/25	1/20	4/24	3/19	6/20	5/16	8/18	7/16	10/15	9/15
		2/26	1/21	4/25	3/20	6/21	5/17	8/19	7/17	10/16	9/16
1951		2/27	1/22	4/26	3/21	6/22	5/18	8/20	7/18	10/17	9/17
1/1	11/24	2/28	1/23	4/27	3/22	6/23	5/19	8/21	7/19	10/18	9/18
1/2	11/25			4/28	3/23	6/24	5/20	8/22	7/20	10/19	9/19
1/3	11/26	3/1	1/24	4/29	3/24	6/25	5/21	8/23	7/21	10/20	9/20
1/4	11/27	3/2	1/25	4/30	3/25	6/26	5/22	8/24	7/22	10/21	9/21
1/5	11/28	3/3	1/26			6/27	5/23	8/25	7/23	10/22	9/22
1/6	11/29	3/4	1/27	5/1	3/26	6/28	5/24	8/26	7/24	10/23	9/23
1/7	11/30	3/5	1/28	5/2	3/27	6/29	5/25	8/27	7/25	10/24	9/24
1/8	12/1	3/6	1/29	5/3	3/28	6/30	5/26	8/28	7/26	10/25	9/25
1/9	12/2	3/7	1/30	5/4	3/29	7/1	5/27	8/29	7/27	10/26	9/26

Solar	Lunar	Solar	Lunar	Solar	Lunar	Solar	Lunar	Solar	Lunar	Solar	Lunar
10/27	9/27	12/24	11/26	2/14	1/19	4/12	3/18	6/9	5/17	8/5	6/15
10/28	9/28	12/25	11/27	2/15	1/20	4/13	3/19	6/10	5/18	8/6	6/16
10/29	9/29	12/26	11/28	2/16	1/21	4/14	3/20	6/11	5/19	8/7	6/17
10/30	10/1	12/27	11/29	2/17	1/22	4/15	3/21	6/12	5/20	8/8	6/18
10/31	10/2	12/28	12/1	2/18	1/23	4/16	3/22	6/13	5/21	8/9	6/19
		12/29	12/2	2/19	1/24	4/17	3/23	6/14	5/22	8/10	6/20
11/1	10/3	12/30	12/3	2/20	1/25	4/18	3/24	6/15	5/23	8/11	6/21
11/2	10/4	12/31	12/4	2/21	1/26	4/19	3/25	6/16	5/24	8/12	6/22
11/3	10/5			2/22	1/27	4/20	3/26	6/17	5/25	8/13	6/23
11/4	10/6			2/23	1/28	4/21	3/27	6/18	5/26	8/14	6/24
11/5	10/7	Solar Date	Lunar Date	2/24	1/29	4/22	3/28	6/19	5/27	8/15	6/25
11/6	10/8	**1952**		2/25	2/1	4/23	3/29	6/20	5/28	8/16	6/26
11/7	10/9	1/1	12/5	2/26	2/2	4/24	4/1	6/21	5/29	8/17	6/27
11/8	10/10	1/2	12/6	2/27	2/3	4/25	4/2	6/22	5/1	8/18	6/28
11/9	10/11	1/3	12/7	2/28	2/4	4/26	4/3	*(Leap Month)*		8/19	6/29
11/10	10/12			2/29	2/5	4/27	4/4	6/23	5/2	8/20	7/1
11/11	10/13	1/4	12/8			4/28	4/5	6/24	5/3	8/21	7/2
11/12	10/14	1/5	12/9	3/1	2/6	4/29	4/6	6/25	5/4	8/22	7/3
11/13	10/15	1/6	12/10	3/2	2/7	4/30	4/7	6/26	5/5	8/23	7/4
11/14	10/16	1/7	12/11	3/3	2/8			6/27	5/6	8/24	7/5
11/15	10/17	1/8	12/12	3/4	2/9	5/1	4/8	6/28	5/7	8/25	7/6
11/16	10/18	1/9	12/13	3/5	2/10	5/2	4/9	6/29	5/8	8/26	7/7
11/17	10/19	1/10	12/14	3/6	2/11	5/3	4/10	6/30	5/9	8/27	7/8
11/18	10/20	1/11	12/15	3/7	2/12	5/4	4/11			8/28	7/9
11/19	10/21	1/12	12/16	3/8	2/13	5/5	4/12	7/1	5/10	8/29	7/10
11/20	10/22	1/13	12/17	3/9	2/14	5/6	4/13	7/2	5/11	8/30	7/11
11/21	10/23	1/14	12/18	3/10	2/15	5/7	4/14	7/3	5/12	8/31	7/12
11/22	10/24	1/15	12/19	3/11	2/16	5/8	4/15	7/4	5/13		
11/23	10/25	1/16	12/20	3/12	2/17	5/9	4/16	7/5	5/14	9/1	7/13
11/24	10/26	1/17	12/21	3/13	2/18	5/10	4/17	7/6	5/15	9/2	7/14
11/25	10/27	1/18	12/22	3/14	2/19	5/11	4/18	7/7	5/16	9/3	7/15
11/26	10/28	1/19	12/23	3/15	2/20	5/12	4/19	7/8	5/17	9/4	7/16
11/27	10/29	1/20	12/24	3/16	2/21	5/13	4/20	7/9	5/18	9/5	7/17
11/28	10/30	1/21	12/25	3/17	2/22	5/14	4/21	7/10	5/19	9/6	7/18
11/29	11/1	1/22	12/26	3/18	2/23	5/15	4/22	7/11	5/20	9/7	7/19
11/30	11/2	1/23	12/27	3/19	2/24	5/16	4/23	7/12	5/21	9/8	7/20
		1/24	12/28	3/20	2/25	5/17	4/24	7/13	5/22	9/9	7/21
12/1	11/3	1/25	12/29	3/21	2/26	5/18	4/25	7/14	5/23	9/10	7/22
12/2	11/4	1/26	12/30	3/22	2/27	5/19	4/26	7/15	5/24	9/11	7/23
12/3	11/5	1/27	1/1	3/23	2/28	5/20	4/27	7/16	5/25	9/12	7/24
12/4	11/6		(1952)	3/24	2/29	5/21	4/28	7/17	5/26	9/13	7/25
12/5	11/7	1/28	1/2	3/25	2/30	5/22	4/29	7/18	5/27	9/14	7/26
12/6	11/8	1/29	1/3	3/26	3/1	5/23	4/30	7/19	5/28	9/15	7/27
12/7	11/9	1/30	1/4	3/27	3/2	5/24	5/1	7/20	5/29	9/16	7/28
12/8	11/10	1/31	1/5	3/28	3/3	5/25	5/2	7/21	5/30	9/17	7/29
12/9	11/11			3/29	3/4	5/26	5/3	7/22	6/1	9/18	7/30
12/10	11/12	2/1	1/6	3/30	3/5	5/27	5/4	7/23	6/2	9/19	8/1
12/11	11/13	2/2	1/7	3/31	3/6	5/28	5/5	7/24	6/3	9/20	8/2
12/12	11/14	2/3	1/8			5/29	5/6	7/25	6/4	9/21	8/3
12/13	11/15	2/4	1/9	4/1	3/7	5/30	5/7	7/26	6/5	9/22	8/4
12/14	11/16	2/5	1/10	4/2	3/8	5/31	5/8	7/27	6/6	9/23	8/5
12/15	11/17	2/6	1/11	4/3	3/9			7/28	6/7	9/24	8/6
12/16	11/18	2/7	1/12	4/4	3/10	6/1	5/9	7/29	6/8	9/25	8/7
12/17	11/19	2/8	1/13	4/5	3/11	6/2	5/10	7/30	6/9	9/26	8/8
12/18	11/20	2/9	1/14	4/6	3/12	6/3	5/11	7/31	6/10	9/27	8/9
12/19	11/21	2/10	1/15	4/7	3/13	6/4	5/12			9/28	8/10
12/20	11/22	2/11	1/16	4/8	3/14	6/5	5/13	8/1	6/11	9/29	8/11
12/21	11/23	2/12	1/17	4/9	3/15	6/6	5/14	8/2	6/12	9/30	8/12
12/22	11/24	2/13	1/18	4/10	3/16	6/7	5/15	8/3	6/13		
12/23	11/25			4/11	3/17	6/8	5/16	8/4	6/14	10/1	8/13

Solar	Lunar
10/2	8/14
10/3	8/15
10/4	8/16
10/5	8/17
10/6	8/18
10/7	8/19
10/8	8/20
10/9	8/21
10/10	8/22
10/11	8/23
10/12	8/24
10/13	8/25
10/14	8/26
10/15	8/27
10/16	8/28
10/17	8/29
10/18	8/30
10/19	9/1
10/20	9/2
10/21	9/3
10/22	9/4
10/23	9/5
10/24	9/6
10/25	9/7
10/26	9/8
10/27	9/9
10/28	9/10
10/29	9/11
10/30	9/12
10/31	9/13
11/1	9/14
11/2	9/15
11/3	9/16
11/4	9/17
11/5	9/18
11/6	9/19
11/7	9/20
11/8	9/21
11/9	9/22
11/10	9/23
11/11	9/24
11/12	9/25
11/13	9/26
11/14	9/27
11/15	9/28
11/16	9/29
11/17	10/1
11/18	10/2
11/19	10/3
11/20	10/4
11/21	10/5
11/22	10/6
11/23	10/7
11/24	10/8
11/25	10/9
11/26	10/10
11/27	10/11
11/28	10/12
11/29	10/13

Solar	Lunar
11/30	10/14
12/1	10/15
12/2	10/16
12/3	10/17
12/4	10/18
12/5	10/19
12/6	10/20
12/7	10/21
12/8	10/22
12/9	10/23
12/10	10/24
12/11	10/25
12/12	10/26
12/13	10/27
12/14	10/28
12/15	10/29
12/16	10/30
12/17	11/1
12/18	11/2
12/19	11/3
12/20	11/4
12/21	11/5
12/22	11/6
12/23	11/7
12/24	11/8
12/25	11/9
12/26	11/10
12/27	11/11
12/28	11/12
12/29	11/13
12/30	11/14
12/31	11/15

Solar Date / Lunar Date — 1953

Solar	Lunar
1/1	11/16
1/2	11/17
1/3	11/18
1/4	11/19
1/5	11/20
1/6	11/21
1/7	11/22
1/8	11/23
1/9	11/24
1/10	11/25
1/11	11/26
1/12	11/27
1/13	11/28
1/14	11/29
1/15	12/1
1/16	12/2
1/17	12/3
1/18	12/4
1/19	12/5
1/20	12/6
1/21	12/7

Solar	Lunar
1/22	12/8
1/23	12/9
1/24	12/10
1/25	12/11
1/26	12/12
1/27	12/13
1/28	12/14
1/29	12/15
1/30	12/16
1/31	12/17
2/1	12/18
2/2	12/19
2/3	12/20
2/4	12/21
2/5	12/22
2/6	12/23
2/7	12/24
2/8	12/25
2/9	12/26
2/10	12/27
2/11	12/28
2/12	12/29
2/13	12/30
2/14	1/1 (1953)
2/15	1/2
2/16	1/3
2/17	1/4
2/18	1/5
2/19	1/6
2/20	1/7
2/21	1/8
2/22	1/9
2/23	1/10
2/24	1/11
2/25	1/12
2/26	1/13
2/27	1/14
2/28	1/15
3/1	1/16
3/2	1/17
3/3	1/18
3/4	1/19
3/5	1/20
3/6	1/21
3/7	1/22
3/8	1/23
3/9	1/24
3/10	1/25
3/11	1/26
3/12	1/27
3/13	1/28
3/14	1/29
3/15	2/1
3/16	2/2
3/17	2/3
3/18	2/4
3/19	2/5

Solar	Lunar
3/20	2/6
3/21	2/7
3/22	2/8
3/23	2/9
3/24	2/10
3/25	2/11
3/26	2/12
3/27	2/13
3/28	2/14
3/29	2/15
3/30	2/16
3/31	2/17
4/1	2/18
4/2	2/19
4/3	2/20
4/4	2/21
4/5	2/22
4/6	2/23
4/7	2/24
4/8	2/25
4/9	2/26
4/10	2/27
4/11	2/28
4/12	2/29
4/13	2/30
4/14	3/1
4/15	3/2
4/16	3/3
4/17	3/4
4/18	3/5
4/19	3/6
4/20	3/7
4/21	3/8
4/22	3/9
4/23	3/10
4/24	3/11
4/25	3/12
4/26	3/13
4/27	3/14
4/28	3/15
4/29	3/16
4/30	3/17
5/1	3/18
5/2	3/19
5/3	3/20
5/4	3/21
5/5	3/22
5/6	3/23
5/7	3/24
5/8	3/25
5/9	3/26
5/10	3/27
5/11	3/28
5/12	3/29
5/13	4/1
5/14	4/2
5/15	4/3
5/16	4/4

Solar	Lunar
5/17	4/5
5/18	4/6
5/19	4/7
5/20	4/8
5/21	4/9
5/22	4/10
5/23	4/11
5/24	4/12
5/25	4/13
5/26	4/14
5/27	4/15
5/28	4/16
5/29	4/17
5/30	4/18
5/31	4/19
6/1	4/20
6/2	4/21
6/3	4/22
6/4	4/23
6/5	4/24
6/6	4/25
6/7	4/26
6/8	4/27
6/9	4/28
6/10	4/29
6/11	5/1
6/12	5/2
6/13	5/3
6/14	5/4
6/15	5/5
6/16	5/6
6/17	5/7
6/18	5/8
6/19	5/9
6/20	5/10
6/21	5/11
6/22	5/12
6/23	5/13
6/24	5/14
6/25	5/15
6/26	5/16
6/27	5/17
6/28	5/18
6/29	5/19
6/30	5/20
7/1	5/21
7/2	5/22
7/3	5/23
7/4	5/24
7/5	5/25
7/6	5/26
7/7	5/27
7/8	5/28
7/9	5/29
7/10	5/30
7/11	6/1
7/12	6/2
7/13	6/3

Solar	Lunar
7/14	6/4
7/15	6/5
7/16	6/6
7/17	6/7
7/18	6/8
7/19	6/9
7/20	6/10
7/21	6/11
7/22	6/12
7/23	6/13
7/24	6/14
7/25	6/15
7/26	6/16
7/27	6/17
7/28	6/18
7/29	6/19
7/30	6/20
7/31	6/21
8/1	6/22
8/2	6/23
8/3	6/24
8/4	6/25
8/5	6/26
8/6	6/27
8/7	6/28
8/8	6/29
8/9	6/30
8/10	7/1
8/11	7/2
8/12	7/3
8/13	7/4
8/14	7/5
8/15	7/6
8/16	7/7
8/17	7/8
8/18	7/9
8/19	7/10
8/20	7/11
8/21	7/12
8/22	7/13
8/23	7/14
8/24	7/15
8/25	7/16
8/26	7/17
8/27	7/18
8/28	7/19
8/29	7/20
8/30	7/21
8/31	7/22
9/1	7/23
9/2	7/24
9/3	7/25
9/4	7/26
9/5	7/27
9/6	7/28
9/7	7/29
9/8	8/1
9/9	8/2

Solar	Lunar
9/10	8/3
9/11	8/4
9/12	8/5
9/13	8/6
9/14	8/7
9/15	8/8
9/16	8/9
9/17	8/10
9/18	8/11
9/19	8/12
9/20	8/13
9/21	8/14
9/22	8/15
9/23	8/16
9/24	8/17
9/25	8/18
9/26	8/19
9/27	8/20
9/28	8/21
9/29	8/22
9/30	8/23
10/1	8/24
10/2	8/25
10/3	8/26
10/4	8/27
10/5	8/28
10/6	8/29
10/7	8/30
10/8	9/1
10/9	9/2
10/10	9/3
10/11	9/4
10/12	9/5
10/13	9/6
10/14	9/7
10/15	9/8
10/16	9/9
10/17	9/10
10/18	9/11
10/19	9/12
10/20	9/13
10/21	9/14
10/22	9/15
10/23	9/16
10/24	9/17
10/25	9/18
10/26	9/19
10/27	9/20
10/28	9/21
10/29	9/22
10/30	9/23
10/31	9/24
11/1	9/25
11/2	9/26
11/3	9/27
11/4	9/28
11/5	9/29
11/6	9/30

Solar	Lunar
11/7	10/1
11/8	10/2
11/9	10/3
11/10	10/4
11/11	10/5
11/12	10/6
11/13	10/7
11/14	10/8
11/15	10/9
11/16	10/10
11/17	10/11
11/18	10/12
11/19	10/13
11/20	10/14
11/21	10/15
11/22	10/16
11/23	10/17
11/24	10/18
11/25	10/19
11/26	10/20
11/27	10/21
11/28	10/22
11/29	10/23
11/30	10/24
12/1	10/25
12/2	10/26
12/3	10/27
12/4	10/28
12/5	10/29
12/6	11/1
12/7	11/2
12/8	11/3
12/9	11/4
12/10	11/5
12/11	11/6
12/12	11/7
12/13	11/8
12/14	11/9
12/15	11/10
12/16	11/11
12/17	11/12
12/18	11/13
12/19	11/14
12/20	11/15
12/21	11/16
12/22	11/17
12/23	11/18
12/24	11/19
12/25	11/20
12/26	11/21
12/27	11/22
12/28	11/23
12/29	11/24
12/30	11/25
12/31	11/26

Solar Date	Lunar Date
1954	
1/1	11/27
1/2	11/28
1/3	11/29
1/4	11/30
1/5	12/1
1/6	12/2
1/7	12/3
1/8	12/4
1/9	12/5
1/10	12/6
1/11	12/7
1/12	12/8
1/13	12/9
1/14	12/10
1/15	12/11
1/16	12/12
1/17	12/13
1/18	12/14
1/19	12/15
1/20	12/16
1/21	12/17
1/22	12/18
1/23	12/19
1/24	12/20
1/25	12/21
1/26	12/22
1/27	12/23
1/28	12/24
1/29	12/25
1/30	12/26
1/31	12/27
2/1	12/28
2/2	12/29
2/3	1/1 (1954)
2/4	1/2
2/5	1/3
2/6	1/4
2/7	1/5
2/8	1/6
2/9	1/7
2/10	1/8
2/11	1/9
2/12	1/10
2/13	1/11
2/14	1/12
2/15	1/13
2/16	1/14
2/17	1/15
2/18	1/16
2/19	1/17
2/20	1/18
2/21	1/19
2/22	1/20
2/23	1/21

Solar	Lunar
2/24	1/22
2/25	1/23
2/26	1/24
2/27	1/25
2/28	1/26
3/1	1/27
3/2	1/28
3/3	1/29
3/4	1/30
3/5	2/1
3/6	2/2
3/7	2/3
3/8	2/4
3/9	2/5
3/10	2/6
3/11	2/7
3/12	2/8
3/13	2/9
3/14	2/10
3/15	2/11
3/16	2/12
3/17	2/13
3/18	2/14
3/19	2/15
3/20	2/16
3/21	2/17
3/22	2/18
3/23	2/19
3/24	2/20
3/25	2/21
3/26	2/22
3/27	2/23
3/28	2/24
3/29	2/25
3/30	2/26
3/31	2/27
4/1	2/28
4/2	2/29
4/3	3/1
4/4	3/2
4/5	3/3
4/6	3/4
4/7	3/5
4/8	3/6
4/9	3/7
4/10	3/8
4/11	3/9
4/12	3/10
4/13	3/11
4/14	3/12
4/15	3/13
4/16	3/14
4/17	3/15
4/18	3/16
4/19	3/17
4/20	3/18
4/21	3/19
4/22	3/20

Solar	Lunar
4/23	3/21
4/24	3/22
4/25	3/23
4/26	3/24
4/27	3/25
4/28	3/26
4/29	3/27
4/30	3/28
5/1	3/29
5/2	3/30
5/3	4/1
5/4	4/2
5/5	4/3
5/6	4/4
5/7	4/5
5/8	4/6
5/9	4/7
5/10	4/8
5/11	4/9
5/12	4/10
5/13	4/11
5/14	4/12
5/15	4/13
5/16	4/14
5/17	4/15
5/18	4/16
5/19	4/17
5/20	4/18
5/21	4/19
5/22	4/20
5/23	4/21
5/24	4/22
5/25	4/23
5/26	4/24
5/27	4/25
5/28	4/26
5/29	4/27
5/30	4/28
5/31	4/29
6/1	5/1
6/2	5/2
6/3	5/3
6/4	5/4
6/5	5/5
6/6	5/6
6/7	5/7
6/8	5/8
6/9	5/9
6/10	5/10
6/11	5/11
6/12	5/12
6/13	5/13
6/14	5/14
6/15	5/15
6/16	5/16
6/17	5/17
6/18	5/18
6/19	5/19

Solar	Lunar
6/20	5/20
6/21	5/21
6/22	5/22
6/23	5/23
6/24	5/24
6/25	5/25
6/26	5/26
6/27	5/27
6/28	5/28
6/29	5/29
6/30	6/1
7/1	6/2
7/2	6/3
7/3	6/4
7/4	6/5
7/5	6/6
7/6	6/7
7/7	6/8
7/8	6/9
7/9	6/10
7/10	6/11
7/11	6/12
7/12	6/13
7/13	6/14
7/14	6/15
7/15	6/16
7/16	6/17
7/17	6/18
7/18	6/19
7/19	6/20
7/20	6/21
7/21	6/22
7/22	6/23
7/23	6/24
7/24	6/25
7/25	6/26
7/26	6/27
7/27	6/28
7/28	6/29
7/29	6/30
7/30	7/1
7/31	7/2
8/1	7/3
8/2	7/4
8/3	7/5
8/4	7/6
8/5	7/7
8/6	7/8
8/7	7/9
8/8	7/10
8/9	7/11
8/10	7/12
8/11	7/13
8/12	7/14
8/13	7/15
8/14	7/16
8/15	7/17
8/16	7/18

Solar	Lunar	Solar	Lunar	Solar	Lunar	Solar	Lunar	Solar	Lunar	Solar	Lunar
8/17	7/19	10/14	9/18	12/11	11/17	2/1	1/9	4/1	3/9	5/29	4/8
8/18	7/20	10/15	9/19	12/12	11/18	2/2	1/10	4/2	3/10	5/30	4/9
8/19	7/21	10/16	9/20	12/13	11/19	2/3	1/11	4/3	3/11	5/31	4/10
8/20	7/22	10/17	9/21	12/14	11/20	2/4	1/12	4/4	3/12		
8/21	7/23	10/18	9/22	12/15	11/21	2/5	1/13	4/5	3/13	6/1	4/11
8/22	7/24	10/19	9/23	12/16	11/22	2/6	1/14	4/6	3/14	6/2	4/12
8/23	7/25	10/20	9/24	12/17	11/23	2/7	1/15	4/7	3/15	6/3	4/13
8/24	7/26	10/21	9/25	12/18	11/24	2/8	1/16	4/8	3/16	6/4	4/14
8/25	7/27	10/22	9/26	12/19	11/25	2/9	1/17	4/9	3/17	6/5	4/15
8/26	7/28	10/23	9/27	12/20	11/26	2/10	1/18	4/10	3/18	6/6	4/16
8/27	7/29	10/24	9/28	12/21	11/27	2/11	1/19	4/11	3/19	6/7	4/17
8/28	8/1	10/25	9/29	12/22	11/28	2/12	1/20	4/12	3/20	6/8	4/18
8/29	8/2	10/26	9/30	12/23	11/29	2/13	1/21	4/13	3/21	6/9	4/19
8/30	8/3	10/27	10/1	12/24	11/30	2/14	1/22	4/14	3/22	6/10	4/20
8/31	8/4	10/28	10/2	12/25	12/1	2/15	1/23	4/15	3/23	6/11	4/21
		10/29	10/3	12/26	12/2	2/16	1/24	4/16	3/24	6/12	4/22
9/1	8/5	10/30	10/4	12/27	12/3	2/17	1/25	4/17	3/25	6/13	4/23
9/2	8/6	10/31	10/5	12/28	12/4	2/18	1/26	4/18	3/26	6/14	4/24
9/3	8/7			12/29	12/5	2/19	1/27	4/19	3/27	6/15	4/25
9/4	8/8	11/1	10/6	12/30	12/6	2/20	1/28	4/20	3/28	6/16	4/26
9/5	8/9	11/2	10/7	12/31	12/7	2/21	1/29	4/21	3/29	6/17	4/27
9/6	8/10	11/3	10/8			2/22	2/1	4/22	3/1	6/18	4/28
9/7	8/11	11/4	10/9			2/23	2/2	*(Leap Month)*		6/19	4/29
9/8	8/12	11/5	10/10	**Solar**	**Lunar**	2/24	2/3	4/23	3/2	6/20	5/1
9/9	8/13	11/6	10/11	**Date**	**Date**	2/25	2/4	4/24	3/3	6/21	5/2
9/10	8/14	11/7	10/12			2/26	2/5	4/25	3/4	6/22	5/3
9/11	8/15	11/8	10/13	**1955**		2/27	2/6	4/26	3/5	6/23	5/4
9/12	8/16	11/9	10/14	1/1	12/8	2/28	2/7	4/27	3/6	6/24	5/5
9/13	8/17	11/10	10/15	1/2	12/9			4/28	3/7	6/25	5/6
9/14	8/18	11/11	10/16	1/3	12/10	3/1	2/8	4/29	3/8	6/26	5/7
9/15	8/19	11/12	10/17	1/4	12/11	3/2	2/9	4/30	3/9	6/27	5/8
9/16	8/20	11/13	10/18	1/5	12/12	3/3	2/10			6/28	5/9
9/17	8/21	11/14	10/19	1/6	12/13	3/4	2/11	5/1	3/10	6/29	5/10
9/18	8/22	11/15	10/20	1/7	12/14	3/5	2/12	5/2	3/11	6/30	5/11
9/19	8/23	11/16	10/21	1/8	12/15	3/6	2/13	5/3	3/12		
9/20	8/24	11/17	10/22	1/9	12/16	3/7	2/14	5/4	3/13	7/1	5/12
9/21	8/25	11/18	10/23	1/10	12/17	3/8	2/15	5/5	3/14	7/2	5/13
9/22	8/26	11/19	10/24	1/11	12/18	3/9	2/16	5/6	3/15	7/3	5/14
9/23	8/27	11/20	10/25	1/12	12/19	3/10	2/17	5/7	3/16	7/4	5/15
9/24	8/28	11/21	10/26	1/13	12/20	3/11	2/18	5/8	3/17	7/5	5/16
9/25	8/29	11/22	10/27	1/14	12/21	3/12	2/19	5/9	3/18	7/6	5/17
9/26	8/30	11/23	10/28	1/15	12/22	3/13	2/20	5/10	3/19	7/7	5/18
9/27	9/1	11/24	10/29	1/16	12/23	3/14	2/21	5/11	3/20	7/8	5/19
9/28	9/2	11/25	11/1	1/17	12/24	3/15	2/22	5/12	3/21	7/9	5/20
9/29	9/3	11/26	11/2	1/18	12/25	3/16	2/23	5/13	3/22	7/10	5/21
9/30	9/4	11/27	11/3	1/19	12/26	3/17	2/24	5/14	3/23	7/11	5/22
		11/28	11/4	1/20	12/27	3/18	2/25	5/15	3/24	7/12	5/23
10/1	9/5	11/29	11/5	1/21	12/28	3/19	2/26	5/16	3/25	7/13	5/24
10/2	9/6	11/30	11/6	1/22	12/29	3/20	2/27	5/17	3/26	7/14	5/25
10/3	9/7			1/23	12/30	3/21	2/28	5/18	3/27	7/15	5/26
10/4	9/8	12/1	11/7	1/24	1/1	3/22	2/29	5/19	3/28	7/16	5/27
10/5	9/9	12/2	11/8		(1955)	3/23	2/30	5/20	3/29	7/17	5/28
10/6	9/10	12/3	11/9	1/25	1/2	3/24	3/1	5/21	3/30	7/18	5/29
10/7	9/11	12/4	11/10	1/26	1/3	3/25	3/2	5/22	4/1	7/19	6/1
10/8	9/12	12/5	11/11	1/27	1/4	3/26	3/3	5/23	4/2	7/20	6/2
10/9	9/13	12/6	11/12	1/28	1/5	3/27	3/4	5/24	4/3	7/21	6/3
10/10	9/14	12/7	11/13	1/29	1/6	3/28	3/5	5/25	4/4	7/22	6/4
10/11	9/15	12/8	11/14	1/30	1/7	3/29	3/6	5/26	4/5	7/23	6/5
10/12	9/16	12/9	11/15	1/31	1/8	3/30	3/7	5/27	4/6	7/24	6/6
10/13	9/17	12/10	11/16			3/31	3/8	5/28	4/7	7/25	6/7

Solar	Lunar	Solar	Lunar	Solar	Lunar	Solar	Lunar	Solar	Lunar	Solar	Lunar
7/26	6/8	9/22	8/7	11/19	10/6	1/11	11/29	3/8	1/26	5/5	3/25
7/27	6/9	9/23	8/8	11/20	10/7	1/12	11/30	3/9	1/27	5/6	3/26
7/28	6/10	9/24	8/9	11/21	10/8	1/13	12/1	3/10	1/28	5/7	3/27
7/29	6/11	9/25	8/10	11/22	10/9	1/14	12/2	3/11	1/29	5/8	3/28
7/30	6/12	9/26	8/11	11/23	10/10	1/15	12/3	3/12	2/1	5/9	3/29
7/31	6/13	9/27	8/12	11/24	10/11	1/16	12/4	3/13	2/2	5/10	4/1
		9/28	8/13	11/25	10/12	1/17	12/5	3/14	2/3	5/11	4/2
8/1	6/14	9/29	8/14	11/26	10/13	1/18	12/6	3/15	2/4	5/12	4/3
8/2	6/15	9/30	8/15	11/27	10/14	1/19	12/7	3/16	2/5	5/13	4/4
8/3	6/16			11/28	10/15	1/20	12/8	3/17	2/6	5/14	4/5
8/4	6/17	10/1	8/16	11/29	10/16	1/21	12/9	3/18	2/7	5/15	4/6
8/5	6/18	10/2	8/17	11/30	10/17	1/22	12/10	3/19	2/8	5/16	4/7
8/6	6/19	10/3	8/18			1/23	12/11	3/20	2/9	5/17	4/8
8/7	6/20	10/4	8/19	12/1	10/18	1/24	12/12	3/21	2/10	5/18	4/9
8/8	6/21	10/5	8/20	12/2	10/19	1/25	12/13	3/22	2/11	5/19	4/10
8/9	6/22	10/6	8/21	12/3	10/20	1/26	12/14	3/23	2/12	5/20	4/11
8/10	6/23	10/7	8/22	12/4	10/21	1/27	12/15	3/24	2/13	5/21	4/12
8/11	6/24	10/8	8/23	12/5	10/22	1/28	12/16	3/25	2/14	5/22	4/13
8/12	6/25	10/9	8/24	12/6	10/23	1/29	12/17	3/26	2/15	5/23	4/14
8/13	6/26	10/10	8/25	12/7	10/24	1/30	12/18	3/27	2/16	5/24	4/15
8/14	6/27	10/11	8/26	12/8	10/25	1/31	12/19	3/28	2/17	5/25	4/16
8/15	6/28	10/12	8/27	12/9	10/26			3/29	2/18	5/26	4/17
8/16	6/29	10/13	8/28	12/10	10/27	2/1	12/20	3/30	2/19	5/27	4/18
8/17	6/30	10/14	8/29	12/11	10/28	2/2	12/21	3/31	2/20	5/28	4/19
8/18	7/1	10/15	8/30	12/12	10/29	2/3	12/22			5/29	4/20
8/19	7/2	10/16	9/1	12/13	10/30	2/4	12/23	4/1	2/21	5/30	4/21
8/20	7/3	10/17	9/2	12/14	11/1	2/5	12/24	4/2	2/22	5/31	4/22
8/21	7/4	10/18	9/3	12/15	11/2	2/6	12/25	4/3	2/23		
8/22	7/5	10/19	9/4	12/16	11/3	2/7	12/26	4/4	2/24	6/1	4/23
8/23	7/6	10/20	9/5	12/17	11/4	2/8	12/27	4/5	2/25	6/2	4/24
8/24	7/7	10/21	9/6	12/18	11/5	2/9	12/28	4/6	2/26	6/3	4/25
8/25	7/8	10/22	9/7	12/19	11/6	2/10	12/29	4/7	2/27	6/4	4/26
8/26	7/9	10/23	9/8	12/20	11/7	2/11	12/30	4/8	2/28	6/5	4/27
8/27	7/10	10/24	9/9	12/21	11/8	2/12	1/1	4/9	2/29	6/6	4/28
8/28	7/11	10/25	9/10	12/22	11/9		(1956)	4/10	2/30	6/7	4/29
8/29	7/12	10/26	9/11	12/23	11/10	2/13	1/2	4/11	3/1	6/8	4/30
8/30	7/13	10/27	9/12	12/24	11/11	2/14	1/3	4/12	3/2	6/9	5/1
8/31	7/14	10/28	9/13	12/25	11/12	2/15	1/4	4/13	3/3	6/10	5/2
		10/29	9/14	12/26	11/13	2/16	1/5	4/14	3/4	6/11	5/3
9/1	7/15	10/30	9/15	12/27	11/14	2/17	1/6	4/15	3/5	6/12	5/4
9/2	7/16	10/31	9/16	12/28	11/15	2/18	1/7	4/16	3/6	6/13	5/5
9/3	7/17			12/29	11/16	2/19	1/8	4/17	3/7	6/14	5/6
9/4	7/18	11/1	9/17	12/30	11/17	2/20	1/9	4/18	3/8	6/15	5/7
9/5	7/19	11/2	9/18	12/31	11/18	2/21	1/10	4/19	3/9	6/16	5/8
9/6	7/20	11/3	9/19			2/22	1/11	4/20	3/10	6/17	5/9
9/7	7/21	11/4	9/20			2/23	1/12	4/21	3/11	6/18	5/10
9/8	7/22	11/5	9/21	**Solar**	**Lunar**	2/24	1/13	4/22	3/12	6/19	5/11
9/9	7/23	11/6	9/22	**Date**	**Date**	2/25	1/14	4/23	3/13	6/20	5/12
9/10	7/24	11/7	9/23			2/26	1/15	4/24	3/14	6/21	5/13
9/11	7/25	11/8	9/24	**1956**		2/27	1/16	4/25	3/15	6/22	5/14
9/12	7/26	11/9	9/25	1/1	11/19	2/28	1/17	4/26	3/16	6/23	5/15
9/13	7/27	11/10	9/26	1/2	11/20	2/29	1/18	4/27	3/17	6/24	5/16
9/14	7/28	11/11	9/27	1/3	11/21			4/28	3/18	6/25	5/17
9/15	7/29	11/12	9/28	1/4	11/22	3/1	1/19	4/29	3/19	6/26	5/18
9/16	8/1	11/13	9/29	1/5	11/23	3/2	1/20	4/20	3/20	6/27	5/19
9/17	8/2	11/14	10/1	1/6	11/24	3/3	1/21			6/28	5/20
9/18	8/3	11/15	10/2	1/7	11/25	3/4	1/22	5/1	3/21	6/29	5/21
9/19	8/4	11/16	10/3	1/8	11/26	3/5	1/23	5/2	3/22	6/30	5/22
9/20	8/5	11/17	10/4	1/9	11/27	3/6	1/24	5/3	3/23		
9/21	8/6	11/18	10/5	1/10	11/28	3/7	1/25	5/4	3/24	7/1	5/23

Solar	Lunar	Solar	Lunar	Solar	Lunar	Solar	Lunar	Solar	Lunar	Solar	Lunar
7/2	5/24	8/30	7/25	10/27	9/24	12/24	11/23	2/14	1/15	4/13	3/14
7/3	5/25	8/31	7/26	10/28	9/25	12/25	11/24	2/15	1/16	4/14	3/15
7/4	5/26			10/29	9/26	12/26	11/25	2/16	1/17	4/15	3/16
7/5	5/27	9/1	7/27	10/30	9/27	12/27	11/26	2/17	1/18	4/16	3/17
7/6	5/28	9/2	7/28	10/31	9/28	12/28	11/27	2/18	1/19	4/17	3/18
7/7	5/29	9/3	7/29			12/29	11/28	2/19	1/20	4/18	3/19
7/8	6/1	9/4	7/30	11/1	9/29	12/30	11/29	2/20	1/21	4/19	3/20
7/9	6/2	9/5	8/1	11/2	9/30	12/31	11/30	2/21	1/22	4/20	3/21
7/10	6/3	9/6	8/2	11/3	10/1			2/22	1/23	4/21	3/22
7/11	6/4	9/7	8/3	11/4	10/2			2/23	1/24	4/22	3/23
7/12	6/5	9/8	8/4	11/5	10/3	Solar	Lunar	2/24	1/25	4/23	3/24
7/13	6/6	9/9	8/5	11/6	10/4	Date	Date	2/25	1/26	4/24	3/25
7/14	6/7	9/10	8/6	11/7	10/5	1957		2/26	1/27	4/25	3/26
7/15	6/8	9/11	8/7	11/8	10/6	1/1	12/1	2/27	1/28	4/26	3/27
7/16	6/9	9/12	8/8	11/9	10/7	1/2	12/2	2/28	1/29	4/27	3/28
7/17	6/10	9/13	8/9	11/10	10/8	1/3	12/3			4/28	3/29
7/18	6/11	9/14	8/10	11/11	10/9	1/4	12/4	3/1	1/30	4/29	3/30
7/19	6/12	9/15	8/11	11/12	10/10	1/5	12/5	3/2	2/1	4/30	4/1
7/20	6/13	9/16	8/12	11/13	10/11	1/6	12/6	3/3	2/2		
7/21	6/14	9/17	8/13	11/14	10/12	1/7	12/7	3/4	2/3	5/1	4/2
7/22	6/15	9/18	8/14	11/15	10/13	1/8	12/8	3/5	2/4	5/2	4/3
7/23	6/16	9/19	8/15	11/16	10/14	1/9	12/9	3/6	2/5	5/3	4/4
7/24	6/17	9/20	8/16	11/17	10/15	1/10	12/10	3/7	2/6	5/4	4/5
7/25	6/18	9/21	8/17	11/18	10/16	1/11	12/11	3/8	2/7	5/5	4/6
7/26	6/19	9/22	8/18	11/19	10/17	1/12	12/12	3/9	2/8	5/6	4/7
7/27	6/20	9/23	8/19	11/20	10/18	1/13	12/13	3/10	2/9	5/7	4/8
7/28	6/21	9/24	8/20	11/21	10/19	1/14	12/14	3/11	2/10	5/8	4/9
7/29	6/22	9/25	8/21	11/22	10/20	1/15	12/15	3/12	2/11	5/9	4/10
7/30	6/23	9/26	8/22	11/23	10/21	1/16	12/16	3/13	2/12	5/10	4/11
7/31	6/24	9/27	8/23	11/24	10/22	1/17	12/17	3/14	2/13	5/11	4/12
		9/28	8/24	11/25	10/23	1/18	12/18	3/15	2/14	5/12	4/13
8/1	6/25	9/29	8/25	11/26	10/24	1/19	12/19	3/16	2/15	5/13	4/14
8/2	6/26	9/30	8/26	11/27	10/25	1/20	12/20	3/17	2/16	5/14	4/15
8/3	6/27			11/28	10/26	1/21	12/21	3/18	2/17	5/15	4/16
8/4	6/28	10/1	8/27	11/29	10/27	1/22	12/22	3/19	2/18	5/16	4/17
8/5	6/29	10/2	8/28	11/30	10/28	1/23	12/23	3/20	2/19	5/17	4/18
8/6	7/1	10/3	8/29			1/24	12/24	3/21	2/20	5/18	4/19
8/7	7/2	10/4	9/1	12/1	10/29	1/25	12/25	3/22	2/21	5/19	4/20
8/8	7/3	10/5	9/2	12/2	11/1	1/26	12/26	3/23	2/22	5/20	4/21
8/9	7/4	10/6	9/3	12/3	11/2	1/27	12/27	3/24	2/23	5/21	4/22
8/10	7/5	10/7	9/4	12/4	11/3	1/28	12/28	3/25	2/24	5/22	4/23
8/11	7/6	10/8	9/5	12/5	11/4	1/29	12/29	3/26	2/25	5/23	4/24
8/12	7/7	10/9	9/6	12/6	11/5	1/30	12/30	3/27	2/26	5/24	4/25
8/13	7/8	10/10	9/7	12/7	11/6	1/31	1/1	3/28	2/27	5/25	4/26
8/14	7/9	10/11	9/8	12/8	11/7		(1957)	3/29	2/28	5/26	4/27
8/15	7/10	10/12	9/9	12/9	11/8			3/30	2/29	5/27	4/28
8/16	7/11	10/13	9/10	12/10	11/9			3/31	3/1	5/28	4/29
8/17	7/12	10/14	9/11	12/11	11/10	2/1	1/2			5/29	5/1
8/18	7/13	10/15	9/12	12/12	11/11	2/2	1/3	4/1	3/2	5/30	5/2
8/19	7/14	10/16	9/13	12/13	11/12	2/3	1/4	4/2	3/3	5/31	5/3
8/20	7/15	10/17	9/14	12/14	11/13	2/4	1/5	4/3	3/4		
8/21	7/16	10/18	9/15	12/15	11/14	2/5	1/6	4/4	3/5	6/1	5/4
8/22	7/17	10/19	9/16	12/16	11/15	2/6	1/7	4/5	3/6	6/2	5/5
8/23	7/18	10/20	9/17	12/17	11/16	2/7	1/8	4/6	3/7	6/3	5/6
8/24	7/19	10/21	9/18	12/18	11/17	2/8	1/9	4/7	3/8	6/4	5/7
8/25	7/20	10/22	9/19	12/19	11/18	2/9	1/10	4/8	3/9	6/5	5/8
8/26	7/21	10/23	9/20	12/20	11/19	2/10	1/11	4/9	3/10	6/6	5/9
8/27	7/22	10/24	9/21	12/21	11/20	2/11	1/12	4/10	3/11	6/7	5/10
8/28	7/23	10/25	9/22	12/22	11/21	2/12	1/13	4/11	3/12	6/8	5/11
8/29	7/24	10/26	9/23	12/23	11/22	2/13	1/14	4/12	3/13	6/9	5/12

Solar	Lunar	Solar	Lunar	Solar	Lunar	Solar	Lunar	Solar	Lunar	Solar	Lunar
6/10	5/13	8/7	7/12	10/3	8/10	12/1	10/10	1/24	12/5	3/22	2/3
6/11	5/14	8/8	7/13	10/4	8/11	12/2	10/11	1/25	12/6	3/23	2/4
6/12	5/15	8/9	7/14	10/5	8/12	12/3	10/12	1/26	12/7	3/24	2/5
6/13	5/16	8/10	7/15	10/6	8/13	12/4	10/13	1/27	12/8	3/25	2/6
6/14	5/17	8/11	7/16	10/7	8/14	12/5	10/14	1/28	12/9	3/26	2/7
6/15	5/18	8/12	7/17	10/8	8/15	12/6	10/15	1/29	12/10	3/27	2/8
6/16	5/19	8/13	7/18	10/9	8/16	12/7	10/16	1/30	12/11	3/28	2/9
6/17	5/20	8/14	7/19	10/10	8/17	12/8	10/17	1/31	12/12	3/29	2/10
6/18	5/21	8/15	7/20	10/11	8/18	12/9	10/18			3/30	2/11
6/19	5/22	8/16	7/21	10/12	8/19	12/10	10/19	2/1	12/13	3/31	2/12
6/20	5/23	8/17	7/22	10/13	8/20	12/11	10/20	2/2	12/14		
6/21	5/24	8/18	7/23	10/14	8/21	12/12	10/21	2/3	12/15	4/1	2/13
6/22	5/25	8/19	7/24	10/15	8/22	12/13	10/22	2/4	12/16	4/2	2/14
6/23	5/26	8/20	7/25	10/16	8/23	12/14	10/23	2/5	12/17	4/3	2/15
6/24	5/27	8/21	7/26	10/17	8/24	12/15	10/24	2/6	12/18	4/4	2/16
6/25	5/28	8/22	7/27	10/18	8/25	12/16	10/25	2/7	12/19	4/5	2/17
6/26	5/29	8/23	7/28	10/19	8/26	12/17	10/26	2/8	12/20	4/6	2/18
6/27	5/30	8/24	7/29	10/20	8/27	12/18	10/27	2/9	12/21	4/7	2/19
6/28	6/1	8/25	8/1	10/21	8/28	12/19	10/28	2/10	12/22	4/8	2/20
6/29	6/2	8/26	8/2	10/22	8/29	12/20	10/29	2/11	12/23	4/9	2/21
6/30	6/3	8/27	8/3	10/23	9/1	12/21	11/1	2/12	12/24	4/10	2/22
		8/28	8/4	10/24	9/2	12/22	11/2	2/13	12/25	4/11	2/23
7/1	6/4	8/29	8/5	10/25	9/3	12/23	11/3	2/14	12/26	4/12	2/24
7/2	6/5	8/30	8/6	10/26	9/4	12/24	11/4	2/15	12/27	4/13	2/25
7/3	6/6	8/31	8/7	10/27	9/5	12/25	11/5	2/16	12/28	4/14	2/26
7/4	6/7			10/28	9/6	12/26	11/6	2/17	12/29	4/15	2/27
7/5	6/8	9/1	8/8	10/29	9/7	12/27	11/7	2/18	1/1	4/16	2/28
7/6	6/9	9/2	8/9	10/30	9/8	12/28	11/8		(1958)	4/17	2/29
7/7	6/10	9/3	8/10	10/31	9/9	12/29	11/9	2/19	1/2	4/18	2/30
7/8	6/11	9/4	8/11			12/30	11/10	2/20	1/3	4/19	3/1
7/9	6/12	9/5	8/12	11/1	9/10	12/31	11/11	2/21	1/4	4/20	3/2
7/10	6/13	9/6	8/13	11/2	9/11			2/22	1/5	4/21	3/3
7/11	6/14	9/7	8/14	11/3	9/12			2/23	1/6	4/22	3/4
7/12	6/15	9/8	8/15	11/4	9/13	**Solar**	**Lunar**	2/24	1/7	4/23	3/5
7/13	6/16	9/9	8/16	11/5	9/14	**Date**	**Date**	2/25	1/8	4/24	3/6
7/14	6/17	9/10	8/17	11/6	9/15			2/26	1/9	4/25	3/7
7/15	6/18	9/11	8/18	11/7	9/16	**1958**		2/27	1/10	4/26	3/8
7/16	6/19	9/12	8/19	11/8	9/17	1/1	11/12	2/28	1/11	4/27	3/9
7/17	6/20	9/13	8/20	11/9	9/18	1/2	11/13			4/28	3/10
7/18	6/21	9/14	8/21	11/10	9/19	1/3	11/14	3/1	1/12	4/29	3/11
7/19	6/22	9/15	8/22	11/11	9/20	1/4	11/15	3/2	1/13	4/30	3/12
7/20	6/23	9/16	8/23	11/12	9/21	1/5	11/16	3/3	1/14		
7/21	6/24	9/17	8/24	11/13	9/22	1/6	11/17	3/4	1/15	5/1	3/13
7/22	6/25	9/18	8/25	11/14	9/23	1/7	11/18	3/5	1/16	5/2	3/14
7/23	6/26	9/19	8/26	11/15	9/24	1/8	11/19	3/6	1/17	5/3	3/15
7/24	6/27	9/20	8/27	11/16	9/25	1/9	11/20	3/7	1/18	5/4	3/16
7/25	6/28	9/21	8/28	11/17	9/26	1/10	11/21	3/8	1/19	5/5	3/17
7/26	6/29	9/22	8/29	11/18	9/27	1/11	11/22	3/9	1/20	5/6	3/18
7/27	7/1	9/23	8/30	11/19	9/28	1/12	11/23	3/10	1/21	5/7	3/19
7/28	7/2	9/24	8/1	11/20	9/29	1/13	11/24	3/11	1/22	5/8	3/20
7/29	7/3	*(Leap Month)*		11/21	9/30	1/14	11/25	3/12	1/23	5/9	3/21
7/30	7/4	9/25	8/2	11/22	10/1	1/15	11/26	3/13	1/24	5/10	3/22
7/31	7/5	9/26	8/3	11/23	10/2	1/16	11/27	3/14	1/25	5/11	3/23
		9/27	8/4	11/24	10/3	1/17	11/28	3/15	1/26	5/12	3/24
8/1	7/6	9/28	8/5	11/25	10/4	1/18	11/29	3/16	1/27	5/13	3/25
8/2	7/7	9/29	8/6	11/26	10/5	1/19	11/30	3/17	1/28	5/14	3/26
8/3	7/8	9/30	8/7	11/27	10/6	1/20	12/1	3/18	1/29	5/15	3/27
8/4	7/9			11/28	10/7	1/21	12/2	3/19	1/30	5/16	3/28
8/5	7/10	10/1	8/8	11/29	10/8	1/22	12/3	3/20	2/1	5/17	3/29
8/6	7/11	10/2	8/9	11/30	10/9	1/23	12/4	3/21	2/2	5/18	3/30

Solar	Lunar	Solar	Lunar	Solar	Lunar	Solar	Lunar	Solar Date	Lunar Date	Solar	Lunar
5/19	4/1	7/16	5/30	9/12	7/29	11/9	9/28			2/24	1/17
5/20	4/2	7/17	6/1	9/13	8/1	11/10	9/29	**1959**		2/25	1/18
5/21	4/3	7/18	6/2	9/14	8/2	11/11	10/1			2/26	1/19
5/22	4/4	7/19	6/3	9/15	8/3	11/12	10/2	1/1	11/22	2/27	1/20
5/23	4/5	7/20	6/4	9/16	8/4	11/13	10/3	1/2	11/23	2/28	1/21
5/24	4/6	7/21	6/5	9/17	8/5	11/14	10/4	1/3	11/24		
5/25	4/7	7/22	6/6	9/18	8/6	11/15	10/5	1/4	11/25	3/1	1/22
5/26	4/8	7/23	6/7	9/19	8/7	11/16	10/6	1/5	11/26	3/2	1/23
5/27	4/9	7/24	6/8	9/20	8/8	11/17	10/7	1/6	11/27	3/3	1/24
5/28	4/10	7/25	6/9	9/21	8/9	11/18	10/8	1/7	11/28	3/4	1/25
5/29	4/11	7/26	6/10	9/22	8/10	11/19	10/9	1/8	11/29	3/5	1/26
5/30	4/12	7/27	6/11	9/23	8/11	11/20	10/10	1/9	12/1	3/6	1/27
5/31	4/13	7/28	6/12	9/24	8/12	11/21	10/11	1/10	12/2	3/7	1/28
		7/29	6/13	9/25	8/13	11/22	10/12	1/11	12/3	3/8	1/29
6/1	4/14	7/30	6/14	9/26	8/14	11/23	10/13	1/12	12/4	3/9	2/1
6/2	4/15	7/31	6/15	9/27	8/15	11/24	10/14	1/13	12/5	3/10	2/2
6/3	4/16			9/28	8/16	11/25	10/15	1/14	12/6	3/11	2/3
6/4	4/17	8/1	6/16	9/29	8/17	11/26	10/16	1/15	12/7	3/12	2/4
6/5	4/18	8/2	6/17	9/30	8/18	11/27	10/17	1/16	12/8	3/13	2/5
6/6	4/19	8/3	6/18			11/28	10/18	1/17	12/9	3/14	2/6
6/7	4/20	8/4	6/19	10/1	8/19	11/29	10/19	1/18	12/10	3/15	2/7
6/8	4/21	8/5	6/20	10/2	8/20	11/30	10/20	1/19	12/11	3/16	2/8
6/9	4/22	8/6	6/21	10/3	8/21			1/20	12/12	3/17	2/9
6/10	4/23	8/7	6/22	10/4	8/22	12/1	10/21	1/21	12/13	3/18	2/10
6/11	4/24	8/8	6/23	10/5	8/23	12/2	10/22	1/22	12/14	3/19	2/11
6/12	4/25	8/9	6/24	10/6	8/24	12/3	10/23	1/23	12/15	3/20	2/12
6/13	4/26	8/10	6/25	10/7	8/25	12/4	10/24	1/24	12/16	3/21	2/13
6/14	4/27	8/11	6/26	10/8	8/26	12/5	10/25	1/25	12/17	3/22	2/14
6/15	4/28	8/12	6/27	10/9	8/27	12/6	10/26	1/26	12/18	3/23	2/15
6/16	4/29	8/13	6/28	10/10	8/28	12/7	10/27	1/27	12/19	3/24	2/16
6/17	5/1	8/14	6/29	10/11	8/29	12/8	10/28	1/28	12/20	3/25	2/17
6/18	5/2	8/15	7/1	10/12	8/30	12/9	10/29	1/29	12/21	3/26	2/18
6/19	5/3	8/16	7/2	10/13	9/1	12/10	10/30	1/30	12/22	3/27	2/19
6/20	5/4	8/17	7/3	10/14	9/2	12/11	11/1	1/31	12/23	3/28	2/20
6/21	5/5	8/18	7/4	10/15	9/3	12/12	11/2			3/29	2/21
6/22	5/6	8/19	7/5	10/16	9/4	12/13	11/3	2/1	12/24	3/30	2/22
6/23	5/7	8/20	7/6	10/17	9/5	12/14	11/4	2/2	12/25	3/31	2/23
6/24	5/8	8/21	7/7	10/18	9/6	12/15	11/5	2/3	12/26		
6/25	5/9	8/22	7/8	10/19	9/7	12/16	11/6	2/4	12/27	4/1	2/24
6/26	5/10	8/23	7/9	10/20	9/8	12/17	11/7	2/5	12/28	4/2	2/25
6/27	5/11	8/24	7/10	10/21	9/9	12/18	11/8	2/6	12/29	4/3	2/26
6/28	5/12	8/25	7/11	10/22	9/10	12/19	11/9	2/7	12/30	4/4	2/27
6/29	5/13	8/26	7/12	10/23	9/11	12/20	11/10	2/8	1/1 (1959)	4/5	2/28
6/30	5/14	8/27	7/13	10/24	9/12	12/21	11/11			4/6	2/29
		8/28	7/14	10/25	9/13	12/22	11/12	2/9	1/2	4/7	2/30
7/1	5/15	8/29	7/15	10/26	9/14	12/23	11/13	2/10	1/3	4/8	3/1
7/2	5/16	8/30	7/16	10/27	9/15	12/24	11/14	2/11	1/4	4/9	3/2
7/3	5/17	8/31	7/17	10/28	9/16	12/25	11/15	2/12	1/5	4/10	3/3
7/4	5/18			10/29	9/17	12/26	11/16	2/13	1/6	4/11	3/4
7/5	5/19	9/1	7/18	10/30	9/18	12/27	11/17	2/14	1/7	4/12	3/5
7/6	5/20	9/2	7/19	10/31	9/19	12/28	11/18	2/15	1/8	4/13	3/6
7/7	5/21	9/3	7/20			12/29	11/19	2/16	1/9	4/14	3/7
7/8	5/22	9/4	7/21	11/1	9/20	12/30	11/20	2/17	1/10	4/15	3/8
7/9	5/23	9/5	7/22	11/2	9/21	12/31	11/21	2/18	1/11	4/16	3/9
7/10	5/24	9/6	7/23	11/3	9/22			2/19	1/12	4/17	3/10
7/11	5/25	9/7	7/24	11/4	9/23			2/20	1/13	4/18	3/11
7/12	5/26	9/8	7/25	11/5	9/24			2/21	1/14	4/19	3/12
7/13	5/27	9/9	7/26	11/6	9/25			2/22	1/15	4/20	3/13
7/14	5/28	9/10	7/27	11/7	9/26			2/23	1/16	4/21	3/14
7/15	5/29	9/11	7/28	11/8	9/27					4/22	3/15

Solar	Lunar	Solar	Lunar	Solar	Lunar	Solar	Lunar	Solar	Lunar	Solar	Lunar
4/23	3/16	6/20	5/15	8/17	7/14	10/14	9/13	12/11	11/12	2/1	1/5
4/24	3/17	6/21	5/16	8/18	7/15	10/15	9/14	12/12	11/13	2/2	1/6
4/25	3/18	6/22	5/17	8/19	7/16	10/16	9/15	12/13	11/14	2/3	1/7
4/26	3/19	6/23	5/18	8/20	7/17	10/17	9/16	12/14	11/15	2/4	1/8
4/27	3/20	6/24	5/19	8/21	7/18	10/18	9/17	12/15	11/16	2/5	1/9
4/28	3/21	6/25	5/20	8/22	7/19	10/19	9/18	12/16	11/17	2/6	1/10
4/29	3/22	6/26	5/21	8/23	7/20	10/20	9/19	12/17	11/18	2/7	1/11
4/30	3/23	6/27	5/22	8/24	7/21	10/21	9/20	12/18	11/19	2/8	1/12
		6/28	5/23	8/25	7/22	10/22	9/21	12/19	11/20	2/9	1/13
5/1	3/24	6/29	5/24	8/26	7/23	10/23	9/22	12/20	11/21	2/10	1/14
5/2	3/25	6/30	5/25	8/27	7/24	10/24	9/23	12/21	11/22	2/11	1/15
5/3	3/26			8/28	7/25	10/25	9/24	12/22	11/23	2/12	1/16
5/4	3/27	7/1	5/26	8/29	7/26	10/26	9/25	12/23	11/24	2/13	1/17
5/5	3/28	7/2	5/27	8/30	7/27	10/27	9/26	12/24	11/25	2/14	1/18
5/6	3/29	7/3	5/28	8/31	7/28	10/28	9/27	12/25	11/26	2/15	1/19
5/7	3/30	7/4	5/29			10/29	9/28	12/26	11/27	2/16	1/20
5/8	4/1	7/5	5/30	9/1	7/29	10/30	9/29	12/27	11/28	2/17	1/21
5/9	4/2	7/6	6/1	9/2	7/30	10/31	9/30	12/28	11/29	2/18	1/22
5/10	4/3	7/7	6/2	9/3	8/1			12/29	11/30	2/19	1/23
5/11	4/4	7/8	6/3	9/4	8/2	11/1	10/1	12/30	12/1	2/20	1/24
5/12	4/5	7/9	6/4	9/5	8/3	11/2	10/2	12/31	12/2	2/21	1/25
5/13	4/6	7/10	6/5	9/6	8/4	11/3	10/3			2/22	1/26
5/14	4/7	7/11	6/6	9/7	8/5	11/4	10/4			2/23	1/27
5/15	4/8	7/12	6/7	9/8	8/6	11/5	10/5	**Solar Date**	**Lunar Date**	2/24	1/28
5/16	4/9	7/13	6/8	9/9	8/7	11/6	10/6			2/25	1/29
5/17	4/10	7/14	6/9	9/10	8/8	11/7	10/7			2/26	1/30
5/18	4/11	7/15	6/10	9/11	8/9	11/8	10/8	**1960**		2/27	2/1
5/19	4/12	7/16	6/11	9/12	8/10	11/9	10/9	1/1	12/3	2/28	2/2
5/20	4/13	7/17	6/12	9/13	8/11	11/10	10/10	1/2	12/4	2/29	2/3
5/21	4/14	7/18	6/13	9/14	8/12	11/11	10/11	1/3	12/5		
5/22	4/15	7/19	6/14	9/15	8/13	11/12	10/12	1/4	12/6	3/1	2/4
5/23	4/16	7/20	6/15	9/16	8/14	11/13	10/13	1/5	12/7	3/2	2/5
5/24	4/17	7/21	6/16	9/17	8/15	11/14	10/14	1/6	12/8	3/3	2/6
5/25	4/18	7/22	6/17	9/18	8/16	11/15	10/15	1/7	12/9	3/4	2/7
5/26	4/19	7/23	6/18	9/19	8/17	11/16	10/16	1/8	12/10	3/5	2/8
5/27	4/20	7/24	6/19	9/20	8/18	11/17	10/17	1/9	12/11	3/6	2/9
5/28	4/21	7/25	6/20	9/21	8/19	11/18	10/18	1/10	12/12	3/7	2/10
5/29	4/22	7/26	6/21	9/22	8/20	11/19	10/19	1/11	12/13	3/8	2/11
5/30	4/23	7/27	6/22	9/23	8/21	11/20	10/20	1/12	12/14	3/9	2/12
5/31	4/24	7/28	6/23	9/24	8/22	11/21	10/21	1/13	12/15	3/10	2/13
		7/29	6/24	9/25	8/23	11/22	10/22	1/14	12/16	3/11	2/14
6/1	4/25	7/30	6/25	9/26	8/24	11/23	10/23	1/15	12/17	3/12	2/15
6/2	4/26	7/31	6/26	9/27	8/25	11/24	10/24	1/16	12/18	3/13	2/16
6/3	4/27			9/28	8/26	11/25	10/25	1/17	12/19	3/14	2/17
6/4	4/28	8/1	6/27	9/29	8/27	11/26	10/26	1/18	12/20	3/15	2/18
6/5	4/29	8/2	6/28	9/30	8/28	11/27	10/27	1/19	12/21	3/16	2/19
6/6	5/1	8/3	6/29			11/28	10/28	1/20	12/22	3/17	2/20
6/7	5/2	8/4	7/1	10/1	8/29	11/29	10/29	1/21	12/23	3/18	2/21
6/8	5/3	8/5	7/2	10/2	9/1	11/30	11/1	1/22	12/24	3/19	2/22
6/9	5/4	8/6	7/3	10/3	9/2			1/23	12/25	3/20	2/23
6/10	5/5	8/7	7/4	10/4	9/3	12/1	11/2	1/24	12/26	3/21	2/24
6/11	5/6	8/8	7/5	10/5	9/4	12/2	11/3	1/25	12/27	3/22	2/25
6/12	5/7	8/9	7/6	10/6	9/5	12/3	11/4	1/26	12/28	3/23	2/26
6/13	5/8	8/10	7/7	10/7	9/6	12/4	11/5	1/27	12/29	3/24	2/27
6/14	5/9	8/11	7/8	10/8	9/7	12/5	11/6	1/28	1/1	3/25	2/28
6/15	5/10	8/12	7/9	10/9	9/8	12/6	11/7		(1960)	3/26	2/29
6/16	5/11	8/13	7/10	10/10	9/9	12/7	11/8	1/29	1/2	3/27	3/1
6/17	5/12	8/14	7/11	10/11	9/10	12/8	11/9	1/30	1/3	3/28	3/2
6/18	5/13	8/15	7/12	10/12	9/11	12/9	11/10	1/31	1/4	3/29	3/3
6/19	5/14	8/16	7/13	10/13	9/12	12/10	11/11			3/30	3/4

Solar	Lunar	Solar	Lunar	Solar	Lunar	Solar	Lunar	Solar	Lunar	Solar	Lunar
3/31	3/5	5/29	5/5	7/26	6/3	9/23	8/3	11/21	10/3	1/14	11/28
		5/30	5/6	7/27	6/4	9/24	8/4	11/22	10/4	1/15	11/29
4/1	3/6	5/31	5/7	7/28	6/5	9/25	8/5	11/23	10/5	1/16	11/30
4/2	3/7			7/29	6/6	9/26	8/6	11/24	10/6	1/17	12/1
4/3	3/8	6/1	5/8	7/30	6/7	9/27	8/7	11/25	10/7	1/18	12/2
4/4	3/9	6/2	5/9	7/31	6/8	9/28	8/8	11/26	10/8	1/19	12/3
4/5	3/10	6/3	5/10			9/29	8/9	11/27	10/9	1/20	12/4
4/6	3/11	6/4	5/11	8/1	6/9	9/30	8/10	11/28	10/10	1/21	12/5
4/7	3/12	6/5	5/12	8/2	6/10			11/29	10/11	1/22	12/6
4/8	3/13	6/6	5/13	8/3	6/11	10/1	8/11	11/30	10/12	1/23	12/7
4/9	3/14	6/7	5/14	8/4	6/12	10/2	8/12			1/24	12/8
4/10	3/15	6/8	5/15	8/5	6/13	10/3	8/13	12/1	10/13	1/25	12/9
4/11	3/16	6/9	5/16	8/6	6/14	10/4	8/14	12/2	10/14	1/26	12/10
4/12	3/17	6/10	5/17	8/7	6/15	10/5	8/15	12/3	10/15	1/27	12/11
4/13	3/18	6/11	5/18	8/8	6/16	10/6	8/16	12/4	10/16	1/28	12/12
4/14	3/19	6/12	5/19	8/9	6/17	10/7	8/17	12/5	10/17	1/29	12/13
4/15	3/20	6/13	5/20	8/10	6/18	10/8	8/18	12/6	10/18	1/30	12/14
4/16	3/21	6/14	5/21	8/11	6/19	10/9	8/19	12/7	10/19	1/31	12/15
4/17	3/22	6/15	5/22	8/12	6/20	10/10	8/20	12/8	10/20		
4/18	3/23	6/16	5/23	8/13	6/21	10/11	8/21	12/9	10/21	2/1	12/16
4/19	3/24	6/17	5/24	8/14	6/22	10/12	8/22	12/10	10/22	2/2	12/17
4/20	3/25	6/18	5/25	8/15	6/23	10/13	8/23	12/11	10/23	2/3	12/18
4/21	3/26	6/19	5/26	8/16	6/24	10/14	8/24	12/12	10/24	2/4	12/19
4/22	3/27	6/20	5/27	8/17	6/25	10/15	8/25	12/13	10/25	2/5	12/20
4/23	3/28	6/21	5/28	8/18	6/26	10/16	8/26	12/14	10/26	2/6	12/21
4/24	3/29	6/22	5/29	8/19	6/27	10/17	8/27	12/15	10/27	2/7	12/22
4/25	3/30	6/23	5/30	8/20	6/28	10/18	8/28	12/16	10/28	2/8	12/23
4/26	4/1	6/24	6/1	8/21	6/29	10/19	8/29	12/17	10/29	2/9	12/24
4/27	4/2	6/25	6/2	8/22	7/1	10/20	9/1	12/18	11/1	2/10	12/25
4/28	4/3	6/26	6/3	8/23	7/2	10/21	9/2	12/19	11/2	2/11	12/26
4/29	4/4	6/27	6/4	8/24	7/3	10/22	9/3	12/20	11/3	2/12	12/27
4/30	4/5	6/28	6/5	8/25	7/4	10/23	9/4	12/21	11/4	2/13	12/28
		6/29	6/6	8/26	7/5	10/24	9/5	12/22	11/5	2/14	12/29
5/1	4/6	6/30	6/7	8/27	7/6	10/25	9/6	12/23	11/6	2/15	1/1
5/2	4/7			8/28	7/7	10/26	9/7	12/24	11/7		(1961)
5/3	4/8	7/1	6/8	8/29	7/8	10/27	9/8	12/25	11/8	2/16	1/2
5/4	4/9	7/2	6/9	8/30	7/9	10/28	9/9	12/26	11/9	2/17	1/3
5/5	4/10	7/3	6/10	8/31	7/10	10/29	9/10	12/27	11/10	2/18	1/4
5/6	4/11	7/4	6/11			10/30	9/11	12/28	11/11	2/19	1/5
5/7	4/12	7/5	6/12	9/1	7/11	10/31	9/12	12/29	11/12	2/20	1/6
5/8	4/13	7/6	6/13	9/2	7/12			12/30	11/13	2/21	1/7
5/9	4/14	7/7	6/14	9/3	7/13	11/1	9/13	12/31	11/14	2/22	1/8
5/10	4/15	7/8	6/15	9/4	7/14	11/2	9/14			2/23	1/9
5/11	4/16	7/9	6/16	9/5	7/15	11/3	9/15			2/24	1/10
5/12	4/17	7/10	6/17	9/6	7/16	11/4	9/16	Solar	Lunar	2/25	1/11
5/13	4/18	7/11	6/18	9/7	7/17	11/5	9/17	Date	Date	2/26	1/12
5/14	4/19	7/12	6/19	9/8	7/18	11/6	9/18			2/27	1/13
5/15	4/20	7/13	6/20	9/9	7/19	11/7	9/19	1961		2/28	1/14
5/16	4/21	7/14	6/21	9/10	7/20	11/8	9/20	1/1	11/15		
5/17	4/22	7/15	6/22	9/11	7/21	11/9	9/21	1/2	11/16	3/1	1/15
5/18	4/23	7/16	6/23	9/12	7/22	11/10	9/22	1/3	11/17	3/2	1/16
5/19	4/24	7/17	6/24	9/13	7/23	11/11	9/23	1/4	11/18	3/3	1/17
5/20	4/25	7/18	6/25	9/14	7/24	11/12	9/24	1/5	11/19	3/4	1/18
5/21	4/26	7/19	6/26	9/15	7/25	11/13	9/25	1/6	11/20	3/5	1/19
5/22	4/27	7/20	6/27	9/16	7/26	11/14	9/26	1/7	11/21	3/6	1/20
5/23	4/28	7/21	6/28	9/17	7/27	11/15	9/27	1/8	11/22	3/7	1/21
5/24	4/29	7/22	6/29	9/18	7/28	11/16	9/28	1/9	11/23	3/8	1/22
5/25	5/1	7/23	6/30	9/19	7/29	11/17	9/29	1/10	11/24	3/9	1/23
5/26	5/2	7/24	6/1	9/20	7/30	11/18	9/30	1/11	11/25	3/10	1/24
5/27	5/3	(Leap Month)		9/21	8/1	11/19	10/1	1/12	11/26	3/11	1/25
5/28	5/4	7/25	6/2	9/22	8/2	11/20	10/2	1/13	11/27	3/12	1/26

Solar	Lunar	Solar	Lunar	Solar	Lunar	Solar	Lunar	Solar	Lunar	Solar	Lunar
3/13	1/27	5/10	3/26	7/7	5/25	9/3	7/24	11/1	9/23	12/30	11/23
3/14	1/28	5/11	3/27	7/8	5/26	9/4	7/25	11/2	9/24	12/31	11/24
3/15	1/29	5/12	3/28	7/9	5/27	9/5	7/26	11/3	9/25		
3/16	1/30	5/13	3/29	7/10	5/28	9/6	7/27	11/4	9/26		
3/17	2/1	5/14	3/30	7/11	5/29	9/7	7/28	11/5	9/27	Solar	Lunar
3/18	2/2	5/15	4/1	7/12	5/30	9/8	7/29	11/6	9/28	Date	Date
3/19	2/3	5/16	4/2	7/13	6/1	9/9	7/30	11/7	9/29		
3/20	2/4	5/17	4/3	7/14	6/2	9/10	8/1	11/8	10/1	1962	
3/21	2/5	5/18	4/4	7/15	6/3	9/11	8/2	11/9	10/2	1/1	11/25
3/22	2/6	5/19	4/5	7/16	6/4	9/12	8/3	11/10	10/3	1/2	11/26
3/23	2/7	5/20	4/6	7/17	6/5	9/13	8/4	11/11	10/4	1/3	11/27
3/24	2/8	5/21	4/7	7/18	6/6	9/14	8/5	11/12	10/5	1/4	11/28
3/25	2/9	5/22	4/8	7/19	6/7	9/15	8/6	11/13	10/6	1/5	11/29
3/26	2/10	5/23	4/9	7/20	6/8	9/16	8/7	11/14	10/7	1/6	12/1
3/27	2/11	5/24	4/10	7/21	6/9	9/17	8/8	11/15	10/8	1/7	12/2
3/28	2/12	5/25	4/11	7/22	6/10	9/18	8/9	11/16	10/9	1/8	12/3
3/29	2/13	5/26	4/12	7/23	6/11	9/19	8/10	11/17	10/10	1/9	12/4
3/30	2/14	5/27	4/13	7/24	6/12	9/20	8/11	11/18	10/11	1/10	12/5
3/31	2/15	5/28	4/14	7/25	6/13	9/21	8/12	11/19	10/12	1/11	12/6
		5/29	4/15	7/26	6/14	9/22	8/13	11/20	10/13	1/12	12/7
4/1	2/16	5/30	4/16	7/27	6/15	9/23	8/14	11/21	10/14	1/13	12/8
4/2	2/17	5/31	4/17	7/28	6/16	9/24	8/15	11/22	10/15	1/14	12/9
4/3	2/18			7/29	6/17	9/25	8/16	11/23	10/16	1/15	12/10
4/4	2/19	6/1	4/18	7/30	6/18	9/26	8/17	11/24	10/17	1/16	12/11
4/5	2/20	6/2	4/19	7/31	6/19	9/27	8/18	11/25	10/18	1/17	12/12
4/6	2/21	6/3	4/20			9/28	8/19	11/26	10/19	1/18	12/13
4/7	2/22	6/4	4/21	8/1	6/20	9/29	8/20	11/27	10/20	1/19	12/14
4/8	2/23	6/5	4/22	8/2	6/21	9/30	8/21	11/28	10/21	1/20	12/15
4/9	2/24	6/6	4/23	8/3	6/22			11/29	10/22	1/21	12/16
4/10	2/25	6/7	4/24	8/4	6/23	10/1	8/22	11/30	10/23	1/22	12/17
4/11	2/26	6/8	4/25	8/5	6/24	10/2	8/23			1/23	12/18
4/12	2/27	6/9	4/26	8/6	6/25	10/3	8/24	12/1	10/24	1/24	12/19
4/13	2/28	6/10	4/27	8/7	6/26	10/4	8/25	12/2	10/25	1/25	12/20
4/14	2/29	6/11	4/28	8/8	6/27	10/5	8/26	12/3	10/26	1/26	12/21
4/15	3/1	6/12	4/29	8/9	6/28	10/6	8/27	12/4	10/27	1/27	12/22
4/16	3/2	6/13	5/1	8/10	6/29	10/7	8/28	12/5	10/28	1/28	12/23
4/17	3/3	6/14	5/2	8/11	7/1	10/8	8/29	12/6	10/29	1/29	12/24
4/18	3/4	6/15	5/3	8/12	7/2	10/9	8/30	12/7	10/30	1/30	12/25
4/19	3/5	6/16	5/4	8/13	7/3	10/10	9/1	12/8	11/1	1/31	12/26
4/20	3/6	6/17	5/5	8/14	7/4	10/11	9/2	12/9	11/2		
4/21	3/7	6/18	5/6	8/15	7/5	10/12	9/3	12/10	11/3	2/1	12/27
4/22	3/8	6/19	5/7	8/16	7/6	10/13	9/4	12/11	11/4	2/2	12/28
4/23	3/9	6/20	5/8	8/17	7/7	10/14	9/5	12/12	11/5	2/3	12/29
4/24	3/10	6/21	5/9	8/18	7/8	10/15	9/6	12/13	11/6	2/4	12/30
4/25	3/11	6/22	5/10	8/19	7/9	10/16	9/7	12/14	11/7	2/5	1/1
4/26	3/12	6/23	5/11	8/20	7/10	10/17	9/8	12/15	11/8		(1962)
4/27	3/13	6/24	5/12	8/21	7/11	10/18	9/9	12/16	11/9	2/6	1/2
4/28	3/14	6/25	5/13	8/22	7/12	10/19	9/10	12/17	11/10	2/7	1/3
4/29	3/15	6/26	5/14	8/23	7/13	10/20	9/11	12/18	11/11	2/8	1/4
4/30	3/16	6/27	5/15	8/24	7/14	10/21	9/12	12/19	11/12	2/9	1/5
		6/28	5/16	8/25	7/15	10/22	9/13	12/20	11/13	2/10	1/6
5/1	3/17	6/29	5/17	8/26	7/16	10/23	9/14	12/21	11/14	2/11	1/7
5/2	3/18	6/30	5/18	8/27	7/17	10/24	9/15	12/22	11/15	2/12	1/8
5/3	3/19			8/28	7/18	10/25	9/16	12/23	11/16	2/13	1/9
5/4	3/20	7/1	5/19	8/29	7/19	10/26	9/17	12/24	11/17	2/14	1/10
5/5	3/21	7/2	5/20	8/30	7/20	10/27	9/18	12/25	11/18	2/15	1/11
5/6	3/22	7/3	5/21	8/31	7/21	10/28	9/19	12/26	11/19	2/16	1/12
5/7	3/23	7/4	5/22			10/29	9/20	12/27	11/20	2/17	1/13
5/8	3/24	7/5	5/23	9/1	7/22	10/30	9/21	12/28	11/21	2/18	1/14
5/9	3/25	7/6	5/24	9/2	7/23	10/31	9/22	12/29	11/22	2/19	1/15

Solar	Lunar	Solar	Lunar	Solar	Lunar	Solar	Lunar	Solar	Lunar	Solar	Lunar
2/20	1/16	4/19	3/15	6/16	5/15	8/13	7/14	10/10	9/12	12/7	11/11
2/21	1/17	4/20	3/16	6/17	5/16	8/14	7/15	10/11	9/13	12/8	11/12
2/22	1/18	4/21	3/17	6/18	5/17	8/15	7/16	10/12	9/14	12/9	11/13
2/23	1/19	4/22	3/18	6/19	5/18	8/16	7/17	10/13	9/15	12/10	11/14
2/24	1/20	4/23	3/19	6/20	5/19	8/17	7/18	10/14	9/16	12/11	11/15
2/25	1/21	4/24	3/20	6/21	5/20	8/18	7/19	10/15	9/17	12/12	11/16
2/26	1/22	4/25	3/21	6/22	5/21	8/19	7/20	10/16	9/18	12/13	11/17
2/27	1/23	4/26	3/22	6/23	5/22	8/20	7/21	10/17	9/19	12/14	11/18
2/28	1/24	4/27	3/23	6/24	5/23	8/21	7/22	10/18	9/20	12/15	11/19
		4/28	3/24	6/25	5/24	8/22	7/23	10/19	9/21	12/16	11/20
3/1	1/25	4/29	3/25	6/26	5/25	8/23	7/24	10/20	9/22	12/17	11/21
3/2	1/26	4/30	3/26	6/27	5/26	8/24	7/25	10/21	9/23	12/18	11/22
3/3	1/27			6/28	5/27	8/25	7/26	10/22	9/24	12/19	11/23
3/4	1/28	5/1	3/27	6/29	5/28	8/26	7/27	10/23	9/25	12/20	11/24
3/5	1/29	5/2	3/28	6/30	5/29	8/27	7/28	10/24	9/26	12/21	11/25
3/6	2/1	5/3	3/29			8/28	7/29	10/25	9/27	12/22	11/26
3/7	2/2	5/4	4/1	7/1	5/30	8/29	7/30	10/26	9/28	12/23	11/27
3/8	2/3	5/5	4/2	7/2	6/1	8/30	8/1	10/27	9/29	12/24	11/28
3/9	2/4	5/6	4/3	7/3	6/2	8/31	8/2	10/28	10/1	12/25	11/29
3/10	2/5	5/7	4/4	7/4	6/3			10/29	10/2	12/26	11/30
3/11	2/6	5/8	4/5	7/5	6/4	9/1	8/3	10/30	10/3	12/27	12/1
3/12	2/7	5/9	4/6	7/6	6/5	9/2	8/4	10/31	10/4	12/28	12/2
3/13	2/8	5/10	4/7	7/7	6/6	9/3	8/5			12/29	12/3
3/14	2/9	5/11	4/8	7/8	6/7	9/4	8/6	11/1	10/5	12/30	12/4
3/15	2/10	5/12	4/9	7/9	6/8	9/5	8/7	11/2	10/6	12/31	12/5
3/16	2/11	5/13	4/10	7/10	6/9	9/6	8/8	11/3	10/7		
3/17	2/12	5/14	4/11	7/11	6/10	9/7	8/9	11/4	10/8		
3/18	2/13	5/15	4/12	7/12	6/11	9/8	8/10	11/5	10/9		
3/19	2/14	5/16	4/13	7/13	6/12	9/9	8/11	11/6	10/10		
3/20	2/15	5/17	4/14	7/14	6/13	9/10	8/12	11/7	10/11		
3/21	2/16	5/18	4/15	7/15	6/14	9/11	8/13	11/8	10/12		
3/22	2/17	5/19	4/16	7/16	6/15	9/12	8/14	11/9	10/13		
3/23	2/18	5/20	4/17	7/17	6/16	9/13	8/15	11/10	10/14		
3/24	2/19	5/21	4/18	7/18	6/17	9/14	8/16	11/11	10/15		
3/25	2/20	5/22	4/19	7/19	6/18	9/15	8/17	11/12	10/16		
3/26	2/21	5/23	4/20	7/20	6/19	9/16	8/18	11/13	10/17		
3/27	2/22	5/24	4/21	7/21	6/20	9/17	8/19	11/14	10/18		
3/28	2/23	5/25	4/22	7/22	6/21	9/18	8/20	11/15	10/19		
3/29	2/24	5/26	4/23	7/23	6/22	9/19	8/21	11/16	10/20		
3/30	2/25	5/27	4/24	7/24	6/23	9/20	8/22	11/17	10/21		
3/31	2/26	5/28	4/25	7/25	6/24	9/21	8/23	11/18	10/22		
		5/29	4/26	7/26	6/25	9/22	8/24	11/19	10/23		
4/1	2/27	5/30	4/27	7/27	6/26	9/23	8/25	11/20	10/24		
4/2	2/28	5/31	4/28	7/28	6/27	9/24	8/26	11/21	10/25		
4/3	2/29			7/29	6/28	9/25	8/27	11/22	10/26		
4/4	2/30	6/1	4/29	7/30	6/29	9/26	8/28	11/23	10/27		
4/5	3/1	6/2	5/1	7/31	7/1	9/27	8/29	11/24	10/28		
4/6	3/2	6/3	5/2			9/28	8/30	11/25	10/29		
4/7	3/3	6/4	5/3	8/1	7/2	9/29	9/1	11/26	10/30		
4/8	3/4	6/5	5/4	8/2	7/3	9/30	9/2	11/27	11/1		
4/9	3/5	6/6	5/5	8/3	7/4			11/28	11/2		
4/10	3/6	6/7	5/6	8/4	7/5	10/1	9/3	11/29	11/3		
4/11	3/7	6/8	5/7	8/5	7/6	10/2	9/4	11/30	11/4		
4/12	3/8	6/9	5/8	8/6	7/7	10/3	9/5				
4/13	3/9	6/10	5/9	8/7	7/8	10/4	9/6	12/1	11/5		
4/14	3/10	6/11	5/10	8/8	7/9	10/5	9/7	12/2	11/6		
4/15	3/11	6/12	5/11	8/9	7/10	10/6	9/8	12/3	11/7		
4/16	3/12	6/13	5/12	8/10	7/11	10/7	9/9	12/4	11/8		
4/17	3/13	6/14	5/13	8/11	7/12	10/8	9/10	12/5	11/9		
4/18	3/14	6/15	5/14	8/12	7/13	10/9	9/11	12/6	11/10		

Solar Date	Lunar Date
1963	
1/1	12/6
1/2	12/7
1/3	12/8
1/4	12/9
1/5	12/10
1/6	12/11
1/7	12/12
1/8	12/13
1/9	12/14
1/10	12/15
1/11	12/16
1/12	12/17
1/13	12/18
1/14	12/19
1/15	12/20
1/16	12/21
1/17	12/22
1/18	12/23
1/19	12/24
1/20	12/25
1/21	12/26
1/22	12/27
1/23	12/28
1/24	12/29
1/25	1/1 (1963)
1/26	1/2
1/27	1/3
1/28	1/4

Solar	Lunar	Solar	Lunar	Solar	Lunar	Solar	Lunar	Solar	Lunar	Solar	Lunar
1/29	1/5	3/28	3/4	5/24	4/2	7/21	6/1	9/17	7/30	11/14	9/29
1/30	1/6	3/29	3/5	5/25	4/3	7/22	6/2	9/18	8/1	11/15	9/30
1/31	1/7	3/30	3/6	5/26	4/4	7/23	6/3	9/19	8/2	11/16	10/1
		3/31	3/7	5/27	4/5	7/24	6/4	9/20	8/3	11/17	10/2
2/1	1/8			5/28	4/6	7/25	6/5	9/21	8/4	11/18	10/3
2/2	1/9	4/1	3/8	5/29	4/7	7/26	6/6	9/22	8/5	11/19	10/4
2/3	1/10	4/2	3/9	5/30	4/8	7/27	6/7	9/23	8/6	11/20	10/5
2/4	1/11	4/3	3/10	5/31	4/9	7/28	6/8	9/24	8/7	11/21	10/6
2/5	1/12	4/4	3/11			7/29	6/9	9/25	8/8	11/22	10/7
2/6	1/13	4/5	3/12	6/1	4/10	7/30	6/10	9/26	8/9	11/23	10/8
2/7	1/14	4/6	3/13	6/2	4/11	7/31	6/11	9/27	8/10	11/24	10/9
2/8	1/15	4/7	3/14	6/3	4/12			9/28	8/11	11/25	10/10
2/9	1/16	4/8	3/15	6/4	4/13	8/1	6/12	9/29	8/12	11/26	10/11
2/10	1/17	4/9	3/16	6/5	4/14	8/2	6/13	9/30	8/13	11/27	10/12
2/11	1/18	4/10	3/17	6/6	4/15	8/3	6/14			11/28	10/13
2/12	1/19	4/11	3/18	6/7	4/16	8/4	6/15	10/1	8/14	11/29	10/14
2/13	1/20	4/12	3/19	6/8	4/17	8/5	6/16	10/2	8/15	11/30	10/15
2/14	1/21	4/13	3/20	6/9	4/18	8/6	6/17	10/3	8/16		
2/15	1/22	4/14	3/21	6/10	4/19	8/7	6/18	10/4	8/17	12/1	10/16
2/16	1/23	4/15	3/22	6/11	4/20	8/8	6/19	10/5	8/18	12/2	10/17
2/17	1/24	4/16	3/23	6/12	4/21	8/9	6/20	10/6	8/19	12/3	10/18
2/18	1/25	4/17	3/24	6/13	4/22	8/10	6/21	10/7	8/20	12/4	10/19
2/19	1/26	4/18	3/25	6/14	4/23	8/11	6/22	10/8	8/21	12/5	10/20
2/20	1/27	4/19	3/26	6/15	4/24	8/12	6/23	10/9	8/22	12/6	10/21
2/21	1/28	4/20	3/27	6/16	4/25	8/13	6/24	10/10	8/23	12/7	10/22
2/22	1/29	4/21	3/28	6/17	4/26	8/14	6/25	10/11	8/24	12/8	10/23
2/23	1/30	4/22	3/29	6/18	4/27	8/15	6/26	10/12	8/25	12/9	10/24
2/24	2/1	4/23	3/30	6/19	4/28	8/16	6/27	10/13	8/26	12/10	10/25
2/25	2/2	4/24	4/1	6/20	4/29	8/17	6/28	10/14	8/27	12/11	10/26
2/26	2/3	4/25	4/2	6/21	5/1	8/18	6/29	10/15	8/28	12/12	10/27
2/27	2/4	4/26	4/3	6/22	5/2	8/19	7/1	10/16	8/29	12/13	10/28
2/28	2/5	4/27	4/4	6/23	5/3	8/20	7/2	10/17	9/1	12/14	10/29
		4/28	4/5	6/24	5/4	8/21	7/3	10/18	9/2	12/15	10/30
3/1	2/6	4/29	4/6	6/25	5/5	8/22	7/4	10/19	9/3	12/16	11/1
3/2	2/7	4/30	4/7	6/26	5/6	8/23	7/5	10/20	9/4	12/17	11/2
3/3	2/8			6/27	5/7	8/24	7/6	10/21	9/5	12/18	11/3
3/4	2/9	5/1	4/8	6/28	5/8	8/25	7/7	10/22	9/6	12/19	11/4
3/5	2/10	5/2	4/9	6/29	5/9	8/26	7/8	10/23	9/7	12/20	11/5
3/6	2/11	5/3	4/10	6/30	5/10	8/27	7/9	10/24	9/8	12/21	11/6
3/7	2/12	5/4	4/11			8/28	7/10	10/25	9/9	12/22	11/7
3/8	2/13	5/5	4/12	7/1	5/11	8/29	7/11	10/26	9/10	12/23	11/8
3/9	2/14	5/6	4/13	7/2	5/12	8/30	7/12	10/27	9/11	12/24	11/9
3/10	2/15	5/7	4/14	7/3	5/13	8/31	7/13	10/28	9/12	12/25	11/10
3/11	2/16	5/8	4/15	7/4	5/14			10/29	9/13	12/26	11/11
3/12	2/17	5/9	4/16	7/5	5/15	9/1	7/14	10/30	9/14	12/27	11/12
3/13	2/18	5/10	4/17	7/6	5/16	9/2	7/15	10/31	9/15	12/28	11/13
3/14	2/19	5/11	4/18	7/7	5/17	9/3	7/16			12/29	11/14
3/15	2/20	5/12	4/19	7/8	5/18	9/4	7/17	11/1	9/16	12/30	11/15
3/16	2/21	5/13	4/20	7/9	5/19	9/5	7/18	11/2	9/17	12/31	11/16
3/17	2/22	5/14	4/21	7/10	5/20	9/6	7/19	11/3	9/18		
3/18	2/23	5/15	4/22	7/11	5/21	9/7	7/20	11/4	9/19		
3/19	2/24	5/16	4/23	7/12	5/22	9/8	7/21	11/5	9/20	Solar	Lunar
3/20	2/25	5/17	4/24	7/13	5/23	9/9	7/22	11/6	9/21	Date	Date
3/21	2/26	5/18	4/25	7/14	5/24	9/10	7/23	11/7	9/22	**1964**	
3/22	2/27	5/19	4/26	7/15	5/25	9/11	7/24	11/8	9/23	1/1	11/17
3/23	2/28	5/20	4/27	7/16	5/26	9/12	7/25	11/9	9/24	1/2	11/18
3/24	2/29	5/21	4/28	7/17	5/27	9/13	7/26	11/10	9/25	1/3	11/19
3/25	3/1	5/22	4/29	7/18	5/28	9/14	7/27	11/11	9/26	1/4	11/20
3/26	3/2	5/23	4/1	7/19	5/29	9/15	7/28	11/12	9/27	1/5	11/21
3/27	3/3	*(Leap Month)*		7/20	5/30	9/16	7/29	11/13	9/28		

Solar	Lunar	Solar	Lunar	Solar	Lunar	Solar	Lunar	Solar	Lunar	Solar	Lunar
1/6	11/22	3/3	1/20	5/1	3/20	6/29	5/20	8/26	7/19	10/23	9/18
1/7	11/23	3/4	1/21	5/2	3/21	6/30	5/21	8/27	7/20	10/24	9/19
1/8	11/24	3/5	1/22	5/3	3/22			8/28	7/21	10/25	9/20
1/9	11/25	3/6	1/23	5/4	3/23	7/1	5/22	8/29	7/22	10/26	9/21
1/10	11/26	3/7	1/24	5/5	3/24	7/2	5/23	8/30	7/23	10/27	9/22
1/11	11/27	3/8	1/25	5/6	3/25	7/3	5/24	8/31	7/24	10/28	9/23
1/12	11/28	3/9	1/26	5/7	3/26	7/4	5/25			10/29	9/24
1/13	11/29	3/10	1/27	5/8	3/27	7/5	5/26	9/1	7/25	10/30	9/25
1/14	11/30	3/11	1/28	5/9	3/28	7/6	5/27	9/2	7/26	10/31	9/26
1/15	12/1	3/12	1/29	5/10	3/29	7/7	5/28	9/3	7/27		
1/16	12/2	3/13	1/30	5/11	3/30	7/8	5/29	9/4	7/28	11/1	9/27
1/17	12/3	3/14	2/1	5/12	4/1	7/9	6/1	9/5	7/29	11/2	9/28
1/18	12/4	3/15	2/2	5/13	4/2	7/10	6/2	9/6	8/1	11/3	9/29
1/19	12/5	3/16	2/3	5/14	4/3	7/11	6/3	9/7	8/2	11/4	10/1
1/20	12/6	3/17	2/4	5/15	4/4	7/12	6/4	9/8	8/3	11/5	10/2
1/21	12/7	3/18	2/5	5/16	4/5	7/13	6/5	9/9	8/4	11/6	10/3
1/22	12/8	3/19	2/6	5/17	4/6	7/14	6/6	9/10	8/5	11/7	10/4
1/23	12/9	3/20	2/7	5/18	4/7	7/15	6/7	9/11	8/6	11/8	10/5
1/24	12/10	3/21	2/8	5/19	4/8	7/16	6/8	9/12	8/7	11/9	10/6
1/25	12/11	3/22	2/9	5/20	4/9	7/17	6/9	9/13	8/8	11/10	10/7
1/26	12/12	3/23	2/10	5/21	4/10	7/18	6/10	9/14	8/9	11/11	10/8
1/27	12/13	3/24	2/11	5/22	4/11	7/19	6/11	9/15	8/10	11/12	10/9
1/28	12/14	3/25	2/12	5/23	4/12	7/20	6/12	9/16	8/11	11/13	10/10
1/29	12/15	3/26	2/13	5/24	4/13	7/21	6/13	9/17	8/12	11/14	10/11
1/30	12/16	3/27	2/14	5/25	4/14	7/22	6/14	9/18	8/13	11/15	10/12
1/31	12/17	3/28	2/15	5/26	4/15	7/23	6/15	9/19	8/14	11/16	10/13
		3/29	2/16	5/27	4/16	7/24	6/16	9/20	8/15	11/17	10/14
2/1	12/18	3/30	2/17	5/28	4/17	7/25	6/17	9/21	8/16	11/18	10/15
2/2	12/19	3/31	2/18	5/29	4/18	7/26	6/18	9/22	8/17	11/19	10/16
2/3	12/20			5/30	4/19	7/27	6/19	9/23	8/18	11/20	10/17
2/4	12/21	4/1	2/19	5/31	4/20	7/28	6/20	9/24	8/19	11/21	10/18
2/5	12/22	4/2	2/20			7/29	6/21	9/25	8/20	11/22	10/19
2/6	12/23	4/3	2/21	6/1	4/21	7/30	6/22	9/26	8/21	11/23	10/20
2/7	12/24	4/4	2/22	6/2	4/22	7/31	6/23	9/27	8/22	11/24	10/21
2/8	12/25	4/5	2/23	6/3	4/23			9/28	8/23	11/25	10/22
2/9	12/26	4/6	2/24	6/4	4/24	8/1	6/24	9/29	8/24	11/26	10/23
2/10	12/27	4/7	2/25	6/5	4/25	8/2	6/25	9/30	8/25	11/27	10/24
2/11	12/28	4/8	2/26	6/6	4/26	8/3	6/26			11/28	10/25
2/12	12/29	4/9	2/27	6/7	4/27	8/4	6/27	10/1	8/26	11/29	10/26
2/13	1/1	4/10	2/28	6/8	4/28	8/5	6/28	10/2	8/27	11/30	10/27
	(1964)	4/11	2/29	6/9	4/29	8/6	6/29	10/3	8/28		
2/14	1/2	4/12	3/1	6/10	5/1	8/7	6/30	10/4	8/29	12/1	10/28
2/15	1/3	4/13	3/2	6/11	5/2	8/8	7/1	10/5	8/30	12/2	10/29
2/16	1/4	4/14	3/3	6/12	5/3	8/9	7/2	10/6	9/1	12/3	10/30
2/17	1/5	4/15	3/4	6/13	5/4	8/10	7/3	10/7	9/2	12/4	11/1
2/18	1/6	4/16	3/5	6/14	5/5	8/11	7/4	10/8	9/3	12/5	11/2
2/19	1/7	4/17	3/6	6/15	5/6	8/12	7/5	10/9	9/4	12/6	11/3
2/20	1/8	4/18	3/7	6/16	5/7	8/13	7/6	10/10	9/5	12/7	11/4
2/21	1/9	4/19	3/8	6/17	5/8	8/14	7/7	10/11	9/6	12/8	11/5
2/22	1/10	4/20	3/9	6/18	5/9	8/15	7/8	10/12	9/7	12/9	11/6
2/23	1/11	4/21	3/10	6/19	5/10	8/16	7/9	10/13	9/8	12/10	11/7
2/24	1/12	4/22	3/11	6/20	5/11	8/17	7/10	10/14	9/9	12/11	11/8
2/25	1/13	4/23	3/12	6/21	5/12	8/18	7/11	10/15	9/10	12/12	11/9
2/26	1/14	4/24	3/13	6/22	5/13	8/19	7/12	10/16	9/11	12/13	11/10
2/27	1/15	4/25	3/14	6/23	5/14	8/20	7/13	10/17	9/12	12/14	11/11
2/28	1/16	4/26	3/15	6/24	5/15	8/21	7/14	10/18	9/13	12/15	11/12
2/29	1/17	4/27	3/16	6/25	5/16	8/22	7/15	10/19	9/14	12/16	11/13
		4/28	3/17	6/26	5/17	8/23	7/16	10/20	9/15	12/17	11/14
3/1	1/18	4/29	3/18	6/27	5/18	8/24	7/17	10/21	9/16	12/18	11/15
3/2	1/19	4/30	3/19	6/28	5/19	8/25	7/18	10/22	9/17	12/19	11/16

Solar Date	Lunar Date
12/20	11/17
12/21	11/18
12/22	11/19
12/23	11/20
12/24	11/21
12/25	11/22
12/26	11/23
12/27	11/24
12/28	11/25
12/29	11/26
12/30	11/27
12/31	11/28
Solar Date	**Lunar Date**
1965	
1/1	11/29
1/2	11/30
1/3	12/1
1/4	12/2
1/5	12/3
1/6	12/4
1/7	12/5
1/8	12/6
1/9	12/7
1/10	12/8
1/11	12/9
1/12	12/10
1/13	12/11
1/14	12/12
1/15	12/13
1/16	12/14
1/17	12/15
1/18	12/16
1/19	12/17
1/20	12/18
1/21	12/19
1/22	12/20
1/23	12/21
1/24	12/22
1/25	12/23
1/26	12/24
1/27	12/25
1/28	12/26
1/29	12/27
1/30	12/28
1/31	12/29
2/1	12/30
2/2	1/1 (1965)
2/3	1/2
2/4	1/3
2/5	1/4
2/6	1/5
2/7	1/6
2/8	1/7
2/9	1/8

Solar	Lunar
2/10	1/9
2/11	1/10
2/12	1/11
2/13	1/12
2/14	1/13
2/15	1/14
2/16	1/15
2/17	1/16
2/18	1/17
2/19	1/18
2/20	1/19
2/21	1/20
2/22	1/21
2/23	1/22
2/24	1/23
2/25	1/24
2/26	1/25
2/27	1/26
2/28	1/27
3/1	1/28
3/2	1/29
3/3	2/1
3/4	2/2
3/5	2/3
3/6	2/4
3/7	2/5
3/8	2/6
3/9	2/7
3/10	2/8
3/11	2/9
3/12	2/10
3/13	2/11
3/14	2/12
3/15	2/13
3/16	2/14
3/17	2/15
3/18	2/16
3/19	2/17
3/20	2/18
3/21	2/19
3/22	2/20
3/23	2/21
3/24	2/22
3/25	2/23
3/26	2/24
3/27	2/25
3/28	2/26
3/29	2/27
3/30	2/28
3/31	2/29
4/1	2/30
4/2	3/1
4/3	3/2
4/4	3/3
4/5	3/4
4/6	3/5
4/7	3/6
4/8	3/7

Solar	Lunar
4/9	3/8
4/10	3/9
4/11	3/10
4/12	3/11
4/13	3/12
4/14	3/13
4/15	3/14
4/16	3/15
4/17	3/16
4/18	3/17
4/19	3/18
4/20	3/19
4/21	3/20
4/22	3/21
4/23	3/22
4/24	3/23
4/25	3/24
4/26	3/25
4/27	3/26
4/28	3/27
4/29	3/28
4/30	3/29
5/1	4/1
5/2	4/2
5/3	4/3
5/4	4/4
5/5	4/5
5/6	4/6
5/7	4/7
5/8	4/8
5/9	4/9
5/10	4/10
5/11	4/11
5/12	4/12
5/13	4/13
5/14	4/14
5/15	4/15
5/16	4/16
5/17	4/17
5/18	4/18
5/19	4/19
5/20	4/20
5/21	4/21
5/22	4/22
5/23	4/23
5/24	4/24
5/25	4/25
5/26	4/26
5/27	4/27
5/28	4/28
5/29	4/29
5/30	4/30
5/31	5/1
6/1	5/2
6/2	5/3
6/3	5/4
6/4	5/5
6/5	5/6

Solar	Lunar
6/6	5/7
6/7	5/8
6/8	5/9
6/9	5/10
6/10	5/11
6/11	5/12
6/12	5/13
6/13	5/14
6/14	5/15
6/15	5/16
6/16	5/17
6/17	5/18
6/18	5/19
6/19	5/20
6/20	5/21
6/21	5/22
6/22	5/23
6/23	5/24
6/24	5/25
6/25	5/26
6/26	5/27
6/27	5/28
6/28	5/29
6/29	6/1
6/30	6/2
7/1	6/3
7/2	6/4
7/3	6/5
7/4	6/6
7/5	6/7
7/6	6/8
7/7	6/9
7/8	6/10
7/9	6/11
7/10	6/12
7/11	6/13
7/12	6/14
7/13	6/15
7/14	6/16
7/15	6/17
7/16	6/18
7/17	6/19
7/18	6/20
7/19	6/21
7/20	6/22
7/21	6/23
7/22	6/24
7/23	6/25
7/24	6/26
7/25	6/27
7/26	6/28
7/27	6/29
7/28	7/1
7/29	7/2
7/30	7/3
7/31	7/4
8/1	7/5
8/2	7/6

Solar	Lunar
8/3	7/7
8/4	7/8
8/5	7/9
8/6	7/10
8/7	7/11
8/8	7/12
8/9	7/13
8/10	7/14
8/11	7/15
8/12	7/16
8/13	7/17
8/14	7/18
8/15	7/19
8/16	7/20
8/17	7/21
8/18	7/22
8/19	7/23
8/20	7/24
8/21	7/25
8/22	7/26
8/23	7/27
8/24	7/28
8/25	7/29
8/26	7/30
8/27	8/1
8/28	8/2
8/29	8/3
8/30	8/4
8/31	8/5
9/1	8/6
9/2	8/7
9/3	8/8
9/4	8/9
9/5	8/10
9/6	8/11
9/7	8/12
9/8	8/13
9/9	8/14
9/10	8/15
9/11	8/16
9/12	8/17
9/13	8/18
9/14	8/19
9/15	8/20
9/16	8/21
9/17	8/22
9/18	8/23
9/19	8/24
9/20	8/25
9/21	8/26
9/22	8/27
9/23	8/28
9/24	8/29
9/25	9/1
9/26	9/2
9/27	9/3
9/28	9/4
9/29	9/5
9/30	9/6

Solar	Lunar
10/1	9/7
10/2	9/8
10/3	9/9
10/4	9/10
10/5	9/11
10/6	9/12
10/7	9/13
10/8	9/14
10/9	9/15
10/10	9/16
10/11	9/17
10/12	9/18
10/13	9/19
10/14	9/20
10/15	9/21
10/16	9/22
10/17	9/23
10/18	9/24
10/19	9/25
10/20	9/26
10/21	9/27
10/22	9/28
10/23	9/29
10/24	10/1
10/25	10/2
10/26	10/3
10/27	10/4
10/28	10/5
10/29	10/6
10/30	10/7
10/31	10/8
11/1	10/9
11/2	10/10
11/3	10/11
11/4	10/12
11/5	10/13
11/6	10/14
11/7	10/15
11/8	10/16
11/9	10/17
11/10	10/18
11/11	10/19
11/12	10/20
11/13	10/21
11/14	10/22
11/15	10/23
11/16	10/24
11/17	10/25
11/18	10/26
11/19	10/27
11/20	10/28
11/21	10/29
11/22	10/30
11/23	11/1
11/24	11/2
11/25	11/3
11/26	11/4
11/27	11/5
11/28	11/6

Solar	Lunar
11/29	11/7
11/30	11/8
12/1	11/9
12/2	11/10
12/3	11/11
12/4	11/12
12/5	11/13
12/6	11/14
12/7	11/15
12/8	11/16
12/9	11/17
12/10	11/18
12/11	11/19
12/12	11/20
12/13	11/21
12/14	11/22
12/15	11/23
12/16	11/24
12/17	11/25
12/18	11/26
12/19	11/27
12/20	11/28
12/21	11/29
12/22	11/30
12/23	12/1
12/24	12/2
12/25	12/3
12/26	12/4
12/27	12/5
12/28	12/6
12/29	12/7
12/30	12/8
12/31	12/9

Solar Date	Lunar Date
1966	
1/1	12/10
1/2	12/11
1/3	12/12
1/4	12/13
1/5	12/14
1/6	12/15
1/7	12/16
1/8	12/17
1/9	12/18
1/10	12/19
1/11	12/20
1/12	12/21
1/13	12/22
1/14	12/23
1/15	12/24
1/16	12/25
1/17	12/26
1/18	12/27
1/19	12/28
1/20	12/29

Solar	Lunar
1/21	1/1 (1966)
1/22	1/2
1/23	1/3
1/24	1/4
1/25	1/5
1/26	1/6
1/27	1/7
1/28	1/8
1/29	1/9
1/30	1/10
1/31	1/11
2/1	1/12
2/2	1/13
2/3	1/14
2/4	1/15
2/5	1/16
2/6	1/17
2/7	1/18
2/8	1/19
2/9	1/20
2/10	1/21
2/11	1/22
2/12	1/23
2/13	1/24
2/14	1/25
2/15	1/26
2/16	1/27
2/17	1/28
2/18	1/29
2/19	1/30
2/20	2/1
2/21	2/2
2/22	2/3
2/23	2/4
2/24	2/5
2/25	2/6
2/26	2/7
2/27	2/8
2/28	2/9
3/1	2/10
3/2	2/11
3/3	2/12
3/4	2/13
3/5	2/14
3/6	2/15
3/7	2/16
3/8	2/17
3/9	2/18
3/10	2/19
3/11	2/20
3/12	2/21
3/13	2/22
3/14	2/23
3/15	2/24
3/16	2/25
3/17	2/26
3/18	2/27

Solar	Lunar
3/19	2/28
3/20	2/29
3/21	2/30
3/22	3/1
3/23	3/2
3/24	3/3
3/25	3/4
3/26	3/5
3/27	3/6
3/28	3/7
3/29	3/8
3/30	3/9
3/31	3/10
4/1	3/11
4/2	3/12
4/3	3/13
4/4	3/14
4/5	3/15
4/6	3/16
4/7	3/17
4/8	3/18
4/9	3/19
4/10	3/20
4/11	3/21
4/12	3/22
4/13	3/23
4/14	3/24
4/15	3/25
4/16	3/26
4/17	3/27
4/18	3/28
4/19	3/29
4/20	3/30
4/21	3/1 *(Leap Month)*
4/22	3/2
4/23	3/3
4/24	3/4
4/25	3/5
4/26	3/6
4/27	3/7
4/28	3/8
4/29	3/9
4/30	3/10
5/1	3/11
5/2	3/12
5/3	3/13
5/4	3/14
5/5	3/15
5/6	3/16
5/7	3/17
5/8	3/18
5/9	3/19
5/10	3/20
5/11	3/21
5/12	3/22
5/13	3/23
5/14	3/24

Solar	Lunar
5/15	3/25
5/16	3/26
5/17	3/27
5/18	3/28
5/19	3/29
5/20	4/1
5/21	4/2
5/22	4/3
5/23	4/4
5/24	4/5
5/25	4/6
5/26	4/7
5/27	4/8
5/28	4/9
5/29	4/10
5/30	4/11
5/31	4/12
6/1	4/13
6/2	4/14
6/3	4/15
6/4	4/16
6/5	4/17
6/6	4/18
6/7	4/19
6/8	4/20
6/9	4/21
6/10	4/22
6/11	4/23
6/12	4/24
6/13	4/25
6/14	4/26
6/15	4/27
6/16	4/28
6/17	4/29
6/18	4/30
6/19	5/1
6/20	5/2
6/21	5/3
6/22	5/4
6/23	5/5
6/24	5/6
6/25	5/7
6/26	5/8
6/27	5/9
6/28	5/10
6/29	5/11
6/30	5/12
7/1	5/13
7/2	5/14
7/3	5/15
7/4	5/16
7/5	5/17
7/6	5/18
7/7	5/19
7/8	5/20
7/9	5/21
7/10	5/22
7/11	5/23

Solar	Lunar
7/12	5/24
7/13	5/25
7/14	5/26
7/15	5/27
7/16	5/28
7/17	5/29
7/18	6/1
7/19	6/2
7/20	6/3
7/21	6/4
7/22	6/5
7/23	6/6
7/24	6/7
7/25	6/8
7/26	6/9
7/27	6/10
7/28	6/11
7/29	6/12
7/30	6/13
7/31	6/14
8/1	6/15
8/2	6/16
8/3	6/17
8/4	6/18
8/5	6/19
8/6	6/20
8/7	6/21
8/8	6/22
8/9	6/23
8/10	6/24
8/11	6/25
8/12	6/26
8/13	6/27
8/14	6/28
8/15	6/29
8/16	7/1
8/17	7/2
8/18	7/3
8/19	7/4
8/20	7/5
8/21	7/6
8/22	7/7
8/23	7/8
8/24	7/9
8/25	7/10
8/26	7/11
8/27	7/12
8/28	7/13
8/29	7/14
8/30	7/15
8/31	7/16
9/1	7/17
9/2	7/18
9/3	7/19
9/4	7/20
9/5	7/21
9/6	7/22
9/7	7/23

Solar	Lunar
9/8	7/24
9/9	7/25
9/10	7/26
9/11	7/27
9/12	7/28
9/13	7/29
9/14	7/30
9/15	8/1
9/16	8/2
9/17	8/3
9/18	8/4
9/19	8/5
9/20	8/6
9/21	8/7
9/22	8/8
9/23	8/9
9/24	8/10
9/25	8/11
9/26	8/12
9/27	8/13
9/28	8/14
9/29	8/15
9/30	8/16
10/1	8/17
10/2	8/18
10/3	8/19
10/4	8/20
10/5	8/21
10/6	8/22
10/7	8/23
10/8	8/24
10/9	8/25
10/10	8/26
10/11	8/27
10/12	8/28
10/13	8/29
10/14	9/1
10/15	9/2
10/16	9/3
10/17	9/4
10/18	9/5
10/19	9/6
10/20	9/7
10/21	9/8
10/22	9/9
10/23	9/10
10/24	9/11
10/25	9/12
10/26	9/13
10/27	9/14
10/28	9/15
10/29	9/16
10/30	9/17
10/31	9/18
11/1	9/19
11/2	9/20
11/3	9/21
11/4	9/22

Solar Date	Lunar Date	Solar Date	Lunar Date	Solar Date	Lunar Date	Solar Date	Lunar Date	Solar Date	Lunar Date	Solar Date	Lunar Date
11/5	9/23	**1967**		2/24	1/16	4/23	3/14	6/20	5/13	8/17	7/12
11/6	9/24	1/1	11/21	2/25	1/17	4/24	3/15	6/21	5/14	8/18	7/13
11/7	9/25	1/2	11/22	2/26	1/18	4/25	3/16	6/22	5/15	8/19	7/14
11/8	9/26	1/3	11/23	2/27	1/19	4/26	3/17	6/23	5/16	8/20	7/15
11/9	9/27	1/4	11/24	2/28	1/20	4/27	3/18	6/24	5/17	8/21	7/16
11/10	9/28	1/5	11/25			4/28	3/19	6/25	5/18	8/22	7/17
11/11	9/29	1/6	11/26	3/1	1/21	4/29	3/20	6/26	5/19	8/23	7/18
11/12	10/1	1/7	11/27	3/2	1/22	4/30	3/21	6/27	5/20	8/24	7/19
11/13	10/2	1/8	11/28	3/3	1/23			6/28	5/21	8/25	7/20
11/14	10/3	1/9	11/29	3/4	1/24	5/1	3/22	6/29	5/22	8/26	7/21
11/15	10/4	1/10	11/30	3/5	1/25	5/2	3/23	6/30	5/23	8/27	7/22
11/16	10/5	1/11	12/1	3/6	1/26	5/3	3/24			8/28	7/23
11/17	10/6	1/12	12/2	3/7	1/27	5/4	3/25	7/1	5/24	8/29	7/24
11/18	10/7	1/13	12/3	3/8	1/28	5/5	3/26	7/2	5/25	8/30	7/25
11/19	10/8	1/14	12/4	3/9	1/29	5/6	3/27	7/3	5/26	8/31	7/26
11/20	10/9	1/15	12/5	3/10	1/30	5/7	3/28	7/4	5/27		
11/21	10/10	1/16	12/6	3/11	2/1	5/8	3/29	7/5	5/28	9/1	7/27
11/22	10/11	1/17	12/7	3/12	2/2	5/9	4/1	7/6	5/29	9/2	7/28
11/23	10/12	1/18	12/8	3/13	2/3	5/10	4/2	7/7	5/30	9/3	7/29
11/24	10/13	1/19	12/9	3/14	2/4	5/11	4/3	7/8	6/1	9/4	8/1
11/25	10/14	1/20	12/10	3/15	2/5	5/12	4/4	7/9	6/2	9/5	8/2
11/26	10/15	1/21	12/11	3/16	2/6	5/13	4/5	7/10	6/3	9/6	8/3
11/27	10/16	1/22	12/12	3/17	2/7	5/14	4/6	7/11	6/4	9/7	8/4
11/28	10/17	1/23	12/13	3/18	2/8	5/15	4/7	7/12	6/5	9/8	8/5
11/29	10/18	1/24	12/14	3/19	2/9	5/16	4/8	7/13	6/6	9/9	8/6
11/30	10/19	1/25	12/15	3/20	2/10	5/17	4/9	7/14	6/7	9/10	8/7
		1/26	12/16	3/21	2/11	5/18	4/10	7/15	6/8	9/11	8/8
12/1	10/20	1/27	12/17	3/22	2/12	5/19	4/11	7/16	6/9	9/12	8/9
12/2	10/21	1/28	12/18	3/23	2/13	5/20	4/12	7/17	6/10	9/13	8/10
12/3	10/22	1/29	12/19	3/24	2/14	5/21	4/13	7/18	6/11	9/14	8/11
12/4	10/23	1/30	12/20	3/25	2/15	5/22	4/14	7/19	6/12	9/15	8/12
12/5	10/24	1/31	12/21	3/26	2/16	5/23	4/15	7/20	6/13	9/16	8/13
12/6	10/25	2/1	12/22	3/27	2/17	5/24	4/16	7/21	6/14	9/17	8/14
12/7	10/26	2/2	12/23	3/28	2/18	5/25	4/17	7/22	6/15	9/18	8/15
12/8	10/27	2/3	12/24	3/29	2/19	5/26	4/18	7/23	6/16	9/19	8/16
12/9	10/28	2/4	12/25	3/30	2/20	5/27	4/19	7/24	6/17	9/20	8/17
12/10	10/29	2/5	12/26	3/31	2/21	5/28	4/20	7/25	6/18	9/21	8/18
12/11	10/30	2/6	12/27			5/29	4/21	7/26	6/19	9/22	8/19
12/12	11/1	2/7	12/28	4/1	2/22	5/30	4/22	7/27	6/20	9/23	8/20
12/13	11/2	2/8	12/29	4/2	2/23	5/31	4/23	7/28	6/21	9/24	8/21
12/14	11/3	2/9	1/1 (1967)	4/3	2/24			7/29	6/22	9/25	8/22
12/15	11/4	2/10	1/2	4/4	2/25	6/1	4/24	7/30	6/23	9/26	8/23
12/16	11/5	2/11	1/3	4/5	2/26	6/2	4/25	7/31	6/24	9/27	8/24
12/17	11/6	2/12	1/4	4/6	2/27	6/3	4/26			9/28	8/25
12/18	11/7	2/13	1/5	4/7	2/28	6/4	4/27	8/1	6/25	9/29	8/26
12/19	11/8	2/14	1/6	4/8	2/29	6/5	4/28	8/2	6/26	9/30	8/27
12/20	11/9	2/15	1/7	4/9	2/30	6/6	4/29	8/3	6/27		
12/21	11/10	2/16	1/8	4/10	3/1	6/7	4/30	8/4	6/28	10/1	8/28
12/22	11/11	2/17	1/9	4/11	3/2	6/8	5/1	8/5	6/29	10/2	8/29
12/23	11/12	2/18	1/10	4/12	3/3	6/9	5/2	8/6	7/1	10/3	8/30
12/24	11/13	2/19	1/11	4/13	3/4	6/10	5/3	8/7	7/2	10/4	9/1
12/25	11/14	2/20	1/12	4/14	3/5	6/11	5/4	8/8	7/3	10/5	9/2
12/26	11/15	2/21	1/13	4/15	3/6	6/12	5/5	8/9	7/4	10/6	9/3
12/27	11/16	2/22	1/14	4/16	3/7	6/13	5/6	8/10	7/5	10/7	9/4
12/28	11/17	2/23	1/15	4/17	3/8	6/14	5/7	8/11	7/6	10/8	9/5
12/29	11/18			4/18	3/9	6/15	5/8	8/12	7/7	10/9	9/6
12/30	11/19			4/19	3/10	6/16	5/9	8/13	7/8	10/10	9/7
12/31	11/20			4/20	3/11	6/17	5/10	8/14	7/9	10/11	9/8
				4/21	3/12	6/18	5/11	8/15	7/10	10/12	9/9
				4/22	3/13	6/19	5/12	8/16	7/11	10/13	9/10

Solar	Lunar	Solar	Lunar	Solar	Lunar	Solar	Lunar	Solar	Lunar	Solar	Lunar
10/14	9/11	12/11	11/10	2/1	1/3	3/31	3/3	5/28	5/2	7/25	7/1
10/15	9/12	12/12	11/11	2/2	1/4			5/29	5/3	7/26	7/2
10/16	9/13	12/13	11/12	2/3	1/5	4/1	3/4	5/30	5/4	7/27	7/3
10/17	9/14	12/14	11/13	2/4	1/6	4/2	3/5	5/31	5/5	7/28	7/4
10/18	9/15	12/15	11/14	2/5	1/7	4/3	3/6			7/29	7/5
10/19	9/16	12/16	11/15	2/6	1/8	4/4	3/7	6/1	5/6	7/30	7/6
10/20	9/17	12/17	11/16	2/7	1/9	4/5	3/8	6/2	5/7	7/31	7/7
10/21	9/18	12/18	11/17	2/8	1/10	4/6	3/9	6/3	5/8		
10/22	9/19	12/19	11/18	2/9	1/11	4/7	3/10	6/4	5/9	8/1	7/8
10/23	9/20	12/20	11/19	2/10	1/12	4/8	3/11	6/5	5/10	8/2	7/9
10/24	9/21	12/21	11/20	2/11	1/13	4/9	3/12	6/6	5/11	8/3	7/10
10/25	9/22	12/22	11/21	2/12	1/14	4/10	3/13	6/7	5/12	8/4	7/11
10/26	9/23	12/23	11/22	2/13	1/15	4/11	3/14	6/8	5/13	8/5	7/12
10/27	9/24	12/24	11/23	2/14	1/16	4/12	3/15	6/9	5/14	8/6	7/13
10/28	9/25	12/25	11/24	2/15	1/17	4/13	3/16	6/10	5/15	8/7	7/14
10/29	9/26	12/26	11/25	2/16	1/18	4/14	3/17	6/11	5/16	8/8	7/15
10/30	9/27	12/27	11/26	2/17	1/19	4/15	3/18	6/12	5/17	8/9	7/16
10/31	9/28	12/28	11/27	2/18	1/20	4/16	3/19	6/13	5/18	8/10	7/17
		12/29	11/28	2/19	1/21	4/17	3/20	6/14	5/19	8/11	7/18
11/1	9/29	12/30	11/29	2/20	1/22	4/18	3/21	6/15	5/20	8/12	7/19
11/2	10/1	12/31	12/1	2/21	1/23	4/19	3/22	6/16	5/21	8/13	7/20
11/3	10/2			2/22	1/24	4/20	3/23	6/17	5/22	8/14	7/21
11/4	10/3			2/23	1/25	4/21	3/24	6/18	5/23	8/15	7/22
11/5	10/4	**Solar**	**Lunar**	2/24	1/26	4/22	3/25	6/19	5/24	8/16	7/23
11/6	10/5	**Date**	**Date**	2/25	1/27	4/23	3/26	6/20	5/25	8/17	7/24
11/7	10/6			2/26	1/28	4/24	3/27	6/21	5/26	8/18	7/25
11/8	10/7	**1968**		2/27	1/29	4/25	3/28	6/22	5/27	8/19	7/26
11/9	10/8	1/1	12/2	2/28	2/1	4/26	3/29	6/23	5/28	8/20	7/27
11/10	10/9	1/2	12/3	2/29	2/2	4/27	4/1	6/24	5/29	8/21	7/28
11/11	10/10	1/3	12/4			4/28	4/2	6/25	5/30	8/22	7/29
11/12	10/11	1/4	12/5	3/1	2/3	4/29	4/3	6/26	6/1	8/23	7/30
11/13	10/12	1/5	12/6	3/2	2/4	4/30	4/4	6/27	6/2	8/24	7/1
11/14	10/13	1/6	12/7	3/3	2/5			6/28	6/3	*(Leap Month)*	
11/15	10/14	1/7	12/8	3/4	2/6	5/1	4/5	6/29	6/4	8/25	7/2
11/16	10/15	1/8	12/9	3/5	2/7	5/2	4/6	6/30	6/5	8/26	7/3
11/17	10/16	1/9	12/10	3/6	2/8	5/3	4/7			8/27	7/4
11/18	10/17	1/10	12/11	3/7	2/9	5/4	4/8	7/1	6/6	8/28	7/5
11/19	10/18	1/11	12/12	3/8	2/10	5/5	4/9	7/2	6/7	8/29	7/6
11/20	10/19	1/12	12/13	3/9	2/11	5/6	4/10	7/3	6/8	8/30	7/7
11/21	10/20	1/13	12/14	3/10	2/12	5/7	4/11	7/4	6/9	8/31	7/8
11/22	10/21	1/14	12/15	3/11	2/13	5/8	4/12	7/5	6/10		
11/23	10/22	1/15	12/16	3/12	2/14	5/9	4/13	7/6	6/11	9/1	7/9
11/24	10/23	1/16	12/17	3/13	2/15	5/10	4/14	7/7	6/12	9/2	7/10
11/25	10/24	1/17	12/18	3/14	2/16	5/11	4/15	7/8	6/13	9/3	7/11
11/26	10/25	1/18	12/19	3/15	2/17	5/12	4/16	7/9	6/14	9/4	7/12
11/27	10/26	1/19	12/20	3/16	2/18	5/13	4/17	7/10	6/15	9/5	7/13
11/28	10/27	1/20	12/21	3/17	2/19	5/14	4/18	7/11	6/16	9/6	7/14
11/29	10/28	1/21	12/22	3/18	2/20	5/15	4/19	7/12	6/17	9/7	7/15
11/30	10/29	1/22	12/23	3/19	2/21	5/16	4/20	7/13	6/18	9/8	7/16
		1/23	12/24	3/20	2/22	5/17	4/21	7/14	6/19	9/9	7/17
12/1	10/30	1/24	12/25	3/21	2/23	5/18	4/22	7/15	6/20	9/10	7/18
12/2	11/1	1/25	12/26	3/22	2/24	5/19	4/23	7/16	6/21	9/11	7/19
12/3	11/2	1/26	12/27	3/23	2/25	5/20	4/24	7/17	6/22	9/12	7/20
12/4	11/3	1/27	12/28	3/24	2/26	5/21	4/25	7/18	6/23	9/13	7/21
12/5	11/4	1/28	12/29	3/25	2/27	5/22	4/26	7/19	6/24	9/14	7/22
12/6	11/5	1/29	12/30	3/26	2/28	5/23	4/27	7/20	6/25	9/15	7/23
12/7	11/6	1/30	1/1	3/27	2/29	5/24	4/28	7/21	6/26	9/16	7/24
12/8	11/7		(1968)	3/28	2/30	5/25	4/29	7/22	6/27	9/17	7/25
12/9	11/8	1/31	1/2	3/29	3/1	5/26	4/30	7/23	6/28	9/18	7/26
12/10	11/9			3/30	3/2	5/27	5/1	7/24	6/29	9/19	7/27

Solar	Lunar
9/20	7/28
9/21	7/29
9/22	8/1
9/23	8/2
9/24	8/3
9/25	8/4
9/26	8/5
9/27	8/6
9/28	8/7
9/29	8/8
9/30	8/9
10/1	8/10
10/2	8/11
10/3	8/12
10/4	8/13
10/5	8/14
10/6	8/15
10/7	8/16
10/8	8/17
10/9	8/18
10/10	8/19
10/11	8/20
10/12	8/21
10/13	8/22
10/14	8/23
10/15	8/24
10/16	8/25
10/17	8/26
10/18	8/27
10/19	8/28
10/20	8/29
10/21	8/30
10/22	9/1
10/23	9/2
10/24	9/3
10/25	9/4
10/26	9/5
10/27	9/6
10/28	9/7
10/29	9/8
10/30	9/9
10/31	9/10
11/1	9/11
11/2	9/12
11/3	9/13
11/4	9/14
11/5	9/15
11/6	9/16
11/7	9/17
11/8	9/18
11/9	9/19
11/10	9/20
11/11	9/21
11/12	9/22
11/13	9/23
11/14	9/24
11/15	9/25
11/16	9/26

Solar	Lunar
11/17	9/27
11/18	9/28
11/19	9/29
11/20	10/1
11/21	10/2
11/22	10/3
11/23	10/4
11/24	10/5
11/25	10/6
11/26	10/7
11/27	10/8
11/28	10/9
11/29	10/10
11/30	10/11
12/1	10/12
12/2	10/13
12/3	10/14
12/4	10/15
12/5	10/16
12/6	10/17
12/7	10/18
12/8	10/19
12/9	10/20
12/10	10/21
12/11	10/22
12/12	10/23
12/13	10/24
12/14	10/25
12/15	10/26
12/16	10/27
12/17	10/28
12/18	10/29
12/19	10/30
12/20	11/1
12/21	11/2
12/22	11/3
12/23	11/4
12/24	11/5
12/25	11/6
12/26	11/7
12/27	11/8
12/28	11/9
12/29	11/10
12/30	11/11
12/31	11/12

Solar Date	Lunar Date
1969	
1/1	11/13
1/2	11/14
1/3	11/15
1/4	11/16
1/5	11/17
1/6	11/18
1/7	11/19
1/8	11/20

Solar	Lunar
1/9	11/21
1/10	11/22
1/11	11/23
1/12	11/24
1/13	11/25
1/14	11/26
1/15	11/27
1/16	11/28
1/17	11/29
1/18	12/1
1/19	12/2
1/20	12/3
1/21	12/4
1/22	12/5
1/23	12/6
1/24	12/7
1/25	12/8
1/26	12/9
1/27	12/10
1/28	12/11
1/29	12/12
1/30	12/13
1/31	12/14
2/1	12/15
2/2	12/16
2/3	12/17
2/4	12/18
2/5	12/19
2/6	12/20
2/7	12/21
2/8	12/22
2/9	12/23
2/10	12/24
2/11	12/25
2/12	12/26
2/13	12/27
2/14	12/28
2/15	12/29
2/16	12/30
2/17	1/1 (1969)
2/18	1/2
2/19	1/3
2/20	1/4
2/21	1/5
2/22	1/6
2/23	1/7
2/24	1/8
2/25	1/9
2/26	1/10
2/27	1/11
2/28	1/12
3/1	1/13
3/2	1/14
3/3	1/15
3/4	1/16
3/5	1/17
3/6	1/18

Solar	Lunar
3/7	1/19
3/8	1/20
3/9	1/21
3/10	1/22
3/11	1/23
3/12	1/24
3/13	1/25
3/14	1/26
3/15	1/27
3/16	1/28
3/17	1/29
3/18	2/1
3/19	2/2
3/20	2/3
3/21	2/4
3/22	2/5
3/23	2/6
3/24	2/7
3/25	2/8
3/26	2/9
3/27	2/10
3/28	2/11
3/29	2/12
3/30	2/13
3/31	2/14
4/1	2/15
4/2	2/16
4/3	2/17
4/4	2/18
4/5	2/19
4/6	2/20
4/7	2/21
4/8	2/22
4/9	2/23
4/10	2/24
4/11	2/25
4/12	2/26
4/13	2/27
4/14	2/28
4/15	2/29
4/16	2/30
4/17	3/1
4/18	3/2
4/19	3/3
4/20	3/4
4/21	3/5
4/22	3/6
4/23	3/7
4/24	3/8
4/25	3/9
4/26	3/10
4/27	3/11
4/28	3/12
4/29	3/13
4/30	3/14
5/1	3/15
5/2	3/16
5/3	3/17

Solar	Lunar
5/4	3/18
5/5	3/19
5/6	3/20
5/7	3/21
5/8	3/22
5/9	3/23
5/10	3/24
5/11	3/25
5/12	3/26
5/13	3/27
5/14	3/28
5/15	3/29
5/16	4/1
5/17	4/2
5/18	4/2
5/19	4/3
5/20	4/4
5/21	4/5
5/22	4/6
5/23	4/7
5/24	4/8
5/25	4/9
5/26	4/10
5/27	4/11
5/28	4/12
5/29	4/13
5/30	4/14
5/31	4/15
6/1	4/16
6/2	4/17
6/3	4/18
6/4	4/19
6/5	4/20
6/6	4/21
6/7	4/22
6/8	4/23
6/9	4/24
6/10	4/25
6/11	4/26
6/12	4/27
6/13	4/28
6/14	4/29
6/15	5/1
6/16	5/2
6/17	5/3
6/18	5/4
6/19	5/5
6/20	5/6
6/21	5/7
6/22	5/8
6/23	5/9
6/24	5/10
6/25	5/11
6/26	5/12
6/27	5/13
6/28	5/14
6/29	5/15
6/30	5/16

Solar	Lunar
7/1	5/17
7/2	5/18
7/3	5/19
7/4	5/20
7/5	5/21
7/6	5/22
7/7	5/23
7/8	5/24
7/9	5/25
7/10	5/26
7/11	5/27
7/12	5/28
7/13	5/29
7/14	6/1
7/15	6/2
7/16	6/3
7/17	6/4
7/18	6/5
7/19	6/6
7/20	6/7
7/21	6/8
7/22	6/9
7/23	6/10
7/24	6/11
7/25	6/12
7/26	6/13
7/27	6/14
7/28	6/15
7/29	6/16
7/30	6/17
7/31	6/18
8/1	6/19
8/2	6/20
8/3	6/21
8/4	6/22
8/5	6/23
8/6	6/24
8/7	6/25
8/8	6/26
8/9	6/27
8/10	6/28
8/11	6/29
8/12	6/30
8/13	7/1
8/14	7/2
8/15	7/3
8/16	7/4
8/17	7/5
8/18	7/6
8/19	7/7
8/20	7/8
8/21	7/9
8/22	7/10
8/23	7/11
8/24	7/12
8/25	7/13
8/26	7/14
8/27	7/15
8/28	7/16

The chart is arranged in six side-by-side Solar Date / Lunar Date column-pairs, read top-to-bottom and left-to-right.

Solar Date	Lunar Date
8/29	7/17
8/30	7/18
8/31	7/19
9/1	7/20
9/2	7/21
9/3	7/22
9/4	7/23
9/5	7/24
9/6	7/25
9/7	7/26
9/8	7/27
9/9	7/28
9/10	7/29
9/11	7/30
9/12	8/1
9/13	8/2
9/14	8/3
9/15	8/4
9/16	8/5
9/17	8/6
9/18	8/7
9/19	8/8
9/20	8/9
9/21	8/10
9/22	8/11
9/23	8/12
9/24	8/13
9/25	8/14
9/26	8/15
9/27	8/16
9/28	8/17
9/29	8/18
9/30	8/19
10/1	8/20
10/2	8/21
10/3	8/22
10/4	8/23
10/5	8/24
10/6	8/25
10/7	8/26
10/8	8/27
10/9	8/28
10/10	8/29
10/11	9/1
10/12	9/2
10/13	9/3
10/14	9/4
10/15	9/5
10/16	9/6
10/17	9/7
10/18	9/8
10/19	9/9
10/20	9/10
10/21	9/11
10/22	9/12
10/23	9/13
10/24	9/14
10/25	9/15
10/26	9/16
10/27	9/17
10/28	9/18
10/29	9/19
10/30	9/20
11/1	9/21
11/2	9/22
11/3	9/23
11/4	9/24
11/5	9/25
11/6	9/26
11/7	9/27
11/8	9/28
11/9	9/29
11/10	10/1
11/11	10/2
11/12	10/3
11/13	10/4
11/14	10/5
11/15	10/6
11/16	10/7
11/17	10/8
11/18	10/9
11/19	10/10
11/20	10/11
11/21	10/12
11/22	10/13
11/23	10/14
11/24	10/15
11/25	10/16
11/26	10/17
11/27	10/18
11/28	10/19
11/29	10/20
11/30	10/21
12/1	10/22
12/2	10/23
12/3	10/24
12/4	10/25
12/5	10/26
12/6	10/27
12/7	10/28
12/8	10/29
12/9	11/1
12/10	11/2
12/11	11/3
12/12	11/4
12/13	11/5
12/14	11/6
12/15	11/7
12/16	11/8
12/17	11/9
12/18	11/10
12/19	11/11
12/20	11/12
12/21	11/13
12/22	11/14
12/23	11/15
12/24	11/16
12/25	11/17
12/26	11/18
12/27	11/19
12/28	11/20
12/29	11/21
12/30	11/22
12/31	11/23

Solar Date   Lunar Date

1970

Solar Date	Lunar Date
1/1	11/24
1/2	11/25
1/3	11/26
1/4	11/27
1/5	11/28
1/6	11/29
1/7	11/30
1/8	12/1
1/9	12/2
1/10	12/3
1/11	12/4
1/12	12/5
1/13	12/6
1/14	12/7
1/15	12/8
1/16	12/9
1/17	12/10
1/18	12/11
1/19	12/12
1/20	12/13
1/21	12/14
1/22	12/15
1/23	12/16
1/24	12/17
1/25	12/18
1/26	12/19
1/27	12/20
1/28	12/21
1/29	12/22
1/30	12/23
1/31	12/24
2/1	12/25
2/2	12/26
2/3	12/27
2/4	12/28
2/5	12/29
2/6	1/1 (1970)
2/7	1/2
2/8	1/3
2/9	1/4
2/10	1/5
2/11	1/6
2/12	1/7
2/13	1/8
2/14	1/9
2/15	1/10
2/16	1/11
2/17	1/12
2/18	1/13
2/19	1/14
2/20	1/15
2/21	1/16
2/22	1/17
2/23	1/18
2/24	1/19
2/25	1/20
2/26	1/21
2/27	1/22
2/28	1/23
3/1	1/24
3/2	1/25
3/3	1/26
3/4	1/27
3/5	1/28
3/6	1/29
3/7	1/30
3/8	2/1
3/9	2/2
3/10	2/3
3/11	2/4
3/12	2/5
3/13	2/6
3/14	2/7
3/15	2/8
3/16	2/9
3/17	2/10
3/18	2/11
3/19	2/12
3/20	2/13
3/21	2/14
3/22	2/15
3/23	2/16
3/24	2/17
3/25	2/18
3/26	2/19
3/27	2/20
3/28	2/21
3/29	2/22
3/30	2/23
3/31	2/24
4/1	2/25
4/2	2/26
4/3	2/27
4/4	2/28
4/5	2/29
4/6	3/1
4/7	3/2
4/8	3/3
4/9	3/4
4/10	3/5
4/11	3/6
4/12	3/7
4/13	3/8
4/14	3/9
4/15	3/10
4/16	3/11
4/17	3/12
4/18	3/13
4/19	3/14
4/20	3/15
4/21	3/16
4/22	3/17
4/23	3/18
4/24	3/19
4/25	3/20
4/26	3/21
4/27	3/22
4/28	3/23
4/29	3/24
4/30	3/25
5/1	3/26
5/2	3/27
5/3	3/28
5/4	3/29
5/5	4/1
5/6	4/2
5/7	4/3
5/8	4/4
5/9	4/5
5/10	4/6
5/11	4/7
5/12	4/8
5/13	4/9
5/14	4/10
5/15	4/11
5/16	4/12
5/17	4/13
5/18	4/14
5/19	4/15
5/20	4/16
5/21	4/17
5/22	4/18
5/23	4/19
5/24	4/20
5/25	4/21
5/26	4/22
5/27	4/23
5/28	4/24
5/29	4/25
5/30	4/26
5/31	4/27
6/1	4/28
6/2	4/29
6/3	4/30
6/4	5/1
6/5	5/2
6/6	5/3
6/7	5/4
6/8	5/5
6/9	5/6
6/10	5/7
6/11	5/8
6/12	5/9
6/13	5/10
6/14	5/11
6/15	5/12
6/16	5/13
6/17	5/14
6/18	5/15
6/19	5/16
6/20	5/17
6/21	5/18
6/22	5/19
6/23	5/20
6/24	5/21
6/25	5/22
6/26	5/23
6/27	5/24
6/28	5/25
6/29	5/26
6/30	5/27
7/1	5/28
7/2	5/29
7/3	6/1
7/4	6/2
7/5	6/3
7/6	6/4
7/7	6/5
7/8	6/6
7/9	6/7
7/10	6/8
7/11	6/9
7/12	6/10
7/13	6/11
7/14	6/12
7/15	6/13
7/16	6/14
7/17	6/15
7/18	6/16
7/19	6/17
7/20	6/18
7/21	6/19
7/22	6/20
7/23	6/21
7/24	6/22
7/25	6/23
7/26	6/24
7/27	6/25
7/28	6/26
7/29	6/27
7/30	6/28
7/31	6/29
8/1	6/30
8/2	7/1
8/3	7/2
8/4	7/3
8/5	7/4
8/6	7/5

Solar	Lunar
8/7	7/6
8/8	7/7
8/9	7/8
8/10	7/9
8/11	7/10
8/12	7/11
8/13	7/12
8/14	7/13
8/15	7/14
8/16	7/15
8/17	7/16
8/18	7/17
8/19	7/18
8/20	7/19
8/21	7/20
8/22	7/21
8/23	7/22
8/24	7/23
8/25	7/24
8/26	7/25
8/27	7/26
8/28	7/27
8/29	7/28
8/30	7/29
8/31	7/30
9/1	8/1
9/2	8/2
9/3	8/3
9/4	8/4
9/5	8/5
9/6	8/6
9/7	8/7
9/8	8/8
9/9	8/9
9/10	8/10
9/11	8/11
9/12	8/12
9/13	8/13
9/14	8/14
9/15	8/15
9/16	8/16
9/17	8/17
9/18	8/18
9/19	8/19
9/20	8/20
9/21	8/21
9/22	8/22
9/23	8/23
9/24	8/24
9/25	8/25
9/26	8/26
9/27	8/27
9/28	8/28
9/29	8/29
9/30	9/1
10/1	9/2
10/2	9/3
10/3	9/4

Solar	Lunar
10/4	9/5
10/5	9/6
10/6	9/7
10/7	9/8
10/8	9/9
10/9	9/10
10/10	9/11
10/11	9/12
10/12	9/13
10/13	9/14
10/14	9/15
10/15	9/16
10/16	9/17
10/17	9/18
10/18	9/19
10/19	9/20
10/20	9/21
10/21	9/22
10/22	9/23
10/23	9/24
10/24	9/25
10/25	9/26
10/26	9/27
10/27	9/28
10/28	9/29
10/29	9/30
10/30	10/1
10/31	10/2
11/1	10/3
11/2	10/4
11/3	10/5
11/4	10/6
11/5	10/7
11/6	10/8
11/7	10/9
11/8	10/10
11/9	10/11
11/10	10/12
11/11	10/13
11/12	10/14
11/13	10/15
11/14	10/16
11/15	10/17
11/16	10/18
11/17	10/19
11/18	10/20
11/19	10/21
11/20	10/22
11/21	10/23
11/22	10/24
11/23	10/25
11/24	10/26
11/25	10/27
11/26	10/28
11/27	10/29
11/28	10/30
11/29	11/1
11/30	11/2

Solar	Lunar
12/1	11/3
12/2	11/4
12/3	11/5
12/4	11/6
12/5	11/7
12/6	11/8
12/7	11/9
12/8	11/10
12/9	11/11
12/10	11/12
12/11	11/13
12/12	11/14
12/13	11/15
12/14	11/16
12/15	11/17
12/16	11/18
12/17	11/19
12/18	11/20
12/19	11/21
12/20	11/22
12/21	11/23
12/22	11/24
12/23	11/25
12/24	11/26
12/25	11/27
12/26	11/28
12/27	11/29
12/28	12/1
12/29	12/2
12/30	12/3
12/31	12/4

Solar Date	Lunar Date
1971	
1/1	12/5
1/2	12/6
1/3	12/7
1/4	12/8
1/5	12/9
1/6	12/10
1/7	12/11
1/8	12/12
1/9	12/13
1/10	12/14
1/11	12/15
1/12	12/16
1/13	12/17
1/14	12/18
1/15	12/19
1/16	12/20
1/17	12/21
1/18	12/22
1/19	12/23
1/20	12/24
1/21	12/25
1/22	12/26
1/23	12/27

Solar	Lunar
1/24	12/28
1/25	12/29
1/26	12/30
1/27	1/1 (1971)
1/28	1/2
1/29	1/3
1/30	1/4
1/31	1/5
2/1	1/6
2/2	1/7
2/3	1/8
2/4	1/9
2/5	1/10
2/6	1/11
2/7	1/12
2/8	1/13
2/9	1/14
2/10	1/15
2/11	1/16
2/12	1/17
2/13	1/18
2/14	1/19
2/15	1/20
2/16	1/21
2/17	1/22
2/18	1/23
2/19	1/24
2/20	1/25
2/21	1/26
2/22	1/27
2/23	1/28
2/24	1/29
2/25	2/1
2/26	2/2
2/27	2/3
2/28	2/4
3/1	2/5
3/2	2/6
3/3	2/7
3/4	2/8
3/5	2/9
3/6	2/10
3/7	2/11
3/8	2/12
3/9	2/13
3/10	2/14
3/11	2/15
3/12	2/16
3/13	2/17
3/14	2/18
3/15	2/19
3/16	2/20
3/17	2/21
3/18	2/22
3/19	2/23
3/20	2/24
3/21	2/25

Solar	Lunar
3/22	2/26
3/23	2/27
3/24	2/28
3/25	2/29
3/26	2/30
3/27	3/1
3/28	3/2
3/29	3/3
3/30	3/4
3/31	3/5
4/1	3/6
4/2	3/7
4/3	3/8
4/4	3/9
4/5	3/10
4/6	3/11
4/7	3/12
4/8	3/13
4/9	3/14
4/10	3/15
4/11	3/16
4/12	3/17
4/13	3/18
4/14	3/19
4/15	3/20
4/16	3/21
4/17	3/22
4/18	3/23
4/19	3/24
4/20	3/25
4/21	3/26
4/22	3/27
4/23	3/28
4/24	3/29
4/25	4/1
4/26	4/2
4/27	4/3
4/28	4/4
4/29	4/5
4/30	4/6
5/1	4/7
5/2	4/8
5/3	4/9
5/4	4/10
5/5	4/11
5/6	4/12
5/7	4/13
5/8	4/14
5/9	4/15
5/10	4/16
5/11	4/17
5/12	4/18
5/13	4/19
5/14	4/20
5/15	4/21
5/16	4/22
5/17	4/23
5/18	4/24

Solar	Lunar
5/19	4/25
5/20	4/26
5/21	4/27
5/22	4/28
5/23	4/29
5/24	5/1
5/25	5/2
5/26	5/3
5/27	5/4
5/28	5/5
5/29	5/6
5/30	5/7
5/31	5/8
6/1	5/9
6/2	5/10
6/3	5/11
6/4	5/12
6/5	5/13
6/6	5/14
6/7	5/15
6/8	5/16
6/9	5/17
6/10	5/18
6/11	5/19
6/12	5/20
6/13	5/21
6/14	5/22
6/15	5/23
6/16	5/24
6/17	5/25
6/18	5/26
6/19	5/27
6/20	5/28
6/21	5/29
6/22	5/30
6/23	5/1 *(Leap Month)*
6/24	5/2
6/25	5/3
6/26	5/4
6/27	5/5
6/28	5/6
6/29	5/7
6/30	5/8
7/1	5/9
7/2	5/10
7/3	5/11
7/4	5/12
7/5	5/13
7/6	5/14
7/7	5/15
7/8	5/16
7/9	5/17
7/10	5/18
7/11	5/19
7/12	5/20
7/13	5/21
7/14	5/22

Solar	Lunar	Solar	Lunar	Solar	Lunar	Solar Date	Lunar Date	Solar	Lunar	Solar	Lunar
7/15	5/23	9/11	7/22	11/8	9/21			2/24	1/10	4/22	3/9
7/16	5/24	9/12	7/23	11/9	9/22			2/25	1/11	4/23	3/10
7/17	5/25	9/13	7/24	11/10	9/23	**1972**		2/26	1/12	4/24	3/11
7/18	5/26	9/14	7/25	11/11	9/24			2/27	1/13	4/25	3/12
7/19	5/27	9/15	7/26	11/12	9/25	1/1	11/15	2/28	1/14	4/26	3/13
7/20	5/28	9/16	7/27	11/13	9/26	1/2	11/16	2/29	1/15	4/27	3/14
7/21	5/29	9/17	7/28	11/14	9/27	1/3	11/17			4/28	3/15
7/22	6/1	9/18	7/29	11/15	9/28	1/4	11/18	3/1	1/16	4/29	3/16
7/23	6/2	9/19	8/1	11/16	9/29	1/5	11/19	3/2	1/17	4/30	3/17
7/24	6/3	9/20	8/2	11/17	9/30	1/6	11/20	3/3	1/18		
7/25	6/4	9/21	8/3	11/18	10/1	1/7	11/21	3/4	1/19	5/1	3/18
7/26	6/5	9/22	8/4	11/19	10/2	1/8	11/22	3/5	1/20	5/2	3/19
7/27	6/6	9/23	8/5	11/20	10/3	1/9	11/23	3/6	1/21	5/3	3/20
7/28	6/7	9/24	8/6	11/21	10/4	1/10	11/24	3/7	1/22	5/4	3/21
7/29	6/8	9/25	8/7	11/22	10/5	1/11	11/25	3/8	1/23	5/5	3/22
7/30	6/9	9/26	8/8	11/23	10/6	1/12	11/26	3/9	1/24	5/6	3/23
7/31	6/10	9/27	8/9	11/24	10/7	1/13	11/27	3/10	1/25	5/7	3/24
		9/28	8/10	11/25	10/8	1/14	11/28	3/11	1/26	5/8	3/25
8/1	6/11	9/29	8/11	11/26	10/9	1/15	11/29	3/12	1/27	5/9	3/26
8/2	6/12	9/30	8/12	11/27	10/10	1/16	12/1	3/13	1/28	5/10	3/27
8/3	6/13			11/28	10/11	1/17	12/2	3/14	1/29	5/11	3/28
8/4	6/14	10/1	8/13	11/29	10/12	1/18	12/3	3/15	2/1	5/12	3/29
8/5	6/15	10/2	8/14	11/30	10/13	1/19	12/4	3/16	2/2	5/13	4/1
8/6	6/16	10/3	8/15			1/20	12/5	3/17	2/3	5/14	4/2
8/7	6/17	10/4	8/16	12/1	10/14	1/21	12/6	3/18	2/4	5/15	4/3
8/8	6/18	10/5	8/17	12/2	10/15	1/22	12/7	3/19	2/5	5/16	4/4
8/9	6/19	10/6	8/18	12/3	10/16	1/23	12/8	3/20	2/6	5/17	4/5
8/10	6/20	10/7	8/19	12/4	10/17	1/24	12/9	3/21	2/7	5/18	4/6
8/11	6/21	10/8	8/20	12/5	10/18	1/25	12/10	3/22	2/8	5/19	4/7
8/12	6/22	10/9	8/21	12/6	10/19	1/26	12/11	3/23	2/9	5/20	4/8
8/13	6/23	10/10	8/22	12/7	10/20	1/27	12/12	3/24	2/10	5/21	4/9
8/14	6/24	10/11	8/23	12/8	10/21	1/28	12/13	3/25	2/11	5/22	4/10
8/15	6/25	10/12	8/24	12/9	10/22	1/29	12/14	3/26	2/12	5/23	4/11
8/16	6/26	10/13	8/25	12/10	10/23	1/30	12/15	3/27	2/13	5/24	4/12
8/17	6/27	10/14	8/26	12/11	10/24	1/31	12/16	3/28	2/14	5/25	4/13
8/18	6/28	10/15	8/27	12/12	10/25			3/29	2/15	5/26	4/14
8/19	6/29	10/16	8/28	12/13	10/26	2/1	12/17	3/30	2/16	5/27	4/15
8/20	6/30	10/17	8/29	12/14	10/27	2/2	12/18	3/31	2/17	5/28	4/16
8/21	7/1	10/18	8/30	12/15	10/28	2/3	12/19			5/29	4/17
8/22	7/2	10/19	9/1	12/16	10/29	2/4	12/20	4/1	2/18	5/30	4/18
8/23	7/3	10/20	9/2	12/17	10/30	2/5	12/21	4/2	2/19	5/31	4/19
8/24	7/4	10/21	9/3	12/18	11/1	2/6	12/22	4/3	2/20		
8/25	7/5	10/22	9/4	12/19	11/2	2/7	12/23	4/4	2/21	6/1	4/20
8/26	7/6	10/23	9/5	12/20	11/3	2/8	12/24	4/5	2/22	6/2	4/21
8/27	7/7	10/24	9/6	12/21	11/4	2/9	12/25	4/6	2/23	6/3	4/22
8/28	7/8	10/25	9/7	12/22	11/5	2/10	12/26	4/7	2/24	6/4	4/23
8/29	7/9	10/26	9/8	12/23	11/6	2/11	12/27	4/8	2/25	6/5	4/24
8/30	7/10	10/27	9/9	12/24	11/7	2/12	12/28	4/9	2/26	6/6	4/25
8/31	7/11	10/28	9/10	12/25	11/8	2/13	12/29	4/10	2/27	6/7	4/26
		10/29	9/11	12/26	11/9	2/14	12/30	4/11	2/28	6/8	4/27
9/1	7/12	10/30	9/12	12/27	11/10	2/15	1/1	4/12	2/29	6/9	4/28
9/2	7/13	10/31	9/13	12/28	11/11		(1972)	4/13	2/30	6/10	4/29
9/3	7/14			12/29	11/12	2/16	1/2	4/14	3/1	6/11	5/1
9/4	7/15	11/1	9/14	12/30	11/13	2/17	1/3	4/15	3/2	6/12	5/2
9/5	7/16	11/2	9/15	12/31	11/14	2/18	1/4	4/16	3/3	6/13	5/3
9/6	7/17	11/3	9/16			2/19	1/5	4/17	3/4	6/14	5/4
9/7	7/18	11/4	9/17			2/20	1/6	4/18	3/5	6/15	5/5
9/8	7/19	11/5	9/18			2/21	1/7	4/19	3/6	6/16	5/6
9/9	7/20	11/6	9/19			2/22	1/8	4/20	3/7	6/17	5/7
9/10	7/21	11/7	9/20			2/23	1/9	4/21	3/8	6/18	5/8

Solar	Lunar
6/19	5/9
6/20	5/10
6/21	5/11
6/22	5/12
6/23	5/13
6/24	5/14
6/25	5/15
6/26	5/16
6/27	5/17
6/28	5/18
6/29	5/19
6/30	5/20
7/1	5/21
7/2	5/22
7/3	5/23
7/4	5/24
7/5	5/25
7/6	5/26
7/7	5/27
7/8	5/28
7/9	5/29
7/10	5/30
7/11	6/1
7/12	6/2
7/13	6/3
7/14	6/4
7/15	6/5
7/16	6/6
7/17	6/7
7/18	6/8
7/19	6/9
7/20	6/10
7/21	6/11
7/22	6/12
7/23	6/13
7/24	6/14
7/25	6/15
7/26	6/16
7/27	6/17
7/28	6/18
7/29	6/19
7/30	6/20
7/31	6/21
8/1	6/22
8/2	6/23
8/3	6/24
8/4	6/25
8/5	6/26
8/6	6/27
8/7	6/28
8/8	6/29
8/9	7/1
8/10	7/2
8/11	7/3
8/12	7/4
8/13	7/5
8/14	7/6
8/15	7/7

Solar	Lunar
8/16	7/8
8/17	7/9
8/18	7/10
8/19	7/11
8/20	7/12
8/21	7/13
8/22	7/14
8/23	7/15
8/24	7/16
8/25	7/17
8/26	7/18
8/27	7/19
8/28	7/20
8/29	7/21
8/30	7/22
8/31	7/23
9/1	7/24
9/2	7/25
9/3	7/26
9/4	7/27
9/5	7/28
9/6	7/29
9/7	7/30
9/8	8/1
9/9	8/2
9/10	8/3
9/11	8/4
9/12	8/5
9/13	8/6
9/14	8/7
9/15	8/8
9/16	8/9
9/17	8/10
9/18	8/11
9/19	8/12
9/20	8/13
9/21	8/14
9/22	8/15
9/23	8/16
9/24	8/17
9/25	8/18
9/26	8/19
9/27	8/20
9/28	8/21
9/29	8/22
9/30	8/23
10/1	8/24
10/2	8/25
10/3	8/26
10/4	8/27
10/5	8/28
10/6	8/29
10/7	9/1
10/8	9/2
10/9	9/3
10/10	9/4
10/11	9/5
10/12	9/6

Solar	Lunar
10/13	9/7
10/14	9/8
10/15	9/9
10/16	9/10
10/17	9/11
10/18	9/12
10/19	9/13
10/20	9/14
10/21	9/15
10/22	9/16
10/23	9/17
10/24	9/18
10/25	9/19
10/26	9/20
10/27	9/21
10/28	9/22
10/29	9/23
10/30	9/24
10/31	9/25
11/1	9/26
11/2	9/27
11/3	9/28
11/4	9/29
11/5	9/30
11/6	10/1
11/7	10/2
11/8	10/3
11/9	10/4
11/10	10/5
11/11	10/6
11/12	10/7
11/13	10/8
11/14	10/9
11/15	10/10
11/16	10/11
11/17	10/12
11/18	10/13
11/19	10/14
11/20	10/15
11/21	10/16
11/22	10/17
11/23	10/18
11/24	10/19
11/25	10/20
11/26	10/21
11/27	10/22
11/28	10/23
11/29	10/24
11/30	10/25
12/1	10/26
12/2	10/27
12/3	10/28
12/4	10/29
12/5	10/30
12/6	11/1
12/7	11/2
12/8	11/3
12/9	11/4

Solar	Lunar
12/10	11/5
12/11	11/6
12/12	11/7
12/13	11/8
12/14	11/9
12/15	11/10
12/16	11/11
12/17	11/12
12/18	11/13
12/19	11/14
12/20	11/15
12/21	11/16
12/22	11/17
12/23	11/18
12/24	11/19
12/25	11/20
12/26	11/21
12/27	11/22
12/28	11/23
12/29	11/24
12/30	11/25
12/31	11/26

Solar Date	Lunar Date
1973	
1/1	11/27
1/2	11/28
1/3	11/29
1/4	12/1
1/5	12/2
1/6	12/3
1/7	12/4
1/8	12/5
1/9	12/6
1/10	12/7
1/11	12/8
1/12	12/9
1/13	12/10
1/14	12/11
1/15	12/12
1/16	12/13
1/17	12/14
1/18	12/15
1/19	12/16
1/20	12/17
1/21	12/18
1/22	12/19
1/23	12/20
1/24	12/21
1/25	12/22
1/26	12/23
1/27	12/24
1/28	12/25
1/29	12/26
1/30	12/27
1/31	12/28

Solar	Lunar
2/1	12/29
2/2	12/30
2/3	1/1 (1973)
2/4	1/2
2/5	1/3
2/6	1/4
2/7	1/5
2/8	1/6
2/9	1/7
2/10	1/8
2/11	1/9
2/12	1/10
2/13	1/11
2/14	1/12
2/15	1/13
2/16	1/14
2/17	1/15
2/18	1/16
2/19	1/17
2/20	1/18
2/21	1/19
2/22	1/20
2/23	1/21
2/24	1/22
2/25	1/23
2/26	1/24
2/27	1/25
2/28	1/26
3/1	1/27
3/2	1/28
3/3	1/29
3/4	1/30
3/5	2/1
3/6	2/2
3/7	2/3
3/8	2/4
3/9	2/5
3/10	2/6
3/11	2/7
3/12	2/8
3/13	2/9
3/14	2/10
3/15	2/11
3/16	2/12
3/17	2/13
3/18	2/14
3/19	2/15
3/20	2/16
3/21	2/17
3/22	2/18
3/23	2/19
3/24	2/20
3/25	2/21
3/26	2/22
3/27	2/23
3/28	2/24
3/29	2/25
3/30	2/26

Solar	Lunar
3/31	2/27
4/1	2/28
4/2	2/29
4/3	3/1
4/4	3/2
4/5	3/3
4/6	3/4
4/7	3/5
4/8	3/6
4/9	3/7
4/10	3/8
4/11	3/9
4/12	3/10
4/13	3/11
4/14	3/12
4/15	3/13
4/16	3/14
4/17	3/15
4/18	3/16
4/19	3/17
4/20	3/18
4/21	3/19
4/22	3/20
4/23	3/21
4/24	3/22
4/25	3/23
4/26	3/24
4/27	3/25
4/28	3/26
4/29	3/27
4/30	3/28
5/1	3/29
5/2	3/30
5/3	4/1
5/4	4/2
5/5	4/3
5/6	4/4
5/7	4/5
5/8	4/6
5/9	4/7
5/10	4/8
5/11	4/9
5/12	4/10
5/13	4/11
5/14	4/12
5/15	4/13
5/16	4/14
5/17	4/15
5/18	4/16
5/19	4/17
5/20	4/18
5/21	4/19
5/22	4/20
5/23	4/21
5/24	4/22
5/25	4/23
5/26	4/24
5/27	4/25

Solar	Lunar	Solar	Lunar	Solar	Lunar	Solar	Lunar	Solar	Lunar	Solar	Lunar
5/28	4/26	7/25	6/26	9/21	8/25	11/18	10/24	1/10	12/18	3/8	2/15
5/29	4/27	7/26	6/27	9/22	8/26	11/19	10/25	1/11	12/19	3/9	2/16
5/30	4/28	7/27	6/28	9/23	8/27	11/20	10/26	1/12	12/20	3/10	2/17
5/31	4/29	7/28	6/29	9/24	8/28	11/21	10/27	1/13	12/21	3/11	2/18
		7/29	6/30	9/25	8/29	11/22	10/28	1/14	12/22	3/12	2/19
6/1	5/1	7/30	7/1	9/26	9/1	11/23	10/29	1/15	12/23	3/13	2/20
6/2	5/2	7/31	7/2	9/27	9/2	11/24	10/30	1/16	12/24	3/14	2/21
6/3	5/3			9/28	9/3	11/25	11/1	1/17	12/25	3/15	2/22
6/4	5/4	8/1	7/3	9/29	9/4	11/26	11/2	1/18	12/26	3/16	2/23
6/5	5/5	8/2	7/4	9/30	9/5	11/27	11/3	1/19	12/27	3/17	2/24
6/6	5/6	8/3	7/5			11/28	11/4	1/20	12/28	3/18	2/25
6/7	5/7	8/4	7/6	10/1	9/6	11/29	11/5	1/21	12/29	3/19	2/26
6/8	5/8	8/5	7/7	10/2	9/7	11/30	11/6	1/22	12/30	3/20	2/27
6/9	5/9	8/6	7/8	10/3	9/8			1/23	1/1	3/21	2/28
6/10	5/10	8/7	7/9	10/4	9/9	12/1	11/7		(1974)	3/22	2/29
6/11	5/11	8/8	7/10	10/5	9/10	12/2	11/8	1/24	1/2	3/23	2/30
6/12	5/12	8/9	7/11	10/6	9/11	12/3	11/9	1/25	1/3	3/24	3/1
6/13	5/13	8/10	7/12	10/7	9/12	12/4	11/10	1/26	1/4	3/25	3/2
6/14	5/14	8/11	7/13	10/8	9/13	12/5	11/11	1/27	1/5	3/26	3/3
6/15	5/15	8/12	7/14	10/9	9/14	12/6	11/12	1/28	1/6	3/27	3/4
6/16	5/16	8/13	7/15	10/10	9/15	12/7	11/13	1/29	1/7	3/28	3/5
6/17	5/17	8/14	7/16	10/11	9/16	12/8	11/14	1/30	1/8	3/29	3/6
6/18	5/18	8/15	7/17	10/12	9/17	12/9	11/15	1/31	1/9	3/30	3/7
6/19	5/19	8/16	7/18	10/13	9/18	12/10	11/16			3/31	3/8
6/20	5/20	8/17	7/19	10/14	9/19	12/11	11/17	2/1	1/10		
6/21	5/21	8/18	7/20	10/15	9/20	12/12	11/18	2/2	1/11	4/1	3/9
6/22	5/22	8/19	7/21	10/16	9/21	12/13	11/19	2/3	1/12	4/2	3/10
6/23	5/23	8/20	7/22	10/17	9/22	12/14	11/20	2/4	1/13	4/3	3/11
6/24	5/24	8/21	7/23	10/18	9/23	12/15	11/21	2/5	1/14	4/4	3/12
6/25	5/25	8/22	7/24	10/19	9/24	12/16	11/22	2/6	1/15	4/5	3/13
6/26	5/26	8/23	7/25	10/20	9/25	12/17	11/23	2/7	1/16	4/6	3/14
6/27	5/27	8/24	7/26	10/21	9/26	12/18	11/24	2/8	1/17	4/7	3/15
6/28	5/28	8/25	7/27	10/22	9/27	12/19	11/25	2/9	1/18	4/8	3/16
6/29	5/29	8/26	7/28	10/23	9/28	12/20	11/26	2/10	1/19	4/9	3/17
6/30	6/1	8/27	7/29	10/24	9/29	12/21	11/27	2/11	1/20	4/10	3/18
		8/28	8/1	10/25	9/30	12/22	11/28	2/12	1/21	4/11	3/19
7/1	6/2	8/29	8/2	10/26	10/1	12/23	11/29	2/13	1/22	4/12	3/20
7/2	6/3	8/30	8/3	10/27	10/2	12/24	12/1	2/14	1/23	4/13	3/21
7/3	6/4	8/31	8/4	10/28	10/3	12/25	12/2	2/15	1/24	4/14	3/22
7/4	6/5			10/29	10/4	12/26	12/3	2/16	1/25	4/15	3/23
7/5	6/6	9/1	8/5	10/30	10/5	12/27	12/4	2/17	1/26	4/16	3/24
7/6	6/7	9/2	8/6	10/31	10/6	12/28	12/5	2/18	1/27	4/17	3/25
7/7	6/8	9/3	8/7			12/29	12/6	2/19	1/28	4/18	3/26
7/8	6/9	9/4	8/8	11/1	10/7	12/30	12/7	2/20	1/29	4/19	3/27
7/9	6/10	9/5	8/9	11/2	10/8	12/31	12/8	2/21	1/30	4/20	3/28
7/10	6/11	9/6	8/10	11/3	10/9			2/22	2/1	4/21	3/29
7/11	6/12	9/7	8/11	11/4	10/10			2/23	2/2	4/22	4/1
7/12	6/13	9/8	8/12	11/5	10/11	Solar	Lunar	2/24	2/3	4/23	4/2
7/13	6/14	9/9	8/13	11/6	10/12	Date	Date	2/25	2/4	4/24	4/3
7/14	6/15	9/10	8/14	11/7	10/13			2/26	2/5	4/25	4/4
7/15	6/16	9/11	8/15	11/8	10/14	**1974**		2/27	2/6	4/26	4/5
7/16	6/17	9/12	8/16	11/9	10/15	1/1	12/9	2/28	2/7	4/27	4/6
7/17	6/18	9/13	8/17	11/10	10/16	1/2	12/10			4/28	4/7
7/18	6/19	9/14	8/18	11/11	10/17	1/3	12/11	3/1	2/8	4/29	4/8
7/19	6/20	9/15	8/19	11/12	10/18	1/4	12/12	3/2	2/9	4/30	4/9
7/20	6/21	9/16	8/20	11/13	10/19	1/5	12/13	3/3	2/10		
7/21	6/22	9/17	8/21	11/14	10/20	1/6	12/14	3/4	2/11	5/1	4/10
7/22	6/23	9/18	8/22	11/15	10/21	1/7	12/15	3/5	2/12	5/2	4/11
7/23	6/24	9/19	8/23	11/16	10/22	1/8	12/16	3/6	2/13	5/3	4/12
7/24	6/25	9/20	8/24	11/17	10/23	1/9	12/17	3/7	2/14	5/4	4/13

Solar	Lunar	Solar	Lunar	Solar	Lunar	Solar	Lunar	Solar	Lunar	Solar	Lunar
5/5	4/14	7/1	5/12	8/29	7/12	10/26	9/12	12/23	11/10	2/13	1/3
5/6	4/15	7/2	5/13	8/30	7/13	10/27	9/13	12/24	11/11	2/14	1/4
5/7	4/16	7/3	5/14	8/31	7/14	10/28	9/14	12/25	11/12	2/15	1/5
5/8	4/17	7/4	5/15			10/29	9/15	12/26	11/13	2/16	1/6
5/9	4/18	7/5	5/16	9/1	7/15	10/30	9/16	12/27	11/14	2/17	1/7
5/10	4/19	7/6	5/17	9/2	7/16	10/31	9/17	12/28	11/15	2/18	1/8
5/11	4/20	7/7	5/18	9/3	7/17			12/29	11/16	2/19	1/9
5/12	4/21	7/8	5/19	9/4	7/18	11/1	9/18	12/30	11/17	2/20	1/10
5/13	4/22	7/9	5/20	9/5	7/19	11/2	9/19	12/31	11/18	2/21	1/11
5/14	4/23	7/10	5/21	9/6	7/20	11/3	9/20			2/22	1/12
5/15	4/24	7/11	5/22	9/7	7/21	11/4	9/21			2/23	1/13
5/16	4/25	7/12	5/23	9/8	7/22	11/5	9/22	Solar	Lunar	2/24	1/14
5/17	4/26	7/13	5/24	9/9	7/23	11/6	9/23	Date	Date	2/25	1/15
5/18	4/27	7/14	5/25	9/10	7/24	11/7	9/24			2/26	1/16
5/19	4/28	7/15	5/26	9/11	7/25	11/8	9/25	**1975**		2/27	1/17
5/20	4/29	7/16	5/27	9/12	7/26	11/9	9/26	1/1	11/19	2/28	1/18
5/21	4/30	7/17	5/28	9/13	7/27	11/10	9/27	1/2	11/20		
5/22	4/1	7/18	5/29	9/14	7/28	11/11	9/28	1/3	11/21	3/1	1/19
(Leap Month)		7/19	6/1	9/15	7/29	11/12	9/29	1/4	11/22	3/2	1/20
5/23	4/2	7/20	6/2	9/16	8/1	11/13	9/30	1/5	11/23	3/3	1/21
5/24	4/3	7/21	6/3	9/17	8/2	11/14	10/1	1/6	11/24	3/4	1/22
5/25	4/4	7/22	6/4	9/18	8/3	11/15	10/2	1/7	11/25	3/5	1/23
5/26	4/5	7/23	6/5	9/19	8/4	11/16	10/3	1/8	11/26	3/6	1/24
5/27	4/6	7/24	6/6	9/20	8/5	11/17	10/4	1/9	11/27	3/7	1/25
5/28	4/7	7/25	6/7	9/21	8/6	11/18	10/5	1/10	11/28	3/8	1/26
5/29	4/8	7/26	6/8	9/22	8/7	11/19	10/6	1/11	11/29	3/9	1/27
5/30	4/9	7/27	6/9	9/23	8/8	11/20	10/7	1/12	12/1	3/10	1/28
5/31	4/10	7/28	6/10	9/24	8/9	11/21	10/8	1/13	12/2	3/11	1/29
		7/29	6/11	9/25	8/10	11/22	10/9	1/14	12/3	3/12	1/30
6/1	4/11	7/30	6/12	9/26	8/11	11/23	10/10	1/15	12/4	3/13	2/1
6/2	4/12	7/31	6/13	9/27	8/12	11/24	10/11	1/16	12/5	3/14	2/2
6/3	4/13			9/28	8/13	11/25	10/12	1/17	12/6	3/15	2/3
6/4	4/14	8/1	6/14	9/29	8/14	11/26	10/13	1/18	12/7	3/16	2/4
6/5	4/15	8/2	6/15	9/30	8/15	11/27	10/14	1/19	12/8	3/17	2/5
6/6	4/16	8/3	6/16			11/28	10/15	1/20	12/9	3/18	2/6
6/7	4/17	8/4	6/17	10/1	8/16	11/29	10/16	1/21	12/10	3/19	2/7
6/8	4/18	8/5	6/18	10/2	8/17	11/30	10/17	1/22	12/11	3/20	2/8
6/9	4/19	8/6	6/19	10/3	8/18			1/23	12/12	3/21	2/9
6/10	4/20	8/7	6/20	10/4	8/19	12/1	10/18	1/24	12/13	3/22	2/10
6/11	4/21	8/8	6/21	10/5	8/20	12/2	10/19	1/25	12/14	3/23	2/11
6/12	4/22	8/9	6/22	10/6	8/21	12/3	10/20	1/26	12/15	3/24	2/12
6/13	4/23	8/10	6/23	10/7	8/22	12/4	10/21	1/27	12/16	3/25	2/13
6/14	4/24	8/11	6/24	10/8	8/23	12/5	10/22	1/28	12/17	3/26	2/14
6/15	4/25	8/12	6/25	10/9	8/24	12/6	10/23	1/29	12/18	3/27	2/15
6/16	4/26	8/13	6/26	10/10	8/25	12/7	10/24	1/30	12/19	3/28	2/16
6/17	4/27	8/14	6/27	10/11	8/26	12/8	10/25	1/31	12/20	3/29	2/17
6/18	4/28	8/15	6/28	10/12	8/27	12/9	10/26			3/30	2/18
6/19	4/29	8/16	6/29	10/13	8/28	12/10	10/27	2/1	12/21	3/31	2/19
6/20	5/1	8/17	6/30	10/14	8/29	12/11	10/28	2/2	12/22		
6/21	5/2	8/18	7/1	10/15	9/1	12/12	10/29	2/3	12/23	4/1	2/20
6/22	5/3	8/19	7/2	10/16	9/2	12/13	10/30	2/4	12/24	4/2	2/21
6/23	5/4	8/20	7/3	10/17	9/3	12/14	11/1	2/5	12/25	4/3	2/22
6/24	5/5	8/21	7/4	10/18	9/4	12/15	11/2	2/6	12/26	4/4	2/23
6/25	5/6	8/22	7/5	10/19	9/5	12/16	11/3	2/7	12/27	4/5	2/24
6/26	5/7	8/23	7/6	10/20	9/6	12/17	11/4	2/8	12/28	4/6	2/25
6/27	5/8	8/24	7/7	10/21	9/7	12/18	11/5	2/9	12/29	4/7	2/26
6/28	5/9	8/25	7/8	10/22	9/8	12/19	11/6	2/10	12/30	4/8	2/27
6/29	5/10	8/26	7/9	10/23	9/9	12/20	11/7	2/11	1/1	4/9	2/28
6/30	5/11	8/27	7/10	10/24	9/10	12/21	11/8		(1975)	4/10	2/29
		8/28	7/11	10/25	9/11	12/22	11/9	2/12	1/2	4/11	2/30

Solar	Lunar	Solar	Lunar	Solar	Lunar	Solar	Lunar	Solar	Lunar	Solar	Lunar
4/12	3/1	6/9	4/30	8/6	6/29	10/3	8/28	12/1	10/29	1/24	12/24
4/13	3/2	6/10	5/1	8/7	7/1	10/4	8/29	12/2	10/30	1/25	12/25
4/14	3/3	6/11	5/2	8/8	7/2	10/5	9/1	12/3	11/1	1/26	12/26
4/15	3/4	6/12	5/3	8/9	7/3	10/6	9/2	12/4	11/2	1/27	12/27
4/16	3/5	6/13	5/4	8/10	7/4	10/7	9/3	12/5	11/3	1/28	12/28
4/17	3/6	6/14	5/5	8/11	7/5	10/8	9/4	12/6	11/4	1/29	12/29
4/18	3/7	6/15	5/6	8/12	7/6	10/9	9/5	12/7	11/5	1/30	12/30
4/19	3/8	6/16	5/7	8/13	7/7	10/10	9/6	12/8	11/6	1/31	1/1
4/20	3/9	6/17	5/8	8/14	7/8	10/11	9/7	12/9	11/7		(1976)
4/21	3/10	6/18	5/9	8/15	7/9	10/12	9/8	12/10	11/8		
4/22	3/11	6/19	5/10	8/16	7/10	10/13	9/9	12/11	11/9	2/1	1/2
4/23	3/12	6/20	5/11	8/17	7/11	10/14	9/10	12/12	11/10	2/2	1/3
4/24	3/13	6/21	5/12	8/18	7/12	10/15	9/11	12/13	11/11	2/3	1/4
4/25	3/14	6/22	5/13	8/19	7/13	10/16	9/12	12/14	11/12	2/4	1/5
4/26	3/15	6/23	5/14	8/20	7/14	10/17	9/13	12/15	11/13	2/5	1/6
4/27	3/16	6/24	5/15	8/21	7/15	10/18	9/14	12/16	11/14	2/6	1/7
4/28	3/17	6/25	5/16	8/22	7/16	10/19	9/15	12/17	11/15	2/7	1/8
4/29	3/18	6/26	5/17	8/23	7/17	10/20	9/16	12/18	11/16	2/8	1/9
4/30	3/19	6/27	5/18	8/24	7/18	10/21	9/17	12/19	11/17	2/9	1/10
		6/28	5/19	8/25	7/19	10/22	9/18	12/20	11/18	2/10	1/11
5/1	3/20	6/29	5/20	8/26	7/20	10/23	9/19	12/21	11/19	2/11	1/12
5/2	3/21	6/30	5/21	8/27	7/21	10/24	9/20	12/22	11/20	2/12	1/13
5/3	3/22			8/28	7/22	10/25	9/21	12/23	11/21	2/13	1/14
5/4	3/23	7/1	5/22	8/29	7/23	10/26	9/22	12/24	11/22	2/14	1/15
5/5	3/24	7/2	5/23	8/30	7/24	10/27	9/23	12/25	11/23	2/15	1/16
5/6	3/25	7/3	5/24	8/31	7/25	10/28	9/24	12/26	11/24	2/16	1/17
5/7	3/26	7/4	5/25			10/29	9/25	12/27	11/25	2/17	1/18
5/8	3/27	7/5	5/26	9/1	7/26	10/30	9/26	12/28	11/26	2/18	1/19
5/9	3/28	7/6	5/27	9/2	7/27	10/31	9/27	12/29	11/27	2/19	1/20
5/10	3/29	7/7	5/28	9/3	7/28			12/30	11/28	2/20	1/21
5/11	4/1	7/8	5/29	9/4	7/29	11/1	9/28	12/31	11/29	2/21	1/22
5/12	4/2	7/9	6/1	9/5	7/30	11/2	9/29			2/22	1/23
5/13	4/3	7/10	6/2	9/6	8/1	11/3	10/1			2/23	1/24
5/14	4/4	7/11	6/3	9/7	8/2	11/4	10/2	Solar	Lunar	2/24	1/25
5/15	4/5	7/12	6/4	9/8	8/3	11/5	10/3	Date	Date	2/25	1/26
5/16	4/6	7/13	6/5	9/9	8/4	11/6	10/4			2/26	1/27
5/17	4/7	7/14	6/6	9/10	8/5	11/7	10/5	1976		2/27	1/28
5/18	4/8	7/15	6/7	9/11	8/6	11/8	10/6	1/1	12/1	2/28	1/29
5/19	4/9	7/16	6/8	9/12	8/7	11/9	10/7	1/2	12/2	2/29	1/30
5/20	4/10	7/17	6/9	9/13	8/8	11/10	10/8	1/3	12/3		
5/21	4/11	7/18	6/10	9/14	8/9	11/11	10/9	1/4	12/4	3/1	2/1
5/22	4/12	7/19	6/11	9/15	8/10	11/12	10/10	1/5	12/5	3/2	2/2
5/23	4/13	7/20	6/12	9/16	8/11	11/13	10/11	1/6	12/6	3/3	2/3
5/24	4/14	7/21	6/13	9/17	8/12	11/14	10/12	1/7	12/7	3/4	2/4
5/25	4/15	7/22	6/14	9/18	8/13	11/15	10/13	1/8	12/8	3/5	2/5
5/26	4/16	7/23	6/15	9/19	8/14	11/16	10/14	1/9	12/9	3/6	2/6
5/27	4/17	7/24	6/16	9/20	8/15	11/17	10/15	1/10	12/10	3/7	2/7
5/28	4/18	7/25	6/17	9/21	8/16	11/18	10/16	1/11	12/11	3/8	2/8
5/29	4/19	7/26	6/18	9/22	8/17	11/19	10/17	1/12	12/12	3/9	2/9
5/30	4/20	7/27	6/19	9/23	8/18	11/20	10/18	1/13	12/13	3/10	2/10
5/31	4/21	7/28	6/20	9/24	8/19	11/21	10/19	1/14	12/14	3/11	2/11
		7/29	6/21	9/25	8/20	11/22	10/20	1/15	12/15	3/12	2/12
6/1	4/22	7/30	6/22	9/26	8/21	11/23	10/21	1/16	12/16	3/13	2/13
6/2	4/23	7/31	6/23	9/27	8/22	11/24	10/22	1/17	12/17	3/14	2/14
6/3	4/24			9/28	8/23	11/25	10/23	1/18	12/18	3/15	2/15
6/4	4/25	8/1	6/24	9/29	8/24	11/26	10/24	1/19	12/19	3/16	2/16
6/5	4/26	8/2	6/25	9/30	8/25	11/27	10/25	1/20	12/20	3/17	2/17
6/6	4/27	8/3	6/26			11/28	10/26	1/21	12/21	3/18	2/18
6/7	4/28	8/4	6/27	10/1	8/26	11/29	10/27	1/22	12/22	3/19	2/19
6/8	4/29	8/5	6/28	10/2	8/27	11/30	10/28	1/23	12/23	3/20	2/20

Solar	Lunar	Solar	Lunar	Solar	Lunar	Solar	Lunar	Solar	Lunar	Solar Date	Lunar Date
3/21	2/21	5/18	4/20	7/15	6/19	9/11	8/18	11/7	9/16		
3/22	2/22	5/19	4/21	7/16	6/20	9/12	8/19	11/8	9/17		
3/23	2/23	5/20	4/22	7/17	6/21	9/13	8/20	11/9	9/18		
3/24	2/24	5/21	4/23	7/18	6/22	9/14	8/21	11/10	9/19	**1977**	
3/25	2/25	5/22	4/24	7/19	6/23	9/15	8/22	11/11	9/20	1/1	11/12
3/26	2/26	5/23	4/25	7/20	6/24	9/16	8/23	11/12	9/21	1/2	11/13
3/27	2/27	5/24	4/26	7/21	6/25	9/17	8/24	11/13	9/22	1/3	11/14
3/28	2/28	5/25	4/27	7/22	6/26	9/18	8/25	11/14	9/23	1/4	11/15
3/29	2/29	5/26	4/28	7/23	6/27	9/19	8/26	11/15	9/24	1/5	11/16
3/30	2/30	5/27	4/29	7/24	6/28	9/20	8/27	11/16	9/25	1/6	11/17
3/31	3/1	5/28	4/30	7/25	6/29	9/21	8/28	11/17	9/26	1/7	11/18
		5/29	5/1	7/26	6/30	9/22	8/29	11/18	9/27	1/8	11/19
4/1	3/2	5/30	5/2	7/27	7/1	9/23	8/30	11/19	9/28	1/9	11/20
4/2	3/3	5/31	5/3	7/28	7/2	9/24	8/1	11/20	9/29	1/10	11/21
4/3	3/4			7/29	7/3	*(Leap Month)*		11/21	10/1	1/11	11/22
4/4	3/5	6/1	5/4	7/30	7/4	9/25	8/2	11/22	10/2	1/12	11/23
4/5	3/6	6/2	5/5	7/31	7/5	9/26	8/3	11/23	10/3	1/13	11/24
4/6	3/7	6/3	5/6			9/27	8/4	11/24	10/4	1/14	11/25
4/7	3/8	6/4	5/7	8/1	7/6	9/28	8/5	11/25	10/5	1/15	11/26
4/8	3/9	6/5	5/8	8/2	7/7	9/29	8/6	11/26	10/6	1/16	11/27
4/9	3/10	6/6	5/9	8/3	7/8	9/30	8/7	11/27	10/7	1/17	11/28
4/10	3/11	6/7	5/10	8/4	7/9			11/28	10/8	1/18	11/29
4/11	3/12	6/8	5/11	8/5	7/10	10/1	8/8	11/29	10/9	1/19	12/1
4/12	3/13	6/9	5/12	8/6	7/11	10/2	8/9	11/30	10/10	1/20	12/2
4/13	3/14	6/10	5/13	8/7	7/12	10/3	8/10			1/21	12/3
4/14	3/15	6/11	5/14	8/8	7/13	10/4	8/11	12/1	10/11	1/22	12/4
4/15	3/16	6/12	5/15	8/9	7/14	10/5	8/12	12/2	10/12	1/23	12/5
4/16	3/17	6/13	5/16	8/10	7/15	10/6	8/13	12/3	10/13	1/24	12/6
4/17	3/18	6/14	5/17	8/11	7/16	10/7	8/14	12/4	10/14	1/25	12/7
4/18	3/19	6/15	5/18	8/12	7/17	10/8	8/15	12/5	10/15	1/26	12/8
4/19	3/20	6/16	5/19	8/13	7/18	10/9	8/16	12/6	10/16	1/27	12/9
4/20	3/21	6/17	5/20	8/14	7/19	10/10	8/17	12/7	10/17	1/28	12/10
4/21	3/22	6/18	5/21	8/15	7/20	10/11	8/18	12/8	10/18	1/29	12/11
4/22	3/23	6/19	5/22	8/16	7/21	10/12	8/19	12/9	10/19	1/30	12/12
4/23	3/24	6/20	5/23	8/17	7/22	10/13	8/20	12/10	10/20	1/31	12/13
4/24	3/25	6/21	5/24	8/18	7/23	10/14	8/21	12/11	10/21		
4/25	3/26	6/22	5/25	8/19	7/24	10/15	8/22	12/12	10/22	2/1	12/14
4/26	3/27	6/23	5/26	8/20	7/25	10/16	8/23	12/13	10/23	2/2	12/15
4/27	3/28	6/24	5/27	8/21	7/26	10/17	8/24	12/14	10/24	2/3	12/16
4/28	3/29	6/25	5/28	8/22	7/27	10/18	8/25	12/15	10/25	2/4	12/17
4/29	4/1	6/26	5/29	8/23	7/28	10/19	8/26	12/16	10/26	2/5	12/18
4/30	4/2	6/27	6/1	8/24	7/29	10/20	8/27	12/17	10/27	2/6	12/19
		6/28	6/2	8/25	8/1	10/21	8/28	12/18	10/28	2/7	12/20
5/1	4/3	6/29	6/3	8/26	8/2	10/22	8/29	12/19	10/29	2/8	12/21
5/2	4/4	6/30	6/4	8/27	8/3	10/23	9/1	12/20	10/30	2/9	12/22
5/3	4/5			8/28	8/4	10/24	9/2	12/21	11/1	2/10	12/23
5/4	4/6	7/1	6/5	8/29	8/5	10/25	9/3	12/22	11/2	2/11	12/24
5/5	4/7	7/2	6/6	8/30	8/6	10/26	9/4	12/23	11/3	2/12	12/25
5/6	4/8	7/3	6/7	8/31	8/7	10/27	9/5	12/24	11/4	2/13	12/26
5/7	4/9	7/4	6/8			10/28	9/6	12/25	11/5	2/14	12/27
5/8	4/10	7/5	6/9	9/1	8/8	10/29	9/7	12/26	11/6	2/15	12/28
5/9	4/11	7/6	6/10	9/2	8/9	10/30	9/8	12/27	11/7	2/16	12/29
5/10	4/12	7/7	6/11	9/3	8/10	10/31	9/9	12/28	11/8	2/17	12/30
5/11	4/13	7/8	6/12	9/4	8/11			12/29	11/9	2/18	1/1
5/12	4/14	7/9	6/13	9/5	8/12	11/1	9/10	12/30	11/10		(1977)
5/13	4/15	7/10	6/14	9/6	8/13	11/2	9/11	12/31	11/11	2/19	1/2
5/14	4/16	7/11	6/15	9/7	8/14	11/3	9/12			2/20	1/3
5/15	4/17	7/12	6/16	9/8	8/15	11/4	9/13			2/21	1/4
5/16	4/18	7/13	6/17	9/9	8/16	11/5	9/14			2/22	1/5
5/17	4/19	7/14	6/18	9/10	8/17	11/6	9/15			2/23	1/6

Solar	Lunar	Solar	Lunar	Solar	Lunar	Solar	Lunar	Solar	Lunar	Solar	Lunar
2/24	1/7	4/23	3/6	6/20	5/4	8/17	7/3	10/14	9/2	12/11	11/1
2/25	1/8	4/24	3/7	6/21	5/5	8/18	7/4	10/15	9/3	12/12	11/2
2/26	1/9	4/25	3/8	6/22	5/6	8/19	7/5	10/16	9/4	12/13	11/3
2/27	1/10	4/26	3/9	6/23	5/7	8/20	7/6	10/17	9/5	12/14	11/4
2/28	1/11	4/27	3/10	6/24	5/8	8/21	7/7	10/18	9/6	12/15	11/5
		4/28	3/11	6/25	5/9	8/22	7/8	10/19	9/7	12/16	11/6
3/1	1/12	4/29	3/12	6/26	5/10	8/23	7/9	10/20	9/8	12/17	11/7
3/2	1/13	4/30	3/13	6/27	5/11	8/24	7/10	10/21	9/9	12/18	11/8
3/3	1/14			6/28	5/12	8/25	7/11	10/22	9/10	12/19	11/9
3/4	1/15	5/1	3/14	6/29	5/13	8/26	7/12	10/23	9/11	12/20	11/10
3/5	1/16	5/2	3/15	6/30	5/14	8/27	7/13	10/24	9/12	12/21	11/11
3/6	1/17	5/3	3/16			8/28	7/14	10/25	9/13	12/22	11/12
3/7	1/18	5/4	3/17	7/1	5/15	8/29	7/15	10/26	9/14	12/23	11/13
3/8	1/19	5/5	3/18	7/2	5/16	8/30	7/16	10/27	9/15	12/24	11/14
3/9	1/20	5/6	3/19	7/3	5/17	8/31	7/17	10/28	9/16	12/25	11/15
3/10	1/21	5/7	3/20	7/4	5/18			10/29	9/17	12/26	11/16
3/11	1/22	5/8	3/21	7/5	5/19	9/1	7/18	10/30	9/18	12/27	11/17
3/12	1/23	5/9	3/22	7/6	5/20	9/2	7/19	10/31	9/19	12/28	11/18
3/13	1/24	5/10	3/23	7/7	5/21	9/3	7/20			12/29	11/19
3/14	1/25	5/11	3/24	7/8	5/22	9/4	7/21	11/1	9/20	12/30	11/20
3/15	1/26	5/12	3/25	7/9	5/23	9/5	7/22	11/2	9/21	12/31	11/21
3/16	1/27	5/13	3/26	7/10	5/24	9/6	7/23	11/3	9/22		
3/17	1/28	5/14	3/27	7/11	5/25	9/7	7/24	11/4	9/23		
3/18	1/29	5/15	3/28	7/12	5/26	9/8	7/25	11/5	9/24	**Solar**	**Lunar**
3/19	1/30	5/16	3/29	7/13	5/27	9/9	7/26	11/6	9/25	**Date**	**Date**
3/20	2/1	5/17	3/30	7/14	5/28	9/10	7/27	11/7	9/26	**1978**	
3/21	2/2	5/18	4/1	7/15	5/29	9/11	7/28	11/8	9/27	1/1	11/22
3/22	2/3	5/19	4/2	7/16	6/1	9/12	7/29	11/9	9/28	1/2	11/23
3/23	2/4	5/20	4/3	7/17	6/2	9/13	8/1	11/10	9/29	1/3	11/24
3/24	2/5	5/21	4/4	7/18	6/3	9/14	8/2	11/11	10/1	1/4	11/25
3/25	2/6	5/22	4/5	7/19	6/4	9/15	8/3	11/12	10/2	1/5	11/26
3/26	2/7	5/23	4/6	7/20	6/5	9/16	8/4	11/13	10/3	1/6	11/27
3/27	2/8	5/24	4/7	7/21	6/6	9/17	8/5	11/14	10/4	1/7	11/28
3/28	2/9	5/25	4/8	7/22	6/7	9/18	8/6	11/15	10/5	1/8	11/29
3/29	2/10	5/26	4/9	7/23	6/8	9/19	8/7	11/16	10/6	1/9	12/1
3/30	2/11	5/27	4/10	7/24	6/9	9/20	8/8	11/17	10/7	1/10	12/2
3/31	2/12	5/28	4/11	7/25	6/10	9/21	8/9	11/18	10/8	1/11	12/3
		5/29	4/12	7/26	6/11	9/22	8/10	11/19	10/9	1/12	12/4
4/1	2/13	5/30	4/13	7/27	6/12	9/23	8/11	11/20	10/10	1/13	12/5
4/2	2/14	5/31	4/14	7/28	6/13	9/24	8/12	11/21	10/11	1/14	12/6
4/3	2/15			7/29	6/14	9/25	8/13	11/22	10/12	1/15	12/7
4/4	2/16	6/1	4/15	7/30	6/15	9/26	8/14	11/23	10/13	1/16	12/8
4/5	2/17	6/2	4/16	7/31	6/16	9/27	8/15	11/24	10/14	1/17	12/9
4/6	2/18	6/3	4/17			9/28	8/16	11/25	10/15	1/18	12/10
4/7	2/19	6/4	4/18	8/1	6/17	9/29	8/17	11/26	10/16	1/19	12/11
4/8	2/20	6/5	4/19	8/2	6/18	9/30	8/18	11/27	10/17	1/20	12/12
4/9	2/21	6/6	4/20	8/3	6/19			11/28	10/18	1/21	12/13
4/10	2/22	6/7	4/21	8/4	6/20	10/1	8/19	11/29	10/19	1/22	12/14
4/11	2/23	6/8	4/22	8/5	6/21	10/2	8/20	11/30	10/20	1/23	12/15
4/12	2/24	6/9	4/23	8/6	6/22	10/3	8/21			1/24	12/16
4/13	2/25	6/10	4/24	8/7	6/23	10/4	8/22	12/1	10/21	1/25	12/17
4/14	2/26	6/11	4/25	8/8	6/24	10/5	8/23	12/2	10/22	1/26	12/18
4/15	2/27	6/12	4/26	8/9	6/25	10/6	8/24	12/3	10/23	1/27	12/19
4/16	2/28	6/13	4/27	8/10	6/26	10/7	8/25	12/4	10/24	1/28	12/20
4/17	2/29	6/14	4/28	8/11	6/27	10/8	8/26	12/5	10/25	1/29	12/21
4/18	3/1	6/15	4/29	8/12	6/28	10/9	8/27	12/6	10/26	1/30	12/22
4/19	3/2	6/16	4/30	8/13	6/29	10/10	8/28	12/7	10/27	1/31	12/23
4/20	3/3	6/17	5/1	8/14	6/30	10/11	8/29	12/8	10/28		
4/21	3/4	6/18	5/2	8/15	7/1	10/12	8/30	12/9	10/29	2/1	12/24
4/22	3/5	6/19	5/3	8/16	7/2	10/13	9/1	12/10	10/30		

Solar	Lunar	Solar	Lunar	Solar	Lunar	Solar	Lunar	Solar	Lunar	Solar	Lunar
2/2	12/25	4/1	2/24	5/30	4/24	7/27	6/23	9/23	8/21	11/20	10/20
2/3	12/26	4/2	2/25	5/31	4/25	7/28	6/24	9/24	8/22	11/21	10/21
2/4	12/27	4/3	2/26			7/29	6/25	9/25	8/23	11/22	10/22
2/5	12/28	4/4	2/27	6/1	4/26	7/30	6/26	9/26	8/24	11/23	10/23
2/6	12/29	4/5	2/28	6/2	4/27	7/31	6/27	9/27	8/25	11/24	10/24
2/7	1/1	4/6	2/29	6/3	4/28			9/28	8/26	11/25	10/25
	(1978)	4/7	3/1	6/4	4/29	8/1	6/28	9/29	8/27	11/26	10/26
2/8	1/2	4/8	3/2	6/5	4/30	8/2	6/29	9/30	8/28	11/27	10/27
2/9	1/3	4/9	3/3	6/6	5/1	8/3	6/30			11/28	10/28
2/10	1/4	4/10	3/4	6/7	5/2	8/4	7/1	10/1	8/29	11/29	10/29
2/11	1/5	4/11	3/5	6/8	5/3	8/5	7/2	10/2	9/1	11/30	11/1
2/12	1/6	4/12	3/6	6/9	5/4	8/6	7/3	10/3	9/2		
2/13	1/7	4/13	3/7	6/10	5/5	8/7	7/4	10/4	9/3	12/1	11/2
2/14	1/8	4/14	3/8	6/11	5/6	8/8	7/5	10/5	9/4	12/2	11/3
2/15	1/9	4/15	3/9	6/12	5/7	8/9	7/6	10/6	9/5	12/3	11/4
2/16	1/10	4/16	3/10	6/13	5/8	8/10	7/7	10/7	9/6	12/4	11/5
2/17	1/11	4/17	3/11	6/14	5/9	8/11	7/8	10/8	9/7	12/5	11/6
2/18	1/12	4/18	3/12	6/15	5/10	8/12	7/9	10/9	9/8	12/6	11/7
2/19	1/13	4/19	3/13	6/16	5/11	8/13	7/10	10/10	9/9	12/7	11/8
2/20	1/14	4/20	3/14	6/17	5/12	8/14	7/11	10/11	9/10	12/8	11/9
2/21	1/15	4/21	3/15	6/18	5/13	8/15	7/12	10/12	9/11	12/9	11/10
2/22	1/16	4/22	3/16	6/19	5/14	8/16	7/13	10/13	9/12	12/10	11/11
2/23	1/17	4/23	3/17	6/20	5/15	8/17	7/14	10/14	9/13	12/11	11/12
2/24	1/18	4/24	3/18	6/21	5/16	8/18	7/15	10/15	9/14	12/12	11/13
2/25	1/19	4/25	3/19	6/22	5/17	8/19	7/16	10/16	9/15	12/13	11/14
2/26	1/20	4/26	3/20	6/23	5/18	8/20	7/17	10/17	9/16	12/14	11/15
2/27	1/21	4/27	3/21	6/24	5/19	8/21	7/18	10/18	9/17	12/15	11/16
2/28	1/22	4/28	3/22	6/25	5/20	8/22	7/19	10/19	9/18	12/16	11/17
		4/29	3/23	6/26	5/21	8/23	7/20	10/20	9/19	12/17	11/18
3/1	1/23	4/30	3/24	6/27	5/22	8/24	7/21	10/21	9/20	12/18	11/19
3/2	1/24			6/28	5/23	8/25	7/22	10/22	9/21	12/19	11/20
3/3	1/25	5/1	3/25	6/29	5/24	8/26	7/23	10/23	9/22	12/20	11/21
3/4	1/26	5/2	3/26	6/30	5/25	8/27	7/24	10/24	9/23	12/21	11/22
3/5	1/27	5/3	3/27			8/28	7/25	10/25	9/24	12/22	11/23
3/6	1/28	5/4	3/28	7/1	5/26	8/29	7/26	10/26	9/25	12/23	11/24
3/7	1/29	5/5	3/29	7/2	5/27	8/30	7/27	10/27	9/26	12/24	11/25
3/8	1/30	5/6	3/30	7/3	5/28	8/31	7/28	10/28	9/27	12/25	11/26
3/9	2/1	5/7	4/1	7/4	5/29			10/29	9/28	12/26	11/27
3/10	2/2	5/8	4/2	7/5	6/1	9/1	7/29	10/30	9/29	12/27	11/28
3/11	2/3	5/9	4/3	7/6	6/2	9/2	7/30	10/31	9/30	12/28	11/29
3/12	2/4	5/10	4/4	7/7	6/3	9/3	8/1			12/29	11/30
3/13	2/5	5/11	4/5	7/8	6/4	9/4	8/2	11/1	10/1	12/30	12/1
3/14	2/6	5/12	4/6	7/9	6/5	9/5	8/3	11/2	10/2	12/31	12/2
3/15	2/7	5/13	4/7	7/10	6/6	9/6	8/4	11/3	10/3		
3/16	2/8	5/14	4/8	7/11	6/7	9/7	8/5	11/4	10/4		
3/17	2/9	5/15	4/9	7/12	6/8	9/8	8/6	11/5	10/5	Solar	Lunar
3/18	2/10	5/16	4/10	7/13	6/9	9/9	8/7	11/6	10/6	Date	Date
3/19	2/11	5/17	4/11	7/14	6/10	9/10	8/8	11/7	10/7	**1979**	
3/20	2/12	5/18	4/12	7/15	6/11	9/11	8/9	11/8	10/8	1/1	12/3
3/21	2/13	5/19	4/13	7/16	6/12	9/12	8/10	11/9	10/9	1/2	12/4
3/22	2/14	5/20	4/14	7/17	6/13	9/13	8/11	11/10	10/10	1/3	12/5
3/23	2/15	5/21	4/15	7/18	6/14	9/14	8/12	11/11	10/11	1/4	12/6
3/24	2/16	5/22	4/16	7/19	6/15	9/15	8/13	11/12	10/12	1/5	12/7
3/25	2/17	5/23	4/17	7/20	6/16	9/16	8/14	11/13	10/13	1/6	12/8
3/26	2/18	5/24	4/18	7/21	6/17	9/17	8/15	11/14	10/14	1/7	12/9
3/27	2/19	5/25	4/19	7/22	6/18	9/18	8/16	11/15	10/15	1/8	12/10
3/28	2/20	5/26	4/20	7/23	6/19	9/19	8/17	11/16	10/16	1/9	12/11
3/29	2/21	5/27	4/21	7/24	6/20	9/20	8/18	11/17	10/17	1/10	12/12
3/30	2/22	5/28	4/22	7/25	6/21	9/21	8/19	11/18	10/18	1/11	12/13
3/31	2/23	5/29	4/23	7/26	6/22	9/22	8/20	11/19	10/19		

Solar	Lunar	Solar	Lunar	Solar	Lunar	Solar	Lunar	Solar	Lunar	Solar	Lunar
1/12	12/14	3/10	2/12	5/7	4/12	7/4	6/11	8/31	7/9	10/28	9/8
1/13	12/15	3/11	2/13	5/8	4/13	7/5	6/12			10/29	9/9
1/14	12/16	3/12	2/14	5/9	4/14	7/6	6/13	9/1	7/10	10/30	9/10
1/15	12/17	3/13	2/15	5/10	4/15	7/7	6/14	9/2	7/11	10/31	9/11
1/16	12/18	3/14	2/16	5/11	4/16	7/8	6/15	9/3	7/12		
1/17	12/19	3/15	2/17	5/12	4/17	7/9	6/16	9/4	7/13	11/1	9/12
1/18	12/20	3/16	2/18	5/13	4/18	7/10	6/17	9/5	7/14	11/2	9/13
1/19	12/21	3/17	2/19	5/14	4/19	7/11	6/18	9/6	7/15	11/3	9/14
1/20	12/22	3/18	2/20	5/15	4/20	7/12	6/19	9/7	7/16	11/4	9/15
1/21	12/23	3/19	2/21	5/16	4/21	7/13	6/20	9/8	7/17	11/5	9/16
1/22	12/24	3/20	2/22	5/17	4/22	7/14	6/21	9/9	7/18	11/6	9/17
1/23	12/25	3/21	2/23	5/18	4/23	7/15	6/22	9/10	7/19	11/7	9/18
1/24	12/26	3/22	2/24	5/19	4/24	7/16	6/23	9/11	7/20	11/8	9/19
1/25	12/27	3/23	2/25	5/20	4/25	7/17	6/24	9/12	7/21	11/9	9/20
1/26	12/28	3/24	2/26	5/21	4/26	7/18	6/25	9/13	7/22	11/10	9/21
1/27	12/29	3/25	2/27	5/22	4/27	7/19	6/26	9/14	7/23	11/11	9/22
1/28	1/1	3/26	2/28	5/23	4/28	7/20	6/27	9/15	7/24	11/12	9/23
	(1979)	3/27	2/29	5/24	4/29	7/21	6/28	9/16	7/25	11/13	9/24
1/29	1/2	3/28	3/1	5/25	4/30	7/22	6/29	9/17	7/26	11/14	9/25
1/30	1/3	3/29	3/2	5/26	5/1	7/23	6/30	9/18	7/27	11/15	9/26
1/31	1/4	3/30	3/3	5/27	5/2	7/24	6/1	9/19	7/28	11/16	9/27
		3/31	3/4	5/28	5/3	*(Leap Month)*		9/20	7/29	11/17	9/28
2/1	1/5			5/29	5/4	7/25	6/2	9/21	8/1	11/18	9/29
2/2	1/6	4/1	3/5	5/30	5/5	7/26	6/3	9/22	8/2	11/19	9/30
2/3	1/7	4/2	3/6	5/31	5/6	7/27	6/4	9/23	8/3	11/20	10/1
2/4	1/8	4/3	3/7			7/28	6/5	9/24	8/4	11/21	10/2
2/5	1/9	4/4	3/8	6/1	5/7	7/29	6/6	9/25	8/5	11/22	10/3
2/6	1/10	4/5	3/9	6/2	5/8	7/30	6/7	9/26	8/6	11/23	10/4
2/7	1/11	4/6	3/10	6/3	5/9	7/31	6/8	9/27	8/7	11/24	10/5
2/8	1/12	4/7	3/11	6/4	5/10			9/28	8/8	11/25	10/6
2/9	1/13	4/8	3/12	6/5	5/11	8/1	6/9	9/29	8/9	11/26	10/7
2/10	1/14	4/9	3/13	6/6	5/12	8/2	6/10	9/30	8/10	11/27	10/8
2/11	1/15	4/10	3/14	6/7	5/13	8/3	6/11			11/28	10/9
2/12	1/16	4/11	3/15	6/8	5/14	8/4	6/12	10/1	8/11	11/29	10/10
2/13	1/17	4/12	3/16	6/9	5/15	8/5	6/13	10/2	8/12	11/30	10/11
2/14	1/18	4/13	3/17	6/10	5/16	8/6	6/14	10/3	8/13		
2/15	1/19	4/14	3/18	6/11	5/17	8/7	6/15	10/4	8/14	12/1	10/12
2/16	1/20	4/15	3/19	6/12	5/18	8/8	6/16	10/5	8/15	12/2	10/13
2/17	1/21	4/16	3/20	6/13	5/19	8/9	6/17	10/6	8/16	12/3	10/14
2/18	1/22	4/17	3/21	6/14	5/20	8/10	6/18	10/7	8/17	12/4	10/15
2/19	1/23	4/18	3/22	6/15	5/21	8/11	6/19	10/8	8/18	12/5	10/16
2/20	1/24	4/19	3/23	6/16	5/22	8/12	6/20	10/9	8/19	12/6	10/17
2/21	1/25	4/20	3/24	6/17	5/23	8/13	6/21	10/10	8/20	12/7	10/18
2/22	1/26	4/21	3/25	6/18	5/24	8/14	6/22	10/11	8/21	12/8	10/19
2/23	1/27	4/22	3/26	6/19	5/25	8/15	6/23	10/12	8/22	12/9	10/20
2/24	1/28	4/23	3/27	6/20	5/26	8/16	6/24	10/13	8/23	12/10	10/21
2/25	1/29	4/24	3/28	6/21	5/27	8/17	6/25	10/14	8/24	12/11	10/22
2/26	1/30	4/25	3/29	6/22	5/28	8/18	6/26	10/15	8/25	12/12	10/23
2/27	2/1	4/26	4/1	6/23	5/29	8/19	6/27	10/16	8/26	12/13	10/24
2/28	2/2	4/27	4/2	6/24	6/1	8/20	6/28	10/17	8/27	12/14	10/25
		4/28	4/3	6/25	6/2	8/21	6/29	10/18	8/28	12/15	10/26
3/1	2/3	4/29	4/4	6/26	6/3	8/22	6/30	10/19	8/29	12/16	10/27
3/2	2/4	4/30	4/5	6/27	6/4	8/23	7/1	10/20	8/30	12/17	10/28
3/3	2/5			6/28	6/5	8/24	7/2	10/21	9/1	12/18	10/29
3/4	2/6	5/1	4/6	6/29	6/6	8/25	7/3	10/22	9/2	12/19	11/1
3/5	2/7	5/2	4/7	6/30	6/7	8/26	7/4	10/23	9/3	12/20	11/2
3/6	2/8	5/3	4/8			8/27	7/5	10/24	9/4	12/21	11/3
3/7	2/9	5/4	4/9	7/1	6/8	8/28	7/6	10/25	9/5	12/22	11/4
3/8	2/10	5/5	4/10	7/2	6/9	8/29	7/7	10/26	9/6	12/23	11/5
3/9	2/11	5/6	4/11	7/3	6/10	8/30	7/8	10/27	9/7	12/24	11/6

12/25	11/7
12/26	11/8
12/27	11/9
12/28	11/10
12/29	11/11
12/30	11/12
12/31	11/13

Solar Date **Lunar Date**

1980

Solar Date	Lunar Date
1/1	11/14
1/2	11/15
1/3	11/16
1/4	11/17
1/5	11/18
1/6	11/19
1/7	11/20
1/8	11/21
1/9	11/22
1/10	11/23
1/11	11/24
1/12	11/25
1/13	11/26
1/14	11/27
1/15	11/28
1/16	11/29
1/17	11/30
1/18	12/1
1/19	12/2
1/20	12/3
1/21	12/4
1/22	12/5
1/23	12/6
1/24	12/7
1/25	12/8
1/26	12/9
1/27	12/10
1/28	12/11
1/29	12/12
1/30	12/13
1/31	12/14
2/1	12/15
2/2	12/16
2/3	12/17
2/4	12/18
2/5	12/19
2/6	12/20
2/7	12/21
2/8	12/22
2/9	12/23
2/10	12/24
2/11	12/25
2/12	12/26
2/13	12/27
2/14	12/28
2/15	12/29
2/16	1/1 (1980)
2/17	1/2
2/18	1/3
2/19	1/4
2/20	1/5
2/21	1/6
2/22	1/7
2/23	1/8
2/24	1/9
2/25	1/10
2/26	1/11
2/27	1/12
2/28	1/13
2/29	1/14
3/1	1/15
3/2	1/16
3/3	1/17
3/4	1/18
3/5	1/19
3/6	1/20
3/7	1/21
3/8	1/22
3/9	1/23
3/10	1/24
3/11	1/25
3/12	1/26
3/13	1/27
3/14	1/28
3/15	1/29
3/16	1/30
3/17	2/1
3/18	2/2
3/19	2/3
3/20	2/4
3/21	2/5
3/22	2/6
3/23	2/7
3/24	2/8
3/25	2/9
3/26	2/10
3/27	2/11
3/28	2/12
3/29	2/13
3/30	2/14
3/31	2/15
4/1	2/16
4/2	2/17
4/3	2/18
4/4	2/19
4/5	2/20
4/6	2/21
4/7	2/22
4/8	2/23
4/9	2/24
4/10	2/25
4/11	2/26
4/12	2/27
4/13	2/28
4/14	2/29
4/15	3/1
4/16	3/2
4/17	3/3
4/18	3/4
4/19	3/5
4/20	3/6
4/21	3/7
4/22	3/8
4/23	3/9
4/24	3/10
4/25	3/11
4/26	3/12
4/27	3/13
4/28	3/14
4/29	3/15
4/30	3/16
5/1	3/17
5/2	3/18
5/3	3/19
5/4	3/20
5/5	3/21
5/6	3/22
5/7	3/23
5/8	3/24
5/9	3/25
5/10	3/26
5/11	3/27
5/12	3/28
5/13	3/29
5/14	4/1
5/16	4/2
5/17	4/3
5/18	4/4
5/19	4/5
5/20	4/6
5/21	4/7
5/22	4/8
5/23	4/9
5/24	4/10
5/25	4/11
5/26	4/12
5/27	4/13
5/28	4/14
5/29	4/15
5/30	4/16
5/31	4/17
6/1	4/18
6/2	4/19
6/3	4/20
6/4	4/21
6/5	4/22
6/6	4/23
6/7	4/24
6/8	4/25
6/9	4/26
6/10	4/27
6/11	4/28
6/12	4/29
6/13	5/1
6/14	5/2
6/15	5/3
6/16	5/4
6/17	5/5
6/18	5/6
6/19	5/7
6/20	5/8
6/21	5/9
6/22	5/10
6/23	5/11
6/24	5/12
6/25	5/13
6/26	5/14
6/27	5/15
6/28	5/16
6/29	5/17
6/30	5/18
7/1	5/19
7/2	5/20
7/3	5/21
7/4	5/22
7/5	5/23
7/6	5/24
7/7	5/25
7/8	5/26
7/9	5/27
7/10	5/28
7/11	5/29
7/12	6/1
7/13	6/2
7/14	6/3
7/15	6/4
7/16	6/5
7/17	6/6
7/18	6/7
7/19	6/8
7/20	6/9
7/21	6/10
7/22	6/11
7/23	6/12
7/24	6/13
7/25	6/14
7/26	6/15
7/27	6/16
7/28	6/17
7/29	6/18
7/30	6/19
7/31	6/20
8/1	6/21
8/2	6/22
8/3	6/23
8/4	6/24
8/5	6/25
8/6	6/26
8/7	6/27
8/8	6/28
8/9	6/29
8/10	6/30
8/11	7/1
8/12	7/2
8/13	7/3
8/14	7/4
8/15	7/5
8/16	7/6
8/17	7/7
8/18	7/8
8/19	7/9
8/20	7/10
8/21	7/11
8/22	7/12
8/23	7/13
8/24	7/14
8/25	7/15
8/26	7/16
8/27	7/17
8/28	7/18
8/29	7/19
8/30	7/20
8/31	7/21
9/1	7/22
9/2	7/23
9/3	7/24
9/4	7/25
9/5	7/26
9/6	7/27
9/7	7/28
9/8	7/29
9/9	8/1
9/10	8/2
9/11	8/3
9/12	8/4
9/13	8/5
9/14	8/6
9/15	8/7
9/16	8/8
9/17	8/9
9/18	8/10
9/19	8/11
9/20	8/12
9/21	8/13
9/22	8/14
9/23	8/15
9/24	8/16
9/25	8/17
9/26	8/18
9/27	8/19
9/28	8/20
9/29	8/21
9/30	8/22
10/1	8/23
10/2	8/24
10/3	8/25
10/4	8/26
10/5	8/27
10/6	8/28
10/7	8/29
10/8	8/30
10/9	9/1
10/10	9/2
10/11	9/3
10/12	9/4
10/13	9/5
10/14	9/6
10/15	9/7
10/16	9/8
10/17	9/9
10/18	9/10
10/19	9/11
10/20	9/12
10/21	9/13
10/22	9/14
10/23	9/15
10/24	9/16
10/25	9/17
10/26	9/18
10/27	9/19
10/28	9/20
10/29	9/21
10/30	9/22
10/31	9/23
11/1	9/24
11/2	9/25
11/3	9/26
11/4	9/27
11/5	9/28
11/6	9/29
11/7	9/30
11/8	10/1
11/9	10/2
11/10	10/3
11/11	10/4
11/12	10/5
11/13	10/6
11/14	10/7
11/15	10/8
11/16	10/9
11/17	10/10
11/18	10/11
11/19	10/12
11/20	10/13
11/21	10/14
11/22	10/15
11/23	10/16
11/24	10/17
11/25	10/18
11/26	10/19
11/27	10/20
11/28	10/21
11/29	10/22
11/30	10/23
12/1	10/24

12/2	10/25	1/25	12/20	3/23	2/18	5/20	4/17	7/17	6/16	9/13	8/16
12/3	10/26	1/26	12/21	3/24	2/19	5/21	4/18	7/18	6/17	9/14	8/17
12/4	10/27	1/27	12/22	3/25	2/20	5/22	4/19	7/19	6/18	9/15	8/18
12/5	10/28	1/28	12/23	3/26	2/21	5/23	4/20	7/20	6/19	9/16	8/19
12/6	10/29	1/29	12/24	3/27	2/22	5/24	4/21	7/21	6/20	9/17	8/20
12/7	11/1	1/30	12/25	3/28	2/23	5/25	4/22	7/22	6/21	9/18	8/21
12/8	11/2	1/31	12/26	3/29	2/24	5/26	4/23	7/23	6/22	9/19	8/22
12/9	11/3			3/30	2/25	5/27	4/24	7/24	6/23	9/20	8/23
12/10	11/4	2/1	12/27	3/31	2/26	5/28	4/25	7/25	6/24	9/21	8/24
12/11	11/5	2/2	12/28			5/29	4/26	7/26	6/25	9/22	8/25
12/12	11/6	2/3	12/29	4/1	2/27	5/30	4/27	7/27	6/26	9/23	8/26
12/13	11/7	2/4	12/30	4/2	2/28	5/31	4/28	7/28	6/27	9/24	8/27
12/14	11/8	2/5	1/1	4/3	2/29			7/29	6/28	9/25	8/28
12/15	11/9		(1981)	4/4	2/30	6/1	4/29	7/30	6/29	9/26	8/29
12/16	11/10	2/6	1/2	4/5	3/1	6/2	5/1	7/31	7/1	9/27	8/30
12/17	11/11	2/7	1/3	4/6	3/2	6/3	5/2			9/28	9/1
12/18	11/12	2/8	1/4	4/7	3/3	6/4	5/3	8/1	7/2	9/29	9/2
12/19	11/13	2/9	1/5	4/8	3/4	6/5	5/4	8/2	7/3	9/30	9/3
12/20	11/14	2/10	1/6	4/9	3/5	6/6	5/5	8/3	7/4		
12/21	11/15	2/11	1/7	4/10	3/6	6/7	5/6	8/4	7/5	10/1	9/4
12/22	11/16	2/12	1/8	4/11	3/7	6/8	5/7	8/5	7/6	10/2	9/5
12/23	11/17	2/13	1/9	4/12	3/8	6/9	5/8	8/6	7/7	10/3	9/6
12/24	11/18	2/14	1/10	4/13	3/9	6/10	5/9	8/7	7/8	10/4	9/7
12/25	11/19	2/15	1/11	4/14	3/10	6/11	5/10	8/8	7/9	10/5	9/8
12/26	11/20	2/16	1/12	4/15	3/11	6/12	5/11	8/9	7/10	10/6	9/9
12/27	11/21	2/17	1/13	4/16	3/12	6/13	5/12	8/10	7/11	10/7	9/10
12/28	11/22	2/18	1/14	4/17	3/13	6/14	5/13	8/11	7/12	10/8	9/11
12/29	11/23	2/19	1/15	4/18	3/14	6/15	5/14	8/12	7/13	10/9	9/12
12/30	11/24	2/20	1/16	4/19	3/15	6/16	5/15	8/13	7/14	10/10	9/13
12/31	11/25	2/21	1/17	4/20	3/16	6/17	5/16	8/14	7/15	10/11	9/14
		2/22	1/18	4/21	3/17	6/18	5/17	8/15	7/16	10/12	9/15
		2/23	1/19	4/22	3/18	6/19	5/18	8/16	7/17	10/13	9/16
		2/24	1/20	4/23	3/19	6/20	5/19	8/17	7/18	10/14	9/17
Solar	**Lunar**	2/25	1/21	4/24	3/20	6/21	5/20	8/18	7/19	10/15	9/18
Date	**Date**	2/26	1/22	4/25	3/21	6/22	5/21	8/19	7/20	10/16	9/19
		2/27	1/23	4/26	3/22	6/23	5/22	8/20	7/21	10/17	9/20
1981		2/28	1/24	4/27	3/23	6/24	5/23	8/21	7/22	10/18	9/21
1/1	11/26			4/28	3/24	6/25	5/24	8/22	7/23	10/19	9/22
1/2	11/27	3/1	1/25	4/29	3/25	6/26	5/25	8/23	7/24	10/20	9/23
1/3	11/28	3/2	1/26	4/30	3/26	6/27	5/26	8/24	7/25	10/21	9/24
1/4	11/29	3/3	1/27			6/28	5/27	8/25	7/26	10/22	9/25
1/5	11/30	3/4	1/28	5/1	3/27	6/29	5/28	8/26	7/27	10/23	9/26
1/6	12/1	3/5	1/29	5/2	3/28	6/30	5/29	8/27	7/28	10/24	9/27
1/7	12/2	3/6	2/1	5/3	3/29			8/28	7/29	10/25	9/28
1/8	12/3	3/7	2/2	5/4	4/1	7/1	5/30	8/29	8/1	10/26	9/29
1/9	12/4	3/8	2/3	5/5	4/2	7/2	6/1	8/30	8/2	10/27	9/30
1/10	12/5	3/9	2/4	5/6	4/3	7/3	6/2	8/31	8/3	10/28	10/1
1/11	12/6	3/10	2/5	5/7	4/4	7/4	6/3			10/29	10/2
1/12	12/7	3/11	2/6	5/8	4/5	7/5	6/4	9/1	8/4	10/30	10/3
1/13	12/8	3/12	2/7	5/9	4/6	7/6	6/5	9/2	8/5	10/31	10/4
1/14	12/9	3/13	2/8	5/10	4/7	7/7	6/6	9/3	8/6		
1/15	12/10	3/14	2/9	5/11	4/8	7/8	6/7	9/4	8/7	11/1	10/5
1/16	12/11	3/15	2/10	5/12	4/9	7/9	6/8	9/5	8/8	11/2	10/6
1/17	12/12	3/16	2/11	5/13	4/10	7/10	6/9	9/6	8/9	11/3	10/7
1/18	12/13	3/17	2/12	5/14	4/11	7/11	6/10	9/7	8/10	11/4	10/8
1/19	12/14	3/18	2/13	5/15	4/12	7/12	6/11	9/8	8/11	11/5	10/9
1/20	12/15	3/19	2/14	5/16	4/13	7/13	6/12	9/9	8/12	11/6	10/10
1/21	12/16	3/20	2/15	5/17	4/14	7/14	6/13	9/10	8/13	11/7	10/11
1/22	12/17	3/21	2/16	5/18	4/15	7/15	6/14	9/11	8/14	11/8	10/12
1/23	12/18	3/22	2/17	5/19	4/16	7/16	6/15	9/12	8/15	11/9	10/13
1/24	12/19										

Solar Date	Lunar Date	Solar Date	Lunar Date	Solar Date	Lunar Date	Solar Date	Lunar Date	Solar Date	Lunar Date	Solar Date	Lunar Date
11/10	10/14	1/2	12/8	3/1	2/6	4/29	4/6	6/25	5/5	8/22	7/4
11/11	10/15	1/3	12/9	3/2	2/7	4/30	4/7	6/26	5/6	8/23	7/5
11/12	10/16	1/4	12/10	3/3	2/8			6/27	5/7	8/24	7/6
11/13	10/17	1/5	12/11	3/4	2/9	5/1	4/8	6/28	5/8	8/25	7/7
11/14	10/18	1/6	12/12	3/5	2/10	5/2	4/9	6/29	5/9	8/26	7/8
11/15	10/19	1/7	12/13	3/6	2/11	5/3	4/10	6/30	5/10	8/27	7/9
11/16	10/20	1/8	12/14	3/7	2/12	5/4	4/11			8/28	7/10
11/17	10/21	1/9	12/15	3/8	2/13	5/5	4/12	7/1	5/11	8/29	7/11
11/18	10/22	1/10	12/16	3/9	2/14	5/6	4/13	7/2	5/12	8/30	7/12
11/19	10/23	1/11	12/17	3/10	2/15	5/7	4/14	7/3	5/13	8/31	7/13
11/20	10/24	1/12	12/18	3/11	2/16	5/8	4/15	7/4	5/14		
11/21	10/25	1/13	12/19	3/12	2/17	5/9	4/16	7/5	5/15	9/1	7/14
11/22	10/26	1/14	12/20	3/13	2/18	5/10	4/17	7/6	5/16	9/2	7/15
11/23	10/27	1/15	12/21	3/14	2/19	5/11	4/18	7/7	5/17	9/3	7/16
11/24	10/28	1/16	12/22	3/15	2/20	5/12	4/19	7/8	5/18	9/4	7/17
11/25	10/29	1/17	12/23	3/16	2/21	5/13	4/20	7/9	5/19	9/5	7/18
11/26	11/1	1/18	12/24	3/17	2/22	5/14	4/21	7/10	5/20	9/6	7/19
11/27	11/2	1/19	12/25	3/18	2/23	5/15	4/22	7/11	5/21	9/7	7/20
11/28	11/3	1/20	12/26	3/19	2/24	5/16	4/23	7/12	5/22	9/8	7/21
11/29	11/4	1/21	12/27	3/20	2/25	5/17	4/24	7/13	5/23	9/9	7/22
11/30	11/5	1/22	12/28	3/21	2/26	5/18	4/25	7/14	5/24	9/10	7/23
		1/23	12/29	3/22	2/27	5/19	4/26	7/15	5/25	9/11	7/24
12/1	11/6	1/24	12/30	3/23	2/28	5/20	4/27	7/16	5/26	9/12	7/25
12/2	11/7	1/25	1/1	3/24	2/29	5/21	4/28	7/17	5/27	9/13	7/26
12/3	11/8		(1982)	3/25	3/1	5/22	4/29	7/18	5/28	9/14	7/27
12/4	11/9	1/26	1/2	3/26	3/2	5/23	4/1	7/19	5/29	9/15	7/28
12/5	11/10	1/27	1/3	3/27	3/3	*(Leap Month)*		7/20	5/30	9/16	7/29
12/6	11/11	1/28	1/4	3/28	3/4	5/24	4/2	7/21	6/1	9/17	8/1
12/7	11/12	1/29	1/5	3/29	3/5	5/25	4/3	7/22	6/2	9/18	8/2
12/8	11/13	1/30	1/6	3/30	3/6	5/26	4/4	7/23	6/3	9/19	8/3
12/9	11/14	1/31	1/7	3/31	3/7	5/27	4/5	7/24	6/4	9/20	8/4
12/10	11/15					5/28	4/6	7/25	6/5	9/21	8/5
12/11	11/16	2/1	1/8	4/1	3/8	5/29	4/7	7/26	6/6	9/22	8/6
12/12	11/17	2/2	1/9	4/2	3/9	5/30	4/8	7/27	6/7	9/23	8/7
12/13	11/18	2/3	1/10	4/3	3/10	5/31	4/9	7/28	6/8	9/24	8/8
12/14	11/19	2/4	1/11	4/4	3/11			7/29	6/9	9/25	8/9
12/15	11/20	2/5	1/12	4/5	3/12	6/1	4/10	7/30	6/10	9/26	8/10
12/16	11/21	2/6	1/13	4/6	3/13	6/2	4/11	7/31	6/11	9/27	8/11
12/17	11/22	2/7	1/14	4/7	3/14	6/3	4/12			9/28	8/12
12/18	11/23	2/8	1/15	4/8	3/15	6/4	4/13	8/1	6/12	9/29	8/13
12/19	11/24	2/9	1/16	4/9	3/16	6/5	4/14	8/2	6/13	9/30	8/14
12/20	11/25	2/10	1/17	4/10	3/17	6/6	4/15	8/3	6/14		
12/21	11/26	2/11	1/18	4/11	3/18	6/7	4/16	8/4	6/15	10/1	8/15
12/22	11/27	2/12	1/19	4/12	3/19	6/8	4/17	8/5	6/16	10/2	8/16
12/23	11/28	2/13	1/20	4/13	3/20	6/9	4/18	8/6	6/17	10/3	8/17
12/24	11/29	2/14	1/21	4/14	3/21	6/10	4/19	8/7	6/18	10/4	8/18
12/25	11/30	2/15	1/22	4/15	3/22	6/11	4/20	8/8	6/19	10/5	8/19
12/26	12/1	2/16	1/23	4/16	3/23	6/12	4/21	8/9	6/20	10/6	8/20
12/27	12/2	2/17	1/24	4/17	3/24	6/13	4/22	8/10	6/21	10/7	8/21
12/28	12/3	2/18	1/25	4/18	3/25	6/14	4/23	8/11	6/22	10/8	8/22
12/29	12/4	2/19	1/26	4/19	3/26	6/15	4/24	8/12	6/23	10/9	8/23
12/30	12/5	2/20	1/27	4/20	3/27	6/16	4/25	8/13	6/24	10/10	8/24
12/31	12/6	2/21	1/28	4/21	3/28	6/17	4/26	8/14	6/25	10/11	8/25
		2/22	1/29	4/22	3/29	6/18	4/27	8/15	6/26	10/12	8/26
		2/23	1/30	4/23	3/30	6/19	4/28	8/16	6/27	10/13	8/27
Solar **Lunar**		2/24	2/1	4/24	4/1	6/20	4/29	8/17	6/28	10/14	8/28
Date **Date**		2/25	2/2	4/25	4/2	6/21	5/1	8/18	6/29	10/15	8/29
		2/26	2/3	4/26	4/3	6/22	5/2	8/19	7/1	10/16	8/30
1982		2/27	2/4	4/27	4/4	6/23	5/3	8/20	7/2	10/17	9/1
1/1	12/7	2/28	2/5	4/28	4/5	6/24	5/4	8/21	7/3	10/18	9/2

Solar	Lunar	Solar	Lunar	Solar	Lunar	Solar	Lunar	Solar	Lunar	Solar	Lunar
10/19	9/3	12/16	11/2	2/7	12/25	4/5	2/22	6/2	4/21	7/31	6/22
10/20	9/4	12/17	11/3	2/8	12/26	4/6	2/23	6/3	4/22		
10/21	9/5	12/18	11/4	2/9	12/27	4/7	2/24	6/4	4/23	8/1	6/23
10/22	9/6	12/19	11/5	2/10	12/28	4/8	2/25	6/5	4/24	8/2	6/24
10/23	9/7	12/20	11/6	2/11	12/29	4/9	2/26	6/6	4/25	8/3	6/25
10/24	9/8	12/21	11/7	2/12	12/30	4/10	2/27	6/7	4/26	8/4	6/26
10/25	9/9	12/22	11/8	2/13	1/1	4/11	2/28	6/8	4/27	8/5	6/27
10/26	9/10	12/23	11/9		(1983)	4/12	2/29	6/9	4/28	8/6	6/28
10/27	9/11	12/24	11/10	2/14	1/2	4/13	3/1	6/10	4/29	8/7	6/29
10/28	9/12	12/25	11/11	2/15	1/3	4/14	3/2	6/11	5/1	8/8	6/30
10/29	9/13	12/26	11/12	2/16	1/4	4/15	3/3	6/12	5/2	8/9	7/1
10/30	9/14	12/27	11/13	2/17	1/5	4/16	3/4	6/13	5/3	8/10	7/2
10/31	9/15	12/28	11/14	2/18	1/6	4/17	3/5	6/14	5/4	8/11	7/3
		12/29	11/15	2/19	1/7	4/18	3/6	6/15	5/5	8/12	7/4
11/1	9/16	12/30	11/16	2/20	1/8	4/19	3/7	6/16	5/6	8/13	7/5
11/2	9/17	12/31	11/17	2/21	1/9	4/20	3/8	6/17	5/7	8/14	7/6
11/3	9/18			2/22	1/10	4/21	3/9	6/18	5/8	8/15	7/7
11/4	9/19			2/23	1/11	4/22	3/10	6/19	5/9	8/16	7/8
11/5	9/20	Solar	Lunar	2/24	1/12	4/23	3/11	6/20	5/10	8/17	7/9
11/6	9/21	Date	Date	2/25	1/13	4/24	3/12	6/21	5/11	8/18	7/10
11/7	9/22	**1983**		2/26	1/14	4/25	3/13	6/22	5/12	8/19	7/11
11/8	9/23	1/1	11/18	2/27	1/15	4/26	3/14	6/23	5/13	8/20	7/12
11/9	9/24	1/2	11/19	2/28	1/16	4/27	3/15	6/24	5/14	8/21	7/13
11/10	9/25	1/3	11/20			4/28	3/16	6/25	5/15	8/22	7/14
11/11	9/26	1/4	11/21	3/1	1/17	4/29	3/17	6/26	5/16	8/23	7/15
11/12	9/27	1/5	11/22	3/2	1/18	4/30	3/18	6/27	5/17	8/24	7/16
11/13	9/28	1/6	11/23	3/3	1/19			6/28	5/18	8/25	7/17
11/14	9/29	1/7	11/24	3/4	1/20	5/1	3/19	6/29	5/19	8/26	7/18
11/15	10/1	1/8	11/25	3/5	1/21	5/2	3/20	6/30	5/20	8/27	7/19
11/16	10/2	1/9	11/26	3/6	1/22	5/3	3/21			8/28	7/20
11/17	10/3	1/10	11/27	3/7	1/23	5/4	3/22	7/1	5/21	8/29	7/21
11/18	10/4	1/11	11/28	3/8	1/24	5/5	3/23	7/2	5/22	8/30	7/22
11/19	10/5	1/12	11/29	3/9	1/25	5/6	3/24	7/3	5/23	8/31	7/23
11/20	10/6	1/13	11/30	3/10	1/26	5/7	3/25	7/4	5/24		
11/21	10/7	1/14	12/1	3/11	1/27	5/8	3/26	7/5	5/25	9/1	7/24
11/22	10/8	1/15	12/2	3/12	1/28	5/9	3/27	7/6	5/26	9/2	7/25
11/23	10/9	1/16	12/3	3/13	1/29	5/10	3/28	7/7	5/27	9/3	7/26
11/24	10/10	1/17	12/4	3/14	1/30	5/11	3/29	7/8	5/28	9/4	7/27
11/25	10/11	1/18	12/5	3/15	2/1	5/12	3/30	7/9	5/29	9/5	7/28
11/26	10/12	1/19	12/6	3/16	2/2	5/13	4/1	7/10	6/1	9/6	7/29
11/27	10/13	1/20	12/7	3/17	2/3	5/14	4/2	7/11	6/2	9/7	8/1
11/28	10/14	1/21	12/8	3/18	2/4	5/15	4/3	7/12	6/3	9/8	8/2
11/29	10/15	1/22	12/9	3/19	2/5	5/16	4/4	7/13	6/4	9/9	8/3
11/30	10/16	1/23	12/10	3/20	2/6	5/17	4/5	7/14	6/5	9/10	8/4
		1/24	12/11	3/21	2/7	5/18	4/6	7/15	6/6	9/11	8/5
12/1	10/17	1/25	12/12	3/22	2/8	5/19	4/7	7/16	6/7	9/12	8/6
12/2	10/18	1/26	12/13	3/23	2/9	5/20	4/8	7/17	6/8	9/13	8/7
12/3	10/19	1/27	12/14	3/24	2/10	5/21	4/9	7/18	6/9	9/14	8/8
12/4	10/20	1/28	12/15	3/25	2/11	5/22	4/10	7/19	6/10	9/15	8/9
12/5	10/21	1/29	12/16	3/26	2/12	5/23	4/11	7/20	6/11	9/16	8/10
12/6	10/22	1/30	12/17	3/27	2/13	5/24	4/12	7/21	6/12	9/17	8/11
12/7	10/23	1/31	12/18	3/28	2/14	5/25	4/13	7/22	6/13	9/18	8/12
12/8	10/24			3/29	2/15	5/26	4/14	7/23	6/14	9/19	8/13
12/9	10/25			3/30	2/16	5/27	4/15	7/24	6/15	9/20	8/14
12/10	10/26	2/1	12/19	3/31	2/17	5/28	4/16	7/25	6/16	9/21	8/15
12/11	10/27	2/2	12/20			5/29	4/17	7/26	6/17	9/22	8/16
12/12	10/28	2/3	12/21	4/1	2/18	5/30	4/18	7/27	6/18	9/23	8/17
12/13	10/29	2/4	12/22	4/2	2/19	5/31	4/19	7/28	6/19	9/24	8/18
12/14	10/30	2/5	12/23	4/3	2/20			7/29	6/20	9/25	8/19
12/15	11/1	2/6	12/24	4/4	2/21	6/1	4/20	7/30	6/21	9/26	8/20

Solar	Lunar	Solar	Lunar	Solar	Lunar	Solar	Lunar	Solar	Lunar	Solar	Lunar
9/27	8/21	11/24	10/20	1/16	12/14	3/13	2/11	5/10	4/10	7/7	6/9
9/28	8/22	11/25	10/21	1/17	12/15	3/14	2/12	5/11	4/11	7/8	6/10
9/29	8/23	11/26	10/22	1/18	12/16	3/15	2/13	5/12	4/12	7/9	6/11
9/30	8/24	11/27	10/23	1/19	12/17	3/16	2/14	5/13	4/13	7/10	6/12
		11/28	10/24	1/20	12/18	3/17	2/15	5/14	4/14	7/11	6/13
10/1	8/25	11/29	10/25	1/21	12/19	3/18	2/16	5/15	4/15	7/12	6/14
10/2	8/26	11/30	10/26	1/22	12/20	3/19	2/17	5/16	4/16	7/13	6/15
10/3	8/27			1/23	12/21	3/20	2/18	5/17	4/17	7/14	6/16
10/4	8/28	12/1	10/27	1/24	12/22	3/21	2/19	5/18	4/18	7/15	6/17
10/5	8/29	12/2	10/28	1/25	12/23	3/22	2/20	5/19	4/19	7/16	6/18
10/6	9/1	12/3	10/29	1/26	12/24	3/23	2/21	5/20	4/20	7/17	6/19
10/7	9/2	12/4	11/1	1/27	12/25	3/24	2/22	5/21	4/21	7/18	6/20
10/8	9/3	12/5	11/2	1/28	12/26	3/25	2/23	5/22	4/22	7/19	6/21
10/9	9/4	12/6	11/3	1/29	12/27	3/26	2/24	5/23	4/23	7/20	6/22
10/10	9/5	12/7	11/4	1/30	12/28	3/27	2/25	5/24	4/24	7/21	6/23
10/11	9/6	12/8	11/5	1/31	12/29	3/28	2/26	5/25	4/25	7/22	6/24
10/12	9/7	12/9	11/6			3/29	2/27	5/26	4/26	7/23	6/25
10/13	9/8	12/10	11/7	2/1	12/30	3/30	2/28	5/27	4/27	7/24	6/26
10/14	9/9	12/11	11/8	2/2	1/1	3/31	2/29	5/28	4/28	7/25	6/27
10/15	9/10	12/12	11/9		(1984)			5/29	4/29	7/26	6/28
10/16	9/11	12/13	11/10	2/3	1/2	4/1	3/1	5/30	4/30	7/27	6/29
10/17	9/12	12/14	11/11	2/4	1/3	4/2	3/2	5/31	5/1	7/28	7/1
10/18	9/13	12/15	11/12	2/5	1/4	4/3	3/3			7/29	7/2
10/19	9/14	12/16	11/13	2/6	1/5	4/4	3/4	6/1	5/2	7/30	7/3
10/20	9/15	12/17	11/14	2/7	1/6	4/5	3/5	6/2	5/3	7/31	7/4
10/21	9/16	12/18	11/15	2/8	1/7	4/6	3/6	6/3	5/4		
10/22	9/17	12/19	11/16	2/9	1/8	4/7	3/7	6/4	5/5	8/1	7/5
10/23	9/18	12/20	11/17	2/10	1/9	4/8	3/8	6/5	5/6	8/2	7/6
10/24	9/19	12/21	11/18	2/11	1/10	4/9	3/9	6/6	5/7	8/3	7/7
10/25	9/20	12/22	11/19	2/12	1/11	4/10	3/10	6/7	5/8	8/4	7/8
10/26	9/21	12/23	11/20	2/13	1/12	4/11	3/11	6/8	5/9	8/5	7/9
10/27	9/22	12/24	11/21	2/14	1/13	4/12	3/12	6/9	5/10	8/6	7/10
10/28	9/23	12/25	11/22	2/15	1/14	4/13	3/13	6/10	5/11	8/7	7/11
10/29	9/24	12/26	11/23	2/16	1/15	4/14	3/14	6/11	5/12	8/8	7/12
10/30	9/25	12/27	11/24	2/17	1/16	4/15	3/15	6/12	5/13	8/9	7/13
10/31	9/26	12/28	11/25	2/18	1/17	4/16	3/16	6/13	5/14	8/10	7/14
		12/29	11/26	2/19	1/18	4/17	3/17	6/14	5/15	8/11	7/15
11/1	9/27	12/30	11/27	2/20	1/19	4/18	3/18	6/15	5/16	8/12	7/16
11/2	9/28	12/31	11/28	2/21	1/20	4/19	3/19	6/16	5/17	8/13	7/17
11/3	9/29			2/22	1/21	4/20	3/20	6/17	5/18	8/14	7/18
11/4	9/30			2/23	1/22	4/21	3/21	6/18	5/19	8/15	7/19
11/5	10/1	Solar	Lunar	2/24	1/23	4/22	3/22	6/19	5/20	8/16	7/20
11/6	10/2	Date	Date	2/25	1/24	4/23	3/23	6/20	5/21	8/17	7/21
11/7	10/3			2/26	1/25	4/24	3/24	6/21	5/22	8/18	7/22
11/8	10/4	**1984**		2/27	1/26	4/25	3/25	6/22	5/23	8/19	7/23
11/9	10/5	1/1	11/29	2/28	1/27	4/26	3/26	6/23	5/24	8/20	7/24
11/10	10/6	1/2	11/30	2/29	1/28	4/27	3/27	6/24	5/25	8/21	7/25
11/11	10/7	1/3	12/1			4/28	3/28	6/25	5/26	8/22	7/26
11/12	10/8	1/4	12/2	3/1	1/29	4/29	3/29	6/26	5/27	8/23	7/27
11/13	10/9	1/5	12/3	3/2	1/30	4/30	3/30	6/27	5/28	8/24	7/28
11/14	10/10	1/6	12/4	3/3	2/1			6/28	5/29	8/25	7/29
11/15	10/11	1/7	12/5	3/4	2/2	5/1	4/1	6/29	6/1	8/26	7/30
11/16	10/12	1/8	12/6	3/5	2/3	5/2	4/2	6/30	6/2	8/27	8/1
11/17	10/13	1/9	12/7	3/6	2/4	5/3	4/3			8/28	8/2
11/18	10/14	1/10	12/8	3/7	2/5	5/4	4/4	7/1	6/3	8/29	8/3
11/19	10/15	1/11	12/9	3/8	2/6	5/5	4/5	7/2	6/4	8/30	8/4
11/20	10/16	1/12	12/10	3/9	2/7	5/6	4/6	7/3	6/5	8/31	8/5
11/21	10/17	1/13	12/11	3/10	2/8	5/7	4/7	7/4	6/6		
11/22	10/18	1/14	12/12	3/11	2/9	5/8	4/8	7/5	6/7	9/1	8/6
11/23	10/19	1/15	12/13	3/12	2/10	5/9	4/9	7/6	6/8	9/2	8/7

Solar	Lunar	Solar	Lunar	Solar	Lunar	Solar	Lunar	Solar	Lunar	Solar	Lunar
9/3	8/8	11/1	10/9	12/29	11/8	2/20	1/1	4/18	2/29	6/15	4/27
9/4	8/9	11/2	10/10	12/30	11/9		(1985)	4/19	2/30	6/16	4/28
9/5	8/10	11/3	10/11	12/31	11/10	2/21	1/2	4/20	3/1	6/17	4/29
9/6	8/11	11/4	10/12			2/22	1/3	4/21	3/2	6/18	5/1
9/7	8/12	11/5	10/13			2/23	1/4	4/22	3/3	6/19	5/2
9/8	8/13	11/6	10/14	Solar	Lunar	2/24	1/5	4/23	3/4	6/20	5/3
9/9	8/14	11/7	10/15	Date	Date	2/25	1/6	4/24	3/5	6/21	5/4
9/10	8/15	11/8	10/16			2/26	1/7	4/25	3/6	6/22	5/5
9/11	8/16	11/9	10/17	**1985**		2/27	1/8	4/26	3/7	6/23	5/6
9/12	8/17	11/10	10/18	1/1	11/11	2/28	1/9	4/27	3/8	6/24	5/7
9/13	8/18	11/11	10/19	1/2	11/12			4/28	3/9	6/25	5/8
9/14	8/19	11/12	10/20	1/3	11/13	3/1	1/10	4/29	3/10	6/26	5/9
9/15	8/20	11/13	10/21	1/4	11/14	3/2	1/11	4/30	3/11	6/27	5/10
9/16	8/21	11/14	10/22	1/5	11/15	3/3	1/12			6/28	5/11
9/17	8/22	11/15	10/23	1/6	11/16	3/4	1/13	5/1	3/12	6/29	5/12
9/18	8/23	11/16	10/24	1/7	11/17	3/5	1/14	5/2	3/13	6/30	5/13
9/19	8/24	11/17	10/25	1/8	11/18	3/6	1/15	5/3	3/14		
9/20	8/25	11/18	10/26	1/9	11/19	3/7	1/16	5/4	3/15	7/1	5/14
9/21	8/26	11/19	10/27	1/10	11/20	3/8	1/17	5/5	3/16	7/2	5/15
9/22	8/27	11/20	10/28	1/11	11/21	3/9	1/18	5/6	3/17	7/3	5/16
9/23	8/28	11/21	10/29	1/12	11/22	3/10	1/19	5/7	3/18	7/4	5/17
9/24	8/29	11/22	10/30	1/13	11/23	3/11	1/20	5/8	3/19	7/5	5/18
9/25	9/1	11/23	10/1	1/14	11/24	3/12	1/21	5/9	3/20	7/6	5/19
9/26	9/2	(Leap Month)		1/15	11/25	3/13	1/22	5/10	3/21	7/7	5/20
9/27	9/3	11/24	10/2	1/16	11/26	3/14	1/23	5/11	3/22	7/8	5/21
9/28	9/4	11/25	10/3	1/17	11/27	3/15	1/24	5/12	3/23	7/9	5/22
9/29	9/5	11/26	10/4	1/18	11/28	3/16	1/25	5/13	3/24	7/10	5/23
9/30	9/6	11/27	10/5	1/19	11/29	3/17	1/26	5/14	3/25	7/11	5/24
		11/28	10/6	1/20	11/30	3/18	1/27	5/15	3/26	7/12	5/25
10/1	9/7	11/29	10/7	1/21	12/1	3/19	1/28	5/16	3/27	7/13	5/26
10/2	9/8	11/30	10/8	1/22	12/2	3/20	1/29	5/17	3/28	7/14	5/27
10/3	9/9			1/23	12/3	3/21	2/1	5/18	3/29	7/15	5/28
10/4	9/10	12/1	10/9	1/24	12/4	3/22	2/2	5/19	3/30	7/16	5/29
10/5	9/11	12/2	10/10	1/25	12/5	3/23	2/3	5/20	4/1	7/17	5/30
10/6	9/12	12/3	10/11	1/26	12/6	3/24	2/4	5/21	4/2	7/18	6/1
10/7	9/13	12/4	10/12	1/27	12/7	3/25	2/5	5/22	4/3	7/19	6/2
10/8	9/14	12/5	10/13	1/28	12/8	3/26	2/6	5/23	4/4	7/20	6/3
10/9	9/15	12/6	10/14	1/29	12/9	3/27	2/7	5/24	4/5	7/21	6/4
10/10	9/16	12/7	10/15	1/30	12/10	3/28	2/8	5/25	4/6	7/22	6/5
10/11	9/17	12/8	10/16	1/31	12/11	3/29	2/9	5/26	4/7	7/23	6/6
10/12	9/18	12/9	10/17			3/30	2/10	5/27	4/8	7/24	6/7
10/13	9/19	12/10	10/18	2/1	12/12	3/31	2/11	5/28	4/9	7/25	6/8
10/14	9/20	12/11	10/19	2/2	12/13			5/29	4/10	7/26	6/9
10/15	9/21	12/12	10/20	2/3	12/14	4/1	2/12	5/30	4/11	7/27	6/10
10/16	9/22	12/13	10/21	2/4	12/15	4/2	2/13	5/31	4/12	7/28	6/11
10/17	9/23	12/14	10/22	2/5	12/16	4/3	2/14			7/29	6/12
10/18	9/24	12/15	10/23	2/6	12/17	4/4	2/15	6/1	4/13	7/30	6/13
10/19	9/25	12/16	10/24	2/7	12/18	4/5	2/16	6/2	4/14	7/31	6/14
10/20	9/26	12/17	10/25	2/8	12/19	4/6	2/17	6/3	4/15		
10/21	9/27	12/18	10/26	2/9	12/20	4/7	2/18	6/4	4/16	8/1	6/15
10/22	9/28	12/19	10/27	2/10	12/21	4/8	2/19	6/5	4/17	8/2	6/16
10/23	9/29	12/20	10/28	2/11	12/22	4/9	2/20	6/6	4/18	8/3	6/17
10/24	10/1	12/21	10/29	2/12	12/23	4/10	2/21	6/7	4/19	8/4	6/18
10/25	10/2	12/22	11/1	2/13	12/24	4/11	2/22	6/8	4/20	8/5	6/19
10/26	10/3	12/23	11/2	2/14	12/25	4/12	2/23	6/9	4/21	8/6	6/20
10/27	10/4	12/24	11/3	2/15	12/26	4/13	2/24	6/10	4/22	8/7	6/21
10/28	10/5	12/25	11/4	2/16	12/27	4/14	2/25	6/11	4/23	8/8	6/22
10/29	10/6	12/26	11/5	2/17	12/28	4/15	2/26	6/12	4/24	8/9	6/23
10/30	10/7	12/27	11/6	2/18	12/29	4/16	2/27	6/13	4/25	8/10	6/24
10/31	10/8	12/28	11/7	2/19	12/30	4/17	2/28	6/14	4/26	8/11	6/25

Solar	Lunar	Solar	Lunar	Solar	Lunar	Solar	Lunar	Solar	Lunar	Solar	Lunar
8/12	6/26	10/9	8/25	12/6	10/25	1/29	12/20	3/27	2/18	5/24	4/16
8/13	6/27	10/10	8/26	12/7	10/26	1/30	12/21	3/28	2/19	5/25	4/17
8/14	6/28	10/11	8/27	12/8	10/27	1/31	12/22	3/29	2/20	5/26	4/18
8/15	6/29	10/12	8/28	12/9	10/28			3/30	2/21	5/27	4/19
8/16	7/1	10/13	8/29	12/10	10/29	2/1	12/23	3/31	2/22	5/28	4/20
8/17	7/2	10/14	9/1	12/11	10/30	2/2	12/24			5/29	4/21
8/18	7/3	10/15	9/2	12/12	11/1	2/3	12/25	4/1	2/23	5/30	4/22
8/19	7/4	10/16	9/3	12/13	11/2	2/4	12/26	4/2	2/24	5/31	4/23
8/20	7/5	10/17	9/4	12/14	11/3	2/5	12/27	4/3	2/25		
8/21	7/6	10/18	9/5	12/15	11/4	2/6	12/28	4/4	2/26	6/1	4/24
8/22	7/7	10/19	9/6	12/16	11/5	2/7	12/29	4/5	2/27	6/2	4/25
8/23	7/8	10/20	9/7	12/17	11/6	2/8	12/30	4/6	2/28	6/3	4/26
8/24	7/9	10/21	9/8	12/18	11/7	2/9	1/1	4/7	2/29	6/4	4/27
8/25	7/10	10/22	9/9	12/19	11/8		(1986)	4/8	2/30	6/5	4/28
8/26	7/11	10/23	9/10	12/20	11/9	2/10	1/2	4/9	3/1	6/6	4/29
8/27	7/12	10/24	9/11	12/21	11/10	2/11	1/3	4/10	3/2	6/7	5/1
8/28	7/13	10/25	9/12	12/22	11/11	2/12	1/4	4/11	3/3	6/8	5/2
8/29	7/14	10/26	9/13	12/23	11/12	2/13	1/5	4/12	3/4	6/9	5/3
8/30	7/15	10/27	9/14	12/24	11/13	2/14	1/6	4/13	3/5	6/10	5/4
8/31	7/16	10/28	9/15	12/25	11/14	2/15	1/7	4/14	3/6	6/11	5/5
		10/29	9/16	12/26	11/15	2/16	1/8	4/15	3/7	6/12	5/6
9/1	7/17	10/30	9/17	12/27	11/16	2/17	1/9	4/16	3/8	6/13	5/7
9/2	7/18	10/31	9/18	12/28	11/17	2/18	1/10	4/17	3/9	6/14	5/8
9/3	7/19			12/29	11/18	2/19	1/11	4/18	3/10	6/15	5/9
9/4	7/20	11/1	9/19	12/30	11/19	2/20	1/12	4/19	3/11	6/16	5/10
9/5	7/21	11/2	9/20	12/31	11/20	2/21	1/13	4/20	3/12	6/17	5/11
9/6	7/22	11/3	9/21			2/22	1/14	4/21	3/13	6/18	5/12
9/7	7/23	11/4	9/22			2/23	1/15	4/22	3/14	6/19	5/13
9/8	7/24	11/5	9/23	**Solar**	**Lunar**	2/24	1/16	4/23	3/15	6/20	5/14
9/9	7/25	11/6	9/24	**Date**	**Date**	2/25	1/17	4/24	3/16	6/21	5/15
9/10	7/26	11/7	9/25			2/26	1/18	4/25	3/17	6/22	5/16
9/11	7/27	11/8	9/26	**1986**		2/27	1/19	4/26	3/18	6/23	5/17
9/12	7/28	11/9	9/27	1/1	11/21	2/28	1/20	4/27	3/19	6/24	5/18
9/13	7/29	11/10	9/28	1/2	11/22			4/28	3/20	6/25	5/19
9/14	7/30	11/11	9/29	1/3	11/23	3/1	1/21	4/29	3/21	6/26	5/20
9/15	8/1	11/12	10/1	1/4	11/24	3/2	1/22	4/30	3/22	6/27	5/21
9/16	8/2	11/13	10/2	1/5	11/25	3/3	1/23			6/28	5/22
9/17	8/3	11/14	10/3	1/6	11/26	3/4	1/24	5/1	3/23	6/29	5/23
9/18	8/4	11/15	10/4	1/7	11/27	3/5	1/25	5/2	3/24	6/30	5/24
9/19	8/5	11/16	10/5	1/8	11/28	3/6	1/26	5/3	3/25		
9/20	8/6	11/17	10/6	1/9	11/29	3/7	1/27	5/4	3/26	7/1	5/25
9/21	8/7	11/18	10/7	1/10	12/1	3/8	1/28	5/5	3/27	7/2	5/26
9/22	8/8	11/19	10/8	1/11	12/2	3/9	1/29	5/6	3/28	7/3	5/27
9/23	8/9	11/20	10/9	1/12	12/3	3/10	2/1	5/7	3/29	7/4	5/28
9/24	8/10	11/21	10/10	1/13	12/4	3/11	2/2	5/8	3/30	7/5	5/29
9/25	8/11	11/22	10/11	1/14	12/5	3/12	2/3	5/9	4/1	7/6	5/30
9/26	8/12	11/23	10/12	1/15	12/6	3/13	2/4	5/10	4/2	7/7	6/1
9/27	8/13	11/24	10/13	1/16	12/7	3/14	2/5	5/11	4/3	7/8	6/2
9/28	8/14	11/25	10/14	1/17	12/8	3/15	2/6	5/12	4/4	7/9	6/3
9/29	8/15	11/26	10/15	1/18	12/9	3/16	2/7	5/13	4/5	7/10	6/4
9/30	8/16	11/27	10/16	1/19	12/10	3/17	2/8	5/14	4/6	7/11	6/5
		11/28	10/17	1/20	12/11	3/18	2/9	5/15	4/7	7/12	6/6
10/1	8/17	11/29	10/18	1/21	12/12	3/19	2/10	5/16	4/8	7/13	6/7
10/2	8/18	11/30	10/19	1/22	12/13	3/20	2/11	5/17	4/9	7/14	6/8
10/3	8/19			1/23	12/14	3/21	2/12	5/18	4/10	7/15	6/9
10/4	8/20	12/1	10/20	1/24	12/15	3/22	2/13	5/19	4/11	7/16	6/10
10/5	8/21	12/2	10/21	1/25	12/16	3/23	2/14	5/20	4/12	7/17	6/11
10/6	8/22	12/3	10/22	1/26	12/17	3/24	2/15	5/21	4/13	7/18	6/12
10/7	8/23	12/4	10/23	1/27	12/18	3/25	2/16	5/22	4/14	7/19	6/13
10/8	8/24	12/5	10/24	1/28	12/19	3/26	2/17	5/23	4/15	7/20	6/14

Solar	Lunar	Solar	Lunar	Solar	Lunar	Solar	Lunar	Solar	Lunar	Solar	Lunar
7/21	6/15	9/17	8/14	11/14	10/13	1/6	12/7	3/4	2/5	5/1	4/4
7/22	6/16	9/18	8/15	11/15	10/14	1/7	12/8	3/5	2/6	5/2	4/5
7/23	6/17	9/19	8/16	11/16	10/15	1/8	12/9	3/6	2/7	5/3	4/6
7/24	6/18	9/20	8/17	11/17	10/16	1/9	12/10	3/7	2/8	5/4	4/7
7/25	6/19	9/21	8/18	11/18	10/17	1/10	12/11	3/8	2/9	5/5	4/8
7/26	6/20	9/22	8/19	11/19	10/18	1/11	12/12	3/9	2/10	5/6	4/9
7/27	6/21	9/23	8/20	11/20	10/19	1/12	12/13	3/10	2/11	5/7	4/10
7/28	6/22	9/24	8/21	11/21	10/20	1/13	12/14	3/11	2/12	5/8	4/11
7/29	6/23	9/25	8/22	11/22	10/21	1/14	12/15	3/12	2/13	5/9	4/12
7/30	6/24	9/26	8/23	11/23	10/22	1/15	12/16	3/13	2/14	5/10	4/13
7/31	6/25	9/27	8/24	11/24	10/23	1/16	12/17	3/14	2/15	5/11	4/14
		9/28	8/25	11/25	10/24	1/17	12/18	3/15	2/16	5/12	4/15
8/1	6/26	9/29	8/26	11/26	10/25	1/18	12/19	3/16	2/17	5/13	4/16
8/2	6/27	9/30	8/27	11/27	10/26	1/19	12/20	3/17	2/18	5/14	4/17
8/3	6/28			11/28	10/27	1/20	12/21	3/18	2/19	5/15	4/18
8/4	6/29	10/1	8/28	11/29	10/28	1/21	12/22	3/19	2/20	5/16	4/19
8/5	6/30	10/2	8/29	11/30	10/29	1/22	12/23	3/20	2/21	5/17	4/20
8/6	7/1	10/3	8/30			1/23	12/24	3/21	2/22	5/18	4/21
8/7	7/2	10/4	9/1	12/1	10/30	1/24	12/25	3/22	2/23	5/19	4/22
8/8	7/3	10/5	9/2	12/2	11/1	1/25	12/26	3/23	2/24	5/20	4/23
8/9	7/4	10/6	9/3	12/3	11/2	1/26	12/27	3/24	2/25	5/21	4/24
8/10	7/5	10/7	9/4	12/4	11/3	1/27	12/28	3/25	2/26	5/22	4/25
8/11	7/6	10/8	9/5	12/5	11/4	1/28	12/29	3/26	2/27	5/23	4/26
8/12	7/7	10/9	9/6	12/6	11/5	1/29	1/1	3/27	2/28	5/24	4/27
8/13	7/8	10/10	9/7	12/7	11/6		(1987)	3/28	2/29	5/25	4/28
8/14	7/9	10/11	9/8	12/8	11/7	1/30	1/2	3/29	3/1	5/26	4/29
8/15	7/10	10/12	9/9	12/9	11/8	1/31	1/3	3/30	3/2	5/27	5/1
8/16	7/11	10/13	9/10	12/10	11/9			3/31	3/3	5/28	5/2
8/17	7/12	10/14	9/11	12/11	11/10	2/1	1/4			5/29	5/3
8/18	7/13	10/15	9/12	12/12	11/11	2/2	1/5	4/1	3/4	5/30	5/4
8/19	7/14	10/16	9/13	12/13	11/12	2/3	1/6	4/2	3/5	5/31	5/5
8/20	7/15	10/17	9/14	12/14	11/13	2/4	1/7	4/3	3/6		
8/21	7/16	10/18	9/15	12/15	11/14	2/5	1/8	4/4	3/7	6/1	5/6
8/22	7/17	10/19	9/16	12/16	11/15	2/6	1/9	4/5	3/8	6/2	5/7
8/23	7/18	10/20	9/17	12/17	11/16	2/7	1/10	4/6	3/9	6/3	5/8
8/24	7/19	10/21	9/18	12/18	11/17	2/8	1/11	4/7	3/10	6/4	5/9
8/25	7/20	10/22	9/19	12/19	11/18	2/9	1/12	4/8	3/11	6/5	5/10
8/26	7/21	10/23	9/20	12/20	11/19	2/10	1/13	4/9	3/12	6/6	5/11
8/27	7/22	10/24	9/21	12/21	11/20	2/11	1/14	4/10	3/13	6/7	5/12
8/28	7/23	10/25	9/22	12/22	11/21	2/12	1/15	4/11	3/14	6/8	5/13
8/29	7/24	10/26	9/23	12/23	11/22	2/13	1/16	4/12	3/15	6/9	5/14
8/30	7/25	10/27	9/24	12/24	11/23	2/14	1/17	4/13	3/16	6/10	5/15
8/31	7/26	10/28	9/25	12/25	11/24	2/15	1/18	4/14	3/17	6/11	5/16
		10/29	9/26	12/26	11/25	2/16	1/19	4/15	3/18	6/12	5/17
9/1	7/27	10/30	9/27	12/27	11/26	2/17	1/20	4/16	3/19	6/13	5/18
9/2	7/28	10/31	9/28	12/28	11/27	2/18	1/21	4/17	3/20	6/14	5/19
9/3	7/29			12/29	11/28	2/19	1/22	4/18	3/21	6/15	5/20
9/4	8/1	11/1	9/29	12/30	11/29	2/20	1/23	4/19	3/22	6/16	5/21
9/5	8/2	11/2	10/1	12/31	12/1	2/21	1/24	4/20	3/23	6/17	5/22
9/6	8/3	11/3	10/2			2/22	1/25	4/21	3/24	6/18	5/23
9/7	8/4	11/4	10/3			2/23	1/26	4/22	3/25	6/19	5/24
9/8	8/5	11/5	10/4	**Solar**	**Lunar**	2/24	1/27	4/23	3/26	6/20	5/25
9/9	8/6	11/6	10/5	**Date**	**Date**	2/25	1/28	4/24	3/27	6/21	5/26
9/10	8/7	11/7	10/6			2/26	1/29	4/25	3/28	6/22	5/27
9/11	8/8	11/8	10/7	**1987**		2/27	1/30	4/26	3/29	6/23	5/28
9/12	8/9	11/9	10/8	1/1	12/2	2/28	2/1	4/27	3/30	6/24	5/29
9/13	8/10	11/10	10/9	1/2	12/3			4/28	4/1	6/25	5/30
9/14	8/11	11/11	10/10	1/3	12/4	3/1	2/2	4/29	4/2	6/26	6/1
9/15	8/12	11/12	10/11	1/4	12/5	3/2	2/3	4/30	4/3	6/27	6/2
9/16	8/13	11/13	10/12	1/5	12/6	3/3	2/4			6/28	6/3

Solar	Lunar	Solar	Lunar	Solar	Lunar	Solar	Lunar	Solar	Lunar	Solar	Lunar
6/29	6/4	8/25	7/2	10/22	8/30	12/19	10/29	2/10	12/23	4/7	2/21
6/30	6/5	8/26	7/3	10/23	9/1	12/20	10/30	2/11	12/24	4/8	2/22
		8/27	7/4	10/24	9/2	12/21	11/1	2/12	12/25	4/9	2/23
7/1	6/6	8/28	7/5	10/25	9/3	12/22	11/2	2/13	12/26	4/10	2/24
7/2	6/7	8/29	7/6	10/26	9/4	12/23	11/3	2/14	12/27	4/11	2/25
7/3	6/8	8/30	7/7	10/27	9/5	12/24	11/4	2/15	12/28	4/12	2/26
7/4	6/9	8/31	7/8	10/28	9/6	12/25	11/5	2/16	12/29	4/13	2/27
7/5	6/10			10/29	9/7	12/26	11/6	2/17	1/1	4/14	2/28
7/6	6/11	9/1	7/9	10/30	9/8	12/27	11/7		(1988)	4/15	2/29
7/7	6/12	9/2	7/10	10/31	9/9	12/28	11/8	2/18	1/2	4/16	3/1
7/8	6/13	9/3	7/11			12/29	11/9	2/19	1/3	4/17	3/2
7/9	6/14	9/4	7/12	11/1	9/10	12/30	11/10	2/20	1/4	4/18	3/3
7/10	6/15	9/5	7/13	11/2	9/11	12/31	11/11	2/21	1/5	4/19	3/4
7/11	6/16	9/6	7/14	11/3	9/12			2/22	1/6	4/20	3/5
7/12	6/17	9/7	7/15	11/4	9/13			2/23	1/7	4/21	3/6
7/13	6/18	9/8	7/16	11/5	9/14	Solar	Lunar	2/24	1/8	4/22	3/7
7/14	6/19	9/9	7/17	11/6	9/15	Date	Date	2/25	1/9	4/23	3/8
7/15	6/20	9/10	7/18	11/7	9/16	1988		2/26	1/10	4/24	3/9
7/16	6/21	9/11	7/19	11/8	9/17	1/1	11/12	2/27	1/11	4/25	3/10
7/17	6/22	9/12	7/20	11/9	9/18	1/2	11/13	2/28	1/12	4/26	3/11
7/18	6/23	9/13	7/21	11/10	9/19	1/3	11/14	2/29	1/13	4/27	3/12
7/19	6/24	9/14	7/22	11/11	9/20	1/4	11/15			4/28	3/13
7/20	6/25	9/15	7/23	11/12	9/21	1/5	11/16	3/1	1/14	4/29	3/14
7/21	6/26	9/16	7/24	11/13	9/22	1/6	11/17	3/2	1/15	4/30	3/15
7/22	6/27	9/17	7/25	11/14	9/23	1/7	11/18	3/3	1/16		
7/23	6/28	9/18	7/26	11/15	9/24	1/8	11/19	3/4	1/17	5/1	3/16
7/24	6/29	9/19	7/27	11/16	9/25	1/9	11/20	3/5	1/18	5/2	3/17
7/25	6/30	9/20	7/28	11/17	9/26	1/10	11/21	3/6	1/19	5/3	3/18
7/26	7/1	9/21	7/29	11/18	9/27	1/11	11/22	3/7	1/20	5/4	3/19
7/27	7/2	9/22	7/30	11/19	9/28	1/12	11/23	3/8	1/21	5/5	3/20
7/28	7/3	9/23	8/1	11/20	9/29	1/13	11/24	3/9	1/22	5/6	3/21
7/29	7/4	9/24	8/2	11/21	10/1	1/14	11/25	3/10	1/23	5/7	3/22
7/30	7/5	9/25	8/3	11/22	10/2	1/15	11/26	3/11	1/24	5/8	3/23
7/31	7/6	9/26	8/4	11/23	10/3	1/16	11/27	3/12	1/25	5/9	3/24
		9/27	8/5	11/24	10/4	1/17	11/28	3/13	1/26	5/10	3/25
8/1	7/7	9/28	8/6	11/25	10/5	1/18	11/29	3/14	1/27	5/11	3/26
8/2	7/8	9/29	8/7	11/26	10/6	1/19	12/1	3/15	1/28	5/12	3/27
8/3	7/9	9/30	8/8	11/27	10/7	1/20	12/2	3/16	1/29	5/13	3/28
8/4	7/10			11/28	10/8	1/21	12/3	3/17	1/30	5/14	3/29
8/5	7/11	10/1	8/9	11/29	10/9	1/22	12/4	3/18	2/1	5/15	3/30
8/6	7/12	10/2	8/10	11/30	10/10	1/23	12/5	3/19	2/2	5/16	4/1
8/7	7/13	10/3	8/11			1/24	12/6	3/20	2/3	5/17	4/2
8/8	7/14	10/4	8/12	12/1	10/11	1/25	12/7	3/21	2/4	5/18	4/3
8/9	7/15	10/5	8/13	12/2	10/12	1/26	12/8	3/22	2/5	5/19	4/4
8/10	7/16	10/6	8/14	12/3	10/13	1/27	12/9	3/23	2/6	5/20	4/5
8/11	7/17	10/7	8/15	12/4	10/14	1/28	12/10	3/24	2/7	5/21	4/6
8/12	7/18	10/8	8/16	12/5	10/15	1/29	12/11	3/25	2/8	5/22	4/7
8/13	7/19	10/9	8/17	12/6	10/16	1/30	12/12	3/26	2/9	5/23	4/8
8/14	7/20	10/10	8/18	12/7	10/17	1/31	12/13	3/27	2/10	5/24	4/9
8/15	7/21	10/11	8/19	12/8	10/18			3/28	2/11	5/25	4/10
8/16	7/22	10/12	8/20	12/9	10/19			3/29	2/12	5/26	4/11
8/17	7/23	10/13	8/21	12/10	10/20	2/1	12/14	3/30	2/13	5/27	4/12
8/18	7/24	10/14	8/22	12/11	10/21	2/2	12/15	3/31	2/14	5/28	4/13
8/19	7/25	10/15	8/23	12/12	10/22	2/3	12/16			5/29	4/14
8/20	7/26	10/16	8/24	12/13	10/23	2/4	12/17	4/1	2/15	5/30	4/15
8/21	7/27	10/17	8/25	12/14	10/24	2/5	12/18	4/2	2/16	5/31	4/16
8/22	7/28	10/18	8/26	12/15	10/25	2/6	12/19	4/3	2/17		
8/23	7/29	10/19	8/27	12/16	10/26	2/7	12/20	4/4	2/18	6/1	4/17
8/24	7/1	10/20	8/28	12/17	10/27	2/8	12/21	4/5	2/19	6/2	4/18
(Leap Month)		10/21	8/29	12/18	10/28	2/9	12/22	4/6	2/20	6/3	4/19

Solar	Lunar	Solar	Lunar	Solar	Lunar	Solar	Lunar	Solar	Lunar	Solar	Lunar
6/4	4/20	8/1	6/19	9/29	8/19	11/26	10/18	1/18	12/11	3/16	2/9
6/5	4/21	8/2	6/20	9/30	8/20	11/27	10/19	1/19	12/12	3/17	2/10
6/6	4/22	8/3	6/21			11/28	10/20	1/20	12/13	3/18	2/11
6/7	4/23	8/4	6/22	10/1	8/21	11/29	10/21	1/21	12/14	3/19	2/12
6/8	4/24	8/5	6/23	10/2	8/22	11/30	10/22	1/22	12/15	3/20	2/13
6/9	4/25	8/6	6/24	10/3	8/23			1/23	12/16	3/21	2/14
6/10	4/26	8/7	6/25	10/4	8/24	12/1	10/23	1/24	12/17	3/22	2/15
6/11	4/27	8/8	6/26	10/5	8/25	12/2	10/24	1/25	12/18	3/23	2/16
6/12	4/28	8/9	6/27	10/6	8/26	12/3	10/25	1/26	12/19	3/24	2/17
6/13	4/29	8/10	6/28	10/7	8/27	12/4	10/26	1/27	12/20	3/25	2/18
6/14	5/1	8/11	6/29	10/8	8/28	12/5	10/27	1/28	12/21	3/26	2/19
6/15	5/2	8/12	7/1	10/9	8/29	12/6	10/28	1/29	12/22	3/27	2/20
6/16	5/3	8/13	7/2	10/10	8/30	12/7	10/29	1/30	12/23	3/28	2/21
6/17	5/4	8/14	7/3	10/11	9/1	12/8	10/30	1/31	12/24	3/29	2/22
6/18	5/5	8/15	7/4	10/12	9/2	12/9	11/1			3/30	2/23
6/19	5/6	8/16	7/5	10/13	9/3	12/10	11/2	2/1	12/25	3/31	2/24
6/20	5/7	8/17	7/6	10/14	9/4	12/11	11/3	2/2	12/26		
6/21	5/8	8/18	7/7	10/15	9/5	12/12	11/4	2/3	12/27	4/1	2/25
6/22	5/9	8/19	7/8	10/16	9/6	12/13	11/5	2/4	12/28	4/2	2/26
6/23	5/10	8/20	7/9	10/17	9/7	12/14	11/6	2/5	12/29	4/3	2/27
6/24	5/11	8/21	7/10	10/18	9/8	12/15	11/7	2/6	1/1	4/4	2/28
6/25	5/12	8/22	7/11	10/19	9/9	12/16	11/8		(1989)	4/5	2/29
6/26	5/13	8/23	7/12	10/20	9/10	12/17	11/9	2/7	1/2	4/6	3/1
6/27	5/14	8/24	7/13	10/21	9/11	12/18	11/10	2/8	1/3	4/7	3/2
6/28	5/15	8/25	7/14	10/22	9/12	12/19	11/11	2/9	1/4	4/8	3/3
6/29	5/16	8/26	7/15	10/23	9/13	12/20	11/12	2/10	1/5	4/9	3/4
6/30	5/17	8/27	7/16	10/24	9/14	12/21	11/13	2/11	1/6	4/10	3/5
		8/28	7/17	10/25	9/15	12/22	11/14	2/12	1/7	4/11	3/6
7/1	5/18	8/29	7/18	10/26	9/16	12/23	11/15	2/13	1/8	4/12	3/7
7/2	5/19	8/30	7/19	10/27	9/17	12/24	11/16	2/14	1/9	4/13	3/8
7/3	5/20	8/31	7/20	10/28	9/18	12/25	11/17	2/15	1/10	4/14	3/9
7/4	5/21			10/29	9/19	12/26	11/18	2/16	1/11	4/15	3/10
7/5	5/22	9/1	7/21	10/30	9/20	12/27	11/19	2/17	1/12	4/16	3/11
7/6	5/23	9/2	7/22	10/31	9/21	12/28	11/20	2/18	1/13	4/17	3/12
7/7	5/24	9/3	7/23			12/29	11/21	2/19	1/14	4/18	3/13
7/8	5/25	9/4	7/24	11/1	9/22	12/30	11/22	2/20	1/15	4/19	3/14
7/9	5/26	9/5	7/25	11/2	9/23	12/31	11/23	2/21	1/16	4/20	3/15
7/10	5/27	9/6	7/26	11/3	9/24			2/22	1/17	4/21	3/16
7/11	5/28	9/7	7/27	11/4	9/25			2/23	1/18	4/22	3/17
7/12	5/29	9/8	7/28	11/5	9/26	**Solar**	**Lunar**	2/24	1/19	4/23	3/18
7/13	5/30	9/9	7/29	11/6	9/27	**Date**	**Date**	2/25	1/20	4/24	3/19
7/14	6/1	9/10	7/30	11/7	9/28			2/26	1/21	4/25	3/20
7/15	6/2	9/11	8/1	11/8	9/29	**1989**		2/27	1/22	4/26	3/21
7/16	6/3	9/12	8/2	11/9	10/1	1/1	11/24	2/28	1/23	4/27	3/22
7/17	6/4	9/13	8/3	11/10	10/2	1/2	11/25			4/28	3/23
7/18	6/5	9/14	8/4	11/11	10/3	1/3	11/26	3/1	1/24	4/29	3/24
7/19	6/6	9/15	8/5	11/12	10/4	1/4	11/27	3/2	1/25	4/30	3/25
7/20	6/7	9/16	8/6	11/13	10/5	1/5	11/28	3/3	1/26		
7/21	6/8	9/17	8/7	11/14	10/6	1/6	11/29	3/4	1/27	5/1	3/26
7/22	6/9	9/18	8/8	11/15	10/7	1/7	11/30	3/5	1/28	5/2	3/27
7/23	6/10	9/19	8/9	11/16	10/8	1/8	12/1	3/6	1/29	5/3	3/28
7/24	6/11	9/20	8/10	11/17	10/9	1/9	12/2	3/7	1/30	5/4	3/29
7/25	6/12	9/21	8/11	11/18	10/10	1/10	12/3	3/8	2/1	5/5	4/1
7/26	6/13	9/22	8/12	11/19	10/11	1/11	12/4	3/9	2/2	5/6	4/2
7/27	6/14	9/23	8/13	11/20	10/12	1/12	12/5	3/10	2/3	5/7	4/3
7/28	6/15	9/24	8/14	11/21	10/13	1/13	12/6	3/11	2/4	5/8	4/4
7/29	6/16	9/25	8/15	11/22	10/14	1/14	12/7	3/12	2/5	5/9	4/5
7/30	6/17	9/26	8/16	11/23	10/15	1/15	12/8	3/13	2/6	5/10	4/6
7/31	6/18	9/27	8/17	11/24	10/16	1/16	12/9	3/14	2/7	5/11	4/7
		9/28	8/18	11/25	10/17	1/17	12/10	3/15	2/8	5/12	4/8

Solar	Lunar	Solar	Lunar	Solar	Lunar	Solar	Lunar	Solar	Lunar	Solar	Lunar
5/13	4/9	7/10	6/8	9/6	8/7	11/3	10/6	Solar	Lunar	2/24	1/29
5/14	4/10	7/11	6/9	9/7	8/8	11/4	10/7	Date	Date	2/25	2/1
5/15	4/11	7/12	6/10	9/8	8/9	11/5	10/8	1990		2/26	2/2
5/16	4/12	7/13	6/11	9/9	8/10	11/6	10/9			2/27	2/3
5/17	4/13	7/14	6/12	9/10	8/11	11/7	10/10	1/1	12/5	2/28	2/4
5/18	4/14	7/15	6/13	9/11	8/12	11/8	10/11	1/2	12/6		
5/19	4/15	7/16	6/14	9/12	8/13	11/9	10/12	1/3	12/7	3/1	2/5
5/20	4/16	7/17	6/15	9/13	8/14	11/10	10/13	1/4	12/8	3/2	2/6
5/21	4/17	7/18	6/16	9/14	8/15	11/11	10/14	1/5	12/9	3/3	2/7
5/22	4/18	7/19	6/17	9/15	8/16	11/12	10/15	1/6	12/10	3/4	2/8
5/23	4/19	7/20	6/18	9/16	8/17	11/13	10/16	1/7	12/11	3/5	2/9
5/24	4/20	7/21	6/19	9/17	8/18	11/14	10/17	1/8	12/12	3/6	2/10
5/25	4/21	7/22	6/20	9/18	8/19	11/15	10/18	1/9	12/13	3/7	2/11
5/26	4/22	7/23	6/21	9/19	8/20	11/16	10/19	1/10	12/14	3/8	2/12
5/27	4/23	7/24	6/22	9/20	8/21	11/17	10/20	1/11	12/15	3/9	2/13
5/28	4/24	7/25	6/23	9/21	8/22	11/18	10/21	1/12	12/16	3/10	2/14
5/29	4/25	7/26	6/24	9/22	8/23	11/19	10/22	1/13	12/17	3/11	2/15
5/30	4/26	7/27	6/25	9/23	8/24	11/20	10/23	1/14	12/18	3/12	2/16
5/31	4/27	7/28	6/26	9/24	8/25	11/21	10/24	1/15	12/19	3/13	2/17
		7/29	6/27	9/25	8/26	11/22	10/25	1/16	12/20	3/14	2/18
6/1	4/28	7/30	6/28	9/26	8/27	11/23	10/26	1/17	12/21	3/15	2/19
6/2	4/29	7/31	6/29	9/27	8/28	11/24	10/27	1/18	12/22	3/16	2/20
6/3	4/30			9/28	8/29	11/25	10/28	1/19	12/23	3/17	2/21
6/4	5/1	8/1	6/30	9/29	8/30	11/26	10/29	1/20	12/24	3/18	2/22
6/5	5/2	8/2	7/1	9/30	9/1	11/27	10/30	1/21	12/25	3/19	2/23
6/6	5/3	8/3	7/2			11/28	11/1	1/22	12/26	3/20	2/24
6/7	5/4	8/4	7/3	10/1	9/2	11/29	11/2	1/23	12/27	3/21	2/25
6/8	5/5	8/5	7/4	10/2	9/3	11/30	11/3	1/24	12/28	3/22	2/26
6/9	5/6	8/6	7/5	10/3	9/4			1/25	12/29	3/23	2/27
6/10	5/7	8/7	7/6	10/4	9/5	12/1	11/4	1/26	12/30	3/24	2/28
6/11	5/8	8/8	7/7	10/5	9/6	12/2	11/5	1/27	1/1	3/25	2/29
6/12	5/9	8/9	7/8	10/6	9/7	12/3	11/6		(1990)	3/26	2/30
6/13	5/10	8/10	7/9	10/7	9/8	12/4	11/7	1/28	1/2	3/27	3/1
6/14	5/11	8/11	7/10	10/8	9/9	12/5	11/8	1/29	1/3	3/28	3/2
6/15	5/12	8/12	7/11	10/9	9/10	12/6	11/9	1/30	1/4	3/29	3/3
6/16	5/13	8/13	7/12	10/10	9/11	12/7	11/10	1/31	1/5	3/30	3/4
6/17	5/14	8/14	7/13	10/11	9/12	12/8	11/11			3/31	3/5
6/18	5/15	8/15	7/14	10/12	9/13	12/9	11/12	2/1	1/6		
6/19	5/16	8/16	7/15	10/13	9/14	12/10	11/13	2/2	1/7	4/1	3/6
6/20	5/17	8/17	7/16	10/14	9/15	12/11	11/14	2/3	1/8	4/2	3/7
6/21	5/18	8/18	7/17	10/15	9/16	12/12	11/15	2/4	1/9	4/3	3/8
6/22	5/19	8/19	7/18	10/16	9/17	12/13	11/16	2/5	1/10	4/4	3/9
6/23	5/20	8/20	7/19	10/17	9/18	12/14	11/17	2/6	1/11	4/5	3/10
6/24	5/21	8/21	7/20	10/18	9/19	12/15	11/18	2/7	1/12	4/6	3/11
6/25	5/22	8/22	7/21	10/19	9/20	12/16	11/19	2/8	1/13	4/7	3/12
6/26	5/23	8/23	7/22	10/20	9/21	12/17	11/20	2/9	1/14	4/8	3/13
6/27	5/24	8/24	7/23	10/21	9/22	12/18	11/21	2/10	1/15	4/9	3/14
6/28	5/25	8/25	7/24	10/22	9/23	12/19	11/22	2/11	1/16	4/10	3/15
6/29	5/26	8/26	7/25	10/23	9/24	12/20	11/23	2/12	1/17	4/11	3/16
6/30	5/27	8/27	7/26	10/24	9/25	12/21	11/24	2/13	1/18	4/12	3/17
		8/28	7/27	10/25	9/26	12/22	11/25	2/14	1/19	4/13	3/18
7/1	5/28	8/29	7/28	10/26	9/27	12/23	11/26	2/15	1/20	4/14	3/19
7/2	5/29	8/30	7/29	10/27	9/28	12/24	11/27	2/16	1/21	4/15	3/20
7/3	6/1	8/31	8/1	10/28	9/29	12/25	11/28	2/17	1/22	4/16	3/21
7/4	6/2			10/29	10/1	12/26	11/29	2/18	1/23	4/17	3/22
7/5	6/3	9/1	8/2	10/30	10/2	12/27	11/30	2/19	1/24	4/18	3/23
7/6	6/4	9/2	8/3	10/31	10/3	12/28	12/1	2/20	1/25	4/19	3/24
7/7	6/5	9/3	8/4			12/29	12/2	2/21	1/26	4/20	3/25
7/8	6/6	9/4	8/5	11/1	10/4	12/30	12/3	2/22	1/27	4/21	3/26
7/9	6/7	9/5	8/6	11/2	10/5	12/31	12/4	2/23	1/28	4/22	3/27

Solar	Lunar
4/23	3/28
4/24	3/29
4/25	4/1
4/26	4/2
4/27	4/3
4/28	4/4
4/29	4/5
4/30	4/6
5/1	4/7
5/2	4/8
5/3	4/9
5/4	4/10
5/5	4/11
5/6	4/12
5/7	4/13
5/8	4/14
5/9	4/15
5/10	4/16
5/11	4/17
5/12	4/18
5/13	4/19
5/14	4/20
5/15	4/21
5/16	4/22
5/17	4/23
5/18	4/24
5/19	4/25
5/20	4/26
5/21	4/27
5/22	4/28
5/23	4/29
5/24	5/1
5/25	5/2
5/26	5/3
5/27	5/4
5/28	5/5
5/29	5/6
5/30	5/7
5/31	5/8
6/1	5/9
6/2	5/10
6/3	5/11
6/4	5/12
6/5	5/13
6/6	5/14
6/7	5/15
6/8	5/16
6/9	5/17
6/10	5/18
6/11	5/19
6/12	5/20
6/13	5/21
6/14	5/22
6/15	5/23
6/16	5/24
6/17	5/25
6/18	5/26
6/19	5/27

Solar	Lunar
6/20	5/28
6/21	5/29
6/22	5/30
6/23	5/1
(Leap Month)	
6/24	5/2
6/25	5/3
6/26	5/4
6/27	5/5
6/28	5/6
6/29	5/7
6/30	5/8
7/1	5/9
7/2	5/10
7/3	5/11
7/4	5/12
7/5	5/13
7/6	5/14
7/7	5/15
7/8	5/16
7/9	5/17
7/10	5/18
7/11	5/19
7/12	5/20
7/13	5/21
7/14	5/22
7/15	5/23
7/16	5/24
7/17	5/25
7/18	5/26
7/19	5/27
7/20	5/28
7/21	5/29
7/22	6/1
7/23	6/2
7/24	6/3
7/25	6/4
7/26	6/5
7/27	6/6
7/28	6/7
7/29	6/8
7/30	6/9
7/31	6/10
8/1	6/11
8/2	6/12
8/3	6/13
8/4	6/14
8/5	6/15
8/6	6/16
8/7	6/17
8/8	6/18
8/9	6/19
8/10	6/20
8/11	6/21
8/12	6/22
8/13	6/23
8/14	6/24
8/15	6/25

Solar	Lunar
8/16	6/26
8/17	6/27
8/18	6/28
8/19	6/29
8/20	7/1
8/21	7/2
8/22	7/3
8/23	7/4
8/24	7/5
8/25	7/6
8/26	7/7
8/27	7/8
8/28	7/9
8/29	7/10
8/30	7/11
8/31	7/12
9/1	7/13
9/2	7/14
9/3	7/15
9/4	7/16
9/5	7/17
9/6	7/18
9/7	7/19
9/8	7/20
9/9	7/21
9/10	7/22
9/11	7/23
9/12	7/24
9/13	7/25
9/14	7/26
9/15	7/27
9/16	7/28
9/17	7/29
9/18	7/30
9/19	8/1
9/20	8/2
9/21	8/3
9/22	8/4
9/23	8/5
9/24	8/6
9/25	8/7
9/26	8/8
9/27	8/9
9/28	8/10
9/29	8/11
9/30	8/12
10/1	8/13
10/2	8/14
10/3	8/15
10/4	8/16
10/5	8/17
10/6	8/18
10/7	8/19
10/8	8/20
10/9	8/21
10/10	8/22
10/11	8/23
10/12	8/24

Solar	Lunar
10/13	8/25
10/14	8/26
10/15	8/27
10/16	8/28
10/17	8/29
10/18	9/1
10/19	9/2
10/20	9/3
10/21	9/4
10/22	9/5
10/23	9/6
10/24	9/7
10/25	9/8
10/26	9/9
10/27	9/10
10/28	9/11
10/29	9/12
10/30	9/13
10/31	9/14
11/1	9/15
11/2	9/16
11/3	9/17
11/4	9/18
11/5	9/19
11/6	9/20
11/7	9/21
11/8	9/22
11/9	9/23
11/10	9/24
11/11	9/25
11/12	9/26
11/13	9/27
11/14	9/28
11/15	9/29
11/16	9/30
11/17	10/1
11/18	10/2
11/19	10/3
11/20	10/4
11/21	10/5
11/22	10/6
11/23	10/7
11/24	10/8
11/25	10/9
11/26	10/10
11/27	10/11
11/28	10/12
11/29	10/13
11/30	10/14
12/1	10/15
12/2	10/16
12/3	10/17
12/4	10/18
12/5	10/19
12/6	10/20
12/7	10/21
12/8	10/22
12/9	10/23

Solar	Lunar
12/10	10/24
12/11	10/25
12/12	10/26
12/13	10/27
12/14	10/28
12/15	10/29
12/16	10/30
12/17	11/1
12/18	11/2
12/19	11/3
12/20	11/4
12/21	11/5
12/22	11/6
12/23	11/7
12/24	11/8
12/25	11/9
12/26	11/10
12/27	11/11
12/28	11/12
12/29	11/13
12/30	11/14
12/31	11/15

Solar Date	Lunar Date
1991	
1/1	11/16
1/2	11/17
1/3	11/18
1/4	11/19
1/5	11/20
1/6	11/21
1/7	11/22
1/8	11/23
1/9	11/24
1/10	11/25
1/11	11/26
1/12	11/27
1/13	11/28
1/14	11/29
1/15	11/30
1/16	12/1
1/17	12/2
1/18	12/3
1/19	12/4
1/20	12/5
1/21	12/6
1/22	12/7
1/23	12/8
1/24	12/9
1/25	12/10
1/26	12/11
1/27	12/12
1/28	12/13
1/29	12/14
1/30	12/15
1/31	12/16

Solar	Lunar
2/1	12/17
2/2	12/18
2/3	12/19
2/4	12/20
2/5	12/21
2/6	12/22
2/7	12/23
2/8	12/24
2/9	12/25
2/10	12/26
2/11	12/27
2/12	12/28
2/13	12/29
2/14	12/30
2/15	1/1 (1991)
2/16	1/2
2/17	1/3
2/18	1/4
2/19	1/5
2/20	1/6
2/21	1/7
2/22	1/8
2/23	1/9
2/24	1/10
2/25	1/11
2/26	1/12
2/27	1/13
2/28	1/14
3/1	1/15
3/2	1/16
3/3	1/17
3/4	1/18
3/5	1/19
3/6	1/20
3/7	1/21
3/8	1/22
3/9	1/23
3/10	1/24
3/11	1/25
3/12	1/26
3/13	1/27
3/14	1/28
3/15	1/29
3/16	2/1
3/17	2/2
3/18	2/3
3/19	2/4
3/20	2/5
3/21	2/6
3/22	2/7
3/23	2/8
3/24	2/9
3/25	2/10
3/26	2/11
3/27	2/12
3/28	2/13
3/29	2/14
3/30	2/15

Solar	Lunar	Solar	Lunar	Solar	Lunar	Solar	Lunar	Solar	Lunar	Solar	Lunar
3/31	2/16	5/28	4/15	7/25	6/14	9/21	8/14	11/18	10/13	1/10	12/6
		5/29	4/16	7/26	6/15	9/22	8/15	11/19	10/14	1/11	12/7
4/1	2/17	5/30	4/17	7/27	6/16	9/23	8/16	11/20	10/15	1/12	12/8
4/2	2/18	5/31	4/18	7/28	6/17	9/24	8/17	11/21	10/16	1/13	12/9
4/3	2/19			7/29	6/18	9/25	8/18	11/22	10/17	1/14	12/10
4/4	2/20	6/1	4/19	7/30	6/19	9/26	8/19	11/23	10/18	1/15	12/11
4/5	2/21	6/2	4/20	7/31	6/20	9/27	8/20	11/24	10/19	1/16	12/12
4/6	2/22	6/3	4/21			9/28	8/21	11/25	10/20	1/17	12/13
4/7	2/23	6/4	4/22	8/1	6/21	9/29	8/22	11/26	10/21	1/18	12/14
4/8	2/24	6/5	4/23	8/2	6/22	9/30	8/23	11/27	10/22	1/19	12/15
4/9	2/25	6/6	4/24	8/3	6/23			11/28	10/23	1/20	12/16
4/10	2/26	6/7	4/25	8/4	6/24	10/1	8/24	11/29	10/24	1/21	12/17
4/11	2/27	6/8	4/26	8/5	6/25	10/2	8/25	11/30	10/25	1/22	12/18
4/12	2/28	6/9	4/27	8/6	6/26	10/3	8/26			1/23	12/19
4/13	2/29	6/10	4/28	8/7	6/27	10/4	8/27	12/1	10/26	1/24	12/20
4/14	2/30	6/11	4/29	8/8	6/28	10/5	8/28	12/2	10/27	1/25	12/21
4/15	3/1	6/12	5/1	8/9	6/29	10/6	8/29	12/3	10/28	1/26	12/22
4/16	3/2	6/13	5/2	8/10	7/1	10/7	8/30	12/4	10/29	1/27	12/23
4/17	3/3	6/14	5/3	8/11	7/2	10/8	9/1	12/5	10/30	1/28	12/24
4/18	3/4	6/15	5/4	8/12	7/3	10/9	9/2	12/6	11/1	1/29	12/25
4/19	3/5	6/16	5/5	8/13	7/4	10/10	9/3	12/7	11/2	1/30	12/26
4/20	3/6	6/17	5/6	8/14	7/5	10/11	9/4	12/8	11/3	1/31	12/27
4/21	3/7	6/18	5/7	8/15	7/6	10/12	9/5	12/9	11/4		
4/22	3/8	6/19	5/8	8/16	7/7	10/13	9/6	12/10	11/5	2/1	12/28
4/23	3/9	6/20	5/9	8/17	7/8	10/14	9/7	12/11	11/6	2/2	12/29
4/24	3/10	6/21	5/10	8/18	7/9	10/15	9/8	12/12	11/7	2/3	12/30
4/25	3/11	6/22	5/11	8/19	7/10	10/16	9/9	12/13	11/8	2/4	1/1
4/26	3/12	6/23	5/12	8/20	7/11	10/17	9/10	12/14	11/9		(1992)
4/27	3/13	6/24	5/13	8/21	7/12	10/18	9/11	12/15	11/10	2/5	1/2
4/28	3/14	6/25	5/14	8/22	7/13	10/19	9/12	12/16	11/11	2/6	1/3
4/29	3/15	6/26	5/15	8/23	7/14	10/20	9/13	12/17	11/12	2/7	1/4
4/30	3/16	6/27	5/16	8/24	7/15	10/21	9/14	12/18	11/13	2/8	1/5
		6/28	5/17	8/25	7/16	10/22	9/15	12/19	11/14	2/9	1/6
5/1	3/17	6/29	5/18	8/26	7/17	10/23	9/16	12/20	11/15	2/10	1/7
5/2	3/18	6/30	5/19	8/27	7/18	10/24	9/17	12/21	11/16	2/11	1/8
5/3	3/19			8/28	7/19	10/25	9/18	12/22	11/17	2/12	1/9
5/4	3/20	7/1	5/20	8/29	7/20	10/26	9/19	12/23	11/18	2/13	1/10
5/5	3/21	7/2	5/21	8/30	7/21	10/27	9/20	12/24	11/19	2/14	1/11
5/6	3/22	7/3	5/22	8/31	7/22	10/28	9/21	12/25	11/20	2/15	1/12
5/7	3/23	7/4	5/23			10/29	9/22	12/26	11/21	2/16	1/13
5/8	3/24	7/5	5/24	9/1	7/23	10/30	9/23	12/27	11/22	2/17	1/14
5/9	3/25	7/6	5/25	9/2	7/24	10/31	9/24	12/28	11/23	2/18	1/15
5/10	3/26	7/7	5/26	9/3	7/25			12/29	11/24	2/19	1/16
5/11	3/27	7/8	5/27	9/4	7/26	11/1	9/25	12/30	11/25	2/20	1/17
5/12	3/28	7/9	5/28	9/5	7/27	11/2	9/26	12/31	11/26	2/21	1/18
5/13	3/29	7/10	5/29	9/6	7/28	11/3	9/27			2/22	1/19
5/14	4/1	7/11	5/30	9/7	7/29	11/4	9/28			2/23	1/20
5/15	4/2	7/12	6/1	9/8	8/1	11/5	9/29	**Solar**	**Lunar**	2/24	1/21
5/16	4/3	7/13	6/2	9/9	8/2	11/6	10/1	**Date**	**Date**	2/25	1/22
5/17	4/4	7/14	6/3	9/10	8/3	11/7	10/2			2/26	1/23
5/18	4/5	7/15	6/4	9/11	8/4	11/8	10/3	**1992**		2/27	1/24
5/19	4/6	7/16	6/5	9/12	8/5	11/9	10/4	1/1	11/27	2/28	1/25
5/20	4/7	7/17	6/6	9/13	8/6	11/10	10/5	1/2	11/28	2/29	1/26
5/21	4/8	7/18	6/7	9/14	8/7	11/11	10/6	1/3	11/29		
5/22	4/9	7/19	6/8	9/15	8/8	11/12	10/7	1/4	11/30	3/1	1/27
5/23	4/10	7/20	6/9	9/16	8/9	11/13	10/8	1/5	12/1	3/2	1/28
5/24	4/11	7/21	6/10	9/17	8/10	11/14	10/9	1/6	12/2	3/3	1/29
5/25	4/12	7/22	6/11	9/18	8/11	11/15	10/10	1/7	12/3	3/4	2/1
5/26	4/13	7/23	6/12	9/19	8/12	11/16	10/11	1/8	12/4	3/5	2/2
5/27	4/14	7/24	6/13	9/20	8/13	11/17	10/12	1/9	12/5	3/6	2/3

Solar	Lunar	Solar	Lunar	Solar	Lunar	Solar	Lunar	Solar	Lunar	Solar	Lunar
3/7	2/4	5/4	4/2	7/1	6/2	8/29	8/2	10/26	10/1	12/23	11/30
3/8	2/5	5/5	4/3	7/2	6/3	8/30	8/3	10/27	10/2	12/24	12/1
3/9	2/6	5/6	4/4	7/3	6/4	8/31	8/4	10/28	10/3	12/25	12/2
3/10	2/7	5/7	4/5	7/4	6/5			10/29	10/4	12/26	12/3
3/11	2/8	5/8	4/6	7/5	6/6	9/1	8/5	10/30	10/5	12/27	12/4
3/12	2/9	5/9	4/7	7/6	6/7	9/2	8/6	10/31	10/6	12/28	12/5
3/13	2/10	5/10	4/8	7/7	6/8	9/3	8/7			12/29	12/6
3/14	2/11	5/11	4/9	7/8	6/9	9/4	8/8	11/1	10/7	12/30	12/7
3/15	2/12	5/12	4/10	7/9	6/10	9/5	8/9	11/2	10/8	12/31	12/8
3/16	2/13	5/13	4/11	7/10	6/11	9/6	8/10	11/3	10/9		
3/17	2/14	5/14	4/12	7/11	6/12	9/7	8/11	11/4	10/10		
3/18	2/15	5/15	4/13	7/12	6/13	9/8	8/12	11/5	10/11	**Solar**	**Lunar**
3/19	2/16	5/16	4/14	7/13	6/14	9/9	8/13	11/6	10/12	**Date**	**Date**
3/20	2/17	5/17	4/15	7/14	6/15	9/10	8/14	11/7	10/13	**1993**	
3/21	2/18	5/18	4/16	7/15	6/16	9/11	8/15	11/8	10/14	1/1	12/9
3/22	2/19	5/19	4/17	7/16	6/17	9/12	8/16	11/9	10/15	1/2	12/10
3/23	2/20	5/20	4/18	7/17	6/18	9/13	8/17	11/10	10/16	1/3	12/11
3/24	2/21	5/21	4/19	7/18	6/19	9/14	8/18	11/11	10/17	1/4	12/12
3/25	2/22	5/22	4/20	7/19	6/20	9/15	8/19	11/12	10/18	1/5	12/13
3/26	2/23	5/23	4/21	7/20	6/21	9/16	8/20	11/13	10/19	1/6	12/14
3/27	2/24	5/24	4/22	7/21	6/22	9/17	8/21	11/14	10/20	1/7	12/15
3/28	2/25	5/25	4/23	7/22	6/23	9/18	8/22	11/15	10/21	1/8	12/16
3/29	2/26	5/26	4/24	7/23	6/24	9/19	8/23	11/16	10/22	1/9	12/17
3/30	2/27	5/27	4/25	7/24	6/25	9/20	8/24	11/17	10/23	1/10	12/18
3/31	2/28	5/28	4/26	7/25	6/26	9/21	8/25	11/18	10/24	1/11	12/19
		5/29	4/27	7/26	6/27	9/22	8/26	11/19	10/25	1/12	12/20
4/1	2/29	5/30	4/28	7/27	6/28	9/23	8/27	11/20	10/26	1/13	12/21
4/2	2/30	5/31	4/29	7/28	6/29	9/24	8/28	11/21	10/27	1/14	12/22
4/3	3/1			7/29	6/30	9/25	8/29	11/22	10/28	1/15	12/23
4/4	3/2	6/1	5/1	7/30	7/1	9/26	9/1	11/23	10/29	1/16	12/24
4/5	3/3	6/2	5/2	7/31	7/2	9/27	9/2	11/24	11/1	1/17	12/25
4/6	3/4	6/3	5/3			9/28	9/3	11/25	11/2	1/18	12/26
4/7	3/5	6/4	5/4	8/1	7/3	9/29	9/4	11/26	11/3	1/19	12/27
4/8	3/6	6/5	5/5	8/2	7/4	9/30	9/5	11/27	11/4	1/20	12/28
4/9	3/7	6/6	5/6	8/3	7/5			11/28	11/5	1/21	12/29
4/10	3/8	6/7	5/7	8/4	7/6	10/1	9/6	11/29	11/6	1/22	12/30
4/11	3/9	6/8	5/8	8/5	7/7	10/2	9/7	11/30	11/7	1/23	1/1
4/12	3/10	6/9	5/9	8/6	7/8	10/3	9/8				(1993)
4/13	3/11	6/10	5/10	8/7	7/9	10/4	9/9	12/1	11/8	1/24	1/2
4/14	3/12	6/11	5/11	8/8	7/10	10/5	9/10	12/2	11/9	1/25	1/3
4/15	3/13	6/12	5/12	8/9	7/11	10/6	9/11	12/3	11/10	1/26	1/4
4/16	3/14	6/13	5/13	8/10	7/12	10/7	9/12	12/4	11/11	1/27	1/5
4/17	3/15	6/14	5/14	8/11	7/13	10/8	9/13	12/5	11/12	1/28	1/6
4/18	3/16	6/15	5/15	8/12	7/14	10/9	9/14	12/6	11/13	1/29	1/7
4/19	3/17	6/16	5/16	8/13	7/15	10/10	9/15	12/7	11/14	1/30	1/8
4/20	3/18	6/17	5/17	8/14	7/16	10/11	9/16	12/8	11/15	1/31	1/9
4/21	3/19	6/18	5/18	8/15	7/17	10/12	9/17	12/9	11/16		
4/22	3/20	6/19	5/19	8/16	7/18	10/13	9/18	12/10	11/17		
4/23	3/21	6/20	5/20	8/17	7/19	10/14	9/19	12/11	11/18	2/1	1/10
4/24	3/22	6/21	5/21	8/18	7/20	10/15	9/20	12/12	11/19	2/2	1/11
4/25	3/23	6/22	5/22	8/19	7/21	10/16	9/21	12/13	11/20	2/3	1/12
4/26	3/24	6/23	5/23	8/20	7/22	10/17	9/22	12/14	11/21	2/4	1/13
4/27	3/25	6/24	5/24	8/21	7/23	10/18	9/23	12/15	11/22	2/5	1/14
4/28	3/26	6/25	5/25	8/22	7/24	10/19	9/24	12/16	11/23	2/6	1/15
4/29	3/27	6/26	5/26	8/23	7/25	10/20	9/25	12/17	11/24	2/7	1/16
4/30	3/28	6/27	5/27	8/24	7/26	10/21	9/26	12/18	11/25	2/8	1/17
		6/28	5/28	8/25	7/27	10/22	9/27	12/19	11/26	2/9	1/18
5/1	3/29	6/29	5/29	8/26	7/28	10/23	9/28	12/20	11/27	2/10	1/19
5/2	3/30	6/30	6/1	8/27	7/29	10/24	9/29	12/21	11/28	2/11	1/20
5/3	4/1			8/28	8/1	10/25	9/30	12/22	11/29	2/12	1/21

Solar	Lunar	Solar	Lunar	Solar	Lunar	Solar	Lunar	Solar	Lunar	Solar	Lunar
2/13	1/22	4/12	3/21	6/8	4/19	8/5	6/18	10/2	8/17	11/30	10/17
2/14	1/23	4/13	3/22	6/9	4/20	8/6	6/19	10/3	8/18		
2/15	1/24	4/14	3/23	6/10	4/21	8/7	6/20	10/4	8/19	12/1	10/18
2/16	1/25	4/15	3/24	6/11	4/22	8/8	6/21	10/5	8/20	12/2	10/19
2/17	1/26	4/16	3/25	6/12	4/23	8/9	6/22	10/6	8/21	12/3	10/20
2/18	1/27	4/17	3/26	6/13	4/24	8/10	6/23	10/7	8/22	12/4	10/21
2/19	1/28	4/18	3/27	6/14	4/25	8/11	6/24	10/8	8/23	12/5	10/22
2/20	1/29	4/19	3/28	6/15	4/26	8/12	6/25	10/9	8/24	12/6	10/23
2/21	2/1	4/20	3/29	6/16	4/27	8/13	6/26	10/10	8/25	12/7	10/24
2/22	2/2	4/21	3/30	6/17	4/28	8/14	6/27	10/11	8/26	12/8	10/25
2/23	2/3	4/22	3/1	6/18	4/29	8/15	6/28	10/12	8/27	12/9	10/26
2/24	2/4	*(Leap Month)*		6/19	4/30	8/16	6/29	10/13	8/28	12/10	10/27
2/25	2/5	4/23	3/2	6/20	5/1	8/17	6/30	10/14	8/29	12/11	10/28
2/26	2/6	4/24	3/3	6/21	5/2	8/18	7/1	10/15	9/1	12/12	10/29
2/27	2/7	4/25	3/4	6/22	5/3	8/19	7/2	10/16	9/2	12/13	11/1
2/28	2/8	4/26	3/5	6/23	5/4	8/20	7/3	10/17	9/3	12/14	11/2
		4/27	3/6	6/24	5/5	8/21	7/4	10/18	9/4	12/15	11/3
3/1	2/9	4/28	3/7	6/25	5/6	8/22	7/5	10/19	9/5	12/16	11/4
3/2	2/10	4/29	3/8	6/26	5/7	8/23	7/6	10/20	9/6	12/17	11/5
3/3	2/11	4/30	3/9	6/27	5/8	8/24	7/7	10/21	9/7	12/18	11/6
3/4	2/12			6/28	5/9	8/25	7/8	10/22	9/8	12/19	11/7
3/5	2/13	5/1	3/10	6/29	5/10	8/26	7/9	10/23	9/9	12/20	11/8
3/6	2/14	5/2	3/11	6/30	5/11	8/27	7/10	10/24	9/10	12/21	11/9
3/7	2/15	5/3	3/12			8/28	7/11	10/25	9/11	12/22	11/10
3/8	2/16	5/4	3/13	7/1	5/12	8/29	7/12	10/26	9/12	12/23	11/11
3/9	2/17	5/5	3/14	7/2	5/13	8/30	7/13	10/27	9/13	12/24	11/12
3/10	2/18	5/6	3/15	7/3	5/14	8/31	7/14	10/28	9/14	12/25	11/13
3/11	2/19	5/7	3/16	7/4	5/15			10/29	9/15	12/26	11/14
3/12	2/20	5/8	3/17	7/5	5/16	9/1	7/15	10/30	9/16	12/27	11/15
3/13	2/21	5/9	3/18	7/6	5/17	9/2	7/16	10/31	9/17	12/28	11/16
3/14	2/22	5/10	3/19	7/7	5/18	9/3	7/17			12/29	11/17
3/15	2/23	5/11	3/20	7/8	5/19	9/4	7/18	11/1	9/18	12/30	11/18
3/16	2/24	5/12	3/21	7/9	5/20	9/5	7/19	11/2	9/19	12/31	11/19
3/17	2/25	5/13	3/22	7/10	5/21	9/6	7/20	11/3	9/20		
3/18	2/26	5/14	3/23	7/11	5/22	9/7	7/21	11/4	9/21		
3/19	2/27	5/15	3/24	7/12	5/23	9/8	7/22	11/5	9/22	**Solar**	**Lunar**
3/20	2/28	5/16	3/25	7/13	5/24	9/9	7/23	11/6	9/23	**Date**	**Date**
3/21	2/29	5/17	3/26	7/14	5/25	9/10	7/24	11/7	9/24	**1994**	
3/22	2/30	5/18	3/27	7/15	5/26	9/11	7/25	11/8	9/25	1/1	11/20
3/23	3/1	5/19	3/28	7/16	5/27	9/12	7/26	11/9	9/26	1/2	11/21
3/24	3/2	5/20	3/29	7/17	5/28	9/13	7/27	11/10	9/27	1/3	11/22
3/25	3/3	5/21	4/1	7/18	5/29	9/14	7/28	11/11	9/28	1/4	11/23
3/26	3/4	5/22	4/2	7/19	6/1	9/15	7/29	11/12	9/29	1/5	11/24
3/27	3/5	5/23	4/3	7/20	6/2	9/16	8/1	11/13	9/30	1/6	11/25
3/28	3/6	5/24	4/4	7/21	6/3	9/17	8/2	11/14	10/1	1/7	11/26
3/29	3/7	5/25	4/5	7/22	6/4	9/18	8/3	11/15	10/2	1/8	11/27
3/30	3/8	5/26	4/6	7/23	6/5	9/19	8/4	11/16	10/3	1/9	11/28
3/31	3/9	5/27	4/7	7/24	6/6	9/20	8/5	11/17	10/4	1/10	11/29
		5/28	4/8	7/25	6/7	9/21	8/6	11/18	10/5	1/11	11/30
4/1	3/10	5/29	4/9	7/26	6/8	9/22	8/7	11/19	10/6	1/12	12/1
4/2	3/11	5/30	4/10	7/27	6/9	9/23	8/8	11/20	10/7	1/13	12/2
4/3	3/12	5/31	4/11	7/28	6/10	9/24	8/9	11/21	10/8	1/14	12/3
4/4	3/13			7/29	6/11	9/25	8/10	11/22	10/9	1/15	12/4
4/5	3/14	6/1	4/12	7/30	6/12	9/26	8/11	11/23	10/10	1/16	12/5
4/6	3/15	6/2	4/13	7/31	6/13	9/27	8/12	11/24	10/11	1/17	12/6
4/7	3/16	6/3	4/14			9/28	8/13	11/25	10/12	1/18	12/7
4/8	3/17	6/4	4/15	8/1	6/14	9/29	8/14	11/26	10/13	1/19	12/8
4/9	3/18	6/5	4/16	8/2	6/15	9/30	8/15	11/27	10/14	1/20	12/9
4/10	3/19	6/6	4/17	8/3	6/16			11/28	10/15	1/21	12/10
4/11	3/20	6/7	4/18	8/4	6/17	10/1	8/16	11/29	10/16		

Solar	Lunar
1/22	12/11
1/23	12/12
1/24	12/13
1/25	12/14
1/26	12/15
1/27	12/16
1/28	12/17
1/29	12/18
1/30	12/19
1/31	12/20
2/1	12/21
2/2	12/22
2/3	12/23
2/4	12/24
2/5	12/25
2/6	12/26
2/7	12/27
2/8	12/28
2/9	12/29
2/10	1/1 (1994)
2/11	1/2
2/12	1/3
2/13	1/4
2/14	1/5
2/15	1/6
2/16	1/7
2/17	1/8
2/18	1/9
2/19	1/10
2/20	1/11
2/21	1/12
2/22	1/13
2/23	1/14
2/24	1/15
2/25	1/16
2/26	1/17
2/27	1/18
2/28	1/19
3/1	1/20
3/2	1/21
3/3	1/22
3/4	1/23
3/5	1/24
3/6	1/25
3/7	1/26
3/8	1/27
3/9	1/28
3/10	1/29
3/11	1/30
3/12	2/1
3/13	2/2
3/14	2/3
3/15	2/4
3/16	2/5
3/17	2/6
3/18	2/7
3/19	2/8

Solar	Lunar
3/20	2/9
3/21	2/10
3/22	2/11
3/23	2/12
3/24	2/13
3/25	2/14
3/26	2/15
3/27	2/16
3/28	2/17
3/29	2/18
3/30	2/19
3/31	2/20
4/1	2/21
4/2	2/22
4/3	2/23
4/4	2/24
4/5	2/25
4/6	2/26
4/7	2/27
4/8	2/28
4/9	2/29
4/10	2/30
4/11	3/1
4/12	3/2
4/13	3/3
4/14	3/4
4/15	3/5
4/16	3/6
4/17	3/7
4/18	3/8
4/19	3/9
4/20	3/10
4/21	3/11
4/22	3/12
4/23	3/13
4/24	3/14
4/25	3/15
4/26	3/16
4/27	3/17
4/28	3/18
4/29	3/19
4/30	3/20
5/1	3/21
5/2	3/22
5/3	3/23
5/4	3/24
5/5	3/25
5/6	3/26
5/7	3/27
5/8	3/28
5/9	3/29
5/10	3/30
5/11	4/1
5/12	4/2
5/13	4/3
5/14	4/4
5/15	4/5
5/16	4/6

Solar	Lunar
5/17	4/7
5/18	4/8
5/19	4/9
5/20	4/10
5/21	4/11
5/22	4/12
5/23	4/13
5/24	4/14
5/25	4/15
5/26	4/16
5/27	4/17
5/28	4/18
5/29	4/19
5/30	4/20
5/31	4/21
6/1	4/22
6/2	4/23
6/3	4/24
6/4	4/25
6/5	4/26
6/6	4/27
6/7	4/28
6/8	4/29
6/9	5/1
6/10	5/2
6/11	5/3
6/12	5/4
6/13	5/5
6/14	5/6
6/15	5/7
6/16	5/8
6/17	5/9
6/18	5/10
6/19	5/11
6/20	5/12
6/21	5/13
6/22	5/14
6/23	5/15
6/24	5/16
6/25	5/17
6/26	5/18
6/27	5/19
6/28	5/20
6/29	5/21
6/30	5/22
7/1	5/23
7/2	5/24
7/3	5/25
7/4	5/26
7/5	5/27
7/6	5/28
7/7	5/29
7/8	5/30
7/9	6/1
7/10	6/2
7/11	6/3
7/12	6/4
7/13	6/5

Solar	Lunar
7/14	6/6
7/15	6/7
7/16	6/8
7/17	6/9
7/18	6/10
7/19	6/11
7/20	6/12
7/21	6/13
7/22	6/14
7/23	6/15
7/24	6/16
7/25	6/17
7/26	6/18
7/27	6/19
7/28	6/20
7/29	6/21
7/30	6/22
7/31	6/23
8/1	6/24
8/2	6/25
8/3	6/26
8/4	6/27
8/5	6/28
8/6	6/29
8/7	7/1
8/8	7/2
8/9	7/3
8/10	7/4
8/11	7/5
8/12	7/6
8/13	7/7
8/14	7/8
8/15	7/9
8/16	7/10
8/17	7/11
8/18	7/12
8/19	7/13
8/20	7/14
8/21	7/15
8/22	7/16
8/23	7/17
8/24	7/18
8/25	7/19
8/26	7/20
8/27	7/21
8/28	7/22
8/29	7/23
8/30	7/24
8/31	7/25
9/1	7/26
9/2	7/27
9/3	7/28
9/4	7/29
9/5	7/30
9/6	8/1
9/7	8/2
9/8	8/3
9/9	8/4

Solar	Lunar
9/10	8/5
9/11	8/6
9/12	8/7
9/13	8/8
9/14	8/9
9/15	8/10
9/16	8/11
9/17	8/12
9/18	8/13
9/19	8/14
9/20	8/15
9/21	8/16
9/22	8/17
9/23	8/18
9/24	8/19
9/25	8/20
9/26	8/21
9/27	8/22
9/28	8/23
9/29	8/24
9/30	8/25
10/1	8/26
10/2	8/27
10/3	8/28
10/4	8/29
10/5	9/1
10/6	9/2
10/7	9/3
10/8	9/4
10/9	9/5
10/10	9/6
10/11	9/7
10/12	9/8
10/13	9/9
10/14	9/10
10/15	9/11
10/16	9/12
10/17	9/13
10/18	9/14
10/19	9/15
10/20	9/16
10/21	9/17
10/22	9/18
10/23	9/19
10/24	9/20
10/25	9/21
10/26	9/22
10/27	9/23
10/28	9/24
10/29	9/25
10/30	9/26
10/31	9/27
11/1	9/28
11/2	9/29
11/3	10/1
11/4	10/2
11/5	10/3
11/6	10/4

Solar	Lunar
11/7	10/5
11/8	10/6
11/9	10/7
11/10	10/8
11/11	10/9
11/12	10/10
11/13	10/11
11/14	10/12
11/15	10/13
11/16	10/14
11/17	10/15
11/18	10/16
11/19	10/17
11/20	10/18
11/21	10/19
11/22	10/20
11/23	10/21
11/24	10/22
11/25	10/23
11/26	10/24
11/27	10/25
11/28	10/26
11/29	10/27
11/30	10/28
12/1	10/29
12/2	10/30
12/3	11/1
12/4	11/2
12/5	11/3
12/6	11/4
12/7	11/5
12/8	11/6
12/9	11/7
12/10	11/8
12/11	11/9
12/12	11/10
12/13	11/11
12/14	11/12
12/15	11/13
12/16	11/14
12/17	11/15
12/18	11/16
12/19	11/17
12/20	11/18
12/21	11/19
12/22	11/20
12/23	11/21
12/24	11/22
12/25	11/23
12/26	11/24
12/27	11/25
12/28	11/26
12/29	11/27
12/30	11/28
12/31	11/29

Solar Date	Lunar Date
1995	
1/1	12/1
1/2	12/2
1/3	12/3
1/4	12/4
1/5	12/5
1/6	12/6
1/7	12/7
1/8	12/8
1/9	12/9
1/10	12/10
1/11	12/11
1/12	12/12
1/13	12/13
1/14	12/14
1/15	12/15
1/16	12/16
1/17	12/17
1/18	12/18
1/19	12/19
1/20	12/20
1/21	12/21
1/22	12/22
1/23	12/23
1/24	12/24
1/25	12/25
1/26	12/26
1/27	12/27
1/28	12/28
1/29	12/29
1/30	12/30
1/31	1/1 (1995)
2/1	1/2
2/2	1/3
2/3	1/4
2/4	1/5
2/5	1/6
2/6	1/7
2/7	1/8
2/8	1/9
2/9	1/10
2/10	1/11
2/11	1/12
2/12	1/13
2/13	1/14
2/14	1/15
2/15	1/16
2/16	1/17
2/17	1/18
2/18	1/19
2/19	1/20
2/20	1/21
2/21	1/22
2/22	1/23
2/23	1/24

Solar	Lunar
2/24	1/25
2/25	1/26
2/26	1/27
2/27	1/28
2/28	1/29
3/1	2/1
3/2	2/2
3/3	2/3
3/4	2/4
3/5	2/5
3/6	2/6
3/7	2/7
3/8	2/8
3/9	2/9
3/10	2/10
3/11	2/11
3/12	2/12
3/13	2/13
3/14	2/14
3/15	2/15
3/16	2/16
3/17	2/17
3/18	2/18
3/19	2/19
3/20	2/20
3/21	2/21
3/22	2/22
3/23	2/23
3/24	2/24
3/25	2/25
3/26	2/26
3/27	2/27
3/28	2/28
3/29	2/29
3/30	2/30
3/31	3/1
4/1	3/2
4/2	3/3
4/3	3/4
4/4	3/5
4/5	3/6
4/6	3/7
4/7	3/8
4/8	3/9
4/9	3/10
4/10	3/11
4/11	3/12
4/12	3/13
4/13	3/14
4/14	3/15
4/15	3/16
4/16	3/17
4/17	3/18
4/18	3/19
4/19	3/20
4/20	3/21
4/21	3/22
4/22	3/23

Solar	Lunar
4/23	3/24
4/24	3/25
4/25	3/26
4/26	3/27
4/27	3/28
4/28	3/29
4/29	3/30
4/30	4/1
5/1	4/2
5/2	4/3
5/3	4/4
5/4	4/5
5/5	4/6
5/6	4/7
5/7	4/8
5/8	4/9
5/9	4/10
5/10	4/11
5/11	4/12
5/12	4/13
5/13	4/14
5/14	4/15
5/15	4/16
5/16	4/17
5/17	4/18
5/18	4/19
5/19	4/20
5/20	4/21
5/21	4/22
5/22	4/23
5/23	4/24
5/24	4/25
5/25	4/26
5/26	4/27
5/27	4/28
5/28	4/29
5/29	5/1
5/30	5/2
5/31	5/3
6/1	5/4
6/2	5/5
6/3	5/6
6/4	5/7
6/5	5/8
6/6	5/9
6/7	5/10
6/8	5/11
6/9	5/12
6/10	5/13
6/11	5/14
6/12	5/15
6/13	5/16
6/14	5/17
6/15	5/18
6/16	5/19
6/17	5/20
6/18	5/21
6/19	5/22

Solar	Lunar
6/20	5/23
6/21	5/24
6/22	5/25
6/23	5/26
6/24	5/27
6/25	5/28
6/26	5/29
6/27	5/30
6/28	6/1
6/29	6/2
6/30	6/3
7/1	6/4
7/2	6/5
7/3	6/6
7/4	6/7
7/5	6/8
7/6	6/9
7/7	6/10
7/8	6/11
7/9	6/12
7/10	6/13
7/11	6/14
7/12	6/15
7/13	6/16
7/14	6/17
7/15	6/18
7/16	6/19
7/17	6/20
7/18	6/21
7/19	6/22
7/20	6/23
7/21	6/24
7/22	6/25
7/23	6/26
7/24	6/27
7/25	6/28
7/26	6/29
7/27	7/1
7/28	7/2
7/29	7/3
7/30	7/4
7/31	7/5
8/1	7/6
8/2	7/7
8/3	7/8
8/4	7/9
8/5	7/10
8/6	7/11
8/7	7/12
8/8	7/13
8/9	7/14
8/10	7/15
8/11	7/16
8/12	7/17
8/13	7/18
8/14	7/19
8/15	7/20
8/16	7/21

Solar	Lunar
8/17	7/22
8/18	7/23
8/19	7/24
8/20	7/25
8/21	7/26
8/22	7/27
8/23	7/28
8/24	7/29
8/25	7/30
8/26	8/1
8/27	8/2
8/28	8/3
8/29	8/4
8/30	8/5
8/31	8/6
9/1	8/7
9/2	8/8
9/3	8/9
9/4	8/10
9/5	8/11
9/6	8/12
9/7	8/13
9/8	8/14
9/9	8/15
9/10	8/16
9/11	8/17
9/12	8/18
9/13	8/19
9/14	8/20
9/15	8/21
9/16	8/22
9/17	8/23
9/18	8/24
9/19	8/25
9/20	8/26
9/21	8/27
9/22	8/28
9/23	8/29
9/24	8/30
9/25	8/1
(Leap Month)	
9/26	8/2
9/27	8/3
9/28	8/4
9/29	8/5
9/30	8/6
10/1	8/7
10/2	8/8
10/3	8/9
10/4	8/10
10/5	8/11
10/6	8/12
10/7	8/13
10/8	8/14
10/9	8/15
10/10	8/16
10/11	8/17
10/12	8/18

Solar	Lunar
10/13	8/19
10/14	8/20
10/15	8/21
10/16	8/22
10/17	8/23
10/18	8/24
10/19	8/25
10/20	8/26
10/21	8/27
10/22	8/28
10/23	8/29
10/24	9/1
10/25	9/2
10/26	9/3
10/27	9/4
10/28	9/5
10/29	9/6
10/30	9/7
10/31	9/8
11/1	9/9
11/2	9/10
11/3	9/11
11/4	9/12
11/5	9/13
11/6	9/14
11/7	9/15
11/8	9/16
11/9	9/17
11/10	9/18
11/11	9/19
11/12	9/20
11/13	9/21
11/14	9/22
11/15	9/23
11/16	9/24
11/17	9/25
11/18	9/26
11/19	9/27
11/20	9/28
11/21	9/29
11/22	10/1
11/23	10/2
11/24	10/3
11/25	10/4
11/26	10/5
11/27	10/6
11/28	10/7
11/29	10/8
11/30	10/9
12/1	10/10
12/2	10/11
12/3	10/12
12/4	10/13
12/5	10/14
12/6	10/15
12/7	10/16
12/8	10/17
12/9	10/18

Solar	Lunar	Solar	Lunar	Solar	Lunar	Solar	Lunar	Solar	Lunar	Solar	Lunar
12/10	10/19	2/1	12/13	3/30	2/12	5/27	4/11	7/24	6/10	9/20	8/9
12/11	10/20	2/2	12/14	3/31	2/13	5/28	4/12	7/25	6/11	9/21	8/10
12/12	10/21	2/3	12/15			5/29	4/13	7/26	6/12	9/22	8/11
12/13	10/22	2/4	12/16	4/1	2/14	5/30	4/14	7/27	6/13	9/23	8/12
12/14	10/23	2/5	12/17	4/2	2/15	5/31	4/15	7/28	6/14	9/24	8/13
12/15	10/24	2/6	12/18	4/3	2/16			7/29	6/15	9/25	8/14
12/16	10/25	2/7	12/19	4/4	2/17	6/1	4/16	7/30	6/16	9/26	8/15
12/17	10/26	2/8	12/20	4/5	2/18	6/2	4/17	7/31	6/17	9/27	8/16
12/18	10/27	2/9	12/21	4/6	2/19	6/3	4/18			9/28	8/17
12/19	10/28	2/10	12/22	4/7	2/20	6/4	4/19	8/1	6/18	9/29	8/18
12/20	10/29	2/11	12/23	4/8	2/21	6/5	4/20	8/2	6/19	9/30	8/19
12/21	10/30	2/12	12/24	4/9	2/22	6/6	4/21	8/3	6/20		
12/22	11/1	2/13	12/25	4/10	2/23	6/7	4/22	8/4	6/21	10/1	8/20
12/23	11/2	2/14	12/26	4/11	2/24	6/8	4/23	8/5	6/22	10/2	8/21
12/24	11/3	2/15	12/27	4/12	2/25	6/9	4/24	8/6	6/23	10/3	8/22
12/25	11/4	2/16	12/28	4/13	2/26	6/10	4/25	8/7	6/24	10/4	8/23
12/26	11/5	2/17	12/29	4/14	2/27	6/11	4/26	8/8	6/25	10/5	8/24
12/27	11/6	2/18	12/30	4/15	2/28	6/12	4/27	8/9	6/26	10/6	8/25
12/28	11/7	2/19	1/1	4/16	2/29	6/13	4/28	8/10	6/27	10/7	8/26
12/29	11/8		(1996)	4/17	2/30	6/14	4/29	8/11	6/28	10/8	8/27
12/30	11/9	2/20	1/2	4/18	3/1	6/15	4/30	8/12	6/29	10/9	8/28
12/31	11/10	2/21	1/3	4/19	3/2	6/16	5/1	8/13	6/30	10/10	8/29
		2/22	1/4	4/20	3/3	6/17	5/2	8/14	7/1	10/11	8/30
		2/23	1/5	4/21	3/4	6/18	5/3	8/15	7/2	10/12	9/1
Solar	**Lunar**	2/24	1/6	4/22	3/5	6/19	5/4	8/16	7/3	10/13	9/2
Date	**Date**	2/25	1/7	4/23	3/6	6/20	5/5	8/17	7/4	10/14	9/3
		2/26	1/8	4/24	3/7	6/21	5/6	8/18	7/5	10/15	9/4
1996		2/27	1/9	4/25	3/8	6/22	5/7	8/19	7/6	10/16	9/5
1/1	11/11	2/28	1/10	4/26	3/9	6/23	5/8	8/20	7/7	10/17	9/6
1/2	11/12	2/29	1/11	4/27	3/10	6/24	5/9	8/21	7/8	10/18	9/7
1/3	11/13			4/28	3/11	6/25	5/10	8/22	7/9	10/19	9/8
1/4	11/14	3/1	1/12	4/29	3/12	6/26	5/11	8/23	7/10	10/20	9/9
1/5	11/15	3/2	1/13	4/30	3/13	6/27	5/12	8/24	7/11	10/21	9/10
1/6	11/16	3/3	1/14			6/28	5/13	8/25	7/12	10/22	9/11
1/7	11/17	3/4	1/15	5/1	3/14	6/29	5/14	8/26	7/13	10/23	9/12
1/8	11/18	3/5	1/16	5/2	3/15	6/30	5/15	8/27	7/14	10/24	9/13
1/9	11/19	3/6	1/17	5/3	3/16			8/28	7/15	10/25	9/14
1/10	11/20	3/7	1/18	5/4	3/17	7/1	5/16	8/29	7/16	10/26	9/15
1/11	11/21	3/8	1/19	5/5	3/18	7/2	5/17	8/30	7/17	10/27	9/16
1/12	11/22	3/9	1/20	5/6	3/19	7/3	5/18	8/31	7/18	10/28	9/17
1/13	11/23	3/10	1/21	5/7	3/20	7/4	5/19			10/29	9/18
1/14	11/24	3/11	1/22	5/8	3/21	7/5	5/20	9/1	7/19	10/30	9/19
1/15	11/25	3/12	1/23	5/9	3/22	7/6	5/21	9/2	7/20	10/31	9/20
1/16	11/26	3/13	1/24	5/10	3/23	7/7	5/22	9/3	7/21		
1/17	11/27	3/14	1/25	5/11	3/24	7/8	5/23	9/4	7/22	11/1	9/21
1/18	11/28	3/15	1/26	5/12	3/25	7/9	5/24	9/5	7/23	11/2	9/22
1/19	11/29	3/16	1/27	5/13	3/26	7/10	5/25	9/6	7/24	11/3	9/23
1/20	12/1	3/17	1/28	5/14	3/27	7/11	5/26	9/7	7/25	11/4	9/24
1/21	12/2	3/18	1/29	5/15	3/28	7/12	5/27	9/8	7/26	11/5	9/25
1/22	12/3	3/19	2/1	5/16	3/29	7/13	5/28	9/9	7/27	11/6	9/26
1/23	12/4	3/20	2/2	5/17	4/1	7/14	5/29	9/10	7/28	11/7	9/27
1/24	12/5	3/21	2/3	5/18	4/2	7/15	6/1	9/11	7/29	11/8	9/28
1/25	12/6	3/22	2/4	5/19	4/3	7/16	6/2	9/12	8/1	11/9	9/29
1/26	12/7	3/23	2/5	5/20	4/4	7/17	6/3	9/13	8/2	11/10	9/30
1/27	12/8	3/24	2/6	5/21	4/5	7/18	6/4	9/14	8/3	11/11	10/1
1/28	12/9	3/25	2/7	5/22	4/6	7/19	6/5	9/15	8/4	11/12	10/2
1/29	12/10	3/26	2/8	5/23	4/7	7/20	6/6	9/16	8/5	11/13	10/3
1/30	12/11	3/27	2/9	5/24	4/8	7/21	6/7	9/17	8/6	11/14	10/4
1/31	12/12	3/28	2/10	5/25	4/9	7/22	6/8	9/18	8/7	11/15	10/5
		3/29	2/11	5/26	4/10	7/23	6/9	9/19	8/8	11/16	10/6

Solar	Lunar	Solar	Lunar	Solar	Lunar	Solar	Lunar	Solar	Lunar	Solar	Lunar
11/17	10/7	1/9	12/1	3/7	1/29	5/4	3/28	7/1	5/27	8/29	7/27
11/18	10/8	1/10	12/2	3/8	1/30	5/5	3/29	7/2	5/28	8/30	7/28
11/19	10/9	1/11	12/3	3/9	2/1	5/6	3/30	7/3	5/29	8/31	7/29
11/20	10/10	1/12	12/4	3/10	2/2	5/7	4/1	7/4	5/30		
11/21	10/11	1/13	12/5	3/11	2/3	5/8	4/2	7/5	6/1	9/1	7/30
11/22	10/12	1/14	12/6	3/12	2/4	5/9	4/3	7/6	6/2	9/2	8/1
11/23	10/13	1/15	12/7	3/13	2/5	5/10	4/4	7/7	6/3	9/3	8/2
11/24	10/14	1/16	12/8	3/14	2/6	5/11	4/5	7/8	6/4	9/4	8/3
11/25	10/15	1/17	12/9	3/15	2/7	5/12	4/6	7/9	6/5	9/5	8/4
11/26	10/16	1/18	12/10	3/16	2/8	5/13	4/7	7/10	6/6	9/6	8/5
11/27	10/17	1/19	12/11	3/17	2/9	5/14	4/8	7/11	6/7	9/7	8/6
11/28	10/18	1/20	12/12	3/18	2/10	5/15	4/9	7/12	6/8	9/8	8/7
11/29	10/19	1/21	12/13	3/19	2/11	5/16	4/10	7/13	6/9	9/9	8/8
11/30	10/20	1/22	12/14	3/20	2/12	5/17	4/11	7/14	6/10	9/10	8/9
		1/23	12/15	3/21	2/13	5/18	4/12	7/15	6/11	9/11	8/10
12/1	10/21	1/24	12/16	3/22	2/14	5/19	4/13	7/16	6/12	9/12	8/11
12/2	10/22	1/25	12/17	3/23	2/15	5/20	4/14	7/17	6/13	9/13	8/12
12/3	10/23	1/26	12/18	3/24	2/16	5/21	4/15	7/18	6/14	9/14	8/13
12/4	10/24	1/27	12/19	3/25	2/17	5/22	4/16	7/19	6/15	9/15	8/14
12/5	10/25	1/28	12/20	3/26	2/18	5/23	4/17	7/20	6/16	9/16	8/15
12/6	10/26	1/29	12/21	3/27	2/19	5/24	4/18	7/21	6/17	9/17	8/16
12/7	10/27	1/30	12/22	3/28	2/20	5/25	4/19	7/22	6/18	9/18	8/17
12/8	10/28	1/31	12/23	3/29	2/21	5/26	4/20	7/23	6/19	9/19	8/18
12/9	10/29			3/30	2/22	5/27	4/21	7/24	6/20	9/20	8/19
12/10	10/30	2/1	12/24	3/31	2/23	5/28	4/22	7/25	6/21	9/21	8/20
12/11	11/1	2/2	12/25			5/29	4/23	7/26	6/22	9/22	8/21
12/12	11/2	2/3	12/26	4/1	2/24	5/30	4/24	7/27	6/23	9/23	8/22
12/13	11/3	2/4	12/27	4/2	2/25	5/31	4/25	7/28	6/24	9/24	8/23
12/14	11/4	2/5	12/28	4/3	2/26			7/29	6/25	9/25	8/24
12/15	11/5	2/6	12/29	4/4	2/27	6/1	4/26	7/30	6/26	9/26	8/25
12/16	11/6	2/7	1/1	4/5	2/28	6/2	4/27	7/31	6/27	9/27	8/26
12/17	11/7		(1997)	4/6	2/29	6/3	4/28			9/28	8/27
12/18	11/8	2/8	1/2	4/7	3/1	6/4	4/29	8/1	6/28	9/29	8/28
12/19	11/9	2/9	1/3	4/8	3/2	6/5	5/1	8/2	6/29	9/30	8/29
12/20	11/10	2/10	1/4	4/9	3/3	6/6	5/2	8/3	7/1		
12/21	11/11	2/11	1/5	4/10	3/4	6/7	5/3	8/4	7/2	10/1	8/30
12/22	11/12	2/12	1/6	4/11	3/5	6/8	5/4	8/5	7/3	10/2	9/1
12/23	11/13	2/13	1/7	4/12	3/6	6/9	5/5	8/6	7/4	10/3	9/2
12/24	11/14	2/14	1/8	4/13	3/7	6/10	5/6	8/7	7/5	10/4	9/3
12/25	11/15	2/15	1/9	4/14	3/8	6/11	5/7	8/8	7/6	10/5	9/4
12/26	11/16	2/16	1/10	4/15	3/9	6/12	5/8	8/9	7/7	10/6	9/5
12/27	11/17	2/17	1/11	4/16	3/10	6/13	5/9	8/10	7/8	10/7	9/6
12/28	11/18	2/18	1/12	4/17	3/11	6/14	5/10	8/11	7/9	10/8	9/7
12/29	11/19	2/19	1/13	4/18	3/12	6/15	5/11	8/12	7/10	10/9	9/8
12/30	11/20	2/20	1/14	4/19	3/13	6/16	5/12	8/13	7/11	10/10	9/9
12/31	11/21	2/21	1/15	4/20	3/14	6/17	5/13	8/14	7/12	10/11	9/10
		2/22	1/16	4/21	3/15	6/18	5/14	8/15	7/13	10/12	9/11
		2/23	1/17	4/22	3/16	6/19	5/15	8/16	7/14	10/13	9/12
Solar	**Lunar**	2/24	1/18	4/23	3/17	6/20	5/16	8/17	7/15	10/14	9/13
Date	**Date**	2/25	1/19	4/24	3/18	6/21	5/17	8/18	7/16	10/15	9/14
1997		2/26	1/20	4/25	3/19	6/22	5/18	8/19	7/17	10/16	9/15
1/1	11/22	2/27	1/21	4/26	3/20	6/23	5/19	8/20	7/18	10/17	9/16
1/2	11/23	2/28	1/22	4/27	3/21	6/24	5/20	8/21	7/19	10/18	9/17
1/3	11/24			4/28	3/22	6/25	5/21	8/22	7/20	10/19	9/18
1/4	11/25	3/1	1/23	4/29	3/23	6/26	5/22	8/23	7/21	10/20	9/19
1/5	11/26	3/2	1/24	4/30	3/24	6/27	5/23	8/24	7/22	10/21	9/20
1/6	11/27	3/3	1/25			6/28	5/24	8/25	7/23	10/22	9/21
1/7	11/28	3/4	1/26	5/1	3/25	6/29	5/25	8/26	7/24	10/23	9/22
1/8	11/29	3/5	1/27	5/2	3/26	6/30	5/26	8/27	7/25	10/24	9/23
		3/6	1/28	5/3	3/27			8/28	7/26	10/25	9/24

Solar	Lunar	Solar	Lunar	Solar	Lunar	Solar	Lunar	Solar	Lunar	Solar	Lunar
10/26	9/25	12/23	11/24	2/13	1/17	4/12	3/16	6/9	5/15	8/5	6/14
10/27	9/26	12/24	11/25	2/14	1/18	4/13	3/17	6/10	5/16	8/6	6/15
10/28	9/27	12/25	11/26	2/15	1/19	4/14	3/18	6/11	5/17	8/7	6/16
10/29	9/28	12/26	11/27	2/16	1/20	4/15	3/19	6/12	5/18	8/8	6/17
10/30	9/29	12/27	11/28	2/17	1/21	4/16	3/20	6/13	5/19	8/9	6/18
10/31	10/1	12/28	11/29	2/18	1/22	4/17	3/21	6/14	5/20	8/10	6/19
		12/29	11/30	2/19	1/23	4/18	3/22	6/15	5/21	8/11	6/20
11/1	10/2	12/30	12/1	2/20	1/24	4/19	3/23	6/16	5/22	8/12	6/21
11/2	10/3	12/31	12/2	2/21	1/25	4/20	3/24	6/17	5/23	8/13	6/22
11/3	10/4			2/22	1/26	4/21	3/25	6/18	5/24	8/14	6/23
11/4	10/5			2/23	1/27	4/22	3/26	6/19	5/25	8/15	6/24
11/5	10/6	Solar	Lunar	2/24	1/28	4/23	3/27	6/20	5/26	8/16	6/25
11/6	10/7	Date	Date	2/25	1/29	4/24	3/28	6/21	5/27	8/17	6/26
11/7	10/8			2/26	1/30	4/25	3/29	6/22	5/28	8/18	6/27
11/8	10/9	**1998**		2/27	2/1	4/26	4/1	6/23	5/29	8/19	6/28
11/9	10/10	1/1	12/3	2/28	2/2	4/27	4/2	6/24	5/1	8/20	6/29
11/10	10/11	1/2	12/4			4/28	4/3	*(Leap Month)*		8/21	6/30
11/11	10/12	1/3	12/5	3/1	2/3	4/29	4/4	6/25	5/2	8/22	7/1
11/12	10/13	1/4	12/6	3/2	2/4	4/30	4/5	6/26	5/3	8/23	7/2
11/13	10/14	1/5	12/7	3/3	2/5			6/27	5/4	8/24	7/3
11/14	10/15	1/6	12/8	3/4	2/6	5/1	4/6	6/28	5/5	8/25	7/4
11/15	10/16	1/7	12/9	3/5	2/7	5/2	4/7	6/29	5/6	8/26	7/5
11/16	10/17	1/8	12/10	3/6	2/8	5/3	4/8	6/30	5/7	8/27	7/6
11/17	10/18	1/9	12/11	3/7	2/9	5/4	4/9			8/28	7/7
11/18	10/19	1/10	12/12	3/8	2/10	5/5	4/10	7/1	5/8	8/29	7/8
11/19	10/20	1/11	12/13	3/9	2/11	5/6	4/11	7/2	5/9	8/30	7/9
11/20	10/21	1/12	12/14	3/10	2/12	5/7	4/12	7/3	5/10	8/31	7/10
11/21	10/22	1/13	12/15	3/11	2/13	5/8	4/13	7/4	5/11		
11/22	10/23	1/14	12/16	3/12	2/14	5/9	4/14	7/5	5/12	9/1	7/11
11/23	10/24	1/15	12/17	3/13	2/15	5/10	4/15	7/6	5/13	9/2	7/12
11/24	10/25	1/16	12/18	3/14	2/16	5/11	4/16	7/7	5/14	9/3	7/13
11/25	10/26	1/17	12/19	3/15	2/17	5/12	4/17	7/8	5/15	9/4	7/14
11/26	10/27	1/18	12/20	3/16	2/18	5/13	4/18	7/9	5/16	9/5	7/15
11/27	10/28	1/19	12/21	3/17	2/19	5/14	4/19	7/10	5/17	9/6	7/16
11/28	10/29	1/20	12/22	3/18	2/20	5/15	4/20	7/11	5/18	9/7	7/17
11/29	10/30	1/21	12/23	3/19	2/21	5/16	4/21	7/12	5/19	9/8	7/18
11/30	11/1	1/22	12/24	3/20	2/22	5/17	4/22	7/13	5/20	9/9	7/19
		1/23	12/25	3/21	2/23	5/18	4/23	7/14	5/21	9/10	7/20
12/1	11/2	1/24	12/26	3/22	2/24	5/19	4/24	7/15	5/22	9/11	7/21
12/2	11/3	1/25	12/27	3/23	2/25	5/20	4/25	7/16	5/23	9/12	7/22
12/3	11/4	1/26	12/28	3/24	2/26	5/21	4/26	7/17	5/24	9/13	7/23
12/4	11/5	1/27	12/29	3/25	2/27	5/22	4/27	7/18	5/25	9/14	7/24
12/5	11/6	1/28	1/1	3/26	2/28	5/23	4/28	7/19	5/26	9/15	7/25
12/6	11/7		(1998)	3/27	2/29	5/24	4/29	7/20	5/27	9/16	7/26
12/7	11/8	1/29	1/2	3/28	3/1	5/25	4/30	7/21	5/28	9/17	7/27
12/8	11/9	1/30	1/3	3/29	3/2	5/26	5/1	7/22	5/29	9/18	7/28
12/9	11/10	1/31	1/4	3/30	3/3	5/27	5/2	7/23	6/1	9/19	7/29
12/10	11/11			3/31	3/4	5/28	5/3	7/24	6/2	9/20	7/30
12/11	11/12	2/1	1/5			5/29	5/4	7/25	6/3	9/21	8/1
12/12	11/13	2/2	1/6	4/1	3/5	5/30	5/5	7/26	6/4	9/22	8/2
12/13	11/14	2/3	1/7	4/2	3/6	5/31	5/6	7/27	6/5	9/23	8/3
12/14	11/15	2/4	1/8	4/3	3/7			7/28	6/6	9/24	8/4
12/15	11/16	2/5	1/9	4/4	3/8	6/1	5/7	7/29	6/7	9/25	8/5
12/16	11/17	2/6	1/10	4/5	3/9	6/2	5/8	7/30	6/8	9/26	8/6
12/17	11/18	2/7	1/11	4/6	3/10	6/3	5/9	7/31	6/9	9/27	8/7
12/18	11/19	2/8	1/12	4/7	3/11	6/4	5/10			9/28	8/8
12/19	11/20	2/9	1/13	4/8	3/12	6/5	5/11	8/1	6/10	9/29	8/9
12/20	11/21	2/10	1/14	4/9	3/13	6/6	5/12	8/2	6/11	9/30	8/10
12/21	11/22	2/11	1/15	4/10	3/14	6/7	5/13	8/3	6/12		
12/22	11/23	2/12	1/16	4/11	3/15	6/8	5/14	8/4	6/13	10/1	8/11

Solar	Lunar	Solar	Lunar	Solar	Lunar	Solar	Lunar	Solar	Lunar	Solar	Lunar
10/2	8/12	11/30	10/12	1/22	12/6	3/20	2/3	5/17	4/3	7/14	6/2
10/3	8/13			1/23	12/7	3/21	2/4	5/18	4/4	7/15	6/3
10/4	8/14	12/1	10/13	1/24	12/8	3/22	2/5	5/19	4/5	7/16	6/4
10/5	8/15	12/2	10/14	1/25	12/9	3/23	2/6	5/20	4/6	7/17	6/5
10/6	8/16	12/3	10/15	1/26	12/10	3/24	2/7	5/21	4/7	7/18	6/6
10/7	8/17	12/4	10/16	1/27	12/11	3/25	2/8	5/22	4/8	7/19	6/7
10/8	8/18	12/5	10/17	1/28	12/12	3/26	2/9	5/23	4/9	7/20	6/8
10/9	8/19	12/6	10/18	1/29	12/13	3/27	2/10	5/24	4/10	7/21	6/9
10/10	8/20	12/7	10/19	1/30	12/14	3/28	2/11	5/25	4/11	7/22	6/10
10/11	8/21	12/8	10/20	1/31	12/15	3/29	2/12	5/26	4/12	7/23	6/11
10/12	8/22	12/9	10/21			3/30	2/13	5/27	4/13	7/24	6/12
10/13	8/23	12/10	10/22	2/1	12/16	3/31	2/14	5/28	4/14	7/25	6/13
10/14	8/24	12/11	10/23	2/2	12/17			5/29	4/15	7/26	6/14
10/15	8/25	12/12	10/24	2/3	12/18	4/1	2/15	5/30	4/16	7/27	6/15
10/16	8/26	12/13	10/25	2/4	12/19	4/2	2/16	5/31	4/17	7/28	6/16
10/17	8/27	12/14	10/26	2/5	12/20	4/3	2/17			7/29	6/17
10/18	8/28	12/15	10/27	2/6	12/21	4/4	2/18	6/1	4/18	7/30	6/18
10/19	8/29	12/16	10/28	2/7	12/22	4/5	2/19	6/2	4/19	7/31	6/19
10/20	9/1	12/17	10/29	2/8	12/23	4/6	2/20	6/3	4/20		
10/21	9/2	12/18	10/30	2/9	12/24	4/7	2/21	6/4	4/21	8/1	6/20
10/22	9/3	12/19	11/1	2/10	12/25	4/8	2/22	6/5	4/22	8/2	6/21
10/23	9/4	12/20	11/2	2/11	12/26	4/9	2/23	6/6	4/23	8/3	6/22
10/24	9/5	12/21	11/3	2/12	12/27	4/10	2/24	6/7	4/24	8/4	6/23
10/25	9/6	12/22	11/4	2/13	12/28	4/11	2/25	6/8	4/25	8/5	6/24
10/26	9/7	12/23	11/5	2/14	12/29	4/12	2/26	6/9	4/26	8/6	6/25
10/27	9/8	12/24	11/6	2/15	12/30	4/13	2/27	6/10	4/27	8/7	6/26
10/28	9/9	12/25	11/7	2/16	1/1	4/14	2/28	6/11	4/28	8/8	6/27
10/29	9/10	12/26	11/8		(1999)	4/15	2/29	6/12	4/29	8/9	6/28
10/30	9/11	12/27	11/9	2/17	1/2	4/16	3/1	6/13	4/30	8/10	6/29
10/31	9/12	12/28	11/10	2/18	1/3	4/17	3/2	6/14	5/1	8/11	7/1
		12/29	11/11	2/19	1/4	4/18	3/3	6/15	5/2	8/12	7/2
11/1	9/13	12/30	11/12	2/20	1/5	4/19	3/4	6/16	5/3	8/13	7/3
11/2	9/14	12/31	11/13	2/21	1/6	4/20	3/5	6/17	5/4	8/14	7/4
11/3	9/15			2/22	1/7	4/21	3/6	6/18	5/5	8/15	7/5
11/4	9/16			2/23	1/8	4/22	3/7	6/19	5/6	8/16	7/6
11/5	9/17	Solar	Lunar	2/24	1/9	4/23	3/8	6/20	5/7	8/17	7/7
11/6	9/18	Date	Date	2/25	1/10	4/24	3/9	6/21	5/8	8/18	7/8
11/7	9/19			2/26	1/11	4/25	3/10	6/22	5/9	8/19	7/9
11/8	9/20	1999		2/27	1/12	4/26	3/11	6/23	5/10	8/20	7/10
11/9	9/21	1/1	11/14	2/28	1/13	4/27	3/12	6/24	5/11	8/21	7/11
11/10	9/22	1/2	11/15			4/28	3/13	6/25	5/12	8/22	7/12
11/11	9/23	1/3	11/16	3/1	1/14	4/29	3/14	6/26	5/13	8/23	7/13
11/12	9/24	1/4	11/17	3/2	1/15	4/30	3/15	6/27	5/14	8/24	7/14
11/13	9/25	1/5	11/18	3/3	1/16			6/28	5/15	8/25	7/15
11/14	9/26	1/6	11/19	3/4	1/17	5/1	3/16	6/29	5/16	8/26	7/16
11/15	9/27	1/7	11/20	3/5	1/18	5/2	3/17	6/30	5/17	8/27	7/17
11/16	9/28	1/8	11/21	3/6	1/19	5/3	3/18			8/28	7/18
11/17	9/29	1/9	11/22	3/7	1/20	5/4	3/19	7/1	5/18	8/29	7/19
11/18	9/30	1/10	11/23	3/8	1/21	5/5	3/20	7/2	5/19	8/30	7/20
11/19	10/1	1/11	11/24	3/9	1/22	5/6	3/21	7/3	5/20	8/31	7/21
11/20	10/2	1/12	11/25	3/10	1/23	5/7	3/22	7/4	5/21		
11/21	10/3	1/13	11/26	3/11	1/24	5/8	3/23	7/5	5/22	9/1	7/22
11/22	10/4	1/14	11/27	3/12	1/25	5/9	3/24	7/6	5/23	9/2	7/23
11/23	10/5	1/15	11/28	3/13	1/26	5/10	3/25	7/7	5/24	9/3	7/24
11/24	10/6	1/16	11/29	3/14	1/27	5/11	3/26	7/8	5/25	9/4	7/25
11/25	10/7	1/17	12/1	3/15	1/28	5/12	3/27	7/9	5/26	9/5	7/26
11/26	10/8	1/18	12/2	3/16	1/29	5/13	3/28	7/10	5/27	9/6	7/27
11/27	10/9	1/19	12/3	3/17	1/30	5/14	3/29	7/11	5/28	9/7	7/28
11/28	10/10	1/20	12/4	3/18	2/1	5/15	4/1	7/12	5/29	9/8	7/29
11/29	10/11	1/21	12/5	3/19	2/2	5/16	4/2	7/13	6/1	9/9	7/30

Solar	Lunar	Solar	Lunar	Solar Date	Lunar Date	Solar	Lunar	Solar	Lunar	Solar	Lunar
9/10	8/1	11/6	9/29	**2000**		2/23	1/19	4/21	3/17	6/17	5/16
9/11	8/2	11/7	9/30	1/1	11/25	2/24	1/20	4/22	3/18	6/18	5/17
9/12	8/3	11/8	10/1	1/2	11/26	2/25	1/21	4/23	3/19	6/19	5/18
9/13	8/4	11/9	10/2	1/3	11/27	2/26	1/22	4/24	3/20	6/20	5/19
9/14	8/5	11/10	10/3	1/4	11/28	2/27	1/23	4/25	3/21	6/21	5/20
9/15	8/6	11/11	10/4	1/5	11/29	2/28	1/24	4/26	3/22	6/22	5/21
9/16	8/7	11/12	10/5	1/6	11/30			4/27	3/23	6/23	5/22
9/17	8/8	11/13	10/6	1/7	12/1	3/1	1/25	4/28	3/24	6/24	5/23
9/18	8/9	11/14	10/7	1/8	12/2	3/2	1/26	4/29	3/25	6/25	5/24
9/19	8/10	11/15	10/8	1/9	12/3	3/3	1/27	4/30	3/26	6/26	5/25
9/20	8/11	11/16	10/9	1/10	12/4	3/4	1/28			6/27	5/26
9/21	8/12	11/17	10/10	1/11	12/5	3/5	1/29	5/1	3/27	6/28	5/27
9/22	8/13	11/18	10/11	1/12	12/6	3/6	2/1	5/2	3/28	6/29	5/28
9/23	8/14	11/19	10/12	1/13	12/7	3/7	2/2	5/3	3/29	6/30	5/29
9/24	8/15	11/20	10/13	1/14	12/8	3/8	2/3	5/4	4/1		
9/25	8/16	11/21	10/14	1/15	12/9	3/9	2/4	5/5	4/2	7/1	5/30
9/26	8/17	11/22	10/15	1/16	12/10	3/10	2/5	5/6	4/3	7/2	6/1
9/27	8/18	11/23	10/16	1/17	12/11	3/11	2/6	5/7	4/4	7/3	6/2
9/28	8/19	11/24	10/17	1/18	12/12	3/12	2/7	5/8	4/5	7/4	6/3
9/29	8/20	11/25	10/18	1/19	12/13	3/13	2/8	5/9	4/6	7/5	6/4
9/30	8/21	11/26	10/19	1/20	12/14	3/14	2/9	5/10	4/7	7/6	6/5
		11/27	10/20	1/21	12/15	3/15	2/10	5/11	4/8	7/7	6/6
10/1	8/22	11/28	10/21	1/22	12/16	3/16	2/11	5/12	4/9	7/8	6/7
10/2	8/23	11/29	10/22	1/23	12/17	3/17	2/12	5/13	4/10	7/9	6/8
10/3	8/24	11/30	10/23	1/24	12/18	3/18	2/13	5/14	4/11	7/10	6/9
10/4	8/25			1/25	12/19	3/19	2/14	5/15	4/12	7/11	6/10
10/5	8/26	12/1	10/24	1/26	12/20	3/20	2/15	5/16	4/13	7/12	6/11
10/6	8/27	12/2	10/25	1/27	12/21	3/21	2/16	5/17	4/14	7/13	6/12
10/7	8/28	12/3	10/26	1/28	12/22	3/22	2/17	5/18	4/15	7/14	6/13
10/8	8/29	12/4	10/27	1/29	12/23	3/23	2/18	5/19	4/16	7/15	6/14
10/9	9/1	12/5	10/28	1/30	12/24	3/24	2/19	5/20	4/17	7/16	6/15
10/10	9/2	12/6	10/29	1/31	12/25	3/25	2/20	5/21	4/18	7/17	6/16
10/11	9/3	12/7	10/30			3/26	2/21	5/22	4/19	7/18	6/17
10/12	9/4	12/8	11/1	2/1	12/26	3/27	2/22	5/23	4/20	7/19	6/18
10/13	9/5	12/9	11/2	2/2	12/27	3/28	2/23	5/24	4/21	7/20	6/19
10/14	9/6	12/10	11/3	2/3	12/28	3/29	2/24	5/25	4/22	7/21	6/20
10/15	9/7	12/11	11/4	2/4	12/29	3/30	2/25	5/26	4/23	7/22	6/21
10/16	9/8	12/12	11/5	2/5	1/1	3/31	2/26	5/27	4/24	7/23	6/22
10/17	9/9	12/13	11/6		(2000)			5/28	4/25	7/24	6/23
10/18	9/10	12/14	11/7	2/6	1/2	4/1	2/27	5/29	4/26	7/25	6/24
10/19	9/11	12/15	11/8	2/7	1/3	4/2	2/28	5/30	4/27	7/26	6/25
10/20	9/12	12/16	11/9	2/8	1/4	4/3	2/29	5/31	4/28	7/27	6/26
10/21	9/13	12/17	11/10	2/9	1/5	4/4	2/30			7/28	6/27
10/22	9/14	12/18	11/11	2/10	1/6	4/5	3/1	6/1	4/29	7/29	6/28
10/23	9/15	12/19	11/12	2/11	1/7	4/6	3/2	6/2	5/1	7/30	6/29
10/24	9/16	12/20	11/13	2/12	1/8	4/7	3/3	6/3	5/2	7/31	7/1
10/25	9/17	12/21	11/14	2/13	1/9	4/8	3/4	6/4	5/3		
10/26	9/18	12/22	11/15	2/14	1/10	4/9	3/5	6/5	5/4	8/1	7/2
10/27	9/19	12/23	11/16	2/15	1/11	4/10	3/6	6/6	5/5	8/2	7/3
10/28	9/20	12/24	11/17	2/16	1/12	4/11	3/7	6/7	5/6	8/3	7/4
10/29	9/21	12/25	11/18	2/17	1/13	4/12	3/8	6/8	5/7	8/4	7/5
10/30	9/22	12/26	11/19	2/18	1/14	4/13	3/9	6/9	5/8	8/5	7/6
10/31	9/23	12/27	11/20	2/19	1/15	4/14	3/10	6/10	5/9	8/6	7/7
		12/28	11/21	2/20	1/16	4/15	3/11	6/11	5/10	8/7	7/8
11/1	9/24	12/29	11/22	2/21	1/17	4/16	3/12	6/12	5/11	8/8	7/9
11/2	9/25	12/30	11/23	2/22	1/18	4/17	3/13	6/13	5/12	8/9	7/10
11/3	9/26	12/31	11/24			4/18	3/14	6/14	5/13	8/10	7/11
11/4	9/27					4/19	3/15	6/15	5/14	8/11	7/12
11/5	9/28					4/20	3/16	6/16	5/15	8/12	7/13

8/13	7/14	9/7	8/10	10/1	9/4	10/26	9/29	11/19	10/24	12/13	11/18
8/14	7/15	9/8	8/11	10/2	9/5	10/27	10/1	11/20	10/25	12/14	11/19
8/15	7/16	9/9	8/12	10/3	9/6	10/28	10/2	11/21	10/26	12/15	11/20
8/16	7/17	9/10	8/13	10/4	9/7	10/29	10/3	11/22	10/27	12/16	11/21
8/17	7/18	9/11	8/14	10/5	9/8	10/30	10/4	11/23	10/28	12/17	11/22
8/18	7/19	9/12	8/15	10/6	9/9	10/31	10/5	11/24	10/29	12/18	11/23
8/19	7/20	9/13	8/16	10/7	9/10			11/25	10/30	12/19	11/24
8/20	7/21	9/14	8/17	10/8	9/11	11/1	10/6	11/26	11/1	12/20	11/25
8/21	7/22	9/15	8/18	10/9	9/12	11/2	10/7	11/27	11/2	12/21	11/26
8/22	7/23	9/16	8/19	10/10	9/13	11/3	10/8	11/28	11/3	12/22	11/27
8/23	7/24	9/17	8/20	10/11	9/14	11/4	10/9	11/29	11/4	12/23	11/28
8/24	7/25	9/18	8/21	10/12	9/15	11/5	10/10	11/30	11/5	12/24	11/29
8/25	7/26	9/19	8/22	10/13	9/16	11/6	10/11			12/25	11/30
8/26	7/27	9/20	8/23	10/14	9/17	11/7	10/12	12/1	11/6	12/26	12/1
8/27	7/28	9/21	8/24	10/15	9/18	11/8	10/13	12/2	11/7	12/27	12/2
8/28	7/29	9/22	8/25	10/16	9/19	11/9	10/14	12/3	11/8	12/28	12/3
8/29	8/1	9/23	8/26	10/17	9/20	11/10	10/15	12/4	11/9	12/29	12/4
8/30	8/2	9/24	8/27	10/18	9/21	11/11	10/16	12/5	11/10	12/30	12/5
8/31	8/3	9/25	8/28	10/19	9/22	11/12	10/17	12/6	11/11	12/31	12/6
9/1	8/4	9/26	8/29	10/20	9/23	11/13	10/18	12/7	11/12		
9/2	8/5	9/27	8/30	10/21	9/24	11/14	10/19	12/8	11/13		
9/3	8/6	9/28	9/1	10/22	9/25	11/15	10/20	12/9	11/14		
9/4	8/7	9/29	9/2	10/23	9/26	11/16	10/21	12/10	11/15		
9/5	8/8	9/30	9/3	10/24	9/27	11/17	10/22	12/11	11/16		
9/6	8/9			10/25	9/28	11/18	10/23	12/12	11/17		

Notes

Introduction

1. Further information on the history and development of the three-by-three magic square can be found in *Numerology Magic* by Richard Webster (Llewellyn Publications, St. Paul, 1995).

2. *The Numerology Workbook* by Julia Line (Aquarian Press, Wellingborough, 1985), 74–79.

3. *Numbers and Their Influence* by Hettie Templeton (DeVorss and Company, Marina del Rey, 1940). *Mark Gruner's Numbers of Life* by Mark Gruner and Christopher K. Brown (Taplinger Publishing Company, New York, 1978). *Secrets of the Inner Self* by Dr. David A. Phillips (Angus and Robertson Publishers, Sydney, 1980).

Chapter 4

1. *Numbers and Their Influence* by Hettie Templeton (DeVorss and Company, Marina del Rey, 1940), 42–58.

Chapter 9

1. In fact, with true lunation, the months vary from twenty-nine days, eight hours to twenty-nine days, nineteen hours. The length of the months is determined by selecting the closest number of days to the actual time of lunation. This means that the lunar months are either twenty-nine or thirty days long.

2. Intercalation, which means bringing the lunar calendar into line with the solar one, was practiced from at least the time of Wu-ting, who reigned from 1324 to 1266 B.C.E. He is believed to have added an intercalary month at the end of the year, creating a thirteen-month year whenever necessary. His son, Tsu-chia, placed the intercalary month after any month when it was required, and called it the same as the preceding month. This created the leap months. (*Encyclopedia Britannica*, Macropedia, Volume 4, page 302. Fifteenth edition, 1983.)

   Other cultures also practice(d) intercalation. The current Jewish calendar, for instance, intercalates a thirteenth month seven times during the nineteen-year cycle. However, the Muslim calendar makes no attempt to keep aligned with the solar calendar, so has no need for intercalary months.

3. *Feng Shui for Beginners* by Richard Webster (Llewellyn Publications, St. Paul, 1997), 79. In feng shui the number four is frequently favorable.

4. *Feng Shui for Beginners*, 81.

5. *Numerology* by Austin Coates (Citadel Press, Secaucus, NJ, 1974), 10.

6. *Feng Shui for Beginners*, 14. Also *Numerology Magic*, 29.

   It is interesting to note that the ancient Chinese did not include air as one of their five elements, especially since ch'i, the universal life energy of feng shui, is basically air.

   Another interesting fact is that every system of Chinese divination derives from yin and yang and the five elements.

Chapter 10

1. *Chinese Astrology* by Derek Walters (Aquarian Press, Wellingborough, 1987), 257.

2. *Numerology Magic*, page 21.

3. *The Key of It All, Book One: The Eastern Mysteries* by David Allen Hulse (Llewellyn Publications, St. Paul, MN, 1993), 350. Hulse includes many examples of yin-yang combinations in his book.

4. *Chinese Astrology* by Derek Walters. On pages 256 and 257 he shows examples of colored magic squares dating from A.D. 982.

Chapter 11

1. Not all authorities agree that the Natal Month number is of lesser importance than the Natal Year. Takashi Yoshikawa, in his book *The Ki* (St. Martin's Press, New York, 1986), considers the Natal Month number to be much more important than the Natal Year.

Suggested Reading

Western Interpretations of Chinese Numerology

Coates, Austin. *Numerology*. The Citadel Press, Secaucus, NJ, 1974.

Gruner, Mark and Christopher Brown. *Mark Gruner's Numbers of Life*. Taplinger Publishing Company, New York, 1978.

Phillips, Dr. David A. *Secrets of the Inner Self*. Angus and Robertson Publishers, Sydney, 1980.

Stein, Robin. *The Numbers of Love*. Penguin Books, Victoria, 1990.

Stein, Robin. *Your Child's Numerology*. Greenhouse Publications, Pty. Ltd., Richmond, Victoria, 1985.

Templeton, Hettie. *Numbers and their Influence*. DeVorss and Company, Marina del Rey, California, 1940.

Webster, Richard. *Quick Readings with Numerology*. Brookfield Press, Auckland, 1979.

The Ki

Kushi, Michio. *Nine Star Ki*. One Peaceful World Press, Becket, MA, 1991.

Sachs, Bob. *The Complete Guide to Nine Star Ki*. Element Books Ltd., Longmead, Dorset, and Element, Inc., Rockport, MA, 1992.

Yoshikawa, Takashi. *The Ki*. St Martin's Press, New York, 1986.

Magic Squares

Andrews, W. S. *Magic Squares and Cubes*. Dover Publications, New York, 1960. Originally published by Open Court Publishing Company, 1917.

Barrett, Francis. *The Magus*. First published in 1801. Numerous versions are still available, including a facsimile edition published by The Aquarian Press, Wellingborough, 1989.

Hulse, David Allen. *The Key of It All, Book One: The Eastern Mysteries*. Llewellyn Publications, St. Paul, MN, 1994.

Webster, Richard. *Numerology Magic*. Llewellyn Publications, St. Paul, MN, 1995.

The Inclusion

Avery, Kevin Quinn. *The Numbers of Life*. Doubleday and Company, Garden City, NY, 1977. (Originally published by Freeway Press, Inc., 1974.)

Shine, Norman. *Numerology: Your Character and Future Revealed in Numbers*. Simon and Schuster Australia, East Roseville, NSW, 1994.

General

Hean-Tatt, Ong. *The Chinese Pakua*. Pelanduk Publications, Malaysia, 1991.

Schimmel, Annemarie. *The Mystery of Numbers*. Oxford University Press, New York, 1993.

Walters, Derek. *Chinese Astrology*. Aquarian Press, Wellingborough, 1987.

Index

REACH FOR THE MOON

Llewellyn publishes hundreds of books on your favorite subjects! To get these exciting books, including the ones on the following pages, check your local bookstore or order them directly from Llewellyn.

ORDER BY PHONE

- Call toll-free within the U.S. and Canada, 1-800-THE MOON
- In Minnesota, call (612) 291-1970
- We accept VISA, MasterCard, and American Express

ORDER BY MAIL

- Send the full price of your order (MN residents add 7% sales tax) in U.S. funds, plus postage & handling to:

  Llewellyn Worldwide
  P.O. Box 64383, Dept. K804-4
  St. Paul, MN 55164–0383, U.S.A.

POSTAGE & HANDLING

(For the U.S., Canada, and Mexico)

- $4.00 for orders $15.00 and under
- $5.00 for orders over $15.00
- No charge for orders over $100.00

We ship UPS in the continental United States. We ship standard mail to P.O. boxes. Orders shipped to Alaska, Hawaii, The Virgin Islands, and Puerto Rico are sent first-class mail. Orders shipped to Canada and Mexico are sent surface mail.

International orders: Airmail—add freight equal to price of each book to the total price of order, plus $5.00 for each non-book item (audio tapes, etc.).

Surface mail—Add $1.00 per item.

Allow 2 weeks for delivery on all orders.
Postage and handling rates subject to change.

DISCOUNTS

We offer a 20% discount to group leaders or agents. You must order a minimum of 5 copies of the same book to get our special quantity price.

FREE CATALOG

Get a free copy of our color catalog, *New Worlds of Mind and Spirit.* Subscribe for just $10.00 in the United States and Canada ($30.00 overseas, airmail). Many bookstores carry *New Worlds*—ask for it!

Visit our web site at www.llewellyn.com for more information.

Feng Shui for Apartment Living

Richard Webster

Don't think that just because you live in an apartment complex, a one-room studio, or a tiny dormitory that you can't benefit from the ancient art of feng shui. You can indeed make subtle changes to your living area that will literally transform your life. Those who practice feng shui are noticing marked improvements in all areas—romantic, financial, career, family, health, even fame. This latest book in Richard Webster's Feng Shui series addresses the special ways that you can improve the harmony and balance in your apartment, at little or no expense.

Learn what to look for when selecting an apartment. Find out where your four positive and four negative locations are, and avoid pointing your bed toward the "disaster" location. Discover the best places for other furniture, and how to remedy negative areas with plants, mirrors, crystals and wind chimes. You will also learn how to conduct a feng shui evaluation for others.

1-56718-794-3, 192 pp., 5 ³/₁₆ x 8, illus., softcover   **$9.95**

To order, call 1-800-THE MOON
Prices subject to change without notice

Spirit Guides & Angel Guardians

Contact Your Invisible Helpers

Richard Webster

They come to our aid when we least expect it, and they disappear as soon as their work is done. Invisible helpers are available to all of us; in fact, we all regularly receive messages from our guardian angels and spirit guides but usually fail to recognize them. This book will help you to realize when this occurs. And when you carry out the exercises provided, you will be able to communicate freely with both your guardian angels and spirit guides.

You will see your spiritual and personal growth take a huge leap forward as soon as you welcome your angels and guides into your life. This book contains numerous case studies that show how angels have touched the lives of others, just like yourself. Experience more fun, happiness and fulfillment than ever before. Other people will also notice the difference as you become calmer, more relaxed and more loving than ever before.

- Learn the important differences between a guardian angel and a spirit guide
- Invoke the Archangels for help in achieving your goals
- Discover the different ways your guardian angel speaks to you
- Create your own guardian angel from within
- Use your guardian angel to aid in healing yourself and others
- Enhance your creativity by calling on angelic assistance
- Find your life's purpose through your guardian angel
- Use time-tested methods to contact your spirit guides
- Use your spirit guides to help you release negative emotions
- Call on specific guides for nurturing, support, fun, motivation, wisdom
- Visit your guides through past-life regression

1-56718-795-1, 368 pp., 5 ³/₁₆ x 8, softcover   **$9.95**

Feng Shui for Beginners

Successful Living by Design

Richard Webster

Not advancing fast enough in your career? Maybe your desk is located in a "negative position." Wish you had a more peaceful family life? Hang a mirror in your dining room and watch what happens. Is money flowing out of your life rather than into it? You may want to look to the construction of your staircase!

For thousands of years, the ancient art of feng shui has helped people harness universal forces and lead lives rich in good health, wealth and happiness. The basic techniques in *Feng Shui for Beginners* are very simple, and you can put them into place immediately in your home and work environments. Gain peace of mind, a quiet confidence, and turn adversity to your advantage with feng shui remedies.

1-56718-803-6, 240 pgs., 5 ^{3}/$_{16}$ x 8, photos, diagrams, softcover $12.95